Industry 4.0 Technologies for Education

The transformative digital technologies developed for Industry 4.0 are proving to be disruptive change drivers in higher education. Industry 4.0 technologies are forming the basis of Education 4.0. *Industry 4.0 Technologies for Education: Transformative Technologies and Applications* examines state-of-the-art tools and technologies that comprise Education 4.0. Higher education professionals can turn to this book to guide them in curriculum development aimed at helping produce the workforce for Industry 4.0.

The book discusses the tools and technologies required to make Education 4.0 a reality. It covers online content creation, learning management systems, and tools for teaching, learning, and evaluating. Also covered are disciplines that are being transformed by Industry 4.0 and form the core of Education 4.0 curricula. These disciplines include social work, finance, medicine, and healthcare. Mobile technologies are critical components of Industry 4.0, as well as Education 4.0. The book looks at the roles of the Internet of Things (IoT), 5G, and cloud applications in creating the Education 4.0 environment.

Highlights of the book include:

- Technological innovations for virtual classrooms to empower students
- Emerging technological advancements for educational institutions
- Online content creation tools
- Moodle as a teaching, learning, and evaluation tool
- Gamification in higher education
- A design thinking approach to developing curriculum in Education 4.0
- Industry 4.0 for Service 4.0 and Research 4.0 as a framework for higher education institutions
- Eye-tracking technology for Education 4.0
- The challenges and issues of the Internet of Things (IoT) in teaching and learning

Industry 4.0 Technologies for Education

Transformative Technologies and Applications

Edited by
P. Kaliraj and T. Devi

CRC Press
Taylor & Francis Group
Boca Raton London New York

CRC Press is an imprint of the
Taylor & Francis Group, an **informa** business
AN AUERBACH BOOK

First edition published 2023
by CRC Press
6000 Broken Sound Parkway NW, Suite 300, Boca Raton, FL 33487–2742

and by CRC Press
4 Park Square, Milton Park, Abingdon, Oxon, OX14 4RN

CRC Press is an imprint of Taylor & Francis Group, LLC

Library of Congress Cataloging-in-Publication Data
Names: Kaliraj, P., editor. | Thirupathi, Devi, editor.
Title: Industry 4.0 technologies for education : transformative technologies and applications / Edited by P. Kaliraj and T. Devi.
Description: First edition | Boca Raton : CRC Press, 2022. | Includes bibliographical references and index.
Identifiers: LCCN 2022015463 (print) | LCCN 2022015464 (ebook) | ISBN 9781032139142 (hardback) | ISBN 9781032331416 (paperback) | ISBN 9781003318378 (ebook)
Subjects: LCSH: Educational technology. | Industry 4.0. | Education—Effect of technological innovations on. | Web-based instruction.
Classification: LCC LB1028.3 .I5192 2022 (print) | LCC LB1028.3 (ebook) | DDC 371.33—dc23/eng/20220622
LC record available at https://lccn.loc.gov/2022015463
LC ebook record available at https://lccn.loc.gov/2022015464

ISBN: 978-1-032-13914-2 (hbk)
ISBN: 978-1-032-33141-6 (pbk)
ISBN: 978-1-003-31837-8 (ebk)

DOI: 10.1201/9781003318378

Typeset in Times
by Apex CoVantage, LLC

Prof. P. Kaliraj *dedicates this book to*

esteemed Bharathiar University,

his father Mr. M. Perumal,

mother Mrs. P. Rathinammal,

and grandchildren Prithika Karthikeyan,

Kayan Karthikeyan,

Ayaan Prashanth, *and*

Akira Prashanth.

Prof. T. Devi *dedicates this book to*

Department of Computer Applications, Bharathiar University,

her husband Mr. D. Ravi,

her mother Mrs. Suseela Thirupathi,

mother-in-law Mrs. Singari Doraiswamy,

son-in-law Mr. Vishnu Prakhash Devaraj,

daughter Mrs. Deepiga Vishnu Prakhash,

son R. Surya, *and*

grandson V. Deera.

Contents

Preface

Education is evolving over a period of time based on industrial revolutions and this has an impact on global economic growth. Based on the Fourth Industrial Revolution, Industry 4.0 that encompasses digital technologies for transformation, a new form of disruptive reformed higher learning institutions are emerging to impart Education 4.0.

The Fourth Industrial Revolution, Industry 4.0, is tremendously changing the world around us. Students are to be equipped to face, embrace and live in this new technology which envisions the need for Education 4.0, to be at par with Industry 4.0. Though Industry 4.0 was suggested only for the manufacturing industry, the presence today of powerful networks, sensors, and devices force universities to prepare students to face the unprecedented and uncertain future world. Hence, it is imperative that universities design guidelines for Curriculum 4.0 and prepare new syllabi for all subjects intertwining Industry 4.0 tools into various disciplines such as science, social science, arts, and education, leading to Education 4.0. This book will help to familiarize students with the state-of-art tools and technologies that comprise Education 4.0 and help universities and colleges to help produce the workforce for the world of Industry 4.0 and the student experience to match it.

The awareness and practice on Industry 4.0 and its tools, skill development to face Industry 4.0, and technologically advanced infrastructure become the keys for successful development of future pillars of our globe. Linking the tools of Industry 4.0 with arts and science education is the need of the hour. Today, the rate at which the transformation happening is very disruptive in nature, and exponential changes are being witnessed. Educational institutions have to be way ahead of the requirement and prepare their students to meet the new challenges to be created by Industry 4.0. Currently, educational institutions are at a crossroads and do not know how to interweave the Industry 4.0 tools into the arts, science, social science, and teacher education programs in universities. This book can aid in imparting the concepts and knowledge of Industry 4.0 among graduates studying in higher education institutions as it highlights the framework of higher education in the era of Industry 4.0 and the digital technologies for transformation. It also describes the Curriculum 4.0 to be adopted by the different disciplines of higher education, and the applications of Education 4.0 in various sectors such as finance, education, electronics, and healthcare.

Artificial Intelligence and machine learning, automation and robotics, Big Data, Internet of Things and augmented reality and virtual reality, and creativity are the tools of Industry 4.0. Worldwide, universities and colleges should prepare students for facing this transformed world and hence it is imperative to align higher education with Industry 4.0 by imparting knowledge on how the educational field is getting transformed with Industry 4.0. It is also very much necessary that the skills necessary to face this transformation are imparted to the students so that they can confidently face the volatile, uncertain, complex, and ambiguous (VUCA) world around them.

Technological advancements are growing at an incredible pace and Industry 4.0 put smart technology at the forefront of manufacturing. Increased collaboration between humans and smart systems are being achieved by merging the high-speed accuracy of industrial automation with the cognitive, critical thinking skills of humans. Since applying the cognitive skills of humans to the pillars of Industry 4.0 will further revolutionize the world, this book devotes ample space to discuss how these skills can be utilized in Education 4.0 and help students face the VUCA world. Moreover, how education in universities can be transformed to Education 4.0 is also discussed across various chapters of the book. This is much essential since majority of the university education was imparted in traditional ways before COVID-19 days. It is high time that education becomes Education 4.0 and this book discusses how the change can be made.

The latest technological innovations for modern classrooms are: artificial intelligence, machine learning, augmented reality, virtual reality and mobile learning technologies. The book discusses the 'Transformation to Education 4.0'—tools and technologies required to make Education 4.0 a reality and details on tools required for online content creation, homework tools, learning management tools, and even the teaching learning and evaluation tool Moodle. When industry goes through the fourth wave of transformation, and education is all set to get aligned with it, the next question is about the career prospects of students. When most of the tasks that humans do get automated, obviously there will be speculation about the jobs students can aspire for and industry can offer them. In this context, the chapters dealing with jobs and job prospects are highly relevant for this time. The chapters discuss about the various skills required for students of the future and the nature of jobs awaiting them. Moreover, detailed discussions on even how faculty can be empowered to equip students for the jobs of coming years find a place in the book. The job roles awaiting students and the educational and skill set requirements for job roles are also discussed in detail. When the educational arena is all set to transform students to be armed with resources to run with the new transformation, the book discusses the diverse types of courses that could be delivered to students in universities and a design thinking approach for the curriculum framework in higher education institutions, and highlights the future strategy for curriculum development. How research can help in the educational transformation and how research outcomes can be implemented for a better society is also discussed in another chapter.

In this era of artificial intelligence and smart computing, whereby machines do most of the work in almost all walks of life, the book is an eye-opener on how disruptive innovation takes over supportive innovation. There are chapters in the book that deal with application areas of Education 4.0. The application areas and impacts of Industry 4.0 on academic writing and product naming are taken under consideration and given ample space for deliberation. Some application areas such as social work, finance, precision medicine, and health care are specifically addressed and detailed. Moreover, since Industry 4.0 would be impossible without mobile applications, as they play an essential role to ensure seamless way to connect with machines and communicate with cloud applications, another chapter discusses mobile applications that leverage 5G technology that enables the rapid adoption of Industry 4.0 and thus brings enormous benefits to manufacturing sectors.

In a world driven by automation, it is imperative that humans don't lose their innate human nature. Therefore, cognitive flexibility for Education 4.0 is covered in the book. A discussion on facilitating one's emotional abilities through empathy, resilience, communication, and social interaction to attain personal, academic, and work/life success comes under the umbrella of this book. Again, another chapter discusses various strategies and ways of improving cognitive flexibility to adapt oneself to the different novel situations—personally and professionally—to solve problems and thus succeed in the fast changing, technologically advancing complex world. Another highlight of the book is a chapter on theoretical frameworks on tone of cognition and metacognition in digital learning environments, where the significance of metacognition for teachers are analysed, the importance of cognitive presence in online community is examined, and the relationship of metacognition with information literacy and metaliteracy in social learning environment is described. Since facilitating one's emotional abilities through empathy, resilience, communication and social interaction is the key to attaining personal, academic and work/life success, a detailed discourse on emotional intelligence is also discussed in a chapter.

Currently, there are no books on Industry 4.0 and its applications that can be used in the curriculum of higher education. This book fills this gap and has a huge scope to be included in the higher education curriculum. The book will be useful for the graduates and higher education institutions as long as the curriculum of higher education institutions focuses on the development of Industry 4.0 skills. The students, scholars, and teachers can be from arts and sciences universities, engineering institutions and teacher education universities. Practitioners—scientists, engineers, and software developers who are interested in adopting Industry 4.0 and its tools—can also use this book for reference.

Chapter 1 entitled "Innovating Higher Education 4.0 in the Era of Industry 4.0" provides the means and methods to align higher education with Industry 4.0 through education on the digital transformation tools of Industry 4.0. This chapter details a framework for Education 4.0 and courses that intertwine Industry 4.0 tools into various disciplines such as science, social science, arts, and education that can be offered to enhance the skill set of students to face the volatile, uncertain, complex, and ambiguous (VUCA) world.

Chapter 2 entitled "Student Talent Management in the Era of Industry 4.0" discusses how students can be prepared for Industry 4.0 through efficient management of their versatile talents. This chapter focuses on talent identification, deployment, and development strategies specific to Industry 4.0, and addresses the challenges in managing student talents. It also details on the possibilities of emerging technologies in classroom talent management.

Chapter 3 entitled "Latest Technological Innovations for the Virtual Classroom: Empowering the Learners" explores how the recent technologies influence the learning environment and illustrates the importance and usage of the latest technologies that changed learning mechanisms. It highlights the implications of artificial intelligence and machine learning towards the education domain, and briefs how augmented reality and virtual reality can transform the education platforms.

Chapter 4 entitled "Industry 4.0: The Need of Industry 4.0 and the Technologies Revolutionizing it" discusses the industrial revolutions that have transformed the world and the need for the Fourth Industrial Revolution—Industry 4.0—and analyses the factors that led to this change. The chapter examines the goals and design principles to be followed in Industry 4.0 and exposes the drivers of Industry 4.0. It also deliberates on the various technologies that revolutionize Industry 4.0 and their impact and progress.

Chapter 5 entitled "Digital Transformation" proposes how to bring about digital transformation in the prevailing business methods, procedures, customs, and customer/user experiences. The chapter discusses why digital transformation is needed, how it is done, and provides some definitions. The application areas of digital transformation, its vital trends and the tools available are also discussed within the chapter.

Chapter 6 entitled "Emerging Technological Advancements for Educational Institutions" explores how educational institutions can leverage emerging technologies such as data analytics, IOT, the cloud, and AR/VR in the teaching and learning process to expand the reach of the university. It analyses how student engagement and retention rates can be improved, and supports employers with competency-based accreditation.

Chapter 7 entitled "Industry 4.0: Application Areas, Impacts, and the Utilities for Creating Applications" identifies the sectors where each of the Industry 4.0 technologies are utilised, and how these technologies affect and boost the various sectors by examining some use-cases. The chapter explores how Industry 4.0 benefits society, and identifies the potential impacts of Industry 4.0 on the society. A study on few tools available used to implement the Industry 4.0 technologies is also provided in the chapter.

Chapter 8 entitled "Technologies, Challenges, and Tools for Education 4.0" explores the tools and technologies needed to make Education 4.0 a reality. It shows how digital learning aids Education 4.0 and explores the profile that students and teachers need for Education 4.0. The chapter also discusses the different modes in which digital learning can be imparted to students and the technologies available for the same. The chapter also discusses the challenges that can come in the way of imparting this new-age learning.

Chapter 9 entitled "Homework Tools" reiterates that the innovation in teaching and evaluation is the stepping stone of online homework tools. This chapter examines the various online homework tools available and explores how they can be used to schedule assignments, grade them, and communicate it to the students.

Chapter 10 entitled "Online Content Creation Tools" explores how online content creation tools with the integration of technology can assist online and classroom-based courses. The chapter justifies how online learning capabilities combined with video collaboration and messaging services give users a best-of-breed combination, enabling them to cater to all academic eLearning use-cases.

Chapter 11 entitled "Moodle: Teaching Learning and Evaluation Tool" provides an overview of how to use Moodle in an educational institution. The chapter discusses the features of Moodle, its advantages, and how it became so popular. The various activities that can be created in Moodle and the resources that can be set up by teachers for students are also discussed.

Chapter 12 entitled "Learning Management Tools" discusses how classroom management strategies using learning management tools help to create an organized classroom environment that is conducive to teaching and learning. The chapter deliberates how effective utilisation of learning management tools help to reduce misbehaviour in the classroom and also explores cost effective methods to evaluate the performance of students and collect their feedback.

Chapter 13 entitled "Industry 4.0 and Jobs 2030" provides a perspective on the nature of jobs in the light of the Fourth Industrial Revolution. The chapter gives a description of what is the mission of the universities for 2030 and discusses what is meant by Education 4.0 and Curriculum 4.0. It also elaborates how the faculty can be trained to match themselves with Education 4.0 and Curriculum 4.0. and further discusses on the various skills required for students in the future, and the challenges of Mission 2030 and briefs on the nature of jobs in 2030.

Chapter 14 entitled "Gamification: A Boon for Higher Education" explains how gamification motivates students in enriching knowledge and understanding the concept, the importance of including gamification in curriculum, framing activities and designs to implement gamification in the teaching and learning process to identify and apply gamification. It envisages that gamification is the need of the hour to revamp higher education.

Chapter 15 entitled "Curriculum 4.0 for Incorporating Industry 4.0 Tools in Higher Education" provides a brief knowledge on the new higher education degree programmes and the corresponding syllabi relevant to Industry 4.0 in Education 4.0 to realize Chancellor's Vision 2030. Moreover, it provides guidelines for incorporating Industry 4.0 tools across various disciplines of arts and science education.

Chapter 16 entitled "Curriculum for Education 4.0: A Design Thinking Approach" proposes the concept of using the design thinking approach for the curriculum framework in higher educational institutions. It shows how design thinking can build and develop the right kind of curriculum for the future to bridge the existing gap between academia and industry.

Chapter 17 entitled "Education 4.0: Curriculum Development for Educational Framework" highlights the feature strategy for curriculum development for the Education Revolution 4.0 in Industry 4.0.

Chapter 18 entitled "Industry 4.0 for Service 4.0 through Research 4.0: A Framework for Higher Education Institutions" shows how Education 4.0 is brought about by Curriculum 4.0 and Faculty 4.0 for Student 4.0. It sheds light into what Curriculum 4.0 is, what the profile of Faculty 4.0 and Student 4.0 are, and how Research 4.0 should be carried out. The paper concludes with how Service 4.0 can be redefined in the context of Education 4.0 and how it can be of benefit to the entire humanity.

Chapter 19 entitled "Electronics in 2030" explores the two types of technology innovation: namely, supporting innovation and disruptive innovation. This chapter makes a study on how new smart products in both these technological innovations will penetrate the market by 2030.

Chapter 20 entitled "Framework for Academic Writing and Product Naming through Software Assistance" provides a summary of the internal process, meaning, transformation, structural, and conceptual implications of writing, nature, and future of academic writing in various disciplines and writing styles of science and technology. It provides an innovative idea for writing manuscripts of various researches through software. This chapter also introduces the model of a new software that can handle finding new names for the research products and methods.

Chapter 21 entitled "Perception on Industry 4.0 and Education in Teaching and Learning" shows that due to Industry 4.0, industrial production and information and communication technology converge, and industries are going through a transformation to full digitization and intelligent production in education. The "drivers of Industry 4.0"—augmented reality, artificial intelligence, the Internet of Things, cloud computing, Big Data analysis, mobile learning and cybersecurity are detailed, along with the high influence of Industry 4.0 on Education 4.0 in teaching and learning process.

Chapter 22 entitled "Education 4.0: Revisiting Contemporary Paradigms in Social Work Education" analyses how social workers can harness technology accelerating the digital revolution to address the accentuating problems in the society and how social work education should be amended to face the emerging challenges.

Chapter 23 entitled "Fintech Application in Commerce" provides a detailed analysis of financial technology and makes the reader understand fintech industry innovations. The chapter also examines how competitive interests will affect how fintech reshapes conventional banking, how fintech companies shift the conventional currency regime, and evaluates the improvements, challenges, and modifications arising from the emergence of fintech solutions. It also discusses how fintech has altered funding through new ways and models and provides a description of the various application areas where financial technology is used.

Chapter 24 entitled "Mobile Cloud Computing in Healthcare" gives the readers a clear understanding of the potential applications in healthcare for mobile cloud computing. The chapter provides a case study where mobile cloud computing has been successfully deployed to improve patient outcomes. It also addresses some of the challenges in using mobile cloud computing for healthcare delivery.

Chapter 25 entitled "Eye-Tracking Technology for Education 4.0" provides a detailed description on what eye-tracking is, its history, eye-tracking in HCI, review of eye-tracking in educational research, cognitive load in learning, eye-based techniques for Education 4.0, and types of eye-trackers available today. The chapter also provides details on eye-tracking metrics and indicators, eye-tracking for Industry 4.0 and the application of eye-tracking technology in Education 4.0.

Chapter 26 entitled "Mobile Applications for Industrial Use" shows how Industry 4.0 would be impossible without mobile applications as they play an essential role to ensure a seamless way to connect with machines and communicate with cloud applications that create an agile, responsive, and truly collaborative environment. Mobile communication technologies, mobile application platforms, how mobile applications can be employed to unlimited use cases of Industry 4.0 such as paperwork eliminations, employee tracking, inventory and asset management, work order management, quality control, remote monitoring and diagnosis, workplace safety, and automation of company processes such as purchase, sales, human resources, production, and accounting are detailed.

Chapter 27 entitled "Cognitive Flexibility: Know-How" summarizes the definition of cognitive flexibility and its related theories. The characteristics of cognitive flexibility, its neuronal perspectives and the different ways to improve cognitive flexibility for educational applications are discussed in detail in this chapter.

Chapter 28 entitled "Education 4.0: Cognitive Flexibility" gives the readers a clear understanding of cognitive flexibility and its meaning, definitions, and its importance in life. The chapter also provides an overview of neural mechanisms of cognitive flexibility, aspects of cognitive flexibility, age and cognitive flexibility, and how to measure it using different tools and tests. It also presents simple case studies highlighting the necessity of possessing this skill.

Chapter 29 entitled "Tone of Cognition and Metacognition in Digital Learning Environments" provides a summary of the theoretical frameworks on tone of cognition and metacognition in digital learning environments. It provides an overview of the theory of learning environment, and metacognitive knowledge in e-learning environments, and explores the theoretical constructs related to three ways of act of remembering in realizing cognition. This chapter also examines the importance of cognitive presence in online community and some theoretical evidence regarding metaliteracy, multiliteracies, and digital metaliteracies.

Chapter 30 entitled "The Role of the Internet of Things (IoT) in Teaching and Learning: Challenges and Issues" details how the incorporation of IoT into the education system facilitates the information exchange and utilizes the information for student interaction, as well as provides involvement to actively participate in the classroom activities. The role of IoT, its influence on education and its advantages, and comparison with the traditional education system are discussed. Additionally, IoT-based educational applications and opportunities are elaborated.

Chapter 31 entitled "Integrative Analysis of Host–Microbiota-Based Multi-Omics Data: A Novel Path towards Precision Medicine" describes the current status and implications of host microbiota–based multi-omics analysis on clinical practice particularly on precision medicine. In addition, the limitations and challenges of translation of these multi-omics information from lab bench to clinical bedside are highlighted.

Chapter 32 entitled "Emotional Intelligence: The Complex Innate Traits of Humankind" serves as a brief knowledge guide about emotional intelligence for the benefit of anyone who thrives to achieve more. It shows how emotional intelligence is the key to attain personal, academic, and work/life success.

The primary audiences for this book are students, scholars, and teachers of higher education institutions who need a reference resource on Industry 4.0, tools and their applications, and Education 4.0. The students, scholars, and teachers can be from arts and science universities and teacher education universities. Practitioners who are interested in applying Industry 4.0 and its tools to solve real-world problems can also use this book for reference. It is also meant for the administrative community of universities and colleges who intend to equip their graduates with the skills of Industry 4.0.

Highlights of the Book

This book introduces Industry 4.0 and its tools such as Big Data, artificial intelligence (AI), IoT, AR and cybersecurity and its applications in the fields of higher education, healthcare, finance (fintech), cognition, learning management, and social work education. The book helps the readers identify strategies to redesign their curriculum in line with Industry 4.0., i.e., to align education with Industry 4.0 tools. Detailed curriculum guidelines are also provided. Forty percent of the authors have international exposure in teaching and research. Most of the authors have experience of more than two decades. All the authors are practitioners of either Industry 4.0 in industries or Education 4.0 in research labs in academic institutions.

How to Use the Book

The method and purpose of using this book depend on the role that you play in an educational institution or in an industry or depend on the focus of your interest. We propose five types of roles: student, software developer, teacher, member of board of Studies, researcher, and administrator of educational and training institutions.

If you are a student: Students can use the book to get a basic understanding of Industry 4.0 and its tools and applications. Students belonging to any of the arts, science base, engineering, education, paramedical care, or social science disciplines will find useful information from chapters on Industry 4.0 technologies, digital transformation, technological advancements for educational institutions, utilities for creating applications, technologies, challenges and tools for Education 4.0, homework tools, Industry 4.0 and Jobs 2030, electronics in 2030, software assistance frameworks, Education 4.0 in teaching and learning, social work education, fintech application, mobile cloud computing in healthcare, mobile applications, and Industry 4.0 for precision medicine. This book will serve as a starting point for beginners. Students will benefit from the chapters on applications of Industry 4.0 in healthcare, commerce, education, medicine, and social work education.

If you are a software developer: Software developers can use the book to get a basic understanding of Industry 4.0 tools and their applications. Readers with software development background will find useful information from chapters on fundamentals and applications. They will benefit from the chapters that deal with the various Industry 4.0 tools such as homework tools, online content creation tools, Moodle, learning management tools, fintech application in commerce, mobile cloud computing in healthcare, and eye-tracking technology for Education 4.0.

If you are a teacher: The book is useful as a text for several different university level and college-level undergraduate and postgraduate courses besides doctoral programs. Chapters on methods to align higher education with Industry 4.0, integrating Education 4.0 with Industry 4.0, modern classroom: empowering the learners, digital transformation, technological advancements for educational institutions, utilities for creating applications, technologies, challenges and tools for Education 4.0, homework tools, online content creation tools, teaching learning evaluation tools, learning management tools, Research 4.0, Education 4.0 in teaching and learning, mobile cloud computing in healthcare, eye-tracking technology for Education 4.0, cognitive flexibility, cognition and metacognition in digital learning, and Internet of Things provide good inputs to the teachers in imparting knowledge on Industry 4.0 in Education. A graduate course on Industry 4.0 or Education 4.0 can use this book as a primary textbook. It is important to equip the learners with a basic understanding on Industry 4.0, tools of Industry 4.0, and how to align higher education with Industry 4.0 through the education on the digital transformation tools of Industry 4.0. This book serves such a purpose. To teach the applications of Industry 4.0 in various sectors, say healthcare, commerce, education, and precision medicine, teachers will find useful information from chapters on healthcare, fintech, gamification, social work education, and biomedicine. A course on Industry 4.0 for science could also use the chapters on healthcare and biomedicine. A course on Industry 4.0 and education could use the chapters that deal with application of Industry 4.0 and its tools in Education 4.0 and social work education.

If you are a member of a Board of Studies: Innovating the education to align with Industry 4.0 requires that the curriculum be revisited. Universities are looking for methods of incorporating Industry 4.0 tools across various disciplines of arts, science, and social science education. This book helps in incorporating Industry 4.0 across science and education. The book is useful while framing the syllabus for new courses that cut across components of Industry 4.0 and disciplines of arts or science or social science education. Chapter 15 presents the various programs that can be introduced in higher education institutions, the relevant digital transformation technology courses for the programs and the method of framing syllabi for interdisciplinary and multidisciplinary courses by intertwining the components of Industry 4.0 onto the respective discipline or domain. For example, syllabi for courses entitled Industry 4.0 in Science, Industry 4.0 in Healthcare, Industry 4.0 in Medical Biotechnology, or Education 4.0 may be framed using the chapters in the book. Industry infusion into curriculum is given much importance by involving more industry experts—research and development managers, product development managers, and technical managers as special invitees in the board of studies. Chapters given by industrial experts in this book will be very helpful to infuse the application part of Industry 4.0 into the curriculum.

If you are a researcher: A crucial area where innovation is required is the research work carried out by universities and research institutions so that innovative, creative, and useful products and services are made available to society through translational research. This book can serve as a comprehensive reference guide for researchers in the development of experimental Industry 4.0 applications. The chapters on Research 4.0; eye-tracking technology for Education 4.0; technologies, challenges, and tools for Education 4.0; and social work education provide researchers, scholars, and students with a list of important research questions to be addressed using Industry 4.0 and Education 4.0.

If you are an administrator of an educational and training institution: Currently, there is no book that guides administrators on how to align higher education with digital transformation technologies, especially Industry 4.0. This book provides frameworks, degree programs, courses, curriculum and syllabi, and methods to frame the syllabi by intertwining components of Industry 4.0 and various disciplines, tools and technologies. Based on this, an administrator can plan, design, and develop the educational institutions of tomorrow so as to make the future pillars of the Globe ready to face the VUCA world.

Acknowledgments

From Prof. P. Kaliraj:

First and foremost, I express my sincere gratitude to Hon'ble Shri. Banwarilal Purohit, former governor of Tamil Nadu, India, who was instrumental in organizing the conference on Innovating Education in the era of Industry 4.0 during 19–20 Dec. 2019 in Ooty, which paved the way for further work in the Industry 4.0 knowledge world, and Hon'ble Shri. R.N. Ravi, governor of Tamil Nadu, India, who was instrumental in organizing the Conference of Vice-Chancellors of State, Central and Private Universities in Tamil Nadu at Raj Bhavan, Ooty during 25–26 Apr 2022, which paved way to redefine the future course of action particularly in education and sustainable developments.

My heartfelt thanks go to Hon'ble Chief Minister of Tamil Nadu, India, and Hon'ble Minister for Higher Education, Government of Tamil Nadu. I thank Principal Secretary to Government, Higher Education Department, Government of Tamil Nadu.

I would like to express my thanks to Secretary to Governor, and Deputy Secretary to Governor, Universities Governor's Secretariat, Raj Bhavan, Chennai.

I thank my wife Dr. Vanaja Kaliraj, my son-in-law Mr. M. Karthikeyan, daughter Mrs. Ratna Priya Karthikeyan, son Dr. K. Siva Prashanth, daughter-in-law Dr. Ratna Priya Prashanth, grandchildren Prithika Karthikeyan, Kayan Karthikeyan, Ayaan Prashanth, Akira Prashanth, and family members for their support and being patient.

From Prof. T. Devi:

I record my sincere thanks to Prof. P. Kaliraj, Hon'ble vice-chancellor of Bharathiar University, who identified the gap in the knowledge world when the professor searched for a book on Industry 4.0 and triggered the process of writing and editing books in the Industry 4.0 series. His continuous motivation during the lockdown period due to COVID-19, sensitization, and encouragement are unmatchable.

I express my profound thanks to the vice-chancellor and registrar for the administrative support. Heartfelt thanks are due to the authors of the chapters for their contributions, continuous co-operation in improvising the chapters as and when requested, and for timely communication. I thank all the expert members who served as reviewers for providing quality and swift reviews.

We wish to thank Mr. John Wyzalek, senior acquisitions editor, Taylor & Francis Group/CRC Press, who believed in the idea of this book and helped us in realizing our dream.

Special thanks are due to Mr. Glenon C. Butler, production editor, Taylor-& Francis Group/CRC Press, Florida, for his coordination and Mr. Balaji karuppanan, project manager, Apex CoVantage for his untiring and swift support.

Thanks to Ms. Stephanie Kiefer, editorial assistant, Taylor & Francis Group/CRC Press, Boca Raton, FL, for her efforts and communications during the project.

Heartfelt thanks go to Prof. R. Sathishkumar, professor and head, Department of Biotechnology, who stressed on the idea of bringing out individual books for each of the components of Industry 4.0 which is all about digital transformation technologies.

Thanks are due to Dr. R. Rajeswari, associate professor, Department of Computer Applications, for her continuous support; Sister Italia Joseph Maria, Ms. M. Lissa, and Mrs. Shalini, project assistants, for providing earnest support; Mrs. P. Sudhandradevi, Research Scholar, for providing timely support.

Thanks to the faculty members Prof. M. Punithavalli, Dr. T. Amudha, Dr. J. Satheeshkumar, Dr. V. Bhuvaneswari, Dr. R. Balu, and Dr. J. Ramsingh.

Thanks to the assistant technical officers Mr. A. Elanchezian, Mr. A. Sivaraj, Mrs. B. Priyadarshini, and office staff Mr. A. Kalidas of the Department of Computer Applications of Bharathiar University, India.

Thanks are due to Mrs. K. Kowsalya, assistant registrar; Mr. R. Karthick, assistant section officer; Mr. A. Prasanth and Mr. Vijayakumar of the office of the vice-chancellor and staff of the office of the Registrar of Bharathiar University, India.

I thank my husband Mr. D. Ravi, daughter Mrs. R. Deepiga, son Mr. R. Surya, son-in-law Mr. D. Vishnu Prakhash, grandson V. Deera, and family members for their encouragement and support.

Editors

Prof. P. Kaliraj, Hon'ble vice-chancellor, Bharathiar University, a visionary and an eminent leader leading big academic teams, has had more than three decades of teaching and research experience. He has held various renowned positions, such as officiating vice-chancellor of Anna University, head of the Centre for Biotechnology of Anna University, dean of faculty at A C College of Technology, and member of the syndicate for two decades at Anna University. Professor Kaliraj had research collaborations with the National Institute of Health in Maryland, USA; Glasgow University in Scotland, UK; and University of Illinois in Rockford, USA. University Grants Commission BSR Faculty Award and the Lifetime Achievement Award from the Biotechnology Research Society of India adorn the professor. Forty-two scholars were gifted to receive the highest academic degree under his distinguished guidance. His remarkable patent in the area of filariasis is a boon in healthcare and saving the lives of humankind. He is a great motivator and very good at sensitizing the faculty, scholars, and students towards achieving academic excellence and institutional global ranking. Professor Kaliraj is a recipient of the Life Time Achievement Award and Sir J.C. Bose Memorial Award for his outstanding contribution in higher education—research. He is the promoter of Industry 4.0 in Bharathiar University (email: vc@buc.edu.in, pkaliraj@gmail.com).

Prof. T. Devi, professor, Centre for Research and Evaluation, former dean of research, professor and head, Department of Computer Applications, Bharathiar University, focuses on state-of-the-art technology that industries adopt in order to make students ready for the future world. She is a Gold Medallist (1981–1984) from University of Madras and a Commonwealth Scholar (1994–1998) for her PhD from the University of Warwick, UK. She has more than three decades of teaching and research experience from Bharathiar University, Indian Institute of Foreign Trade, New Delhi, and University of Warwick, UK. Professor Devi is good at team building and setting goals and achieving them. Her research interests include integrated data modelling and framework, meta-modelling, computer-assisted concurrent engineering, and speech processing. Professor Devi has visited the United Kingdom, Tanzania, and Singapore for academic collaborations. She has received a Commonwealth Scholarship and the Best Alumni Award from PSGR Krishnammal College for Women (PSGRKCW), a Proficiency Award from PSG College of Technology, and awards from Bharathiar University for serving on BU-NIRF, Curriculum 4.0, and Roadmap 2030, as well as guiding 23 PhD scholars. Prof. T. Devi may be contacted at (email: tdevi@buc.edu.in, tdevi5@gmail.com).

Contributors

Kochumol Abraham
PG Department of Computer Applications
Marian College, Kuttikkanam
Kerala, India

Thomas Alexander
Department of Cardiology
Kovai Medical Center and Hospital
Coimbatore, India

T. Amudha
Department of Computer Applications
Bharathiar University
Coimbatore, India

V. Bhuvaneswari
Department of Computer Applications
Bharathiar University
Coimbatore, India

M. Daniel
Chief Executive Office
SNS Group of Institutions
Coimbatore, India

T. Devi
Department of Computer Applications
Bharathiar University
Coimbatore, India

M. Dhanabhakyam
Department of Commerce
Bharathiar University
Coimbatore, India

F.X. Lovelina Little Flower
Department of Social Work
Bharathiar University
Coimbatore, India

Manika Garg
Senior Consultant
Infosys
Bangalore, India

Juby George
PG Department of Computer Applications
Marian College, Kuttikkanam
Kerala, India

R. K. Gowthami
RK Model Group of Institutions
Chittoor, Andhra Pradesh

Win Mathew John
PG Department of Computer Applications
Marian College, Kuttikkanam
Kerala, India

Antony William Joseph
Department of Computer Science
Madurai Kamaraj University
Madurai, India

P. Kaliraj
Bharathiar University
Coimbatore, India

G. S. Karthick
Department of Computer Science
Bharathiar University
Coimbatore, India

Italia Joseph Maria
Department of Computer Applications
Bharathiar University
Coimbatore, India

C. Vishnu Mohan
Department of Computer
Applications
Bharathiar University
Coimbatore, India

Sumathy Mohan
Department of Commerce
Bharathiar University
Coimbatore, India

Dr. Varshini Neethi Mohan
STEMI India
Coimbatore, India

Dr. S. Muruganand
Department of Electronics and Instrumentation
Bharathiar University
Coimbatore, India

Dr. Ramaswamy Murugesh
Department of Computer Science
Madurai Kamaraj University
Madurai, India

Dr. D. Napoleon
Department of Computer Science
Bharathiar University
Coimbatore, India

Dr. K. Prem Nazeer
Principal
Dr. SNS Rajalakshmi College of Arts and Science,
Coimbatore, India

Dr. P. B. Pankajavalli
Department of Computer Science
Bharathiar University
Coimbatore, India

Ms. N. Priya
Department of Computer Science
Bharathiar University
Coimbatore, India

Prof. M. Punithavalli
Department of Computer Applications
Bharathiar University
Coimbatore, India

Dr. R. Rajeswari
Department of Computer Applications
Bharathiar University
Coimbatore, India

Dr. V. Ramanujam
Bharathiar School of Management and Entrepreneurship
Bharathiar University
Coimbatore, India

Ms. N. P. Komala Raveendra
Founder Correspondent
RK Model Group of Institutions
Andhra Pradesh, India

Dr. P. Janardhanakumar Reddy
Department of Education
Bharathiar University
Coimbatore, India

Mr. Devaraj Sambandan
Department of Computer Applications
Bharathiar University
Coimbatore, India

Dr. S. Sarala
Department of Computer Applications
Bharathiar University
Coimbatore, India

Dr. V. Saravanan
Dean-Computer Studies
Dr. SNS Rajalakshmi College of Arts and Science
Coimbatore, India

Dr. J. Satheeshkumar
Department of Computer Applications
Bharathiar University
Coimbatore, India

Mrs. S. Shalini
Department of Computer Applications
Bharathiar University
Coimbatore, India

Dr. S. Sharmila
Department of Computer Science
Bharathiar University
Coimbatore, India

Prof. G. Singaravelu
Department of Education
Bharathiar University
Coimbatore, India

Dr. N. Subramanian
S Veerasamy Chettiar College of Education
Tenkasi, India

Mr. Sadhasivam Subramaniam
Dept. of Extension and Career Guidance
Bharathiar University
Coimbatore, India

V. M. Subramanian
Department of Linguistics
Bharathiar University
Coimbatore, India

J. Tresa Sugirtha
Department of Social Work
PSG College of Arts & Science
Coimbatore, India

Krishnan Swaminathan
Department of Biochemistry and Microbiology
KMCH Research Foundation
Coimbatore, India

Binu Thomas
PG Department of Computer Applications
Marian College, Kuttikkanam
Kerala, India

Ganesan Velmurugan
Department of Biochemistry and Microbiology
KMCH Research Foundation,
Coimbatore, India

S. R. Vijayalakshmi
Department of Electronics and Instrumentation
Bharathiar University
Coimbatore, India

S. Vijayarani
Department of Computer Science
Bharathiar University
Coimbatore, India

1

Innovating Higher Education 4.0 in the Era of Industry 4.0

P. Kaliraj and T. Devi

CONTENTS

Objectives

As an outcome of reading this chapter, the learner will gain knowledge on the following:

1. Concepts and tools of Industry 4.0.
2. Need for innovating education in the era of Industry 4.0.
3. A framework and the relevant components and processes.
4. New higher education degree programmes.
5. Courses and the corresponding syllabi relevant to Industry 4.0 in Education 4.0.

1.1 Industry 4.0

The Fourth and Fifth Industrial Revolutions, Industry 4.0 and Industry 5.0, are changing the world around us. Artificial intelligence (AI) and machine learning, automation and robotics, Big Data, Internet of Things (IoT) and augmented reality (AR) and virtual reality (VR), and creativity are the tools of Industry 4.0 (Figure 1.1). The Fourth Industrial Revolution is affecting the roles that Indian universities and colleges prepare students for, and educational institutions are ideally placed to help produce the workforce for this new world and the student experience to match it. It is necessary to align higher education with Industry 4.0 through education on the tools of Industry 4.0. It is also very essential to impart the skills that are necessary to develop the students to face the volatile, uncertain, complex and ambiguous (VUCA) world around us. Thus, awareness and practice on Industry 4.0 tools, skill development to face

DOI: 10.1201/9781003318378-1

FIGURE 1.1 Industry 4.0.

the VUCA world and technological advanced infrastructure become the keys for successful development of future pillars of our globe, linking Industry 4.0 with arts and science education, medical education, fisheries education, law education, teacher education, physical education and sports education.

1.2 Higher Education in Tamil Nadu, India

The main goal of higher education institutions in Tamil Nadu is to become hubs of eminence, innovation and development. They aim to create future pillars of the nation with a most vigorous knowledgeable society by providing everyone equal access to higher education. According to the policy note of Higher Education Department, Government of Tamil Nadu [1], the gross enrolment ratio (GER) in Tamil Nadu is 48.6%, while the national average GER is only 25.8%. The policy note also states that 21 institutions from Tamil Nadu are among the top 100 universities in the National Institutional Ranking Framework (NIRF) for 2019, out of which seven institutions are state universities. The Chancellor's vision 2030 aims to implement an education model in higher education which will enable the graduates to be skilled for the Industry 4.0 era.

1.2.1 State Universities in Tamil Nadu, India

The number of colleges and universities in Tamil Nadu is higher than other states in the country. There are 22 state universities in Tamil Nadu, of which one is exclusively for women students [2]. Out of 22 universities, Anna University (www.annauniv.edu) offers engineering education, Tamil Nadu Music and Fine Arts University (http://tnmfau.ac.in/) offers music and fine arts education, Tamil Nadu Open University (www.tnou.ac.in) offers only distance education mode, and the remaining 19 universities offer arts and science education, medical education, law education, teacher education, fisheries education and physical education and sports education. These 19 universities are Alagappa University (http://alagappauniversity.ac.in/), Annamalai University (www.annamalaiuniversity.ac.in), Bharathiar University (www.b-u.ac.in), Bharathidasan University (www.bdu.ac.in), University of Madras (www.unom.ac.in), Madurai Kamaraj University (www.mkuniversity.org), Manonmaniam Sundaranar University (www.msuniv.ac.in/), Mother Teresa Women's University (www. motherteresawomenuniv.ac.in), Periyar University (http://periyaruniversity.ac.in), Tiruvalluvar University (www.thiruvalluvaruniversity.ac.in), Tamil Nadu Fisheries Universities (www.tnfu.org.in/university/wp/), Tamil Nadu Teacher Education University (http://tnteu.ac.in/), Tamil University (www.tamiluniversity.ac.in), Tamil Nadu Agricultural University (www.tnau.ac.in), Tamil Nadu Dr. Ambedkar Law University (www.tndalu.org), Tamil Nadu Dr. MGR Medical University (www.tnmgrmu.ac.in), Tamil Nadu National Law University (www.tnnlu.ac.in), Tamil Nadu Physical Education and Sports University (www.tnpesu.org), and Tamil Nadu Veterinary and Animal Sciences University (www.tanuvas.ac.in). These universities always encourage students to pursue higher education without any obstacles. They care for economically and socially struggling youngsters by offering free education, scholarships for PhD scholars, community-based scholarships, free hostels and free laptops.

Arts and science education includes degree programmes such as bachelor of arts, master of arts, bachelor of science, master of science, doctor of philosophy (PhD) in arts and PhD in science disciplines. Medical education involves MBBS and MD. Law education includes bachelor of law, master of law and doctor of philosophy in law. Teacher education institutions offer bachelor of education, master of education and PhD in education. Physical education includes bachelor of physical education, master of physical education and PhD in physical education.

1.3 Education in the Era of Industry 4.0

In order to prepare students for the VUCA world through Education 4.0, the focus has to be linking university education with Industry 4.0 through applications, case studies, teaching support tools, learner support tools and evaluation tools (Figure 1.2). For example, in case of arts and science university education, courses may include the following topics or courses may be offered with the following titles.

- Applications of Big Data Analytics in Social Work
- Applications of Machine Learning in Framing Economic Policies
- Augmented Reality–Based Chemistry Practicals
- Artificial Intelligence for Arts Education
- Big Data Analytics in Marketing
- Design of AR Courses in Science Education
- Mobile Apps for Language Teaching
- Augmented Reality in Apparel Design
- Cyber Security in Education

In law education, while linking law education with Industry 4.0 through design of new courses with syllabi, applications, case studies, teaching support tools, learner support tools and evaluation tools, courses may be given in the following areas.

- Applications of Big Data Analytics in Law
- Automation for Legal and Compliance
- Predictive Data Analytics in IP Law
- Augmented Reality–Based Lawyer Training
- Artificial Intelligence for Law Education
- Big Data Analytics in Criminal Law
- Design of AR Courses in Law Education
- Mobile Apps for Law Teaching
- Augmented Reality in Training Business Lawyers

In the case of medical education, while linking the medical education with Industry 4.0 through design of new courses with syllabi, applications, case studies, teaching support tools, learner support tools and evaluation tools, the following topics or courses would add value.

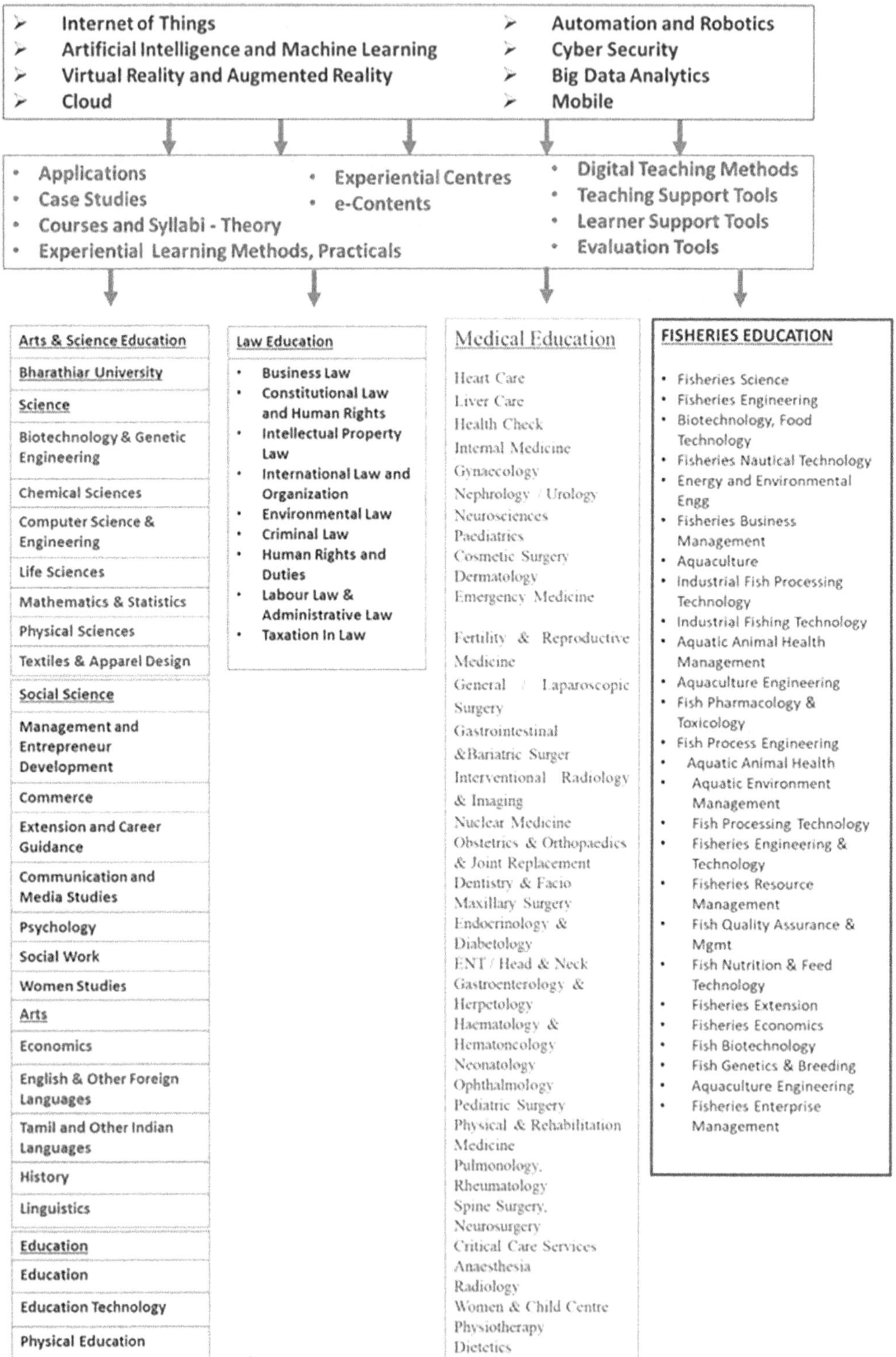

FIGURE 1.2 Education in the era of Industry 4.0.

- Applications of Big Data Analytics in Viral Diseases
- Predictive Data Analytics in Diabetics Care
- Augmented Reality–Based Medical Training
- Artificial Intelligence for Diagnosis
- Big Data Analytics for Personalised Medicine
- Design of AR Courses in Medical Education
- Mobile Apps for Medical Teaching
- Augmented Reality in Training Medical Practitioners
- Robotic Process Automation in Healthcare
- Machine Learning for Healthcare
- Cyber Security in Healthcare

In fisheries Education 4.0, the tools of Industry 4.0 can be applied through design of new courses with syllabi, applications, case studies, teaching support tools, learner support tools and evaluation tools. For example, courses may be as follow.

- Inshore Fisheries Optimisation Using Big Data Analytics
- Fishery Production Prediction Using Predictive analytics
- IoT-based Fisheries Management Systems
- IoT for Aquaculture 4.0
- IoT Technology for the Global Fishing Economy
- Augmented Reality–Based Fisheries Training
- Artificial Intelligence for Successful Fishing
- Sustainable Aquaculture with AI and IoT
- Design of AR Courses in Fisheries Education
- Mobile Apps for Fisheries Teaching
- Augmented Reality in Training Fisheries Practitioners
- Mapping Global Fishing Activity with Machine Learning

Teacher education plays a vital role when digital transformation in education is taking place around the world (Figure 1.3). Teachers are to be given enough training on how to use the technological tools such

Teacher Education

- Pedagogical Sciences
- Value Education
- Educational Psychology
- Educational Technology
- Curriculum Planning & Evaluation
- Educational Planning & Administration

Physical Education and Sports

- Physical Education
- Yoga
- Health Centre
- Sports Management and Sports
- Advanced Sports Training & Technology
- Exercise Psychology & Sociology
- Statistics & Computer Application
- Exercise Physiology & Biomechanics

FIGURE 1.3 Specialisations in universities.

as massive open online courses, learning management systems, digital tools in class room, mobile-based learning tools and assessing using digital technology. When the focus is on linking teacher education with Industry 4.0 through design of new courses with syllabi, applications, case studies, teaching support tools, learner support tools and evaluation tools, the courses may be of the following nature.

- Artificial Intelligence and Modern Teacher Education Technology
- Personalised Learning for All Using Big Data and IoT
- Adaptive Learning Using Machine Learning Techniques
- Learning Analytics in Education Using Big Data Analytics
- Predicative Analytics in Education Using AI
- AI towards Improved Learning and Equity
- Data Analytics in Education Management Systems
- Evolution of Learning Management Systems (LMSs)
- Curriculum for a Digital- and AI-Powered World
- Digital Content Creation
- Creativity and Digital Technlogies
- Computational Thinking
- Massively Open Online Courses (MOOCs)
- Artificial Intelligence in Education: Challenges and Policy Implications
- Challenges in Online Delivery of Lectures
- Framework to Measure Digital Literacy
- Data-Driven Education Systems
- New Curriculum for Industry 4.0–Based Teacher Education
- Computational Thinking in Education
- AI Market in Indian Education
- AI Market in Global Education
- Intelligent Tutoring Systems by and for the Developing World
- IoT applications in Education
- Wearable IoT (Sensor–Based) Devices for Learner Performance Analysis
- Data Analytics and IoT for Predicting Learner's Talent
- IoT–Based Teacher Education Management System
- IoT for Health Management of Teachers and Learners
- IoT Technology for Teacher Education
- Augmented Reality–Based Teacher (Education) Training
- Design of AR Courses in Teacher Education
- Virtual Reality for Learner Training
- Mobile Apps for Teacher Education
- Impact of Education 4.0 on Global Education
- Wearable Technology and Learners
- Student Assessment Using Machine Learning
- Digital Infrastructure for Teacher Education
- Digital Infrastructure for Education 4.0
- Cloud–Based Systems for Education
- Augmented Reality Tools for the Classroom
- IoT Tools for the Classroom
- Open Learning Environment Using Augmented Reality

While linking physical education and sports (Figure 1.3) with Industry 4.0 through design of new courses with syllabi, applications, case studies, teaching support tools, learner support tools and evaluation tools, the courses may be the following.

- Artificial Intelligence and Modern Sports Education Technology
- AI and Individualised Education in Physical Education
- Wearable IoT (Sensor–Based) Devices for Performance Analysis
- Data Analytics and IoT for Predicting Sports Talent
- IoT–Based Physical Education Management System
- IoT for Health Management of Athletes
- IoT Technology for Physical Education
- Augmented Reality–Based Physical Education Training
- Artificial Intelligence for Successful Sports Personality Development
- Sustainable Health with AI and IoT
- Design of AR Courses in Physical Education
- Virtual Reality for Player Training and Fan Engagement
- Mobile Apps for Physical Education
- Augmented Reality in Training Physical Education Practitioners
- Global Sports Analytics with Machine Learning
- Wearable Technology and Athletes

1.3.1 Skill Set Development

Apart from these courses linking Industry 4.0 tools with the domain, the skill set that is to be imparted to students and required to face Jobs 2030 are: critical thinking, people management, emotional intelligence, critical judgement, negotiation, cognitive flexibility, knowledge production and management. Methods and practices to impart and develop these skills to students are also of important concern.

1.3.2 Digital Support Systems

Technological advancements and digital tools have revealed a world of possibilities for higher education institutions. Whether through online learning, VR, MOOCs or AI with its variety of new teaching and learning approaches, higher education has evolved tremendously in the past decade [3]. This rapid evolution has inspired change in many institutions, with universities leveraging new technologies, exploring innovative teaching approaches and implementing meaningful change across their operations. Knowledge on the critical technological advancements that educational institution needs to implement has to be imparted. The advancements may include enterprise resource planning (ERP) for educational institutions, smart classrooms, video conferencing, studios for e-content development and cloud-based delivery systems.

1.4 Education 4.0

Education 4.0 is innovating education in the era of Industry 4.0. Education 4.0 embraces the advanced analytics and uses it to treat each student as an individual, understanding that everyone's learning needs and desired outcomes will be different. The Education 4.0 process adopts each individual student to achieve 5Cs: *communication*, *collaboration*, *competence*, *creativity* and *critical thinking* (Pinnamaneni, 2020). This is only possible using extended reality (XR), whereby the virtual labs can dynamically be changed in such a way that the practical experiments will be aligned to the needs of the industry and the needs of the individual learner, i.e., personalised learning 4.0.

1.4.1 Framework for Bharathiar University Education

While aligning Education 4.0 with Industry 4.0, keeping in mind the university's Vision 2030, the focus has to be on the tools of Industry 4.0. The Fourth Industrial Revolution, Industry 4.0, is already changing the world around us. AI and machine learning, automation and robotics, Big Data, IoT and AR/VR, cybersecurity and mobile computing are its new tools. At the same time, Industry 5.0 has also started influencing daily lives. If Industry 4.0 emerged with automation, smart factories and IoT, Industry 5.0 takes the next step. It involves leveraging the collaboration between increasingly powerful and accurate machinery and the unique creative potential of the human being. Hence, education too has to align with these emerging technologies.

The key elements of realising the ten years vision include: ensure student excellence, achieve sustained academic excellence, ensure faculty excellence, achieve excellence in research and scholarship, enhance international opportunities and experiences for students, achieve sustained staff excellence, ensure excellence in governance and management, and honouring student/institutional diversity. In view of implementing this multi-faceted vision, Bharathiar University has already worked upon and prepared the following framework for Education 4.0.

1.4.2 Curriculum 4.0

When education is spearheading towards Education 4.0, it is inevitable that curriculum revamp follows. It implies quite a variety of aspects such as industry exposure, international exposure, advanced learning pathways, interdisciplinary programmes and digital academic repositories. Ensuring the involvement of industry experts like research and development managers, product development managers, technical managers, etc., as special invitees in board of studies (BoS) can ensure that the curriculum prepared stands up to date with industry requirements. With their expertise and experience in industry, these experts can ensure that the curriculum incorporates the latest know-how which enables students to be industry-ready. International exposure provides a global outlook to the students and helps them to come out of their limited outlook and restricted views. There are a variety of learning pathways like experiential learning, case study–based approach, problem-solving approach, practicals, team-based project work, etc., incorporated into the syllabus to stand instead of the traditional classroom approach, which exploits the digital skills of the current generation and keeps them engaged and interesting. Revised curriculum also includes the use of ICT, e-learning resources and self-learning courses, and encourages the teaching modes of blended learning, digital and online learning, etc. Another aspect of the new curriculum is the increased importance given to field-based training, internship, visits to industries and projects. The new curriculum promotes multiple approaches of learning and the portions where these approaches are to be used are clearly mentioned.

The new curriculum of Bharathiar University has an industry component in all its undergraduate and post-graduate programmes. It has also integrated interdisciplinary programmes so that the versatile skill set of students can be polished and they gain expertise in whatever areas they are interested in. Though there are many digital academic repositories available now at the click of a mouse, their potential has to be leveraged. Bharathiar University is in the process of digital content development by building a repository of curricular materials and learning resources on its own. Credits are given for certificate programmes and training in skills required for global competency also are included in the new curriculum.

1.4.3 Faculty Development

Faculty development for Education 4.0 envisions continuous professional development and induction programmes for all the faculty. They will be encouraged to obtain industrial exposure to enhance their skills and align them with recent trends and advancements in the industry. They will be provided training for digital content development, thus equipping themselves with the resources they need. Faculty will be motivated to earn global reachability and global recognition and they will be provided training for attaining global competency skills. Moreover, faculty will have options to improve themselves based on student feedback and peer assessment. The output of student satisfaction surveys also will be a motivator to the faculty for improvement and upgradation.

FIGURE 1.4 Model Framework for Education 4.0 at Bharathiar University.

1.4.4 Importance of Industrial Collaboration

Bharathiar University considers industrial collaboration as an important component in its framework for Education 4.0, and industry interface is hence given sufficient importance in is curriculum. Collaborating with industries enables to systematically include additional development and training for students. It is essential to prepare the students with new skills and competencies to ensure they remain relevant and are able to thrive in the digital era. Bharathiar University is aware of the fact that a mismatch of skills required by the industry has always been the root of unemployment of many graduates. That is the reason why academia-industry linkages for academic engagement via curriculum, lectures and internships are promoted. By working on projects from the industry, students develop critical skills including teamwork, creativity, communication and critical thinking. Moreover, by infusing industry-based skills into education, the university ensure that students gain the practical know-how to match theories, and they graduate with a holistic view of the specialisations provided.

1.5 Conclusions

The Fourth Industrial Revolution, Industry 4.0, is tremendously changing the world around us. Students are to be equipped to face, embrace and live in this new technology which envisions the need for Education 4.0 to be at par with Industry 4.0. Though Industry 4.0 was suggested only for the manufacturing industry, today the presence of powerful networks, sensors and devices force universities to prepare students to face the unprecedented and uncertain future world. Hence it is imperative that universities design guidelines for Curriculum 4.0 and prepare new syllabi for all subjects intertwining Industry 4.0 tools onto various disciplines such as science, social science, arts and education. This chapter has detailed the education in the era of Industry 4.0 and 5.0, and introduced a framework for Education 4.0 which can be used as a model for universities and colleges across the globe.

REFERENCES

1. PN_HED, https://cms.tn.gov.in/sites/default/files/documents/hedu_e_pn_2019_20.pdf, Policy Note of Higher Education Department—2019–2020, 27.4.2020.
2. UGC, www.ugc.ac.in/stateuniversitylist.aspx?id=31&Unitype=2, UGC Website, 28.4.2020.
3. www.qs.com
4. Pinnamaneni Bhanu Prasad, Discussions on Industry 4.0 and 5.0 with Pinnamaneni, Bharathiar University, Coimbatore, 2020.

2

Student Talent Management in the Era of Industry 4.0

M. Dhanabhakyam

CONTENTS

Objectives

1. To prepare students for Industry 4.0 through efficient management of their *versatile talents.*
2. To focus on *talent identification*, *deployment*, and *development* strategies specific to Industry 4.0.
3. To address the *challenges* in managing students' talent.
4. To discuss the possibilities and *emerging technologies* in classroom talent management.
5. To develop *case study*–based discussions on the relevance of talent management among students for Industry 4.0.

DOI: 10.1201/9781003318378-2

2.1 Introduction

The world is continuously evolving to face unprecedented growth and challenges. The changes from animal to human beings are further moving into the human to human-less environment and workplaces. Mechanization, globalization, and increased knowledge mobility and portability have already fueled the growth of Industry 4.0 in many developed economies. This phase of industrial revolution induces massive transformations in analyzing data across machines, efficient and flexible production standards necessitating massive modifications in the profile of the workplace. Industry 4.0 upholds different sets of skills and capabilities for enhancing the candidate's competencies across regions and companies. Major technologies transforming in Industry 4.0 include Big Data analytics, autonomous robots, simulations, horizontal and vertical system integration, the industrial Internet of Things (IoT), cybersecurity, cloud, additive manufacturing, augmented reality, etc. (Boston Consultancy Group). To build and sustain in Industry 4.0, employers demand candidates with high practical knowledge about digital technologies equipped with state-of-the-art talent system.

Managing the talent of the students prima facie involves bringing tremendous change in the skill sets and capabilities of the budding employees to make them adapt to the changing work culture (Ejovwokeoghene et al., 2018). The concept of managing talent among students aims at creating a talent pool attractive to employers across the globe. Student talent which varies across the humanistic and demographic perspective needs to be pumped as high performers for Industry 4.0. Talent management in educational institutions sought to produce highly competent performers that cater to specific organizational needs. The major aim of student talent management is to enable steady employability that can bring tantamount changes in organizational performance, either through immediate contribution or in the long term by demonstrating high levels of potential. Talent management acts as an espoused and enacted commitment in implementing integrated, strategic, and technology-enabled approaches to managing the inherent talent of students to face the prospects and challenges of Industry 4.0 (Daubner-Siva, 2018). Talented students are the primary source of competitive advantage for educational institutions. Thus, efforts of educational institutions should be on producing students to occupy the upcoming challenges in emerging workplaces.

This chapter attracts relevance for the emphasis it delves in. Education is the major sector in India that lacks thoughtful reforms and amplified pedagogies for the overall development of the child. The stakeholders of higher educational institutions are very often fascinated by the precocious benefits of technology and the jubilation of Western methods. We lack a congruent methodology to address the needs of Industry 4.0 in a more lucrative and legitimate style (Whysall et al., 2019). Rather than being a bandwagon of Western cultures, it is high time for higher educational institutions to develop their specific talent pools with broad focus on the needs of changing industries.

2.2 The need for Student Talent Management in the Era of Industry 4.0

Managing the talent of students should aim at a high level of practical engagement, focusing on the surfacing needs of Industry 4.0. Talent management endorses an undifferentiated approach toward students that manages the capabilities and skills of all students alike. Further, talent management based in educational institutions should dwell on teachings of inclusivity. Exclusive talent strategies will result in in-group favoritism and in-group bolstering among students which may have unintended consequences over student performance (Claus, 2019). Exclusive talent philosophies may result in self-prophecy of declining competence and derailed training and development initiatives. Talent management interventions inclusive of all students overcome the cultural and systematic issues involved in talent development, whereas the principle of exclusivity leads to a culture of arrogance, invincibility, and poor decision making among students. The need for a robust system of talent management among students is highlighted in what follows.

1. Talent management helps to align learning and development activities that complement the strategic business needs and demands. It also offers a diversification of learning delivery options among students, such as e-learning, m-learning, and electronic performance support systems.

2. Managing talent concentrates on achieving efficiency and responsiveness among students through streamlining developmental interventions. Talent management realizes the interdependency between learning and work, thereby improving compliance measures.
3. Talent management ensures sustainable progress among the students, whereby the major aim is the creation of value among all students. Talent management is viewed as a collective endeavor of all faculties and students that requires conjoint actions to conquer the workplace of Industry 4.0. It ensures dependence, interdependence, and mutuality among all parties concerned in this process. Talent management drives a process called talent which drives fruitful and mutually beneficial interaction between students and between students and teachers.
4. Talent management is fundamentally a new approach that points toward managing uncertainties in the future. Industry 4.0, with its multipurpose nature of demand, is highly uncertain regarding the quality of manpower it requires. Talent management is not an end in itself but rather aids in achieving broader objectives of higher educations which includes the employability of its wards (Painter-Morland et al., 2019).
5. Talent management assists in just-in-time production of talent in demand according to the needs of Industry 4.0. This talent-on-demand framework is further driven by the operations-based tools that are customized for meeting changing needs. Talent management remains focused on various elements that drive efficiencies and excellence among the students.
6. Talent management acts as an advisor to the faculties, mentors, and university administrators by providing insights about students regarding their emotional connections and their behaviors. In other words, talent management also helps the educational institutions to manage emotional wallets among students which are necessary for the current workplace.
7. Talent management also aims at enhancing the professional competencies among the students and make them ready for Industry 4.0. Professional competencies include various technical and functional knowledge regarding Industry 4.0, skills, time management, conflict resolution, executive development, and the capabilities that the students need to develop for the transformed workplaces (Schreuder & Noorman, 2019).
8. Moreover, talent management assists the educational institutions to emerge as a talent hub of students. Successful educational institutions emerge as a talent brand which is most preferred by the employers during Industry 4.0. This upgrades the educational institution's image as an ideal learning place for the students, domestically and globally. Those institutions that endorse their value, image, and prestige to develop the student's talent through internal and external talent branding emerge as learning centers of high repute. Internal branding deals with the identification of inherent talent among students and developing them, whereas external branding involving attracting prospective employers to recruit their students.
9. Prudent talent management framework helps in developing a student community with inimitable human capital. The focus of talent management should be on fulfilling the needs and expectations of their students and developing them through continuous learning and career development opportunities.
10. Offering a congruent talent management framework makes the students enthusiastic, and they start to reciprocate emerging as a valuable asset to the educational institutions and resonate the same in the job market specifically Industry 4.0. Universities must act as brand representatives, deliver brand promises, and shape the educational institution as a talent hub, which adds to the competitive advantage of the whole economy.

Thus, it is evident that the present education system requires a choiceful revamping of its existing pedagogy and should infuse the latest skill among the students to be successful in Industry 4.0. According to the World Economic Forum's "Future of Jobs" reports, there exists a drastic difference in the various skill set in demand across 2015 and 2020. Table 2.1 lists some of the key differences in required competencies.

Table 2.1 highlights the need for managing student talent in the wake of Industry 4.0. The students become what they see, what they think, and finally what they are taught. The complex and technology-oriented Education 4.0 can be achieved only through managing the holistic talent of all the students

TABLE 2.1

Difference in Required Skills and Competence over Five Years

SI No.	2020	2015
1	Critical thinking	Thinking
2	Creativity	Herd behavior
3	People management	Money management
4	Coordinating with others	Self-sustenance
5	Emotional intelligence	Intelligence quotient
6	Judgment and decision making	Relying on information
7	Service orientation	Extrinsic support
8	Negotiation	Active listening
9	Cognitive flexibility	Quality control

Source: "Future of Jobs" reports, World Economic Forum

from their basic-level education. Education 4.0 should aim at improving the specific skills of the students which will be in demand for a longer period of time. The management of student talent is not an easy approach for the kind of diversity and skill embedded in the student community. Hence, this chapter paves a road forward in building a strong and sustainable talent management culture in the educational institutions that incentivize the student talent and assist them in succeeding in the tough blocks of Industry 4.0.

2.3 Talent Management Strategies for Students

The unprecedented pace and velocity of changes offered by Industry 4.0 offer both boon and bane regarding the employability of the graduates, and it outpaces the individual ability to adapt. The changes created by Industry 4.0 are considered as a perfect storm in the workplace in which candidates without skills, competencies, and talent will easily get washed away. The work environment under Industry 4.0 will be constantly changing, highly challenging, and complex in nature. The educational institutions and government have the onus of promoting talent management among the students, thereby making them attractive and wanted by major employers. The proposed talent management system consists of a broad mindset and considerations on talent identification, deployment and development of students.

2.3.1 Talent Identification among Students

This process forms the foundation for managing talent among the students. A comprehensive talent identification process is based on two major elements: the performance and potential of the students (Shahi et al., 2020). Effective talent identification and assessment strategy should be adopted by the educational institutions, as it helps in designing the developmental interventions among the students. This process must be considered as a dynamic and ongoing process, and it should not simply be viewed as a student labeling process.

2.3.1.1 Performance Management and Potential Identification

In a well-defined performance management system, the mentor or the faculty focused on the goal setting undertakes unbiased evaluation of the student's performance within a coherent unified framework that aims to align and balance between the existing curriculums and Industry 4.0. Performance management should be done concretely with a thorough student evaluation, and it should be executed on a three-layer basis: the actual result achieved by the student should be compared with their preset targets to identify any major deviations. The responsibility quotient applied by the students apart from achieving their goals should be also assessed to determine their level of commitment. Finally, faculties should also assess the conditionality under which the results were achieved by the students.

Potential identification involves the systematic determination of whether the students have the capabilities or potential for advancement in a career relating to Industry 4.0. It also measures the responsibility of managing ability and technical expertise among the students relating to Industry 4.0. In other words, potential identification helps the institution to evaluate and understand the needs of the students based on what they have and what they lack. Potential identification can be done based on contextual factors including student performance, prior knowledge, knowledge mobility, and demographics. The judgment factors include the speed of work completion by students, specific talents among them, and their destination targets. Finally, the content domain includes personality, motivation, leadership competencies, functional knowledge, values, etc.

2.3.2 Talent Deployment Strategies

This part ensures talent mobility and talent autonomy for all learners. Talent deployment is concerned with the application of identified talent among the students for their success in Industry 4.0. As globalization accelerates the need for talent rises worldwide, teachers and institutional authorities should develop the application possibilities of their inherent talent. The major solution for effective talent deployment focuses on the principle of inclusive talent management. Teachers should focus on the inclusivity and talent development of all the students, rather than focusing on very few 'high performers' and start talents (Gallardo-Gallardo et al., 2020). The development of an inclusive talent atmosphere also leads to an effective psychological contract between the students and between the students and the teachers. No two persons have some potential and capability level,; hence, the teachers should ensure a tailor-made approach in managing the capabilities of students. The principle of inclusivity caters to the needs of all category students, regardless of the talent they pose (Daubner-Siva et al., 2017).

2.3.3 Talent Development Strategies

The most successful talent development process is the one that is customized for each student and integrated according to the needs of Industry 4.0. The talent developmental initiatives should be designed based on the needs of the industry, the behavior of students, and the demands of prospective employers. The educational institutions should devoid themselves from relying on managing the student talent in a most simple manner, neglecting the long-term benefits. Any development initiative should balance impact and simplicity with science and data. The talent development of students should consist of five major factors: developmental relationships, developmental assignments, formal programs, feedback activities, and self-development activities.

2.3.3.1 Developmental Relationships

The talent management activities in educational institutions should focus on a healthy relationship between the students and teachers. This healthy relationship can be achieved through mentoring and coaching activities. The teachers should act as a mentor in delivering necessary knowledge among the students. The institutions can rely on both internal mentoring and external mentoring. The institutions should rely on extensive coaching to prepare the students for Industry 4.0. Coaching should unleash the practical knowledge need to work in a technology-oriented workplace. One-to-one coaching should be provided to the students to train them to face the challenges in the workplace.

2.3.3.2 Developmental Assignments

Learning should be the prime focus of the activities included in the developmental assignments. There should be rotations in the activities given to students. They must be exposed to various tasks that involve risk-taking, responsibility management, and emotional involvement. Project assignment is another initiative that relies on student talent development. The students should be provided assignments and projects with attainable deadlines that offer an insight into Industry 4.0. The institutions should also engage in student exchange programs that enable collaborations with institutes of national reputation and international institutions. The student exchange programs will facilitate the students to acquire standardized knowledge and global exposure.

2.3.3.3 Formal Programs

Formal programs include the executive education system and training interventions by the educational institutions. The executive education system should prepare the students for vertical and horizontal career movement in the phase of Industry 4.0. Apart from the traditional routine education process, teachers should focus on developing the students particularly for enjoying the benefits of Industry 4.0 through Education 4.0. Students should also be introduced to both formal and informal training programs focusing on individual change management for sustained performance during their careers.

2.3.3.4 Feedback Process

This is an effective process while developing talent among students. Proper talent reviews must be conducted periodically that evaluate the progress and performance of the students in the talent development process. These results should be communicated to the students periodically. An effective feedback system helps the students to regularize and standardize their performance, thereby resulting in appropriate goal setting. The teachers should exercise due care to consider both positive and negative feedback hand in hand, thereby facilitating both the personality and emotional development of the students.

2.3.3.5 Self-Development Activities

Educational institutions should offer self-development activities such as personality development, emotional management, stress management, anger management, yoga, meditation, etc., that have a positive contribution toward the talent development of the students. Entertainment and refreshers should also be made part of the curriculum as these offer intrinsic motivation to achieve more. The workplace created by Industry 4.0 is not just machinery and a human-less environment, but it necessitates a high degree of emotional regulation among the employees. Students should be trained to evaluate themselves not in terms of marks only, but also in terms of their potential talents.

Figure 2.1 posturizes the mapping of elements in Industry 4.0 and Education 4.0. A sudden shift to Education 4.0 seems practically impossible, but universities and colleges should take considerable efforts

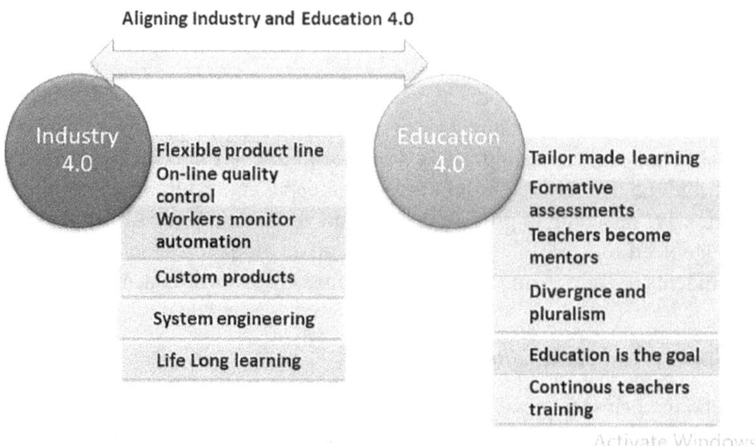

FIGURE 2.1 Aligning Industry 4.0 and Education 4.0: the path ahead.

to tap the potential of their young talents who are already fascinated by the latest technologies. Managing student talent is—to a great extent—a psychological phenomenon that should be exercised with much caution to avoid its debilitating and irreversible impacts (Rotolo et al., 2018).

2.4 Addressing the Challenges of Talent Management in Industry 4.0

The ways in which workplaces get transformed in Industry 4.0 pose a serious challenge in ensuring leak-proof talent development among the students. The velocities within which the changes are happening globally make bewildering the kind of talent management activities to be adopted for the students. These very often create a skill and capability gap among the students, prompting more effective and proactive talent management initiatives. Confronting these challenges suggests the need for the evolution of talent management practices in the classroom, enabling all the students to keep up with technological changes. Common challenges of talent management and coping mechanisms are discussed in the following subsections.

2.4.1 Critical Skill Shortages

Industry 4.0 comes with rapidly plugging resource gaps in the industries, as it involves technologies that combine the physical, biological, and digital worlds impacting several disciplines across the landscape. The major concern of universities will be on developing app developers, cloud computing specialists, data scientists, drone operators, driverless car engine designers, and the like, which were not even in existence a decade ago. The authorities should extend faculty enrichment programs on the developmental initiatives of Industry 4.0 through which necessary training can be provided to the student community. Mentoring by the drivers of Industry 4.0 and successful entrepreneurs should be initiated periodically that boosts the mental capabilities among the students. The universities should adopt an internal talent network system and holistic talent management practices.

2.4.2 Identification of Critical Talent for Industry 4.0

Industry 4.0 which is characterized by the global knowledge economy does not specify which type of talent is reflected as critical for the employability of the student. Some industries consider 'high performers' as talented, whereas filling 'pivotal positions for competitive advantage' is considered as talent management by a few. The kinds of positions that are considered strategically important within the ambits of Industry 4.0 are still unclear. The only viable solution is that the universities and colleges must rely highly on internal talent development activities that focus on the paradigm shift relating to Industry 4.0.

2.4.3 New Core Competencies

Industry 4.0 requires a new set of competencies that even the trainers and teachers are ill-equipped to teach. Students should be imparted a new kind of mindset and skill set, and a broader set of competencies beyond the usual academic technological know-how. Industry 4.0 readiness demands cross-discipline and interdisciplinary interactions between university departments. Some of the core competencies expected in the Industry 4.0 job market include commerciality, client management skills, relationship and communication skills, collaboration, system thinking, and a strong external market focus.

2.4.4 Pivotal Talent Management—The Neglected Medium Students

It is quite common to have in-group favoritism among students and between students and teachers that will hamper the talent development process. If the teachers consider exclusivity philosophy in talent development, only 'high performers' in classrooms will be considered talented, with the inherent potential for mediocre students to be neglected and thereby having a negative consequence on their psychological contracts. There can be growing divisions in the classrooms between 'best performers', 'average students', and the 'poor wards'. The concept of cross-functional mobility should be made familiar between all clusters of students to achieve the visions of Education 4.0 and to face the challenges of Industry 4.0.

2.4.5 Transforming Talent Management

Teachers or mentors sometimes have the fallacy of focusing on current performance, neglecting long-term efficiency. Sometimes satisfactory delivery of projects in the immediate term was more embraced than the student's capability for the long-term benefit. The teachers should motivate the students to think beyond deadlines, beyond time, and to think strategically. The teachers should strive to achieve a shift from short-term tactical resources to long-term strategic resources. The higher educational institution should ultimately build a strong talent pipeline, which encourages the students to take appropriate risks for the benefit of their long-term development. Student recognition should be considered as an integrated approach to talent development (Moghaddas et al., 2020).

2.5 Emerging Technologies for Classroom Talent Management Activities

The learning styles and expectations of the present and upcoming generations of students are far different from those of their predecessors. Technology has shaped how the students will learn and process available information. Along with a well-structured curriculum, teamwork and experiential activities of the educational institutions should add technology-based learning, entertainment, and excitement in Industry 4.0–oriented training. Technology should be used to reflect the real-world activities of Industry 4.0 which make the curriculum customizable and flexible.

2.5.1 Audiovisual Interfaces

Educational institutions should utilize the latest technology to deliver audiovisual-rich content to the learners, and multi-tasking challenges requiring a collaborative approach. Mentoring and training sessions can also be handled through this audiovisual platform to enrich student experience and knowledge.

2.5.2 PaaS (Platform-as-a-Service) for Talent Management

Plateau system is the first PaaS for the talent management industry, launched by Heath Williams in Europe. Similarly, higher educational institutions should implement PaaS-oriented talent management systems to prepare the students for Industry 4.0. These solutions must have the functional breadth and flexibility to build, manage, and develop student skills. This platform must be designed to induce specific competencies and fill the skill gap emerging in Industry 4.0. This will help the educational institutions in making the right sort of progress at the right time.

2.5.3 Artificial Intelligence–Powered On-Demand Talent Platforms

Rather than using artificial intelligence platforms for plug and play purposes, the students must be trained for rapid prototyping, iterative feedback, working in multidisciplinary teams of Industry 4.0. These types of technologies will assist the students in managing agility in the transformed workplaces.

2.5.4 Gaming among Students

The educational institution should manage to develop talent-based games that focus on shaping and re-engineering the inherent talent among students. The games should be designed and developed in such a way that it induces critical thinking and problem-solving skills among the students. Gaming also involves a high level of engagement among the students with necessary deadlines. The games can also be developed using AI-based technologies.

2.5.5 Talent Management Software and Applications

Talent management software helps students to accurately manage, develop, and evaluate their talent with increased mobility and simplicity. The educational institutions can either offer all talent management interventions and methodologies in one platform or develop separate software for training, student engagement and student recognition, etc. Some of the talent management software prominent among corporates include BizMerlin, CEIPAL Talent Hire, Appreiz, etc.

2.6 Case Studies

2.6.1 Bharat Heavy Electrical Limited (BHEL)

BHEL is a public company under Navaratna status in India. Like other Navaratna Companies, BHEL also competes based on their employability skills and their excellence in delivery services. The mission statement of the company emphasizes enhancing value to their employees for achieving the dual objectives of business quality and quality of work/life to the employees. The changing landscape in the labor market—including the phenomenal changes in the quality of labor with the advent of millennial workers—had posed a major challenge to the human resource management of the company. The exponential changes in the labor market are always a cause of worry in the public sector enterprises, especially regarding employee retention. BHEL, recognized for its huge investment in training and development activities adopted a well-defined talent management process that combines the needs of all silos of the workforce. Moreover, talent interventions at BHEL are a combination of the following recruitment and sound retention strategies.

1. Balance scorecards and e-maps: Each department in BHEL approves its balanced scorecard to evaluate the performance of the employees to achieve its operational objectives. Balance scorecards act as an effective evaluation tool that focuses on four parameters: customers, business process, learning, and growth.
2. Online performance planning: This platform offers online communication of objectives, goals, and performance targets for each employee, and continuous feedback to improve their performance.
3. Performance counseling and final review: This acts as a vital component of the company's talent management system in which the supervisor continuously monitors the performance of the employees and closely checks for any deviations and related solutions if necessary.
4. Reward system: BHEL implements an active reward payment system which acts as a major motivation for the employees. Apart from this, the company has leadership development programs, individual-level competency mapping, participation of employees in important meetings, etc. The company also adopts vigorous knowledge management and knowledge transfer systems. An intranet-based service is available in all departments to share best practices, alternative solutions, etc.

BHEL considers talent management as a strategic business priority rather than as a talent management intervention. The sophisticated talent management interventions target the retention of employees for the development of the company.

2.6.2 ICICI Bank

Major private financial institution ICICI Bank has nourished a healthy talent management atmosphere. The bank has succeeded in developing a talent pool and a well-defined leadership pipeline. The talent

FIGURE 2.2 Kamath model of talent management in ICICI bank.

management process established by the founder CEO and MD K.V. Kamath had led the bank ahead in managing its human resources. The talent management process in the bank was centered on two major human resource interventions: leadership development and mentoring of young talent. Pioneering the formal leadership development process, the bank emphasized a robust talent screening process. With the number of employees rising and the bank expanding to various national and international markets, efficient talent screening was the only viable way to recruit talented employees. Since the onus for selection of potential leaders was on top management, talent screening was considered as a way to list and spot the leadership talent. In ICICI Bank, mentoring was used as a major tool to channelize the talent of the younger generation.

Along with mentoring, succession planning was used as a major tool to groom the employees for future roles. While the formal leadership development system was effectively in place to nourish the talent of young professionals at the bank, ICICI Bank also took responsibility in developing people to the senior management levels. For instance, ICICI Bank came up with a new leadership program called 'Mentoring the Mentors' for professionals at the senior management level which offered tremendous possibilities to the employees of all levels to become the best leaders of the future. The program aimed to hone the mentoring abilities of professionals so that they stay longer with the organization and the organization can gain maximum advantage. To accentuate better mentoring, the bank also invites corporate elites from other sectors to share their paths to success and the secret behind them. To date, the bank believes that despite being in global exposure due to many crises, it is commitment to its employees is that keeps them leaping ahead.

REFERENCES

Brian Elliott., & Boston Consulting Group. (2020). Revolutionizing how we work.

Claus, L. (2019). HR disruption—Time already to reinvent talent management. *BRQ Business Research Quarterly*, *22*(3), 207–215.

Daubner-Siva, D. (2018). The talent paradox: Talent management as a mixed blessing. *Journal of Organizational Ethnography*, *7*(1), 74–86.

Daubner-Siva, D., Vinkenburg, C. J., & Jansen, P. G. W. (2017). Dovetailing talent management and diversity management: The exclusion-inclusion paradox. *Journal of Organizational Effectiveness: People and Performance*, *4*(4), 315–331.

Ejovwokeoghene, M., A, Oluseye Ogunnaike, O., & Oluseye, O. (2018). Talent management as a determinant of firm performance : A conceptual approach. *Business and Social Science Journal*, *3*(1), 21–32.

Gallardo-Gallardo, E., Thunnissen, M., & Scullion, H. (2020). Talent management: Context matters. *International Journal of Human Resource Management*, *31*(4), 457–473.

Moghaddas, A., Jajarmizadeh, M., & Abbasi, N. (2020). Investigating relationship between talent management and human resource productivity with the mediation role of organizational creativity in ABFA. *International Journal of Management, Accounting & Economics*, *7*(1), 20–29.

Painter-Morland, M., Kirk, S., Deslandes, G., & Tansley, C. (2019). Talent management: The good, the bad, and the possible. *European Management Review*, *16*(1), 135–146.

Rotolo, C. T., Church, A. H., Adler, S., Smither, J. W., Colquitt, A. L., Shull, A. C., . . . Foster, G. (2018). Putting an end to bad talent management: A call to action for the field of industrial and organizational psychology. *Industrial and Organizational Psychology*, *11*(2), 176–219.

Schreuder, R., & Noorman, S. (2019). Strategic talent management: Creating strategic value by placing top talents in key positions. *Development and Learning in Organizations*, *33*(1), 1–4.

Shahi, T., Farrokhsheresht, B., Taghipourian, M. J., & Aghajani, H. A. (2020). Behavioral factors affecting talent management: Meta-synthesis technique. *Iranian Journal of Management Studies*, *13*(1), 117–137.

Whysall, Z., Owtram, M., Brittain, S., Whysall, Z., Owtram, M., & Brittain, S. (2019). The new talent management challenges of industry 4.0. *Journal of Management Development*, *38*(2), 118–129.

World Economic Forum, "The Future of Job Reports", October 2020.

3

Latest Technological Innovations for the Virtual Classroom: Empowering the Learners

P. B. Pankajavalli, G. S. Karthick and N. Priya

CONTENTS

DOI: 10.1201/9781003318378-3

Objectives

1. To explore how recent technologies influenced the learning environment.
2. To illustrate the importance and usage of the latest technologies that changed learning mechanisms.
3. To highlight the implications of artificial intelligence and machine learning in the education domain.
4. To exemplify how augmented reality and virtual reality transformed the education platforms.
5. To signify the importance of social media in education.

3.1 Introduction

In today's world, ideas spread fast and wide. Technological advancements have allowed hardware companies to produce affordable laptops, tablets, and other devices that are explicitly designed to meet specific educational needs. Further, intense competition has pushed them to create products with cutting-edge technology at a rapid pace. Many cutting-edge technologies are ruling today's learning domain. The further sections in this chapter will cover a few of those cutting-edge technologies

1. Virtual reality in education
2. Artificial intelligence and machine learning
3. Social media in education
4. Augmented reality
5. Multi-touch LCD screens
6. Game-based learning

3.2 Virtual Reality in Education

Virtual Reality (VR) works on the premise of creating a virtual world that can be real or imagined. The users can see it and also interact with it. VR uses computer technology to simulate an environment. In it, the users are immersed in a virtual world with which they can interact. It stimulates senses such as vision, touch, hearing, and even smell. It simulates a real environment in a convincing manner (Babich, 2019).

It enhances the learning process by immersing the learner in whatever they are learning. Not only does it help the learner understand even the most complex subjects, but it also requires less cognitive load to process the information (MacGillivray, 2017).

Whatever the student learns, they wish to experience it. When a student wants to learn about a place, VR facilitates learning by literally allowing the student to live in that place. This remarkably engages the mind. This virtual experiential learning can revolutionize the teaching and learning processes.

Following are some ways that VR can be used in education.

3.2.1 Field Trips

Many educational institutes have started using the Google Expedition app to transport students to far away and hard-to-get places. This app is a free download and is available for iOS or Android operating systems. Inexpensive headphones or earbuds can be attached to the smartphone for audio. With this, the students can feel far-off places such as the polar regions, historical monuments, space, and even the deep sea. It is an effective way to learn about different places (Hernandez, 2019).

3.2.2 Training in Different Skills

Practical skills can be learned effectively using VR. The students can learn from realistic scenarios, which also negates any risk involved while learning an unfamiliar skill in an uncontrolled real-life situation. In an experiment carried out by Google's Daydream labs, it was found that students who used VR learned much faster than those who did not. This interactive experiment attempted to teach coffee making using a YouTube video and VR with two sets of students. After the training, which allowed the students to train as long as they liked, the students from both groups were asked to make coffee in real life. It was found that the group that used VR performed better and was quicker than the group that did not use VR.

3.2.3 Language Learning

Immersion is one of the best and quickest ways to learn a new language. Since it is impossible for most to go to a different country to immerse themselves in learning a new language, VR is the best option. It provides a simulated immersion that tricks the brain into believing that the experiences are real. Nowadays, several language learning apps that use VR have been developed. One such app is the Unimersiv. When paired with an Oculus Rift headset, it allows the user to interact with people worldwide and practice language skills while playing games and connecting with others in a virtual world.

3.2.4 Design and Architecture

VR is a great way to ignite a student's creativity. It is engaging and beneficial when it comes to design and architecture. It opens up many possibilities in this field. The plans of the students can be brought to life using Oculus Rift hardware. In Ireland, students of a school have been using VR to construct historical Irish sites and visit them virtually.

3.2.5 Distance Education

VR has immense potential in distance education. In a recent study conducted by Penn State University researchers, it was found that VR improved learning outcomes for online students. Stanford School of Business offers a certificate program delivered entirely through VR. Students at the University of British Columbia Law School enjoy virtual lectures using a VR social application called VR Chat. This app, along with a VR headset, allows students to project themselves virtually and interact with lecturers and other students in the virtual online chat spaces (Stenger, 2017).

3.2.6 Improved Student-Teacher Collaboration

Student-teacher collaboration is greatly enhanced in both classroom-based and distance learning with the use of VR technology. Research indicates that virtual and AR simulations increase student motivation and improve collaboration and knowledge. Second Life, a study conducted in the virtual world, allowed teachers to design, create, and use collaborative activities to introduce exchange students to the Chinese language and culture before they went to China. This helped students show improvement in their language skills and supported better social interaction between students when they went to China.

3.2.7 Learning through Games

Games are engaging and motivation of the learner. VR will revolutionize this area by taking this to the next level. Jane Wilde, an instructor at Marlboro College in Vermont, has been using games and simulations in her lessons for quite some time (Maseko, 2019). Her observations reveal that VR being fun and engaging, can make a substantial difference to learning outcomes.

3.3 Artificial Intelligence and Machine Learning

3.3.1 Implications of Artificial Intelligence in Education

Artificial intelligence (AI) has been analyzed in the context of education for about fifty years, and it is initiated into the education stream as a core curriculum. AI has improved the online tutoring and teacher training system. Today, education-based AI applications are increasing exponentially in the context of education. An AI-driven system is designed with personalized instructions and dialogues to facilitate the educators in teaching aspects. AI assists in learning, supporting services through chatbots, analyzing the writing skill of the students, and tutor-matching systems for students, and offers a game-based atmosphere. One-to-one interaction and the whole school system are also made by AI to conveniently facilitate the learning process through gadgets. In education, AI has played a prominent role and has also enhanced the practices of learning and teaching.

In the context of educational analysis, (Holmes et al., 2019) shows that every student poses unique characteristics and suffers from learning difficulties. To offer appropriate teaching methods for students with learning issues and the identification of exact features of every individual student is a complex process for a teacher. The computer-assisted environment offers educational analysis in a regular school environment. An expert system is employed in analyzing the students based on the data and recommends an appropriate teaching scheme. The academic skills and progression history of the student are taken into account for the analysis by an expert system. The expert system provides complete guidance to the teacher across various learning stages of the student, and the skill sets of the students are also improved in the process.

The AI-based education system is an innovative and derivative approach. It also uses the methodologies and theories from the field of cognitive science. AI tools support the teaching and learning processes based on cognitive behavior. Through learning science, the learning process and other related issues are investigated, and decision-making is accomplished. A newly developed educational approach is applied directly in the environment of the classroom, whether or not AI is determined with the help of learning science. For example, problem-solving behavior and the misconception identification of the student is an unknown factor for educators. Educators and researchers started to observe the learning process of students, and it, in turn, played a major role in the learning outcome.

The AI-based education system provides coaching in any individual area. For example, in in-game playing, the information related to the situation is initiated, which provides coaching on a particular ability, the required solving strategy, and required manipulation behavior for the environment. The reasoning knowledge of the student is improved with questioning and through discussion. The activity responses of the students are tested to identify the misconceptions of the student. The main intent behind AI in the education system is to develop the learning process and the observational behavior of the students, according to Jones (1985).

3.3.2 Machine Learning

From the perspective of AI, a complete set of rules is stored in the system, and the rules are used in performing a complete task that exactly follows the set rules. In machine learning, algorithms are programmed for performing the task. In other words, it will learn the situation and perform accordingly. In machine learning, the novel outcome is predicted from a huge amount of input data and programming. Direct commands for decision-making are not permitted in this system, and it allows the system to learn the nature of the data for making any decision. The outline of machine learning with the AI data is explained in Figure 3.1.

Machine learning algorithms examine data to discover the nature of the patterns and to design a model that is then incorporated into the system to predict the needed future values. The process of

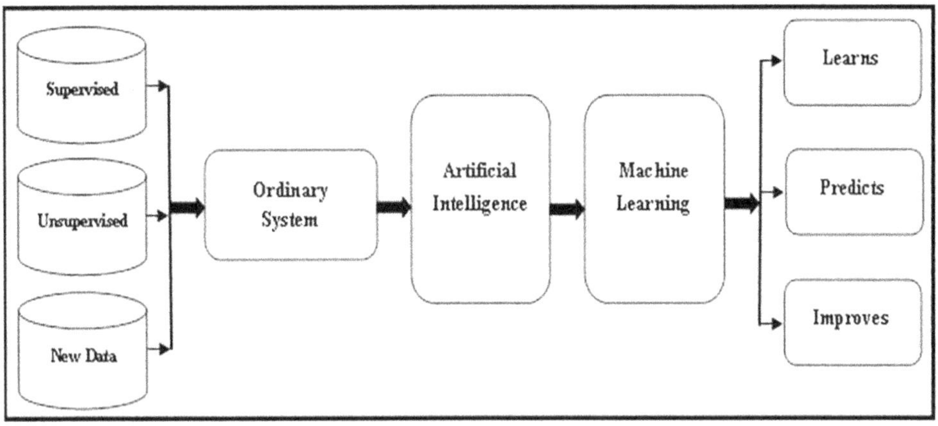

FIGURE 3.1 Outline of a machine learning system with AI.

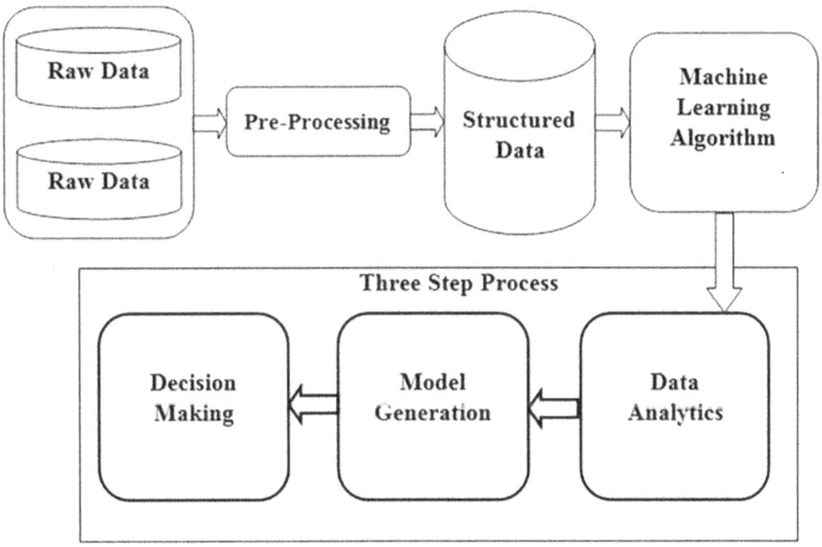

FIGURE 3.2 Three-step process of a machine learning algorithm.

machine learning is composed of three steps; they are data analysis, construction of the model, and undertaking a decision which is shown in Figure 3.2. In the first step, the input data is learned, and the relevant model is constructed. In the subsequent process, decisions are made from the completed model.

Many of the current applications are developed based on machine learning algorithms such as self-driving cars, AlphaGo and Google's DeepMind. Machine learning and AI act in a synchronous manner whereby machine learning is a sub-domain of AI. For example, AI identifies the movement of the future stock exchange with the assistance of patterns in the previous stock data and machine learning. The system learns from the previous data, and the prediction is carried out based on the situation (Apte et al., 2000). In the last decade, AI has shown exponential development and renaissance, which is due to the considerable advances in machine learning. Machine learning is categorized into three categories: supervised, unsupervised, and reinforcement learning.

3.3.2.1 Supervised Learning

The key objective of supervised learning is discovering the needed function that links the data to the relevant labels. From the discovery, a new model is constructed, and the new model is applied to identify new data. In Facebook, every photograph is labeled with a unique label value. The algorithm is applied to spot the relevant people in the photograph, and automatic identification is initiated for new data.

3.3.2.2 Unsupervised Learning

In this method, AI provides the data that are classified instead of being labeled. To uncover the required hidden patterns, the classified data is analyzed. From the schema of the data, new clusters are formed, and the clusters are further classified. Google uses unsupervised learning to group the customers for posting relevant advertisements based on their recent searches.

3.3.3.3 Reinforcement Learning

In supervised and unsupervised learning, the model generation is based on the nature of the data. Once the data changes to a new format, the process of analysis is carried to generate a new model. Reinforcement learning uses the continuous learning process to construct a model based on the generated feedback. The reinforcement-based model is iteratively developed, meaning that it is continuously learned and evolving.

3.3.3.4 Impact of Machine Learning in Education

Machine learning has shown an enormous impact on education, and it is used in the prediction of future education systems. With the help of new education supporting technologies, machine learning uncovers the nature of future circumstances of education. The nature, aptitude level, response-ability, and skill set of the student are considered for the analysis. Through the analyzed data, a proficient model is generated to enrich the education system, as well as the ability of the student. Via real-time data analysis, the generated model assists educators to easily identify the nature of the student and the progression level of the student. A customized teaching method initiated and pedagogical syllabus is framed for the students based on necessity (Asthana & Hazela, 2020). For educators, a self-evaluation system is also provided for making any further improvement in their teaching level. Self-assessment and suggestions were provided based on the teaching of the educators. Machine learning has revolutionized the education system in numerous aspects is shown by Duzhin and Gustafsson (2018).

3.4 Social Media in Education

Social media are websites and/or mobile applications that allow users to communicate, share, create content, and enable social networking. Social media had conquered the impact of human life in all aspects. Abraham and Saini (2015) have shown that social media in education has a great impact on day-to-day life of students' teachers and institutions. Social media in education helps students to gather information on particular topics through learning forums, posing queries, engaging in discussions, and interactions with subject experts. Learners from the school level to higher education have a great impact using various social media platforms like Facebook, Twitter, Solo, YouTube, and so on (LCIBS, 2014).

3.4.1 Role of Social Media in Education

In the past few years, many institutions of higher education are motivating students to complete online courses as part of their curriculum. The institutions encourage academia to deliver the content via online webinars and other tools. The impact of computer technology and its development plays a significant role in layering a platform for social media–based education. This section focuses on the impact of social media in education from an individual point of view, various approaches in learning, technological development, and tools that support an education platform.

3.4.2 Technological Support

The rapid development of the computer, changing curriculum, and availability of high-speed internet have made social media a major platform for students, teachers, learners, and educational institutions. Due to technology support, the traditional classroom teaching has a transformation in classroom structures, turning them into smart classrooms and improvising teachers as technology teachers (Kumi-Yebaoh & Blankson, 2014).

The advanced communication tools involved in social media for education designed (Devi et al., 2019) to enhance the communication through audio and video capturing, connection, and extracting features are the following (Meyer, 2015).

1. Collaborative tools enable document sharing and editing features to multiple users.
2. Blogs help to publish works and get feedback and likes.
3. Social book markings allow tagging their favorite sites.
4. Academic collaboration creates a common platform for the educators.
5. VoiceThread allows sharing images, videos, and documents, and also has features for online conversations.
6. Diigo is a social bookmarking tool that allows learners to create bookmarks for websites and store them in the cloud.
7. Scoop is an online content publishing tool that allows posting on their page, along with a note.
8. Feedly is an online feed aggregator that allows them to receive updates fed by teachers on their blogs so students can know recent technological developments.

3.4.3 Popular Web-Based Platforms

Learners and the students use global social networks for learning outside the college or school environment. In the current scenario, the popular and trending learning tools in social media are Google Classroom, massive open online courses (MOOCs), Facebook, Twitter, and Skype (Mukhaini et al., 2014).

3.4.3.1 Google Classroom

Google Classroom is a free web service available to enable paperless sharing of files between a teacher and a student. Based on the survey done by Azhar and Iqbal (2018), the findings show that teachers with experience of 2–15 years have used Google Classroom for a period of 5–10 months. The main purpose of using Google Classroom by teachers are for assigning, uploading, and assessing assignments.

3.4.3.2 MOOCs

MOOCs are platforms that offer courses online containing video lessons, readings, assessments, and discussion forums. MOOC courses are offered by various providers like Coursera and edX, and in India, the MOOC courses are offered mostly via NPTEL and SWAYAM portals (Bowden, 2019). Zawacki-Richter et al. (2018) explored the study of MOOCs on the following four aspects.

1. The potential and challenges of MOOCs for universities
2. MOOC platforms
3. Learners and content in MOOCs
4. The quality of MOOCs and instructional design issues

3.4.3.3 Facebook

Facebook is a popular tool for sharing information with people worldwide. Facebook is a common tool for sharing information on different disciplines like engineering, medical, library science, marketing, psychology, and so on. It attracts people of all age groups to make them active by sharing information and making friends. Shaw (2017) found that there are wide benefits of using Facebook as an educational tool. The author has highlighted the following potential benefits of using Facebook as an educational tool.

1. A collaboration environment can be set
2. Communication between student and teacher can be enhanced
3. Improvement in computer literacy and language skills
4. Improvising the current student learning culture

3.4.3.4 YouTube

YouTube is a social network tool to download and upload videos. It includes a wide variety of videos from all domains. For use in education, it has videos that explain the concepts from basic understanding level to advanced level. Based on the study, YouTube features concepts, lectures, programs, and conference information related to education. In his study (Dixit, 2013), the author mentioned that around 90% of viewers view videos from YouTube, and videos viewed other than YouTube follow at approximately 7.6% only. Based on the article, YouTube has categorized education as primary and secondary, university, and lifelong learning (Dixit, 2013).

3.4.4 Positive and Negative Impacts

In social media–based education, the connectedness and learning process happens among the teachers and the student's community. This has its own positive and negative impacts (Devi et al., 2019), as follows.

3.4.4.1 Positive Impacts

1. Students communicate with each other to come out with quality projects and assignments.
2. Social media tools help teachers to get connected with students, as well as parents.
3. Students who have difficulty expressing their thoughts have the perfect platform to improve their confidence level.
4. Students can learn at their convenient place and time.

3.4.4.2 Negative Impacts

1. Students get easily distracted, and their focus will be changed.
2. Students lack face-to-face communication, which may reduce their attention.
3. Students sometimes post irrelevant content due to mood fluctuations.

3.5 Augmented Reality

Augmented Reality (AR) offers an enriched vision of the physical world that adds layers with needed contextual information. The wearable and handheld gadgets assist in delivering visual information and stimulating the senses. AR is widely applied in manufacturing (Nee et al., 2012), robotics (Mourtzis et al., 2017), education (Bernhardt et al., 2017), and the medical (Akçayir et al., 2016), and aerospace industries (Stone et al., 2011). In the field of education, AR plays a vital role in improving the learner's skills in various aspects. Two-dimensional media is preferred in the traditional education system that is static. Three-dimensional media created by computers for real-world vision is AR, which is introduced to achieve betterment in education. It offers dynamic content and immerses the viewers in the virtual world. The learners will be able to experience the real world via modeled virtual things.

Nowadays, augmentation of the natural world is attained by plotting the virtual objects in an ordinary place. AR interfaces with the educational content and provides the combination of scenes in a composite view to the learners. AR helps in the effectiveness of the teaching and effectively engages learners. AR assists the learners in understanding complex problems with ease. AR designers superimpose graphical objects over the real physical world, which permits the students direct interaction with the digital content (Azuma et al., 2001) (Kiyokawa et al., 2002) (Billinghurst & Duenser, 2012).

3.5.1 Blending Augmented Reality with Traditional Education

AR has shown effectiveness in teaching and acts as a complement for traditional learning progress. When the augmented books (where graphical scenes displayed over the printed material were streamed with audio effects) along with printed books to teach storytelling, teachers observed increased attention of students. Augmented book technology offered a multisensory scheme to learn the content—as well as the format—of motivational communication. The problem-solving skills and the understanding of the information highly improved among the students. AR-based teaching delivered an improved medium of education with education and entertainment. Figure 3.3 shows the design of AR.

The novel learning approach is brought about due to mobile AR applications. Researchers are showing interest in developing innovative AR educational applications. Through mobile applications, students can actively engage in the process of learning without geographical restrictions (Billinghurst et al., 2001). The MagicBook is an example of an augmented book developed with a transitional interface in a handheld device. Readers can explore the virtual environment of the real content, and it can be viewed by two or more people.

MagicBook comes with two buttons that provide certain display options and navigation directions. MagicBook transformed the reading experience into a multistate visual experience. Interactivity is one of the foremost experiences of augmented books, and it is attractive to the students because of its virtual scenes.

3.5.2 Design Principles of AR

In the context of AR for education, design principles are developed to optimize the usability and the requirements of the teacher. AR system must be user-friendly enough for the teacher to adapt it to the necessities of the students. The visual content should be based on the curriculum and delivered precisely over other lessons. AR system must satisfy the constraints of the educational context. The general principle behind the design of AR-based education is "Classroom usability raises if the learning circumstance fulfills all classroom constraints" (Bower et al., 2013).

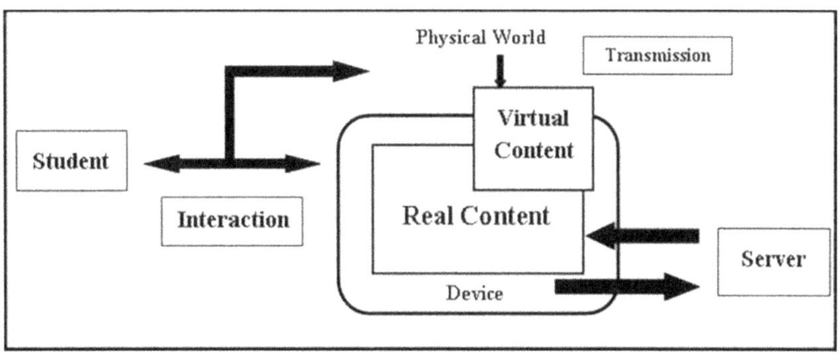

FIGURE 3.3 Design of augmented reality.

The design principle is accompanied by the learning behavior of the student (intrinsic) and the effective use of technology in teaching (extrinsic). While designing AR-based teaching aids, the classroom constraints need to be considered, and the designer must focus on the violating choices in the AR system. To design a system without affecting the context of classroom education, five design principles have been considered that are shown in Figure 3.4.

1. Integration: The learning atmosphere is included in the workflow, and the strength of the student decreases. AR supports one activity among a diverse set of educational activities. In the context of education, the students involved in activity will vary—namely: individual, group, higher and lower levels.
2. Empowerment: The learning atmosphere permits the educator as a central point that facilitates the governing of the group of students. The students may be distracted due to various factors, and a teacher cannot make all the students focus on the teaching. A guided identification of activity and smart teacher assistance is being offered by AR technology.
3. Awareness: Awareness about the state and the observation level of the students present in the classroom is provided by AR technology.
4. Flexibility: The learning context should be flexible to meet the needs of the educator. It should be adaptve to unexpected events and evolving scenarios.
5. Minimalism: If the learning atmosphere does not offer the needed amount of information at a preferred time, the teaching method should not be affected. The technology should be tangible to the load.

These five principles were framed based on external factors, and the learning science is neglected. The instructional design is framed based on the intrinsic constraint, and the factors like safety and relevance of the educational activity are not included. For the effective implementation of AR, the principle should be deployed through the teacher to the classroom with a flawless design.

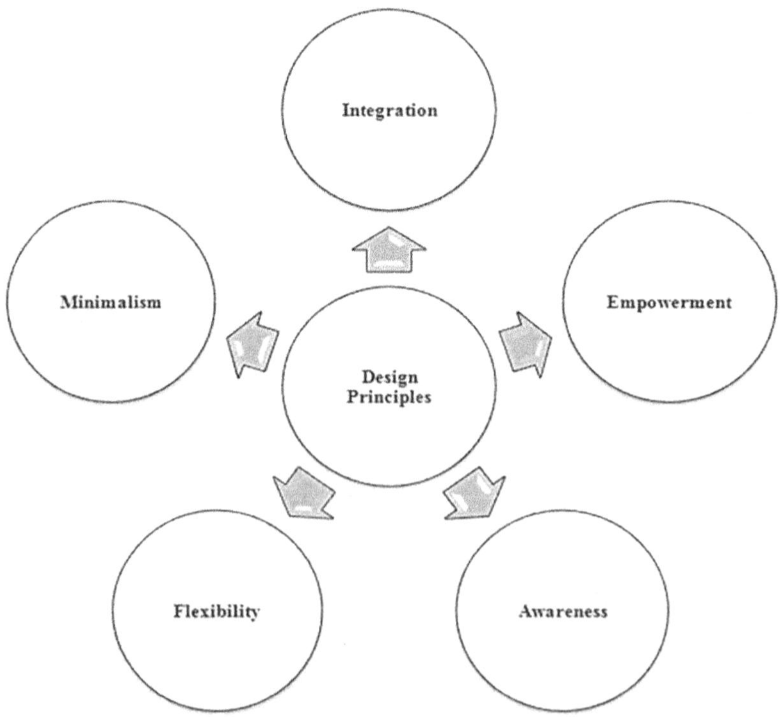

FIGURE 3.4 Design principles of augmented reality.

3.6 Multi-Touch LCD Screens

Multi-touch technology is currently dominating higher education, especially in the smart classroom. It allows the individual to interact in different ways. In particular, large-screen displays with multi-touch technology hold new opportunities for the learning process through the dialogic interaction between students and the physical interaction with the screen (Agostini & Di Biase, 2012). The multi-touch liquid crystal display (LCD) screens have replaced the traditional whiteboards with options like zooming, scrolling, and selecting. Nowadays, accurate multi-touch screens are available in LCD screens with high performance and reliability. By using multi-touch LCD screens, one can zoom in or zoom out by pinching or expanding two fingers across a touch screen. These kinds of screens are suitable for all kinds of displays with high brightness, and it helps to increase student's involvement participation in the classroom environment. Therefore, having multi-touch LCD screens in the classrooms is an effective aid to both the teachers and the learners.

3.6.1 Effectiveness of Multi-Touch LCD Screens

Nowadays, children are well versed with the multimedia digital world and are comfortable with technologies to communicate: for entertainment, for knowledge and for exploring, etc. Moving to higher education, they expect to learn from an active learning method. In that aspect, a multi-touch LCD screen has an inherent ability to enhance learning skills. It helps the students to interact with their peers to develop a relationship and critical life skills. Moreover, the students are motivated to pay more attention, to observe, analyze, and arrive at a smart solution. Demonstrations create attention among students. The presentations on the big screen, along with the multi-touch capabilities, let several students manipulate onscreen content as a team. As it is the latest emerging technology, the touch screen is essential, and it is simple to learn and easy to navigate for people who have little or no experience (Kamalakannan & Saikiran, 2014). Benefits of using the multi-touch screen include ease of use and the device's user-friendly nature, which helps to save time.

3.6.2 Role of Multi-Touch Technology in Education

Martinez-Maldonado et al. (2014) designed multi-tabletop classrooms and applications that focused on meeting teaching goals. Figure 3.5 shows the technological and process set up for designing a multi-tabletop classroom.

Agostini and Di Biase (2012) applied multi-touch displays for digital storytelling in primary schools to increase student involvement and participation. The authors designed an application, and based on their experiment, they concluded that the level of attention and participation of the students was higher than in the traditional lesson-taking approach.

3.6.3 Single Touch vs. Multi-Touch

The demand for touch screens is improving day by day because of their uniqueness and reliability (Jain et al., 2013). It allows the user to interact with the electronic device by touching the screen physically.

In earlier days, touch screen technology devices were limited to single touch functions, which are lack versatility. Since a user can only touch once at a time, if randomly touched at another place, it will not work further. Technology is evolving and today's multi-touch screens have become better because they support two or more simultaneous touch operations. This has become very popular in many classrooms. Zoom in and zoom out are the best features of the multi-touch screen. The basic principle behind these two technologies is to support user input via touch. It is a widely accepted technology by the end-users due to its promising features and ease of use. Efficient mechanisms provide the settings to work multi-touch screens effectively to read and interpret the multiple pressure points, including gestures with high precision.

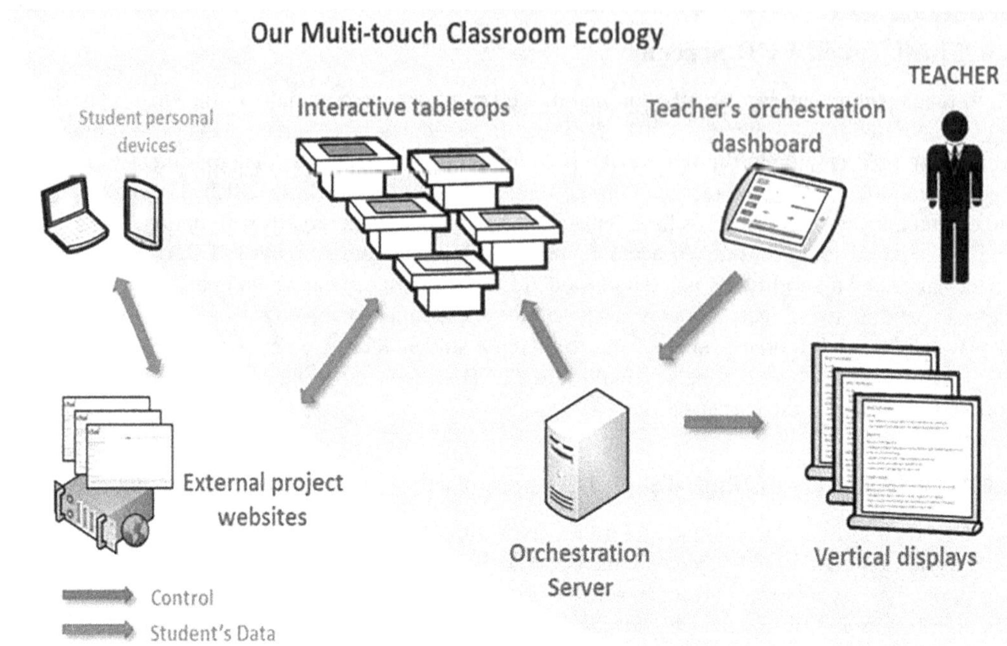

FIGURE 3.5 Multi-touch technology in education.

3.6.4 Advantages and Disadvantages of Multi-Touch Screens

The advantages and disadvantages of multi-touch screens applied in the classroom are summarized as follows (Lindemann, 2010).

> The touch screens devices usually have a simple user interface. Multi-touch facilitates use by multiple individuals at the same which helps in time-saving aspects to complete the given task within the stipulated time. It supports multi-touch functions/operations like scrolling, zooming, gesture-based multi-touch, etc. The integrated display and input spaces are more effective and space-saving with design flexibility in multi-touch screens. It is much simpler and faster than using a mouse.

There are also some disadvantages with the multi-touch screen, and cost effectiveness is one of the main drawbacks of this technology. Since a display is directly contacted by the user, the screen can become dirty and less visible; also, malfunctions are possible due to any scratches on the screen. Moreover, if a touch screen device crashes, the entire screen would be unresponsive and would have to be replaced. Multi-touch screens will not recognize touch from thick (gloved) hands. "Fingers on" is one of the major disadvantages of multi-touch screens, especially drawing applications and design.

3.7 Game-Based Learning

Game-based learning (GBL) and gamification is the trend that has been implemented in various settings including workplace, training, education and social media. The motivation behind GBL is to make the students engage with educational materials playfully and dynamically. The concept is defined as the learning activities that incrementally establish the concepts and guide users to achieve an end goal (Pho & Dinscore, 2015). GBL approach is a constructive type of approach which helps to promote challenge and enjoyment in learning. In this approach, the students are expected to learn by playing games and building the games using computers. Figure 3.6 depicts the processing model of GBL. The outcome

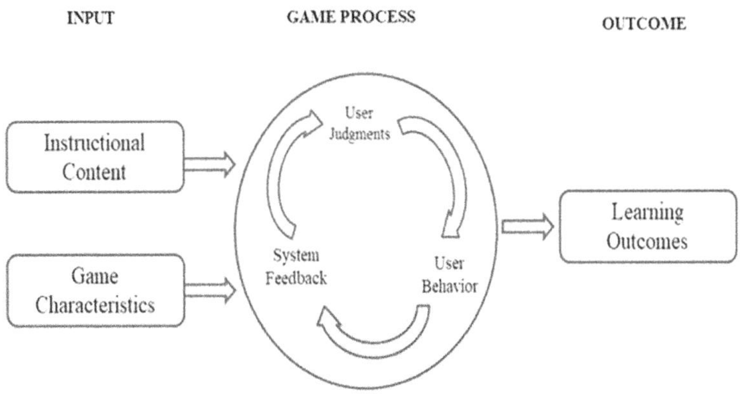

FIGURE 3.6 Model of game-based learning.

Sources: Garris et al. (2002)

was successfully achieved by repetitive teaching methods, failures, and the accomplishment of goals. The video games concept was followed in GBL; in video games initially, the players start slower and reach the most difficult level by their skillful navigations. Games are designed perceptively to offer acceptable difficulties to the player for keeping it challenging but easy enough to win. Similarly, in GBL, students work toward a goal, choosing actions and experiencing the consequences of those actions leading to active learning and practice. The best example for GBL is flight simulators, which pilots commonly use during their training. They have specific goals, and they practice until they attain them—the learning outcome is better than the conventional lectures and theory.

3.7.1 Categorization of Games

In recent years, more and more GBL is used in higher studies due to its effectiveness. Game developers apply varying classification to classify games based on the following seven genres (Gros, 2007).

1. Action games: Response-based video games that highlight physical challenges like hand-eye coordination and motor skills.
2. Adventure games: The player solves problems to progress through levels within a virtual world.
3. Fighting games: These involve fighting with computer-controlled characters or those controlled by other players. Most of the fighting games feature a large number of playable characters and a competitive multiplayer mode.
4. Role-playing games: Players assume the roles of fictional characters with a predetermined storyline.
5. Simulations: Games are modeled subsequently based on natural or man-made systems in which players have to achieve pre-specified goals. Here, strategic planning and learning exercises were considered.
6. Sports games: These are based on different kinds of sports which involve physical and tactical challenges.
7. Strategy games: These recreate historical scenes or fictional scenarios in which players must devise an appropriate strategy to achieve the goal. Almost all strategy games require typical situation awareness skills.

3.7.2 Game-Based Learning vs. Textbook Learning

Games are designed to deliver an optimal experience to the user, and they can be used to solve problems more effectively and quickly. GBL becomes one of the most successful methods to improve learning and teaching ability because of the attractiveness of games. The knowledge attained by the GBL is retained longer than the other learning methods. Moreover, positive results have been found with GBL in various disciplines like health sciences, architecture and construction, pilot training, etc. Medical students use a computer game to make decisions about a particular drug action (Boreham et al., 2010). Playing computer games helps to learn and reduces student stress. The aforementioned pilots are commonly using flight simulators during their training to achieve their desired goal. On the other hand, the traditional learning method contains all the information and methods in a theoretical format. The limitation of the textbook learning method is the lack of "information update" in the rapidly changing technological world. Learners are expecting an updated version that has the latest information about a particular topic, but there is a substantial delay before the curriculum changes and comes in the booking form to reach the students. To overcome the shortcomings in the textbook learning method, the GBL method is implemented in higher education as an adaptive approach. While creating a game, it will be tested and adjusted for effectiveness as new information gets updated periodically. In addition, these kinds of games have student monitoring analysis tools which helps the teachers to monitor the students.

3.7.3 Advantages of Game-Based Learning

GBL can take place in a virtual environment or simulated environment with multiple benefits where certain concepts can teach easily via gamification. One of the key aspects of the GBL is that each student as a player will receive feedback based on their performance. GBL method of learning offers the opportunity to learn by doing experimentally. Besides, the game provides a safe and contextual environment to help students learn different skills from basic to more complex. In this method, students finish each game level, making tasks progressively challenging (Vlachopoulos & Makri, 2017). An important element of this effective learning method lies in ensuring that students can move at their own pace. The skills acquired during the GBL method must be applied to real-time practice to fully achieve the learning outcome.

3.8 Conclusion

This chapter dwelt on the relationship between modern technologies and their uses in learning. This study also established that all these modern technologies have a positive impact on the learning outcome of the students. Technologies such as artificial intelligence, machine learning, augmented reality, and virtual reality have paved the way for innovative applications in the classroom. Apart from being immensely beneficial to students, modern technology has many uses for the teacher, too. The article also dwells on how social media and game-based learning are used by students as well as teachers to enhance the teaching and learning process. There is no doubt that these technologies are empowering the learner like never before. The impact of the latest technological innovations in the virtual classroom is definitely worthy of further study.

REFERENCES

Abraham, J., & Saini, C. 2015. Using Social Media for Educational Purposes: Approaches and Challenges. In: *International Educational Conference 2015 Learning Technologies in Education*. Jamia Millia Islamia: Excel India Publishers, pp. 484–489.

Agostini, A., & Di Biase, E. 2012. Large Multi-Touch Screens to Enhance Collaboration in the Classroom of the 21st Century: An Italian Experiment. *Interaction Design and Architecture(s) Journal—IxD&A*, 15, 40–56.

Akçayir, M., et al. 2016 Augmented Reality in Science Laboratories: The Effects of Augmented Reality on University Students' Laboratory Skills and Attitudes Toward Science Laboratories. *Computers in Human Behavior*, 57, 334–342.

Apté, C., Morgenstern, L., & Hong, S. 2000. AI at IBM Research. *IEEE Intelligent Systems*, 15, 51–57.

Asthana, P., & Hazela, B. 2020. Applications of Machine Learning in Improving Learning Environment. In: *Multimedia Big Data Computing for IoT Applications*. Singapore: Springer, pp. 417–433.

Azhar, K., & Iqbal, N. 2018. Effectiveness of Google Classroom: Teachers' Perceptions. *Prizren Social Science Journal*, 2(2), 52–66.

Azuma, R., Baillot, Y., Behringer, R., & Feiner, S. 2001. Recent Advances in Augmented Reality. *Computer Graphics and Applications, IEEE*, 21(6), 34–47.

Babich, N. 2019. How VR In Education Will Change How We Learn And Teach. https://xd.adobe.com/ideas/principles/emerging-technology/virtual-reality-will-change-learn-teach/ [accessed on 14 April 2020]

Bernhardt, S., et al. 2017. The Status of Augmented Reality in Laparoscopic Surgery as of 2016. *Medical Image Analysis*, 37, 66–90.

Billinghurst, M., & Duenser, A. 2012. Augmented Reality in the Classroom. *Computer*, 45(7), 56–63.

Billinghurst, M., Kato, H., & Poupyrev, I. 2001. The Magic- Book—Moving Seamlessly Between Reality and Virtuality. *IEEE Computer Graphics and Applications*, 2001, 6–8.

Boreham, N., Foster, R., & Mawer, G. 2010. The Phenytoin Game: Its Effect on Decision Skills. *Simulation Games*, 20(3), 292–299.

Bowden, P. 2019. Beginners Guide to Massive Open Online Courses (MOOCs). www.classcentral.com/help/moocs/ [accessed on 12 April 2020]

Bower, M., Howe, C., McCredie, N., Robinson, A., & Grover, D. 2013. Augmented Reality in Education – Cases, Places, and Potentials. In: *2013 IEEE 63rd Annual Conference International Council for Education Media (ICEM)*, pp. 1–11. doi: 10.1109/CICEM.2013.6820176.

Devi, K., Gouthami, E., & Lakshmi, V. 2019. Role of Social Media in Teaching-Learning Process. *JETIR*, 6, 96–103.

Dixit, V. 2013. The Importance of YouTube in Education. www.queryfloor.com/blog/why-youtube-is-important-for-teachers-and-students [accessed on 12 April 2020]

Duzhin, F., & Gustafsson, A. 2018. Machine Learning-Based App for Self-Evaluation of Teacher-Specific Instructional Style and Tools. *Education Sciences*, 8(1), 7.

Garris, R., Ahlers, R., & Driskell, J.E. 2002. Games, Motivation and Learning. *Simulation & Gaming: An Interdisciplinary Journal of Theory, Practice and Research*, 33(4).

Gros, B. 2007. Digital Games in Education: The Design of Games Based Learning Environments. *Journal of Research on Technology in Education*, 40(1), 23–39.

Hernandez, B. 2019. 4 Inventive Examples of Virtual Reality in Education. https://arpost.co/2019/12/04/4-inventive-examples-virtual-reality-education-learning/ [accessed on 14 April 2020]

Holmes, W., Bialik, M., & Fadel, C. 2019. *Artificial Intelligence in Education: Promises and Implications for Teaching and Learning.* Boston, MA: Center for Curriculum Redesign, 39pp.

Jain, A., Bhargava, D., & Rajput, A. 2013.Touch-Screen Technology. *International Journal of Advanced Research in Computer Science and Electronics Engineering*, 2(1).

Jones, M. 1985. Applications of Artificial Intelligence within Education. *Computers & Mathematics with Applications*, 11(5), 517–526.

Kamalakannan, J., & Saikiran, C. 2014. *Different Paradigm for Touch-Screen Technology: A Survey*, 5pp.

Kiyokawa, K., Billinghurst, M., Hayes, S., Gupta, A., Sannohe, Y., & Kato, H. 2002. Communication Behaviors of Co-Located Users in Collaborative AR Interfaces. In: *IEEE and ACM International Symposium on Mixed and Augmented Reality.* Darmstadt, Germany: IEEE Press, pp. 139–148.

Kumi-Yebaoh, A., & Blankson, H. 2014. Social Media and Use of Technology in Higher Education. In: *Handbook of Research on Education and Technology in a Changing Society*, pp. 217–234. DOI: 10.4018/978-1-4666-6046-5.ch017.

LCIBS. 2014. Role of Social Media in Education. www.lcibs.co.uk/the-role-of-social-media-in-education/.

Lindemann, P. 2010. *A Short Report on Multi-Touch User Interfaces*, London, UK: London College of International Business Studies, pp. 1–3.

MacGillivray, Ian. 2017. Daydream Labs: Teaching Skills in VR. www.blog.google/products/google-vr/daydream-labs-teaching-skills-vr/ [accessed on 13 April 2020]

Martinez-Maldonado, R., Kay, J., Clayphan, A., & Ackad, C. 2014. Multi-touch Technology in a Higher-Education Classroom: Lessons In-The-Wild. DOI:10.1145/2686612.2686647.

Maseko, F. 2019. Virtual Reality in education: Welcome to the new age of learning. news@itnewsafrica.com.

Meyer, L. 2015. 6 Alternative Social Media Tools for Teaching and Learning. https://campustechnology.com/articles/2015/01/07/6-alternative-social-media-tools-for-teaching-and-learning.aspx [accessed on 12 April 2020].

Mourtzis, D., Zogopoulos, V., & Vlachou, E. 2017. Augmented Reality Application to Support Remote Maintenance as a Service in the Robotics Industry. *Procedia CIRP*, 63, 46–51.

Mukhaini, E., Al-Qayoudhi, W., & Al-Badi, A. 2014. The Adoption of Social Networking in Education: A Study of the Use of Social Networks by Higher Education Students in Oman. *Journal of International Education Research*, 10. DOI: 19030/jier.v10i2.8516.

Nee, A.Y.C., et al. 2012. Augmented Reality Applications in Design and Manufacturing. *CIRP Annals - Manufacturing Technology*, 61(2), 657–679.

Pho, A., & Dinscore, A. 2015. *Game Based Learning*. Association of College and Research Libraries and American Library Association, USA, 5pp.

Shaw, C. 2017. *Using Facebook as an Educational Resource in the Classroom*. Oxford Research Encyclopedia of International Studies, 18pp. DOI: 10.1093/acrefore/9780190846626.013.11

Stenger, M. 2017. 10 Ways Virtual Reality Is Already Being Used in Education. www.opencolleges.edu.au/informed/edtech-integration/10-ways-virtual-reality-already-used-education/ [accessed on 13 April 2020]

Stone, R.J., Panfilov, P.B., & Shukshunov, V.E. 2011. Evolution of Aerospace Simulation: From Immersive Virtual Reality to Serious Games. In: *RAST 2011 — IEEE, Proceedings of 5th International Conference on Recent Advances in Space Technologies*, Turkey, pp. 655–662.

Vlachopoulos, D., & Makri, A. 2017. The Effect of Games and Simulations Onhigher Education: A Systematic Literature Review. *International Journal of EducationalTechnology in Higher Education*, 14, 22. DOI: 10.1186/s41239-017-0062-1.

Zawacki-Richter, O., Bozkurt, A., Alturki, U., & Aldraiweesh., A. 2018. What Research Says About MOOCs—An Explorative Content Analysis. *The International Review of Research in Open and Distributed Learning*, 19(1). https://doi.org/10.19173/irrodl.v19i1.3356.

4

Industry 4.0: The Need of Industry 4.0 and the Technologies Revolutionizing It

C. Vishnu Mohan and T. Devi

CONTENTS

Objectives

1. To understand the Industrial Revolutions that have transformed the world and thus identify the need for the Fourth Industrial Revolution—Industry 4.0.
2. To analyze the factors that lead to the revolution.
3. To understand why the companies should adapt to Industry 4.0 and its standards.
4. To understand the differences between traditional industries and Industry 4.0.
5. To learn what Industry 4.0 is and how it is useful.

DOI: 10.1201/9781003318378-4

6. To understand the goals and design principles to be followed in Industry 4.0.
7. To know the drivers of Industry 4.0.
8. To learn about the various technologies that revolutionize Industry 4.0
9. To understand the impact and progress of Industry 4.0 technologies.

4.1 The Need of Industry 4.0

Automations have made life much comfortable for humanity. It can be a mechanical or electronic automation that has transformed society. Technology has always helped people to make their lives easier and adapt to the next level of their living standard. The concept of the Industrial Revolution started in this way. At present, we travel through the Fourth Industrial Revolution, or Industry 4.0 (I4.0) (Pouspourika, 2013).

Industrial revolutions started in the 18th century when steam power and mechanization were used in many areas, especially in the fields of manufacturing and agriculture, and it emerged to be the backbone of the economy. Following this, in the 19th century, electricity was discovered and emerged to be the major source of power. Mass production was so common in the manufacturing units and thus resulted in increased productivity (Crandall, 2017). In the last few decades of the 20th century, the invention and manufacturing of several electronic devices such as transistors and integrated circuits, and services such as the internet, made it possible to reduce human effort and automate the production process.

Although automated systems were in place, this period still relied on human input and intervention. Also, as the demands and needs of the economy dynamically changed mostly in terms of quantity and quality, existing technologies proved slower and sometimes crashed. To adapt to the changes in the market, manufacturers had to be innovative and faster in their production (Immerman, 2017). To compete in the market and to provide better services to society, industries need to be customer-centric, cost-efficient, and agile.

In this digital age, to adapt to the changing needs of society, these factors such as cost-effectiveness and customer-centric service need to be well addressed. With the advent of technologies evolving, it is aimed that these technologies can be relied on for better livelihood.

People across the globe are currently enjoying the benefits of I4.0. This is due to the fact that many advanced technologies with the base of data and automation are applied to industry standards, commonly known as Industry 4.0 or I4.0. It is built on the developments and outcomes of Industry 3.0. If systems were earlier just embedded with simpler technologies, now they are advanced to the next level through networking and have a digital twin on the internet, so to speak. They allow communication with other services and facilities, and hence, this leads to the next phase—automating the production. The interconnection of these systems leads to cyber-physical systems. This establishes autonomous smart factories, where efficient output is achieved through the communication of production systems, their elements, workforce, and the end users across a network.

Establishing the standards of Industry 4.0 is not a simple task when compared to implementing an alternate technological solution. The implementation is dependent on the interaction of people with the technology so that industrial automation becomes more efficient. However, there are people who believe that by implementing Industry 4.0 technologies, it is always possible to get the maximum benefit (Koshy, 2019). This thought backfires most times. The best solution to it is to understand exactly what the workforce problems are, rather than focusing on the collected data alone. An amicable solution has to be then proposed and implemented by utilizing the I4.0 technologies consisting of cloud computing, robotics, the Industrial Internet of Things (IIoT), etc. To generate greater profits, new concepts can be added to the industrial processes or integrated with the existing processes, or the old processes can be replaced by the new ones.

Factories and their components are connected by various technologies which are further connected to make a universal solution through making use of the collected data. Following are the reasons that signify the need to implement Industry 4.0 solutions.

1. **Payback**

   Industrialists expect that they will get better results and increased revenue for whatever huge amount is invested.
2. **Market Competition**

   Many countries and companies have already invested a huge amount for the implementation of Industry 4.0 standards to increase productivity and earn better profits.
3. **Create a New Type of Product**

   In addition to saving costs, it is also possible to develop a new type of product through the increased use of technologies.
4. **Create New Models in Business**

   When new methods of industrialization are adopted, there is a reduction in the need for manpower. Hence, manual labor can be utilized in creating new ideas that provide better services.
5. **Increase Productivity**

   There is a growing pressure for companies to increase productivity with less consumption of energy and reduced raw materials. Estimates show that there will be a more than 3% increase in the efficiencies of companies resulting in around the same percentage of annual cost savings.

A brief comparison of traditional industries and Industry 4.0 is shown in Table 4.1.

4.1.1 Industry 4.0—The Need to Adopt

Various studies have shown that adopting I4.0 technologies assists business establishments and countries to achieve sustainable growth through the use of innovative products, reduction of industrial waste, better designs, condensed risk, etc.; the population has grown rapidly over the years and has become rich, advanced, and seeking better solutions in every vertical. At present, more than two billion of the world's population have access to mobile phones, which increases each year by 10%. Creations like voice assistants and several Internet of Things (IoT) products are influencing the purchasing habits of people, thus narrowing down the gaps between the situations that a product will be purchased and how it will be purchased by the consumers.

Following the sequence, e-commerce has achieved a growth rate of 18% across the world with a more widened space in items like cosmetics, pet care and beauty kits, pharmaceutical products, and sports products. Factors such as reduced prices, free or low shipping costs, and other product offers are areas of concern in the retail sector. Hence, to encircle the needs of consumers, companies have framed new models, thereby attracting fresh competitors. The daily-use consumer products section is passing through a huge revolution. To emerge as the front runner in this area, companies must focus on investment in technologies. The integration of production followed by its marketing, and trade, which should be built on a well-developed architecture, should be considered as the primary step. The architecture should be created and maintained in such a way that it is constantly adaptable to the changes in customer requirements.

TABLE 4.1

Traditional Industry vs. Industry 4.0

What Changes Does the Company Make with Industry 4.0?	
Traditional Industry	**Industry 4.0**
Mass production	Customization according to customer requirements
Large factories to manufacture big volumes of a specific product	Smart factories with flexible production at a competitive cost
Orderly planning based on anticipation with a stock	Dynamic production according to demand
Product purchase	Use of the product as a service
Minimization of costs	Maximization of return on capital employed
Work rigidity	Flexibility in work organization

Simulation and modeling are to be applied for designing products, improving customer ratings, and enhancing the logistics network. It was observed that sales and population-based information predicted customer shopping trends and how this helped companies to optimize production to target their customers. The outcomes of such studies result in getting better insights on how to carry out their business, advising what steps should be taken to enable valued services to customers and promote business to the next level.

The rapid evolution of consumer stipulations has uplifted the entire logistics process. As a result, the handover time is bound to be shorter, delivering products within a day or even an hour. Consumers can often set the delivery timings and delivery options according to their convenience, rather than admitting to the company's demand for delivery. Thus, the traditional ways of industrial processes have now become obsolete. A new customer-centric contemporized logistics network is required, whereby all the parties—starting from the raw material suppliers, through the manufacturers to the end-customers—cooperate in a unified environment. This interconnected logistics network should have a self-learning nature with the ability to model or remodel itself, reduce the workloads, and regulate redundant processes. Such kinds of systems can increase productivity and optimizes the cost.

Computerization, collaborative robots (cobots), and drone products have become central to supply chain automation, digitized production, warehouse management, and sales. Using the data collected from these sections, it is possible to investigate and identify meaningful patterns, which in turn assist in forecasting and optimally addressing customer requests. For this, many prediction algorithms are developed that make use of these data to find product susceptibilities when the mode of operation changes from un-automated to partially or fully automated systems. For example, geovisualization or geofencing systems can detect vehicle locations and can inform them about a shipment that is ready to be delivered (Tassel, 2019).

The change of trends in Industry 4.0 is based on the following characteristics.

1. **Localization**

   This refers to the capability of the architecture of various components and sub-tasks to work independently and making decisions of their own with minimal interference.
2. **Virtualization**

   Through gathering data from various elements, processes, architectures, and previous products, the system should be able to make virtual blueprints of the products.
3. **Interoperability**

   This refers to the property by which all the components of a system such as physical devices, robots, embedded systems, cloud-based applications, IoT products, employees, experts, and external systems communicate with each other and share information for collective goal achievement.
4. **Adaptability and Modularity**

   Adaptability refers to scaling the processes to meet business and customer needs by measuring the technical capabilities of the systems involved. Modularity refers to the capability of various sub-tasks or components to process independently and later integrate them into the complete system.
5. **Real-Time Analytics**

   This is the process involved in dynamically collecting and analyzing huge volumes of data called Big Data, in turn allowing good control over the processes.
6. **Service Orientation**

   This refers to delivering quality products to customers by making use of new models created and new technologies implemented.

4.1.2 Industry 4.0 Drivers

Data and its analysis are the core capabilities that all the components have in common. Also, the following three main factors form the core of I4.0.

1. **Product Digitization and Services Offered**
   For the digitization of products, new and advanced ways to collect data and its analysis should be considered. For example, the innovations done in certain products that have low customer transaction value helps companies to increase earnings through the implementation of advanced digital technologies.
2. **Digitized Business Infrastructure**
   An updated digitized business model is required to produce quality products that satisfy customers and stay alive in the market space. This is a continuous process, as customer requirements and trends change dynamically.
3. **Digitization of Horizontal and Vertical Entity Chains**
   Horizontally, Industry 4.0 connects various levels of authorities from the stakeholders, partners, and raw material providers to manufacturers and employees, whereas vertically, it unifies all the operations that take place throughout the life cycle of product development such as the operations involved in designing, manufacturing, marketing, supply chains, servicing, etc. All of these valued entities should integrate themselves and work together as a system.

4.2 The Roadmap to Industry 4.0

Technology is now a common driver of our daily lives, but the seamless connected environment and principles we rely on and the culture we live in is also impacting the world of industry. I4.0 is associated with the fourth revolution that takes place in industries of various sectors. It is the term ascribed to the emerging association of old, conventional production and industrial principles, as well as routines with more advanced technologies.

The First Industrial Revolution started in the 1760s with the advent of mechanization, steam power, and water power. It was a shift from our reliance on animals and high utilization of manpower, along with a shift in the use of biomass which was used as the primary source of power to the usage of mechanized methods. The Second Industrial Revolution that revolved around mass production and assembly lines using electricity came into force in the 1850s. The Third Industrial Revolution that emerged in 1950 made use of electronics and information technology (IT) systems, and rapid advances in computing power. These gradually led to the Fourth Industrial Revolution—Industry 4.0—that gives importance in implementing technologies including cyber-physical systems (CPS), IoT, and computer networks (Figure 4.1).

The first pillar denotes Industry 1.0 with major growth in mechanization, steam power, and the weaving loom. The second pillar denotes Industry 2.0, where the focus was on mass production, assembly lines, and electrical energy. Industry 3.0 is denoted by the third pillar, which has given importance to automation, computers, and electronics. The fourth pillar shows Industry 4.0, which labels technologies such as cyber-physical systems, IoT, and networks.

Each of these first three industrial revolutions represented reflective changes across the world. Life transformed from the farms to the factories, and people relocated themselves to the towns by introducing mechanical production. The discovery of electricity and mass production changed the way people lived and worked. At the latest, the digital revolution has altered every industry in all sectors, once again dynamically transforming how people live, work, and communicate.

The terms "Fourth Industrial Revolution", "Industry 4.0", and "I4.0" are often used interchangeably, featuring factories with machines that are integrated with sensors and wireless connectivity, integrated with software for visualizing the complete processes to decide and implement solutions independently. I4.0 shows how companies are rethinking and changing their methodologies in industrial processes. I4.0 technologies include Big Data and data analytics, artificial intelligence (AI), cloud computing, CPS, IoT, robotics, simulation, augmented reality (AR), and virtual reality (VR).

The intention behind I4.0 has not aroused from an individual's brain, an establishment, or a company. It is from the government of Germany itself in 2013 through a memo from the government mentioning the term "Industrie 4.0". This memo contained a well-structured plan to nearly completely automate

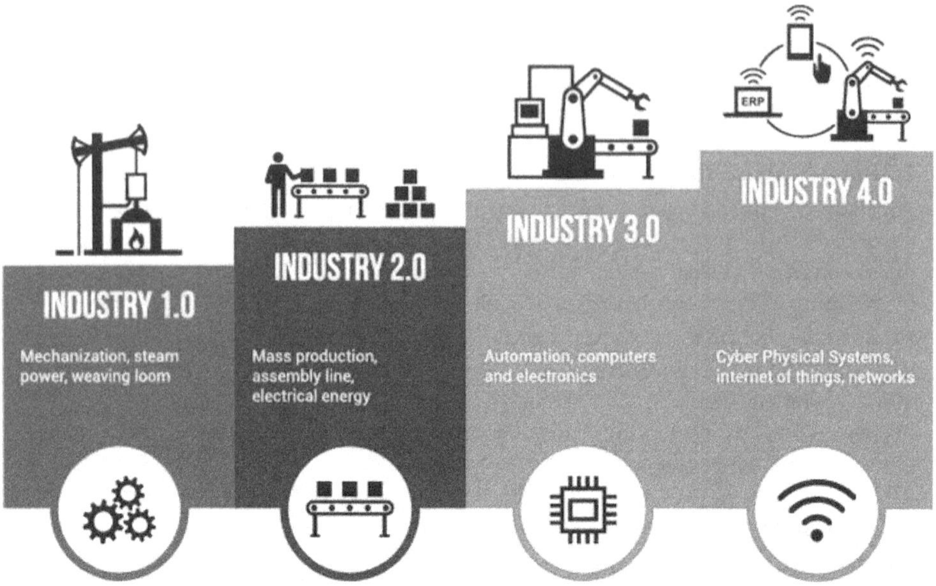

FIGURE 4.1 The industrial revolutions. Four pillars displaying various industrial revolutions from Industry 1.0 through Industry 4.0. The technologies or inventions which form the foundation of each revolution are given inside the pillars.

the production section without much human interference. This idea then hit the newspaper headlines and online news when then-Chancellor Angela Merkel delivered a vivid speech about the plan in 2015, at the World Economic Forum in Davos, Switzerland, terming I4.0 as the way to quickly synchronize production with the internet world. Then, the government invested €200 million for the researchers to explore the concept mainly in the areas of academics, governance, and business sectors. These revolutions are not a part of Germany alone. The Smart Manufacturing Leadership Coalition (SMLC), United States—a non-profit organization made up of universities, suppliers, government agencies, manufacturers, technology firms, and laboratories—also has the common goal of advancing the way of migrating to Industry 4.0.

I4.0 brings in smart cyber-physical systems, which provide fresh and advanced efficiencies to the workforce and systems. Even though these efficiencies are cultivated based on technology and models of the Third Industrial Revolution, I4.0 focuses on fresh methods with technology is the core. Examples include machine learning applications, gene engineering, applications based on cryptography, etc. (Davis, 2016). Even though, in general, the world is experiencing the benefits of I4.0, many areas across the globe are still in the previous revolutions. Mobile phones were very popular and more people had access to them than they did to basic sanitation. Similarly, Industry 4.0 has started to arise parallel with the Third Industrial Revolution that has started ripening in many locations.

Many companies and people believe that Industry 4.0 is hostile and inexperienced due to the complexity that these technologies expose and their slow-growing nature. Therefore, it should be kept in mind that the individual and collective choices of people are ultimately driving all the industrial revolutions. In this regard, more than the adoptions by developers, designers, and research and development teams, they are the choices of authorities, investors, government policies, experts, and people that matter to how these technologies are implemented.

4.2.1 Goals and Design Paradigms

The design paradigms of I4.0 assist many organizations to understand where they stand in terms of technology-related aspects and what steps are to be followed to migrate to I4.0 standards.

1. **Data Clarity**

   This refers to the open nature of data that various technologies should provide from the enormous collection of valuable data so that it aids in making better solutions. Data collection can be made flexible by the use of interconnected systems and operations, followed by examining the trends to reveal meaningful derivations that help businesses.
2. **Interconnectivity**

   This refers to the capability that each component of the industrial processes such as devices, sensors, software, and employees possess to share the information and intermediate results through a networked architecture.
3. **Decentralized Decision-Making**

   Each component in the industrial floor should be able to make judgments of its own after analyzing the data, without any human assistance. If any exceptional cases are encountered, they should identify them and pass them on to the authority level.
4. **Scientific Aid**

   Assistance related to technological implementations is required in two verticals. First, these digitized systems should be able to provide meaningful information to humans in various processes through accumulation and visualization of information so that even minor issues get solved quickly. Second, it should physically support humans by identifying and involving them in tasks that may be unfriendly, draining, and risky for the employees.

Industry 4.0 also predicts the processes as environment-friendly and tidy by maximizing the reduction in physical waste in production as well as logistics. A transparent, go-green standard for digital systems is to be constructed (Moore, 2019). It is expected that this platform will eventually enable manufacturing units to gain easy and affordable access to modeling and analytical technologies that can be customized to meet customer needs.

4.3 Technologies Involved in Industry 4.0

The advent of I4.0 brings in a transformation that gathers and analyzes data from various machines or processes, thus accelerating flexible and efficient operations that yield high-value products at a low cost. It improves the industry potential and growth, as well as boosts the abilities of employees, and finally makes companies more competitive in the marketplace. It also defines the emergent trend toward knowledge sharing and automation of processes within the industry.

When the First Industrial Revolution was piloted by the use of steam engines, the Fourth Industrial Revolution is led by the digitization of industries. The world is changing very rapidly with the increased adoption of applied science concepts like IIoT, augmentation, and virtualization. Digital technology was already in use as a part of the Third Industrial Revolution in production, but as I4.0 standards are applied, it transforms the production sector. As a result, increased efficiency—as well as the enhanced relationship among the producers, vendors, and consumers—can be achieved. When digitization is integrated into industrial systems and operations, it creates a space to generate huge potentials. These interconnected systems communicate with each other, visualize the production processes, and make autonomous and automatic decisions.

There are nine pillars that various industries use to improvise their entire industrial operations. They are the technologies that form the components of I4.0 which are estimated to have an extensive effect all over society. Already many companies have started updating to these technologies, as updated by the Boston Consulting Group (BCG), a global management consulting firm and the world's prominent advisor on business strategies.

4.3.1 Big Data and Its Analytics

The foundation of all I4.0 technologies lies in the collection of data and its evaluation. Enormous collections of unexploited data exist in the industrial system; hence, the data collection and its analysis are a concerning factor when considering the implementation of digitization in the industries. Here, the primary area of concern is in the amount of data, because when they are present in large volumes, careful analysis of the significant data which is required in making decisions is time-consuming. Big Data and its analytics are essential at this stage to detect and understand how each module or component performs and identify the boundaries of operations to avoid concerns.

Data analytics is the procedure involved in evaluating huge diverse datasets to discover uncovered trends, consumer purchasing trends, unknown correlations, or any other valid pattern which might be beneficial for business. An analysis of these data can optimize production quality, improve services, save energy, and allow real-time decision-making (Figure 4.2). Considering an example, semiconductor manufacturer Infineon Technologies was able to reduce defects in products by associating single-chip data collected at the end of the production process in the testing phase with processing data collected previously (Rubmann et al., 2015). This allowed them to identify trends early in the production process that helps to deal with defective chips and thus increase the quality of the production process.

Companies have to pressure their research teams in understanding the importance of I4.0, which enables them to do further research in addition to technical research. Every company is now almost fully digitized, and they should exist not only to survive but also to flourish with advanced potential to analyze data of high importance. Analyzing has to be implemented in all the corners of business such as human resources, manufacturing, marketing, and trade. Such data have an unsettling nature, and it is difficult to predict when and where the next new idea will emerge and how it influences and affect lives.

The manufacturers should have tools like dashboards, which aid to remove unwanted data, and classify and flexibly visualize enormous classes of information so that, finally, it reduces the time taken in analysis, visualization, and refining unproductive operations (Essentra Components, 2018). The integration and assessment of multi-sourced data from devices and systems, enterprises, and CRM systems shall exceptionally boost dynamic decision-making.

4.3.2 Autonomous Robots

Although robotics is in its infant phase in the industry, it is noted that there is a gradual rise in its application in certain production-related activities; for example, robots are used in activities such as the movement of materials and management of product inventory. Robots are created to be involved in a greater

FIGURE 4.2 Big Data analytics in I4.0. A radial cluster that shows the benefits of Big Data analytics. The central circle labels the technology Big Data analytics, to which three of its benefits—new products and services; faster, better decision-making; and cost reduction are connected and labeled inside circular shapes.

utility, becoming more independent and autonomous, cooperative, and flexible. Many manufacturers now use robots for finding solutions to complex tasks in many industries, but robots are evolving to prove much more potential making use of their independent decision-making capability, flexibility, and associative nature. Also, robots can communicate with other devices, processes, and components—as well as with themselves—and work safely along with humans. Such kinds of robots are known as collaborative robots or cobots. Comparatively, they are less expensive to implement and possess higher proficiencies compared to ordinary industrial components.

An example of a robot is the KUKA robot. The European robot producer manufactures robots which are capable of communicating among themselves. Figure 4.3 shows the KUKA robots welding ladder frames for the automotive sector. Their interconnection allows them to spontaneously balance their movements to complete the robotic operation. To enable collaboration with humans, they are equipped with control units and top-end sensors. Similarly, ABB, a robot equipment vendor, has manufactured a cobot named YuMi, which has just two arms to gather electronic goods and assists workers. In addition, it has a visualization ability to see and communicate.

STAR is another example, applied in the healthcare sector: a surgical robot set by The Children's National Health System in Washington, DC (Figure 4.4). With a $1.5 million fundraising, it has developed this bold robot, which is truly an autonomous system for surgery. Designed by the hospital's Sheikh Zayed Institute for Pediatric Surgical Innovation, the autonomous soft tissue surgery technology has proven itself capable of suturing pig tissue, as well as live pigs, with better precision than a human hand (Bold Business, 2017).

4.3.3 Simulations and Virtualizations

Computer simulations have been used for years to develop the best possible designs for production process and distribution systems. Considering the large capital invested, as well as changes occurring in the processes and consideration to be given to the staff and suppliers, the question that arises: How can manufacturers choose the right strategy to implement Industry 4.0 technologies? Every manufacturing system is unique, and hence, there is no single solution that can be implemented in all approaches to

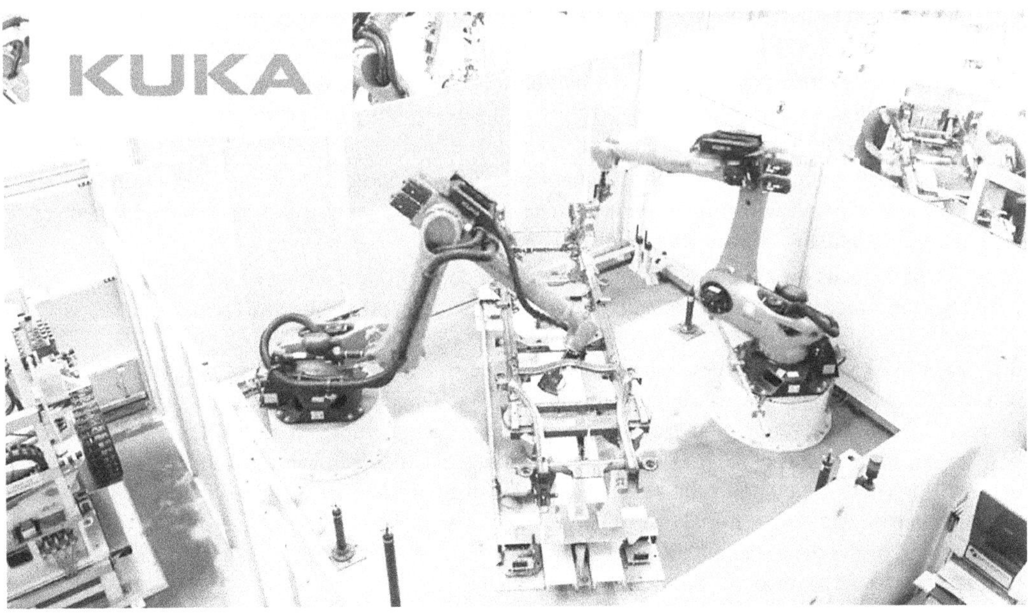

FIGURE 4.3 Two KUKA robots welding a ladder frame for the automobile sector. The robot arms are engaged in welding inside a closed cabin thus making the assembly line fully automated.

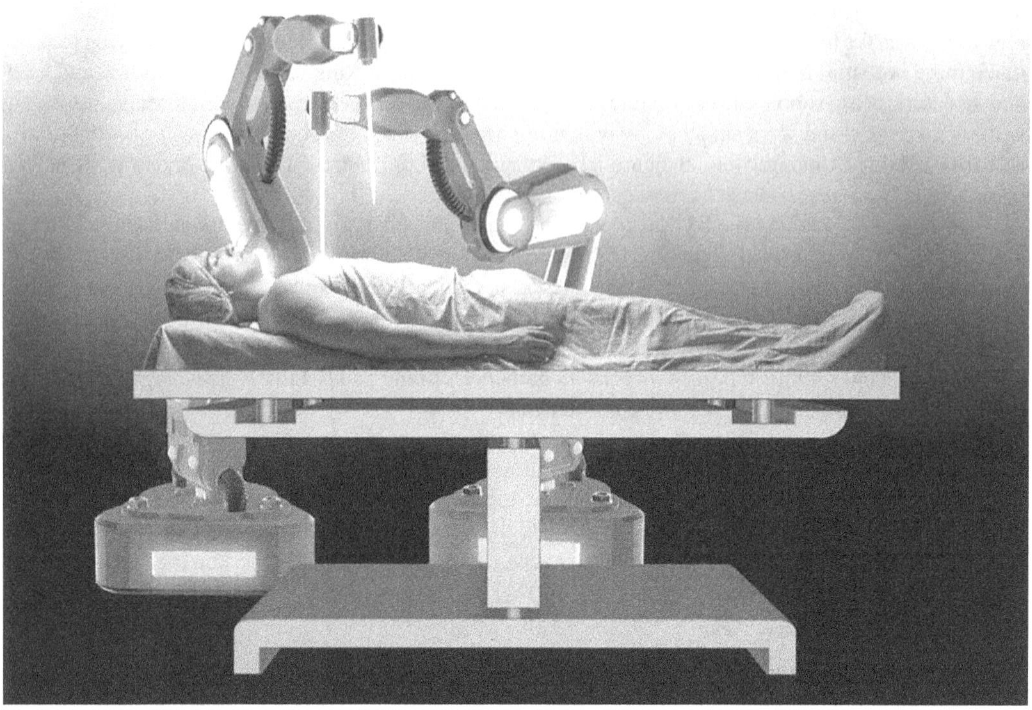

FIGURE 4.4 STAR Surgical Robot. Two STAR surgical robots are seen performing surgery for a patient lying on the bed. They stitch sutures tissues in the body using their robotic arms.

create a connected digitized industry. Following are a few reasons why simulation is one of the best technologies (SIMUL8, 2020).

- It enables various devices and people to communicate with each other and process the required information via the IoT.
- It helps in a virtualized vision of the real physical world using data captured through sensors which further enables to represent a full working environment, such as a manufacturing plant or contact center.
- It provides technical assistance that supports decision-making through the quick accumulation of data and its visualization when it is processed, as well as physical tools that help to replace or reduce human effort in demanding or risky tasks.
- It can make its own decisions autonomously in a decentralized manner for regular events in a system, which requires only a human oversight when exceptional events occur.

Simulations can virtually reproduce industrial ecosystems and environments of organizations. Hence, this visualization can narrow down the gap between the real and digital environments, alongside monitoring and processing, verifying outputs, and standardizing fragile operations. These functionalities can be achieved without causing degradation of production goals, reducing waste in industries and ensuring that each processing—unimportant or critical—takes place inside the digitized platforms. Generally, simulations can help decision-makers by depicting a clear understanding of the capital, the enhancements required, and the payback that is expected as a return, so that they need not delay or cancel any of their projects as they previously did.

Simulation software is under rapid development and many people use the existing simulations as learning and experimental aids. By making use of simulated platforms, analyzing information can be made easy, with a decent error rate allowed—whereas, in the case of non-simulated environments, even a minor error can result in degradation in quality. Therefore, through analyzing data by the simulations, obstructions in processing can be easily identified and suitable actions can be formulated. For all these actions to be performed, data collection should be expanded from all the integrated corners of the industry. Various simulations of intermediate outputs and operations allow the real-world data to be visualized digitally so that it will be easy for workers to check whether any devices are malfunctioning or any procedure results in generating incorrect outcomes.

A virtual machine (Figure 4.5), which simulates the working environment of a factory, was manufactured by Siemens and resulted in a reduction of the initial setting time to 80%.

The Center for Immersive and Simulation-based Learning of Stanford Medicine has developed simulator models that are used as learning tools for medical students. One such example is shown in Figure 4.6.

Similar to simulation, virtualization (or VR) is also plays a dominant part in I4.0. It creates opportunities for manufacturers on how to utilize intelligent data effectively thereby improvising manufacturing abilities.

A few uses of VR include the following.

1. **Inspection**

   Every device and industrial operation can be inspected in detail using VR applications. This is of great importance because when devices are manually checked, there is a higher chance of unnoticed errors.
2. **Training**

   VR applications can provide training to the workforce with a virtual atmosphere created so that they can understand the issues that may happen in the future.
3. **Plant Planning**

   When the current plant has to be revamped or a fresh one has to be built, virtualizations can aid in the situations where the models created are tested repeatedly.

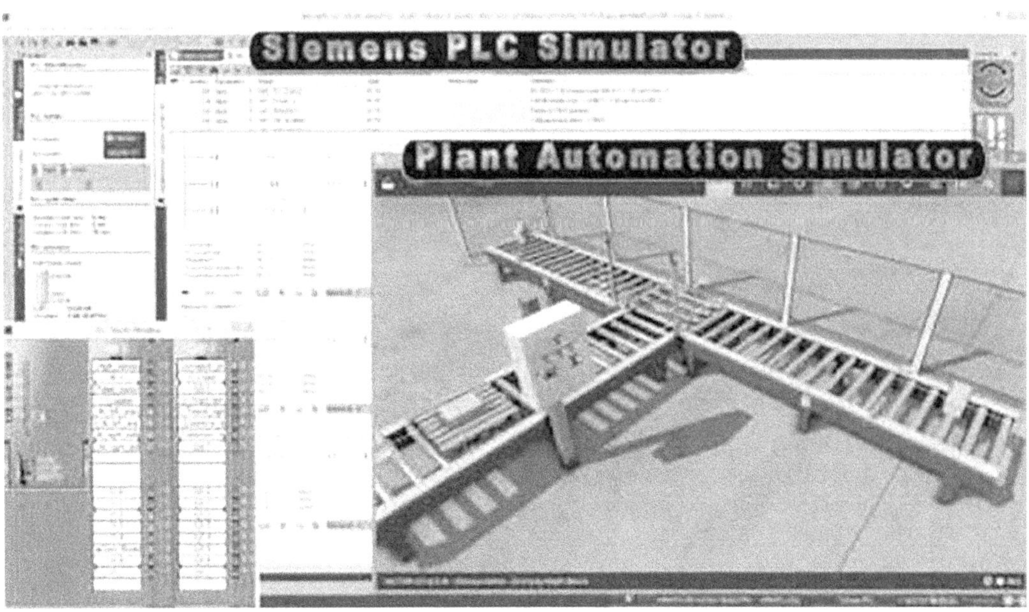

FIGURE 4.5 Siemens automation simulator. A plant automation simulator screen is embedded inside the press line simulation (PLS) simulator interface. The plant automation simulator consists of a T-shaped track where items are moved through the assembly line. The PLS simulator interface shows the integrated development environment (IDE) where options associated with simulation are shown.

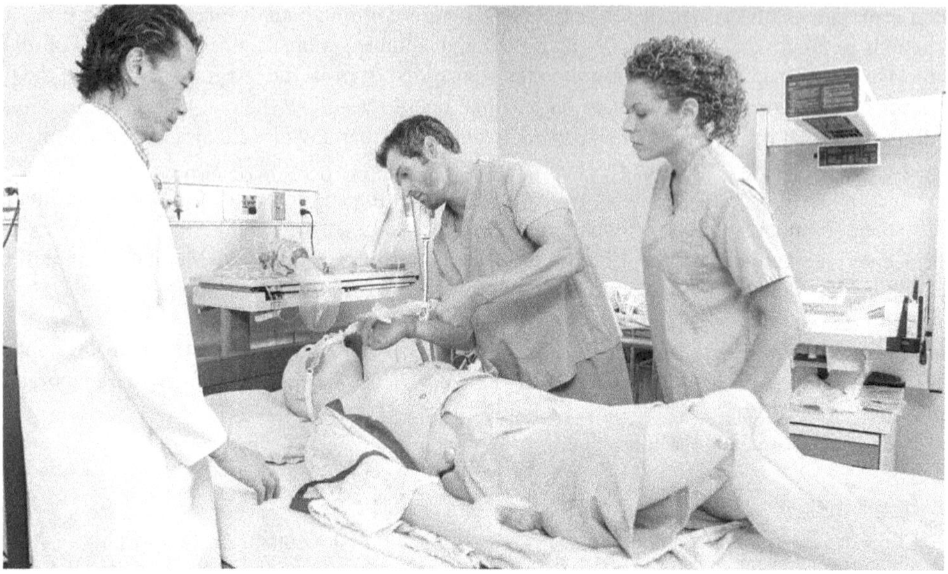

FIGURE 4.6 Simulator used as a learning tool in healthcare. A simulator representing a patient is placed on the patient's bed for learning. Two medical students are seen to be learning by intubating (penetrating a tube through the mouth of) the simulator body under the supervision of a doctor standing nearby.

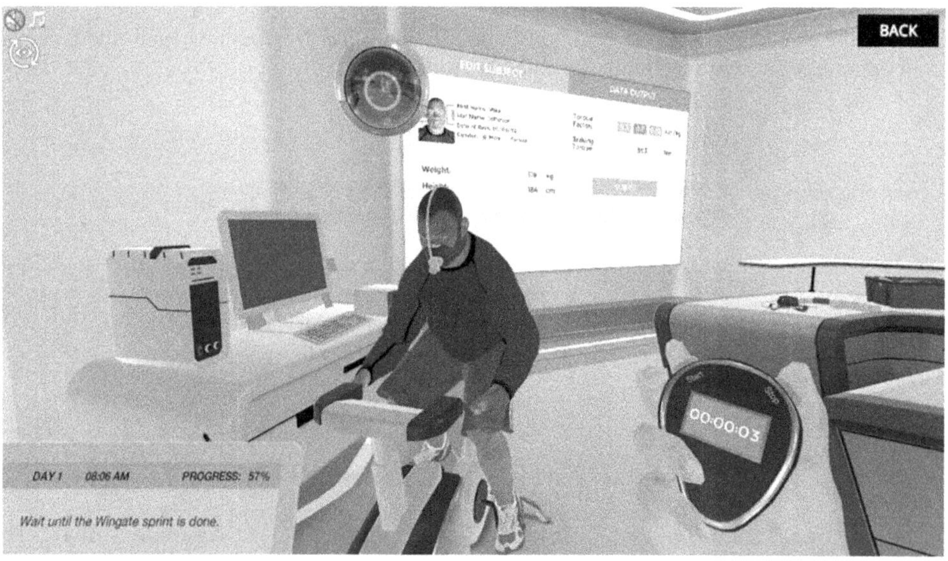

FIGURE 4.7 Labster VR. A virtual lab with Labster VR tool is displayed for learning STEM (science, technology, engineering, and mathematics) subjects. The interface shows a boy sprinting on a stationary bicycle where his progress is monitored using a timer. Another projection screen showing the data output and subject details are also displayed within the VR interface.

VR is extensively used in the educational sector, also. For instance, if a virtual laboratory can be set up for students for subject learning, it would be one of the best aids in providing an intuitive and interactive environment. An example of such an application provider is the Labster VR (Figure 4.7), which delivers 100-plus types of virtual laboratories in various educational institutions with exceptional service feedback.

4.3.4 System Integration

The automated environment that I4.0 provides is greatly dependent on the interconnection between machines, devices, and procedures, and as the systems become more integrated, the production processes are revamped and taken to the next level.

In IT systems, not all machines are completely integrated. In many systems, the vendors, manufacturers, and consumers are not connected in the chain, and even the internal elements of various sectors of the organization lack integration—but when implementing I4.0, these industrial components and process flows tend to show increased consistency, by way of inter-organizational data network development assisting the internal operations. For example, for the European aerospace and defense sector, an alliance between BoostAeroSpace and Dassault Systèmes had set up a platform called AirDesign (Figure 4.8). It offers cloud-based services for automated design and manufacture. The platform serves as an exceptional carrier of information that is to be shared among various manufacturing companies within the partnership.

Individually, many components may be fully digitized to do specific functions, but in many cases, they cannot share data with other systems. The transparent platform of integrated systems assists in sharing data and resources among all the entities involved. As a part of data sharing, to smoothen the communication, certain standards and formats for the data are also defined.

System integration can be performed both horizontally and vertically. Horizontal integration is the networked integration among the participating machines, equipment, or production bases, whereas vertical integration refers to the communication of all the parties involved in the trade such as vendors, producers, and consumers. The impact of these integrations is that the entire organization will be interconnected and integrations out of the company can also be created, thus enabling truly automated value chains.

4.3.4.1 Challenges Faced by Integration

System integration also brings in a few concerns, and hence, industries have to be more creative and should come up with the growing pace alongside technological aspects. The first major challenge is in maintaining systems and monitoring their functions. Second, there exist bulky overloaded data records,

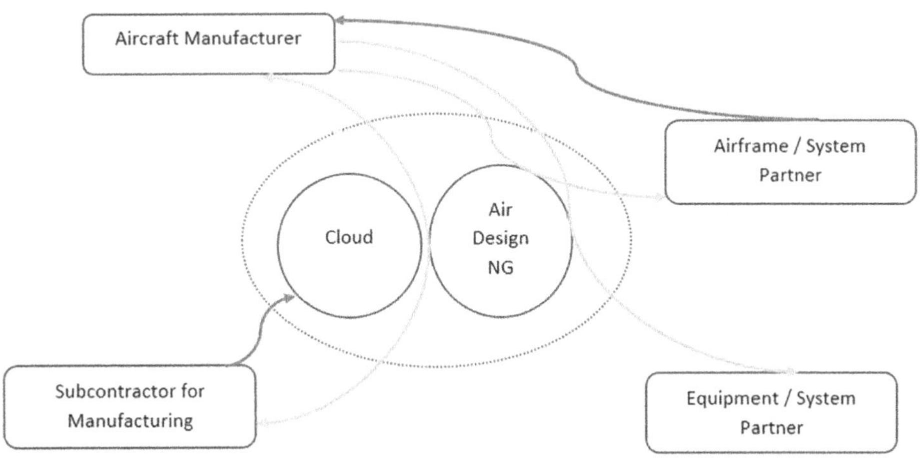

FIGURE 4.8 AirDesign collaboration platform. The figure shows the AirDesign collaboration platform with AirDesign NG and its cloud service as the central component. The other components shown are aircraft manufacturer, airframe/system partner, subcontractor for manufacturing, and equipment/system partner. Aircraft manufacturer and subcontractors are bidirectionally connected through the AirDesign NG. The former also connects to airframe/system partner and equipment/system partner through AirDesign NG. The manufacturer can receive components directly through airframe/system partner. The subcontractor is directly connected with the cloud services.

such that accessing them is a herculean process because most data access mechanisms require specialized programs. Following it, the accessed data needs to be stored and analyzed to convert it into knowledge.

The third challenge lies in the security when permissions are granted to access data. As systems become increasingly connected, there is a high chance that gaining access to a particular system can further result in accessing other systems, as well. As all these issues prevail in many industries, experts are being employed to find solutions to issues raised by system integration.

Whatever be the sector, whether it be logistics, transportation, education, or production, companies require access to data from their previous products or literature to facelift their industry and stay ahead of competitors. This modernization is not often simple, and it requires shutting down the systems rather than performing it while the system operates (Boughton, 2015). There are solutions implemented by various industrialists, but they may not be a single-fit solution, and it is hence up to the industrialists to find it. Flexibility is an indispensable factor among good systems integrators. The industrialists and their workforce have to learn a lot working with rangy systems of different products, performing smart work while also updating with the latest blooming technologies.

4.3.5 The Industrial Internet of Things (IIoT)

IoT refers to inter-connectivity and data sharing of smart equipment and systems, as well as platforms. The IoT is a key functionality and is utilized as a service in Industry 4.0–driven solutions. The data from the networked physical devices are collected and are then combined and analyzed by the IoT for the decision-making process. It is a form of embedded computing that nourishes the functionality and value of the product that is being manufactured. IoT devices can be common devices such as smartphones, tablets, and laptops, extending to wearable, automotive, or any communicable devices. When IoT is implemented in the world of production, it becomes the IIoT. It is a standard method of integrating various industrial machines and equipment, data analytics, and personnel at work. It is a network of a large number of smart devices linked using communication systems, which in turn form a system, which accumulates, observes, interchanges, explores, and conveys precious unexplored information and perceptions and intuitions.

In the manufacturing sector, sensors are attached to devices on the production floor so that they can capture data that are liable to make impacts and those that are capable to influence decisions in real time, thus leading to increased productivity and efficiency. In a statement, BCG comments that currently, only some manufacturers use IoT products that are interconnected (Rubmann et al., 2015). Typically, their arrangement is in the form of an automated vertically stacked pyramid whereby the data from sensors and other automated devices with limited intelligence are fed into a predominant manufacturing process control system. However, when IIoT is implemented, more devices can be connected which can communicate among themselves with controls being centralized.

There is a greater potential when Industrial IoT is implemented; even an intermediate product can be enhanced using IoT. It can be achieved when the devices on the floor are permitted to interact and communicate. Higher association, competence, improved safety, reduction in time and costs through predictive maintenance, real-time responses, and other operational efficiencies are the benefits. Consider an example of IIoT in transportation—most companies in the automotive sector have started their research foreseeing the future of motors. Here, the IoT and IIoT technologies make vehicles "smart", developing alternatives identical to Mass Rapid Transit (MRT), thus giving a few substantial improvements to private cars. The maximum efficiency is attained by observing and gaining better control over similar and related infrastructure and the structural in-born faults in vehicle transport. However, IoT enhances private motors as non-public spaces. IoT brings customization and identical enhancements as those inside the home to these smart vehicles (Figure 4.9). Remote area monitoring, automatic fleet monitoring, public transportation management, geofencing, inventory management, etc., are some other examples where IIoT is implemented in transportation.

4.3.5.1 IIoT and the Manufacturing Industry

The IIoT, when applied to the manufacturing sector, deals with integrating manufacturing machines, AI-aided automation, and strengthened data analysis to make factories and workers productive. IIoT

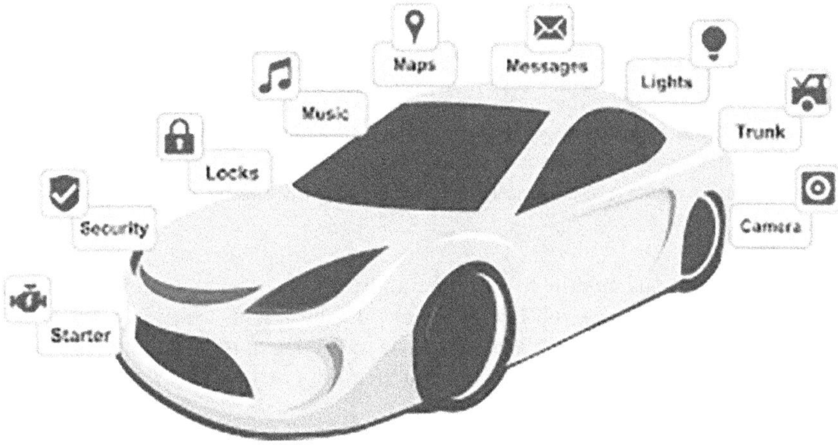

FIGURE 4.9 IoT-enabled car (smart car). A sedan-class smart car is displayed with all the smart features labeled around it. The features labeled are starter, security, locks, music, maps, messages, lights, trunk, and camera.

transforms the production sector by acquiring and accessing huge databases at a greater speed, hence guiding producers to install IoT devices in their workplaces and warehouses. The advantage is that IoT products tend to collect and analyze data much faster than do traditional processing elements. Even though the aim is to be more operationally efficient, the exact procedure of how this technology is implemented varies, depending on the company that implements it. For example, companies can collect advanced analytical data by providing wearable technology to the warehouse workers so that they can train warehouse workers in the operations related to a warehouse.

The revolution of using IIoT in the manufacturing sector began long ago. In a survey report by the Industry Development Corporation, it is found that the production industry has provided the capital of above $175 billion on IoT in 2016, whereas in a report by MarketWatch, the production industry investments are supposed to bud at 29.68% each year (i-SCOOP, 2016). It can be inferred that IIoT has boosted the sector by providing, a better vision of the entire production operations.

The principal idea behind IIoT is to make machines smarter and more efficient than manual efforts by constantly collecting, analyzing, and processing data. With the advent of blooming digitized systems to gather data, the collected data can be utilized by AI to predict future production. Systems and IoT devices are directed to identify trends that may cause a failure in the near future. The applications which perform these tasks have helped companies to optimize profits in millions—or even billions—of dollars. Another big area of utility for IIoT is in revolutionizing the existing legacy infrastructure and protocols within the industrial and manufacturing processes. For example, tire manufacturer Michelin used built-in sensors that can automatically monitor tire pressure. This helped truck drivers in understanding how they can save cost and fuel.

4.3.5.2 Present IIoT Challenges

IIoT also faces certain challenges in its implementation. The first significant challenge is all about interoperability. There is no single IIoT solution that can be implemented in all enterprises because protocols and architectures may be different in most machines. Also, within an enterprise, there can be a conflict of protocol among the machines or devices. API (application programming interface) calls can be used for the machines to communicate in order to solve the issue.

Security is another concern that needs to be addressed. When IoT is implemented, more reliance is given to cloud storage and computing—and hence, many companies will be quite concerned about the possibility of disruptive operations, cyberattacks, and data thefts (Smith, 2018). Companies, stakeholders, and decision-makers will need to coordinate and discuss to alleviate this risk.

4.3.5.3 IIoT Use Cases

4.3.5.3.1 Airbus

Airbus is a European aircraft manufacturer that uses IIoT technology to manufacture planes, and tools for their ground staff to use in aircraft manufacture. "Factory of the Future" is a recent initiative launched by Airbus to control the operations and improvise production (CMS CONNECTED, 2018). Airbus has installed sensors in their systems and workers are provided with wearable technology.

4.3.5.2 Caterpillar

Caterpillar has signed a partnership with a data analytics company called Uptake to create IoT products to monitor the fault rate and life of factory devices. With the aid of AR as an addition, they have developed applications to obtain a virtualized display of the machine parts. Also, when a particular component needs a replacement, the system guides on how to do it (Internet of Business, 2016).

4.3.5.3 Amazon

Customer orders are at most times fulfilled by Amazon warehouses through the use of drones and robotics. Since 2012, Amazon has been using robots to identify the location of products and transport them to the employees for further processing. These robotic technology implementations have reduced operating costs by 20% (Kim Bhasin et al., 2022).

4.3.6 Cybersecurity

The risk of cyberattacks also increases alongside the increase in systems connectivity. Starting from the supply chains to the operations, multiple areas of the business could be damaged if any security breach occurs. The information systems and production lines should be protected from cyberthreats by companies making necessary preparations.

Newer challenges, particularly of cybersecurity, are brought in by the IT-based operational technology with I4.0. Cybersecurity is considered as the core issue that all governments follow; it deals with preventing unauthorized access, abuse, and theft by adopting methodologies to protect the networked systems. As there exists a high tendency of misusing data, cyberattacks have become more dominant with the expansion of network connections. The primary areas of importance have to be given to automation and the dependence that society has on it. Apart from the growing nature of networks, the tools that hackers use are becoming more effective, and as a result, there is a rapid increase in the count of cyberattackers and the growth in the size of the network. Therefore, to achieve a decent performance ability, protection should be guaranteed from vulnerabilities and threats.

The new forms of defending cybercrimes are brought in by the extensive use of IoT services. Recent decades have seen a tremendous increase in cyberattacks and threats, and directly or indirectly, the decision-makers are affected by the issue. Serious financial burdens, data loss, virus attacks, market losses, etc., have resulted from the exposure to malicious attacks in large companies. Cybersecurity is considered an issue related to technology in many organizations. Access to sensitive business details such as targets, funds invested, employee and customer-centric details, etc., are considered as the potential areas by many public and private company authorities, and they do not want the attackers to access them. In recent years, cybersecurity capabilities are strengthened by most large companies that are making good profits. In order to bring down the damage caused due to cyber-attack, many companies have invested millions of dollars in deploying new and advanced policies in the domain of cybersecurity. As technologies such as IoT are achieving a large growth by 2020, these systems seem to be more prune to cyberattacks.

The rate of victims attacked through the cyberworld ranges from individuals to governments is growing rapidly due to the increase in cyberattacks. Considering the damage caused by the cyberattacks, as seen from the general perspective, organizations should come in front to create awareness among the consumers related to the safety procedures that should be kept in mind when using a networked system.

4.3.6.1 Vulnerabilities and Security Threats

Generally, there exist four major levels in Industry 4.0 architecture. Figure 4.10 shows the various levels and components at each level.

1. **Perception Layer**
   The perception layer (sensing layer) comprises of sensors and physical devices including RFID sensors. They allow devices to sense and collect data about other objects.
2. **Network Layer**
   The wired or wireless connections among various sensing components and the automated system are established by the infrastructure provided by this layer.
3. **Service Layer**
   This layer provides and controls the services needed by applications and users of the system, and is also responsible for linking to databases of the enterprise.
4. **Application Layer**
   The application layer (interface layer) establishes the interaction mechanisms between users and applications whose aim is to provide user-beneficial services.

4.3.6.2 Strategic Principles of Cybersecurity

When building an effective security solution, the following six characteristics are to be considered which must be assured to guarantee security in the entire system.

1. **Confidentiality**
   The critical information and other device outputs should be hidden from people who are not authorized to access it. This ability of information systems to hide information is known as confidentiality. Examples of such sensitive data include patient data, sales data, user authentication keys, digital signatures, military data, etc.

	Perception layer	Network layer	Service layer	Application layer
Components	• Barcodes • RFID tags • RFID reader-writers • Intelligent sensors, GPS • BLE devices	• Wireless sensor networks (WSNs) • WLAN • Social networks • Cloud network	• Service management • Database • Service APIs	• Smart applications and management • Interfaces
Security threats & vulnerabilities	• Unauthorized access • Confidentiality • Availability • Noisy data • Malicious code attacks	• Denial of Services (DoS) • Routing attack • Transmission threats • Data breach • Network congestion	• Manipulation • Spoofing • Unauthorized access • Malicious information • DoS attacks	• Configuration threats • Malicious code (Malware) attacks • Phishing Attacks

FIGURE 4.10 Components, vulnerabilities, and security threats by layer. A table figure with column labels perception layer, network layer, service layer, and application layer is given with values listed against components and security threats and vulnerabilities as row headings of the first and second row in each of the four layers.

2. **Integrity**

   While confidentiality deals with hiding information, integrity deals with protecting it from unauthorized access or alteration. To provide reliable services to users, ensuring integrity is mandatory and integrity needs to change depending on the systems implementing it.
3. **Availability**

   The data, information, or resources should be made available to its users, devices, or systems whenever required or requested to avoid significant losses.
4. **Authenticity**

   Only authorized persons or devices are allowed to perform certain operations, and there should be a limit on the number of operations to be performed in a connected environment. This feature is called authenticity, and different kinds of authentication with different solutions can be implemented. For example, in systems dealing with finance, a strong authentication mechanism should be implemented.
5. **Nonrepudiation**

   Nonrepudiation ensures that all the parties involved in sending and receiving data should claim mutually. At a later stage, the sender should not deny that a message is not sent, and the receiver cannot deny it is received. This guarantee is provided by the property of nonrepudiation.
6. **Privacy**

   Any participating entities in an automated environment have the right to determine up to what extent they can interact with its environment, what should be hidden from outside access, and what information is to be shared with others.

Some of the security challenges faced by certain sectors are given in Table 4.2.

4.3.6.3 Cybersecurity Measures

To reduce cyber risks, certain measures need to be taken by businessmen. To prevent cyberattacks, following are a few precautions and measures.

1. A machine should not be directly connected to a network or the internet. Many enterprises do not give much importance to it and this gap is enough for a cyberattacker to access and exploit control systems, thus causing damages. Hence, connection media among the devices should be disconnected.
2. The number of connections or routes in the network should be reduced by using specialized protocols, and the network boundaries and segments should be established. Firewalls should be installed to monitor the network traffic, and mechanisms should be implemented to check

TABLE 4.2

Challenges across Various Industries

Businesses	Adding security shied for critical information.
	Making all types of agreements and contracts with third parties securely.
Energy	Adding security shield for critical information.
	Lack of cyber-awareness.
	Fear of component data loss in energy systems.
Healthcare	User privacy should be protected. According to the HIPAA Act, all healthcare establishments need to assure data privacy and security to patient data, including the details of transactions.
	Medical equipment issues.
	Managing third-party risk.
Logistics and Transportation	Ensuring information security and privacy.
	DoS and Spoofing attacks.

the network limit restrictions and manage the communication flows to monitor suspicious communication flows.

3. Virtual methods like virtual private networks (VPNs) can be advantageous, as attackers do not get easy access to systems.
4. Based on the business routines, role-based access control can be implemented, which will allow or deny resource access through the network. This security mechanism can restrict unauthorized users from accessing file systems.
5. Strong passwords should be applied wherever applicable. Care should be taken that personal and critical information not be used in creating passwords, and character combinations that are close together on the keyboard are not used, to help prevent hackers from using brute force attack mechanisms. Besides, it would be safer if there exists a password policy that also includes password reset or modification functionalities.
6. The hard-coded default credentials which are used by many networked devices are freely available on the internet. Such information may be known to many people. These credentials can be used by attackers to inject malware and make the entire system dysfunction.
7. The systems must be updated on a timely basis. Based on certain positive impacts affecting an organization, hackers try to utilize such opportunities and perform phishing attacks. Proper precautions are needed in such cases, and all the critical updates should be performed whenever necessary.
8. Awareness should be created on the part of the workforce about the impact and vulnerability that each security breach can lead to. Training regularly should be given to the employees about safe online habits and practices.
9. Laptops and other portable systems expose a security risk due to their portable nature, and hence, to protect the sensitive data, extra steps must be taken. The easiest way is to encrypt the portables with a secure password.
10. Smartphones and laptops are commonly used in every organization, and it has become a habit that humans store more sensitive data in them. They should be valued, and care should be taken to keep them locked. To enforce security, encryption software, password protection, fingerprint sensors, and location detection can be used.
11. The impacts of threats and the importance of cybersecurity may not be generally known to organizational heads or external stakeholders. They should be properly informed about the aftereffects of a security breach and the need of implementing security mechanisms.
12. In addition to anti-virus software, firewalls and intrusion detection mechanisms should be installed and servers should be examined to check whether there is an infection or an abnormal network flow.

Cayir Ervural & Bilal Ervural (2019)

4.3.7 Cloud Computing

Cloud technology, which is a critical enabler of Industry 4.0, provides mechanisms to store and access information and applications over the internet. Along with all the data they generate, cloud services make use of a wide range of devices and provide scalability and real-time information services. In the era of I4.0, cloud technology stands effectively supporting other technologies like the IoT, robotics, and automation.

The technology is termed "cloud" computing because of its virtual visualization that information that is stored or made available seems to be in a virtual imaginable cloud space. The users can store and access their information and applications from remotely located servers, and many companies have come up to help the users in providing cloud services. This provides an advantage for the users to access these cloud resources from remote locations and according to their convenience. This eliminates the burden of transferring enormous data among various devices through physical transportation media and spending a huge time on it (Nayyar & Kumar, 2020). All of these works are stored in huge servers which are located remotely in cyberspace. All devices that have internet access, regardless of their physical location, can access these data, and applications as the internet act inside the cloud. Because of this reason, there is a major shift in the IT industry with the contribution of cloud computing.

The technical characteristics of the cloud are as follows.

1. **The Certainty of Performance**

   Performance can be guaranteed regardless of whether the cloud has a single or multitude of users with predetermined contracts at the service level.
2. **The Infrastructure Abstraction**

   The data, resources, and applications are no longer residing in individual devices, so they can be accessed from the cloud anytime and from anywhere required.
3. **Payments Based on Requirements**

   Cloud services can be made available based on paying only for the services required by a company with only a minimal initial investment cost. It requires only an internet connection and an internet-enabled device.
4. **Vertical Scalability**

   The resources are made available on demand and instantly, without checking any forecast.

Red Reply (2020)

From these characteristics, the following series of benefits can be realized by industries.

1. **Agile and Flexible**

   It is natural for a company that there can arise a need for increased cloud service utility because of sudden changes in company activities. The advantage of the cloud is that even if more services are required by the companies, they can be provided with ease.
2. **Increased Operational Efficiency**

   It takes minimal time to deploy and provide cloud services to the users.
3. **Shorter Innovation Cycles**

   When new or updated services are required by the users, the cloud can provide it easily and with maximum simplification because of the fact that service updating is continuously made by the cloud providers.
4. **Cost Reduction**

   Implementing cloud services can reduce the costs involved in managing power, connectivity, personnel, etc.

Setting up an IT environment is a herculean task that includes the purchase of servers, hardware, and software and its licenses, as well as installation of these. This task is considered to be hectic, time-consuming, and also incurs additional costs. With the advent of cloud computing and its services occupying Industry 4.0, this entire process can be made into a commonplace: the cloud. As examples that are implemented already, storages, backups of data, email apps, production processes, etc., are a few components that are now moved on to the cloud.

When a few leading companies have started this setup, the trend has influenced others also, leading to a centralized way and reaping of benefits. The various components of the cloud in Industry 4.0 can be seen in Figure 4.11.

A few impacts that benefit organizations by incorporating cloud services are the following.

1. **Need of Advanced IT Skills**

   Before cloud integration, employee skills revolved around the physical infrastructure environment and they had to deal with a lot of technical issues. As fresh skills and specialty skills are blooming, the copybook skills are to be revamped to fit with the cloud technology. The IT staff needs to acquire additional skills such as understanding the benefits of cloud platforms and the methods to assemble them with traditional industry architecture.

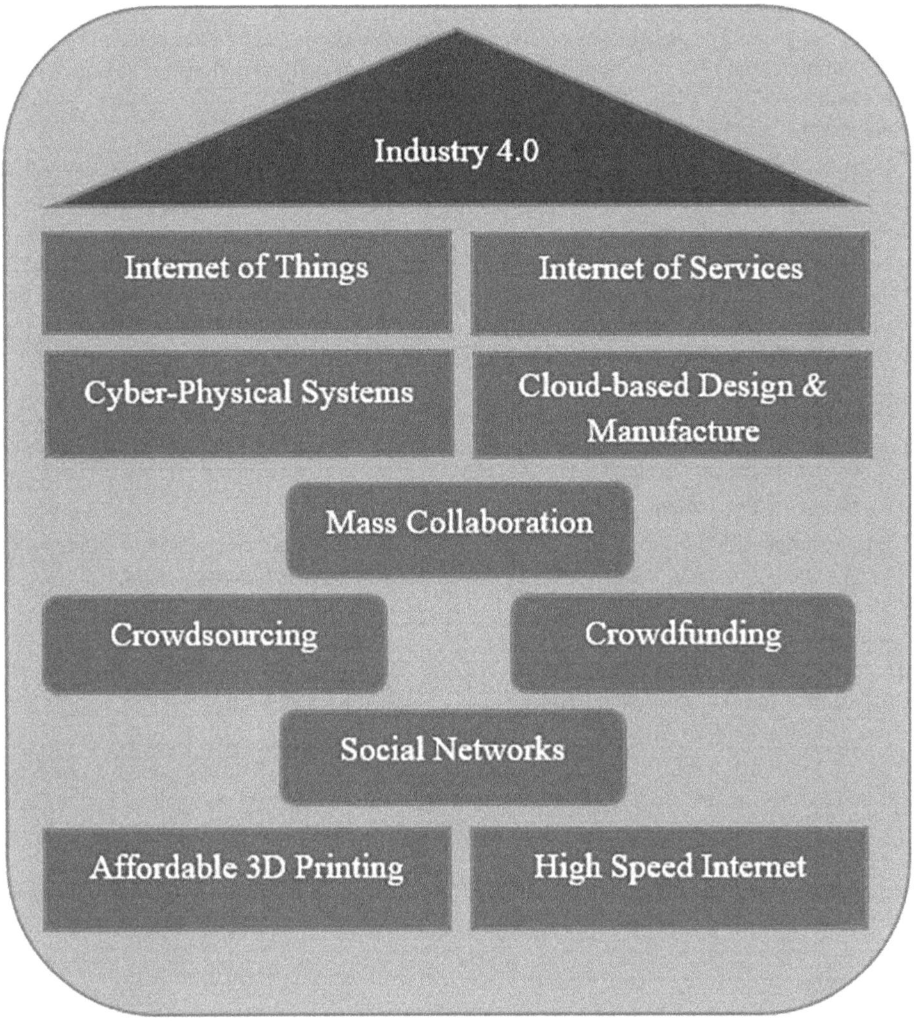

FIGURE 4.11 Contribution of cloud computing in industry. A diagram showing the sectors of Industry 4.0 where cloud computing is applied is given inside blocks under the main block named Industry 4.0. The blocks labeled are IoT, internet of services, cyber-physical systems, cloud-based design and manufacture, mass collaboration, crowdsourcing, crowdfunding, social networks, affordable 3D printing, and high-speed internet.

2. **Significant Updates in the IT Infrastructure**

   The IT infrastructure undergoes commendable updates when applications are hosted from the cloud platform. The IT managers and staff should examine and take decisions about how these applications are created and made available for use.
3. **Support Staff**

   When migrating to the cloud platform, the requirement of staff got reduced as the core of the operation is on the cloud side. However, the existing staff needs to be trained in understanding the cloud technology and working with it.
4. **Maintaining Data**

   Usage of the traditional physical systems has an advantage and a drawback. As an advantage, it was possible to have control over the systems by directly measuring the needed variables and manually having control over them. However, the drawback is in the effort, time, and cost needed to do so. The shifting of data records to the cloud reduces the overhead of effort to maintain data and resources, since the majority of the security functions are taken care of by the cloud.

5. **Security**

   Security experts are being assigned by the firms who provide the cloud facility so that they can handle security-related issues from time to time.

6. **Customization in Software**

   The usual software used in the industry is incompatible with the cloud standards. Hence, this issue has to be addressed by the software developers by including pieces of code to make applications run on the cloud platform. However, most cloud providers are also serving enterprises to make the applications cloud-appropriate.

Cloud computing is evolving rapidly, such that many sectors such as banking, insurance, etc., are already in it. Having a cloud platform is advantageous in many respects because of the following capabilities.

1. **The Power to Transform**

   Cloud technologies can transform the scalability of their resources up and down, depending on the demand fluctuations. This opens up a comfort zone for business establishments and consumers.

2. **Cost Savings**

   The only costs incurred by the cloud provider when moving to a cloud platform occurs when the customer makes use of the platform.

3. **Ease of Collaborative Alliance**

   Various locations across the globe are interconnected by the cloud, based on a deadline to expand the customers to cover more geographical locations. This opens up information sharing and dealing businesses to more users through the platform.

Cloud computing also faces certain challenges. A few challenges in some domains are listed in what follows.

1. **Insurance**

   Most insurance companies prefer private clouds, as they believe that private clouds offer more security compared to public clouds. However, studies suggest that community clouds will be emergent in the industry in the coming years.

2. **Banking**

   Most banks have confusion and feel uneasy regarding the security aspect of clouds. Hence, most banks limit the use of the cloud as a service for emails, file transfer, and other administrative functions.

3. **Governments**

   Governments have a multitude of opportunities using cloud technology, but they are still lacking ideas on how to effectively use the cloud as a platform for governance.

4.3.8 Augmented Reality

AR, or augmentation, is the technology involving specialized software installed onto devices—such as smartphones, eyeglasses, or smartwatches—for displaying digital content in the real world. Operations like sending repair instructions over mobile devices, selecting materials from a warehouse, etc., can be done through AR-based systems. The scope of this technology is that most companies will have much reliance on these systems, as they can provide real-time information for the employees to improve the decision-making process. Examples of AR applications include displaying a 3D view of an information transfer when repairing a part of it, or the 3D display of a simulator device and training personnel through it.

The 20th century has witnessed great advances in researches in the field of VR and AR. The major difference between VR and AR is that the latter allows us to add information to the display field. Considering the physical world, these visuals are put alongside the visible environment. Consider the following VR scenario in the mechanical sector. When a device with pointing equipment is integrated with an AR tool, a certain list of operations is displayed in the field of view of the operator. Therefore, the operator can quickly interfere based on the information displayed.

AR in industrial applications is renovating the way new products are designed, and it brings in new possibilities. The behavior of various objects and in the real world can be provided using computer simulations. The benefits of implementing VR are proper use of materials, execution of the right task at the right time, eliminating manual operations, and optimization of handling and operation times.

An example of AR in the healthcare sector is shown in Figure 4.12. This AR application aids in surgery by displaying 3D anatomical information of the human body. The nerves, major blood vessels, and

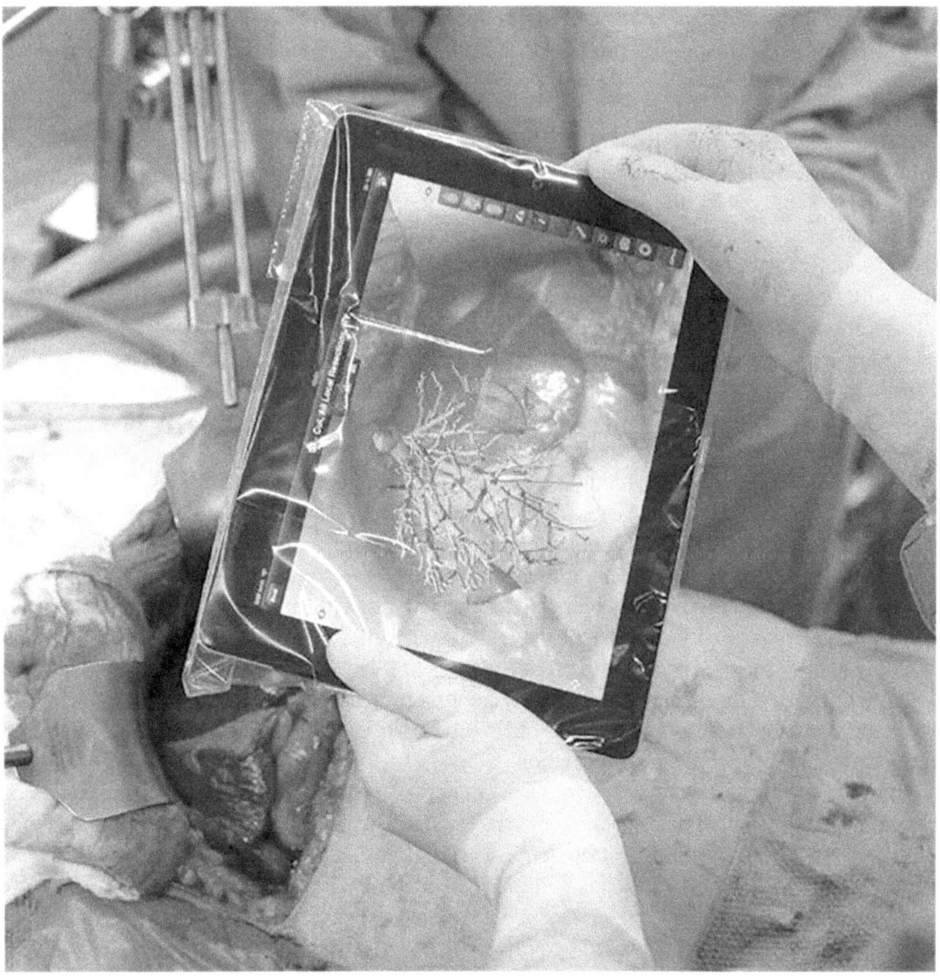

FIGURE 4.12 AR Application displaying a 3D view of the liver. A surgeon holds an AR-enabled tablet computer above the liver of the open body of a patient and visualizes the plans for the patient's liver surgery. The 3D structure of nerves and body sections belonging to the captured area of the body is displayed in the AR window.

ducts are highlighted and color-coded. The tumor is similarly outlined in AR, showing its relationship to surrounding vital anatomy.

A striking feature of AR applications is that it combines reality with virtual information (Mercadie, 2019). As a result, it is possible to explain complex environments while relating them to the real world. Another advantage is that it provides a platform to identify and work on the elements. Hence, it is possible to relate it to the gaming platform with still focusing on the kinesthetic real environment. A few use cases of AR applications include the following.

1. **Training**
   Newly appointed staff may be unfamiliar with the industry environment, devices, machines, and processes. Hence, for safety, they should be well trained. Here, AR can be used to make them understand the functioning of the industry by projecting real-world information through AR apps.
2. **Streamlined Logistics**
   In warehouses, AR can be applied to automate processes, thus reducing the errors, saving money, time, and resources in contrast to manual checks.
3. **Maintenance**
   As AR projects real-time information, it reduces the guesswork of the maintenance team, and hence, it can save time. It can provide details about the equipment, potential issues, service history of the machine, etc.

It is observed that, in general, AR-enabled applications are found to be far ahead of traditional applications in that they take less time to complete tasks with a minimal error rate. However, when the complexity of the tasks increases, the AR technology takes more time compared to smaller AR applications. Thus, tasks should be selected in such a way that it best fits an AR solution. Also, the experience of the workers is another factor that influences the performance of AR applications. It is more productive when working with trained workers than untrained workers.

AR offers a wide range of possibilities in various industries. In manufacturing, AR can be used to design and operate processes, training modules for operators, and so on. "Pick by vision" is a concept that is used in the logistics sector to select pick locations and the quantity to be picked up. Other noticeable fields of applications include warehouse operations, maintenance, data acquisition, quality assurance, supervisory control, and visualization of instructions. AR is also implemented in the robotics field as a part of collaborative robot functions such as safety enrichment and case studies.

AR systems require a device with capturing capability (camera), a visualization technology like hand-held devices, a tracking system to connect to the physical world, and a user interface as its components. There are four visualization technologies available for AR systems: hand-held devices (HHDs), head-mounted displays (HMDs), projectors, and static screens. The visualization can be either statically placed or portable, based on the nature of the task. Devices like static screens and projectors are used for assembly applications. Projectors directly display the information on the projection window whereas static screens are used for displaying standard operating procedures (SOPs). The academic sector and other industries are much focused on the use of HMDs because the operators can transport these devices wherever they want and access the information.

The tracking function in the AR system enables inert-correlating digital objects using markers with the physical world objects. Physical markers attached to certain places are then used to calculate the accurate location for placing a digital object. The methodology—even though simple—is affected by certain issues like dust and dirt, which will affect readability. Because of this drawback, markerless systems—i.e., cameras—are used as the sensors of the physical environment. One such example of using a camera as the sensor is HoloLens used by Microsoft.

The AR user interface provides bidirectional communication, i.e., from the system to the user, as well as feedback from the user back to the system (Masooda & Egger, 2019). The main part is the visualization system relaying information to the user. Other technologies, like forceful feedback or acoustic cues are also in use. Even though the main part is visualization technology, user input interaction methods such as gesture recognition, speech recognition, and discrete hardware solutions such as the mouse, keyboard, and hand-held scanner are also important. At the consumer level, compared to VR applications, even though AR applications are on the verge of infancy in the Industry 4.0 era, they tend to make a footprint much faster. AR offers an increase in productivity through collecting real-time real-world information, and experiments prove that the error rate of AR applications is much less.

4.3.9 Artificial Intelligence (AI)

AI illustrates the ability of machines and software systems to simulate human mental expertise. The system, software, and good internet connectivity with data sources and the cloud are the three main components of AI. Machines represent physical equipment such as robots and are not only programmed for decision-making but also to learn with experience. Software mechanisms are being managed by the software part of AI solely for decision-making purposes.

It was estimated by Forbes that 44–49% of automotive manufacturers rated AI as their critical factor for success. Also, 56% of the manufacturers were planning to enhance their production environment with AI. In another survey by TrendForce, it was expected that by end of 2020, AI-enhanced manufacturing will make a growth rate of above 12% (Wright, 2019).

AI is an extensive field of research that associates itself with the areas of machine learning, IoT, natural language processing, and Big Data analytics. Machine learning and AI are interrelated, and together, these technologies achieve a greater potential for the industries and maximize investment returns. A factor that adds to the success rate of AI-based applications is the knowledge that AI developers possess in bringing out the best possible solutions for the industries. Also, another blooming discipline called industrial AI has set its base by deploying machine learning algorithms in various industrial applications. It narrows down the gap in collaborating both industrial and academic researches and also enhances the potential of AI developers by providing them industrial AI experience.

Productivity growth has not been significantly impacted by AI-driven automation. Also, industries face certain challenges as more industries gain industrial AI exposure. Attaining a remarkable level of efficiency and flexibility in industrial operations is now possible by integrating other I4.0 technologies with AI. Even though there are industries that have already implemented industrial AI, it is still in the early days of development. Hence, parameters like methodologies and challenges should be well defined in the industry that has a plan to migrate to industrial AI.

One of the issues with many organizations is the difficulty in finding manpower potential in all areas of industrial AI in order to draw observations from whatever data they have to work with. Industrial sectors like healthcare, logistics, and transportation require plenty of manual labor. Thus, when migrating to industrial AI, the results produced by AI-based applications should be effective as they deal with larger databases.

Platforms using bots that make use of fractal science technology can be attempted in the manufacturing industry even to carry out administration duties. This requires only minimal computing power working under a thin foundation base, but offers improved performance.

In industrial AI, whereby bots are involved in industrial operations, most infrastructures deploy multiple bots performing dedicated tasks operating on a single system simultaneously. These bots gather, process, and derive knowledge out of even the unstructured data dynamically. In addition, the manual laborers can use these systems in performing other activities even if bots are assigned tasks in these systems. This enhances the skill set of the manual workforce in performing operations which they might not have performed earlier. A few industries like the automotive industry have already implemented this concept. As a result, in addition to performing complex operations at the production unit, bots provide experience to the human workforce spent their talent in decision-making.

The advantage of most industrial AI-based platforms is that bots are capable of working efficiently with unstructured data, even in the form of daily paperwork. As bots make use of fractal science technology, the time required for a product's manufacture is reduced, without compromising the efficiency of the development line. For example, it is seen that original equipment manufacturers who have applied industrial AI have revolutionized their manufacturing lines to attain better production efficiency. Thus, it can be inferred that those industries that underwent digitization can achieve better quality control by making use of the AI-embedded machine learning procedures through exploring the available data sources. But it should be made sure that the data sets are well organized and utilized for prediction routines. With many companies creating success stories, more companies are now attracted to AI platforms.

AI's impact on manufacturing can be analyzed with respect to five main parameters: quality, design, collaboration, adaptability, and maintenance. Quality is the topmost priority among all these parameters, as it is the main factor that attracts customers. Quality issues can be informed to the manufacturing controllers by using advanced machine learning algorithms. Designing with the aid of AI is widely used in the industry. The machine learning algorithms are efficient enough to explore all possible design combinations with just a brief design fed as the input.

The collaborative operations among the bots and workforce improve the efficiency of the production lines and skills of the workforce, and enhances decision-making. Based on the data collected from market analysis, AI applications can improve production to better adapt to market conditions. Prediction algorithms are extensively used to predict when there are chances of failure of a device or a system, when the personnel associated with the components are alerted about the maintenance. These algorithms replace the conventional method of scheduling timely system maintenance (Seebo, 2020).

4.3.10 AI's Impact on Healthcare

In healthcare, AI uses complex algorithms and software to emulate human intellect in the analysis of complicated medical data. Specifically, computer algorithms can predict results without direct human input. The traditional technologies in healthcare differ from AI-driven healthcare in the ability to gather information, process it, and give a well-defined output to the end user. This is accomplished through machine learning algorithms which recognize patterns in behavior and create their logic. To reduce the margin of error, these algorithms are tested repeatedly.

The primary aim of health-related AI applications is to analyze relationships between treatment techniques and patient test outcomes. Actions like treatment protocol, diagnosing procedures, drug evolution, patient monitoring, and personalized medicine are being transformed by AI applications. Many AI-based applications are being developed by tech giants like Google for the healthcare sector. In addition, to enhance patient satisfaction, many hospitals have implemented AI-based applications for hospital procedures and internal operations. As a consequence, many companies have come forward to develop predictive analytics solutions to be implemented in hospitals to enhance their business. The benefits of implementing AI in healthcare include efficient data collection, faster processing, an e-health record system, enhanced computer vision, robotics-based surgical procedures, and in-depth learning about diseases.

4.4 Conclusion

There is a drastic change in people's lives with the emergence of Industry 4.0 technology standards. Even though each of the previous industrial revolutions has contributed much to the economy, the impact made by the Fourth Industrial Revolution is quite big and is still elevating. Real-time market analysis, product analysis, and deploying advanced digitized technologies have enabled most industries to achieve what they strive for. Advancements in the areas of IIoT, robotics, virtualization, artificial intelligence, and maching learning have nourished the processing capabilities of industries and organizations in all sectors.

REFERENCES

Bold Business. 2017. STAR Surgical Robot, a Robotic Surgery Breakthrough. www.boldbusiness.com/health/star-surgical-robot/. [accessed 26 March, 2020]

Boughton, Nick. 2015. Systems Integration for Industry 4.0. *Automation.com*. www.automation.com/en-us/articles/2015-2/systems-integration-for-industry-40. [accessed 26 March, 2020]

CMS CONNECTED. 2018. What Is iIoT (Industrial IoT)? *Industrial Insights.* https://www.cms-connected.com/PromoNews/What-is-Industry-IoT-4-0. [accessed 25 March, 2020]

Crandall, Richard E. 2017. Industry 1.0 to 4.0: The Evolution of Smart Factories. *APICS Magazine.* www.apics.org/apics-for-individuals/apics-magazine-home/magazine-detail-page/2017/09/20/industry-1.0-to-4.0-the-evolution-of-smart-factories. [accessed 25 March, 2020]

Davis, Nicholas. 2016. What Is the Fourth Industrial Revolution? *World Economic Forum.* www.weforum.org/agenda/2016/01/what-is-the-fourth-industrial-revolution/. [accessed 25 March, 2020]

Ervural, B. Cayir & Ervural, Bilal. 2019. Overview of Cyber Security in the Industry 4.0 Era. In: *Industry 4.0: Managing the Digital Transformation.* pp. 270–274. Springer International, Switzerland. doi: 10.1007/978-3-319-57870-5_16.

Essentra Components. 2018. The 9 Technologies Behind Industry 4.0. www.essentracomponents.com/en-gb/news/news-articles/the-9-technologies-behind-industry-40. [accessed 25 March, 2020]

Immerman, Graham. 2017. Why Industry 4.0 Is Important. *MachineMetrics.* www.machinemetrics.com/blog/why-industry-4-0-is-important. [accessed 25 March, 2020]

Internet of Business. 2016. 9 Examples of Manufacturers Making IIoT Work for Them. https://internetofbusiness.com/9-examples-manufacturers-iiot/. [accessed 25 March, 2020]

i-SCOOP. 2016. The Internet of Things in Manufacturing: Benefits, Use Cases and Trends. https://www.i--scoop.eu/internet-of-things-iot/internet-of-things-in-manufacturing/. [accessed 26 March, 2020]

Kim Bhasin, Patrick Clark, How Amazon triggered a Robot Arms Race, https://www.livemint.com/Industry/ITsEIiLFTUBX8eGd5gGJ9L/How-Amazon-triggered-a-robot-arms-race.html, [accessed 6 Sep, 2022]

Koshy, Kevin. 2019. Why Is Industry 4.0 Important in Manufacturing? *Capgemini.* www.capgemini.com/gb-en/2019/06/why-is-industry-4-0-important-in-manufacturing/. [accessed 25 March, 2020]

Masooda, Tariq & Egger, Johannes. 2019. Augmented Reality in Support of Industry 4.0 — Implementation Challenges and Success Factors. *Robotics and Computer-Integrated Manufacturing*, 58: 181–195. doi: 10.1016/j.rcim.2019.02.003.

Mercadie, Simon. 2019. Augmented Reality in Industry 4.0. *Insights.* www.leyton.com/blog/?p=3671-augmented-reality-industry-4-0. [accessed 26 March, 2020]

Moore, Mike. 2019. What Is Industry 4.0? Everything You Need to Know. *Techradar News.* www.techradar.com/in/news/what-is-industry-40-everything-you-need-to-know. [accessed 25 March, 2020]

Nayyar, Anand & Kumar, Akshi. 2020. *A Roadmap to Industry 4.0: Smart Production, Sharp Business, and Sustainable Development.* Advances in Science, Technology & Innovation. Springer, Switzerland. doi: 10.1007/978-3-030-14544-6.

Pouspourika, Katerina. 2013. The 4 Industrial Revolutions. *Institute of Entrepreneurship Development.* https://ied.eu/project-updates/the-4-industrial-revolutions. [accessed 25 March, 2020]

Red Reply. 2020. How to Take Advantage of Cloud Computing for Industrie 4.0 and Enterprise 4.0. www.reply.com/red-reply/en/Shared%20Documents/Red-Reply-How-to-take-advantage-of-cloud-for-Industrie4.0-and-enterprise4.0.pdf. [accessed 26 March, 2020]

Rubmann, Michael, Lorenz, Markus, Gerbert, Philipp, Waldner, Manuela, Justus, Jan, Engel, Pascal & Harnisch, Michael. 2015. Industry 4.0—The Future of Productivity and Growth in Manufacturing Industries. *The Boston Consulting Group.* www.bcg.com/en-in/publications/2015/ engineered_products_project_business_industry_4_future_productivity_growth_manufacturing_industries.aspx. [accessed 25 March, 2020]

Seebo. 2020. Artificial Intelligence—The Driving Force of Industry 4.0. www.seebo.com/industrial-ai/. [accessed 26 March, 2020]

SIMUL8. 2020. Planning for Industry 4.0 with Simulation. www.simul8.com/manufacturing/implementing-industry-4-0-with-simulation. [accessed 26 March, 2020]

Smith, Jason. 2018. What Is iIoT (Industrial IoT)? *CMSCMedia.* www.cms-connected.com/PromoNews/What-is-Industry-IoT-4-0. [accessed 26 March, 2020]

Tassel, Loic. 2019. Why Strive for Industry 4.0. *World Economic Forum.* www.weforum.org/agenda/2019/01/why-companies-should-strive-for-industry-4-0/. [accessed 25 March, 2020]

Wright, Ian. 2019. Artificial Intelligence & Industry 4.0. *MAcerta.* https://medium.com/acerta/artificial-intelligence-industry-4-0-aec8282f3543. [accessed 26 March, 2020]

5

Digital Transformation

S. Shalini and T. Devi

CONTENTS

DOI: 10.1201/9781003318378-5

Objective

5.1 Introduction

Digital transformation is defined as organizational, operational and cultural modifications of a business or industry, ecosystem or organization via a wise integration or combination of digital techniques, competencies and processes across all stages and functions in a compiled method. This chapter includes the following topics in various sections.

1. Why a Digital Information Revolution is needed
2. Digital transformation definitions
3. How digital transformation is done
4. Where digital transformation is applied
5. Vital trends in digital transformation
6. What the tools are available for digital transformation

5.2 Why a Digital Information Revolution Is Needed

The "Digital Information Revolution" is the reason for dynamic innovation and it enables people to lead better lives. Vast and enhanced processing of data and information forever could have improved life for people. Progress in information technology (IT) has happened entirely throughout the record—from Guttenberg's innovation of moving type, to the new invention typewriter and then the telegraph, to the most useful telephone and ultimately the Xerox machine—making it cheaper and easier to generate, manipulate, systematize, transmit, save and operate with processed data. With every information and innovation advance, idealists and experts indicated a novel and new period. Hence, for instance, with the emergence of the push for information advancement in the 19th century, "an agent is at hand to bring everything into harmonious cooperation, triumphing over space and time, to subdue prejudice and unite every part of our land in rapid and friendly communication and that great motive agent is steam," sociologist Charles Fraser stated in 1880 (Atkinson & Castro, 2008).

After World War II, information stayed limited and was difficult to use and share, but many information innovations occurred during that period. The dealing and dispensation of information depended on "atoms" to save or share processed data in analog format rather than "bits" (binary digits consisting of 1s and 0s where 1 represents "on" whereas 0 represents "off"), utilized to save or share the information in digital format. Pen and pencil, photocopy machines and offset printers recorded information on paper, then light is captured through a camera lens to stimulate imprinted photo paper with chemicals and telephones converted voices into electric waves that would also be listened to again with the help of speakers. In the era of their preamble, many technologies with analog information were taken care of with well-deserved elation (Atkinson & Castro, 2008).

Considering the quantum advancements, technologies with analog information are now considered as outdated as cuneiform should have appeared to those in the period of industries. The revolution involving digital information ensures a massive amount of voice's digital form information over a telephone, to a wireless sensor signal of pollution in a place, to processed data on medical origins—to be more simply produced, shared and then analyzed (Atkinson & Castro, 2008).

What makes the Digital Information Revolution powerful? Nowadays, huge amounts of processed data are in digital formats, and when it is not expensive and easily created, manipulated, arranged, shared, saved and acted on, that is the information one could talk of being there in the age of digital information. The truth is that one's shoes can even interact with their iPod now, which in turn is a Digital Information Revolution. Both individual lives and society as a whole became radically different and better because of the Digital Information Revolution. But in having the revolution of information in the digital platform to the norms, "Does it generate novel things which are big?" The skeptics miss the key point of the revolution, which is that most of the big innovations in "things" is over. Many of the things that people think of developing have been developed already. But the thing that is done is beginning from scratching the surface to make the world alive with information (Atkinson & Castro, 2008). The Digital Information Revolution is the groundwork and key strategy of trending digital transformation.

5.3 Digital Transformation Definitions

Digital transformation is the process of using digital technologies to create new—or modify existing—business processes, culture, and customer experiences to meet changing business and market requirements. This reimagining of business in the digital age is digital transformation (Salesforce, 2020).

Digital transformation is the cultural, organizational and operational change of an organization, industry or ecosystem through smart integration of digital technologies, processes and competencies across all levels and functions in a staged way. Digital transformation (also DX or DT) leverages technologies to create value for various stakeholders (customers in the broadest possible sense) to innovate and adapt to changing circumstances (i-scoop, 2019).

DT or DX is the use of new, fast and frequently changing digital technology to solve problems. One of the examples of digital transformation is cloud computing, which reduces reliance on user-owned hardware and increases reliance on subscription-based cloud services. Some of these digital solutions enhance the capabilities of traditional software products (e.g., Microsoft Office compared to Office 365), while others are entirely cloud based (e.g., Google Docs) (Wikipedia(Definitions,2020a)).

5.4 How Digital Transformation Is Done

Effective digital transformation is in need of a strategy that is well visualized for modifying customs and serving customers with innovative methods, even if it is meant as a vital distraction from the previous methods of executing a business. What are the ones which lead to an efficient digital transformation strategy? (import.io, 2018). Following are the six elements required for success.

5.4.1 Lead from the Front

The digital transformation is in need of a planned and managerial vision with good management. Since the distraction to a company's customs and business is so insightful, there is a need for the executive team to be digitally intellectual. The *Harvard Business Review* states that digital transformations should have a strong management right from the top else it will be informal and untidy.

> As it is significant to appreciate the possession of projects and ideas, making them into changers of the game requires obvious but sometimes difficult direction from the core with which projects to grow and in which array. The CEOs have the sole authority to give this type of instruction across the whole enterprise. For doing it efficiently, CEOs of the companies required a holistic view of the pressure in a digital platform, opportunities and risks leading to major divisions of the company, and a path to associate them to a general idea for how digital platform is redesigning the landscape with competitiveness.
>
> (Nathan Furr et al., 2022)

Unequal digital transformation proposals could be gathered, compiled, joined, designated and appropriately synchronized for an utmost force with the executive vision and endorsement in place. It is significant to see that executives are not necessarily experts or technologists for providing such a level of digital leadership. It is more significant for digital executives to constantly articulate a visualization of improving its procedures, returns, consumer experience and competitive position if digitally transforming an organization will come into the picture. Typically, the CMO leads this initiative and should focus on KPIs such as return on marketing investments, reduction customer acquisition costs, and generation of a large amount of valuable data that can be used to acquire new customers and better serve existing customers (Nathan Furr et al., 2022).

5.4.2 Set Strategy Ahead of Technology

A well-built planned management must be combined with a convincing and time-bounded strategy of digital transformation. Companies could start by recording evidently the ultimate stage of how the digital transformation seems like, with specific concentration on the sting spots and customer experiences. The customer experience revolution has made possible usage specific measure to understand better what the organization should be doing (Agility CMS, 2022).

5.4.3 Promote New Cultural Norms

A vital encouragement associated with digital transformation is continued existence. Companies should have a vision beyond the normal paradigms of the typical competitors and markets, lending models of the business from other industries. Risk-taking disruptive innovation is all that digital transformation needs, and it can be encouraged and rewarded. Consider a manufacturer, say General Electric (GE), has taken advice from experts on the Internet of Things (IoT) and adjoined monitoring remotely, digital platform and optimization of the system products; this novelty would have helped in improving GE's position in the market (Craig Resnick, 2016).

A culture of calculated risk-taking is one on which companies rely to make such large innovations. Digital executives like managers and staff can cultivate the concept of "failing fast," which is a precious mindset.

As Dr. John Halamka (Deloitte, 2022), Beth Israel Deaconess Medical Center's chief information officer, said in a Deloitte Consulting paper,

> Failure is a valid outcome. Wearable computing is great, but Google Glass wearable computing devices turned out not to be for us right now. We may discover that patients love the Apple Watch wrist-wearable device and it becomes a platform. It's hard to know. But even if it doesn't, it's OK.
>
> (Gerald C. Kane, 2015)

The learning is that in the middle of a transformation which is digital, most of the stuff will be not be known; hence the finest route to fetch clarity is to attempt small experiments, collect stakeholder's reviews, plan e upcoming small experiments and repeat the process until an efficient and sustainable strategy is achieved (import.io, 2018).

5.4.4 Rethink the Customer Journey

Efficient digital transformations use information-based processes and procedures to find out the pain points of the customer and then proceed in reverse into valuable features, propositions and—ultimately—the customer's experience with an approach on the spot and cultural realignment underway. Social media engagement, online customer surveys, text analytics tools, data mining and advanced analytics are some of the ways to understand customer pain points that are offered by digital media. When the data is processed into executable customer visions, the company can bring out new user journeys, and at the end statements are arrived at like "the customers of the firm will have X product selection and purchasing experience" (import.io, 2018).

The ultimate aim is tools like multichannel integration through self-service applications of customer and customer relationship management (CRM) systems that help in creating convincing customer experiences (Wesley Chai et al., 2020).

5.4.5 Interrupt Your Own Business

Companies are in a position to transform their operational processes digitally by keeping new customer experiences in mind. Collaboration tools, enterprise analytics platforms and digital automation pave the path to alter old processes with deeper and more integrated ways of executing at various stages of the companies. As the MIT Sloan Management Review noted,

> Transformed customer experiences are the most visible—and arguably the most exciting—aspects of transformation, companies are also realizing very strong benefits from transforming internal processes through process digitization, worker enablement and performance management.
>
> (George Westerman, et al., 2014)

The company-wide digitally transforming process creates a way to transform the business digitally. The organization or company can proceed with new digital products with less interference from incompatible data or operational silos. Amazon is a prime example of an enterprise that is digitally enabled inducting and supporting novel business in a digital platform, beginning with books, and then to other consumer fields like cloud storage. Another example is an automobile repair shop that would provide services like online tracking and online appointment fixing to augment the car service they provide normally (Markus Menz et al., 2021).

5.4.6 Proceed with New Technology

The later realization in digital transformation should be the technology. Companies can then estimate present skill gaps against the paths of the digital transformation to discover data gaps or functionality with a novel culture, method and model of business in execution. Normally, this assessment process involves comparing present abilities to the issues that are required to be resolved in digital transformation, and results given by the requirements and strategy of novel experiences of customers could support prioritizing the roadmap of technology for all the transformations in the digital platform (Chris Angevine et al., 2021).

Along with the planning of technology, companies and industries would make efforts to connect the insights of analytics with new techniques and technologies to ensure the digital transformation. Appropriately defined analytics rooted into staff member's usual workflows enable essential features for digital transformation, including the following.

1. Increased productivity
2. Improved Resource Management
3. More competitive Innovations
4. Improved responsiveness
5. Improved revenue
6. Increased customer satisfaction

(Mary K. Pratt, 2021)

As digital transformation begins at the pinnacle, it would be viewed as a repetitive series that anticipates inspection, a breakdown at an early stage and adaptation of processes. It begins with digitally committed and sensible executives, who then take the entire approach. The cultural transformation would arrange the company's procedures with the risk acceptance which is required to define the persuasive new experiences of the customer. Models of new business and operational processes arise, which, in turn, create need for investments on technologies around the experiences.

5.5 Where Digital Transformation is Applied

In the Big Data–driven market, the IoT and applications with cloud connectivity have become the ones used to record everything, even the platform used to communicate with clients, dealers and smart things.

Irrespective of whether the businesses use the public or private cloud, on-premise systems or a merger of both, digital transformation is happening and a big role is played by applications, writes Gavin Holme, country head, Africa at Wipro. Data is a precious benefit and tool for any company. Recording data for usage is more and more vital (IT-ONLINE, 2017).

The ideal system for the recording and sourcing is applications via which the data commitment with multiple fields—from customers to dealers to staff members and even opponents—happens. If it is seen as an entire scheme of record and an intermediate medium for systems of commitment, it is possible to view how applications are placed at the center of digital transformation. Businesses today are ruled by customers and companies are continually determined for superior and a unique experience of customers to make the businesses distant from competitions (IT-ONLINE, 2017).

Customer experience is the core of any company, and applications facilitate customer experience, regardless of the medium. The applications with a system of engagement, allow everybody—like staff, dealers and clients alike—to communicate virtually from any place. Data collected and saved from communications across various applications could be analyzed to evaluate various things, from purchasing and ordering trends to consumer requirements. It provides businesses a sole view of their customers, allowing companies to streamline and sketch a business strategy (IT-ONLINE, 2017). Applications for supplier collaboration and business networks, applications for workforce management and applications for IoT are certain trending applications of digital transformation.

5.5.1 Applications for Supplier Collaboration and Business Networks

A business should have the ability to automatically refill its typical stocks as supplies diminish, assuring the business never runs out of stocks and can meet out all orders and needs. Consider a business that has an outline of all the suppliers and their cost terms which let them place orders with effective cost controls. Consider a business that never misses the fees and knows where exactly what is to be delivered at any given time. All these cases can happen in reality. The reality is facilitated by applications, providing businesses a way to interact with suppliers as if they are a sole entity yet being able to split them for practical purposes. Vendors and suppliers can be handled with ease, while data can be used to calculate future trends and habits of suppliers (IT-ONLINE, 2017).

5.5.2 Applications for Workforce Management

The usage of applications in a business infrastructure is to help a business not only to hire and retain the best fitted human resources for any particular program, but they can also help to find the limitations and repetitions in a workforce. Informative and simple interface applications can also help to encourage and encourage employees, helping businesses to maximize performance and reduce staff turnover. Management would use the applications to interact with human resources and even incentivize them through lending programs with in-house loyalty programs. An application used for recruiting and employing the staff can also ensure that the business hires only apt candidates (IT-ONLINE, 2017).

5.5.3 Applications for IoT

Most businesses are investigating IoT, if they are not already involved in progressing out an IoT strategy as the world is constantly getting more intellectual and smarter. There is an engagement between smart devices and management systems driven by applications, finding and solving issues, and sorting and providing data in return. Smart devices are assets to the business and prevail to give precious information to the business. Applications (apps) allow to keep track of the business assets and requirements. At the back end, applications make certain that data is available to analyze for records and trends; hence, the businesses can strategize and prepare with forethought (IT-ONLINE, 2017).

Digital transformation could be viewed in such a way as to collect the best potential values of business from the huge quantity of datasets that exist presently. Digital transformation is enabled by applications to happen between all sections of a business. The applications enabling digital transformation ensure that an organization sees, serves and retrieves the utmost value from clients, customers, suppliers, individual entities and workers or assets. Further progress and expansion by the applications is ensured to an organization through predictive and cognitive analytics. Either within an organization or in the cloud platform, accurate applications provide businesses to digitally transform, stay in the present and stay at the forefront of global competition (IT-ONLINE, 2017).

5.6 Vital Trends in Digital Transformation

Stephanie Overby of The Enterprises Project recently reported that "ongoing digital transformation across industries became a given in 2019. At the same time, digital transformation fatigue also became very real" (The Enterprisers Project, 2020). Organizations that proceed to undervalue the requirement for custom changes do so at self threat. Steve Hall, president and partner of global technology research and advisory firm ISG, predicted that "2020 will still see the rapid scaling of digital initiatives across industries" (The Enterprisers Project, 2020). The following are the eight key digital transformation trends that industrial people should be aware of.

1. A shakeout for industrial people who have spent on Big Data governance and analytics
2. Integrated cross-functional teams which are included in the fast adoption of digital operating models
3. Acquisition activity and continued merger in the outsourcing companies of the IT industry
4. Better use of artificial intelligence (AI) and machine learning
5. New digital partnerships formed by consultancies
6. Increasing public cloud adoption
7. Winning metrics of new digital transformation
8. Awareness of the long-term value of digital initiatives

(The Enterprisers Project, 2020)

Apart from these points, many of the discussion topics are about the upcoming year's trends of digital transformation are all about cloud, edge computing, the IoT and augmented reality. While the same core technologies proceed to be an initial basic foundation to our combined digital transformation path, the upcoming year will be defined class of technologies like 5G, AI and advanced data analytics. The most significant trends and technologies in 2020 were 5G, faster wi-fi, data analytics, machine learning and AI, robotic process automation, blockchain, conversational AI, Everything-as-a-Service (XaaS), user and customer experience, and privacy and digital privacy (Newman, 2019).

5.6.1 5G

Some of the biggest names in telecommunications are ensuring that global deployments of 5G (fifth-generation broadband) is timely, and the release of 5G phones has already been started by the best manufacturers in the world. In 2020, 5G was to be hitting the ground running. The propagation of 5G would speed up progress in smart manufacturing, smart vehicles and smart city. IoT-intensive technologies will work far better on 5G. To say it differently, the real value of 5G will not be restricted only to mobile phones. All of the industries that are used in day-to-day lives will be altered by the evolution of the technology that will, in turn, define 2020 (Newman, 2019).

5.6.2 Faster Wi-Fi

5G and Wi-Fi 6 are entirely different from each other; both will be making sure to take people much faster meting out the faster wireless connection. Wi-Fi 6 and 5G working in concert will lead to the ultra-fast connectivity with end-to-end combination perfectly. The true value of Wi-Fi 6 is in its capability to deliver speedy and faster data much better than the devices connected with Wi-Fi 5. And this is significant for two major reasons. First and foremost is that the number of devices with wi-fi network connectivity is anticipated to increase from ten to about 50 in the upcoming years, and that growth will end up in wi-fi capabilities which are more capable, smarter and faster. The second cause is that the volume and quality of data used via wi-fi networks are mounting but Wi-Fi 5 could not handle and hold the increasing load better. Wi-Fi 6 would tend to eradicate both of these points (Newman, 2019).

5.6.3 Data Analytics

Valuable and significant customer data are gathered, processed and formed into insights for a business to remain spirited in the wide global market without making entire usage of tools of analytics with recent trends. Every big information technical company has found out already that data is the future—and most particularly, processing of it in real time—and so, regardless of the type of industry, data analytics becomes one of the foremost central points of digital transformation (Newman, 2019).

5.6.4 Machine Learning and Artificial Intelligence

If people are ready to make their investments in analytics, they also happen to invest in machine learning and AI, and these will ensure the ability to move on to the huge churning seas of data and processed data, i.e., information. The value of machine learning and AI to data analytics could be classified based on three distinct propositions: speed, scale and convenience. In the mentioned value prepositions, scale and speed relate to the benefit of automation of analysis of vast data sets. AI and machine learning help in analyzing complex data sets in a fraction of the time. This is because algorithms with AI and machine learning of recent trends have gotten better at data analysis (Newman, 2019).

5.6.5 Blockchain

Many other global leaders are utilizing blockchain technology with the Blockchain-as-a-Service platform based on subscription including Amazon Web Services (AWS). Beyond payments and cryptocurrencies, there are many other real use cases for the technology. Blockchain shall be used in real estate/asset management, food safety, intellectual property, and intellectual royalties. The beginning of the true ascent of the blockchain was preditecd to be 2020 (Newman, 2019).

5.6.6 Robotic Process Automation

Robotic Process Automation (RPA) is said to be the nearest hanging fruit on the AI tree and it is not new, but it is nevertheless a very centric topic at every manufacturing and tech conference. Cisco and other enterprise companies are already using RPA to assist the creation of room to upskill and enhance the power of existing manpower resources, and also their model is firm to rapidly progress into a successful strategy (Newman, 2019).

5.6.7 Conversational Artificial Intelligence

Companies are working to pursue composite interactions and grasp the degrees of sentiment and emotion, while ongoing improvisation is happening over time. On the side of silicon, the chipsets that developed exclusively for the smart devices are fetching remarkably well at separating voices of mankind from noises at the backgrounds, and they are capable of exactly processing real-time natural language (Newman, 2019).

5.6.8 User and Customer Experience, XaaS (Everything-as-a-Service) and Digital Privacy

Digital transformation is greater because of the combination of its technical aspects. Undergoing change is the major stimulator for digital transformation. Change nearly forever excels the tools that facilitate it. Some of the technology-adjoining trends that may rule the discussions of digital transformation in 2020 are

XaaS (i.e., Everything-as a-Service), UX/CX (i.e., experience of users/customers) and digital privacy (Newman, 2019).

5.6.8.1 User and Customer Experience

Progress in transformation in the digital platform is closely related to the experience of users/customers, and this importance will lead to prolonging investments or deposits of the company in the domain of digital transformation. On one side, this is particularly real, as companies are more and more transiting from constructing internal skill sets and increasing competence in running on the company's idea. On the other side, progress in connectivity—like 5G or Wi-Fi 6, computing abilities like edge, cloud and machine learning, smart automation like RPA and AI and intuitive user interfaces like gesture analysis, conversational AI and augmented reality—will together make inflection viewpoint for user/customer experience across a range of industries from hospitality and retail to healthcare and transportation (Newman, 2019).

5.6.8.2 XaaS

Everything-as-a-Service would get even more thrust in the most technical industries/sectors driven by hardware. As continued to view the progress of off-side, onsite, cloud and hybrid "large IT" would shift to on-premises as-a-service, exactly at the side of analytics, blockchain, Big Data and more (Newman, 2019).

5.6.8.3 Digital Privacy

Companies will take on transparency and privacy as a trademark, thereby making the customers choose in or out of data compilation schemes easily and with responsiveness. Apart from that, the opportunities for legacy high-technology companies to produce some original and meaningful organization around data privacy and security, there is way to pave the path to digital privacy regeneration (Newman, 2019).

5.7 What Are the Tools Available for Digital Transformation?

There are many tools available in the market to serve the progress of the digital future. The applications, tools, products and platforms that may support the digital journey include: chatbots, TensorFlow, Node.js, Quick Base, Hootsuite, Slack, Xero, Trello, SAP Concur and Stripe.

5.7.1 Chatbots

Chatbots are the most eminent tools of technology available nowadays, states Carlos Melendez, chief operating officer (COO) of nearshore software engineering services firm Wovenware (DeNisco Rayome, 2018):

> Their ability to interact with customers, and answer basic questions and route inquiries appropriately, allow companies with a limited staff to seem much larger and improve customer service-even providing 24/7 call center support when it would be impossible to hire enough people to do this.

The expense of constructing a chatbot of solo principle is also within the affordable limits of the majority of mid-market concerns, and they need not pay much for hiring a representative for customer service, Melendez said (DeNisco Rayome, 2018). Figure 5.1 includes a representation of the chatbot and its flow of conversation.

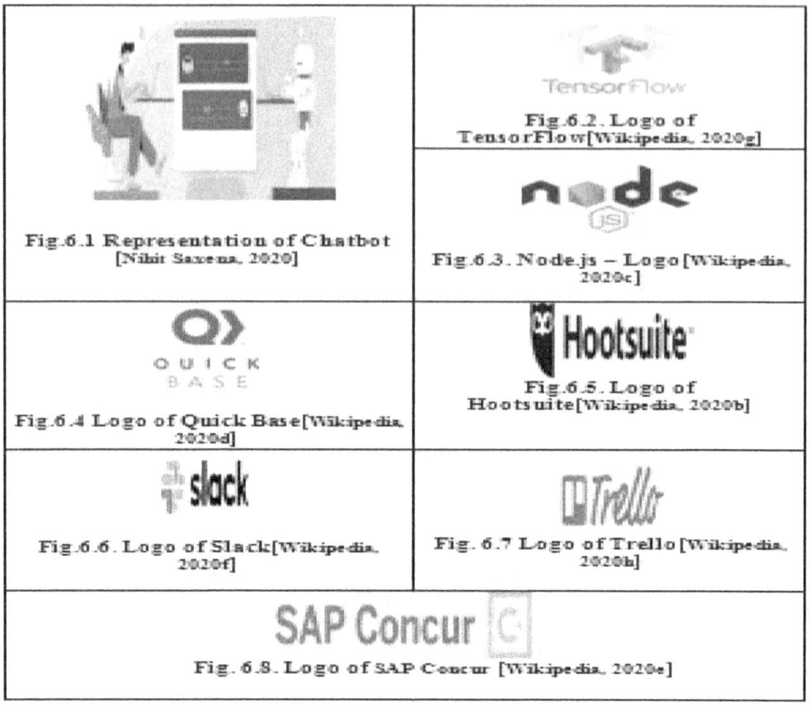

FIGURE 5.1 Applications, tools, products and platforms for digital transformation.

5.7.2 TensorFlow

Google researchers developed TensorFlow, a framework of machine learning. TensorFlow is a framework tool and is open-source (Wikipedia, 2020g). MejorTrato.com, a site for comparison of financial products, started utilizing the platform; it can computerize queries around 57%, responding to customers for general questions quicker within a few seconds, thereby allowing the team to give responses to harder questions. The sales of the company also increased greater than 24% since it has been into function. Cristian Rennella, CTO, MejorTrato.com, stated that they are "honestly surprised with the results and very happy because on the way to digital transformation, the boring, manual and repetitive business processes today can be performed automatically" and Cristian Rennella also thanked AI technology (DeNisco Rayome, 2018). Figure 5.1 shows the icon of TensorFlow (Wikipedia, 2020g).

5.7.3 Node.js

There exists gravitation toward Node.js when digital transformation is considered, as this platform allows using the same language on both the back end as well as front end (Wikipedia, 2020c). This makes the teams working for smaller development spend only minimum time in writing as well as reworking code. "With minimal training, these developers can quickly use Node.js to get a web server up and running and, from there, they can expand out to APIs, devices and front end," said Keith Chester, research and development lead and senior application developer for Fusion Marketing (DeNisco Rayome, 2018). Figure 5.1 shows the logo of Node.js. (Wikipedia, 2020c).

5.7.4 Quick Base

The Quick Base platform (Wikipedia, 2020d), with a low code for clients, helps the professionals who are not from a technical background to easily build applications for business. Quick Base is specifically for business users who use spreadsheets which could twist out of control when users are doing modifications and building newer editions of the application.

Joe Marchillo, a member of the IT solutions team at Apex Imaging Services, said:

> With Quick Base, we get a view of the high level of everything we need to know in a single snapshot All of our project managers (who don't know how to code) are now using Quick Base as their new Excel spreadsheet. It definitely streamlines efficiency; for example, if we call stores and say we're going to be there for the project in two days, we have a log of all that in case there's any push back.
>
> (DeNisco Rayome, 2018)

Figure 5.1 shows the logo of Quick Base (Wikipedia, 2020d).

5.7.5 Hootsuite

Hootsuite is a social media platform used by more than 15 million people worldwide (Wikipedia, 2020b). The social media marketing and management platform, can help to take control of a social media presence. The Hootsuite platform provides various resources, including the top ten tips of social media for small businesses, and it also helps on how owners of small businesses could make use of social media to make progress in the business and stay competitive (DeNisco Rayome, 2018). Figure 5.1 shows the logo of Hootsuite (Wikipedia, 2020b).

5.7.6 Slack

In recent years, a tool for messaging in the workplace called Slack has progressed in enterprises (Wikipedia, 2020f). "Slack is a great tool for SMBs (small- and medium-sized businesses), particularly if team members or vendors are geographically scattered," Kim McCumber, founder of Floodlight Training & Consulting, said. "It's great for communication and sharing files with one or multiple individuals at a company". It also integrates well with Zapier, a tool that can take a large number of Software-as-a-Service (SaaS) platforms and connect them to work along, said McCumber (DeNisco Rayome, 2018). Figure 5.1 shows the logo of Slack (Wikipedia, 2020f).

5.7.7 Xero

Cloud-based Xero is an accounting platform that can be used by accountants, bookkeepers and small businesses. This platform launched a chatbot for Facebook messenger called Hey Xero in order to help small businesses to locate bookkeepers and accountants, as per Alexandra Zelenko, technical writer and marketer of DDI Development. Xero was enabled to apply AWS AI service and machine learning service for tasks such as invoices coding for payment purposes, as Xero has also moved the platform to AWS, Zelenko said (DeNisco Rayome, 2018).

5.7.8 Trello

SaaS for project management called Trello (Wikipedia, 2020h) is a significant element for efforts in a digital platform, stated Evan Tarver, a tech analyst working for FitSmallBusiness.com. The product in this platform paves a way for numerous teams across different operational groups to collaborate on projects, and manage multiple project pipelines. "Using Trello brings your business processes into the digital age, and makes your company run more efficiently," Tarver stated (DeNisco Rayome, 2018). Figure 5.1 shows the logo of Trello (Wikipedia, 2020h).

5.7.9 SAP Concur

Software for invoice management is provided by SAP Concur (Wikipedia, 2020e) to help small businesses to save time on administrative tasks, keep the headcount down and avoid faults. "It's easier than ever for small businesses to adopt enterprise tools," said Christal Bemont, general manager and senior vice president of the small, midsized and nationals business unit at SAP Concur.

> Historically, enterprise tools have come with an enterprise cost, and often entail lengthy deployments. However, thanks to the rise of the cloud, small businesses can quickly and easily deploy less expensive apps based on the web to position them better for rapid growth.
>
> (DeNisco Rayome, 2018)

Figure 5.1 shows the logo of SAP Concur (Wikipedia, 2020e).

5.7.10 Stripe

An economic infrastructure will be built by Stripe for the wide network called the internet, thereby allowing running financial operations and allowing payments and transactions online. The platforms that are generally used include Shopify and Squarespace. "After 36 hours live on the newly integrated-with-Stripe Snowvation platform, one Snowvation partner ski resort processed 10% of its entire 2016 volume," said Michael Stocker, CEO and founder of ski resort software provider Snowvation. "In an industry where most revenue is restricted to only four months of the year, making payments as faster and easier as possible, online particularly, is key" (DeNisco Rayome, 2018).

5.8 Conclusion

This chapter described the need for a Digital Information Revolution, definitions of digital transformation, the process by which digital transformation is done, applications of digital transformation, the key trends and technologies in digital transformation, and the tools and technologies available for digital transformation. The progressing technologies like chatbots, 5G, faster wi-fi and conversational artificial intelligence has been explained with the mode of digital transformation. Thus, digital transformation is the driving force for various upcoming technologies and trends in information technology, as well as in many other domains and streams which are based on digitization.

REFERENCES

Agility CMS, 2022, Agility, How Digital Transformation Can Overcome the Customer Experience Revolution, https://agilitycms.com/resources/posts/how-digital-transformation-can-overcome-the-customer-experience-revolution

Atkinson, Robert D. & Castro, Daniel D., 2008, Digital Quality of Life, https://itif.org/files/DQOL.pdf [Accessed October, 2008]

Chris Angevine, Jacklyne Keomany, Jannick Thomsen, and Rodney Zemmel, 2021, Implementing a digital transformation at industrial companies, https://www.mckinsey.com/industries/advanced-electronics/our-insights/implementing-a-digital-transformation-at-industrial-companies

Craig Resnick, 2016, ARC VIEW, GE's Industrial Internet of Things Journey, https://www.ge.com/digital/sites/default/files/download_assets/GE%20Industrial%20Internet%20of%20Things%20Journey%20%281%29.pdf

Deloitte, Strategy, not technology, drives digital transformation Becoming a digitally mature enterprise, https://www2.deloitte.com/us/en/insights/topics/digital-transformation/digital-transformation-strategy-digitally-mature.html, [Accessed 7 Sep, 2022]

DeNisco Rayome, Alison., 2018, TechRepublic, 10 Tech Tools That Will Help Bring Digital Transformation to Your SMB (Small- and Medium-Sized Businesses), www.techrepublic.com/article/10-tech-tools-that-will-help-bring-digital-transformation-to-your-smb/ [Accessed 15 February, 2018]

George Westerman, Didier Bonnet, and Andrew McAfe, 2014, MIT Sloan Management Review, The Nine Elements of Digital Transformation, https://sloanreview.mit.edu/article/the-nine-elements-of-digital-transformation/

Enterprisers Project, 2020, What Are the Key Trends in Digital Transformation in 2020? https://enterprisers-project.com/what-is-digital-transformation [Accessed 02 April, 2020]

Gerald C. Kane, Doug Palmer, Anh Nguyen Phillips, David Kiron and Natasha Buckley, 2015, Strategy, not Technology, Drives Digital Transformation, https://www2.deloitte.com/content/dam/Deloitte/fr/Documents/strategy/dup_strategy-not-technology-drives-digital-transformation.pdf [Accessed 24 March, 2020]

i-scoop, 2019, Digital Transformation: Online Guide to Digital Business Transformation, www.i-scoop.eu/digital-transformation/ [Accessed 26 December, 2019]

IT-ONLINE, 2017, The Role of Applications in Digital Transformation, https://it-online.co.za/2017/02/03/the-role-of-applications-in-digital-transformation/#:~:text=Applications%20enable%20digital%20transformation%20to,assets%20as%20single%2C%20individual%20entities [Accessed 03 February, 2017]

Markus Menz,Sven Kunisch,Julian Birkinshaw, David J. Collis, Nicolai J. Foss,Robert E. Hoskisson, John E. Prescott, 2021, Journal of Management Studies, Corporate Strategy and the Theory of the Firm in the Digital Age, https://onlinelibrary.wiley.com/doi/10.1111/joms.12760

Mary K. Pratt, 2021, Tech Target, 10 digital transformation benefits for business, https://www.techtarget.com/searchcio/tip/Top-10-digital-transformation-benefits-for-business

Nathan Furr, Andrew Shipilov, Didier Rouillard, Antoine Hemon-Laurens, Harvard Business Review, 2022, Digital Transformation, https://hbr.org/2022/01/the-4-pillars-of-successful-digital-transformations

Newman, Daniel., 2019, Top 10 Digital Transformation Trends for 2020, Forbes, www.forbes.com/sites/danielnewman/2019/07/14/top-10-digital-transformation-trends-for-2020/#6d5374f76beb [Accessed 14 July, 2019]

Salesforce, 2020, What Is Digital Transformation? www.salesforce.com/products/platform/what-is-digital-transformation/ [Accessed 24 March, 2020]

Saxena, Nihit., 2020, Chatbot Architecture Tutorial, Towards Data Science, https://towardsdatascience.com/chatbot-tutorial-choosing-the-right-chatbot-architecture-5539c8489def [Accessed 15 February, 2020]

Wesley Chai, Tim Ehrens, Karolina Kiwak, 2020, Tech Target, https://www.techtarget.com/searchcustomerexperience/definition/CRM-customer-relationship-management

Wikipedia(Definitions,2020a), digital transformation, https://www.definitions.net/definition/digital+transfor mation, [Accessed 23 March, 2020]

Wikipedia, 2020b, Hootsuite, https://en.wikipedia.org/wiki/Hootsuite#/media/File:Hootsuite_logo.svg [Accessed 05 April, 2020]

Wikipedia, 2020c, Node.js, https://en.wikipedia.org/wiki/Node.js#/media/File:Node.js_logo.svg, [Accessed 05 April, 2020]

Wikipedia, 2020d, QuickBase, https://en.wikipedia.org/wiki/QuickBase,_Inc.#/media/File:Primary_Logo_RGB_Purple_HighRes800x800.png [Accessed 05 April, 2020]

Wikipedia, 2020e, SAP_Concur, https://en.wikipedia.org/wiki/SAP_Concur#/media/File:Concur_logo.png [Accessed 05 April, 2020

Wikipedia, 2020f, Slack, https://upload.wikimedia.org/wikipedia/commons/b/b9/Slack_Technologies_Logo.svg [Accessed 05 April, 2020]

Wikipedia, 2020g, TensorFlow, https://en.wikipedia.org/wiki/TensorFlow#/media/File:TensorFlowLogo.svg [Accessed 05 April, 2020]

Wikipedia, 2020h, Trello, https://en.wikipedia.org/wiki/Trello#/media/File:Trello_logo.svg [Accessed 05 April, 2020]

6

Emerging Technological Advancements for Educational Institutions

Manika Garg

CONTENTS

Objectives

1. To introduce the emerging vital methods for educational institutions
2. To make students aware of the impact of technology on educational institutions
3. To introduce the key components such as AI, AR, Cloud for education delivery

DOI: 10.1201/9781003318378-6

6.1 Introduction to Emerging Imperatives for Educational Institutions

During the span of the past few decades, we find ourselves surrounded by technology and networks all around us, and it is marching—as well as transforming—at a breakneck speed. With the adoption of technology by business firms, healthcare, start-ups, and almost all government institutions across the globe, an environment has evolved whereby no walk of life that can be imagined can afford to remain outside its purview. It has resulted in a steep demand for sufficiently trained resources who can not only skilfully handle but also keep pace with this monster. And since it has been the primary responsibility of educational institutions for ages to impart or facilitate the acquisition of necessary knowledge and skills as per the demands of that particular era, this time around also the onus is on these very institutions to rise to the occasion and brace themselves up for the onerous task ahead. Educational institutions today confront the twin tasks of needing not only to adapt and be dextrous in handling the educational tools that technology has put at their disposal, but also being able to roll out sufficient resources to cater to the needs of the environment outside. The gap between the demand and supply of trained resources needs to be filled up. The need of the hour is to create an education system wherein educational institutions cease to operate within their respective cocoons and at the same time throw open their gates wide open to potential hirers who can regularly engage with the teacher as well as the taught. The educational ecosystem, in short, needs a paradigm shift.

The present era education system involves a digital, non-static approach to learning, a fully equipped faculty, a broader coalition among various beneficiaries as well as stakeholders, and adequate levels of funding. It will be crucial to devise innovative solutions to accelerate the performance of the higher education sector to satisfy market demands, improve access to students, and drive operational efficiency.

The importance of social skills like cooperation, empathy, social awareness, and global citizenship cannot be underestimated, along with technical skills such as software development, decision science, etc. The blurring of boundaries between the physical, digital, and biological worlds, and the advent of artificial intelligence (AI), quantum computing, genetic engineering, etc., has thrown open a new chapter in human development, and rationally learning this chapter is a challenge as well as an opportunity.

The World Economic Forum proposes a global framework for education, as shown in Figure 6.1. It has defined learning for new age and economy through eight key changes in traditional learning. Educational institutions can adopt these changes as a guiding light to provide students with skills needed at work, in society, and in economy of the future.

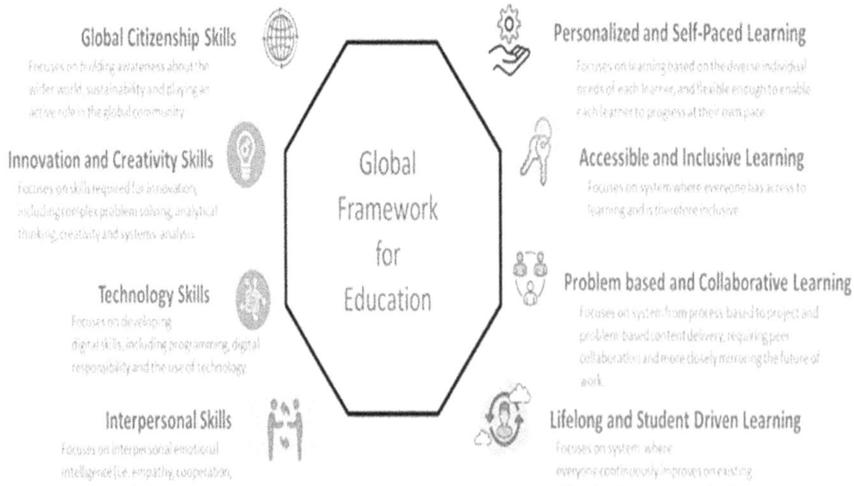

FIGURE 6.1 World Economic Forum global framework for education.

6.1.1 Global Citizenship Skills

Children must be aware of global challenges and have the skills to initiate, participate in, and review the campaigns and programs addressing such challenges. They are expected to emerge as agents of positive change.

Creating future citizens would require school systems to help children in developing global awareness, comprehension of global interdependencies of issues, and their role and responsibilities within the global community. These skills can be imparted through formal and informal mechanisms.

A project, in technology and science, can teach awareness and sustainability by highlighting historical moments through different perspectives from a diverse set of people across the globe. Outside the classroom, activities such as community service, social activism, and volunteering assignments can help students learn global citizenship skills. For example, climate change protests in 2019 taught students from many schools about the methods of addressing issues of public concern.

Emerging technologies such as virtual classrooms, social media, and cyber-physical systems can be used for global citizenship education. Students can interact and exchange ideas with students across the globe through the use of video conferences and virtual classrooms. It helps them learn from different perspectives and through different approaches. Such classrooms with a global presence allow students to understand their roles in the global ecosystem and develop empathy and respect toward other communities and countries, supporting the feeling and idea of one world. Governments and national curricula should promote global citizenship learning—as done by Italy, where all students must study climate change and sustainability.

6.1.2 Innovation and Creativity Skills

All-encompassing change being the hallmark of this era, adaptation to it through innovation and creativity has become the key driver of growth and value creation in the Fourth Industrial Revolution (World Economic Forum, 2020).

The development of innovation and ideation skills in children is a must for children to productively contribute to a future economy. They should have the capability to translate ideas into solutions, products, and systems which are scalable, practically feasible, and adaptable. Skills such as curiosity, creativity, critical thinking, problem-solving and systems analysis, etc., enable innovation. Innovative skills can also be enabled by play activities which can be applied in both formal and informal education. Play activities enable children to tap into their natural curiosity, learn through trial and error, and explore new solutions to challenges.

Innovation skills can be developed through collaboration, both between students and teachers from diverse backgrounds and between industry and academia. Industry can help bring the needs of the real world and academia can assist with research and inventions.

Students/children get a chance to channel their creative energy while learning through digital modes such as programming games and activities, such activities also contextualize and solidify the learning. For example, students can learn to use design and engineering skills with applications such as Dassault Systems' SolidWorks. Another example of a team that gamifies innovation and creativity learning is Real Play Coalition, which is formed by the partnership of learning companies and international organizations such as LEGO Foundation, National Geographic, Unilever, the Ingka Group, and UNICEF.

6.1.3 Technology Skills

Students must develop technology skills to become the workforce of the future; the onus of developing these skills falls on educational institutions. Educational institutes should not only help students develop hard technical skills such as software development, technical design, etc., but should also help students understand their responsibilities in the digital world. The student should also be sensitized toward the risks, security, and potential hazards of the digital world, to help them develop a healthy relationship with technology. The combination of these skills will help students use technology effectively for societal and economic growth.

Technology skills can be developed with the help of new age digital learning channels. Students can learn programming, animation skills, and story building from online web applications such as CodeAcademy and Code.org. Educational institutes should be technologically capable of enabling digital learning of technical skills which will be relevant in the industry in near future. To do so and gain deep insights into the job market, education institutes should collaborate with industry bodies, experts, e.g., Verizon's Innovative Learning Program think tank DQ Institute. Government education departments and bodies can play a fundamental role in developing technology skills, for example by launching programming and technology competitions.

6.1.4 Interpersonal Skills

Interpersonal skills, also known as people skills—qualities like leadership, social influence, empathy, teamwork, and emotional intelligence, etc.—are among the high-demand interpersonal skills of the future.

These skills can help students appreciate different perspectives and viewpoints, and develop long-lasting meaningful relationships with fellow beings. For example, students can learn to appreciate the perspectives of fellow people with disabilities or people with non-binary gender identities. With such sensitization, students can help create a more inclusive society in the future and innovate to develop new solutions to address the needs of people with special needs.

Interpersonal skills can also be developed informally through the exposure of students to a diverse set of peers, allowing students to become culturally aware and respectful of diversity and—in return—improving interpersonal skills. Students can be exposed to diverse peers spread across the globe through communication and video conferencing technologies such as Skype.

6.1.5 Personalized and Self-Paced Learning

Recourse to personalized and self-paced learning through flexible learning environments has a significant positive effect on students. One of the multiple methods to deliver personalized learning is to limit the class size and enable educators to spend more time with each student. This method has been followed and promoted by many educational institutes. Another method is to provide the flexibility of channel (physical or digital, flexibility in curriculum and choice of areas, and flexibility in the choice of assessment mode, as well), presentations, oral assessments, live projects, etc. Personalized experience can be enabled by new age web/cloud-based learning platforms that provide online courses or MOOCs (massive open online courses). Byjus, Khan Academy, Coursera, Udemy, and Edx are some of the prominent platforms that allow students to undertake the digital course in the subjects of their choice and flexibility of time and pace.

6.1.6 Accessible and Inclusive Learning

Learning ecosystems and educational institutions must make education and opportunities more accessible and inclusive. Education is a key determinant in overall quality of life and ability to socialize and contribute to the economy. Education can also be more engaging through the inclusion of other modalities of learning such as visual, audial, tactile, and kinesthetic methods. Learning can be made more accessible to children from different backgrounds by ensuring diverse representation in learning material, such as book characters and historical figures. Technology can also help increase the level of access to education for students with special needs. For example, visually impaired students can leverage text-to-speech solutions. EdTech companies such as Labster and Praxilabs have designed online lab simulations, which help to teach science subjects when access to science facilities is not available.

6.1.7 Problem-Based and Collaborative Learning

Today's economy is driven by innovation—creation of new ideas, solutions, services, and products—and there is no single panacea for doing that. To inculcate innovation and promote such thinking, the learning process in educational institutions has to shift from a process-based to a problem-based approach.

To make this shift, education institutions have to take an open-ended path rather than a single-answer approach. Students can be given problems that are closer to the real world to implement problem-based learning. Collaborative projects can be assigned to them to solve real-world challenges. For example, in a typical classroom, cubic volume is taught by teaching a formula—length multiplied by height and width—and then asking them to apply this abstract procedure, which they have just memorized, to find the volume of different box sizes. A problem-based approach to the same concept can be to design a box which is water-resistant and can hold 25 toys of a certain size so that toys can be transported from one place to another in a rainy season. With such an approach, children will inculcate problem-solving skills. They will research different water-resistant materials, will estimate the size of the box differently (thus, each box will looking different), while still solving the same problem.

Problem-based, collaborative learning approaches can certainly be facilitated by technology. Cloud-based tools, for example, can facilitate accessibility globally, hence allowing students to work from different locations on the same document, and build on each other's work. Augmented reality (AR) and virtual reality (VR) can provide a different context and add a layer of challenge to problem-solving by taking students to new geographies and environments and solve problems in their contexts. Here again, the private sector can play a key role. Microsoft, for example, has partnered with The Knowledge Society (TKS)—an extracurricular program in the United Kingdom—to provide their high school students with real challenges that the company is facing.

6.1.8 Lifelong and Student-Driven Learning

Traditional education systems did not take into consideration the dynamism of the job industry. These were designed to impart the knowledge until a certain age and then use that during life. But with future job disruptions, lifelong learning is required to acquire new skills to fulfill the demands of industry. Open-ended methods of teaching—inquiry-based learning, etc.—can support lifelong learning. For example, to demonstrate the knowledge acquired on any topic like personal hygiene, students can be given an option to showcase it by giving a speech, through a presentation, creating a work of art, writing an essay, or creating a film. With all these varied formats, teachers and families will not only know about the child's understanding of the concept but can also know the child's interests and personality.

Digital courseware gives students multiple options for the course material. Students have the flexibility to choose the material and the mode of presentation they would like to engage in, so digital education helps facilitate learner-driven approaches. Teachers can also leverage learning management systems to keep track of the multiple learning journeys undertaken by students. Governments can play a major role in facilitating this shift to lifelong and student-driven learning. Finland, for example, has given away the practice of national standardized tests and evaluates the learning by just pulling the sample of students. This system has resulted in better understanding as children enjoy learning, rather than feeling the pressure of assessment.

6.2 Impact of Technology on Educational Institution Value Chains

As swift advancements in technology are transforming the civil space and the working society, the gap between the education systems and the needs of global economies and societies is continuously increasing. In the dynamic world, all education establishments should respond favorably to changing societal needs. In the disruptive job industry, demand for new skills and socioeconomic polarization is increasing day by day. Here, education systems have a critical role to play in preparing the workforces of the future. Education institutions are hence seemingly under intense pressure to create value and focus their efforts and scarce funds on activities that drive up value for their respective customers and other stakeholders (Goldsworthy, 2008). Time and experience have proven that if the universities improve upon the quality of their services, they can provide the best services to the community. The transformation of higher learning institutions into competitive enterprises is underway.

One of the models which can be of significant help in improving the quality of educational institutions is the value chain model. In this model, an organization can define its core competencies and activities and can focus on having a competitive advantage of differentiation and cost in these activities. According to Michael Porter's study in 1985, the value chain model is based upon the process approach of an organization (Porter Michael, 1985; Dorria, Mahsa et al., 2012). For the creation of value under the value chain model, the organization has to segregate its activities into different components so that analysis of the value chain can be performed (Pathak Virendra, Kavit Pathak, 2010). Earlier, this segregation was not possible with traditional schools of learning, but with recent trends in higher education, educational activities can be segregated. Hence, the academic process has to be disaggregated into different components which have well-developed measures.

The value chain of a university in today's era, as shown in Figure 6.2, can be defined as a conjunction of activities performed around research, teaching, and community service. Teaching involves processes like educational delivery, educational design, and assessment, while research function involves research grants and publications, research training, and development services. As part of community service function, various processes include outreach activities, brand development, managing alumni, employer, and funding agencies relations. These processes are further supported by activities like recruitment, admission, enrollment, academic service, and alumni support.

Each of these processes when combined adds value to the total educational package provided to students. Let us have a look at some of these activities, as follows.

- **Enrollment of Students and Recruitment of Teaching/Research Staff**

  The new age institutions must derive value out of numbers. The student-teacher ratio in education institutions thus may vary from *just-in-case* (conservative student-to- staff ratios which constrain the demand for faculty and the number of students to be admitted) to *just-in-time* (flexible inventory of staff, more contractual, casual, and part-time employment to adjust the capacity for demand) and *just-for-me* (menu-driven virtual education customized for each student, with no demand for staff resources) (Duderstadt, 1999).

- **Teaching and Learning**

  With the disruptive technological advancements, the business models for education institutions have changed. Three emerging business models are brick and mortar (physical campus), brick and click (physical as well as virtual campus), and click only (virtual campus) (Levine, 2001).

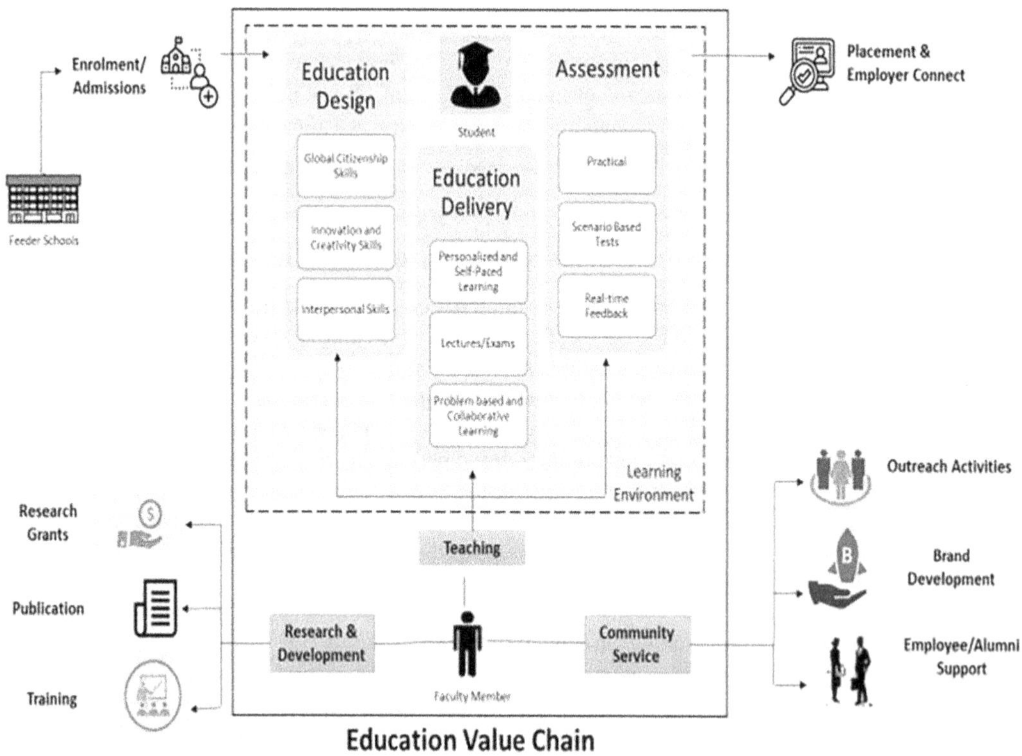

FIGURE 6.2 Education value chain.

Now the teachers can manage the student's overall learning experience, i.e., driving up student (customer) satisfaction. They are playing a key role as one of the many content providers (industry experts, thought leaders) for the new education customer.

- **Research Training and Development**

  To retain intellectual capital and to survive in the future, research publications and grants have become the most important measures for higher educational institutions. The value from this activity can be derived by training teachers to produce more commercially relevant and better-quality research publications. The researcher can be empowered to deliver high-quality research outcomes, get their work published in the best possible academic journals, commercialize their research, and develop an intellectual property portfolio.

- **Community Service—Visibility**

  The market is enormously expanding with a diverse set of customers; hence, institutions are looking forward to active brand building and differentiation. This can be achieved by creating a highly skilled human resource: identifying the incumbent student/teacher/researcher and equipping them with the right resources. Alumni can also play the role of brand ambassadors/mascots. Marketing the right way by efficiently using these components can contribute to the educational institutions' rankings at national and international levels. These rankings directly impact the research grants and funds that organizations receive. So, the operations for higher education institutions have to be reconfigured to ensure smooth research activities and to maintain national/international credibility by accommodating the other two critical customers, i.e., funding agencies and ranking agencies.

The core activities which add the most value to educational institutions are educational delivery and design. But when we analyze the educational institution of higher learning using the value chain model, the educational "supply chain" includes relationships with feeder schools and employers. The students who come from these feeder schools get trained in higher education institutions so that they can be consumed in the industry by employers. The overall system performance of an educational institution can be greatly improved by looping in these entities within the educational package. Considering this whole system together will benefit society directly by providing valuable feedback for educational redesign.

Research and development in technology can come as a support service in education either by automating the activities in the value chain or by provisioning the tools that facilitate the planning, organizing, and monitoring of activities in the value chain. It is changing the ways education is delivered by the development of curriculum, assessment plans, new pedagogy, flipped classrooms, blended learning, etc.

In value chain activities, technology can play a significant role. It can facilitate student enrollments and attract qualified academic/research staff. Institutions of higher learning today are using disruptive technology (simulation-ready software, the development of virtual content broken into fine grain) to render tangibility, separability, inventory, and standardization to the academic process (Noble, 1998; Poon, 2006; Levine, 2001). Since the education system has to serve a diverse pool of users—faculty, students, administrators, guidance counselors, alumni, student organizations, the office of career services, companies, and feeder schools—technology tools like collaboration platforms, learning management systems, etc., can play a vital role.

6.3 Key Components of Education Delivery, Their Evolution, and Emerging Technology Applications

Education 4.0—which focuses on the individual learner, lifelong learning, and uses technology for the in-formalization of education—is built upon four pillars: educational content, learning environment, assessment, and accreditation.

- **Educational Content**

  In a robust learning environment, the educational content is knowledge centered, meaning that it is built upon the core concepts along with innovative ideas. The main focus here is to transfer the knowledge based on the context of the individual learner.

- **Learning Environment**

  A powerful learning environment should be designed to cater to the skills, knowledge, needs, and attitudes brought in by each learner. Today's learner-centered approach emphasizes the need of bringing in multiple perspectives and using them within the context of the training activity to create a personalized learning environment.
- **Assessments**

  Assessment-centered elements help make capabilities and thinking visible to students, teachers, and others in the learning community. Furthermore, these elements support an ongoing process of labor and revision that is focused on deepening understanding.
- **Accreditation**

  Accreditation-centered elements ensure quality in activities of an educational organization and fix accountability. They provide public confidence or trust in the system by developing the credibility of the institution. Accreditation unites the professionals and brings together teachers, practitioners, and students in an activity that focuses on improving professional preparation and practice.

6.3.1 Content

In the post-industrial era, the skill sets which were obtained in university or college helped one to serve for a lifetime—one could cope up with them throughout one's career. However, over the period, the duration of time for which the skill remains relevant has declined. Unfortunately, educational institutions have not kept up with these changes. One of the challenges for the higher education sector today is the widening gap between college curricula and market demands. It has led to a skill mismatch for the talent entering the market. To bridge this gap, educational content plays a very important role. Tailoring the content to serve market demands and incorporating new age technologies in the creation and delivery of content can lead to more accomplished learning. Students can be motivated to learn about subject content by activating their prior knowledge of the subject topic. Once this is done successfully, one can start presenting new concepts and content vocabulary.

Over time, the content has evolved, as shown in Figure 6.3, with technological advancements. For a long time, books (print media in general) were the only source of knowledge. Knowledge seekers would spend hours in the libraries reading books, magazines, articles, and journals educating themselves in

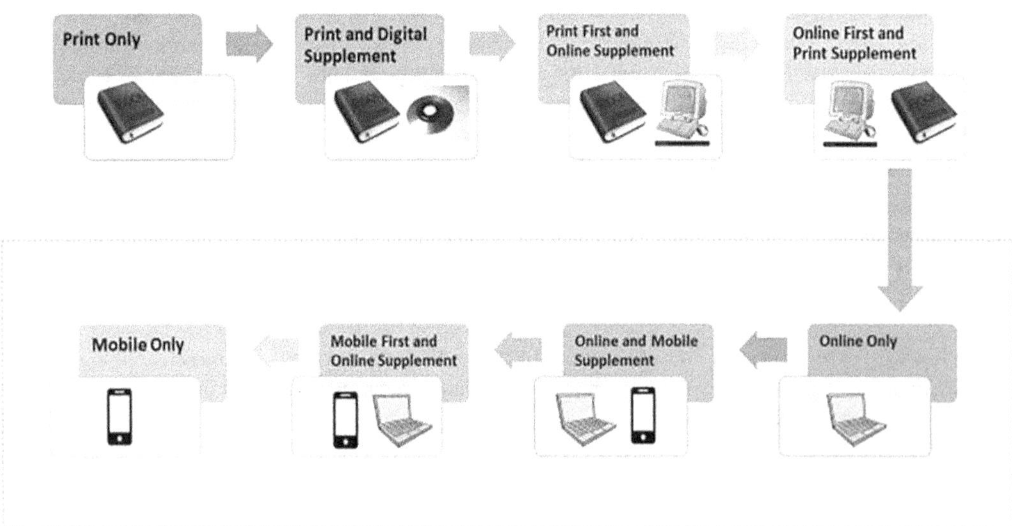

FIGURE 6.3 Evolution of learning content.

their areas of interest. With the advent of the personal computer, education companies saw the need to open a second channel—a digital channel. We started seeing CDs and DVDs packed at the very end of the books. While the book was still the primary product here, the CDs or DVDs would often contain supplementary content such as video snippets, additional quizzes, etc.

As the internet became popular, CDs and DVDs slowly faded away and were replaced with an "online access code" that users could redeem to access content online. It was the same content as in the CDs or DVDs, but available online, so that the content could be updated regularly without having to ship a whole new disc again.

With the internet becoming ubiquitous in most parts of the world, people are starting to prefer online content over print media. Most of us today read our morning news online, access digital versions of our favorite magazines, and buy and access e-books instead of printed books. Education companies are being forced to flip their business models. The online product is now becoming the primary product, and printed books—for the first time—are a supplementary offering.

With more and more people preferring online learning products over books, many education companies are being forced to roll out their first set of "online only" products, which do not come with any print offerings. Publishing companies that traditionally printed books are focused on building digital online products and creating digital learning experiences. The advent of the "smartphone" has opened up yet another digital channel that can be used to engage learners beyond the online experience, with supplementary quizzes, extended reading, and video snippets that can be consumed anytime anywhere on personal devices. Learners typically get free access to mobile content along with their online product purchases.

With the increasing popularity and growing adoption of smartphones, we will soon be seeing many "mobile first" products that would be targeted to the growing population of smartphone users. All the traditional online content will now have to be tweaked to work responsively on mobile or be completely re-designed for a mobile-first experience.

The most natural way of consuming digital content today is a smartphone. If one wants to learn anything, all that is needed is a phone with an internet connection. With the help of smartphones, the content is accessible now anytime, anywhere, on the go. These days, this channel is effectively leveraged for learning and education. We have an enormous number of smartphone-based education products in the market, and this will only grow in the years to come.

6.3.1.1 Applications of Artificial Intelligence for Educational Content

Education today is moving toward personalized learning, a learning experience customized for each student with her/his unique needs. Learning can be personalized by adjusting the learning components, such as content, pace, or sequence of content, learning environment, etc., according to the learners' needs and purpose. AI has been applied to areas of content abstraction and sequencing as discussed in what follows.

Educational content has traditionally been created in form of books, and now with the proliferation of the internet and the need for quick and enjoyable learning, the content is being created in audio and video formats. Whatever be the format—books, audio, or video—the creation of content requires immense human expertise and effort. However, things are slowly changing as AI capabilities have been developed which can produce digital content of quality at par with human experts. AI, today, is being used to create condensed content by breaking down the existing body of textbooks into manageable bite-sized pieces of information, which accelerate the learner's journey to learn and master content. Condensed content is useful for a quick review of content and has an impact on all levels from elementary to the corporate environment.

An example of such a solution, Cram101, uses AI to make textbook content easier to navigate and more comprehensible. It breaks down the textbook content into a small, understandable "smart" study guide, which includes chapter summaries, flashcards, and true/false and multiple-choice practice tests. The content is hierarchically structured from textbook, author, and chapter. It allows the reader to quickly get the gist of the content without having to read the entire content. Another similar application, developed by Content Technologies Inc., allows the users to highlight important content from the textbook chapters. It also generates chapter-specific summaries (Content Technologies Inc., 2022).

Content sequencing is to organize the content in a certain order to ensure overall comprehension and achievement of educational objectives through the learning activities of the students. Custom content sequencing and assembly is a time-consuming process and can, at times, result in gaps in the course structure which the teachers may be unaware of. AI can be used to evaluate content sequence by generating content recommendations after each module and checking for coverage of the topics suggested by the AI recommendation and existing course structure.

Online portals such as Project Management Institute, American Psychological Association, various news websites, and social media websites such as Medium, allow users to create an account on their website and read the content. Such portals actively use content recommendation engines powered by AI which allow them to analyze the historical content read by the user and content read by other users, as shown in Figure 6.4, to suggest related or next best articles/news/journals, etc. The use of content recommendation engines enhances the customer experience by providing them personalized content and alerts, and increases traffic on the platform, translating into increased revenues.

6.3.1.2 Applications of Augmented Reality to Enhance Content

The famous proverb "Tell me and I forget. Show me and I remember. Involve me and I understand" is the underlying principle for use of AR in education, an emerging area that has the potential to cause significant changes in teaching methods and the students' learning processes. The use of AR transforms the education experience from an ordinary textbook reading to an interactive and engaging experience that lasts longer in the learner's memory. AR adds virtual objects to the real world, and it helps students to virtually see, feel, and interact with objects in three dimensions—like seeing and interacting with real objects, but without the physical and other limitations of the real world.

From an educational institution's perspective, AR provides a huge opportunity to scale up its educational content without investing in expensive physical laboratories, experiment centers, and training labs. Educational institutes can leverage the state-of-the-art AR technology mobile devices and applications, which university students are generally accustomed to using for communication and leisure. Apart from saving heavy capital investments, Augmented reality also helps universities save operational expenses in form of lesser employee requirements for training and supervision in laboratories, etc. AR applications can be used to deliver required content to the students without exposing students or others to potential hazards. The use of AR in the field of education has a multi-fold impact on student engagement, retention, and experience as we will see through the following examples.

Engineering Graphics (EG) is a subject that allows engineers to convey information about a three-dimensional (3D) object such as shape, size, surface, etc., into two dimensions (2D). Engineers,

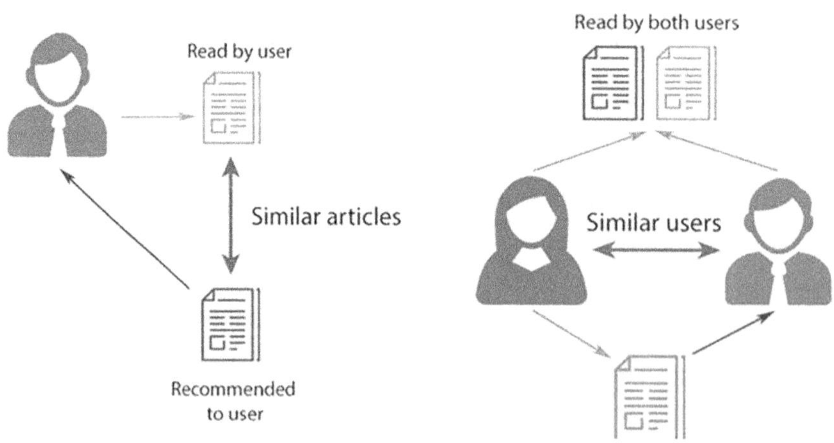

FIGURE 6.4 Recommendation engines for content recommendation.

especially mechanical and civil engineers, must essentially develop the capability to create and understand graphical representations of engineering structures. Therefore, engineering drawing and graphics are an important part of the engineer's curriculum. However, there are limited resources available with teachers to effectively and highlight the relationship between the 3D geometry and their 2D projection. AR solutions are being studied and developed, specifically FOR EG instruction, with an aim at improving learning effectiveness, the interest of the students, and spatial awareness. AR allows students to comprehend complex spatial relationships quickly and influence their academic performance and motivation.

The AR-based method is proved to be effective teaching aids for EG courses as proved by researchers at the University of La Laguna, Spain. In their research paper "Applying Augmented Reality in Engineering Education to Improve Academic Performance & Student Motivation," they prove the effectiveness of using AR (Jorge Martin-Gutierrez, María Dolores Meneses Fernández, 2014):

> This research yields results that indicate how engineering students obtain better academic results and are more motivated when the new generation of technological tools is incorporated into the learning process. Twenty-five first-year students studying for a Mechanical Engineering degree used AR technology to assist them in the subject of graphic engineering. During the study, a control group of twenty-two fellow students used traditional class notes. All these students took an exam and two surveys to give feedback on the teaching material: one for finding out the effectiveness and efficiency of the material itself, together with the level of student satisfaction; another for assessing the level of student motivation when using the technology available during the study. The results showed a significant statistical difference between their academic performances, proving to be higher in the experimental group; this group also showed a higher level of motivation than the control group.

Medical education and training can leverage AR in multiple ways to enhance both knowledge and skills of medical students. By using AR, medical students can learn anatomy in detail, experiment and practice on virtual patients, and train better with the help of simulations. For example, Human Anatomy Atlas is a mobile application that allows medical students to visualize the human body and understand its functioning. It provides more than 10,000 anatomical models which can be viewed as 3D models, and allows students to rotate and interact with them. Similarly, the HoloAnatomy application developed by Case Western Reserve University and the Cleveland Clinic helps medical students learn anatomy (SonaliBloom, 2017); Touch Surgery specializes in surgical simulation to allow users to practice surgery on virtual patients; and Dynamic Anatomy, by Leiden University and the Leiden University Medical Center, helps students learn human anatomy using their bodies as medical holograms mirror their movements (Leiden University, 2017).

Manufacturing, aeronautics, and marine engineering fields are also leveraging augmented reality to impart training and education. Augmented reality technology is used to create an environment required for training; it helps the trainees by practical hands-on experience in place of just theoretical understanding of the machine's functioning. The use of augmented reality allows users to get step-by-step instructions on how to operate the device/machine, and they can also collaborate with their co-workers. Siemens is including more and more digital content and practices in its training, transforming the way its students learn. They use AR-based solutions to help trainees learn extremely difficult and threatening tasks, such as industrial operations, hot welding, etc. The solutions also allow trainers to review the progress on the display screens, while trainees practice welding. Similarly, NASA has tested the use of HoloLens to provide virtual illustrations and instructions to help crew members perform complex tasks (NASA, 2015).

6.3.1.3 Application of the Cloud and Wikis for Content Creation and Management

Educational institutions need to collaborate with external knowledge communities to keep the educational content updated and relevant; this need can be fulfilled by a platform that enables collaboration and the creation of a knowledge body that can be accessed and amended by anyone. With the emergence of the internet and cloud-based solutions, educators have the freedom to work synchronously on the same content, enhancing collaboration and efficiency of content creation.

Collaboration in content creation, with everyone having edit rights and no single authority, allows different authors to explain the concept from different angles, reducing any biases. Wikis are web-based and allow all viewers of a page to change the content by editing the page online. There are multiple applications of Wikis in educational content creation such as assembling a curriculum and collaborative authoring of articles or project documents. Platforms such as Wiki allow educators from different universities, locations, and cultures to add or edit the contents at any time. It also allows observing the content sequence and evolution of the content and thought processes, through its versioning capability. Version control also facilitates monitoring of content changes and easy restoration of deleted content.

The University of British Columbia uses a Wiki software application called UBC Wiki, as shown in Figure 6.5, as a shared space for use by students, staff, and faculty (university of British Columbia, 2022). The UBC website described it as "a course repository, a personal and collaborative workspace, a documentation depository, and a growing guide to everything and anything UBC." The user of this application—students, staff, and faculty, create expand and annotate the information, resources, and links on the UBC Wiki.

6.3.2 Learning Environment

Learning does not happen on any one single platform. It happens across platforms and experiences. A typical eLearning ecosystem comprises a variety of learning platforms including learning management systems, eBook platforms, assessment platforms, mobile applications, discussion forums, and many more. Apart from these, a significant amount of learning happens in classrooms, during office hours, over social media, and via other "non-learning" channels. With the demands of time, we must revolutionize our learning environments. Let us start with our classrooms. The classroom should no longer be just a place to come and sit for learning; it should be a location where students engage in a rich and interactive experience. These days, the following dramatic changes are being seen in classrooms.

- Touch screen smart boards have replaced the traditional blackboards that help instructors and students to interact.
- More engaging content is being used to teach in the classrooms, such as multimedia content.

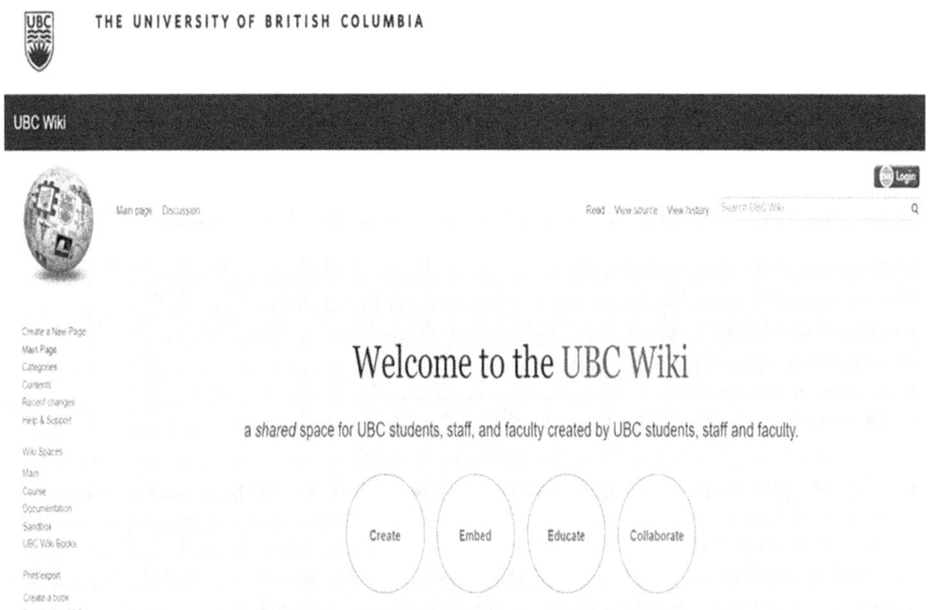

FIGURE 6.5 University of British Columbia Wiki page, https://wiki.ubc.ca/Main_Page

- The architecture of the classroom is changing, which promotes interpersonal skills among students.
- The concept called BYOD (bring your own device) is introduced, whereby students can bring their digital devices into the classroom to enable them to learn.
- Most of the campuses at schools and colleges are providing wi-fi.
- Mainstream schooling systems are introducing new age technologies such as smart science kits, VR headsets, etc., to make the learning experience more engaging.

Learning these days does not happen only in classrooms. It is an era of blended learning when a lot of learning happens outside, as well as in the classroom, through online media like watching videos, reading articles, playing games, and interacting with friends over social platforms. There is a paradigm shift with the help of smartphones in the way we communicate and consume digital content. Conventional education lacks the element of personalization. Imagine a class of 40 students—every single individual is different, comes with different abilities, has varied degrees of prior learning dispositions, has different perspectives and needs, and has different strengths and weaknesses. Some students are quick learners, while others need additional help in grasping a concept. With such diversity, the conventional education system is not able to address every student's individual needs. In the conventional system whereby the students outnumber the instructors, the instructor cannot give personal attention to every single student. All students are treated the same, regardless of their abilities, progress, or performance. The same learning content, set of lectures, homework, and assignments are forced down the throat of all the students.

This problem can be solved through the use of technology. Learning platforms are becoming smarter and smarter with the advances in technology. Technology has made it possible to capture and store the finest details about the progress and performance of students. Based on these inputs the learning paths can be personalized for everyone based on individuals' needs, as shown in Figure 6.6. The learning platform knows the strengths and weaknesses of students and can accordingly push the content and additional practice exercises onto the student's device. The platform also can learn a person's learning styles and habits, and craft content accordingly.

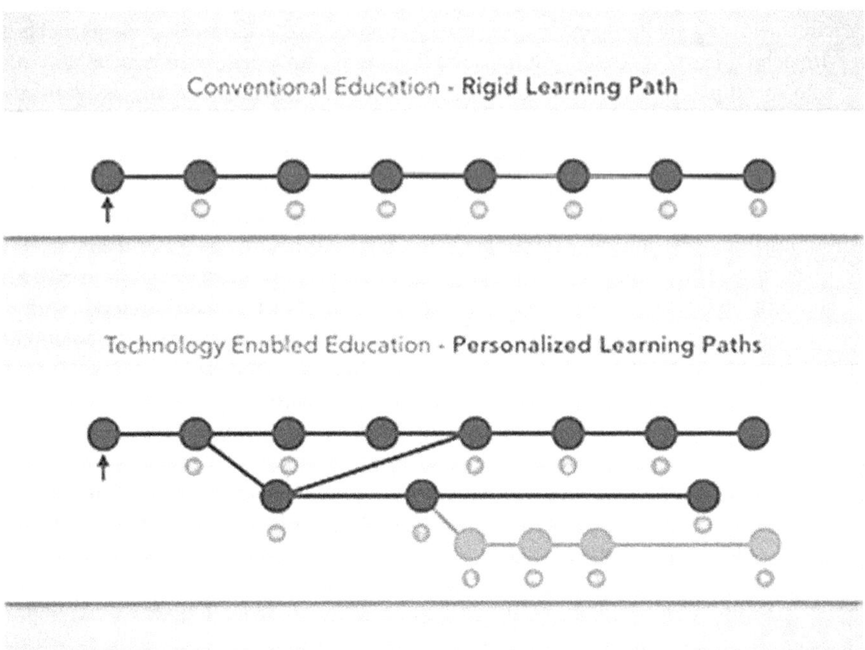

FIGURE 6.6 Technology-enabled personalized learning paths

So, technology is everywhere, both inside and outside the classroom, but technology is just a means to an end, the real magic lies in the hands of educators, instructors, and content creators. They need to work toward the creation of such an environment that most accurately fits the scholar and not an environment that they are comfortable with.

Educators and instructors need to embrace technology and use it effectively to make a change.

6.3.2.1 Cloud-Based New Age Learning Platforms

Cloud computing has been used by educational institutions for multiple purposes including communication exchange, information systems, knowledge management, enterprise resource planning system, and now for online distance learning platforms. Cloud-based platforms offer universities a way to grow beyond the physical boundaries of the campus and cater to students from across the world. Educational organizations can use cloud-based platforms in conjunction with traditional classroom-based delivery to enhance the student's experience. Students today are technology savvy, and they demand education without the constraints of location and time. Cloud platforms are especially more relevant during the unprecedented hard times of temporary and sustained closings due to pandemic COVID-19, etc. In case of a prolonged closure of universities, it will be imperative for the educational institutes to adapt and develop cloud-based learning platforms which allow their students to access courses, documents, and other university content online anywhere and anytime through a secure internet connection.

Blackboard, an education company that provides a virtual learning platform called Collaborate, has helped educational institutions including Mapúa University (Philippines) to advance the university learning environment to digital channels (Blackboard Inc., 2019). Mapúa University, under certain programs, allows students and faculty to participate in online teaching and learning using Blackboard Collaborate. Leading cloud service providers such as Google and Microsoft also offer cloud-based platforms such as Google Classroom which provide universities a unified environment to manage digital channels through a suite of applications and services.

6.3.2.2 Applications of AI Techniques to Improve the Learning Environment

AI and machine learning are being extensively used to improve experiences of students and efficiency of teamers. AI/machine learning–based solutions are helping create a better professional environment for educators who spend plenty of time on administrative activities such as creating assignments, answering frequently asked questions, correcting assignments and essays, etc. Some of these activities can be efficiently handled by virtual teaching assistants. A virtual teaching assistant is an AI-based tool that can take up routine tasks from the educator and free up their time. Virtual teaching assistants can answer common student queries and send filtered unique queries for an educator to answer. They can also be used to grade assignments, not only multiple-choice tests but also essays. For example, Educational Testing Service, in the United States, developed an AI-based assessment tool to grade essays in standardized tests; similarly, in China, an automatic essay correction solution has been developed with a precision of correction matching humans in over 90%. Another firm in China is developing a solution to answer student queries; it boasts of a capability to answer 500 million simultaneous questions from students. AI solutions are used to monitor course discussion groups and identify key discussion topics and student concerns, allowing educators to focus on these areas and enhance learning.

AI can help personalize learning for students in multiple ways—it can understand the current level of skills, students' strengths and weaknesses, learning preferences and a student's facial expressions, etc., to recommend learning paths and relevant content. All these inputs in tandem significantly improve student's learning, such as the following.

- Daptio, a South African company, uses Deep Learning–based solutions to assess the proficiency level of the student and then suggest relevant content.
- Carnegie Mellon University specialists in the United States have also developed voice recognition and machine learning-based solutions to personalize learning.

- Geekie, a Brazilian edtech company, uses machine learning to flag learning difficulties faced by students and allows teachers to concentrate on those areas.
- IBM's "Simpler Voice: Overcoming Illiteracy" uses AI to translate text into visuals or simple spoken words to enable easy understanding of adult learners with a low level of literacy.
- Hujiang, a Chinese firm, analyzes students' facial expressions and uses image and voice recognition tools to provide online feedback to educators about the student's level of comfort with the content.

6.3.3 Assessment

Assessment is an important aspect of learning. It influences how students learn, their motivation to learn, and how teachers teach. According to Manitoba Education, assessment is used in various contexts for learning the following (Manitoba Education, 2022).

- **Assessment for Learning**
  Assessment helps teachers gain insight into what students understand to plan, guide, instruct, and provide helpful feedback to students. It requires careful design on the part of teachers so that they use the resulting information to determine not only what students know, but also to gain insights into how, when, and whether students apply what they know.
- **Assessment as Learning**
  Students develop an awareness of how they learn and use that awareness to adjust and advance their learning, taking increased responsibility for their learning. When students are active, engaged, and critical assessors, they make sense of information, relate it to prior knowledge, and use it for new learning.
- **Assessment of Learning**
  Assessment informs students, teachers, and parents, as well as the broader educational community, of achievement at a certain point in time to celebrate success, plan interventions, and support continued progress.

Assessment should have a clear purpose and must be planned accordingly. Assessment for, as, and of learning, if appropriately balanced, has significantly improved student learning and plays a major role to play in supporting it. The key aspect of assessment is to test whether the knowledge acquired is appropriately used and interpreted to fulfill the intended purpose.

Assessment is tightly interconnected with curriculum and instruction, and thus is rooted in the learning process. As students work under the guidance of teachers to attain the curriculum outcomes, assessment plays a continuous role in checking progress and achievement, guiding teachers in designing instruction and providing students with the next steps. Teachers can create different strategies and processes for assessing students, and can modify them to suit the individual needs and assessment purposes.

Experience and research have shown that learning has its best outcomes when students are involved in the learning process. When students understand the learning goals and the standards of quality work, they take the steps to adjust their performance by using the descriptive feedback which they have received through assessment.

When the assessment is based on coherent learning goals and is differentiated according to student learning needs, it supports the student learning in the best possible way. Students receive descriptive feedback from assessments and use it to take the steps to improve their performance. When the families and students are well informed about the child's progress through assessment tools, they gain confidence in the system and they support the educational institution to help plan to learn and fulfill the learning goals. This assessment information is also circled back as feedback to improvise and make decisions that support further learning.

Most of the assessment tests today only assess the aptitude and intelligence of students—that is, they fit the prediction and selection model. They primarily predict the performance of an individual in an educational environment or are used as a tool for the selection of individuals into those environments.

Some of these tests fit the accountability and audit model. These tests primarily assess the achievement of students and educational institutes to determine how well they are doing. These assessment models generally focus on the demands of audiences other than the student. They enable the institutions to either select individuals or assess their performance under a certain preset curriculum. They hardly provide any direct feedback to the examinee about their understanding of the concepts, or the core skills required in the industry. The information derived from such instruments is typically used by others who are relatively distal to the process of teaching and learning, and who have purposes other than enhancement of the educational outcomes of individual examinees. But many factors are shaping the current policy for educational assessment. The pursuit of excellence by maintaining high standards for all children, by educational institutions, is directly affecting the assessment. The second factor which is giving a direction to educational assessment is increased public demand for accountability. The need to improve the educational system can be observed in everyday discussions, especially in the media and in political and public forums. Educational professionals, politicians, and citizens have started considering a value-added approach to assess the system and to hold various entities accountable.

Assessment has become one of the most pervasive aspects of the educational landscape. More is needed in the improvement of academic achievement instead of constantly assessing it. Assessment is an integral part of the learning and teaching process, and it can impact achievement significantly. We can use the assessment outcome to improve the teaching process but only when we have better assessment practices. For that, assessment must be designed to focus more on developing academic programs. In other words, the assessment must become an essential part of the design and enactment of contemporary learning environments.

6.3.3.1 Applications of Artificial Intelligence in Educational Assessment

A major share of educators' time is consumed by academic assessment; they spend a lot of time and labor in reading, checking, and grading student essays, homework, and assignments. This adds to educators' overheads and takes away precious time which could be used to research or provide focused additional support to students. AI solutions can be used to assist educators in student assessments. The use of AI for assessment started in the 1990s with automated scoring and computer-generated reports of computer-based tests. Today, AI is used to create tests, assess tests, score answer sheets, check assignments for plagiarism, and identify key improvement areas for students.

For instance, solutions such as Cram101 can be used to create multiple-choice practice tests from given chapter content. Objective tests can help educators assess students' learning and knowledge, and for more subjective assessments such as writing skills, etc.—machine learning and natural language—based solutions can be used. For example, Educational Testing Service, in the United States, developed an AI-based assessment tool to grade essays in standardized tests (Pedró, Francesc, Subosa Miguel, Rivas Axel, Valverde Paula, 2019). Similarly, in China, an automatic essay correction solution has been developed with a precision of correction matching humans in over 90% (Chen, 2018). IntelliMetric® is another such solution that can grade papers and provide immediate adaptive feedback. Researchers are also exploring the application of AI in progressive assessments, personality tests, psychometric assessments, and real-time interviews; one such example is the use of chatbot conversations or AI-based virtual interviews with candidates in situational judgment tests.

AI can be used by students, unfairly also, to create papers and assignments—essays, summaries, and literature reviews of existing content—with minimal inputs from students themselves. Therefore, authenticity checking software needs to be capable of detecting AI-generated texts, which a traditional plagiarism checker cannot detect. AI-enabled plagiarism checkers can verify authorship effectively and provide substantial evidence (EdTechReview Editorial Team, 2020). Emma, by Unicheck, is one such AI-powered cheating prevention assistant. It takes as input three 1,000-word long pieces written by the author; uses models based on NLP (natural language processing) to learn to distinguish their writing style, voice, and pattern; and then classifies another incoming essay as either written by the author or not.

6.3.3.2 Gamification and Scenario Environments for Assessment

Assessment of skills such as critical thinking, decision making, problem solving, and collaboration is critical for determining the employability of a student/candidate. Traditional interview-based or situation-based questionnaires are not very effective to gauge such skills, as candidates can understand the purpose of the question and may tweak their responses accordingly to increase their chances of scoring high. One of the methods to effectively assess candidates in such situations is the use of scenario-based or gamified tests. For instance, security awareness and data leakage prevention training aim at making employees more vigilant about their actions and make fewer security mistakes. Candidates can easily choose the correct action in a test format but are prone to willing/unwilling mistakes in day-to-day operations. Gamification of assessment, in this case, can allow candidates to enter a gamified environment replicating their actual work environment and take actions to achieve the stated goals of the game: performance and productivity. The actions taken by the candidate are observed from a security standpoint, and it allows the assessor to analyze the potential behavior of the candidate in real life. Another example is a platform created by Prof. Patrick Griffin and Esther Care (2014) to test the collaborative problem-solving ability of candidates. In this test, two candidates are presented with a problem statement that requires them to interact with each other through a messaging application and collectively solve the problem. The platform can gauge the candidate's ability through analysis of the records of messaging.

6.3.4 Accreditation

Former IBM chief executive officer (CEO) Ginni Rometty has asserted that "Getting a job at today's IBM does not always require a college degree. What matters most is relevant skills" (Indiatimes, 2020). Jeff Weiner, the executive chairman and former CEO of LinkedIn, has been pushing the same message at his company (American city business journals, 2022).

In today's technology-disrupted and dynamic world, quality education has become a fundamental goal. The universities should not just provide diplomas to the graduates, but should aim at the development of the personalities and intellectual abilities of the students. New emerging technologies such as Big Data analytics, AI, the Internet of Things (IoT), robotics, and quantum computing have posed a demand for continuous learning. Technology disruption has created such an environment that the skills acquired at college become outdated very soon. However, soft skills—such as critical thinking, creativity, innovation, leadership, and effective communication—are always in demand by employers (Quartz, 2022).

The undergraduate college curricula and degrees have not changed much over a hundred years; they are still based on scores, seat time, and credit hours. The general structure of the courses and curricula is remarkably consistent across most institutions. These courses provide the content knowledge and have curricular breadth, but these are loosely connected with learning outcomes. In some disciplines like engineering, courses and outcomes are connected a bit more tightly, but in others, such as those in the arts and sciences, the connections are looser.

Graduate degrees have changed more as compared to undergraduate degrees. The primary structure of these degrees is quite similar and configured around organized courses. These degrees are loosely coupled with learning outcomes. Hence, professional master's degrees are getting more and more popular these days, and professional doctorates are becoming more common. Professional degrees rely on the process of learning by doing. Although professional degrees are more focused than graduate degrees but credit hours and seat time, here as well these constitute a significant part of the learning experience. These days, online models of delivery have come into the picture. With their advent, nothing much has changed in undergraduate/graduate degrees or their structures, just that these are repackaged in online delivery modes. Most online degrees are in line with traditional degrees. Their credit counts, curricular structures, and even individual course content follow the traditional model and remain very similar to the face-to-face courses that have been offered on college campuses for decades.

However, there is a dire need and immense pressure to change the traditional model of education. Higher education has become unreachable for many, learning outcomes have no connection with the course structures, and the widening gap between degrees and jobs calls into question the relevancy and applicability of degrees. To deal with these problems, standards of outcomes and accountability are increasingly being used as the lenses through which the value of a college is judged. An adult student is now a mainstream student, and lifelong learning is not just a luxury or avocation but has become the necessity for employment and economic prosperity. Job competition is global and multidimensional. These days, workers must compete not only with the workers in neighborhoods but also with the workers in other countries. With advancing technologies, workers now must also compete with machines that can do the same work but at lower costs and with more precision sans any human resources issues. As competition continues to rise with technology advancements and globalization, the key factor in increasing the value of higher education degrees is the extent to which it improves one's competitive advantage.

Under this scenario, it is envisioned that along with traditional degrees, more relevant options will emerge such as online badging regimes which will help in keeping the skills relevant and can indicate when someone has mastered a discrete skill and completed an area of study.

Soon, I agree with LinkedIn's Weiner: "It's not skills at the exclusion of degrees." But, increasingly, more importance will be given to the evidence of attainment of the stated skills. Going forward, degrees have to be supported by the practice of inculcating the core skills of innovation, creativity, communication, critical thinking, and leadership. At the same time, we have to incorporate emerging technologies and practices into the curriculum. We have to teach our students so that they can do the technological implementation of solutions and help them cultivate the practice of application of acquired knowledge to new environments.

If higher education degrees are to remain economically and socially important and indispensable, they must contemplate these and other current realities. The degrees of tomorrow must be as relevant as any job training program, as malleable as our fast-changing world, as accessible as any website anywhere in the world, and as ubiquitous as social media. Degrees must, in evincible and direct ways, help people be better, faster, and smarter, and ensure the recognition of qualification and employability of academic personnel. To the extent we can succeed in these areas, we will be able to keep the degrees relevant to both employers and prospective students.

6.3.4.1 Blockchain and Cloud-Enabled Digital Degrees

The purpose of accreditation in higher education is to provide the candidate with a public accountable certificate of achievement/completion. Traditional certificates are paper-based and are prone to tampering and damage over time; they also do not provide an easy way to verify their authenticity. Digital degrees can help overcome these challenges. The Massachusetts Institute of Technology (MIT) in the United States offers its students an option to opt for a digital degree certificate which can be downloaded on a smart device, shared with potential employers, or uploaded on social media (Elizabeth, Durant, Alison Trachy, 2017). MIT uses blockchain technology to protect digital degrees from any kind of tampering. It uses the BlockCerts Wallet mobile application, allowing the students to download, store or share transcripts, certifications & letters.

6.4 Conclusion

Education 4.0 will require shifts in educational content, learning environment, assessment, and accreditation. This shift will be enabled by emerging technologies such as artificial intelligence, machine learning, Internet of Things, augmented reality and virtual reality, cloud computing, gamification, and blockchain. Successful transition to Education 4.0 will help universities provide personalized learning, global citizenship skills, innovation and creativity skills, future technology skills, interpersonal skills, accessible and inclusive learning, and problem-based and collaborative learning.

REFERENCES

Akshay Kumar, Chaturvedi, Recommender System for News Articles Using Supervised Learning. URL: https://arxiv.org/ftp/arxiv/papers/1707/1707.00506.pdf

American city business journals. (2022). LinkedIn CEO says college degrees are overrated and more vocational training is needed Present online at: https://www.bizjournals.com/sanfrancisco/news/2016/11/16/linkedin-ceo-says-college-degrees-are-overrated.html

Blackboard Inc, 2019 Mapúa University Advances Its Digital Learning Environment, Case Study. URL: www.blackboard.com/sites/default/files/2019 - 10/Bb2019_CaseStudy_Mapu%CC%81aUniversity.pdf

Care, Esther et al., 2014 Collaborative Problem-Solving Tasks. In book: Assessment and Teaching of 21st Century Skills: Methods and Approach. (pp. 85–104) Chapter: 4, Springer, DOI: 10.1007/978-94-017-9395-7_4

Chen, 2018 China's Schools Are Quietly Using AI to Mark Students' Essays . . . But do the Robots Make the Grade? *South China Morning Post.* URL: www.scmp.com/news/china/society/article/2147833/chinas-schools-are-quietly-using-ai-mark-students-essays-do

Content Technologies Inc, The Notion of Artificial Intelligence is a Thing of the Past. The Reality of Artificial Intelligence is a Thing of Today. URL: http://contenttechnologiesinc.com/, Accessed on: 11 Sep 2022.

Dorria, Mahsa, Mohammad H. Yarmohammadianb, Mohammad Ali Nadi, 2012 A Review on Value Chain in Higher Education. URL: Available online at www.sciencedirect.com

Duderstadt, J. (1999) 'Can colleges and universities survive in an information age?' In R. N. Katz (ed.), *Dancing with the Devil: Information Technology and the New Competition in Higher Education.* San Francisco, CA: Jossey-Bass, pp. 1–25.

EdTechReview Editorial Team, 2020 Top Five Use Cases of AI in Education: The Good and the Bad. URL: https://edtechreview.in/trends-insights/trends/3856-top-five-use-cases-of-ai-in-education

Elizabeth, Durant, Alison Trachy, 2017 Digital Diploma Debuts at MIT. URL: http://news.mit.edu/2017/mit-debuts-secure-digital-diploma-using-bitcoin-blockchain-technology-1017

Goldsworthy, J., 2008 Research Grant Mania. *Australian Universities Review*, 50(2), 17–24.

Indiatimes, 2020, Not College Degrees But Skills Should Be Hiring Focus, Says Former IBM CEO Present online at https://www.indiatimes.com/technology/news/college-degrees-skills-hiring-jobs-ginni-rometty-526355.html

Jorge Martin-Gutierrez, María Dolores Meneses Fernández, 2014 Applying Augmented Reality in Engineering Education to Improve Academic Performance & Student Motivation. *International Journal of Engineering Education*, 30, 625–635.

Leiden University, 2017 HoloLens-App Brings Mixed Reality to Teaching in Leiden. URL: www.universiteitleiden.nl/en/news/2017/09/hololens-app-brings-mixed-reality-to-teaching-in-leiden

Levine, A. (2001) Privatization in Higher Education, Teachers College, Columbia University. Online: http://www.nga.org/Files/pdf/HIGHEREDPRIVATIZATION.pdf (accessed 15 September 2009).

Manitoba Education, (2022). The Role of Assessment in Learning. URL: www.edu.gov.mb.ca/k12/assess/role.html

NASA, 2015 RELEASE 15–139 NASA, Microsoft Collaborate to Bring Science Fiction to Science Fact. URL: www.nasa.gov/press-release/nasa-microsoft-collaborate-to-bring-science-fiction-to-science-fact

Noble, D. (1998) Digital Diploma Mills: The Automation of Higher Education. Online: http://131.193.153.231/www./issues/issue3_1/noble/index.html (accessed 15 September 2009).

Pathak, Virendra, Kavita Pathak, 2010 Reconfiguring the Higher Education Value Chain. *Management in Education.* URL: https://doi.org/10.1177/0892020610376791

Pedró, Francesc, Subosa Miguel, Rivas Axel, Valverde Paula, 2019 Artificial Intelligence in Education: Challenges and Opportunities for Sustainable Development, UNESDOC Digital Library. URL: https://unesdoc.unesco.org/ark:/48223/pf0000366994

Poon, T.S. (2006) 'The commoditification of higher education: implications for academic work and employment'. *International Journal of Employment Studies*, 14(1), 81–104.

Porter, Michael E., (1985) *Competitive Advantage. Creating and Sustaining Superior Performance.* Free Press, New York, 557 p.

Quartz. (2022). LinkedIn CEO Jeff Weiner says the biggest skills gap in the US is not coding Present online at https://qz.com/work/1423267/linkedin-ceo-jeff-weiner-the-main-us-skills-gap-is-not-coding/

SonaliBloom, 2017 HoloAnatomy: AR Bodies, ARselves. URL: https://digital.hbs.edu/platform-digit/submission/holoanatomy-ar-bodies-arselves/

University of British Columbia Wiki page, 2022, https://wiki.ubc.ca/Main_Page

World Economic Forum, 2020 Schools of the Future Defining New Models of Education for the Fourth Industrial Revolution, Switzerland. URL: http://www3.weforum.org/docs/WEF_Schools_of_the_Future_Report_2019.pdf (accessed 10 May 2020).

7

Industry 4.0: Application Areas, Impacts, and the Utilities for Creating Applications

C. Vishnu Mohan and T. Devi

CONTENTS

DOI: 10.1201/9781003318378-7

Objectives

1. To identify the sectors where each of the Industry 4.0 technologies are utilized.
2. To understand how various Industry 4.0 technologies affect and boost various sectors.
3. To examine a few use case scenarios in various sectors.

4. To understand how Industry 4.0 benefits society.
5. To identify the potential impacts of Industry 4.0 on society.
6. To identify the areas of concern when implementing Industry 4.0.
7. To learn a few utilities available used to implement the Industry 4.0 technologies.

7.1 Areas of Application

7.1.1 Manufacturing Sector

Companies are forced by globalization and competitiveness to change around and innovate their production processes following the Industry 4.0 (I4.0) standard, representing the integration of tools such as Big Data, cloud, robot, 3D printing, simulation, etc., now connected into a global network by transmitting digital data. For companies that are faced with big investments, the implementation of this new paradigm represents a huge change. Companies must have the prerequisites needed to endure changes generated by the "smart" system (Petrillo et al., 2018), to benefit from the opportunities offered by the smart revolution. In addition, without forgetting soft skills, new workers who face the world of Work 4.0 should have new skills in automation, digitization, and information technology.

The manufacturing sector is undergoing a rapid shift in the industry at a constant pace. I4.0 has contributed much to the sector and its benefits are much rewarding. In the sector, it is observed that there is a good market with an average of $175 billion for cybersecurity and augmented reality (AR)-based products, whereas for additive manufacturing and Internet of Things (IoT), the market grows at an average of around $11 billion. It has also been predicted that the market for all the I4.0 products may cross the $4 trillion mark by 2020 (TULIP, 2019).

From centralized to decentralized manufacturing, there is a holistic shift that requires the adaptation of processes, talent, business structure, and technology. As the digital storage capability and processing capability of machines have increased in the sector, new solutions have been identified for various kinds of products. As this revolution progresses, the technologies such as artificial intelligence (AI), IoT, robotics, cloud technology, etc., are blending themselves to contribute to the growth of the sector.

In addition to aim more profit, these technologies also have a scope beyond the production sector and the credit is not taken away by a single technology, and rather, is a combined implementation of many. I4.0 is characterized by broad consensus such as the following.

- Scalable set of technologies that assures good payback on the money invested.
- Maintaining good relationships among the various entities involved in the sector.
- To earn the title "revolution", dispersion and pace are sufficient.

Further, I4.0 in manufacturing has the following three main drivers.

- Concurrent expansion of the technologies used earlier, as well as the implementation of new technologies.
- Development of new solutions for the existing and new products.
- Growingly scalable incorporation of digitization.

In the traditional model of manufacturing, processing was performed either by machines or by humans. There were confusions regarding how to classify machine operators and machine programmers, what all operations are involved in completing a production, etc. When I4.0 was implemented, there was a clear distinction of work among machines and the workforce. A few scenarios in the manufacturing sector are notable with the introduction of I4.0 technologies.

7.1.1.1 Digital Performance Management

In developing I4.0 capabilities and infrastructure, digital performance management should be the primary area of focus. To evaluate the digital performance, much reliance was given to Industrial IoT (IIoT) and cloud technology by measuring the dynamic processing capability. Through the software interfaces and mobile apps, workers can monitor the performance of the entire system.

7.1.1.2 Automatic Maintenance Scheduling

The manufacturing and data analysis software have improved with the introduction of I4.0. However, the tools that are used to track human performances, machine learning, and maintenance have to be updated periodically. With the aid of Deep Learning, the timetables for maintenance can be created with more precision, and through this, machine effectiveness and reduction in down-time can be achieved. This is further enhanced with the introduction of sensing technology that can replace human tasks with machine tasks.

7.1.1.3 Optimization of Processes

In I4.0, the data that is collected automatically from various components involved in the processing are then explored using the latest procedures. This process should not happen for one of the several processes alone, and instead should be applied to all the industrial processes. The companies that have implemented this, along with the pace of technology growth, are already gaining by the integrated use of analysis in all their departments.

7.1.1.4 Extended Automation

It is predicted that robotic technology and robotic process automation are the future of industries in the coming decade. Still, automation cannot rely entirely on robotics, and rather, there should be an interconnected environment to achieve full automation. To cope up with this, many machine learning algorithms, advanced data collection and analysis methods, and extended security mechanisms are deployed.

7.1.1.5 Impact of I4.0 in Manufacturing

The trends show that more than half of industrialists, around 53% of the manufacturers, insisted on adopting I4.0 as a major investment. In industries producing electrical, electronic, and automobile products, around 80% believed in the growth of I4.0; whereas it has the faith of 70% of industrialists overall (Alphacore, 2019).

As a part of integrating I4.0 technologies into manufacturing, the floors are made interconnected and automated. The point here to consider is that whether all of these I4.0 tools are utilized and/or at whether even distribution or utilization. Initially, Big Data analytics, cyber-security, and cloud technology were introduced by most companies, but still, their level of utilization was much less. Later, tools like robotic process automation and augmentation were used as the years progressed.

In any sector, the same kind of strategy cannot be applied for transforming to I4.0 standards. It depends on the company's product, size, location, and competence in the market. When I4.0 standards are applied, companies should include the following.

- Interconnectivity—All the components in the manufacturing unit, such as machines, software, IoT equipment, and workforce should communicate with one another and share knowledge.
- Data sharing—I4.0 systems are usually capable of visualizing products and processing by capturing data through sensors and then converting them to knowledge.
- Technical support—I4.0 tools enable systems to analyze data and aid decision-makers. In addition, they safeguard operators by performing tasks that are risky for people.
- Independent decision-making power—Most components in the industry can work independently by continuously monitoring the processes, and also by working as a part of a bigger system.

Most manufacturers and businessmen do not care much about the changes occurring on the technological side, or about the methods to be adopted to find the best possible solutions to I4.0, while a few are already into it transforming their businesses. Also, I4.0 technologies keep on evolving at a constant pace, and its future is not fully predictable.

7.1.1.6 Use Case in Manufacturing Sector

7.1.1.7 BJC HealthCare Has Adopted IoT for Inventory and Supply Chain Management

BJC HealthCare is a U.S. healthcare service provider that operates 15 hospitals in Missouri and Illinois. It is one of the major manufacturers of RFID sensors used in healthcare. It uses RFID to track medical device data. It senses the data using radio waves, and stores it inside a tag attached to the medical device. Initially, the manual force was employed in managing the inventory data, but monitoring was a concern, because of the increase in purchases of medical devices, which are used for specific procedures. Even tracking the expiry of products was to be done manually and inventory checks were regularly needed.

7.1.2 Healthcare Sector

I4.0 utilizes the applications of data analytics, Big Data, cloud computing, and cryptography for automated systems where data exchange is possible to a greater extent. When the healthcare sector applies I4.0 standards, it is termed Health 4.0. It has transformed the way by which bots operate by developing intelligence that previously only humans possessed. In addition, the adoption of I4.0 has increased the quality of various healthcare products and services. It also visualizes a reduction in cost with increased utilization and reliance on Health 4.0.

I4.0 possesses a greater problem-solving capability in the medical field and yields the best results (Javaid and Haleem, 2019). Due to the flexible design of products, the sector can ensure that the systems are digitally well controlled. Health 4.0 is capable of the following.

- Yield maximum throughput.
- Perform intelligent patient data analysis.
- Automatically store data and predict the future impact of diseases.
- Achieve greater precision in results.
- Reduction in cost of operation and implementation.
- Achieve the best value with reduced time.
- Reduce the use of extra devices or equipment to collect data, and making use of CAD systems for it.
- Eliminate writing works.
- Expand the use of materials and tools.
- Efficiently create implants based on patient data utilizing smart component sensors.
- Handle complex surgeries efficiently.
- Track new types of diseases using sensors.

I4.0 has imposed a huge transformation in traditional healthcare device production by creating a smart factory environment, which is the future. Major optimizations in computing systems, incorporation of cybersecurity, AI, and IoT continue to progress and play a greater role in the smart manufacturing units. The change has been a part of the individual participation of each device and systems developed out of the technologies, applied in decentralized decision-making and problem-solving, with minor human interference, while keeping the control with their operators through real-time collaboration.

The number of electronic devices is seen to be decreasing with migration to Health 4.0. Also, there is a reduction in size for many devices and equipment, making it "handy" and portable, by the use of IoT sensors. These devices individually are performing well to a greater extent and it is expected that as time progress and requirements change, all these smaller pieces of technology can be integrated to set a single standard for the medical sector.

Additive manufacturing is another component of Health 4.0 seen as the future product. This technology is based on layering objects, one after another, combining them to form a three-dimensional (3D) product. A well-known example of additive manufacturing is 3D bioprinting. This application is utilized in creating 3D prints of tissues and organs of people, which in turn aids scientists in developing new types of drugs which can be tested directly on humans rather than on animals. The range of applications assisted by 3D printing is many, such as reconstructive surgery, dental implantation, etc. (Mtshali, 2020).

7.1.2.1 Use Case in Healthcare Sector

RealView Imaging is a start-up company in Israel which takes lead in the area of live holography. It uses digital light shaping technology, providing a natural experience for doctors, to produce 3D holograms accurately. RealView Imaging (Figure 7.1) concentrates on emerging in the 3D medical imaging segment in the marketplace using its holography-based products. After its successful trial first in the world, in this segment in interventional cardiology, it unveiled the first product configuration in 2019.

7.1.3 Education Sector

The influence of I4.0 in society is so huge that it has affected all aspects of life. In the case of businessmen, to achieve, they need to make the right decisions, utilizing the problem-solving ability of machines of I4.0. To achieve it, they need to be educated in their respective areas. The others, who are the end users of I4.0 products, need to be trained right from an early stage of graduation because it influences every sector that they will get used to in the future.

It is very important to educate people to understand what the advantages and drawbacks of using these technologies are, keeping in mind a safer utilization of its products. In addition, it is also necessary to highly educate people in developing skills for at least the technologies which they intend to work with in the future. It should be kept in mind that the ability should not only be on developing the products of technology but also on thorough knowledge on when and where it can be implemented. This thinking should reflect the schooling curriculum itself so that, even at early stages, they can find ways to adapt to future living creating as many opportunities as possible. There should not arise a situation where people lack skills that the new kind of jobs ask for, and this situation can be avoided only by highly educating them and making I4.0 a part of the curriculum.

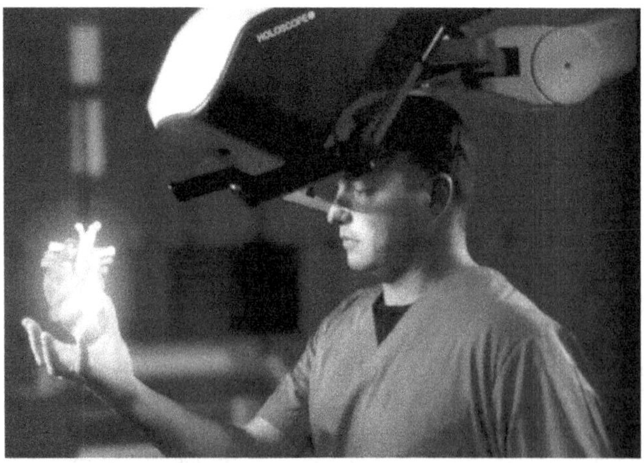

FIGURE 7.1 Hologram using RealView Imaging. A device called a holoscope is placed above a surgeon's head. A 3D display hologram display of the human heart is produced in his hands through a cylindrical pipe coming out of the holoscope using RealView Imaging technology.

It is much important for the youth that they learn, analyze, and apply their I4.0 knowledge in whatever applicable diverse fields. To be more fruitful, the students should learn themselves by getting involved in real projects, and by continuous communication with experts and teachers. They should fully utilize their capabilities working on complex projects and think critically, leading to better problem-solving.

Developing such a kind of an environment leads to a new type of worker, called a knowledge worker (Restart 4.0, 2018). Critical thinking, good problem-solving ability, innovation, and value-enabled work are the core of a knowledge worker.

7.1.3.1 Use Case in Education Sector

AR can help in faster learning and improved communication skills of students. For example, it aids in delivering a better experience to students by way of expanding pedagogy to incorporate visual contexts. It thus develops interest and enthusiasm in students (Figure 7.2).

An AR setup in a classroom can be done by combining an internet connection with a portable device whereby an AR app is installed in it that shows markers on the screen. Teachers can use AR to assist their students in learning skills and concepts within pre-existing and future lessons more efficiently.

7.1.4 Aerospace and Defense Sector

I4.0 brings in a mandatory changeover for the aerospace and defense (A&D) sector, by incorporating digitization completely. Surveys state that more than 80% of A&D companies believe in adopting I4.0 in the sector to stand out in the market, but still the fact is that much lesser companies have adopted it as of now for the real-time decision-making process (Hussain et al., 2019). It has a positive impact on all the areas of A&D, including equipment manufacturers and suppliers. Bringing better changes to the design of existing products or new products and the creation of models are the key areas of concern for A&D, with less than 50% identifying it as the primary focus to be addressed.

Also, even after utilizing I4.0 in sectors such as production and logistics, most A&D companies are denial of or are much slower in extending them to the entire value chains. The major reason behind this is that the A&D industry itself has not set a priority for digitization, and instead tends to concentrate on specific utilizations of I4.0 applications. This kind of approach degrades the collective performance of companies and they tend to be unnoticed. Therefore, the A&D sector should completely identify the need of migrating to I4.0 standards, instead of adding on to existing methods and yield better benefits.

FIGURE 7.2 Augmented reality (AR) used in teaching. An AR-enabled tablet PC is seen focusing a diagram pinned to the wall. Through the AR application installed on the tablet PC, real 3D images are displayed on the AR interface in the tablet.

Application of I4.0 in the A&D sector is coined as A&D 4.0, which aims at developing products involving advanced usage of industrial applications at an efficient cost. A few A&D companies have understood the impact of A&D 4.0 (Table 7.1), which they use to research and identify the multiple dimensions which benefit by it. To cite as an example, deploying sensors in flights can schedule travel, maintain timings, and check fuel consumption. By tracking the data collected from sensors, it can predict failures and also schedule maintenance. Figure 7.3. shows a robot that is used in the aircraft manufacturing unit in the construction of aircraft. Because of robots' reliability, capability, and precision, their popularity in the aerospace industry is growing.

TABLE 7.1

Current and Emerging Application of A&D 4.0

Technology	Current Applications	Emerging Applications
Additive manufacturing	Prototyping, tooling and functional end-use parts manufacturing	Integrating innovative and new materials to improve aerospace parts.
advanced Analytics	Monitoring aircraft system failures and scheduling their timely maintenance	Fully digitizing the data-related maintenances and maintenance schedules of aircraft
Extended robotics and cognitive automation	Enhancing manufacturing using robotics	Simplifying simulations of aircraft, weapons, and satellite performance, avoiding time-consuming analysis and tests of algorithms, software, and hardware
Artificial intelligence	Utilizing AI in automation of tasks, and predictive maintenance	Leveraging AI and computer vision to augment advanced safety features in aircraft, incorporating advanced AI into drones, and replacing human co-pilots in new, autonomous aircraft
Blockchain	Transparent information interchange, enhancing supply chain, reducing order errors	Keeping shared databases among various parties for tracking logistics, reducing fraud using time-stamping, evaluating supplier value and enhancing security
AR/VR/mixed reality	Replacing assembly manuals with smart-glass displays, which substantially reduces wiring production time	Using VR to design factory components, and simulate the factory environment fully, and to provide training to the workforce
IoT	Installing sensors and collecting aircraft data to monitor issues and component performances	Creation of automated manufacturing environments

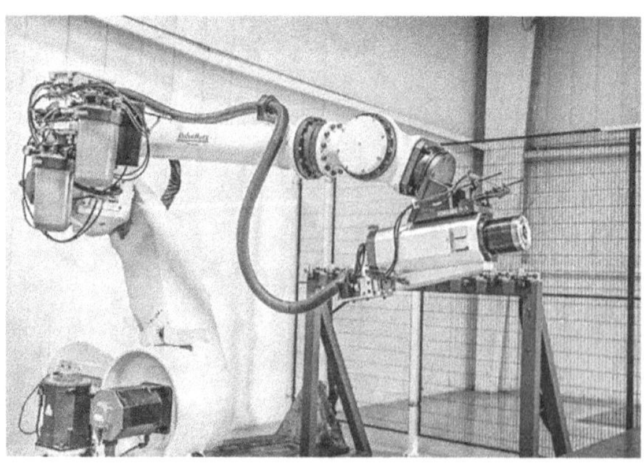

FIGURE 7.3 Robotics in A&D 4.0. A variant of the KUKA robot is seen involved in the construction of an aircraft in a closed environment. It has a robotic arm that holds 3D laser vision equipment.

7.1.5 Agriculture Sector

I4.0 has made a revolutionary impact on production, including the agriculture sector. The main focus is on implementing connectivity and increased usage of IoT devices. Other than IoT, technologies such as Big Data analytics and AI also can enrich the sector well. Along with the usage of advanced technologies, better practices in cooperation, innovations, and mobility also have to be adopted, which further creates smart farms, connected agricultural machines, etc. This in turn affects productivity positively and also adds value to the value chain (Digital Transformation Monitor, 2017).

The fully connected environment in the sector can be made possible by the use of new types of tools and devices manufactured. A forecast of the past, present, and future of Agriculture 4.0 is shown in Figure 7.4.

- **Connected Tractors**
  A tractor is a basic machine used in the agricultural sector. Hence, innovations should start from a tractor. Providing a fully connected system for tractors, usage of GPS, optimization of routes, reduced fuel usage, etc., are a few implementations. It also includes developing IoT devices to scale agricultural production. These tools can monitor crops, and their treatments to increase productivity. Also, by tracking the equipment data, the suppliers can provide better services.
- **Automation**
  Another factor that leads to a big changeover is implementing automation among all the components. This significantly reduces the burdens of human workers. Automation can be applied to processes, tools, vehicles, and robots.
- **New Measurement Tools**
  The point behind implementing applications based on I4.0 relies on the extended collection of data about crops, climate, soil, facilities, threats, etc. This can be achieved by using IoT products and other sensors in the agricultural area, apart from satellite data.

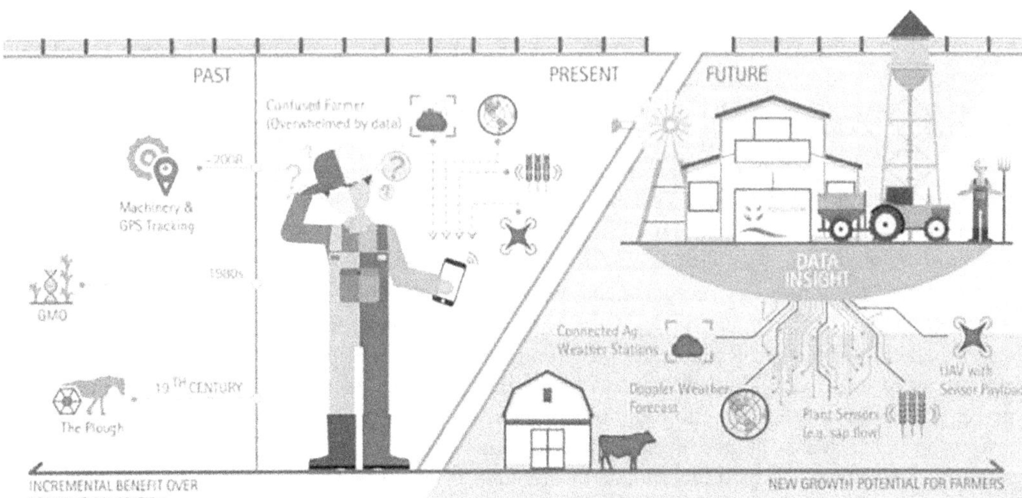

FIGURE 7.4 Agriculture 4.0 Forecast. A diagram showing the past, present, and future of agricultural evolution. The first section shows the agricultural methods used in the past such as plows, GMOs, and machinery. The second section, labeled as the present, shows the image of a confused farmer holding a mobile phone overwhelmed with data. The third section shows the future overcast of deriving data insight in agriculture through connected weather stations, Doppler weather forecasts, plant sensors, and UAVs with sensor payloads.

- **IoT Requirements**

  The development of connected objects is relied upon for the creation of new tools for robustness, connectivity, and legacy technologies and practices in agriculture. Still, in terms of connectivity, the agriculture domain has specific requirements.
- **Covering Rural Areas**

  Rural areas should be efficiently deployed and covered by the communication networks, which stands as the key requirement. The large exposure and low costs for deployment and maintenance are the major connectivity factors of agriculture IoT applications, but it is found that the requirements are less for the majority of applications that collect data based on bandwidth. Thus, for the current deployment, technologies such as the LPWA (low power, wide area) technologies like LoRa and Sigfox, and legacy 2G networks become best suitable. However, guarantee cannot be assured in terms of long-term sustainability, and provided the lifespan of agricultural equipment, a delay in the technological choices is about to occur because of this uncertainty. In certain advanced cases such as the use of video, AR, or full automation, however, either 5G networks have to be deployed or irregular connectivity has to be established. Also, IoT solutions should be able to adhere to the limitations of the environment such as rain, dust, wind, limited power, etc., to be deployed efficiently in rural areas. Technology adoption can be delayed if these factors are not taken into consideration.
- **Connecting Machines and Farms**

  The ability to remotely collect, utilize, and exchange data is the driving factor that affects productivity, besides the introduction of new tools and practices. The use of IoT to collect, process, and publish information on the production processes is one of the primary applications. For this purpose, many activities are done, including the facilitation and automation of legal and tax declarations by the digital tools, publishing detailed information related to goods, quality, and origins for food traceability, etc. As only limited integration with the production environment is required, such cases are easy to adopt and implement.

Another example is how data related to agricultural tools are communicated to manufacturers. For this, AI-driven predictive maintenance is applied. The manufacturers can track how their products are being used through high-speed connectivity and sensor deployment. Low performance can be detected early, and preventive maintenance can thus be performed. Besides, the needs and usages of products and tools can be better understood by their manufacturers. The third use case shows how to improve the production process, practices, crops, and tools utilizing the automated data collection. This enables increased productivity and optimized use of fertilizers, fuels, and herbicides. It is estimated that there is a 20% increase in the income from agriculture even by reducing the fuel consumption and herbicides from 10% to 20% (Norris & Bland, 2015). However, as extensive data collection and exploiting the environment is required, it takes time for the implementation of these scenarios.

A more complex-valued network is created by deploying IoT in the sector that includes new roles in the chain such as connectivity providers and application providers. As the agricultural sector becomes increasingly connected and automated, there is a rise in demand for equipment and tools, thus leading to market competition. Rather than providing traditional and limited products, these tool manufacturers need to provide almost complete farm services to the people to remain competitive in the market. To optimize the production and to achieve better results, pattern recognition and prediction have to be conducted at higher levels rather than analyzing it inside a farm. Hence, extensive data exchange mechanisms—which incorporate information from various actors involved, even with different interests—should be included in it.

7.1.6 Transportation and Logistics Sector

One of the striking features when applying I4.0 technologies is to create connections across various networks in the cloud where information interchange occurs between the people and various objects without intervention. This thinking gives way to the wider IoT. At least three categories of market players are created by users and devices connected by IoT technology in the area of supply chains. Shippers and consignees of products belong to the first category. Their services are used by people throughout the supply chain. People and computer systems used by transport and logistics operators belong to the second category, whereas owners and infrastructure managers—along with their infrastructure such as infrastructure managers of railways in each state—belong to the third category. All of these categories use universal or dedicated software or even semi-automated robots to manage their staff, equipment, operations, and administration.

When applied to the logistics sector, industrialists termed the environment as Logistics 4.0 that integrates all these market players, as well as public market regulators. Primarily, it is concerned with robot implementation and the data exchange among various devices. For this, the consignee first creates an order of the parts or raw materials related to manufacturing or assembling to the suppliers. This is done using the automated IT facilities as a usual procedure. When it reaches the supplier side, these orders are managed by the machines or manually, depending on the nature of the order. For example, if a robot is employed in the supplier warehouse, the order can be sent to the robot which then picks it, packs it, and addresses the shipment to the loading ramp. Next, the shipment is picked by an autonomous vehicle that reaches the ramp, collects it, and transports it to the place of delivery. In the smart factory, this shipment is reloaded and taken to the place where the product is exactly required. Another use case is a 3D printer, which is a kind of robot that can be used at the receiver side, controlled by the supplier. Here, the physical movement of the finished product does not happen from the supplier and instead raw materials for the product are transferred which is handled by the printer. This implies that the movement of raw materials rather than the product can lead to significant cost reduction in the supply chain activities.

However, there are also challenges posed by Logistics 4.0. Automation was previously limited to factories or warehouses alone. Data exchange and significant information transfer also occurs outside the manufacturing environment such as the road infrastructure and its utilization by smart vehicles. For example, an autonomous truck carrying a shipment gets early information that a road is blocked somewhere in its path, and hence it must take another path to reach its destination. This does not happen in the manually controlled truck because the driver comes to know about the block only after reaching the blocked part of the road, which in turn leads to wastage of time and fuel.

The idea of automated communication between robots and smart vehicles can lead to greater efficiency. At present, there are drawbacks caused by the decrease in satisfaction level of the services offered by technical devices. Many managers of the supply chain claim that sometimes shipments have to be controlled and coordinated again manually because robots are inefficient. It is being examined that human controlling procedures are better compared to robot controlling procedures.

Heavy vehicles are in greater demand because they fulfill several kinds of transportation tasks. Operators are interested to implement autonomous heavy vehicles in carrying out local transport, as well as medium and long-range transport. In these cases, the jobs done by a driver are replaced by controllers that can manage vehicle movements and operations with an interaction with the remote control system. In both kinds of road transport, installation of some devices to enable communication between the vehicle and infrastructure is required. There are two use cases for this. Mobile devices that are capable of exchanging data with the vehicles running there are installed in certain sites. In another case, devices that are equipped with IoT are installed in various places, especially roads, so that they can integrate into the common network of vehicles and their infrastructure. In such cases, the infrastructure becomes self-aware and intelligent. Semi-autonomous vehicle implementation is also possible when working as a part of the network integrating both vehicles and infrastructure. In case of failures, the operator of such systems will take control and rectify them (Paprocki, 2017).

Revoolt is a company that has already implemented Logistic 4.0 standards. It is a last-mile delivery company that bases its business on three main pillars: electric vehicles, the IoT, and the cloud. The company controls its fleet using electric vehicles that send and receive data from the OBD port of the car which is then stored and analyzed in the cloud platform. The theory of Logistics 4.0 is built upon 6Rs: right customer, right product, right place, right time, right quantity, and right quality. With the increase in the market demands, companies should implement systems that allow the following.

- Improvement of customer experience.
- Achieving market efficiencies.
- Operating with the environment, studying its impacts.

To do so, many technologies are transforming the logistics industry.

7.1.6.1 Internet of Things (IoT)

IoT, in the logistics sector, aids the following processes and applications.

- Inventory management.
- Safe transportation.
- Vehicle tracking.
- Supply chain monitoring.
- Process automation.
- Predictive maintenance.

In addition, IoT platforms assist in reducing human errors in the following ways.

- Through the alerts when data monitoring fails.
- Through updates done remotely without physical intervention.
- Through remote configuration systems.

7.1.6.2 Data-Driven Technologies

Technologies like AI and Big Data make use of their data analysis capability to improve logistics systems. Data can be collected from many different points through IoT devices. From this huge collection of data, companies can make a series of decisions more accurately, from the moment a product is shipped until it reaches the client. For example, as the product becomes available for shipping, an alert could be issued which calls the closest vehicle and alerts the customer as to the time it will take to reach the customer side.

7.1.6.3 Blockchain

Blockchain technology deals with storing digital information (blocks) in public databases (chain). In the traditional logistic scenario, manual computer entry of data is required, or in the worst case, it is handwritten. Living in this technological era, it is not possible to trust these data because they can be easily manipulated or stolen. Blockchain technology solves this problem by recording the details about goods throughout their flow. Hence, the supply chain achieves transparency and the details are easily traceable at any time. For example, blockchain technology can be used in pharmaceutical products, which may need medicines requiring cold transport.

Technology is widely influencing the way logistics operations are being followed in the industry. They all are aimed at generating more efficiencies and thus improving the customer experience. A use case that develops an efficient outcome is of Amazon Prime Air (Figure 7.5), drones are used to deliver products. Amazon Prime Air uses almost all the combined Logistics 4.0 technologies for serving customers in a better way, whereas a common revolution that is seen around is the smart car which uses technologies to become autonomous and eliminates human involvement.

FIGURE 7.5 Amazon Prime Air. The image shows the prototype of the Amazon Prime Air drone that is used to deliver products to customers. The drone is seen with a landing wheel toward the center of the front side and two stands on both sides of the rear end of the drone. It has a platform at the top for placing goods or products.

7.2 How Is I4.0 Beneficial to Society?—Impacts and Benefits

There are many more advancements in technology in this decade than ever before. A decade ago, it was difficult to imagine many solutions or products that emerge in society. The various industries were slow to adapt to all these innovative technologies. IoT, AI, and Big Data are in the front to transform the entire value chain just like Ford's assembly line contributed to industrial growth (Shkabura, 2019). We live on the edge of a technological revolution that will alter the way we work and live.

To mechanize production, water and steam power were used in the First Industrial Revolution. Mass production aided with electric power was used in the Second Industrial Revolution. The Third Industrial Revolution relied on automation through electronics and information technology applications. At present, the Fourth Industrial Revolution, or the I4.0, is building on the top of these revolutions which is characterized by the fusion of technologies that narrows down the gap between the physical and digital world.

The three reasons why I4.0 is treated as a distinct revolution are its scope, velocity, and systems impact. The pace at which these technologies evolve does not have any historical predecessors, and it evolves at an exponential pace rather than a linear pace. Also, it has made its impact in every industry and has transformed the entire systems of production, management, and governance. Unlimited access to knowledge, storage capacity, and processing power through mobile devices are offered to many people. As the technologies such as robotics, IoT, AI, autonomous vehicles, and quantum computing emerge, the possibilities as further heightened.

AI has played a vital role in offering driverless cars and drones to virtual assistants, software to discover new drugs, and translation software. Driven by the availability of a huge amount of data, and an increase in computer power, remarkable progress has been made by this technology. As the gap between the physical and digital world diminishes, it is to be ensured that the impact these technologies have on society is positive. However, it is not easy to precisely know the impact on different individuals and groups. There are three big areas of concern: inequality, security, and identity.

7.2.1 Inequality

According to Credit Suisse's Global Wealth Report 2015, it is examined that the richest 1% of the global population owns half of all household wealth. Oxfam 2015's report has found out that 62 individuals had more assets than the poorer 3.6 billion people combined (Elliott, 2016). This gap is stunning, and poorer sections thus tend to be violent, suffer from mental stress, and have lower life expectancies and less trust. As the cost of products falls, with stability in its quality, it is observed that consumers tend to gain more. I4.0 makes most of the services and products available to increase the standard of our living or make better profits. Instant access is possible now for services like transport booking, booking restaurants, making payments, watching movies, and buying groceries and other items, at any place and time.

But, the question that is raised here is whether everyone can enjoy these benefits and access, afford, and enjoy these innovations. Our reliance on the digital markets is a potential driver of this inequality. These digital platforms grant rewards or offers to a small number of star products and services. Also, for many people, it is concerning, given the power, influence, and profitability of digital platforms.

One of the striking issues raised by I4.0 is its potential that leads to unemployment to some extent. Newly digitized industries and platforms require less manpower as compared to the older traditional ones. Hence, comparatively, positions are fewer. According to studies by Carl Benedict Frey from the Oxford Martin Programme on Technology and Employment, only 0.5% of the workforce in the United States is employed now in I4.0 adopted sectors, which marks an existence of I4.0 at the beginning of the twentieth century itself. Also, the rate of new jobs, which was 8.2% in the 1980s, was reduced to 4.4% in the 1990s, a trend which is expected to continue. Also, the types of new jobs in the industry require higher educational qualifications and specialized study for which the higher class only could acquire. The jobs such as physical and routine tasks which were done by the lower class of people were taken away. Also, it is predicted that future jobs will increasingly require complex problem-solving capabilities and social and system skills. This kind of bias arising between the rich and poor, educated and the uneducated, disproportionally affects the weaker sections of society (Davis, 2016). This is one of the reasons why many countries still are under-developed and live in the Third Industrial Revolution, whereas the others enjoy their life taking the advantage of I4.0 technologies.

Table 7.2 shows the probability of various occupations to be prone to automation.

TABLE 7.2
Probability of Occupations Prone to Automation

	Probability	Occupation
Most Prone to Automation	0.99	Telemarketers
	0.99	Tax preparers
	0.98	Auto damage, insurance appraisers
	0.98	Referees, umpires, and other sports officials
	0.98	Legal secretaries
	0.97	Restaurants, lounge and coffee shop hosts and hostesses
	0.97	Real estate brokers
	0.97	Farm labor contractors
	0.96	Secretaries and administrative assistants, except legal, medical, and executive
	0.94	Couriers and messengers
Least Prone to Automation	0.0031	Mental health and substance abuse social workers
	0.0040	Choreographers
	0.0042	Physicians and surgeons
	0.0043	Psychologists
	0.0055	Human resource managers
	0.0065	Computer systems analysts
	0.0077	Anthropologists and archaeologists
	0.0100	Marine engineers and naval architects
	0.0130	Sales managers
	0.0150	Chief executives

7.2.2 Security

Inequality affects productiveness, emotional state of mind, and confidence, and in addition, it creates many security concerns for people, companies, and governance systems. A fully connected digital environment with unequal distribution of power and wealth thus creates demoralization and agitation. All these combined concerns can create violence and security breaches driven by power. Also, the I4.0 technologies and digitization brought by it have created the cyberworld as a battlespace for survival and existence. Even though the conflicts among companies may not happen physically, it is most likely that some companies use the cyberworld to gain access to other's technology and information.

In the military, there are a few emerging developments that can even communicate with the human brain of a soldier and control his/her actions. If an area like a neuro-scientific field is exploited, then there is a greater chance that the next war will be using the human brain as a weapon. In addition to these fears, the extensive use of modern technologies makes it difficult for most companies to settle up conflicts and agreement issues. The challenge that is being put up by I4.0 is going to create disputes to a deeper extent, and many companies will have to find more time to settle it.

7.2.3 Identity, Voice, and Community

Other than the issues related to the rise of imbalanced power in society and the safety of properties, I4.0 will also have an impact on the people individually as well as collectively. Thus far, digitization has created the formation of new societies and groups by way of connecting people based on their needs and interests. Also, some of these links go further, above the limits allowed. Extended digitization need not always give way to diversity. There are chances that new products can be used to challenge, demoralize, or harass people. Even in the dominion of medicine and biology, new concerns have been posted on technology's effects on human beings. Here, various technological tools can even change our genes or the way we think. In addition to providing technological products for society, care should be taken that there are fewer concerns about its impacts on livelihood.

7.2.3.1 The Impact on Business

The way how technologies and products based on the upcoming technologies grow is really hard to predict. It is signaled that the I4.0 technologies impose a striking impact on businesses. The vendors see I4.0 as a way to cater to existing needs in an advanced manner, thus exploiting the values. This sudden change in the technology implemented by the opponents and challengers can throw out well-settled companies within a short period. As the customers have advanced access to their needs with the advent of smartphones and networks, there is a shift in the demands, driven by the changes in customers' shopping trends. This has forced the manufacturers to bring in huge changes to their existing systems right from the design until the delivery. The scenario that is seen now is an environment channeling the demand with the supply through the extended use of technology and the internet. This, in turn, enables new and creative ways of accessing the services and products, as well as simplifying the workloads of industrial staff.

In the I4.0 environment, there are as many as four factors that have a consequence on the businesses. First, meeting the expectations of consumers is highly crucial because they are the central point of concern for the existence of industries. Hence, every work done should be to improvise the services offered to consumers. Second, the focus should be on creating products with extended features and capabilities so that there are greater chances of getting them purchased. With data analytics as to the base, these technologies can be utilized to innovate products to the maximum. Hence, the third factor should be collective innovation that is streamlined with other processes and the type of services offered. Finally, as modern technologies and new ways of attracting customers are implemented in the industry, the organizational structure should be revamped, including employee skills and socialization. Therefore, companies should revamp their business models, periodically keeping the base as the same, i.e., experts, stakeholders, and heads of various departments identifying the change and adapting to it by transforming their workforce and the mode of operations.

7.2.3.2 The Impact on Government

With the technologies imposing a much bigger impact on the people through digitization, foundations have been laid for the people to communicate with the governance systems, poll their voices, and even outmaneuver many authority decisions. On the other hand, governments can make a hold on their citizens by using powerful ubiquitous monitoring systems. Also, they are forced to change their existing approaches of governance, managing the citizens, and making policies because of the decentralized distribution of power and digital freedom that the people possess.

The government organizations and public services can survive only if the IT ministry has a vision of extending the existing services through the adoption of new technologies, or by implementing new digitized services for the public. Their systems and services become much ignorable and unreliable if they cannot adapt to modernization. In the governance systems earlier, the authorities or ministers initially learn about a problem, form the action plans, and execute them, taking their own time. This approach follows a sequential pattern, learning the concerns one after the other, and formulating ways to deal with them linearly. Rather than taking public opinions or voices into consideration for sorting out public issues, these systems developed more a kind of imposed solutions that comes out of the thinking from government officials alone.

The old traditional approaches are not realistic and practical in the current generation. The extended technological growth and the acceleration of change brought in by modern technologies are confronting the governance systems to bring in transformation at a high degree for which most governments fail to achieve. In addition, a few governments fail to maintain the well-being of the public while adopting new policies based on the technological revolution. Hence, governments must communicate and work closely with the society and technical team so that they will be able to move on to implement modern governance systems, thereby promoting to the next stage, with continuously collecting feedback and attaining the satisfaction of the public.

I4.0 technologies have made an impact on the nation's security aspects, also, and this is the area where conflicts are more probable to occur. The cold wars between nations; economic growth of countries and states; and the cultural, linguistic, and religion-based separations form the foundations for the thought to innovate the existing methodologies related to security. On the other hand, the innovations that emerge such as biological weapons, or the development of new kinds of micro-organisms through advanced technologies, become flexible for countries to even destroy an opponent's economy. For example, some nations raised allegations that the novel COVID-19 virus that started to spread across the world in December 2019 is a biological weapon of China. Even though it is not yet known whether it is either a bio-weapon to destroy economies or was developed in advanced Chinese laboratories using modern technologies, it has destroyed the world population to a huge extent because it affects only humans with a high spreading rate and there are no treatments for it.

Such kinds of defenselessness are also brought in by the research done using modern technologies in various sectors. Opposing these concerns, these issues can be tackled again by the same technological revolutions either by eliminating the risk completely or by diminishing the impact. For example, in the COVID-19 scenario, the virus spread can be predicted by collecting and analyzing the patient data using data analytics and machine learning techniques. This, in turn, helps the governments to make necessary action plans if a sudden spread occurs.

7.2.3.3 The Impact on People

I4.0 technologies also transform us in addition to making a huge transformation in the way we operate. It is all concerned with the changes brought in by affecting our characteristics and all the issues driven by such changes. Examples include privacy, authority, and possession, consumption trends, monthly expenses, working time, relaxation time, sociability, etc. There arises a question of whether the execution of such inevitable technology-oriented policies in society would weaken classical human values such as benevolence and collaboration. As an example, it can be seen that the use of mobile phones has reduced the time which we once spent to communicate with family, to stay healthy by involving in physical works, etc. Privacy is the biggest matter of concern for the citizens, affected by digital technologies. Even though it is known why such applications are developed, people still fear due to the tracing and sharing of personal data (Schwab, 2016).

Even though I4.0 exposes many concerns in the public, it still possesses many advantages for people as workers. For instance, it creates space for the workforce to learn innovative tasks. The I4.0 environment gives an extended awareness about the use of modern technologies, the operations involved in the workplace, knowledge about machines and other devices, logistics operations, trade processes, the company's performance, and the products you develop. Also, the pay scale of jobs posted by implementing modern technologies is much higher, and hence, the staff is trained to work on the new platforms, which can increase their talents as well as their income.

7.3 Utilities for Creating I4.0 Applications

There is a vast number of tools offered by I4.0 which can be utilized to create software, hardware, and embedded systems. These tools are applied in AI, Automation, Big Data, virtual reality (VR), AR, and IoT. A few leading tools are listed in what follows.

7.3.1 Artificial Intelligence

7.3.1.1 Amazon Web Services (AWS)

AWS is the cloud platform developed by Amazon, which offers a wide set of tools to create machine learning solutions for your businesses efficiently. Hence, it has more than 10,000 clients ranging from big enterprises to start-ups. For AI projects, AWS's Amazon Machine Learning and Apache Spark are in great demand.

7.3.1.2 AI-One

Using AI-One, smart assistants can be built using all software platforms. It is a biological AI tool, which has many APIs, building agents, and libraries. It also can convert data into a set of rules that facilitate AI and machine learning structures.

7.3.1.3 DeepLearning4J

DeepLearning4J or Deep Learning for Java is an open-source DL library for JVM. It runs on Apache Spark and Hadoop. It also includes Doc2vec, Boltzmann machine, recursive neural tensor network, deep autoencoder, Word2vec, deep belief net, and stacked denoising autoencoder.

7.3.1.4 Apache Mahout

Apache Mahout (TM) is a distributed framework for machine learning algorithms based on algebra and has a tool ScalaDSL to easily work out on machine learning algorithms. The back-end commonly used with it is Apache Spark, but other distributed back-ends can also be used.

It runs on top of Apache Hadoop by making use of the MapReduce platform. The Hadoop Distributed File System contains Big Data sets, where the Apache Mahout tools can be used for pattern recognition in much less time (Zola, 2017).

7.3.2 Big Data and Data Analytics

7.3.2.1 Tableau Public

This is a simple and intuitive tool offering valuable insights through data visualization. Tableau Public has a million-row limit. As it is easy to use, it fares better than most of the other players in the data analytics market. With Tableau's visuals, it is possible to investigate a hypothesis and also to explore the data and cross-check the insights. Visualizations published to Tableau Public can be embedded into blogs. Also, web pages and be shared through email or social media. The shared content can be made available for downloads. This makes it the best Big Data analytics tool.

7.3.2.2 OpenRefine

Formerly known as GoogleRefine, the data cleaning software helps to clean up data for analysis. It operates on a row of data. It also has cells under columns, quite similar to relational database tables. OpenRefine could be used for geocoding addresses to geographic coordinates.

7.3.2.3 KNIME

KNIME helps to manipulate, analyze, and model data through visual programming. It is used to integrate various components for data mining and machine learning. Analysis tools like these can be extended to run chemistry data, text mining, Python, and R.

7.3.2.4 RapidMiner

RapidMiner provides machine learning and data mining procedures including data visualization, processing, statistical modeling, and predictive analytics. RapidMiner, written in Java, is fast gaining acceptance as a Big Data analytics tool. It provides an integrated environment for business analytics and predictive analysis. Along with commercial and business applications, it can also be used for application development.

7.3.2.5 Google Fusion Tables

When coming to data tools, this is a larger version of Google Spreadsheets. It is an incredible tool for data analysis, mapping, and large dataset visualization. Also, Google Fusion Tables can be added to the business analytics tools list. This is also one of the best Big Data analytics tools that combine tables with other data on the web and can merge multiple tables to generate a single visualization that includes sets of data. Even it is possible to create a map in minutes.

7.3.2.6 NodeXL

This is a visualization and analysis software of relationships and networks. NodeXL provides exact calculations. It is a free open-source network analysis and visualization software. NodeXL is one of the best statistical tools for data analysis in which includes advanced network metrics. Also, it has access to social media network data importers and automation. This software integrates into Microsoft Excel 2007, 2010, 2013, and 2016, and it opens as a workbook with a variety of worksheets containing the elements of a graph structure.

7.3.2.7 Microsoft HDInsight

Azure HDInsight is a Spark and Hadoop service in the cloud. It provides Big Data cloud offerings in two categories, standard and premium. It provides an enterprise-scale cluster for the organization to run Big Data workloads and offers reliable analytics with an industry-leading service-level agreement (SLA), enterprise-grade security and monitoring, protection of data assets and extends on-premises security and governance controls to the cloud, a high-productivity platform for developers and scientists, integration with leading productivity applications and deployment of Hadoop in the cloud without purchasing new hardware or paying up-front costs (Guru99, 2020).

7.3.3 Virtual Reality

7.3.3.1 Unity

Unity is a VR platform for game development. It also assists in developing VR applications for other purposes. It has tools like HD Render Pipeline for VR, Spatial Audio, Stereo Instancing, XR Interaction toolkit, CAD and collaboration toolkit, and Particle System. The Jaguar's I-Pace, Beat Saber game, and Bonfire VR movie are all Unity-assisted products.

7.3.3.2 Amazon Sumerian

Amazon Sumerian allows easier creation and running of browser-based 3D, AR, and VR applications. It provides interactive 3D front-end created using Sumerian editor, is a part of AWS, and also provides access to ML and chat-bots. Sumerian works with VR platforms like Oculus Go, Oculus Rift, HTC Vive, HTC Vive Pro, Google Daydream, and Lenovo Mirage. In addition, it works on mobile platforms like Android and iOS. Its features include a ready-to-use template set, state machine, and scripting API, and browser-based publishing. Amazon Sumerian supports various VR use cases like 3D web, online education, production and marketing, retail merchandizing, manufacturing, e-commerce and sales, training simulations, data visualization, travel, and hospitality, etc. Its products include an AI-driven web virtual care platform called Electronic Caregiver and AR visualization of air quality index—WeatherBug and Fidelity Labs.

7.3.3.3 Google VR

Google provides many VR tools for developing VR-based applications for its clients, which can be directly accessed from the VR developer portal. These tools support many platforms like Android, Android NDK, Unreal, iOS, Unity, and Web. The guides to develop applications, and the software development kits, based on each of the Google VR tools are also available.

Technologies such as 360⁰ media, Controllers, Seurat, and Resonance Audio assist in empowering the VR experience. A few Google VR products include Daydream, EarthVR, Expeditions, Tilt Brush, VR180 Cameras, Tour Creator, YouTube VR, and Google Cardboard.

7.3.3.4 Unreal Engine 4 (UE4)

Unreal Engine is an open and advanced real-time platform for 3D application development. Started initially for 3D-based games, now it extends the environment for other novel applications. With a rich set of VR development tools, VR apps that run on major VR platforms can be built, such as Sony, Oculus, Samsung Gear VR, Android, iOS, Google VR, etc. It has connections to media production pipelines, with standard Python scripting. Using Datasmith, it can convert entire animation and metadata scenes. The UE4 platform has many features like the following.

- Visual Dataprep—for automatic data preparation workflows.
- LiDAR point cloud support—for larger datasets collection.
- Shotgun integration—for connection between upstream and downstream data.

7.3.3.5 Cryengine

Cryengine is a popular VR-based real-time application development tool, initially focused on developing games. It also has a rich toolkit for VR-based application development. Cryengine has the best-in-class visuals that enrich the visual experience. In addition, its Sandbox—a set of tools—is used to create the best development experiences. AI and animation techniques such as character technology, geometry cache, procedural motion, and parametric skeletal animation; audio technologies such as Audio Controls Editor, audio abstraction, HRTF Audio Spatialization, audio occlusion, and dynamic response system; and visual technologies such as area lights, physically based rendering, tessellation, and volumetric fog shadows (Davies, 2020).

7.3.4 Augmented Reality

7.3.4.1 Vuforia

Vuforia is a platform for creating AR applications. Its rich set of tools allow developers to extend applications by adding computer vision techniques to create a virtual world. In 2017, Vuforia was integrated with Unity, which is a leading platform for AR/VR applications. Vuforia Engine supports Android, iOS, and UWP platforms for application development. The recent version is Vuforia Engine 9.1, released in May 2020. Its features include the following.

- Vuforia model targets—for identifying objects by their shape.
- Vuforia ground plane—for the digital content to be placed on a surface such as a floor, ground, or table.
- Vuforia fusion—for addressing fragmentation issues in AR devices like sensors, chips, cameras, etc.
- Simulation play mode—for visualizing applications in a better way.

7.3.4.2 ARToolKit

ARToolKit is an open-source library for creating AR-based applications. The last stable release is ARToolKit 1.0.6.1 released in April 2020. It works on many platforms including Android, Linux, Windows, iOS, and OS X.

ARToolKit utilizes computer vision to solve the issue of tracking user's viewpoints. The libraries are capable of calculating camera positions more accurately. Its features include the following.

- A simple framework for real-time AR applications.
- Multiplatform library.
- Tracking user's viewpoint.
- Expanded video library with multiple input sources, multiple formats, camera tracking, and GUI initializing interface.
- 6D marker tracking.
- Simple graphics library.
- Fast rendering based on OpenGL.
- Simple application programming interface.

7.3.4.3 Google ARCore

ARCore is the platform offered by Google for the development of AR applications. ARCore APIs are capable of understanding the environment and interact accordingly. It runs on platforms such as iOS, Android (Nougat onwards), etc. The features of ARCore include the following.

- Motion tracking—ARCore utilizes its striking feature called simultaneous localization and mapping to map the phone with the real world. Using its feature detection techniques using feature points, it can calculate the location change. The virtual image is overlayed on the camera-captured image to make it feel virtual on a physical world.
- Environmental understanding—By making use of its motion tracking, ARCore continuously enhances the understanding of the physical world. Transforming the feature point clusters into planes, and deciding the boundaries of planes, makes it possible to see the virtuality in the AR application.
- Light estimation—ARCore is capable of detecting the lighting of the real world, which it focuses on. Taking the camera image as the input, it calculates average intensity and color, and shows the image with nearly the same originality.

7.3.4.4 Apple ARKit

Apple ARKit is an AR platform specially designed for Apple (iOS) devices. AR application developers can easily and quickly create AR applications and games that run on the iOS platform. It requires only the camera and sensors of Apple devices for presenting an interactive AR world. Its initial package came in 2017 with the iOS 11, followed by its second and third versions in iOS 12 and iOS 13, respectively. Its features include the following.

- Visual inertial odometry—To track the physical environment around the device, to sense objects around it.
- Multiplayer—ARKit 2 comes with a feature called multiplayer that enables different AR devices to view the same display environment, having pause and resume options.
- Scene geometry—Identifies each object in the surroundings such as walls, floor, windows, furniture, etc., and creates a detailed scene of the world.
- LiDAR scanner—A few devices use LiDAR Scanner that can quickly detect planes, allowing an instant AR creation.
- Multiple face detection—ARKit can detect multiple faces (up to three) at once using a TrueDepth camera.

7.3.4.5 Wikitude

Wikitude is a mobile-based AR package that came into the industry in 2008. With a browser-based front end, it provides location-based virtual content through the use of motion tracking and location sensing. Its development kit comprises tools for image recognition and tracking, image and video overlaying, etc. Recently, simultaneous localization and mapping were also integrated into the package. It works on multiple platforms such as Android, iOS, Windows, and Smart Glasses (Ahuravlov-Galchenko, 2018), while it supports frameworks such as Flutter, Xamarin, Unity, and Cordova. It was also the first technology to use a localization approach in AR.

Its features include object and scene tracking instantly, image tracking, augmenting multiple objects and images at the same time, cloud-based storage, geo-AR, and cylinder tracking.

7.3.5 Internet of Things (IoT)

7.3.5.1 Tessel 2

Tessel 2 is a platform for developing IoT and robotics solutions and products. It has numerous sensors and modules for providing extended functionality, which includes RFID, GPS, camera, etc. It has ten-pin modules that include accelerometer, ambient display, humidity, and temperature detection, etc.; USB modules such as BLE, MicroSD, camera, etc., and community-created modules for distance sensing, color sensing, motion sensing, etc.

One who has a good knowledge of Java and Node.JS can easily develop devices in a short time. It has two processors—Mediatek MT7620n (580MHz) and Atmel SAMD21 (48MHz). One of the processors runs the applications at a good speed, and the other takes care of input/output functions, control, and power operations.

7.3.5.2 Eclipse IoT

Eclipse IoT is an open-source solution for IoT projects, cloud platforms, and M2M applications, first made available in 2012. It is a working group that collaborates with many industries and academic experts for the development of IoT products, based on creating an open standard, frameworks and protocols, and tools for IoT development. It operates on connectivity protocols such as CoAP, LWM2M, MQTT, and oneM2M. People can get information about Eclipse IoT services from the official website iot.eclipse.org.

7.3.5.3 Arduino

Arduino offers a platform where sensors can be used extensively for data collection and stored in the cloud. Good control over the physical world by even a computer can be achieved by Arduino, such as controlling thermostats, door locks, and other kinds of home automation. It is an open-source, easy-to-use platform for IoT, which makes a better combination of utilizing hardware and software. It relies more on hardware specifications applied to sensors. The platform comes with an interactive IDE along with the Arduino programming language. The Arduino core functions are based on C++, which makes it easy to learn.

7.3.5.4 PlatformIO

PlatformIO is a multiplatform professional environment for IoT and embedded systems. It assists in rapid development using C/C++ code completions and smart code linter. With the support of more than 800 embedded boards, 35-plus development platforms, and more than 20 frameworks, it extends the technologies for embedded application development. With a unified debugger, multiple architectures and development platforms are supported to make debugging easier with more than 250 embedded boards. It also comes with an IDE that supports multiple platforms such as Windows, Mac, and Linux.

7.3.5.5 IBM Watson

IBM Watson is an IoT platform that offers cloud-based services and manages IoT devices. In addition, it also has add-on services of blockchain that can collect and analyze data from devices and sensors, and extract information. It comes with interactive APIs with dashboards and other resources for rich IoT development. Its features include the following.

- Automatic data collection through sensors.
- Data collection on a real-time basis so that critical knowledge is obtained at the earliest.
- Reduced cost of operation and increased productivity by continuous monitoring of IoT devices and visualizing its data.
- Increased revenue generation through efficient communication with customers and users.
- Efficient tools of data analysis.
- Transparent blockchain service.
- Ensures cloud security and privacy.
- Scalable by using IBM cloud services.

7.3.6 Cloud Computing

7.3.6.1 Amazon Cloudwatch

Amazon Cloudwatch is a cloud service that provides data and knowledge for AWS. It can capture and monitor data and performance using logs and metrics. One can check whether anything anomalous occurs, set alerts for them, and monitor the performance in real time. The advantages of Amazon Cloudwatch include the following.

- Ability to collect, analyze, and generate knowledge on a single platform from data across multiple applications.
- For AWS, the easiest way to collect metrics data.
- Increased resource utilization and operational performance.
- Gaining valuable insights in the best possible way.
- Form actions from logs, events, and metrics.

Its use cases include infrastructure monitoring, proactive resource optimization, application monitoring, etc.

7.3.6.2 Enstratius

Enstratius (formerly Enstratus) is a cross-platform cloud infrastructure management for all types of clouds (public, private, or hybrid) that can be used by organizations for data storage, application processing, governance, and security. It was founded in 2009 by George Reese for Enstratius, Inc., US, which has since been acquired by Dell. It offers support for 20-plus clouds and frameworks such as Puppet and Chef. The supported computational platforms include AWS, GoGrid, HP Cloud, IBM SmartCloud Enterprise, etc.; the supported storage platforms include AWS, AT&T, Azure Services Platform, Google, Rackspace, etc.; and cloud platforms include EMC Atmos, Citrix CloudStack, Eucalyptus, OpenStack, vCloud, and vSphere. In Enstratius, there is provision for self-service of cloud resources and misprovision of it, and also it has other features like cost tracking, ability to customize role-based access controls, a single login for management of cloud, supporting authentication systems such as by SAML 2.0 and OpenId (Burns, 2013).

7.3.6.3 CloudHub

CloudHub is an integrated PaaS (Platform-as-a-Service) that allows users to integrate multiple types of cloud applications, create new application programming interfaces over the data sources, migrate existing applications onto clouds, etc. It is Mulesoft's cloud-based integration platform for integrating various applications and data. CloudHub's Anypoint runtime manager can be used to deploy applications to CloudHub. The features of CloudHub include the following.

- Integration with Anypoint Studio—Applications created using Anypoint Studio can be deployed on CloudHub easily. Using a user account, it is possible to access these applications.
- Cloud-enterprise application integration—Anypoint Virtual Private Cloud enables connection to on-premise applications using IPsec virtual private network or Anypoint VPC.
- CloudHub API—This API helps in managing and monitoring cloud applications and scales them.
- Proactive monitoring applications—Using various tools, the application can be monitored by checking the logs, events, dashboards, and set up alerts if anything anomalous occurs. This is a process that is performed 24 hours a day.

Its vendors include MasterCard, Nestle, Nokia, Walmart, and Honeywell.

7.3.6.4 Informatica Cloud

Informatica Cloud is an integration platform for the cloud that works with data and applications as SaaS (Software-as-a-Service). It allows integration and synchronization of all related data, and applications in on-premises systems and within other cloud applications. It offers a platform in which more insights are obtained for decision-making. It integrates with most warehouses such as AWS Redshift, Snowflake, and Azure SQL to provide extended processing capability. It also integrates with cloud applications such as Marketo and Netsuite.

The Informatica Intelligent Cloud Services offers data integration, cloud application integration, API management, B2B gateway services, integration hub, master data management, data quality and governance cloud, data security cloud, and cloud mass ingestion.

7.3.6.5 Microsoft Azure

Microsoft Azure is the cloud computing platform for Microsoft. It can store, analyze, connect, and process cloud data, and also offers many extended services. By offering a wide range of cloud services, it aids businessmen to make better decisions and frame policies. Even though it is a service from Microsoft, it is compatible with many open cloud technologies, providing a better experience for its users. In addition, recently, it has added IaaS, PaaS, and SaaS services through Azure. Also, the users need to pay for only those services or resources that they require.

In addition to its services, various third-party vendors also make applications available to the users in the Azure portal. Once a user subscribes, they can access the Azure resource for cloud services, where they can host applications or databases. Five different support options are provided by Microsoft for Azure—basic, developer, standard, professional direct, and premier. The various category of services of Azure includes mobile, Web, storage, analytics, networking, integration, IoT, AI, security, etc. (Bigelow & Posey, 2020).

7.3.7 Cybersecurity

Most popular Cybersecurity tools are solarwinds security event manager, intruder, mimecast, CIS, snort and simulation (Software Testing Help, 2020b).

7.3.7.1 SolarWinds Security Event Manager

SolarWinds Security Event Manager is a security system that extends the security of existing security mechanisms for various products. It is a SIEM (security information and event management) system that enhances the administration and management of networks and security policies. Previously known as Log & Event Manager, it accesses the log data and aids in managing and monitoring it in real-time, so that if any issues are raised, it can notify quickly. Its features include the following.

- Real-time event correlation—From an enormous number of log messages from multiple sources, it can correlate events and identify threats.
- Active response—As soon as an issue is triggered by real-time event correlation, the SEM processes automated responses to the problems identified.
- Rogue USB data loss and theft protection—Through active responses, accessing data using USB devices can be detected and stopped by SEM. Thus it provides unauthorized access to files and systems.
- Advanced searching mechanisms—SEM uses virtual search and forensic tools to search from a large volume of logs.
- Reporting—It has a powerful reporting engine that can generate reports based on more than 300 built-in reports (Leskiw, 2020).

7.3.7.2 Intruder

Intruder is a vulnerability scanning software made for organizations for finding faults, weaknesses, and anomalies in their systems (Software testing help, 2020b). Developed in 2015, it uses the same foundation as that of governance systems and banks, and it also assists in automatic fraud detection and suggests the methods to solve them. Its features include asset discovery, asset tagging, network scanning, patch management, prioritization, risk management, vulnerability assessment, and web scanning. It integrates with most cloud providers such as AWS, Google Cloud, and Azure, as well as other software tools, to manage and monitor the security aspects of cloud data and applications in real time. More than 9,000 vulnerability checks are performed such as finding missing patches, weaknesses of configurations, application bugs, issues in content management systems, etc.

7.3.7.3 Mimecast

Mimecast, founded in 2003 is a security platform that mainly assures security to email services (cloud-based) for Microsoft, which includes security, efficient searching, and establishing continuity mailing services even after the occurrence of a threat. Mimecast uses a huge grid infrastructure for cloud storage, and its MTA enables efficient routing services. It comes with a secure gateway with spam detection, real-time reporting, secure delivery, content conversion, online queuing, etc., and scans for maliciousness at the gateway. Large files can be sent easily with all security measures for the message. It enables users to search for emails of a particular type or content through the archiving facility, protects from ransomware attacks, and prevents data loss.

7.3.7.4 CIS

The Center for Internet Security (CIS) (Software testing help, 2020b), founded in 2000, is aimed at developing and promoting the best solutions for cybersecurity, and utilize solutions for creating a cyber-environment of trust. Crowd collaboration is identified as the best source of enabling security measures, and as a result, CIS leads in creating the best security policies and decisions. CIS package includes CIS controls, benchmarks, communities, and cybermarket. CIS offers features such as the following.

- Monitoring threats and mitigating them through MS-ISAC, for the governance systems.
- Monitoring threats and mitigating them through EI-ISAC, for the election office systems of the country/state.
- Providing 24-hour security services in a week real-time responses.
- Providing global standards for network security such as CIS controls and benchmarks.

7.3.7.5 Snort

Snort is an open-source system developed by Cisco to prevent intrusions into networks. It is a lightweight system that is capable of controlling the network traffic and analyze the protocols in real time. It also performs content searching, finds new vulnerabilities in the network, and prevents various kinds of threats. It works in three configurations—sniffer mode (tcpdump), packet logger mode (network traffic debugging), and network intrusion detection system mode. When a threat is detected, an alert is sent by Snort to the user. It works next after the firewall, providing an extra shield of security (Software Testing Help, 2020a). It supports many platforms including Windows, Fedora, and Centos.

7.3.8 Simulation

7.3.8.1 AnyLogic

AnyLogic is a cross-platform modeling tool for creating simulations. It provides simulation software for various sectors such as healthcare, road traffic, logistics and supply chain, production, education, etc. It uses the modeling approaches—system dynamics, discrete event simulation, and agent-based modeling. It is designed to work with Windows, MacOS, and Linux. The features of AnyLogic include the following.

- Multimethod modeling—Using the three modeling methods in any combination.
- Animation and visualization—Interactive presentation incorporating 3D graphics and intuitivism.
- Industry-specific libraries—Contains various sets of libraries specifically for creating simulations of each kind of industry.
- GIS map integration—Ability to embed GIS map in simulation software.
- Simulation in the cloud—It provides AnyLogic cloud for cloud-based simulation applications.
- Digital twins—Has powerful models to visualize 3D twins of objects.
- Artificial intelligence—Uses advanced AI techniques for simulation development.

7.3.8.2 FlexSim

FlexSim is a 3D simulation modeling and analysis tool that can visualize any type of system in the real world of various areas of application. Developed in 1993, FlexSim has now set a standard for simulation software development. It recently launched a product called FlexSim HC specifically for the healthcare sector. It is used in various other sectors, including production, logistics and supply chain, and transportation. The main features of FlexSim are a standardized object library for robust application development, easily customizable logic creating tools, and drag-and-drop objects for model creation.

7.3.8.3 SimScale

SimScale, developed by SimScale GmbH in 2012, is a computer-aided engineering product designed to create simulations. It can create simulations based on fluid dynamics, finite element analysis, and thermal simulations. It is based on the open-source platforms—Code_Aster and CalculiX for finite element analysis, and OpenFOAM for computational fluid dynamics. It offers a cloud platform to run simulated applications remotely, and also supports a variety of geometrical file formats. One use case is Tokyowheel, a racing wheel company that uses SimScale to select the best aerodynamic wheel.

7.3.8.4 Simul8

Simul8, a product of SIMUL8 Corporation, is used to model simulations for any intuitive process flows, especially in activities related to a real production environment starting from planning to the service. Simul8 assists companies in decision-making by making use of its simulation software. Its features include the following.

- Ease of use—Comes with a drag-and-drop feature to easily create applications.
- Power—Can create applications of any complexity.
- Value—Ensures good return on investment.
- All-in-one solution—The same set of features and tools can be used across all kinds of platforms.

7.3.8.5 Arena

Arena is an event simulation software, developed in 2000 by Rockwell Automation. SIMAN processor is used as the simulation language. Arena provides an interface where users can place different modules related to their components for development. These modules are connected and formed entities. It is also integrated into Microsoft products such as MS Excel and MS Access. It has flowchart-based modeling that consists of a large number of libraries that can be directly used, defining object paths, report generation, auto-diagnosis, reduced errors, etc. (Biolyse, 2020).

7.3.9 Robotics

7.3.9.1 Blue Prism

Blue Prism is a robotic process automation tool that creates the workforce virtually using robots. Developed by the Blue Prism Group in 2001, it enforces rule-based processing using robots that interoperate with other systems in an organization. The term robotic process automation (RPA) itself is termed by Blue Prism. The technology is based on Java programming and it runs on many platforms. With minimum knowledge in programming, one can easily update and learn RPA in Blue Prism, because of visual designers. The features include the following.

- Security and accuracy.
- Robustness.
- Scalability and resilience.
- Better analytics.
- Cloud support.
- Improved service quality.

7.3.9.2 Nintex RPA

Earlier known as Foxtrot, Nintex RPA is another RPA tool that can perform task automation and optimization. The best feature of Nintex in the industry is the faster creation of bots in a much easier way without code awareness. It comes with three goals—manage, automate, and optimize. Nintex is capable of mapping and managing the business goals and aligning the product development according to the goals. It then identifies what processes are required for automation, achieved mostly using interactive features like drag-and-drop rather than working with codes. Finally, it optimizes the entire business by monitoring the processes. It works along with Sharepoint, Office 365, Adobe, Salesforce, Box, etc.

7.3.9.3 UiPath

UiPath is a leading tool of RPA products, basically for desktop automation. Developed in 2005, UiPath aims to eliminate human hands in processing. The features of UiPath that make it the leading RPA tool in the industry include the following.

- Complete solution provider—UiPath offers UiPath Studio, UiPath Orchestrator, and UiPath Robots for providing a complete solution for its clients.
- Intuitiveness—Creating robots and working with UiPath tools are much easier because of its features like drag-and-drop.
- Activity library—A vast number of libraries available to incorporate any kind of drag-and-drop actions.
- Security—Provides the best security services by encrypting credentials.
- Recording—It can record desktop application activities, Citrix environment, and other activities for easier product development.
- Universal search—Single and fast searching for all resources.
- Third-party integration—Integrates with ABBYY, IBM Watson, Google, and Microsoft.

7.3.9.4 Pega

Pega is a business process RPA tool that incorporates machine learning to a greater extent and automates tasks without human involvement. It develops applications and/or robots that are capable of collecting data from the working environment and manipulating it, further increasing productivity and improving efficiency. A large number of processes can be executed faster, with more accuracy, using Pega RPA. It provides a Pega Robotic Automation Studio for configuring animations. It works with multiple platforms such as Windows, Linux, and MacOS, and also offers cloud-based solutions. Pega RPA uses a faster event-driven approach for development and creates robust applications. A better range of flexibility is attained by distributing works across multiple platforms and users (Software Testing Help, 2020a).

7.4 Conclusion

I4.0 has promulgated in society within a short period, bringing in flexibility in all aspects of life. The chapter briefly walks through the domains and areas where the I4.0 technologies have metastasized. It has helped the manufacturing sector in finding markets, through enabling industries by adapting their business. In the healthcare sector, more and more IoT devices, sensors, and bots are developed which assists in surgery and live imaging of the human body. The products of AR have helped students in empowering their critical thinking and efficiency. Other sectors like agriculture, transportation, etc., also benefit from the revolution of I4.0 technologies. They have made a remarkable impact on society. The chapter also discusses how the technologies affect various sectors and a few utilities that are used to create products using the technologies.

REFERENCES

Ahuravlov-Galchenko, Andrii., 2018. Six Top Tools to Build Augmented Reality Mobile Apps. www.infoq.com/articles/augmented-reality-best-skds/. [accessed 29 March, 2020]

Alphacore., 2019. Industry 4.0 Audit. https://www.alphacore.co.in/industry-4-0-audit/. [accessed 27 March, 2020]

Bigelow, Stephen, and Brien Posey., 2020. Microsoft Azure. *SearchCloud Computing*. https://searchcloud-computing.techtarget.com/definition/Windows-Azure. [accessed 29 April, 2020]

Biolyse., 2020. Top 7 Simulation Software in 2018. www.biolyse.ca/top-7-simulation-software-2018/. [accessed 29 March, 2020]

Burns, Christine., 2013. Top 10 Cloud Tools. www.networkworld.com/article/2164791/top-10-cloud-tools.html. [accessed 29 March, 2020]

Davies, Aran., 2020. 10 Great Tools for VR Development. *DevTeamSpace*. www.devteam.space/blog/10-great-tools-for-vr-development/. [accessed 29 March, 2020]

Davis, Nicholas., 2016. What Is the Fourth Industrial Revolution? *World Economic Forum*. www.weforum.org/agenda/2016/01/what-is-the-fourth-industrial-revolution/. [accessed 25 March, 2020]

Digital Transformation Monitor., 2017. Industry 4.0 in Agriculture: Focus on IoT aspects.

Elliott, Larry., 2016. Richest 62 People as Wealthy as Half of World's Population, Says Oxfam. www.theguardian.com/business/2016/jan/18/richest-62-billionaires-wealthy-half-world-population-combined. [accessed 28 March, 2020]

Guru99., 2020. 11 Best Big Data Analytics Tools in 2020. www.guru99.com/big-data-analytics-tools.html. [accessed 29 March, 2020]

Hussain, Aijaz, Hanley, Tim, Rutgers, Vincent, and Sniderman, Brenna., 2019. Aerospace & Defense 4.0. *Deloitte*. https://www2.deloitte.com/us/en/insights/focus/industry-4-0/aerospace-defense-companies-digital-transformation.html. [accessed 28 March, 2020]

Javaid, Mohd, and Abid Haleem., 2019. Industry 4.0 Applications in Medical Field: A Brief Review. *Current Medicine Research and Practice*. doi: 10.1016/j.cmrp.2019.04.001.

Leskiw, Aaron., 2020. SolarWinds Security Event Manager Review: One Powerful Security Tool. *NetworkManagement Software*. www.networkmanagementsoftware.com/solarwinds-security-and-event-manager-review/. [accessed 29 April, 2020]

Mtshali, Amanda. Health 4.0: The Healthcare Revolution will be Digitized. https://blog.kuduwave.com/what-industry-4.0-means-for-healthcare. [accessed 28 March, 2020]

Norris, Jess, and Bland, Jessica., 2015. Precision Agriculture: Almost 20% Increase in Income Possible from Smart Farming. *Nesta*. https://www.nesta.org.uk/blog/precision-agriculture-almost-20-increase-in-income-possible-from-smart-farming/. [accessed 28 March, 2020]

Paprocki, Wojciech., 2017. *How Transport and Logistics Operators Can Implement the Solutions of "Industry 4.0"*. Sustainable Transport Development, Innovation and Technology. pp. 185–196.

Petrillo, Antonella, Fabio De Felice, Raffaele Cioffi, and Federico Zomparelli., 2018. Fourth Industrial Revolution: Current Practices, Challenges, and Opportunities. *Digital Transformation in Smart Manufacturing*. doi: 10.5772/intechopen.72304.

Restart 4.0., 2018. Industry 4.0 and Its Impact on Education. https://restart-project.eu/industry-4-0-impact-education/. [accessed 28 March, 2020]

Schwab, Klaus., 2016. The 4th Industrial Revolution: What It Means, How to Respond. *GE Reports*. www.ge.com/reports/the-4th-industrial-revolution-what-it-means-how-to-respond/. [accessed 29 March, 2020]

Shkabura, Oleksandr., 2019. The Main Benefits and Challenges of I4.0 Adoption in Manufacturing. *Industry 4.0 Infopulse*. www.infopulse.com/blog/the-main-benefits-and-challenges-of-industry-4-0-adoption-in-manufacturing/. [accessed 29 March, 2020]

Software Testing Help., 2020a. 10 Most Popular Robotic Process Automation RPA Tools in 2020. www.softwaretestinghelp.com/robotic-process-automation-tools/. [accessed 29 March, 2020]

Software Testing Help., 2020b. Top 11 Most Powerful CyberSecurity Software Tools in 2020. www.softwaretestinghelp.com/cybersecurity-software-tools/. [accessed 29 March, 2020]

TULIP., 2019. What Is Industry 4.0? The Ultimate Guide to the Fourth Industrial Revolution. https://tulip.co/ebooks/industry-4-0/. [accessed 28 March, 2020]

Zola, Andrew., 2017. top 5 tools for Artificial Intelligence (AI) and Machine Learning (ML) Development. *Digi117*. https://digi117.com/blog/top-5-tools-for-artificial-intelligence-ai-and-machine-learning-ml-development.html. [accessed 29 March, 2020]

8

Technologies, Challenges, and Tools for Education 4.0

Italia Joseph Maria and T. Devi

CONTENTS

DOI: 10.1201/9781003318378-8

Objectives

Industry 4.0 is all about a fully interconnected society with connected cyber-physical systems fueled by the Internet of Things (IoT) and powered by data. The field of education cannot remain blind to this revolutionary change, and hence it has to adapt itself to Education 4.0, making students—the future citizens—confident to face the volatile, uncertain, complex, and ambiguous (VUCA) world. This chapter explores the tools and technologies needed to make Education 4.0 a reality. It shows how digital learning aids Education 4.0 and explores the profile that students and teachers need for Education 4.0. The chapter also discusses the different modes by which digital learning can be imparted to students and the technologies available for the same. Before concluding, the chapter also discusses the challenges that can come in the way of imparting this new-age learning.

8.1 Introduction

In the wake of Industry 4.0, education is also seeing tremendous changes, the prime one being the implementation of digital learning instead of the traditional ways of classroom teaching (Maria et al., 2019). The technologies behind Education 4.0 are manifold, including 3D printing technologies, biometrics, augmented reality (AR), virtual reality (VR), interactive screens, the Internet of Things (IoT), artificial intelligence (AI), and other cutting-edge technologies. Traditional learning does not include these technologies, and digital learning is hence a need of the hour. Digital learning is a 'continuous' learning process that happens in a scheduled or unscheduled manner with the help of technological devices such as computers, smartphones, or other devices. With the increased skills and talents of students, and a huge repository of resources, this novel platform is changing the face of education in India. Today, it is possible and easy for students to find anything interesting or whatever they have to learn because they are available on the internet, just a click away (Maria et al., 2019). Digital platforms include interactive learning, adaptive software, video games, conventional literature, simulations, and peer discussions which provide students a 'choose-your-own-adventure' kind of learning. This chapter explores the need for digital learning and technological advancements in the field of education, and discusses the profile of a student and teacher for Education 4.0.

8.1.1 Digital Learning and Education 4.0

Each day, it can be seen that digital learning is capable of substituting the conventional modes of education more and more. Even without considering how much technology is inculcated into the classroom, digital learning has come to have an important role in educational practice. By expanding the learning horizons of the students and making them more interested and involved in learning, this type of education empowers the students and expands their potential. Thus, digital learning paves the way for Education 4.0 and provides flexibility to the learners to have control over the time, pace, and place of their education. Enumerated in what follows (Figure 8.1) are some of the reasons why this learning is now pioneering the way education is imparted.

8.1.1.1 Making Students Smarter

Students become smarter and effectively develop self-directed learning skills by using digital tools. They become so efficient that they know what they want to learn, where and how to find online resources, how to use them, how to apply the knowledge they acquired in various situations, how to evaluate the results, and even how to give and take feedback. The productivity and efficiency of such students can be seen to improve exponentially. Another important thing that happens is the sharpening of their critical thinking skills. A positive impact of this is that students get a feeling of accomplishment by gaining mastery in new knowledge and skills, and they build confidence that they can do much more (Panworld Education Inc., 2017).

8.1.1.2 Equity and Inclusion

Digital learning envisions and ensures education for all. Education confined to classrooms does not ensure equity and inclusion for all. As an indispensable part of your life, technology can be seen mastered by even the uneducated elderly and speech-unable toddlers. Digital learning is not just handling technology; it is learning with the help of technology. Completely opening up a new dimension of learning, it provides equal opportunities for learning to each and everyone connected to the internet.

FIGURE 8.1 Need for digital learning.

8.1.1.3 Reachability

Digital learning is reachable to anyone at any time and anywhere. In an era when IITs (Indian institutes of technology) and IIMs (Indian institutes of management) and the like are in big cities, digital learning provides learners even in small towns and remote areas to be privileged with quality and up-to-date education.

8.1.1.4 Digital Tides Everywhere

Digital technology is today seen everywhere, not only in the field of education. Today's students are digital natives who think digitally and are living in a digitally networked universe. Hence, unlike the previous generation of classroom students, today's digital natives require a digitally networked learning environment.

8.1.1.5 Availability of New Digital Resources

The availability of a myriad variety of online resources such as massive online open courses (MOOCs), SWAYAM (study webs of active learning for young aspiring minds), and initiatives such as national digital library (NDL) and SWAYAM PRABHA, which are rich in content and delivery capabilities, can be extended to reach any learner anywhere in the country only through digital education. Again, the treasure hidden within resources such as synchronous presentations, research readings on the web, assessment through e-portfolios, and online discussion forums can be tapped efficiently only via this new medium of learning.

8.2 Technological Advancements in Education 4.0

The efficacy of the teaching and learning process can be improved by incorporating the latest technologies. Education 4.0 can result in benefits from the use of these cutting-edge technologies that were once available only in industries. They are capable of engaging the students in learning and keep inspiring them to learn more (Halili, 2019). The latest advancements in technology for teaching which may bring enormous vicissitudes in every aspect of life from manufacturing to daily life, from learning to social commitment are listed (Keser & Semerci, 2019) in what follows.

8.2.1 3D Printing Technologies

The decrease in the cost of three-dimensional (3D) printing technologies has popularized their use in education, though they were once used only in industries. Using this technology, students can transform their creative ideas into real models, which results in a unique learning experience (Keser & Semerci, 2019) and a deeper understanding of concepts (Halili, 2019). 3D printing can be used for supporting outreach activities and creating assistive technologies, and can be used as a support technology while teaching, apart from producing artifacts that help in the learning process (Ford & Minshall, 2019).

8.2.2 Augmented Reality

AR can induce a passion for learning in students since it shows real-world settings in an indirect manner, thus closing the gap between real and virtual space (Keser & Semerci, 2019). This physical experience is accomplished using graphical elements and sensory inputs (Halili, 2019), by having a transformation in education in terms of timing and location. AR can be applied to classroom learning in subjects like physics, biology, astronomy, mathematics, and chemistry, and can be adopted to augmented books (K. Lee, 2012). Moreover, AR is considered to be a good practice of individualized learning experience by assisting students to interact proactively with course materials, reducing the physical and virtual gap using 3D visualization techniques, and also enabling students to interact with the contents within textbooks (Keser & Semerci, 2019). In recent times, it is seen that enhanced learning achievement is a testified benefit of using AR systems in education (Akcayir & Akcayir, 2017).

8.2.3 Virtual Reality

Creating a simulated environment, VR systems immerse people in the created virtual environment, allowing them to interact with 3D materials. The amount of knowledge imparted to a student using this VR world is enormous when compared to the same imparted reading books (Halili, 2019). VR used in the educational field increases the intrinsic motivation of students (Kavanagh et al., 2017). It can be used as a hands-on tool for learning and can be a solution to some of the challenges in education. It enhances student engagement, allows for constructivist learning, and produces powerful learning opportunities when historical events, scientific environments, and the like are reproduced in a virtual environment (Au & Lee, 2017).

8.2.4 Cloud Computing

Gone are the days when students used to carry their books and other study materials in big bags on their shoulders. Cloud computing enables students to keep their study material in the cloud and access it from anywhere without any cost. A stable internet connection which is very affordable today is the basic requirement needed for using this technology (Halili, 2019). The advantages of implementing cloud computing in the educational field are found to be the following (Almajalid, 2017).

- Students and teachers can have their own workspace.
- Interaction in teaching and learning is enhanced.
- Provides fast access, operations, and computation since processing power is high.
- Backups are not needed since storage will be in the cloud.

8.2.5 Holograms

Holograms, which are photographic recordings of a light field, are used in education to help a student to learn in a real-time environment. Students get a learning experience that is interactive and visual (Halili, 2019). Using holography in interactive learning environments is a way of futuristic learning which enhances the learning process. In the medical and engineering fields, this technology can be used for projecting 3D objects which will be much beneficial to the students (Ramachandiran et al., 2019).

8.2.6 Biometrics

Biometrics can include eye-tracking, fingerprints, or facial recognition. It can be used in education for student recognition in classrooms and the library. It saves the time of taking attendance and aids the attendance marking, and can also be used for security purposes (Halili, 2019). This further gives more quality time for effective teaching and learning, and engaging the students with creative works. The use of biometrics is beneficial even in online learning platforms where the students could be monitored continuously during exams to ensure the authenticity of the student, thus lessening academic fraud (Guillén-Gámez, 2017).

8.2.7 Paper-Thin Smartphones

Standing in the place of a smartphone holding textbooks, playing music or video, and providing opportunities for digital and online learning, paper-thin smartphones with their sleek designs help the students to learn with ease. Operating as a small sheet of interactive paper, students get the feel of reading from a book (Halili, 2019). When used extensively, these smartphones could replace paper and be kept stacked on the table of a teacher.

8.2.8 Interactive LCD Screen

Preparing slides and delivering presentations are an integral part of the teaching and learning process. These interactive liquid crystal display (LCD) screens with multi-touch are a perfect solution to such scenarios. Moreover, students can sit around this multi-touch board, use their fingers to touch and swipe images and other elements, and also use the interactive keyboard for typing notes. There are companies that develop software for interactive presentation boards that teachers can use for their classes. Simulated and explanatory lab experiences, programs that enhance skill development and interactive content, aids the students to acquire knowledge in a very interesting manner.

8.2.9 Internet of Things

The IoT is an advantage to the education sector in the sense that it offers a collaborative and more connected environment where students get easy access to study materials and competent methods of communication. With the increasing popularity of smartphones, this technology helps to establish better communication and interaction with teachers and students (Halili, 2019). The traditional system of education can be transformed into a more efficient e-learning platform, with many physical and virtual interacting objects involved in the learning process (Bajracharya et al., 2018).

8.2.10 Artificial Intelligence

Almost all learning materials are today available through smartphones and computers. Physical presence in classrooms maybe one day be a forgotten dream since education can be imparted more effectively and economically using AI. It can accelerate the process of teaching and learning and improve the learning experience of students. When AI takes over most of the work teachers do, teachers can spend more time with the students, engaging them (Halili, 2019). A study conducted by Holmes et al. (2019) reveals that more than 50% of the proficiency levels of adults have already been matched by AI and it is on the verge of taking over another 36%. AI is showing an exponential rate of growth in the educational scenario in many ways. It is included as a course in the curriculum, to enhance online learning, and as a method for enriching teacher expertise (Holmes et al., 2019). This study sheds light on how AI is impacting the field of education. AI-enabled student-teacher matching, student-support chatbots, intelligent bots in game-based environments, AI-supported learning and dialogue, and instructional systems driven by AI are some examples given (Holmes et al., 2019). In fact, AI is bringing a revolution to the traditional methods of teaching and learning.

8.2.11 Big Data

Educational institutions generate much data that must be managed very carefully and systematically. A lot of insights can be gained from student data if they are analyzed using the right tools. Big data technology enables an institution to use this huge amount of data and analyze it to find the academic performance of students, drop-out patterns, attendance patterns, and the like. 'Datafication—the collection of data into databases for analysis and evaluation—is also largely used in the field of education these days. Recently, data centers and data labs have been established at educational institutions for educational data mining and analysis (Williamson, 2017),

8.2.12 QR Codes

Quick response (QR) codes are digital images that can be scanned by smartphones and used in the classroom to aid students to browse websites (Halili, 2019), engage students in a lesson, and manage the classroom. They are a significant tool that enhances distributed and active learning (Rabu et al., 2019), and provides a substantial answer to digital authentication and security (Goyal et al., 2016).

8.3 Profile of a Student in Education 4.0

In 2016, the International Society for Technical Education (ISTE), which serves educators who use technology in education, set standards for students to make them capable and ready to get involved in a world that is digitally connected. Students in Education 4.0 should be made ready to live in a regularly evolving technological atmosphere. The standards set by ISTE are designed to empower the voice of students and to ensure that learning is a process that is to be done by the student (Iste, 2020). They envision a student of this fourth wave of digital transformation, as an empowered learner, digital citizen, innovative designer, knowledge constructor, creative communicator, global collaborator, and a computational thinker (Iste, 2020; Maria et al., 2019).

8.3.1 Empowered Learner

Digital learning enables one to choose what, how, and when they learn. Having free and direct access to all types of knowledge and resources available online and to one's peers and experts in the field, these empowered learners create a culture of self-directed learning whereby they direct themselves to learning which helps them in a career or to which credits they earn for a better living. Moreover, they are having personalized learning with personal learning goals that cater to their individual needs and preferences.

8.3.2 Digital Citizen

A person who utilizes information technology (IT) effectively for creating blogs, participating in social networks, tapping digital resources, and keeping oneself updated with online news channels can be termed as a digital citizen. Digital citizenship, according to Wikipedia, begins with email signup, online purchase, photo upload, or even by participation in a discussion forum, and will demonstrate and practice responsible, legal, and safe use of technology. In this sense, digital learning will be potentially easy for a digital citizen (Wikipedia Inc, 2020b).

8.3.3 Knowledge Constructor

Having an internet of information at their fingertips, students can easily access needed information and synthesize it to a representation of their understanding. Learners should have the ability to locate digital

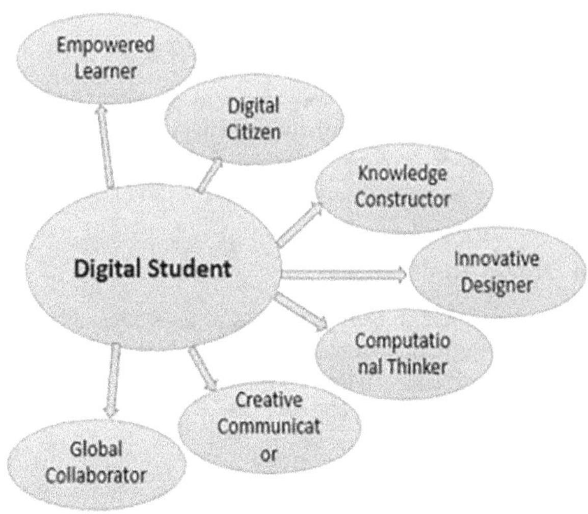

FIGURE 8.2 Profile of a digital student.

tools and resources, skillfully use them, and produce artifacts that showcase their understanding and learning.

8.3.4 Innovative Designer

Independence and creativity are the key factors for free thinking. Students in the digital world are not to be just tested in the classrooms. They can select and use digital tools to plan and improvise their learning process so that they can manage designs even amid constraints and calculated risks. Using their creativity and imagination, innovative designers can identify and find solutions to problems.

8.3.5 Computational Thinker

Traditional chalk-talk classrooms focused on learning and retaining information, whereas digital learning focuses on how students can decipher problems and find innovative solutions. This is a higher-level thought process that can be called computational thinking. Problem-solving and decision-making are made easier by leveraging the power of technological solutions to develop applications and then test them. Once the data is logically sorted and analyzed, automated solutions can be developed for them which enables students to deal with complex problems confidently.

8.3.6 Creative Communicator

As digital learners, students should learn to clearly communicate and creatively express themselves using digital platforms, tools, and formats that are appropriate for them. Producing original works or responsibly remixing digital content into new creations and being able to convey knowledge or positive messages by using a variety of digital tools like simulations, models, or visualizations are bookmarks of a creative communicator.

8.3.7 Global Collaborator

Communicating with one another across the globe is today as easy as face-to-face communication. Students can have a collaborative experience online by communicating with instructors and with peers, clarifying doubts, enhancing knowledge, and even by providing feedback. It benefits the learner with skills such as responsiveness, critical thinking, and reasoning, and polishes his global competencies.

8.4 Profile of a Faculty Member in Education 4.0

To cope with the challenges of Education 4.0 and to train students in the digital learning realm, teachers also should undergo a paradigm shift. They should have an expertise and interest in digital tools, should be able to manage and deliver appropriate content, should be familiar with free and open digital content, and should have a mindset to enhance collaborative learning (Maria et al., 2019) (Figure 8.3).

8.4.1 Proficiency in Digital Tools

As a digital tide is visible everywhere, though digital immigrants, teachers should also be efficiently equipped to swim smoothly in these tidal waves. They should be open to learn and try new things, explore and find new tools, and if possible get trained in these rapidly changing technologies so that they can confidently face this massive challenge of change.

8.4.2 Familiarity with Free and Open Digital Content

There is a myriad of tools available for digital learning today, which puts an increased responsibility on a teacher's shoulders to be skilled in these various tools. The introduction of free and open courses such

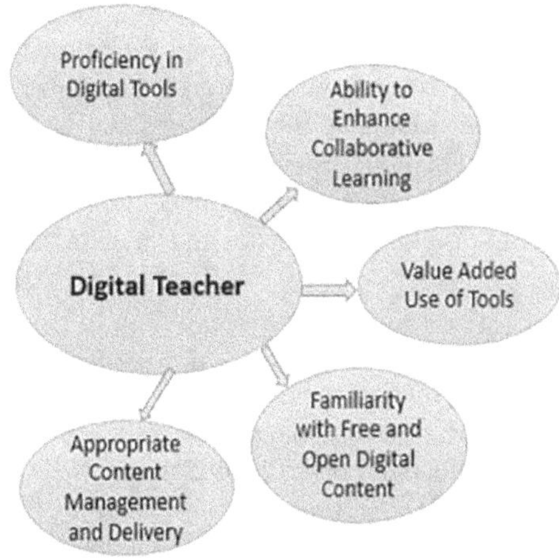

FIGURE 8.3 Digital faculty profile.

as MOOCs and SWAYAM by the Ministry of the Human Resource Development (MHRD), and other online certifications provided by private bodies from time to time, makes teachers in a way liable to be proficient in what these are, what opportunities they provide, which are the ones suited to be included in their course, etc., so that that they can be a true facilitator to their students in this courses they deliver.

8.4.3 Appropriate Content Management and Delivery

Becoming digitally well-versed is not an automatic thing that happens over night. Tremendous efforts are to be made so that teaching methods are focused upon the success of students, individualized learning, and more flexible content delivery. Teachers should be capable of integrating digital skills into the curriculum and use them for evaluation, too.

8.4.4 Ability to Enhance Collaborative Learning

Teaching in a digital world implies meeting and nurturing students sitting at their homes or anywhere at any time, which requires the teacher to design a course by adding collaborative activities, group work including online discussion forums, and even feedback systems. This further requires a teacher to listen and answer them, encourage discussions, enable social media–type interactions, promote online forums, and respond to feedback and restructure course design accordingly, if needed.

8.4.5 Value-Added Use of Tools

In a realm where any information is available to anyone at any time, there is a high chance that learners go beyond what is necessary to them, and teachers hence should be able to deliver sufficient content so that learners have little chance to deviate from them. Moreover, in a networked social environment, students have to learn to understand and respect privacy, treat personal data with respect, and thus have appropriate online behavior. It is the task of the teacher to ensure that ethical know-how is passed along to students.

8.5 The Teaching Mode in Education 4.0

Learning in Education 4.0 is a developmental process, and hence it is not surprising that many students enter college or university without such 'academic' skills. So applying learning methods to these students should be looked at according to the context, not just abstractly. Thinking skills in one subject area may not transfer well to another subject area. Students with good logical skills may not be good painters or efficient leaders. The process of imparting education through digital means should address these areas, enabling out-of-the-box thinking and enhancing the innate standards, logic, and values of the specific subject domain of a learner, thus keeping it learner-centered. That is the reason why the chalk-talk classrooms are realized not to be the best way to engage learners and the following from among a myriad number of teaching strategies are finding their own space and value in the teaching and learning process.

8.5.1 Flipped Classrooms

Learning at home and practicing that in classrooms is the essence behind flipped classrooms. As the name itself implies, it is the opposite of the traditional practice of teaching new content at school and then giving homework and projects to be done at home (TeachThought Staff, 2020). Digital learning envisages conventional classrooms as flipped classrooms whereby absorbing information takes place at home, and practice and discussions take place in classrooms. It brings activities done at home into the openness of a classroom. Students can watch lectures delivered online, participate in online discussions, and even conduct research from home while the implementation of these concepts is carried out with the help of a mentor in the classroom. The interaction of a teacher in such a classroom will be more personalized and less instructive, which enable students to acquire knowledge more effectively (Wikipedia Inc, 2020b) (Figure 8.4).

8.5.2 Blended Learning

This is an approach that combines the traditional classroom model of teaching with online educational materials and opportunities for interaction. Both the teacher and the student should be physically present with control over the place, time, and pace in this mode of learning (Wikipedia Inc, 2020a). Learning which happens online or via technology never degrades the role of a teacher, but rather reinforces the teacher's role as a facilitator who helps learners find the right topics, discuss it with them, and guides and encourages them at their own pace in the learning process, thus enabling them to be equipped for the jobs waiting for them in the knowledge society. Here, though the basic classroom model is maintained, the traditional face-to-face teaching is blended with online teaching (Figure 8.5).

8.5.3 Personalized Learning

This is an educational approach that customizes learning according to the strengths, needs, interests, and skills of each student. A learning plan is given to each student depending on what each knows and how best each learns (Morin, n.d.). The needs of each learner and the instructional approach are optimized

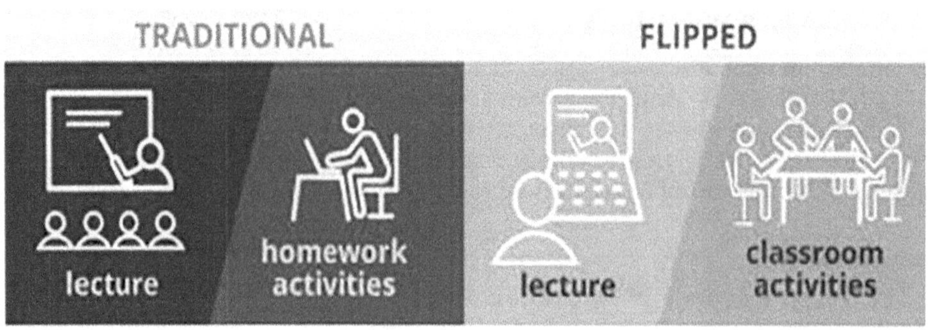

FIGURE 8.4 Flipped classroom concept.

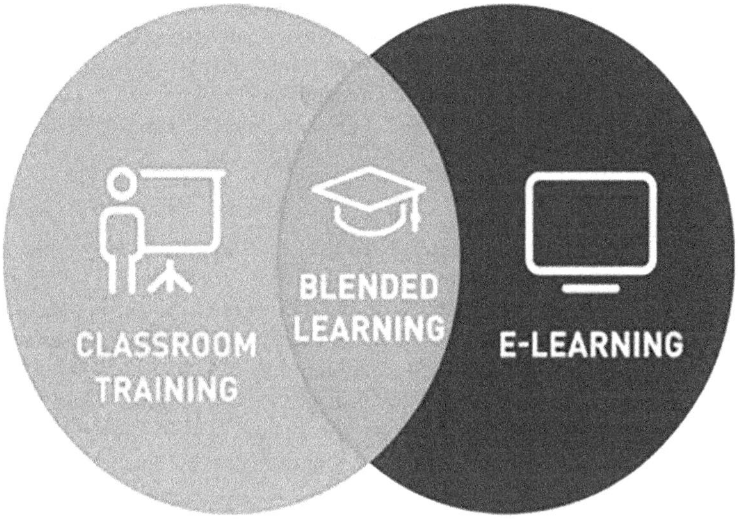

FIGURE 8.5 Blended learning.

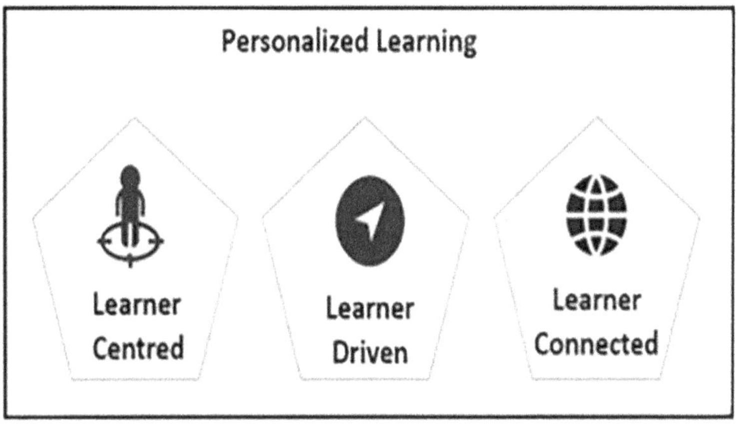

FIGURE 8.6 Personalized learning.

for each learner here. Instructional approaches and content the objectives of learning differ based on the needs of the learners. Moreover, learning activities that are relevant and meaningful to learners are made available to them (Office of Ed Tech, 2017). It is learner centered, learner driven, and learner connected. Skills, talents, and tastes vary across individuals, and digital learning accommodates individual learning by enabling each learner to grasp the topics at the learner's own pace. One can even find topics that suit their flavor and master them in a personalized manner. The benefits of this type of learning are increased student engagement, improved performance of staff and administration, greater student retention, improved test scores, higher grades, and better attendance (Figure 8.6).

8.5.4 Augmented Learning

Augmented learning is the process of taking real-life objects, elements, and experiences, and augmenting those using computer-generated input (Arshavskiy, 2016). It is learning that utilizes context-aware technologies such as tablets and smartphones to enable participants to interact with digital information embedded within the physical environment. As a pedagogical and cognitive tool, augmented learning positions learners in the real world physically and guides and facilitates them in participatory learning processes such as reciprocal teaching, peer coaching, authentic inquiry, active observation, and legitimate peripheral participation with different types of presentation (Dunleavy & Dede, 2014).

8.5.5 Online Learning

Education that happens over the internet is termed online learning. Here, electronic technologies are utilized for education with the help of the internet. Today, there are a variety of platforms that provide online learning through MOOCs, which are available online and aim at open access and unlimited participation through the internet. Most of the MOOCs deliver interactive courses with social media discussions or user forums so that community interactions are supported among students, professors, and teaching assistants. Moreover, they do not neglect the traditional course materials, such as filmed lectures, readings, and problem sets. They are capable of providing immediate feedback to quick quizzes and assignments. MOOCs, a popular tool in distance education, were first introduced in 2008 and later became a regular mode of learning in 2012 (Wikipedia Inc, 2020c). MOOCs from platforms like EdX, NPTEL (National Programme on Technology Enhanced Learning), Udemy, and Coursera which focus on self-paced learning are examples. Most of these also have paid and/or free online certificates.

8.5.6 Innovative Learning

Innovative learning provides an environment that will foster students' love of learning (Schwartz, 2013). Digital learning is innovative in the sense that it catches the attention of learners by delivering video-based, game-based, and mobile-based content, thereby making an otherwise boring concept enjoyable. Innovative learning enables students to become self-regulated learners who can control their emotions and motivations, set goals, and monitor their learning processes.

8.6 Technologies for the Reformation

With no location and time constraints, digital learning can easily adapt to user preferences—and with the introduction of a number of tools, it is practical, too. Some of these tools are MOOCs, SWAYAM, NDL, free and open-source software for education (FOSSEE), and learning management systems (LMSs).

8.6.1 MOOCs (Massive Open Online Courses)

MOOCs aim at unconstrained membership and open access, and they are the result of tremendous research for distance education. Online MOOCs have high-quality content and bring forth a big leap in the realm of interaction in classrooms. They are a means to impart education even to the unreached. Many of the MOOCs provide interactive courses with discussion forums enabling interaction between instructors and learners, or learners among themselves, thus making digital learning a reality (Wikipedia Inc, 2020c).

8.6.2 SWAYAM (Study Webs of Active Learning for Young Aspiring Minds)

SWAYAM is India's indigenous MOOC portal, developed to attain the three main principles of national education policy: access, equity, and quality. It aims to make available the best teaching and learning resources to everyone, including the most disadvantaged (AICTE, 2017). It does so by bridging the digital division for the students who were not touched by the digital revolution This is a sophisticated MOOC platform for distance education that offers all the courses from school level (Class IX) to post-graduation level (Anand, 2017).

8.6.3 National Digital Library (NDL)

This is an initiative of the Ministry of Human Resource Development which provides a digital library platform. It is cost-free for every student in the nation and has more than 2.5 crores of digital learning resources under a single umbrella. It is a framework of a virtual database containing digital learning resources having a single-window search option (GKToday, 2019). This massive repository of knowledge makes multimedia digital educational resources from various subject domains accessible to learners of all ages, regardless of their economic backgrounds. It aims to deliver quality educational resources to all citizens of the country in digital form to encourage, inspire, and empower learning (GKToday, 2019).

8.6.4 Free and Open-Source Software for Education (FOSSEE)

FOSSEE is a project that promotes the use of free and open-source tools to increase the quality of education in our country, thereby trying to reduce the use of proprietary software in educational institutions. Tapping the potential of this project also ensures equity via digital learning.

8.6.5 Learning Management Systems (LMSs)

LMSs are software applications that help a teacher to manage, track, deliver, report, and evaluate educational resources so that the entire teaching and learning process becomes efficient. There are many LMSs in use, of which Modular Object-Oriented Dynamic Learning Environment (Moodle) is the prominent one. These systems are permanent, organized, structured, and accessible at any time, and they can be repeated as many times as needed by the learner.

8.7 Challenges

Digital learning has a lot of advantages in today's teaching and learning environment. Though it allows teaching and learning to happen anywhere and at any time as the teacher and learner wish, it is not without disadvantages. Lack of state-of-the-art infrastructure, poor exposure to the potential of IT, a chance for content misuse, screen distractions of students, challenges for differently abled students, and lack of quality and practical learning are the main challenges that are discussed here (Figure 8.7).

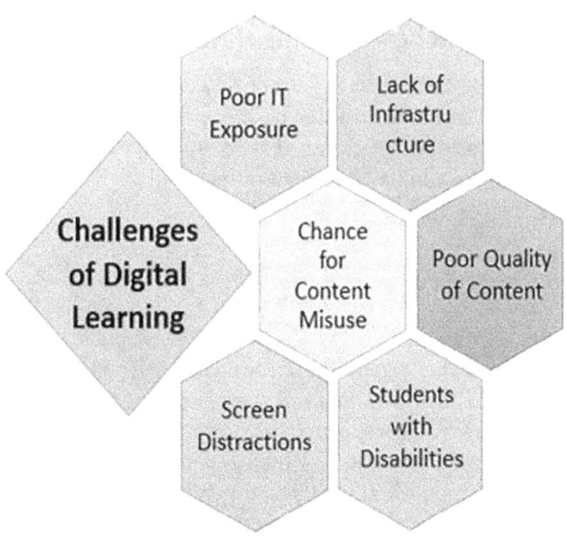

FIGURE 8.7 Challenges of digital learning.

8.7.1 Lack of State-of-the-Art Infrastructure

All initiatives and efforts will be of no use if the learner does not have a digital device and an internet connection, which still is a challenge in the underdeveloped, uneconomic and remote areas of the country. Moreover, giving an exception to urban areas, even with access to digital devices and making internet connection a basic human right, high-speed internet connectivity is a big issue in most parts of India.

8.7.2 Poor Exposure to the Effective Use of IT among Students and Teachers

Though the introduction of MOOCs and other online platforms has made knowledge just a click or tap away, not all are digitally literate. Some teachers still feel hesitant to wake up to the digital advancements, whereas teachers who want to embrace this potential become a beacon of light to their peers. Unless teachers are made experts in these online resources, they will lack the confidence and expertise to facilitate and impart this digital know-how to the learners, and the fact that teachers are digital immigrants while learners are digital natives has to be kept in mind.

8.7.3 Chance for Content Misuse

Having an ocean of information at your fingertips does not imply having access to authentic content. And with open books and open-source tools on the way, still there can be issues of copyright violations.

8.7.4 Screen Distractions of Students

Digital learning implies 'always-on behavior' from learners and instructors. Lack of self-motivation can result in learners shifting their focus from academic materials to other distractions that come in the form of social media interactions, games, news updates, etc.

8.7.5 Students with Disabilities

Ensuring access and equity of education obviously should include the hearing and visually impaired students. There should be provisions to have text and audio options for this kinds of learners. Moreover, courses designed with the well-established standard of UDL (universal design for learning) can address the needs of a wide-ranging group of students, not learners with disabilities (Bates, 2015).

8.7.6 Lack of Quality and Practical Learning through MOOCs

When one learns through MOOCs, the learning is entirely dependent on the effort and the time spent by the learner for the course. The quality, in this case, can be compromised if the learner is not sincere enough in the process of learning. There can also be problems with acquiring practical knowledge through MOOCs. Moreover, there can be fraudulent online courses which, if enrolled in, can result in waste of time and money.

8.8 Conclusion

Education 4.0 is all about using technology in the teaching and learning process, and it benefits students with the opportunity to learn in their personalized ways, thereby making the teaching process more easily adaptable to student diversity. Hence, prime importance must be given to the age-old basic principle of effective teaching, 'know your student', which encompasses knowledge of the similarities and differences of students, their emotional and intellectual potential, their digital skills, what technologies they have access to, and obviously, their taste for the course that is taken. In these modern times, when Industry 4.0 is making Education 4.0 a reality, digital learning is proven to be the mainstream mode of teaching, and teachers—who are digital immigrants—are to be efficient facilitators to students who are the digital natives (Maria et al., 2019). This chapter has given a summary of the technological advancements of Education 4.0, the need for digital learning, the profile needed for a digital student and faculty, and challenges that are to be addressed.

REFERENCES

AICTE, 2017. Swayam, www.aicte-india.org/bureaus/swayam, [Accessed April 27, 2020]

Akcayir, M., & Akcayir, G., 2017. Advantages and Challenges Associated with Augmented Reality for Education: A Systematic Review of the Literature, *Educational Research Review*, 20, pp. 1–11.

Almajalid, R., 2017. A Survey on the Adoption of Cloud Computing in Education Sector. arXiv preprint arXiv:1706.01136.

Anand, S., 2017. Free Mooc Courses at Swayam—Govt's Online Education Platform, www.shiksha.com/engineering/articles/free-mooc-courses-at-swayam-govt-s-online-education-platform-blogId-14716, [Accessed April 25, 2020]

Arshavskiy, M., 2016. 6 Tools You Need to Create Amazing Augmented Learning (at little cost), https://elearningindustry.com/6-tools-need-create-amazing-augmented-learning-little-cost, [Accessed April 23, 2020]

Au, E. H., & Lee, J. J., 2017. Virtual Reality in Education: A Tool for Learning in the Experience Age, *International Journal of Innovation in Education*, 4(4), p. 215.

Bajracharya, B., Blackford, C., & Chelladurai, J., 2018. Prospects of internet of things in education system, *The CTE Journal*, 6(1), pp. 1–7

Bates, A. W., 2015. Teaching in a Digital Age, https://opentextbc.ca/teachinginadigitalage/, [Accessed April 5, 2020]

Dunleavy, M., & Dede, C., 2014. Augmented Reality Teaching and Learning, *Handbook of Research on Educational Communications and Technology*, pp. 735–745.

Ford, S., & Minshall, T., 2019. Where and How 3D Printing Is Used in Teaching and Education, *Additive Manufacturing*, 25, pp. 131–150.

GKToday, 2019. HRD Ministry Launches National Digital Library of India, https://currentaffairs.gktoday.in/hrd-ministry-launches-national-digital-library-india-08201983008.html, [Accessed April 24, 2020]

Goyal, S., Yadav, S., & Mathuria, M., 2016, September. Exploring Concept of qr Code and its Benefits in Digital Education System. 2016 International Conference on Advances in Computing, Communications and Informatics (ICACCI) IEEE, pp. 1141–1147.

Guillén-Gámez, F. D., 2017. Biometrics and Education: A Review about Facial Authentication Software for the Identification and Verification of Students Who Use Virtual Learning Platform, *Advances in Educational Technology and Psychology*, 1, pp. 1–8.

Halili, S. H., 2019. Technological Advancements In Education 4.0, *The Online Journal of Distance Education and e-Learning*, 7(1), pp. 63–69.

Holmes, W., Bialik, M., & Fadel, C., 2019. *Artificial Intelligence in Education*, Boston: Center for Curriculum Redesign.

Iste, 2020. Iste Standards for Students, www.iste.org/standards/for-students, [Accessed April 21, 2020]

Kavanagh, S., Luxton-Reilly, A., Wuensche, B., & Plimmer, B., 2017. A Systematic Review of Virtual Reality in Education, *Themes in Science and Technology Education*, 10(2), pp. 85–119.

Keser, H., & Semerci, A., 2019. Technology Trends, Education 4.0 and Beyond, *Contemporary Educational Researches Journal*, 9(3), pp. 39–49.

Lee, K., 2012. Augmented Reality in Education and Training, *Techtrends*, 56(2), pp. 13–21.

Maria, I. J., Devi, T., et al., 2019. Technologies, Challenges and Tools for Digital Learning, 2019. IEEE Tenth International Conference on Technology for Education (T4E), pp. 268–269.

Morin, A., Personalized Learning: What You Need to Know, www.understood.org/en/school-learning/partnering-with-childs-school/instructional-strategies/personalized-learning-what-you-need-to-know, [Accessed April 20, 2020]

Office of Ed Tech, 2017. What is Personalized Learning? https://medium.com/personalizing-the-learning-experience-insights/what-is-personalized-learning-bc874799b6f, [Accessed April 25, 2020]

Panworld Education Inc., 2017. Benefits of Digital Learning Over Traditional Education Methods, www.panworldeducation.com/2017/03/23/benefits-of-digital-learning-over-traditional-education-methods/, [Accessed April 24, 2020]

Rabu, S. N. A., Hussin, H., & Bervell, B., 2019. QR Code Utilization in a Large Classroom: Higher Education Students' Initial Perceptions, *Education and Information Technologies*, 24(1), pp. 359–384.

Ramachandiran, C. R., Chong, M. M., & Subramanian, P., 2019. 3D Hologram in Futuristic Classroom: A Review, *Periodicals of Engineering and Natural Sciences*, 7(2), pp. 580–586.

Schwartz, K., 2013. 7 Essential Principles of Innovative Learning, www.kqed.org/mindshift/26755/7-essential-principles-of-innovative-learning, [Accessed April 18, 2020]

TeachThought Staff, 2020. The Definition of the Flipped Classroom, www.teachthought.com/learning/the-definition-of-the-flipped-classroom/, [Accessed April 21, 2020]

Williamson, B., 2017. *Big Data in Education: The Digital Future of Learning, Policy and Practice*, London: Sage.

Wikipedia Inc., 2020a. Blended Learning, https://en.wikipedia.org/wiki/Blended_learning, [Accessed March 19, 2020]

Wikipedia Inc., 2020b. Flipped Classroom, https://en.wikipedia.org/wiki/Flipped_classroom, [Accessed April 28, 2020]

Wikipedia Inc., 2020c. Massive Open Online Course, https://en.wikipedia.org/wiki/Massive_open_online_course, [Accessed April 14, 2020]

9

Homework Tools

Win Mathew John

CONTENTS

Objectives

Flexibility in teaching/learning and evaluation has a high impact in the education sector. The innovation in teaching and evaluation becomes the stepping stone of online homework tools. There are many homework tools available. Using these tools, we are able to schedule assignments for the courses we are handling and grade them online, and the students are able to see their grades as well as the overall grade. The students will get notifications about the assignment, they are able to set reminders for the assignments, and there is ability to comment as well as to communicate with the teacher and the students.

9.1 Homework

Homework is defined as being tasked with performing assigned activities to practice, apply newly acquired skills and knowledge, and learn necessary skills of independent study by spending time outside the classroom and an instructional strategy to acquire self-discipline and time management. To correlate

DOI: 10.1201/9781003318378-9

the acquired information from the classroom with real life, learn a new thing by doing and familiarise the procedures are the objectives of homework (Butty, 2010). The design and assigning of homework are done by the teachers; the characteristics of the homework are mainly used to impart knowledge on their perspectives about a topic and to impart significant contribution on the quality of homework. The data of homework provide valuable information to expose the background works of the complex network of relationships between homework and improved grades. The homework is given for refreshing topics covered earlier by reviewing and continuous practicing (Pedro et al., 2019).

9.2 Different Types of Homework

Practice, preparation, and extension are three types of instructional homework purposes. To promote student engagement and effective learning, these practices can be used by teachers while assigning homework assignments. Increasing the speed, mastering the demonstration, review of work, studying for tests, and retaining specific skills over time are the focus of the practice homework tasks. Since practice and preparation homework can be more convenient and less time-consuming, these types of tasks are given more often by teachers. In mathematics, spelling proficiency and fluency in mathematical facts practice homework is used frequently. Preparing students for the next lesson is the main aim of the preparation homework. Students' thinking about a previous topic discussed in class and preparation for future topics are the main advantages of the homework. Extension of homework encourages applying previous learning to new tasks. To encourage students to collaborate with peers and be more creative, teachers use an extension of homework during the learning process of students. To complete extension homework tasks, real-life and hands-on applicable skills are used which incorporate an efficient learning experience for students. The homework with a specific purpose of the extension is valuable for greater achievement among students (Pedro et al., 2015).

9.3 Advantages of Homework

Many discussions and debates exist on homework, the advantages and disadvantages of homework, etc., but the basic purpose of homework is to bridge the gap between learning at school and at home. At school, the learning community is in a monitored environment, whereas at home, students might be learning alone or with minimal intervention of parents. Of course, we should think about how relevant it is to the modern generation. We cover the advantages and disadvantages of homework (Good Education Group, 2020).

9.3.1 Children Can Develop Time Management Skills

Students can manage their time effectively if there is any homework, which is a very useful skill to have in all areas of life. As they grow up, it will be a habit for them to sum up the activities of the day and to fill the gaps if there are any (Good Education Group, 2020).

9.3.2 Students Can Be Busy with Their Studies

Students are able to refresh courses they learned from the school while staying alone in the safety of their home and with their loved ones, and they are also able to be engaged. It also helps parents to get involved in their childrens' school assignments, providing additional insights in a different dimension other than that of an academic (Good Education Group, 2020).

9.3.3 Teachers Can Track the Progress of Students

Teachers can keep track of the progress of the students, which means the teacher can identify if a child is struggling with content or slower than the rest of the cohort. It can be a good point of discussion in parent-teacher meetings, too (Good Education Group, 2020).

9.4 Disadvantages of Homework

9.4.1 Homework Eats Up Free Time

One of the strong and common arguments against homework is that it takes the valuable time the children have to spend with their families, perform extracurricular activities, and play with friends (Good Education Group, 2020).

9.4.2 Excess Homework Causes Children to Feel "Burnt Out"

Completion of the homework after a mix of educational and extracurricular activities seems to be a boring task to students, causing some students to feel exhausted before they reach the final years of school (Good Education Group, 2020).

9.4.3 Homework Is Rarely Valuable

The value of the homework will rarely be productive and informative, even though the teachers work hard to set homework to engage students at home (Good Education Group, 2020).

9.5 Effects of Technology in Homework

Technology has changed the way in which we approach anything and every aspect of our lives, and we are not using anything now as it was used a couple of decades ago. It has changed the nature of offices, the way an office functions, the way in which communication happens, and what else—you name it. The field of education has no exception and the students welcomed the tech revolution with great enthusiasm. The educational institutions also adopted this change very aggressively since improves learning (Google for Education, 2020). The interaction between teachers, schools, and parents is improved, and it becomes a new source of information. Following are some of the technology interventions that help students to learn in a better way (Times Square Chronicles, 2018).

9.5.1 Research Has Become Easier

Many online homework tools already exist, and they allow students to practice what they learn in school and get immediate and focused feedback on their work. Students can see right away whether they did something correctly, and they are prevented from practicing strategies incorrectly because these tools let them know when they are off track. That is vastly better than assigning students homework that does not provide feedback and resembles busy work, be it photocopied word searches in the elementary grades or repetitive math worksheets across the school years. Those dull, outdated assignments do not further learning goals and only serve to disengage students (Heffernan, 2019).

9.5.2 Scheduling and Planning is Efficient and Fast

Today, students live and study in a world guided by technology. Students no longer use print or paper copies of agendas, homework folders, sticky notes, or any paper tools to organise their learning. As a result of the move to planning and engaging students with technology, schools and teachers are getting on board with better ways to connect with their students.

9.5.3 Encourages Active Participation

Online homework portals for students allow teachers to engage students by motivating them; helping them to organise their learning through the use of tools, calendars and reminders; and communicating with them through relevant technologies.

9.5.4 Study Groups Connectedness

Online homework portals are one tool that helps teachers access student motivations and relevant planning and organisational tools, and helps them communicate in more effective and real-time ways with their students. Teachers are a fundamental part of the online learning portal and can post announcements, individual messages and posts, and instructional videos.

9.6 Transition to Online Homework

There are a variety of online homework portals for students, and the research is clear on them (Rutledge, 2019). The three main online homework tools are Seneca, Google Classroom, and Show My Homework.

9.6.1 Seneca

Lukas Feddern is the founder and Stephen Wilks is the CEO of Seneca. The tag line of Seneca is "The fastest, most engaging way to learn". Seneca is an online platform created for both teachers and students for free. Teachers can use Seneca to set tasks for homework and keep track of the progress of their students, while the students will be able to use it for revising the course. Seneca helps students to study faster and enhance by heart learning. Cognitive neuroscience technique is applied in the platform, which makes learning more efficient and entertaining. Seneca offers a large number of free courses covering almost all exam boards. Seneca is more interactive and effective than reading revision guides or making notes (Learn 2x faster for free with Seneca, 2020).

Seneca is best used as an addition to any classroom activities—both as a revision and homework platform. However, nowadays more teachers are using Seneca in the classroom as students generally engage very well with the content. If you have access to a digital board or projector, then you could hold an interactive session in the class. Start any study session on Seneca's student platform and ask the students in the class for answers to each section. This will not only make the students more familiar with the study platform, but will also create a lot of discussion and engagement in the classroom. During the discussion, if any student says something wrong, it offers the opportunity for the teacher to explain the topic (Belham et al., 2019).

Several teachers are keeping the leader boards of their class. These teachers would host regular class sessions during which the students revise on Seneca. At the end of the session, the teacher would then copy the class progress into a spreadsheet. This is currently a manual taskb as it does not yet have an export feature, but it might be a fun way to get your students even more engaged (Belham et al., 2019).

During exam time, the students use more time to study on their own. One of the ways to do this is by letting students freely make progress on their Seneca courses. It is possible to set a homework assignment that the students should complete in a stipulated time or even individual assignments based on the progress of the student (Belham et al., 2019).

9.6.1.1 Seneca Learning

There are basically two options to start with Seneca, as a teacher or as a student, as shown in Figure 9.1. If the teacher option is selected, the platform can be utilised as a teacher.

The steps include:

- Sign up as teacher
- See the course content
- Create a class
- Add courses to your class
- Invite students
- Change personal information or password

After signing up as a teacher, you probably would like to see the course content. To get the student experience and see the structure of the courses, click on the header menu on "Try as a student". This will open a new tab in your browser with the student platform. Here you can try out all the courses and get a feeling for what your students will experience. After you create your first class and course, you can add multiple courses to the same class. From the dashboard, click on your class opening the view shown in Figure 9.2. Here, click on the "Add course" button to add a different course to your class. This is also possible after inviting your students as shown in Figure 9.2 (Belham et al., 2019).

Then, students should be added to the classroom to monitor the progress of the students. The students can be added by sending the link generated by email or by sharing through Google Classroom.

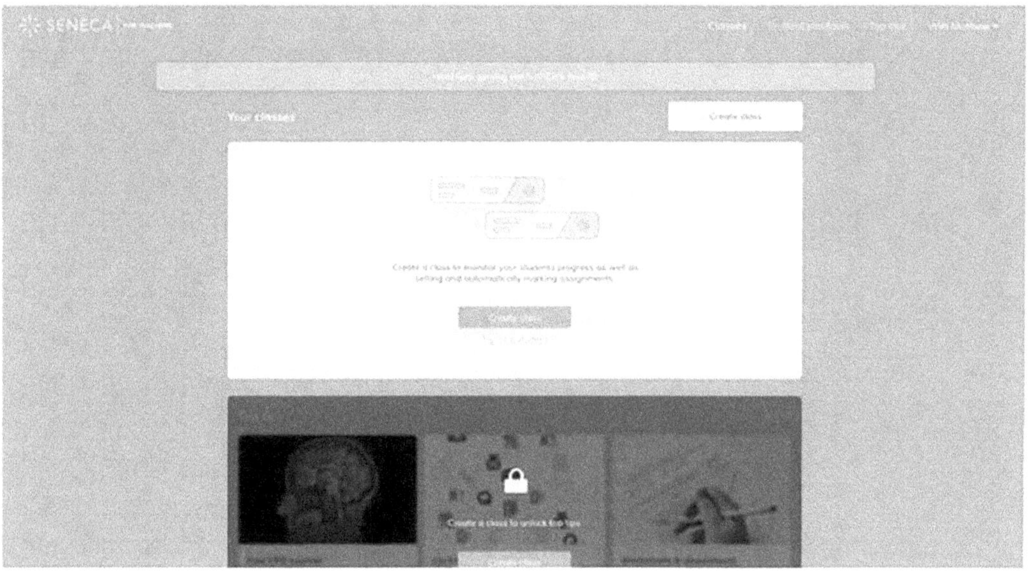

FIGURE 9.1 Opening screen of Seneca Learning.

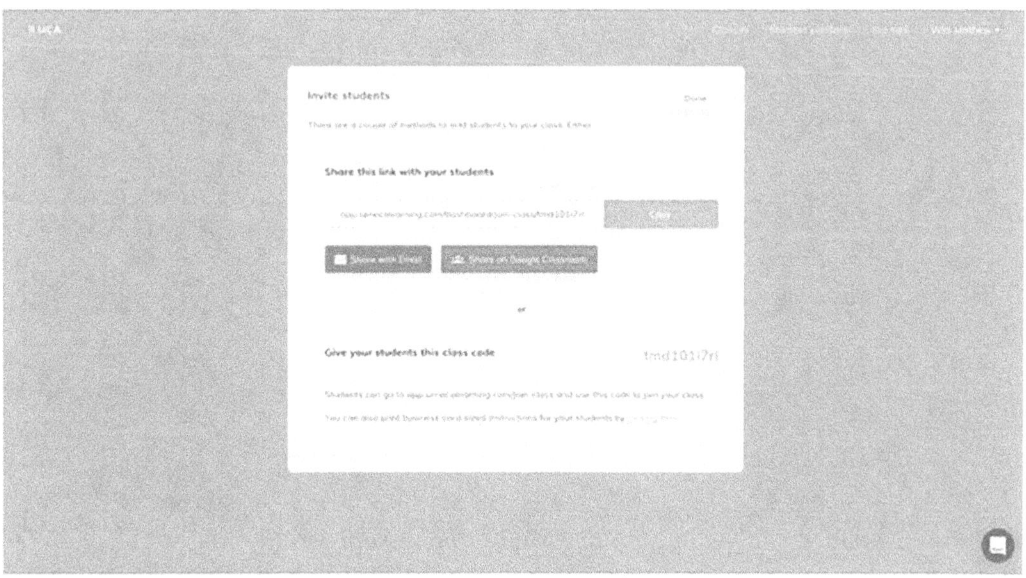

FIGURE 9.2 Inviting students to join the classroom: Seneca Learning.

Another provision is to generate an invitation card with a quick response (QR) code so that students can scan this QR code to join the class. To join with your class, they should enter a class code, which is also generated on the creation of the classroom. The invitation card can be printed or can be sent to the student community via email, or it can be shared over any social media platform (Belham et al., 2019). The format of the invitation card is shown in Figure 9.3.

After enrolling students, the courses can be provided by adding sections and sub-sections in your class content. There is much course content available (Figure 9.4), and you are free to select any board or any subject for your class (Belham et al., 2019).

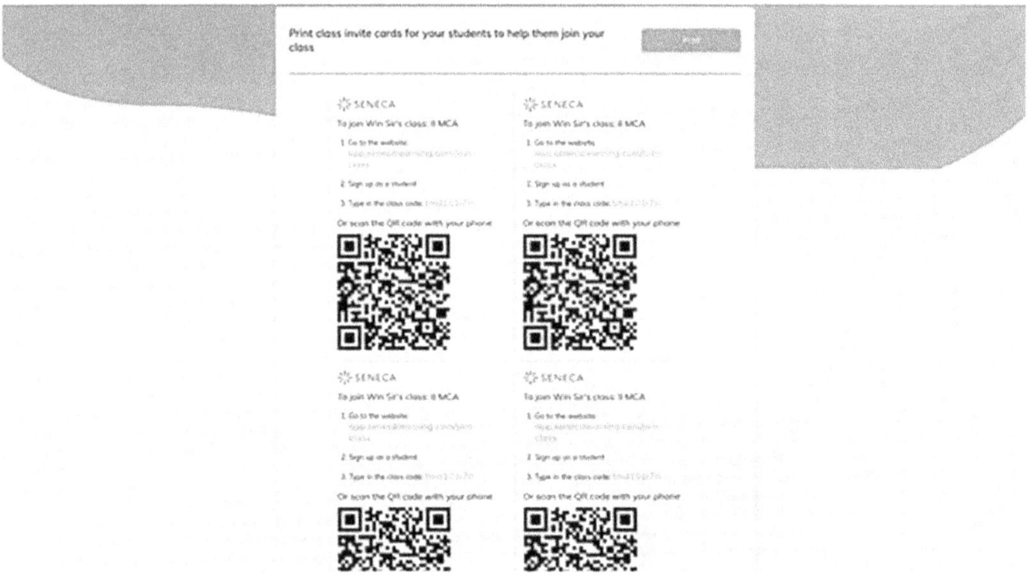

FIGURE 9.3 Invitation card: Seneca Learning.

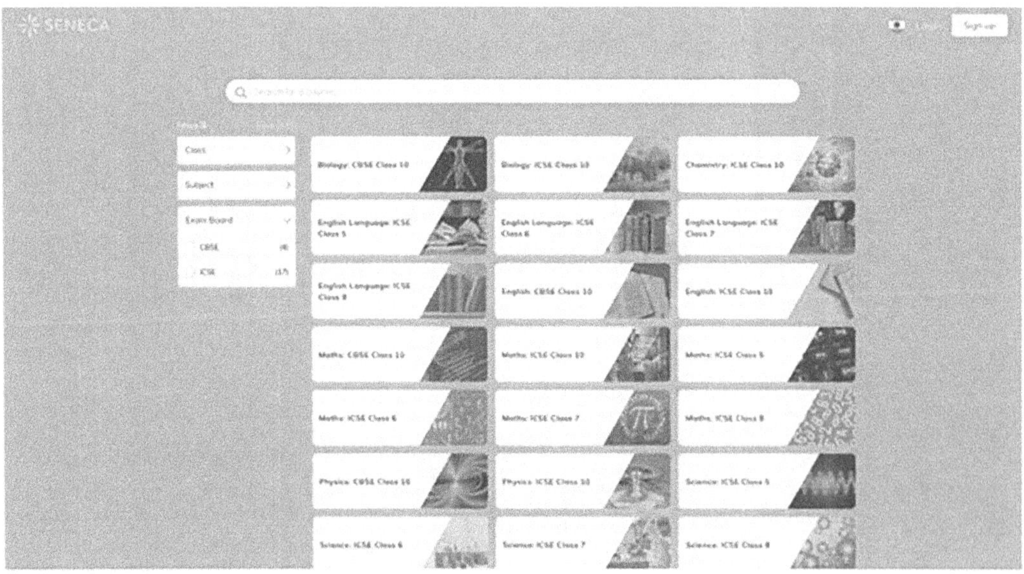

FIGURE 9.4 The available courses: Seneca Learning.

Then you are able to create an assignment on Seneca Learning for the subjects you had assigned for your students. The steps are:

9.6.1.1.1 Step 1: Create an Assignment

First, enter one of your classes and click on "Create assignment".

9.6.1.1.2 Step 2: Assign Sections

Next up is to assign the sections of the right course. You can select entire sections or sub-sections.

9.6.1.1.3 Step 3: Select Students

After selecting the sections, you will have to select the students that you want to complete the assignment. You can either select the entire class or individual students.

9.6.1.1.4 Step 4: Pick Start and Due Dates

The final step is to select start and due dates for the students.

As a student, we can join a class upon getting an invitation from a teacher. After joining the class, we are able to see the classes, upcoming assignments and past assignments. We can start doing assignments as shown in Figure 9.5 given by the teacher (Belham et al., 2019).

9.6.2 Google Classroom

Google Classroom is a free web service developed by Google for schools that aims to make things easier for generating, issuing, and grading assignments. Google Classroom uses the combination of Google Drive for assignment generation and providing the same to the students; for writing, we use Google Docs, Sheets and Slides; communication is done using Gmail; and Google Calendar is used for planning. A private code can be generated and distributed to the students who want to join the class, or automatically imported from a school domain. A separate folder is created in the respective user's Google Drive, where the assignments can be submitted by the students and can be graded by a teacher. The users can take photos and attach them to assignments, share files from other apps, and access information offline using the mobile apps, available for iOS and Android devices. Teachers can monitor and grade the progress of each student, and teachers can return work along with comments (Wikipedia, 2020).

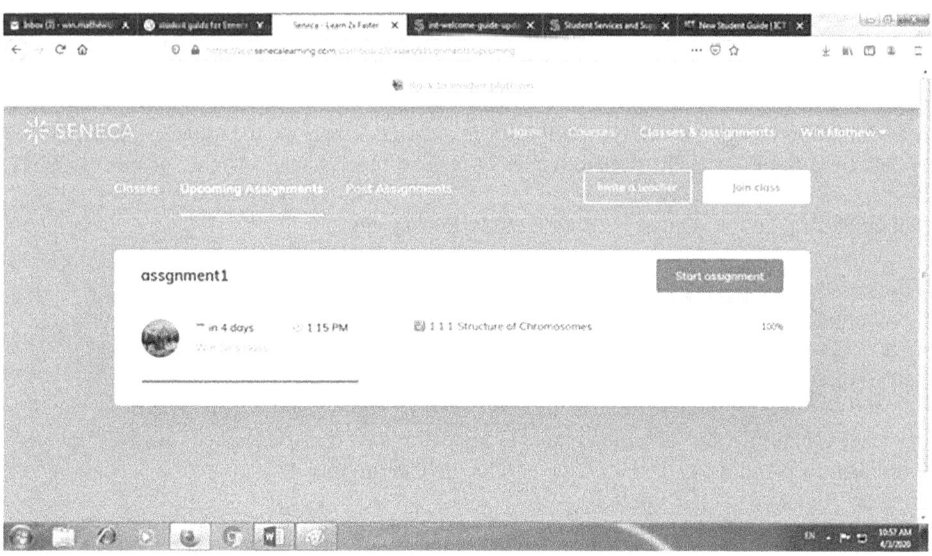

FIGURE 9.5 The student screen: Seneca Learning.

Google Classroom was released on August 12, 2014. In 2015, Google announced a Classroom API, allowing school administrators and developers to further engage with Google Classroom through a share button for websites. Google incorporated Google Calendar into Classroom for scheduling assignments in 2015. In 2017, personal Google users were allowed to join classes without the requirement of having a G Suite for Education account, and in April of the same year, it became possible to create and teach a class by any personal Google user. In 2018, new features like adding a classwork section, improving the grading interface, allowing reuse of classwork from other classes, and adding features for teachers to organise content by topic were also included, and 78 new illustrated themes and the option to drag and drop topics and assignments in the classwork section were introduced in 2019 (Wikipedia, 2020).

Google Drive, Google Docs, Sheets and Slides, and Gmail were tied together in Google Classroom to help educational institutions to become paperless systems. Google Calendar was later incorporated to help with scheduling assignments, field trips, and class speakers. A private code can be generated and distributed to the students who want to join the class, or automatically imported from a school domain. A separate folder is created in the respective user's Google Drive, where the assignments can be submitted by the students and can be graded by a teacher (Wikipedia, 2020).

Google's suite of productivity applications allows collaboration between teachers and students or student to a student whereby the assignments are scored and graded. Instead of sharing documents that reside on the student's Google Drive with the teacher, files are hosted on the student's Google Drive and then submitted for grading. Teachers may choose a file that can then be treated as a template so that every student can edit their own copy and then turn it back in for a grade instead of allowing all students to view, copy, or edit the same document. Students can also choose to attach additional documents from their Google Drive to the assignment (Wikipedia, 2020).

A number of grading schemes are supported by Google Classroom. The students can view, edit, or get an individual copy of the files attached to the assignment by the teacher. If a copy of a file was not created by the teacher, students can create files and then attach them to the assignment. Teachers can monitor the progress of each student on the assignment where they can make comments and edit. Graded assignments can be edited by the teacher only, unless the teacher turns the assignment back into the students (Wikipedia, 2020).

Teachers can post announcements to the class stream which can be commented on by students when two-way communication between teachers and students is allowed. Students can post to their class stream, but the priority will not be as high as an announcement made by a teacher. Teachers can send emails to one or more students in the Google Classroom interface through the options provided by Gmail. At the end of a term or year, Google Classroom allows instructors to archive courses. The "Archived Classes" area helps teachers to keep their current classes organised by removing the archived course from the homepage. Teachers and students can view a course once it is archived, but until it is restored, changes cannot be made (Wikipedia, 2020).

Google Classroom does not show any advertisements in its interface for students, faculty, and teachers, as part of G Suite for Education, and user data is not used for advertising purposes (Wikipedia, 2020).

If you are signing in for the first time, take the following steps.

1. Access classroom.google.com (Figure 9.6) and hit the "Go to classroom" button.
2. Enter your username.
3. Provide your password.
4. Read the welcome message, and hit "Accept".
5. In the G Suite for Education account, you need to choose either "I'm a student" or "I'm a teacher" (Figure 9.7). Note: In personal Google accounts, this option will not be displayed, as you are always supposed to be a teacher (Google Classroom, 2020).
6. Hit on "Get started" (Figure 9.8).

Now you are ready to start using Google Classroom. If you are a teacher, you can create a class, or if you are a student, you can join a class if and only if there is an invitation or with a class code.

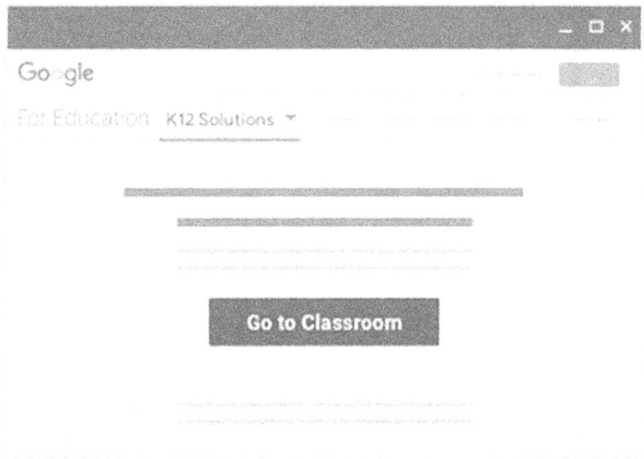

FIGURE 9.6 Initial screen: Google Classroom.

FIGURE 9.7 Screen for selecting the role: Google Classroom.

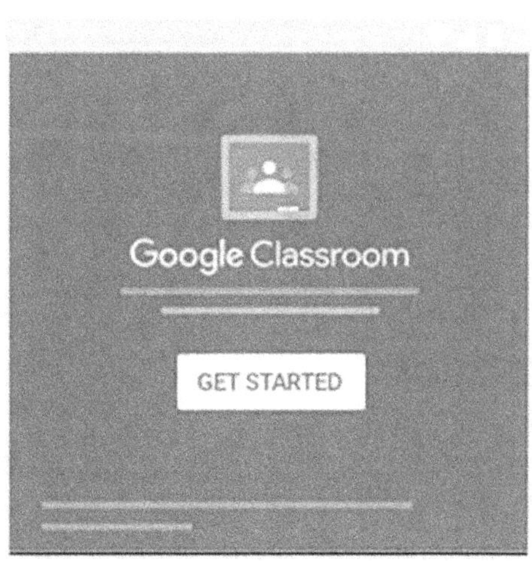

FIGURE 9.8 Starting Google Classroom.

9.6.2.1 How to Create a Class

Creating a class for each class is the first job a teacher can do with Google Classroom. You should use the email of the G Suite for Education account, to create your classes if you have a G Suite account. In your class, you can provide assignments, post announcements, and attach files to the assignment (Google Classroom, 2020).

For creating a class, take the following steps.

1. Use classroom.google.com.
2. On your "Classes" page, click on "Add + > Create class" (Figure 9.9).
3. Enter the class name (Figure 9.10).
4. Click on "Section" and enter the details if you want to enter a short description, grade level, or class time.
5. Click on one from the list that appears when you enter text or hit "Subject" and enter a name if you want to add a subject.
6. Click on "Room" and enter the details, if you need to enter the location for the class.
7. Click on "Create".

Upon creating a class, Google Classroom creates a class code automatically. To invite the students, you can use the generated code. The class code is viewed on the "Stream" page always. You can see a list of all your work on the work page. You can check your grades, review assignments and due dates, and see any work that is late or missing. You can also filter your work by status: "Assigned", "Returned with grade", or "Missing". If you want, you can see additional details, such as comments or attachments (Delhi University, 2019).

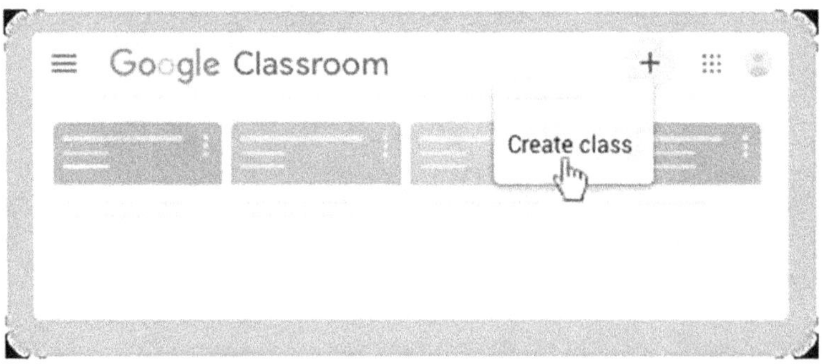

FIGURE 9.9 Creating a Class: Google Classroom.

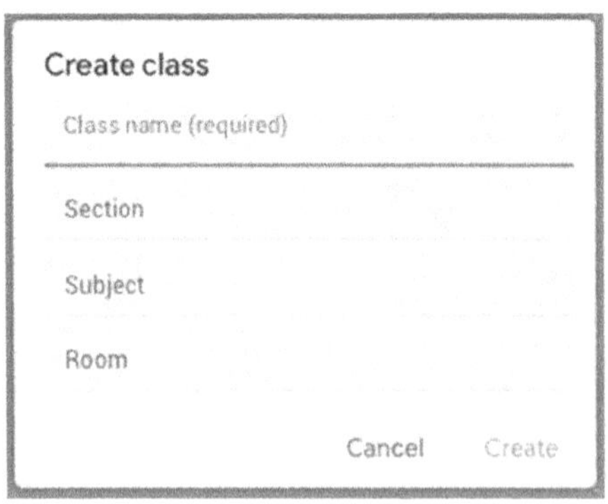

FIGURE 9.10 Specifying the details of the class: Google Classroom.

Google Calendar can be utilised to view all the works you had assigned to different classes. The calendar can be viewed by month, week, or day. The student can use any of the Google Drive provisions for submitting the assignment, and communication can happen through Gmail (Delhi University, 2019).

9.6.3 Show My Homework

The Show My Homework app can make the setting, administering, and monitoring of homework much easier, and it is a part of a school-wide service. The subscribed service can be accessed on mobile devices, tabs, and personal computers by staff, students, and parents. With the app, the student can focus on the task at hand; it is one of the best homework tools. Over half a million parents, teachers, and students are using Show My Homework for Android as the online tool for viewing and setting homework. Students can submit homework, receive notifications for when homework is due, and access their to-do list anytime with Show My Homework. (Eden Boys' School, Preston, 2019).

It is flexible to access the homework. On Android and iOS devices, there is a free-to-download app available. Also, we can log in to a web-based version (Figure 9.11) from any internet-connected computer. Show My Homework ensures that homework is set across the school, with statistics available by year, class, teacher, and subject. It is easy to set homework for teachers, and students can easily keep track of their homework deadlines. It is also great to keep parents informed about homework (N A College, 2019).

Teachers

- Set homework in minutes
- Grade homework quickly
- Track homework in seconds

Students

- See homework on the move
- Stay on top of homework deadlines
- Work smarter and get better results

The first page you see will look something like this (Figure 9.12). Just select "Accept" for now. You can look at these options later.

You are now presented with a screen something like Figure 9.13.

The homework a student needs to do will be listed, along with the day on which it should be submitted on the left. When finishing an assignment, the student will click on the little box on the right. This will

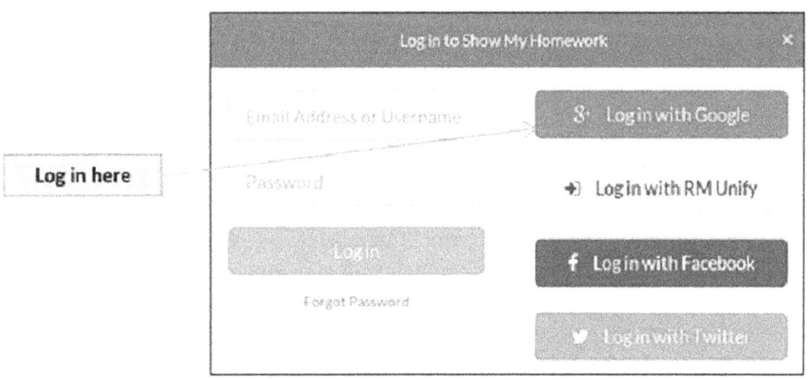

FIGURE 9.11 Login screen of Show My Homework.

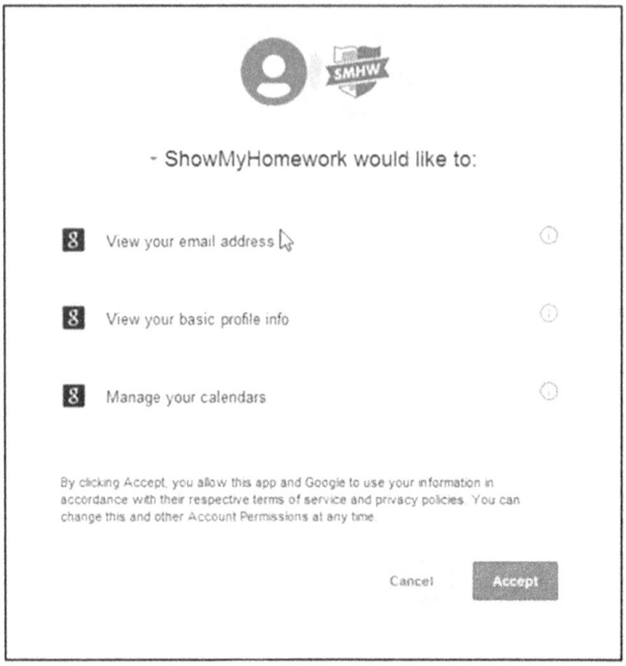

FIGURE 9.12 The opening screen of Show My Homework.

FIGURE 9.13 The basic screen of Show My Homework.

move the homework from the "Issued" list to the "Completed" list. Clicking on the name of the homework will give you more details of the homework (Eden Boys' School, Preston, 2019).

To keep track of your homework, you can use the student calendar (Figure 9.14), which is reliable and fast. By hitting the "Homework" calendar from the left-hand menu and selecting the "My Calendar" tab, you can access your personal student calendar. A highlighted box starting from the issue date ending with the due date specifies the assignment in Show My Homework. The colour specifies the task you need to complete. The solid colours indicate that the assignment is active and the student needs to complete it

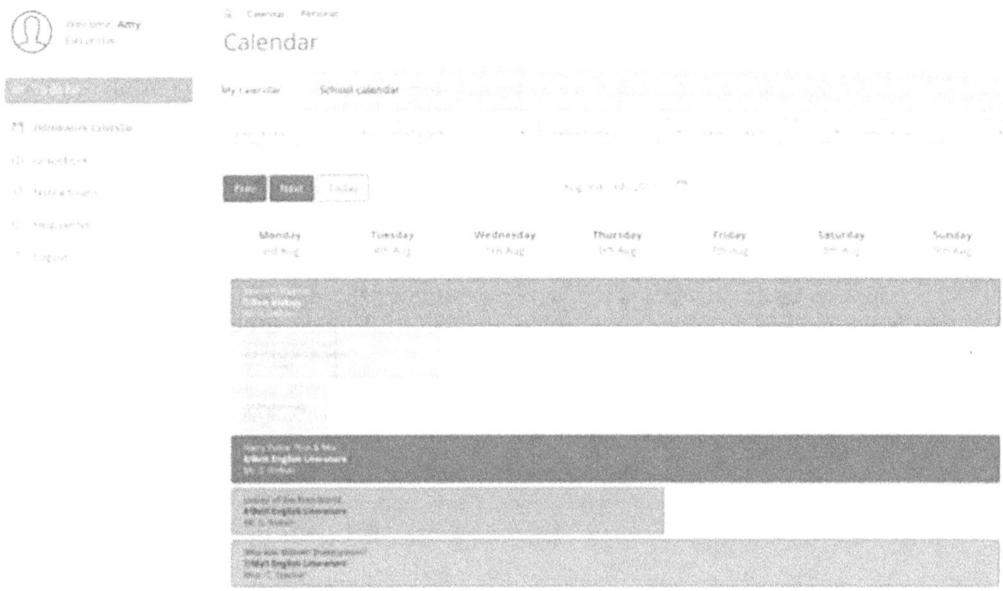

FIGURE 9.14 The calendar of Show My Homework.

before it reaches its due date. The colour will be faded once the due date is over. The title of the homework, the teacher who set it, the class, and the subject are shown on the "Homework" box. Clicking on the box will display the homework description, and also the attachments, if any (N A College, 2019).

Show My Homework will encourage students to study well and improve their final grade if and only if it is a positive experience that helps them to learn. Students learn to work independently and improve self-discipline while doing homework. With Show My Homework, students are encouraged to take initiative and responsibility for completing a task. Parents will have an active role in their child's education while using this tool, and it will support them to evaluate the progress of their child. Since you learn how to use different resources, like libraries, texts, book chapters, and even websites in order to do the homework, it will teach you how to study and work independently. Then, if you face challenges, you know how to manage them and overcome them successfully. More than that, online homework tools set events in a familiar environment to students, who are expected to engage with the electronic world than with paper (Eden Boys' School, Preston, 2019).

REFERENCES

Belham, F., et al., 2019. The Actual Impact Of Seneca On Student Grades, www.senecalearning.com/blog/the-actual-impact-of-seneca-on-student-grades, [Accessed April 9, 2020]

Butty, J.A.M., 2010. Homework. In: C.S. Clauss-Ehlers (eds.) *Encyclopedia of Cross-Cultural School Psychology*. Springer, Boston, MA, [Accessed April 12, 2020]

Delhi University, 2019. Google Classroom on a Computer, Google Classroom User Manual, www.du.ac.in/du/uploads/Google_Classroom_UserGuide.pdf, 3–12pp, [Accessed April 10, 2020]

Eden Boys' School, Preston, 2019. Show My Homework Guide, Eden Boys' School, Preston, Show-My-Homework-Guide-Book-Version-2.0.pdf, 3–7pp, [Accessed April 9, 2020]

Good Education Group, 2020. www.goodschools.com.au/insights/parental-advice/the-advantages-and-disadvantages-of-homework, [Accessed April 11, 2020]

Google Classroom, 2020. Welcome to Your First Day of Classroom, https://classroom.google.com/u/0/h, [Accessed April 10, 2020]

Google for Education, 2020. Teacher Center, https://teachercenter.withgoogle.com/first-day-trainings/welcome-to-classroom, [Accessed April 10, 2020]

Heffernan, N., 2019. OPINION: Online Homework Tools Trade 'Busy Work' for Feedback to Help end Inequities in Schools, https://hechingerreport.org/opinion-online-homework-tools/ [Accessed April 12, 2020]

Learn 2x faster for free with Seneca, 2020. www.senecalearning.com, [Accessed April 9, 2020]

N A College, 2019. A Student's Guide to Show My Homework, www.nacollege.devon.sch.uk/assets/uploads/pdf/Satchel-Show-My-Homework-Guide-for-Students-1.pdf, [Accessed April 9, 2020]

Pedro, R., et al., 2015. Does Homework Design Matter? The Role of Homework's Purpose in Student Mathematics Achievement, *Contemporary Educational Psychology*, 43, 10–24, [Accessed April 12, 2020].

Pedro, R., et al., 2019. Homework Should Be . . . but We Do Not Live in an Ideal World: Mathematics Teachers' Perspectives on Quality Homework and on Homework Assigned in Elementary and Middle Schools, *Frontiers in Psychology*, 10, www.frontiersin.org/article/10.3389/fpsyg.2019.00224, [Accessed April 9, 2020]

Rutledge, M., 2019. The Benefits of Online Homework Portals for Students, https://symboliamag.com/the-benefits-of-online-homework-portals-for-students/, [Accessed April 10, 2020]

Times Square Chronicles, 2018. How Modern Technologies Help Students do Homework, https://t2conline.com/how-modern-technologies-help-students-do-homework/, [Accessed April 11, 2020]

Wikipedia, 2020. https://en.wikipedia.org/wiki/Google_Classroom Google Classroom, [Accessed April 10, 2020]

10

Online Content Creation Tools

Kochumol Abraham

CONTENTS

Objectives

The focus of online content creation tools is to assist with the integration of technology for online and classroom-based courses. Online learning capabilities combined with video collaboration and messaging

DOI: 10.1201/9781003318378-10

services give users a best-of-breed combination, which enables them to cater to all academic e-learning use cases (Roszak et al., 2016).

10.1 Introduction

E-content sharing enables the contribution of informative resources through any media to the online world. The process of generating topic ideas, creating written or visual content around those ideas, and providing global accessibility to it as a blog, video or any other format is known as e-content creation. Even though it is not a substitute for classroom learning, the benefits of online knowledge sharing are immense (Training Industry, 2020).

10.1.1 Relevance of Online Content Creation

With the recent advancements in technology, the way students learn and teachers teach has immensely changed (Redecker et al., 2009). Online teaching and learning tools enable teachers to teach effectively while students enjoy learning (Bhatia, 2011).

10.1.1.1 Expanding the Reach of Information

With the advent of new technological platforms, the scope of online education has made a drastic change globally. There is a possibility for the growth and development of skilled trainers (Booth and Kellogg, 2015). Knowledge from outstanding professors and instructors will be available throughout the world through online education (Williams and Sekret, 2018).

10.1.1.2 Flexibility

Staying updated with the recent advancements, flexibility to refine and refresh knowledge for working professionals, and learning in an advanced environment are some of the factors which promote flexibility in online education (Morze and Kuzminska, 2017). Working professionals and students can improve and update their skills. By removing the geographical barriers from education, online education has set an integral path for future learning (Arkorful and Abaidoo, 2014).

10.2 Online Education

Online education provides a wide range of possibilities for lifelong learning (Sekret et al., 2019). With the emergence of technological aids in telecommunication and computers, online education has become much more affordable at all levels of learning (Sekret et al., 2019). In such a scenario, educational institutions are urged to provide different teaching and learning methods to meet the needs of educators (Sekret, 2012a, 2012b; Sekret and Kommers, 2014). Information and communication technology (ICT)-enabled learning environments grew up, and as a result, instructors are required to revise their professional competencies (Sekret, 2012a, 2012b; Sekret and Kommers, 2014). Instructors are expected to switch their mode of teaching to online tutoring and develop their teaching strategies to an ICT-enabled learning environment (Sekret et al., 2019).

10.3 Collaborative Learning

The traditional student-centered approach of learning focused on structured and well-prepared lessons by a teacher (Mcloughlin et al., 2007). Unless and until instructed by a teacher, students get fewer opportunities to share their experiences and interact with each other. Effective learning includes collaboration, experience sharing, discussions, joint activities and support from others (Mokwa-Tarnowska, 2017). This enables us to build healthy relationships and further learn from one another (Benedek, 2018). With the advent of technological aids, collaborative learning is strengthened by remotely connecting individuals in real time (Kaul, 2018).

10.3.1 Computer-Supported Collaborative Learning

Technology is an enabler that enhances the collaboration among students and teachers. The learning process can be transformed into various modes by a mix of technologies (Redecker et al., 2009).

Technology-enhanced education can be implemented by integrating social media, open educational resources and web-based multimedia production (Mcloughlin et al., 2007). Learning management systems (LMSs) are being used by various institutions to enhance the collaboration among students and teachers (Jesionkowska, 2018). These systems provide discussion forums, assignment submissions and many other interactive activities (Scott, 2015).

10.4 Open Education

Factors like globalization, increasing demand for higher education and changing demographics of students significantly contribute to the ever-changing circumstances in education (Instructional Strategies for Teachers: Help & Review, 2020). Open education provides opportunities and supports the divergent innovations in education, preserving the basic values of education (Smyrnova-Trybulska et al., 2019). It supports an interactive platform for students and teachers whereby a transition from the traditional student-centered approach to knowledge facilitator happens (Smyrnova-Trybulska et al., 2017).

10.5 Tools for Online Education

A number of crucial services such as content creation, which require an authoring tool, support learning environments (Cranefield et al., 2015). The last decade or so has witnessed increased attention on tools for authoring learning content for education.

Three different tools introduced here are Zoom, Loom and Screencastify.

10.5.1 Zoom

Zoom is a platform that enables high-definition (HD) video conferencing, mobility and web meetings together as a free cloud service. A crystal-clear video conversation and high-quality screen sharing are possible anytime, from anywhere, with up to 25 people or rooms. It is available for Windows, Mac, iOS and Android.

10.5.1.1 Install Zoom

Following are the steps to install Zoom.

1. Go to https://zoom.us/download
2. Click "Download" under "Zoom client for meetings".

10.5.1.2 Sign Up

Following are the steps required for signup.

1. Access https://zoom.us/signup and enter on "Sign up, it's free" (Figure 10.1).
2. Enter your email address, or either "Sign in with Google" or "Sign in with Facebook", as shown in the figure.

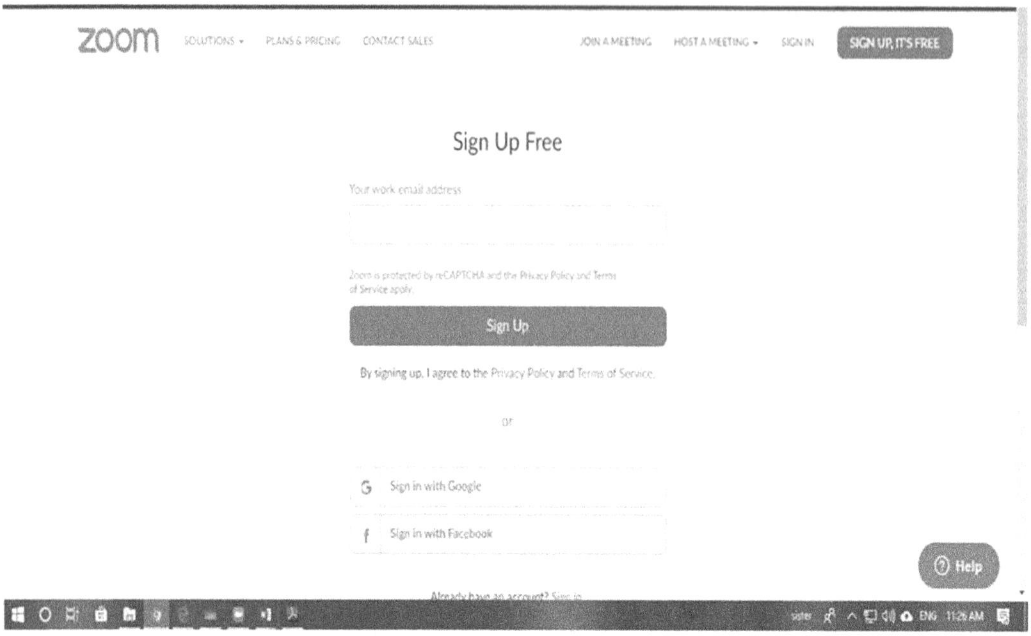

FIGURE 10.1 Interface for "Sign Up".

FIGURE 10.2 Interface for "Sign In".

10.5.1.3 Sign In

1. Click on "Sign in".

   The following interface (Figure 10.2) will appear.
2. Options for "Sign in".

   Enter your email address and password or sign in with SSO, Google or Facebook. Figure 10.3 shows the various options for Sign In.
3. Click the "Launch Zoom" button as shown in Figure 10.4.

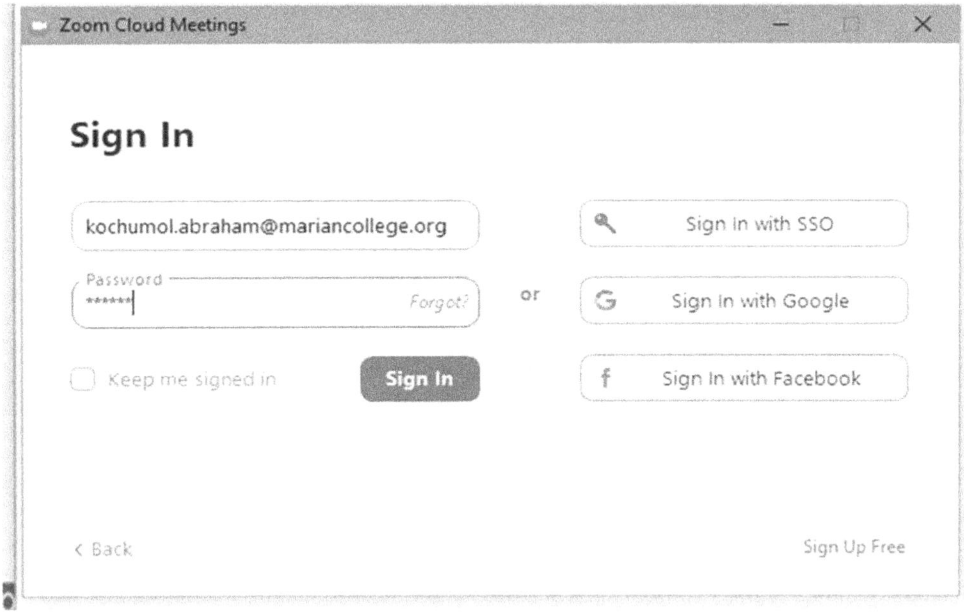

FIGURE 10.3 Interface showing the various options for "Sign In".

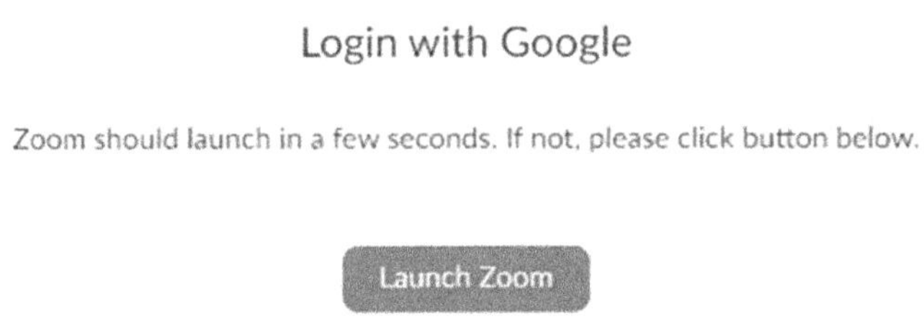

FIGURE 10.4 Interface before launching Zoom.

10.5.1.4 Using Zoom

After the initial login, a dialog box will appear as shown below. The "Home" tab is the default tab. Figure 10.5 shows the initial Home page of Zoom.

a. To start a Zoom meeting, enter the "New meeting" option.
b. Click on "Join" to join a meeting in progress.
c. To schedule a meeting for a later time, click on "Schedule".
d. The "Share Screen" option is used to share your "desktop" or "application" during a meeting.

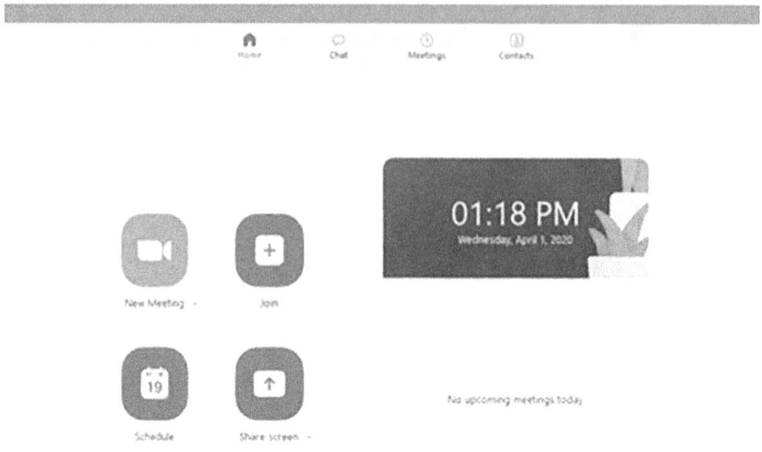

FIGURE 10.5 "Home Page" of Zoom.

FIGURE 10.6 Initial interface of "New meeting".

FIGURE 10.7 Zoom menu bar.

10.5.1.5 New Meeting

Figure 10.6 indicates an interface of the new meeting. We can use Zoom by easily navigating The Zoom menu bar. Figure 10.7 indicates the menu bar of Zoom.

The controls available in The Zoom menu bar.

- Audio: mute/unmute Audio
- Start Video: start/stop video
- Invite: Used to invite persons for a meeting
- Manage Participants: used to "mute" participants.

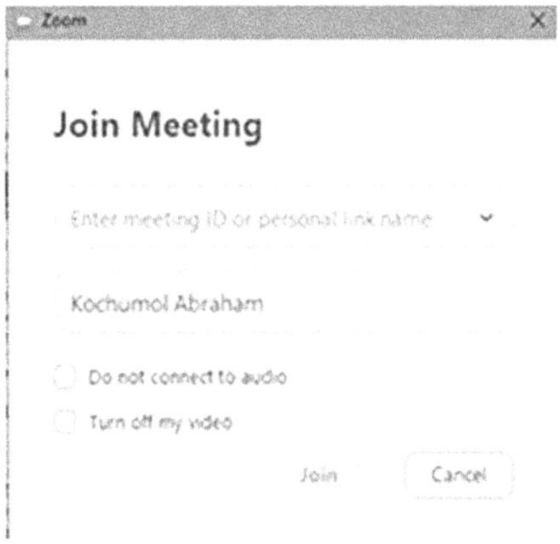

FIGURE 10.8 Interface for "Join Meeting".

- Share Screen: share your screen with other users
- Chat: group or private chat
- Record: save/record your meetings for future use
- Reactions: ,

10.5.1.6 Join

Following are the steps to join a zoom meeting. Figure 10.8 shows the interface for joining a meeting.

1. Enter meeting ID.
2. Enter your name.
3. Click "Join".

10.5.1.7 Schedule

Click "Schedule" on the Home page. The following dialog box (Figure 10.9) will appear.

1. In the "Topic" box, specify the name of the meeting.
2. Enter start date and time, duration and time zone of meeting.
3. Select meeting options:
   - Meeting ID
   - Meeting password
4. Select video/audio options
5. A calendar can be selected from the following options:
   - Outlook
   - Google Calendar
   - Other calendars
6. In the "Advanced" options tab, there are options for
   - Enable waiting room
   - Enable join before host
   - Mute participants on entry
   - Automatically record meetings on the local computer
7. Click "Schedule".
8. Copy and paste the meeting invite in an email or other form of communication and send it to your participants.

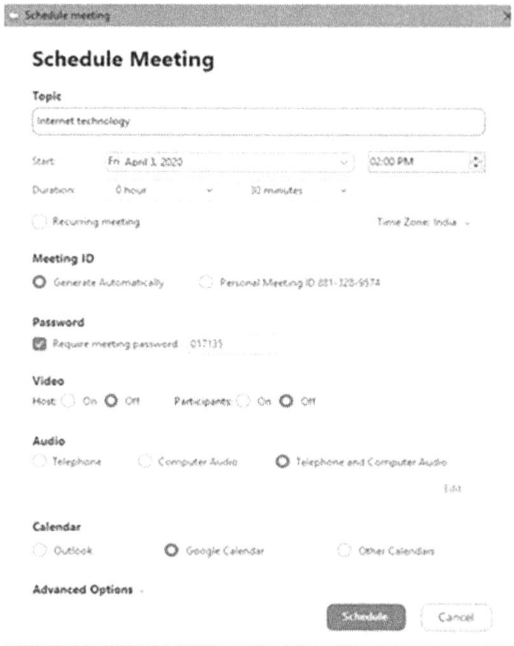

FIGURE 10.9 Interface for "Schedule Meeting".

FIGURE 10.10 Interface for entering meeting ID.

10.5.1.8 Share Screen

Following are the steps for sharing a user screen in zoom (Zoom Help Center/Audio, Video, Sharing, Zoom Video Communications).

1. Click on the "Share Screen" tab on the Home page. The following dialog box (Figure 10.10) will appear.
2. Enter your meeting ID and click on "Share". The following Interface (Figure 10.11) will appear.
3. In the "Basic" tab, the following options are there for sharing.
   - Screen
   - Whiteboard
   - iPhone/iPad
   - Other documents in your local computer
4. In the "Advanced" tab, click on "Portion of the screen" and then the "Share" button at the bottom right of the dialog box.
5. In the "Files" tab, options for sharing documents appear.
6. At the top of the screen, click on "Stop share" to pause sharing as shown in Figure 10.12.

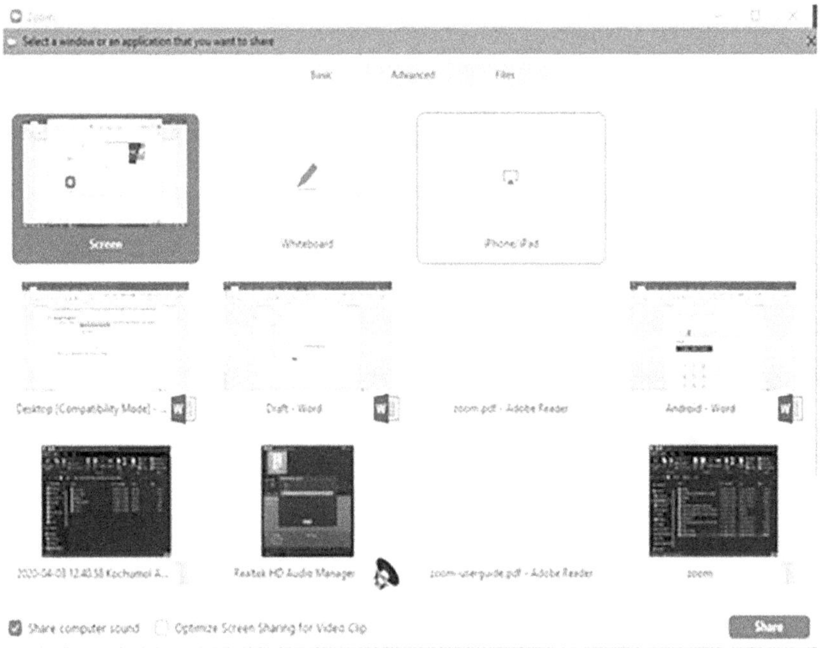

FIGURE 10.11 Interface for selecting the document/screen/whiteboard to be shared.

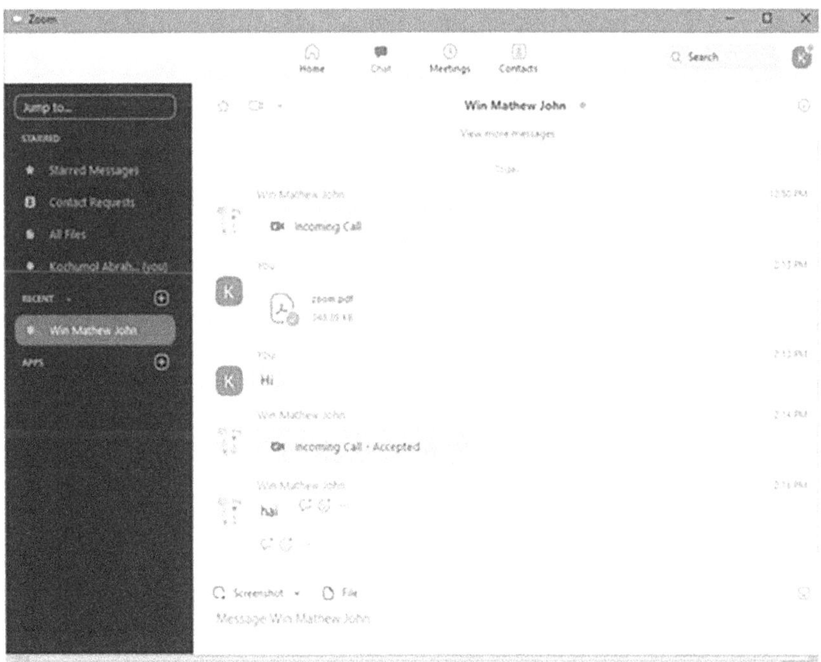

FIGURE 10.12 Interface for "Chat".

10.5.1.9 Chat

The "Chat" tab (Figure 10.12) enables you to share documents and messages with any participants.

10.5.1.10 Meetings

The "Meetings" tab (Figure 10.13) enables you to view the "Upcoming" and "Recorded" meetings.

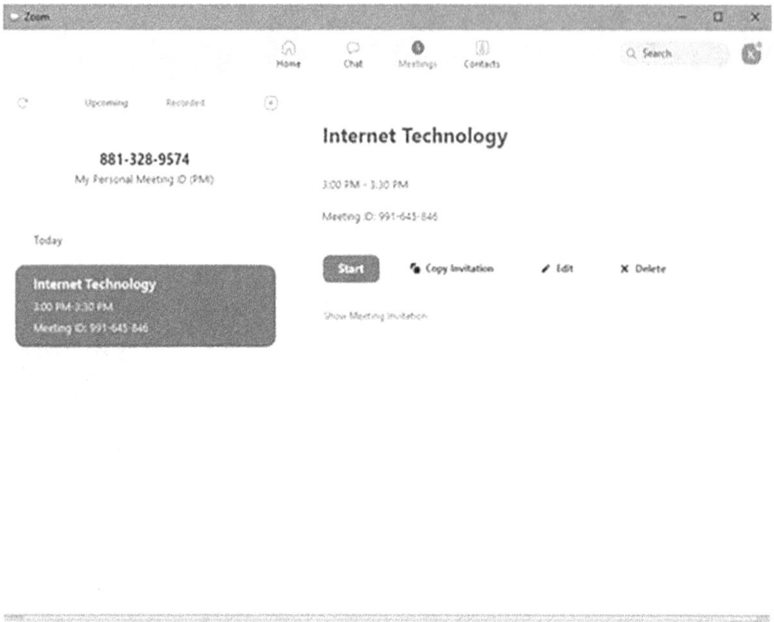

FIGURE 10.13 Interface for "Upcoming" and "Recorded" meetings".

10.5.1.11 Contacts

The "Contacts" tab (Figure 10.14) enables you to chat and message with existing contacts.

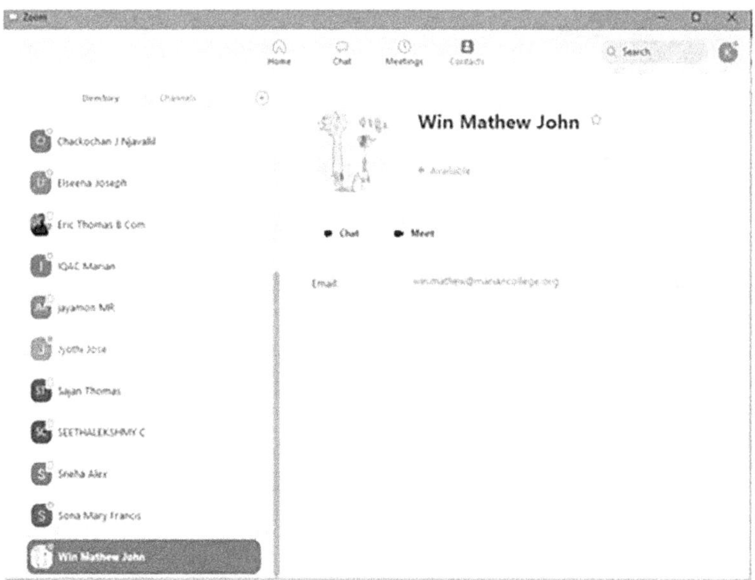

FIGURE 10.14 Interface for "Chatting".

FIGURE 10.15 Interface for downloading Loom.

10.5.2 Loom

Loom is a simple video recording tool that enables you to instantly share videos, record your computer screen, and upload it to your Loom account (Loom Help Center, 2020). It is a screen recording service. By signing up for a Loom account, you can download the desktop client. Alternatively, a Google Chrome extension could be installed. With Loom, you can record your camera, microphone, and desktop simultaneously.

10.5.2.1 Install Loom

Following are the steps for downloading Loom.

1. Go to www.loom.com/download
2. Click on "Download for PC" as shown in Figure 10.15.
3. Click on "Finish Installing".

10.5.2.2 Record Video Using Loom Desktop Client

Following are the steps to record a video using Loom. (HowtoUseLoomVideoRecorder, 2018)

1. Open the Loom desktop client
2. Select recording type from the three primary recording options:
   - Screen + Cam: allows you to record both your screen and your PC camera at the same time
   - Screen only: records only your screen
   - Cam only: records just your PC camera
3. Press "Start Recording" to begin your recording session as shown in Figure 10.16. When the recording begins, a red "recording" button will appear on the left-hand side of the desktop. If you hover on it, it will expand down vertically to reveal three more buttons: "Pause" button, "Delete" button and "Drawing Tool" button, which requires Pro Subscription (Loom Help Center/How to Capture Internal Audio/System Audio, 2020).

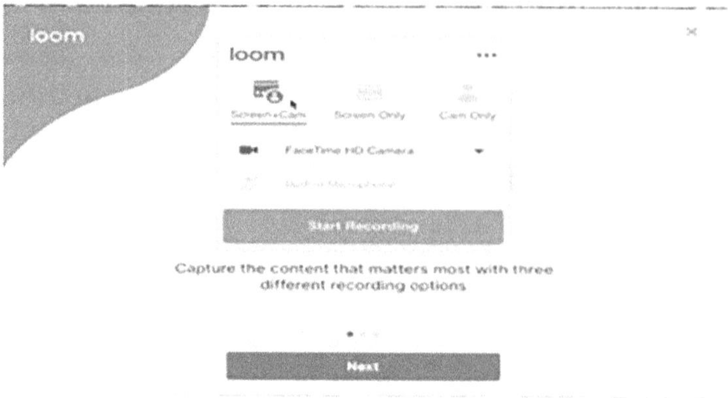

FIGURE 10.16 Interface for recording video (HowtoUseLoomVideoRecorder, 2018).

FIGURE 10.17 Menu for delete and Pause.

10.5.3 Screencastify

Screencastify is a free screen recorder for Chrome. No downloads are required. It enables users to record, edit and share within seconds videos which will be auto-saved to their Google Drive (Screencastify, Initial Setup, 2020).

The Screencastify extension can be installed from the following two places (Screencastify, User Guide, 2020; Screencastify, User Guide, 2020a).

1. The Screencastify website
2. Listing in the Chrome Web Store

You must be using Google Chrome to install and use Screencastify.

10.5.3.1 Install Screencastify

Following are the steps to install Screencastify (Screencastify, User Guide, 2020; Screencastify, User Guide, 2020b).

1. Go to the home page and click the blue install button. A confirmation box appears (Figure 10.18).
2. Click "Add extension". Screencastify will begin downloading.
3. From the Chrome Web Store, enter "Add to Chrome". A confirmation box appears as shown in Figure 10.18.
4. Click on "Add extension". Screencastify will then begin downloading.

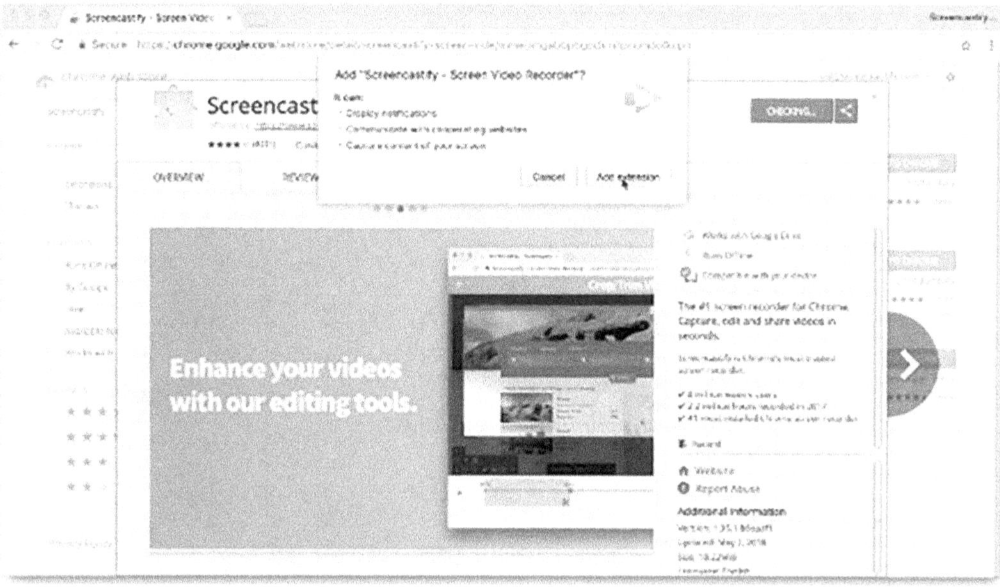

FIGURE 10.18 Initial screen of Screencastify.

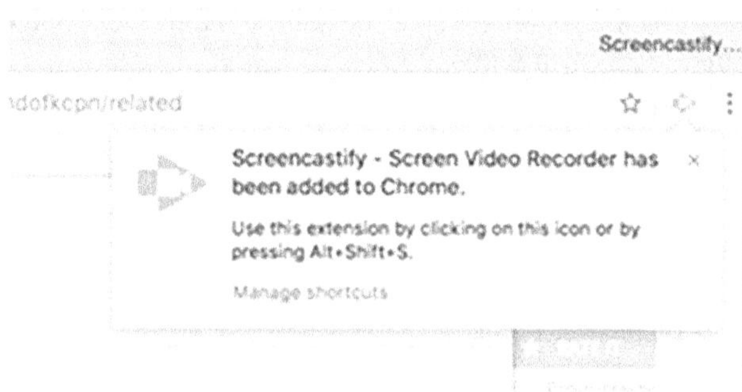

FIGURE 10.19 The Screencastify icon.

Once Screencastify finished recording, an arrow icon () will appear as shown in Figure 10.19. Click the icon to get started.

Now you are ready to create your first recording. The first time you click on the Screencastify extension icon, you will need to complete a setup process. After you sign in with your Google account, you will be asked to allow microphone/camera and tab permissions. Screencastify asks for these permissions so that you are able to narrate over your recordings and embed/record your webcam. If done so, drawing tools can be embedded automatically. Your recordings are saved to your Google Drive in a folder titled "Screencastify". This process could take time to finish after you end a recording.

10.5.3.2 Create and Start a Recording

Following are the steps to create a recording session using Screencastify (Screencastify, User Guide, 2020; Screencastify, User Guide, 2020c).

1. Click the Screencastify extension icon.
2. Select the option for recording: browser tab, entire desktop, or webcam.

FIGURE 10.20 The "Record" option interface.

3. If narration is required, enter the toggle next to the microphone.
4. To record audio from *within* your browser tab or application, click on "Show more options" and turn on "Tab Audio" or "System Audio".
5. To include your webcam, enter on the toggle next to "Embed Webcam".
6. Once you click on "Record", your recording will begin as shown in Figure 10.20.
7. Once you click on the extension icon and then the stop button, the recording will end.

10.5.3.3 Desktop Recording

Screencastify captures everything on the entire screen or in a specific application while recording the desktop.

10.5.3.3.1 Steps to Start a Desktop Recording

Following are steps to start a desktop recording (Screencastify, User Guide, 2020; Screencastify, User Guide, 2020e)

1. Open up the *recording control panel* by entering the extension icon.
2. Select the "Desktop" option.
3. Enable "Microphone" and choose your audio device.
4. Enable "Embed Webcam" and select your camera to embed your webcam into your recording.
5. Click "Record".

10.5.4 Record a Browser Tab

To record a browser tab, select "Tab recording". All annotation tools can be used while recording.

10.5.4.1 Start a Tab Recording

The following steps are required to start a tab recording (Screencastify, User Guide, 2020; Screencastify, User Guide, 2020d).

1. Open the recording control panel by clicking on the extension icon.
2. Click the "Browser tab" option.

3. Enable "Microphone" and choose your audio device.
4. Enable "Embed webcam" and select your camera.
5. To include audio that originates from *within* a browser tab, click on "Show more options" and enable "Tab Audio".
6. Select "Record Tab". A countdown will begin and then Screencastify will begin recording.

During the recording, a red dot will appear in the extension's icon.

10.5.4.2 Steps to Record Webcam

To record your webcam, do the following (Screencastify, User Guide, 2020; Screencastify, User Guide, 2020e):

1. Open the recording control panel by clicking on the extension icon.
2. The "Webcam only" option is then selected
3. Select or enable "Microphone" and choose your audio device.
4. The "Camera" dropdown menu lists the webcam, once Screencastify detects it.
5. Click on "Record".

10.5.4.3 Toggle the Annotation Tools

The annotation toolbar appears in the bottom left-hand corner of the browser tab (Screencastify, User Guide, 2020; Screencastify, User Guide, 2020f). All annotation tools are there for toggling. By pressing Alt + T, this can be hidden.

10.6 Conclusion

Virtual teaching aids enable unlimited access even after real-time sessions. Regardless of location and time, online learning environments provide unlimited access to resources, and break the geographical barriers of education by providing a platform whereby students can connect globally with skilled teachers.

REFERENCES

Arkorful, V., & Abaidoo, N., 2014. The Role of E-learning, the Advantages and Disadvantages of its Adoption in Higher Education, pp. 397–410. www.ijern.com/journal/2014/December-2014/34.pdf. [Accessed April 10, 2020].

Benedek, A., 2018. Digital Transformation in Collaborative Content Development, Advances in Intelligent Systems and Computing 916. In: *The Challenges of the Digital Transformation in Education: Proceedings of the 21st International Conference on Interactive Collaborative Learning*, Springer, Greece, pp. 58–67. [Accessed April 20, 2020].

Bhatia, Ravi P., 2011. Features and Effectiveness of E-learning Tools. *Global Journal of Business Management and Information Technology*, pp. 1–7. www.ripublication.com/gjbmit/gjbmitv1n1_01.pdf. [Accessed April 10, 2020].

Booth, S.E., & Kellogg, S.B., 2015. Value Creation in Online Communities for Educators (Report). *British Journal of Educational Technology*, 46(4), p. 684. [Accessed April 11, 2020].

Cranefield, J., et al., 2015. Rethinking Lurking: Invisible Leading and Following in a Knowledge Transfer Ecosystem. *Journal of the Association for Information Systems*, 16(4), pp. 213–247. [Accessed April 23, 2020].

HowtoUseLoomVideoRecorder, 2018. www.youtube.com/watch?v=3PY6v9s1MU8. [Accessed April 10, 2020].

Instructional Strategies for Teachers: Help & Review, 2020. Working Scholars. https://study.com/academy/lesson/what-are-online-learning-tools-definition-types-examples.html. [Accessed April 10, 2020].

Jesionkowska, Joanna, 2018. Designing Online Environment for Collaborative Learning in a Scientific. In: *Advances in Intelligent Systems and Computing 916: The Challenges of the Digital Transformation in Education: Proceedings of the 21st International Conference on Interactive Collaborative Learning*, Springer, Greece, pp. 176–185. [Accessed April 12, 2020].

Kaul, Manfred, 2018. Student Activation in iOER Maker Spaces, Advances in Intelligent Systems and Computing 916. In: *The Challenges of the Digital Transformation in Education: Proceedings of the 21st International Conference on Interactive Collaborative Learning*, Springer, Greece, pp. 34–45. [Accessed April 18, 2020].

Kołodziejczak, B., & Roszak, M., 2017. ICT Competencies for Academic E-Learning. Preparing Students for Distance Education—Authors' Proposal. *International Journal of Information and Communication Technologies in Education*, pp. 14–25. https://doi.org/10.1515/ijicte-2017-0012. [Accessed April 25, 2020].

Loom Help Center, 2020. https://support.loom.com/hc/en-us/articles/360002158057-What-is-Loom. [Accessed April 10, 2020].

Loom Help Center/How to Capture Internal Audio/System Audio, 2020. https://support.loom.com/hc/en-us/articles/360002449178-How-to-capture-internal-audio-system-audio. [Accessed April 9, 2020].

Mcloughlin, C., et al., 2007. Social Software and Participatory Learning: Pedagogical Choices with Technology Affordances. In: *Web 2.0 Era Introduction: Social Trends and Challenges. Ascilite 2007*, Science and Education, Singapore, pp. 664–675. [Accessed April 24, 2020].

Mokwa-Tarnowska, I., 2015. How to Engage Students in Online Learning—Web-Enhanced and Blended ESP Classes. In: E. Smyrnova-Trybulska (Ed.), *IT Tools—Good Practice of Effective Use in Education*, Springer, Switzerland, pp. 81–88. [Accessed April 25, 2020].

Mokwa-Tarnowska, I., 2017. Higher Interest, Deeper Concentration, More Satisfaction—Web 2.0 Tools to Enhance Technical English Classes. In: M. Sowa, J. Krajka, & P. Lang (Eds.), *Innovations en langues sur objectifs spécifiques: défies actuels et engagements à venir (Innovations in Languages for Specific Purposes: Present Challenges and Future Promises)*, Springer, Switzerland, pp. 156–167. [Accessed April 26, 2020].

Morze, N., & Kuzminska, O., 2017. Blended Learning in Practice of E-Learning Managers Training. In: M. Hrubý (Ed.), *Proceedings (Selected Papers) of Distance Learning, Simulation and Communication 2017*, University of Defence, Brno, pp. 121–126. [Accessed April 27, 2020].

Redecker, C., et al., 2009. Learning 2.0: The Impact of Web 2.0 Innovations on Education and Training in Europe. In: *JRC Scientific and Technical Reports*, JRC European Commission, Luxembourg. [Accessed April 15, 2020].

Roszak, M., et al., 2016. Implementation of E-learning Portal for Academic Education and Lifelong Learning. *International Journal of Continuing Engineering Education and Life-Long Learning*, 26(2), pp. 135–152. https://doi.org/10.1504/IJCEELL.2016.076011. [Accessed April 17, 2020].

Scott, C.L., 2015. The Futures of Learning 3: What Kind of Pedagogies for the 21st Century? *Education Research and Foresight*, pp. 1–21. https://doi.org/10.1016/j.pse.2015.08.005. [Accessed April 21, 2020].

Screencastify, Initial Setup, 2020. https://help.screencastify.com/category/131-initial-setup. [Accessed April 08, 2020].

Screencastify, User Guide, 2020a. https://help.screencastify.com/. [Accessed April 10, 2020].

Screencastify, User Guide, 2020b. https://help.screencastify.com/article/136-install-the-screencastify-extension. [Accessed April 11, 2020].

Screencastify, User Guide, 2020c. https://help.screencastify.com/article/140-record-a-browser-tab. [Accessed April 11, 2020].

Screencastify, User Guide, 2020d. https://help.screencastify.com/article/141-record-your-desktop. [Accessed April 11, 2020].

Screencastify, User Guide, 2020e. https://help.screencastify.com/article/142-record-your-webcam. [Accessed April 11, 2020].

Screencastify, User Guide, 2020f. https://help.screencastify.com/article/143-annotate-a-recording. [Accessed April 11, 2020].

Sekret, I., 2012a. Implementing ICT in a Higher Technical Establishment: Institutional Level. In: *Humanitarian Bulletin—Annex 1 to Issue 27. Vol III (36): Thematic issue "Higher Education of Ukraine in the Context of its Integration to the European Educational Space"*, Springer, Kyiv, pp. 185–193. [Accessed April 23, 2020].

Sekret, I., 2012b. Social Media in Learning. Wyźsza Szkola Humanistyczna Towarzystwa Wiedzy Powszechnej w Szczecinie/EDUKACJA HUMANISTYCZNA/Półrocznik myśli społeczno-pedagogicznej/Nr, 2(27), pp. 179–188, From Face-to-Face Teaching to Online Tutoring: Challenges, Solutions and Perspectives. [Accessed April 24, 2020].

Sekret, I., & Kommers, P., 2014. Conceptual Issues of the Digital Competence Development in the Framework of the Council of the European Union pp, 183–194 DIVAI 2014. The 10th International Scientific Conference on Distance Learning in Applied Informatics. ISBN:978-80-7478-497-2.

Sekret, I., et al., 2019. From Face-to-Face Teaching to Online Tutoring: Challenges, Solutions and Perspectives. In: *Eugenia Smyrnova-Trybulska, Piet Kommers, Nataliia Morze, Josef Malach, Critical Studies of Education: Universities in the Networked Society, Cultural Diversity and Digital Competences in Learning Communities*, Vol. 10. Switzerland: Springer, pp. 171–184. [Accessed April 26, 2020].

Smyrnova-Trybulska, E., et al., 2017. Using Effective and Adequate IT Tools for Developing Teachers' Skills. *International Journal of Continuing Engineering Education and Life-Long Learning (IJCEELL)*, 27(3), pp. 219–245.

Smyrnova-Trybulska, E., et al., 2019. Develop and Implement MOOCs Unit: A Pedagogical Instruction for Academics, Case Study. In: *Critical Studies of Education, Universities in the Networked Society, Cultural Diversity and Digital Competences in Learning Communities*, pp. 103–132, Springer, Switzerland. [Accessed April 21, 2020].

Training Industry, 2020. 5 Advantages of E-Learning. https://trainingindustry.com/articles/e-learning/5-advantages-of-e-learning/. [Accessed April 8, 2020].

Williams, P., & Sekret, I., 2018. Implementation of Social Media for Enhancing Learning Interactivity in Formal Education. In: *Pedagogical Advances in Technology-Mediated Education*, pp. 68–83. www.patme-iatels.com/index.php/patme/article/view/15.

Zoom Help Center/Audio, Video, Sharing, Zoom Video Communications. https://support.zoom.us/hc/en-us/categories/201137166. [Accessed April 10, 2020].

11

Moodle: Teaching, Learning, and Evaluation Tool

Binu Thomas

CONTENTS

Objectives

This chapter introduces Moodle, a tool that will be of great use in the era of Education 4.0. It is capable of providing online digital learning with online activities and repositories. The chapter provides an overview of how to use Moodle in an educational institution. The features of Moodle, its advantages, how it became so popular, and various components are discussed. The various activities that can be created in Moodle and the resources that teachers can set up for students are also introduced. This chapter summarizes Moodle, its features, and its usage in the online learning environment.

11.1 Introduction

In today's interrelated world, the digital revolution is fast evolving. Every day, new technology comes as information and communication technology (ICT) tools in this current scenario. From working to socializing, learning to playing, shopping to online shopping, learning to e-learning, and traditional letters to electronic mail, these are all the impact of ICT that plays significant roles in entertainment, education, business, and workplaces. Today, ICT is seen by many as an agent for change; it can transform working conditions, the way one handles and exchange information, the methods used for teaching and learning, research done in scientific fields, and the way these technologies can be accessed (Aydin and Tirkes, 2010).

Today, the digital age has transformed how those of the young generation access information, get help, learn, network, and communicate. This young generation has become an online population that uses computers, tablets, and other mobile devices to access information. Equipping the students with 21st-century skills and providing them opportunities to learn and apply them in real scenarios are needed.

DOI: 10.1201/9781003318378-11

ICT enhances both teaching and learning, and for teachers, it plays a significant role in creating an environment of pedagogy. Using ICT, teachers can deliver their classes attractively and make the learners learn at any level of academics. These ICT gadgets reduce human work by speeding up communication and learning anytime, anywhere (Godwin-Jones, 2003). It also develops literacy so that the management of schools and education systems are enhanced, the relevance and quality of learning are improved, and the educational opportunities are extended to the vulnerable and marginalized, including those in conflict and crisis areas.

The current group of university students is composed primarily of 'Generation Z', i.e., the generation born since 2000. How Generation Z differs from previous generations and how these differences are shifting higher education approaches have been topics of considerable discussion over the past years.

Generation Z is the most different generation that anyone teaches, and the teaching methods must be diverse. Generation Z expects to be involved in their learning, which means they do not do well as passive learners. If teachers do not have technology that will be part of their learning, they will go anywhere else to be engaged and collaborate with technology. Generation Z recognizes a sharp difference between their comfort level of technology and the technology comfort level of their instructors (Alier et al., 2010). These devices include smartphones, computers, and the Internet. But most of the spending in ICT in Indian educational institutions has resulted in an increase of computers and access to the Internet, with teachers and students still depending on the old-style method of face-to-face education.

The study of the features of education and academic institutions of the twenty-first century demonstrates that features in the forefront are relevance, authenticity, collaboration, inclusiveness, flexibility, and extended restrictions on the part of the institution. The instructor's and participant's roles have changed meaningfully. One way of familiarizing the classroom to meet the present age's needs is to assimilate technology as a learning tool, not as a replacement for effective teaching. Many recognized and developing teaching technologies can be used effectively, including course management systems, student response systems, and learning management systems (LMSs) (Wu, 2012). An LMS is a software system for the management, reporting, tracking documentation, and circulation of electronic educational technology (also called e-learning) training programs and courses. Moodle is the most prevalent LMS available today.

11.2 Learning Management System

LMSs are web-based software, which means they run on a server, and a web browser is needed to access them. The LMS server is possibly located in the university or some department, but it can be anywhere in the cloud. An Internet connection is enough for both the teacher and the student to enter the system (Chung and Babin, 2017).

Primarily, LMSs give instructors software tools to initiate a website and provide access to management so that only participants can view it (Figure 11.1). LMSs also offer a vast collection of tools that enables an online course to be more effective. It provides an environment to manage teaching resources, evaluations and feedback collections, and thereby the performance evaluation of the participants (Godwin-Jones, 2003). The following sections provide a quick overview of each of these features and how they might be helpful.

11.3 Uploading and Sharing of Materials

The tools offered by the LMSs publish content quickly. As an alternative to using an HTML (hypertext markup language) editor and then sending resources to a server using File Transfer Protocol, a web form can be used to keep the syllabus on the server. Many instructors upload documents, assignments, and syllabi so that the students can access them from anywhere. One can distribute files, documents, web resources, folders, and YouTube videos (Figure 11.2).

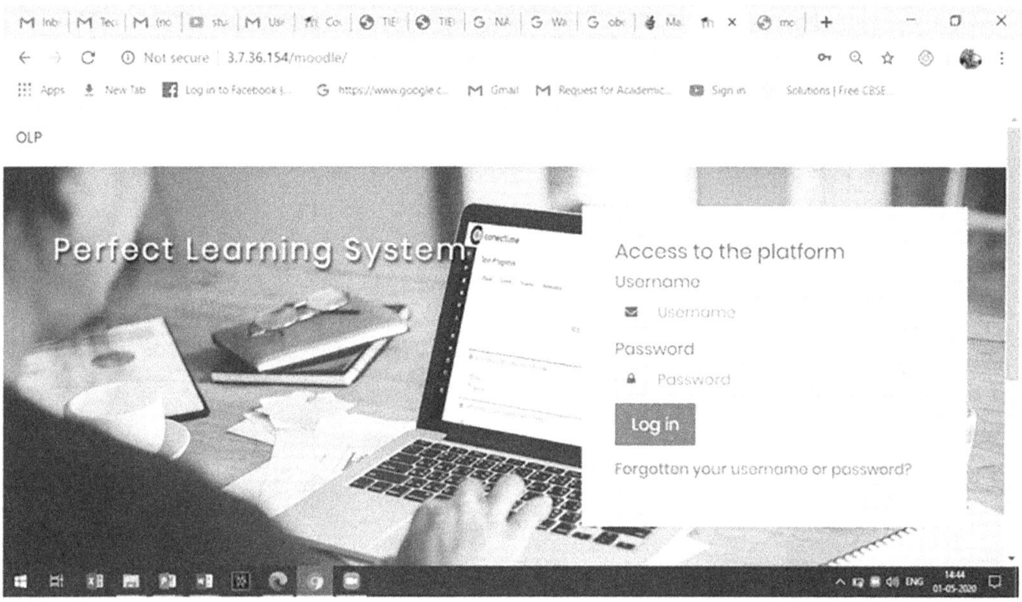

FIGURE 11.1 Moodle login page.

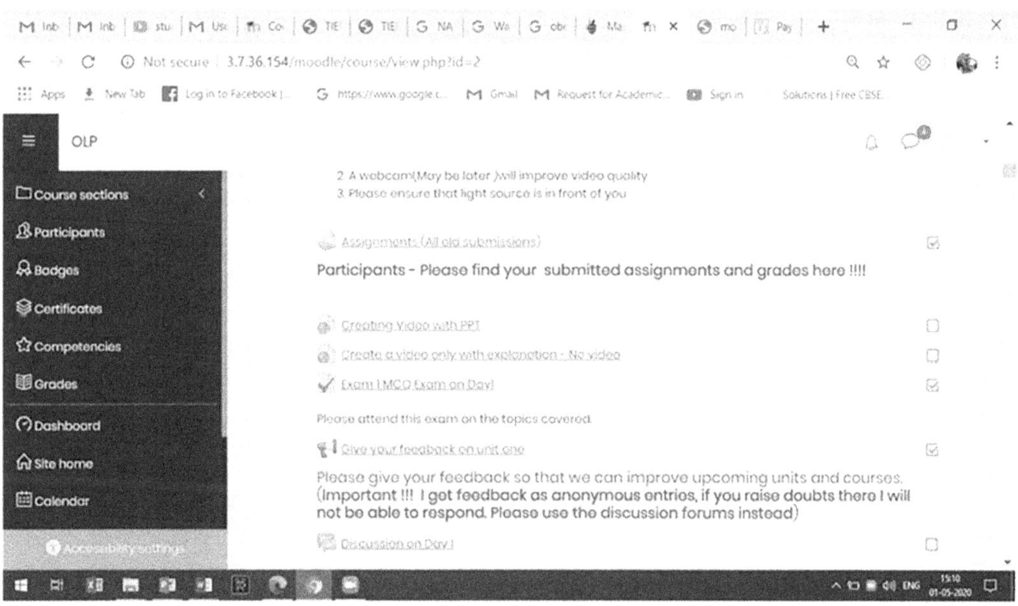

FIGURE 11.2 Sharing resources like files, books, video content, etc., in an LMS.

11.4 Discussion Forums and Chats

Online chats and forums are a means of messaging outside of classroom meetings (Figure 11.3). Students can use enough time so that discussion forums will lead to more valuable thoughts. Chats, instead, provide a way to easily and quickly connect with remote students. They can be utilized for project deliberations between student groups or last-minute questions on the previous day of an exam.

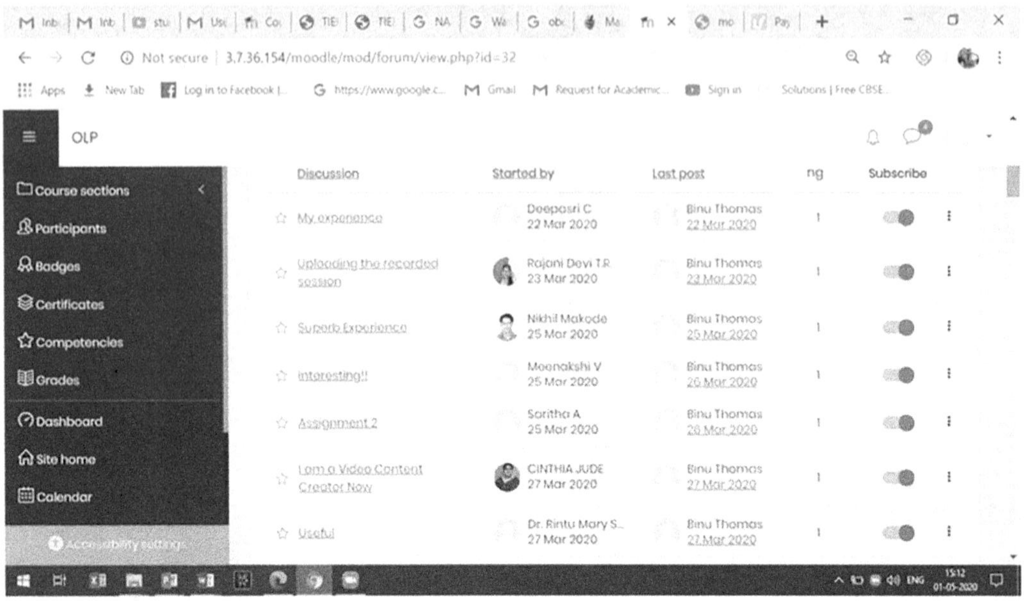

FIGURE 11.3 A discussion forum in Moodle.

11.5 Moodle as a Learning Management System

Moodle (short for modular object-oriented dynamic learning environment) is an open-source software education management system written in the scripting language PHP and circulated under the GNU general public license for software. Developed on educational principles, Moodle is used for flipped classrooms, distance learning, blended learning, and other e-learning projects in schools, higher education institutions, workplaces, and other public sectors. Martin Dougiamas initially developed Moodle to aid teachers in creating online courses focusing on collaborative and interactive content building and is still evolving. The first version is released on 20 August 2002; the Moodle project today is led and coordinated by Moodle HQ, an Australian company that is economically maintained by a network of Moodle partner service companies worldwide. Open-source programmers have contributed much to the development of Moodle (Al-Ajlan and Zedan, 2008).

Moodle is an LMS, an Internet system that could be accessed from anywhere, at any time via the Internet. Moodle allows students and teachers to interconnect and participate in a range of teaching and learning activities using 'courses'. Teachers can use Moodle to provide students with access to resources related to courses. Existing learning environments are replaced and enhanced using Moodle. It has various novel features such as a grade book and calendar as a digital learning tool (Chung and Babin, 2017). Moodle is a virtual learning atmosphere and can be used in various environments such as business, education, and training, and can even be hosted on the cloud (Figure 11.4).

The administration features of Moodle can be customized and hence can be helpful as private websites for educators and trainers to attain learning goals by providing online courses. Moodle allows modifying and extending learning environments using plugins that are supported by the Moodle community. The instructors can make this platform easy for uploading the different types of teaching content. Moodle's built-in media tools permit one to quickly embed images, animation, audio, and video into the courses. This offers learners numerous means of learning stimulation to keep them engaged.

11.6 Features of Moodle

Moodle has numerous features, including Wikis, chats, surveys, forums, workshops, and feedback functions. All these permit content-driven collaborative learning practices. Another essential feature is that

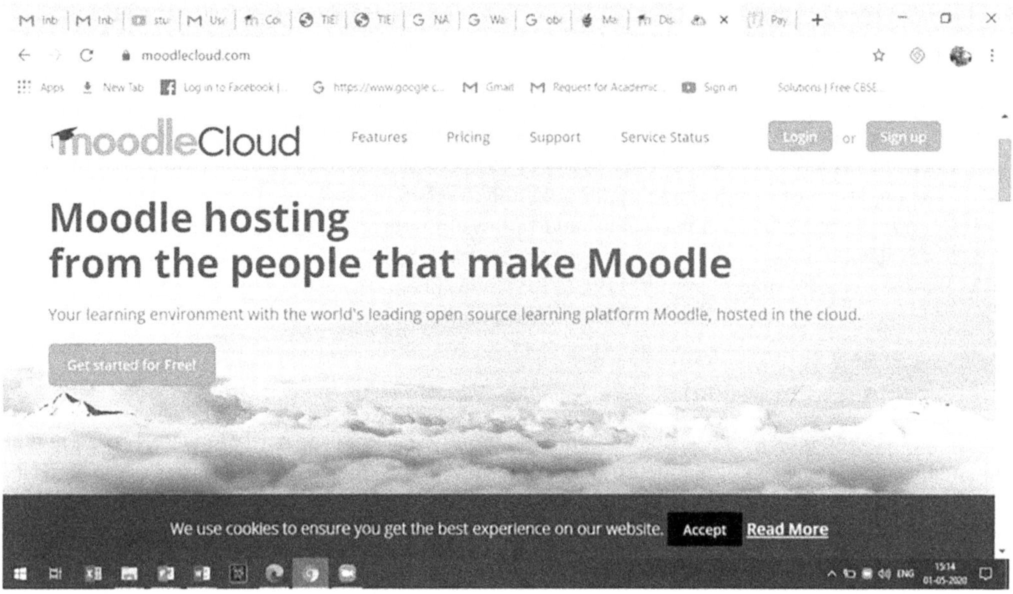

FIGURE 11.4 Moodle cloud site where you can try Moodle for free.

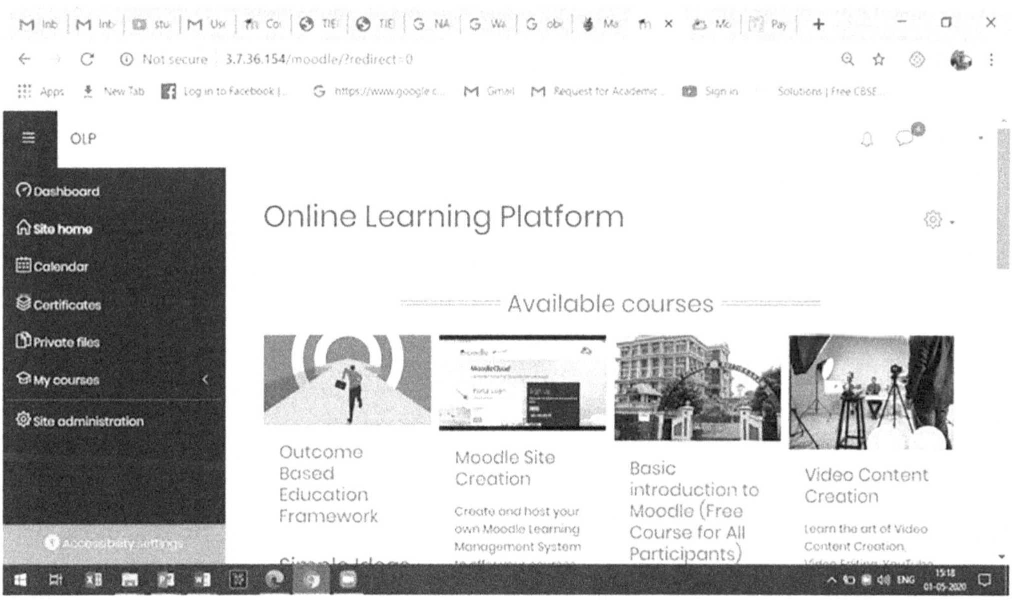

FIGURE 11.5 Moodle Website with course lists.

any number of courses can be added, and teachers and students can be enrolled in their respective courses (Figure 11.5). Teachers can test the learners collaboratively and engagingly using the built-in gaming facilities. Moodle can challenge those who love games with classics such as Snakes and Ladders, Sudoku, and Hangman using quiz questions and dictionary terms. It can also provide a high-quality education experience to remote learners via chat, video, audio, whiteboards, and real-time sharing of slides. The recording is possible for sessions so that students can play them back later. With the incorporation of the 'Big Blue Button', Moodle can directly add webinars as an activity so that students can register and join the webinar session without leaving their courses (Kumar et al., 2011). The basic principles behind the policy and development of Moodle as an e-learning platform are listed as follows.

1. Learning is easy when something is generated or expressed for others to see.
2. Learning is easy when we see the activity of our peers.
3. Teaching is easy by understanding the situation of others.
4. Learning is accessible in a malleable and flexible atmosphere because it can give a fast response to participant needs.
5. Teaching is accessible in a truly cooperative environment.

11.7 Advantages of Moodle

Moodle has progressed as the most successful and popular LMS in the market today. There are manyadvantages of using Moodle as identified by the surveys conducted by eLearning Guild Research (Lapointe, 2012). Some of these advantageous are reduced ownership, high security, advanced flexibility, provision to edit the source code, plugins and third-party components, and extensive documentation support.

The primary advantage of Moodle is lesser cost and the availability of a multitude of advanced tools that can interact with the Moodle platforms. Support from online communities of practice and use of innovative plugins, roles, user management, support of interoperability, and compliance to open standards are some other features that make Moodle so popular (Figure 11.6).

The features like the global community that enhances communication, quality, reliability, collaboration, accountability, and accuracy make Moodle one with the maximum number of users. It is the most popular LMS platform available today. With a strong team of supportive, talented people, Moodle users find the help they always need by connecting with developers or by being able to download patches at any time, anywhere (Quesada et al., 2013). Moreover, Moodle provides its online documentation so that any concerns from users can be addressed at any time (Figure 11.7).

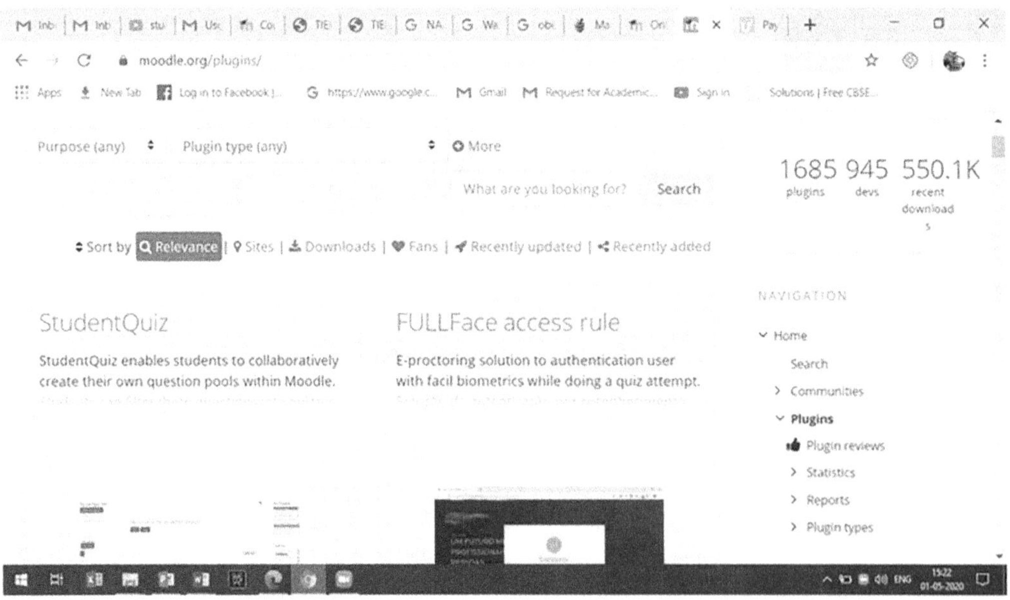

FIGURE 11.6 The vast collection of Moodle plugins to meet any need.

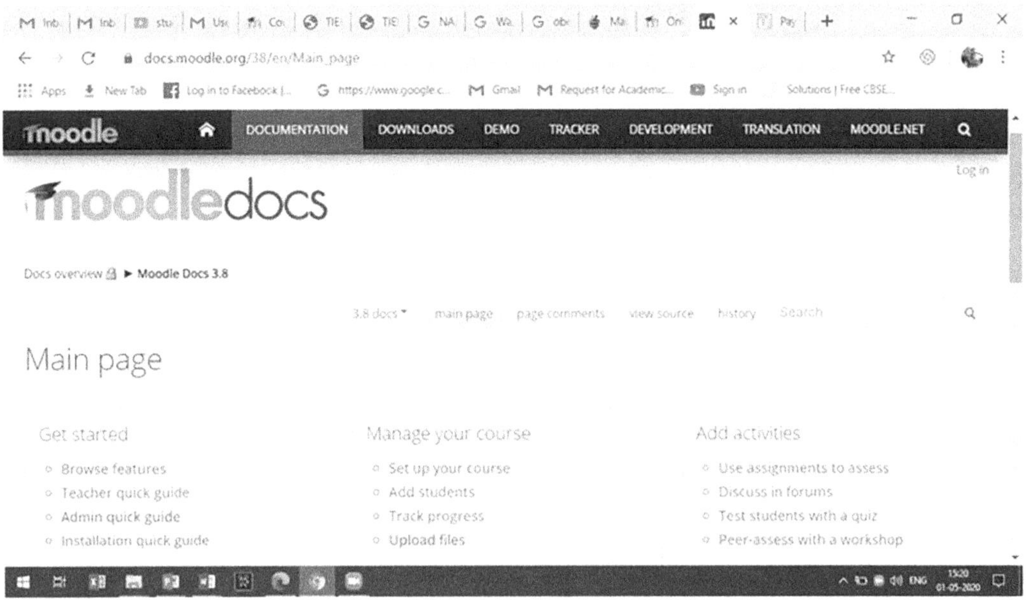

FIGURE 11.7 Moodle documentation support.

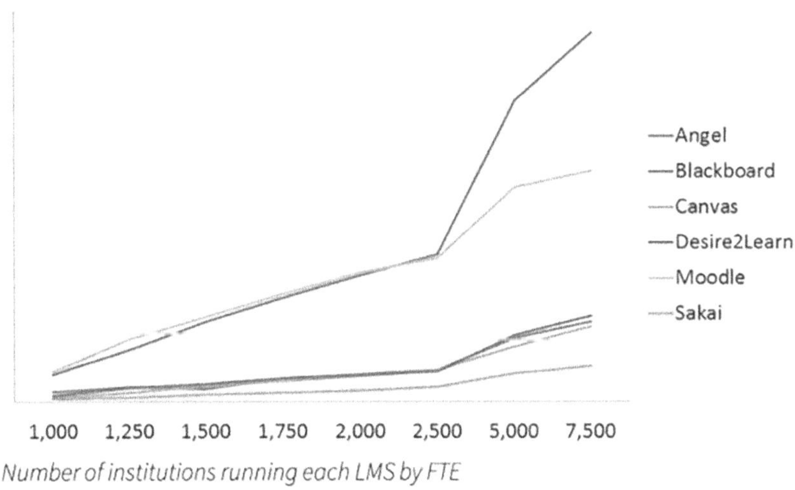

FIGURE 11.8 Popularity of Moodle (Moodle LMS Statistics, 2019).

11.8 Popularity of Moodle

The administrations that have installed and are using Moodle around the globe report easy installation and use, low costs, and high satisfaction rates. The majority of the users—about 95% of them—say that they don't want to find a tool instead of Moodle (Figure 11.8). A very diverse and large community of users are fascinated by Moodle within its first ten years. Moodle developers want to expand their reach and services to underdeveloped, developing, and rich countries by building cost-effective online learning communities (Machado and Tao, 2007).

TABLE 11.1

The Popularity of Moodle across the World (Moodle LMS Statistics, 2019)

Registered Sites	65,545
Countries	224
Courses	9,287,327
Users	81,594,426
Enrolments	237,146,830
Forum posts	166,607,161
Resources	84,428,670
Quiz Questions	407,735,911

Academic communities have the values of information sharing, peer review, and freedom, which is another factor for Moodle's success. Moodle effectively uses pedagogical principles to create an efficient and cooperative online community to aid teachers at a meager cost. Moodle can be installed quickly and almost effortlessly by anyone. It can scale up to incorporate a large community of users and provide the learning structures available in related products. Moodle produces frequent updates, and the support from its developer community provides reliable learning solutions to learners, including support for visually challenged learners (Calvo et al., 2012).

Moodle is used in many educational institutions at large. The Open Polytechnic in New Zealand is one of the best examples of a big Moodle site. Eleven polytechnics, three universities, enormous government departments, and a growing number of schools under it have Moodle installed and used it (Kumar et al., 2011). This means that nearly two lakh students access this platform for the 900 hours of e-learning facilities available on it. The University of Athabasca, Canada's open university, has Moodle installed with nearly 30,000 users for 11 graduate and undergraduate courses.

Moodle is extending the reach of LMSs to teachers worldwide (Table 11.1) because it is available in many different languages. The language can be chosen from a language menu, whereby teachers and students can access it in their language. All the elements within Moodle—like labels, tabs, and menus—will change to the selected language, thus enhancing local preferences. The only restriction is that user-created content will remain as such since Moodle cannot translate such content.

11.9 Advantages of the Latest Release of Moodle

The initial version of Moodle was version 1.0.0, and the Moodle HQ is very keen on developing frequent updates to release newer versions of Moodle. Ever since the first release, there have been 21 significant versions of Moodle, and now we are at version 3.8.2. The major advantages of the present version of Moodle are as follow,

1. **User-friendly, modern interface:** From both mobile and desktop devices, Moodle can easily be accessed with smooth navigation, since it is envisioned as accessible and responsive.
2. **Customized dashboard:** It is straightforward to systematically arrange and display courses as you wish, and easy to provide glimpses of current messages and tasks (Figure 11.9).
3. **Activities and tools to collaborate:** There are database activities, glossaries, Wikis, and forums available for collaborative learning.
4. **Calendar utility:** The calendar utility helps to view course deadlines, track personal or company calendars, and manage group meetings and other teacher-specific activities on the site.
5. **Easy management of files:** It is easy to drag and drop files from cloud storage services such as Google Drive, MS Dropbox, and Skydrive.
6. **Simple and intuitive text editor:** Moodle has a rich text editor where one can enter mathematical equations, multimedia content with images, video, and audio. Even HTML code can be embedded in the text editor (Figure 11.10).

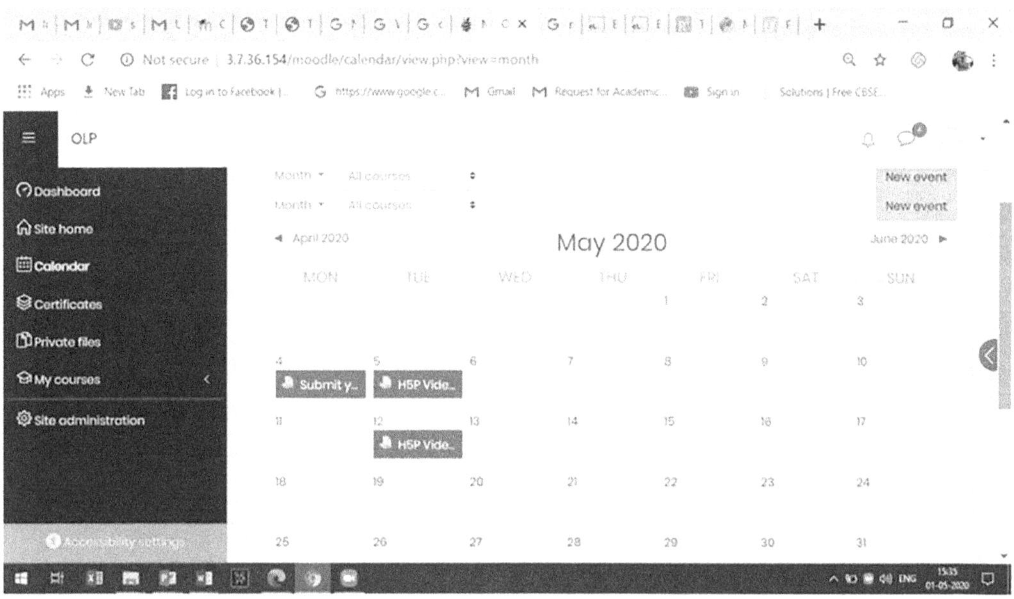

FIGURE 11.9 Moodle dashboard with the calendar.

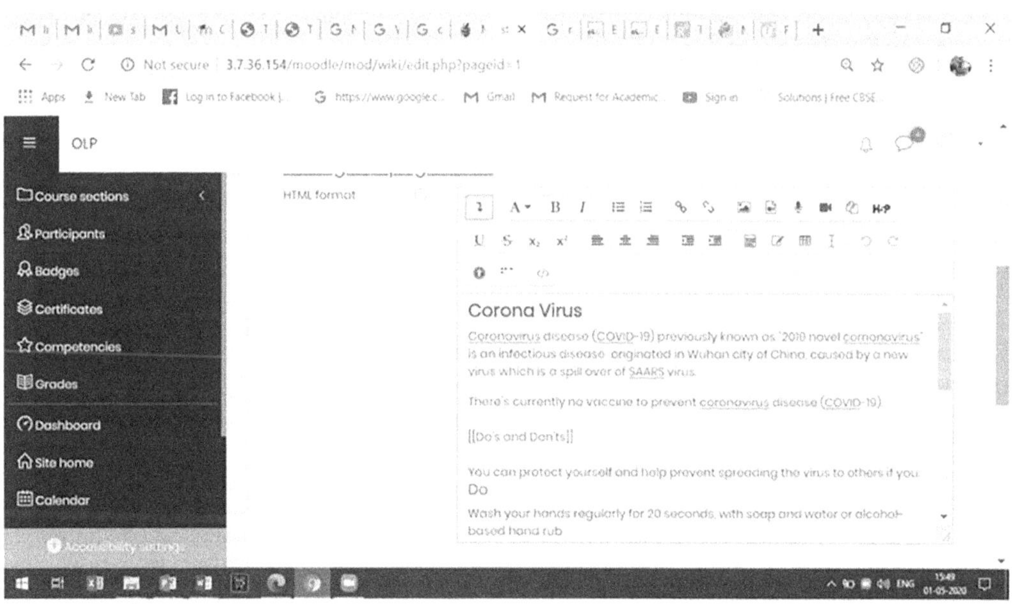

FIGURE 11.10 Feature-rich Moodle built-in editor.

7. **Notifications:** This option enables teachers to give automatic notifications to students on forum posts, deadlines, and new assignments. Students and teachers can send private messages to each other.
8. **Tracking progress:** Individual resources and activities and even courses can be tracked for progress by learners and educators.
9. **Layout and design of site is customizable:** A Moodle theme can be easily customized with the user's logo, colors and styles, and new themes can even be designed.

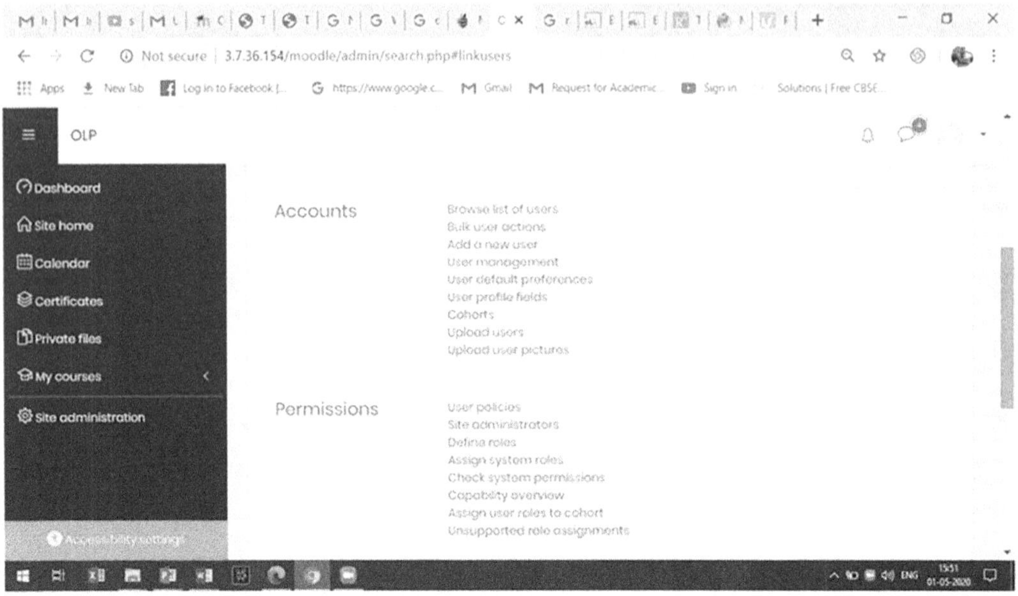

FIGURE 11.11 User management options in Moodle.

10. **Backup and creation of bulk courses easy:** The backup of courses can be quickly taken to be restored at a later stage.
11. **Mass enrollment and secure authentication:** Many enrollments and authentication options are available to add and enroll users to the Moodle site and its courses (Figure 11.11).
12. **Support for multiple languages:** Users across the globe can see the content of courses and learn in their language. Moodle can be set up for multilingual organizations and users.

11.10 Activities in Moodle

A collection of features for a course in Moodle is called an activity. Commonly, it is an activity a student does cooperatively with other students and or the facilitator. In the vocabulary of Moodle, activities such as quizzes, assignments, or forums mean something that students can directly contribute to. These are also resources such as a page or file, which the teacher presents to the students, which may be the reference for the given activities, but commonly, for ease of use and understanding, the term activity is used to refer to both resources and activities as a group. The standard Moodle version contains 14 varieties of activities when the editing option is switched on and upon clicking the 'Add an activity or resource' option (Figure 11.12). These activities can be further enhanced by installing additional plugins through Moodle administration. Attendance is a similar plugin activity (Moodle, Inc., 2020). The common activates in Moodle are as follow.

1. **Assignments:** These are created by students and submitted, whereby teachers could give comments and grade them.
2. **Chat:** Real-time discussions can be done synchronously using this activity.
3. **Choice:** Different responses from students can be collected by teachers in this activity.
4. **Database:** A repository where related information is kept. It is created, searched, and maintained by users.
5. **Feedback:** This activity is used for conducting surveys and collecting feedback regarding the course and instructions.
6. **Forum:** This activity is for online discussions that happen asynchronously.

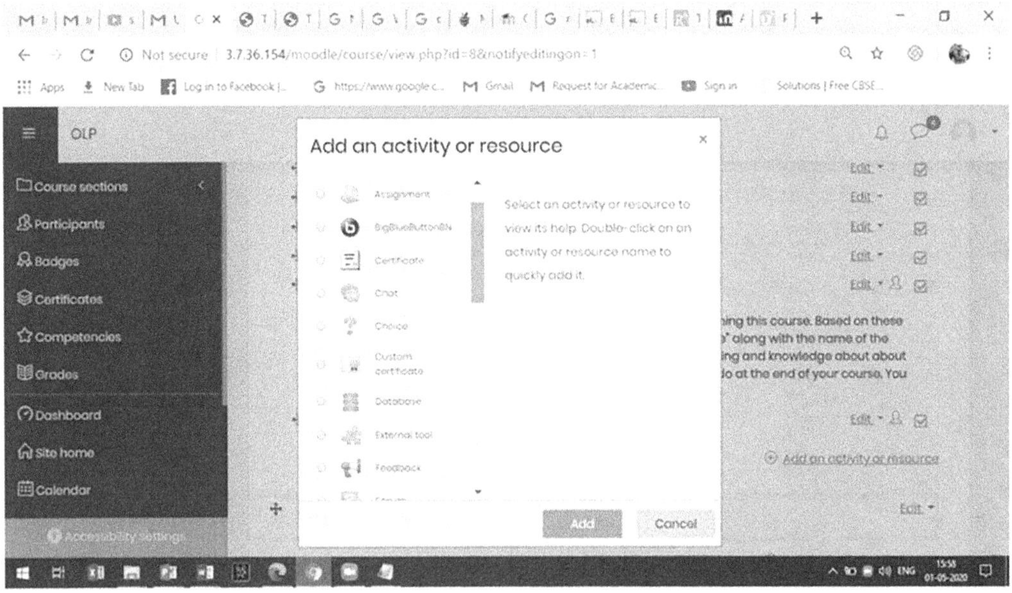

FIGURE 11.12 Adding Moodle activities.

7. **Glossary:** A collection of definitions can be created and maintained by participants using this activity.
8. **Lesson:** This activity allows flexible content delivery, ensures students' engagement, and can be used as either an activity or a resource.
9. **LTI external tool:** This activity allows participants to interact with learning tools interoperability (LTI)-compatible learning activities and resources on other sites.
10. **Quiz:** This activity permits a teacher to design and enable quizzes or online tests, which will later be evaluated automatically, and results and feedback will be available to participants. There are many options to be selected regarding question behavior, choices, and assessments.
11. **SCORM:** Using this activity, SCORM packages can be included as content within courses.
12. **Survey:** This activity collects data from students to provide teachers with comments and feedback so that they can reflect on their teaching and improve. It has pre-created questions.
13. **Wiki:** This is a resource with a collection of web pages that students can add to or edit and can be given as an assignment for advanced learners.
14. **Workshop:** Enables peer assessment so that students can assess the works of others too (Dooley, 2009).

Additional plugins from the plugins directory of Moodle may also be installed on our Moodle site to get other activities and functionalities.

11.11 Resources in Moodle

A resource is an item that a teacher can share to support learning among students, such as a file or link. Moodle supports a variety of resource types that teachers can add to their courses. In edit mode, a teacher can add resources via the 'Add an activity or resource' link (Figure 11.13). Resources appear as a single link with an icon in front of it representing the resource type (Moodle, Inc., 2020). Available resources include the following.

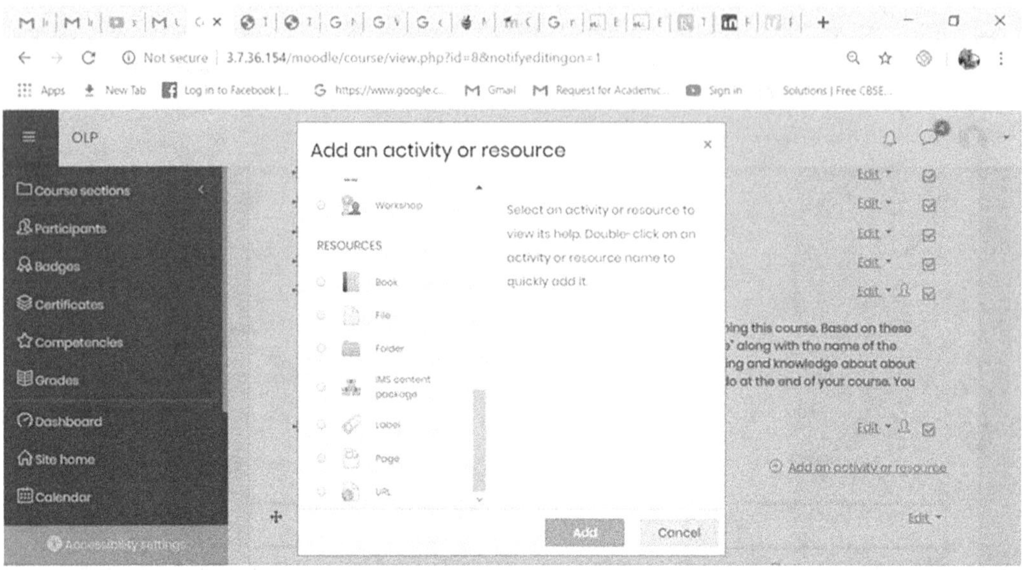

FIGURE 11.13 Adding resources to a Moodle site.

1. **Book:** With a format like that of a book, this is a multi-page resource. Facilitators can export their books as pdf files, also. It is a good tool by which a book can be created for students by collecting files from different sources.
2. **File:** A resource to share video files, sound files, pdf documents, images, or spreadsheets.
3. **Folder:** A resource to systematically organize folders.
4. **IMS content package:** A resource used to add static material from other sources in the standard IMS content package format.
5. **Label:** These resources are used as separators for activities and resources in a topic and can be a few words or an image. or even a bit long description in words.
6. **Page:** This is a resource whereby a single, scrollable screen is visible to the student. It is a page created by the teacher with a user-friendly HTML editor.
7. **URL:** Using this resource, the student can be directed to any other website to get content.

11.12 Conclusion

Moodle has many advantages over its competitors, such as Blackboard, among LMS platforms. The popularity of this system shows that it is the preferred LMS platform for academics worldwide. This is the open-source and cost-effective solution to the current situations prevailing in the higher education scenario. It has rich features to create an assessment and collaborative activities, and to share resources among students. Moodle keeps learning interesting, engaging, and fruitful for the students. It always stands top in integrating everything needed for an online course.

REFERENCES

Al-Ajlan, A., and Zedan, H., 2008, Why Moodle. 2008 12th IEEE International Workshop on Future Trends of Distributed Computing Systems, Kunming, pp. 58–64. Doi: 10.1109/FTDCS.2008.22.

Alier, M., Casañ, M.J., and Piguillem, J., 2010, Moodle 2.0: Shifting from a learning toolkit to an open learning platform. In: Lytras, M.D., et al. (eds) *Technology Enhanced Learning. Quality of Teaching and Educational Reform. TECH-EDUCATION 2010. Communications in Computer and Information Science*, vol. 73. Springer, Berlin, Heidelberg.

Aydin, C. C., and Tirkes, G., 2010, Open source learning management systems in e-learning and moodle. IEEE EDUCON 2010 Conference, Madrid, pp. 593–600. Doi: 10.1109/EDUCON.2010.5492522.

Calvo, R., Iglesias, A., and Moreno, L., 2012, Is moodle accessible for visually impaired people? In: Filipe, J., and Cordeiro, J. (eds) *Web Information Systems and Technologies. WEBIST 2011. Lecture Notes in Business Information Processing*, vol. 101. Springer, Berlin, Heidelberg.

Chung, C., and Babin, L.A., 2017, New technology for education: Moodle. In: Campbell, C.L. (ed) *The Customer is NOT Always Right? Marketing Orientations in a Dynamic Business World. Developments in Marketing Science: Proceedings of the Academy of Marketing Science*. Springer, Cham.

Dooley, J.F., 2009, Peer assessments using the moodle workshop tool. In: Proceedings of the 14th annual ACM SIGCSE Conference on Innovation and Technology in Computer Science Education (ITiCSE' 09). Association for Computing Machinery, New York, NY, p. 344. https://doi.org/10.1145/1562877.1562985

Godwin-Jones, B., 2003, Tools for distance education: Towards convergence and integration. *Language Learning & Technology*, 7(3), 18–22. Retrieved March 20, 2015, from http://llt.msu.edu/vol7num3/emerging/

Kumar, S., Gankotiya, A.K., and Dutta, K., 2011, A comparative study of MOODLE with other e-learning systems. Electronics Computer Technology (ICECT) 2011 3rd International Conference on, 5, pp. 414–418.

Lapointe, L., 2012. The eLearning guild: http://www.elearningguild.com: Visited: Fall 2011. *Public Services Quarterly*, 8(1), 57–58.

Machado, M., and Tao, E., 2007, Blackboard vs. Moodle: Comparing user experience of learning management systems. 2007 37th Annual Frontiers in Education Conference—Global Engineering: Knowledge Without Borders, Opportunities Without Passports, Milwaukee, WI, pp. S4J-7–S4J-12. Doi: 10.1109/FIE.2007.4417910.

Moodle, Inc., 2020, Moodle. https://docs.moodle.org/ [Accessed April 17, 2020].

Moodle LMS Statistics, 2019, Retrieved from https://stats.moodle.org

Quesada, J., Calvo, I., Sancho, J., Sainz, J.A., Sánchez, J., Gil-García, J.M., Sebastián, R., and Castro, M., 2013, Combining MOODLE and redmine as e-learning tools in project based learning of industrial electronics. E-Learning in Industrial Electronics (ICELIE) 2013 7th IEEE International Conference on, pp. 86–91.

Wu, Z., 2012, Integrated mobile learning support service system based on moodle. Proceedings of the 2012 3rd International Conference on E-Business and E-Government—5 (ICEE' 12). IEEE Computer Society, pp. 549–553.

12

Learning Management Tools

Dr Juby George

CONTENTS

Objectives

Classroom management strategies using learning management tools help create an organized classroom environment conducive to teaching and learning. Participants know the expectations in different types of learning situations. An instructor with solid classroom management skills creates consistency for students. Strategies for managing learning can be harmonized with organizational policies and standards. Effective utilization of learning management tools helps to reduce misbehavior in the classroom. Learning content has received particular attention in the past, and learner engagement is now playing an essential role in promoting outcome-based learning. Students nowadays are more exposed to technology and online learning platforms, so learning management tools help an interactive and innovative way to create a tremendous psychological impact to attain learning outcomes. The objective is to find instructors an easy and cost-effective method of assessing student performance and obtaining feedback to improve the teaching method.

DOI: 10.1201/9781003318378-12

12.1 Introduction

Instructors are always interested in evaluating course results. They can ensure student understanding of a topic if the instructor uses different evaluation methods. Evaluation helps performance analysis of participants by storing performance data from students and grading them based on the criteria or rubrics. Assessment is essential, and regular assessments based on rubrics are critical in all teaching, which helps the instructors report the participants' expectations and performance (Bruff, 2017).

When a need arises to assess the level of understanding of a particular skill or understand a topic, instructors regularly use the traditional assessment tools, but instructors spend time grading assignments, surveys, or tests after their administration, which will not reflect instant feedback. Instructors, first of all, consolidate all the data of different assessments by themselves, and grading and analysis happens only after all tests and assignments are complete (Imwold et al., 1982).

Learning management tools facilitate teaching activity interactively by using both hardware and software resources (Imwold et al., 1982). This section explains three learning management tools that will help effective classroom management: 1) Mentimeter; 2) Plickers; and 3) uReply. By using these learning management tools and the assessment data, instructors can decide whether their students should have progressed or revisit the same course module by using an alternative teaching and learning methodology.

Mentimeter is a tool that lets instructors engage and interact with their audiences in real time. Mentimeter has a wide range of areas when usage brings value to a presenter. It helps to understand an audience's view on the subject, with expectation management, and with getting input on advanced questions as discussion reference in a workshop.

Plickers is online software and is accessible. It helps instructors gather instantaneous evaluation and results and decide about effective student involvement and participation in the absence of hardware resources. The Plickers cards used by the audience are scanned and are used to generate the response immediately. It allows all the students to engage and participate in the learning without feeling self-conscious.

uReply is a classroom communication system for use with a smartphone. The system supports the multiple-choice type of questions and short questions, which require students to input text. Student's feedback is collected and analyzed in the form of graphs or tables. Teachers can show performance back to the class right there in the classroom for enhanced learning effect. Records of the class activities are also retrievable in the system by teachers at a later time.

12.2 Usage of Learning Management Tools

Nowadays, technology has transformed the way education is delivered to people across the globe. The emergence of sophisticated communication technologies and digital devices has enabled a new generation of information consumers to satisfy their demands for knowledge without meeting in a physical location. Learning management tools use web-based software resources that provide an interactive online learning environment, assessment, and organization, and the educational content and learner outcomes are delivered and reported at any time. We are discussing three learning management tools that help an interactive way of learning.

12.2.1 Mentimeter

Mentimeter is a tool that lets the instructor engage with the class interactively in real time. Mentimeter allows the students to give their feedback in real time using a digital device. It is a good learning management tool for presentations, and it enables the audience to perform and receive immediate feedback. Following are the steps to use Mentimeter.

Step 1: Create a free account.

Step 2: Create an event.

Step 3: Running the presentation/poll and results.

12.2.1.1 Step 1: Create an Account and Get Started

1. To use Mentimeter, create an account by visiting the website www.memtimeter.com and clicking on the "Sign up" button at the top right (Tech de Monterrey, Mexico, 2020).
2. You are then prompted to choose what you will use Mentimeter mainly for:
   - Workshops
   - Events (10–50 people)
   - Training sessions
   - Education
   - Meetings or team management
   - Conferences or large events
3. You are then greeted by an example quiz using Mentimeter to explain how to participate in a quiz (Tech de Monterrey, Mexico, 2020).

12.2.1.2 Step 2: Create an Event (Create Our Own Presentation/Quiz)

1. Click on "Your presentations" in the options menu as shown in Figure 12.1.
2. Click on the "New presentation" button to start constructing your quiz.
3. Name the presentation.
4. Optional: Change the theme of the quiz to anything you prefer.
5. Optional: Change the voting pace from presenter pace to audience pace. The presenter's pace implies that the audience fills in the questions at the speed of the presenter. Audience pace would lead to the audience members each being able to answer all the questions at their own pace.
6. Optional: Share results with the audience can be turned off.

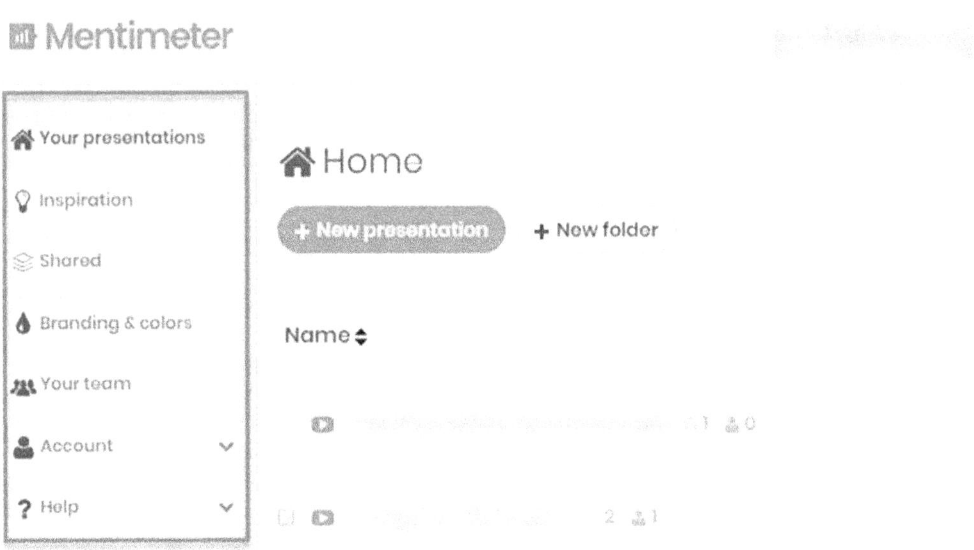

FIGURE 12.1 Mentimeter starting interface.

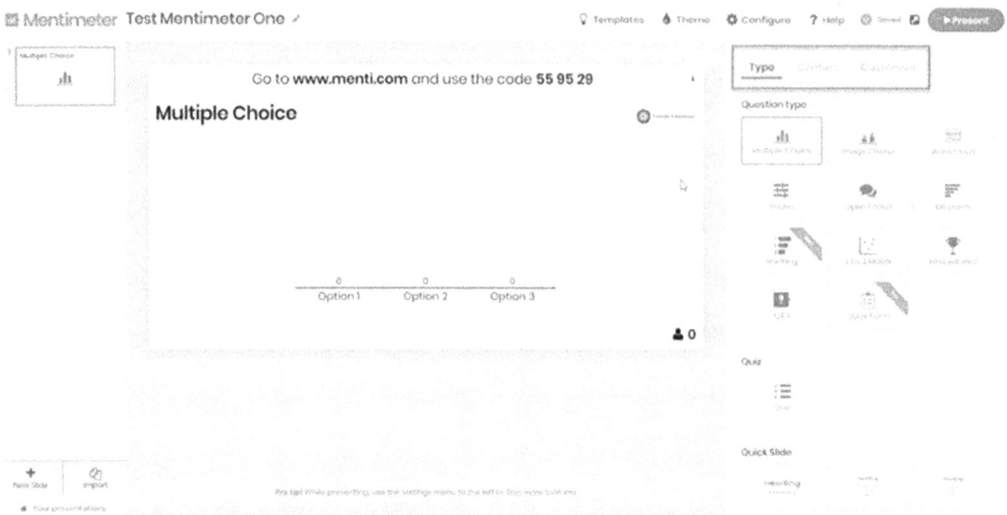

FIGURE 12.2 Different question types in Mentimeter interface.

7. Create a question by choosing type/answers. The different question types are shown in Figure 12.2.
    1. **Multiple Choice:** Allows participants to select several options. It is possible to allow participants to choose more than one answer by rephrasing the question.
    2. **Image Choice:** Similar to multiple choice, but this type allows to add an image per answer.
    3. **Word Cloud:** Allows participants to describe what they think in one word. Example: How can we combat climate change?
    4. **Open-ended:** Participants say something or express themselves, regardless of the question, such as "Nice Talk!"
    5. **100 Points:** Allows participants to assign points to a specific topic. For example: How many points do you assign to Narendra Modi, Donald Trump, and Pinarai Vijayan, respectively?
    6. **Ranking:** Allows participants to rank topics or to make a topic out of the topics presented.
    7. **2 by 2 Matrix:** Allows participants to score answers on two variables. The answers then appear in the form of a matrix.
    8. **Who will win?** Allows participants to select a winner. For example: Which presentation was the most informative?
    9. **Q&A:** Allows participants to ask questions on these slides.
    10. **Quick Form:** With the quick form, you can create a small survey and have participants fill in their details such as email address, date of birth, and other relevant information you would like to know.
    11. **Quiz:** Ask a question with one or more correct answers. The participants fill in their names, and a ranking will be made when they fill in the questions. It is also possible to select an option to make the response time of the participant count for the ranking in the competition. When the participants fill in the questions, a leader board will appear. For more information, see https://help.mentimeter.com/creating-presentations-and-questions/letyour-audience-choose-between-predefined-options/mentimeter-quiz (Tech de Monterrey, Mexico, 2020).

12.2.1.3 Step 3: Running the Presentation/Poll

Press "Show presentation" to start getting responses from the participants. While clicking "Show presentation," you will be brought to a new screen. On this new screen, there will be a reference to the site

FIGURE 12.3 Interface at menti.com for students to start the interaction. The part highlighted with the red box shows a randomly generated code that students have to fill in on their devices when they visit the site.

students have to go to (www.menti.com) and a randomly generated code for them to fill in (Tech de Monterrey, Mexico, 2020), as shown in Figure 12.3.

12.2.1.4 Results

After participants fill in their answers, Mentimeter will immediately show the results for you to interpret.

12.2.2 Plickers

This tool helps instructors to perform polling or response voting in course classes by distributing to each participant a Plickers card and using a handheld device to scan the participants' cards. After scanning, students' responses are automatically collected, assessed, and stored on the website (www.plickers.com). For analysis, the response data collected by participants are used to determine the level of participation and understanding by students. If necessary, specific topics can be revisited if students were not clear about the topic. Before engaging the students, the instructors should be ready with Plickers set up questions. The queries are verbally announced, projected, or given out on a paper or card. Participants hold the cards in different angles and directions to respond with answers. Using mobile or tab, the instructor scans the answers. The Plickers program responds with immediate feedback. With the generated feedback or results, the instructor can check the students' understanding of the topic and decide whether or not to move on to other topics. Instructors can, later on, download all the data and have a thorough analysis of students learning and understanding about the topics (Chng & Gurvitch, 2018).

Using the Plickers program, the steps to follow the formative and summative assessment are described as:

Step 1: App downloading.
Step 2: Account creation.
Step 3: Printing cards.
Step 4: Adding class and students.
Step 5: Adding questions.
Step 6: Staying organized.
Step 7: Implementing real-time assessment.
Step 8: Viewing results.

12.2.2.1 Step 1: App Downloading

As a first step, the instructor is required to download the free app on a digital device, which is then used to scan the answers in class.

12.2.2.2 Step 2: Account Creation

After downloading the Plickers app, the instructor should sign up and create an account on the Plickers homepage. The instructor provides data such as first name, last name, email, and password. On the website, instructors can make a repository of questions to manage their classes. This method allows the instructor to manage the classes anywhere, anytime, using any device, because all pieces of information are stored virtually.

12.2.2.3 Step 3: Print Cards

The instructor needs to print the cards by considering the total number of participating participants in the class. A maximum of 63 responses is scanned at a time. Each student is assigned a unique numbered card. The website www.plickers.com/cards can be used to print the card. The letters A, B, C, or D are represented on each side, as shown in Figure 12.4.

Once presented the topic, the instructor then starts to ask questions with answers denoted as A, B, C, D. The students respond by raising the cards to show the correct letter as the answer. If cards have been printed with fine quality paper, scanning becomes precise, and this ensures the durability of the cards. If the instructor insists the students use laminated cards, the scanning should be affected so that it will not be apparent. Amazon provides these types of cards to purchase (Chng & Gurvitch, 2018).

12.2.2.4 Step 4: Adding Classes and Students

After an account has been established by the instructor, classes are added by the "Classes" tab by providing the primary data regarding the course. Color can also be used to represent a class, as shown in Figure 12.5.

After creating the class and selecting the class, the student's name can be entered by pressing the enter option, as shown in Figure 12.6.

12.2.2.5 Step 5: Add Questions

By pressing the "+" icon, the repository of questions is created. The form of questions can be either true/false or multiple choice. By clicking on "Insert Image," instructors can add images in the question box, as shown in Figure 12.7.

The library folders are arranged in levels, or by game type, or by instructional content. Creating new folders and subfolders helps easy access to the library.

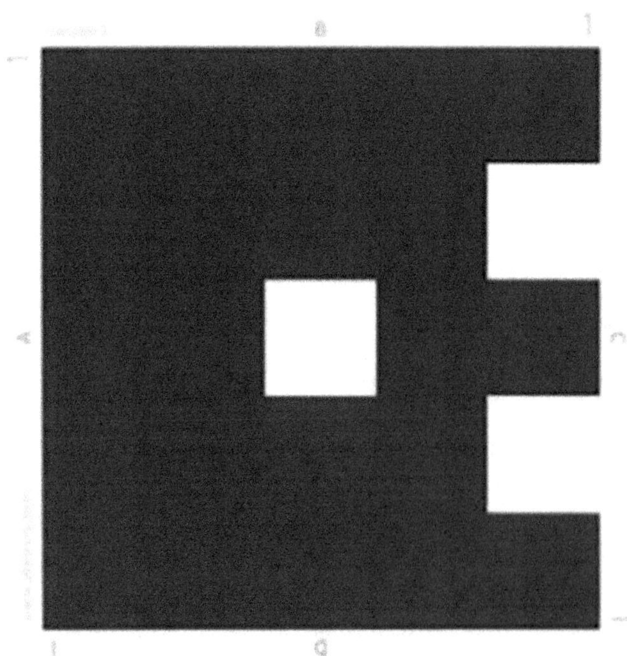

FIGURE 12.4 Plickers card representing the letter B.

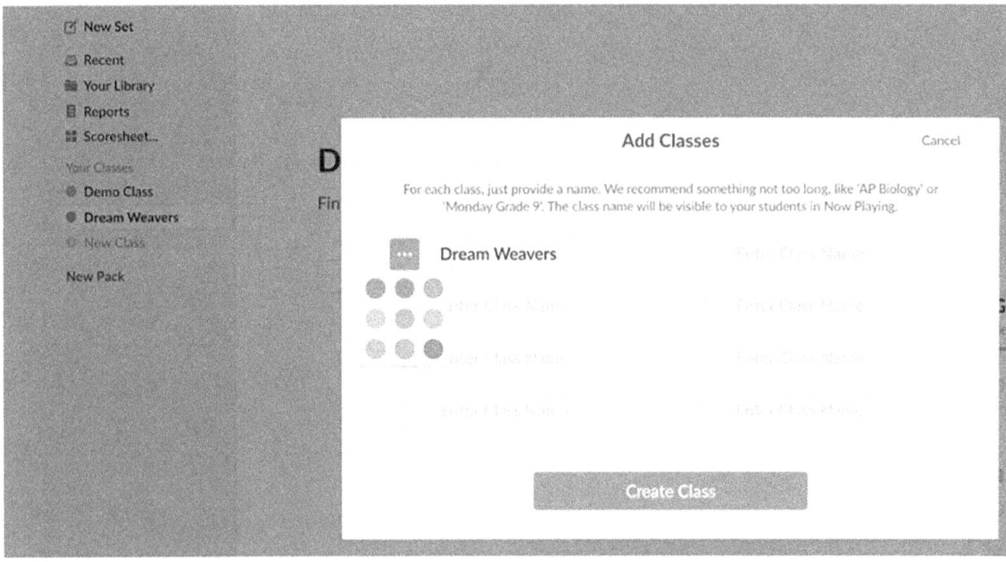

FIGURE 12.5 Color codes can be assigned to each class.

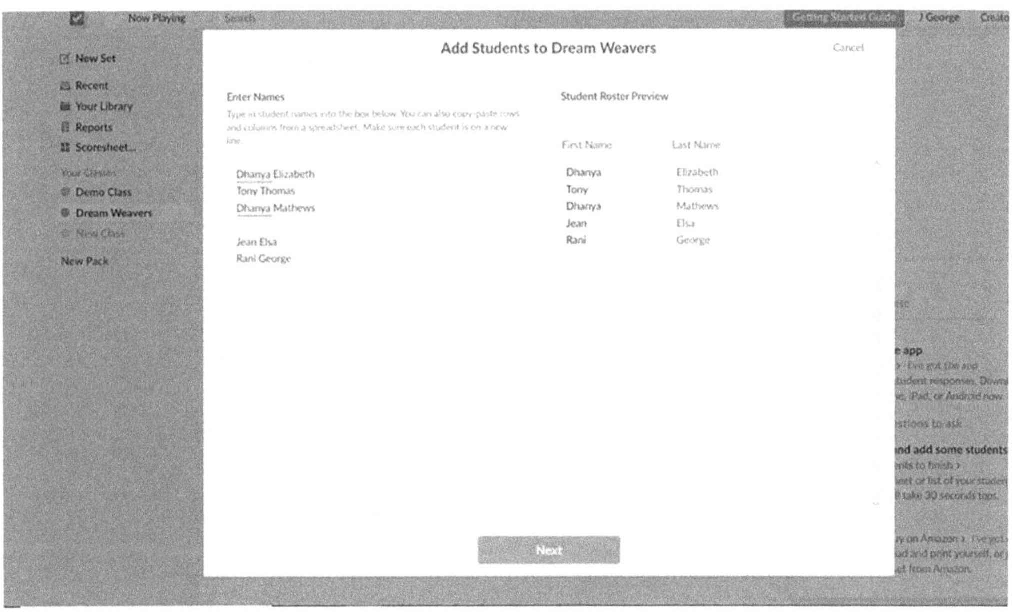

FIGURE 12.6 Interface for adding participant details.

12.2.2.6 Step 6: Stay Organized

Since each student holds a unique card, the instructor must ensure that they have their cards every time. The same card can be reused for different classes by an instructor. Instructors use different innovative methods to organize the cards so that they are arranged systematically, as shown in Figure 12.8.

Instructors take cards for a different batch of participants and recommend the participants place the Plickers cards either in their folder or notebook. This helps the students to be ready with Plickers cards for all topics, and when the instructors need to perform a survey or quiz, they can use it instantaneously

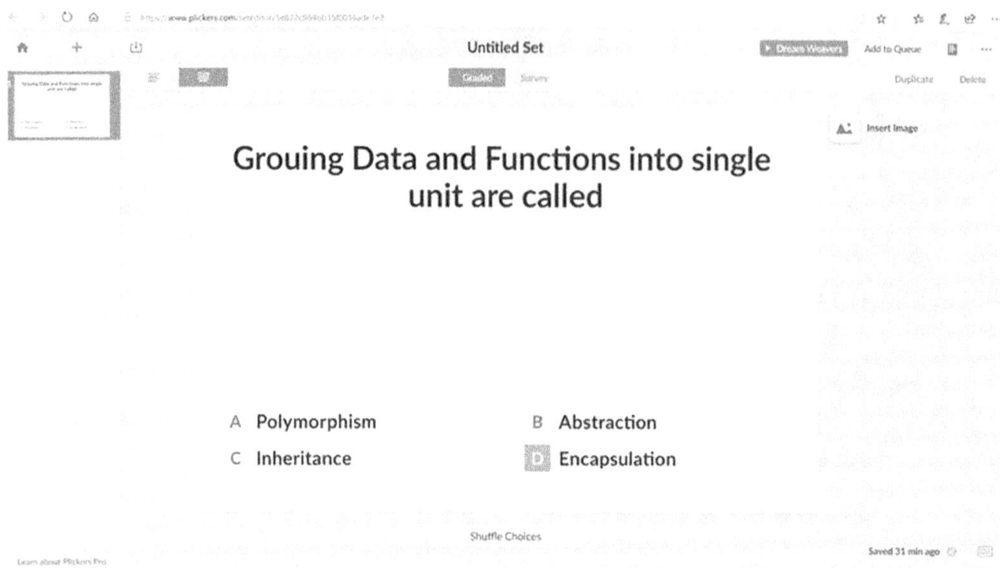

FIGURE 12.7 Sample of question and insert image option.

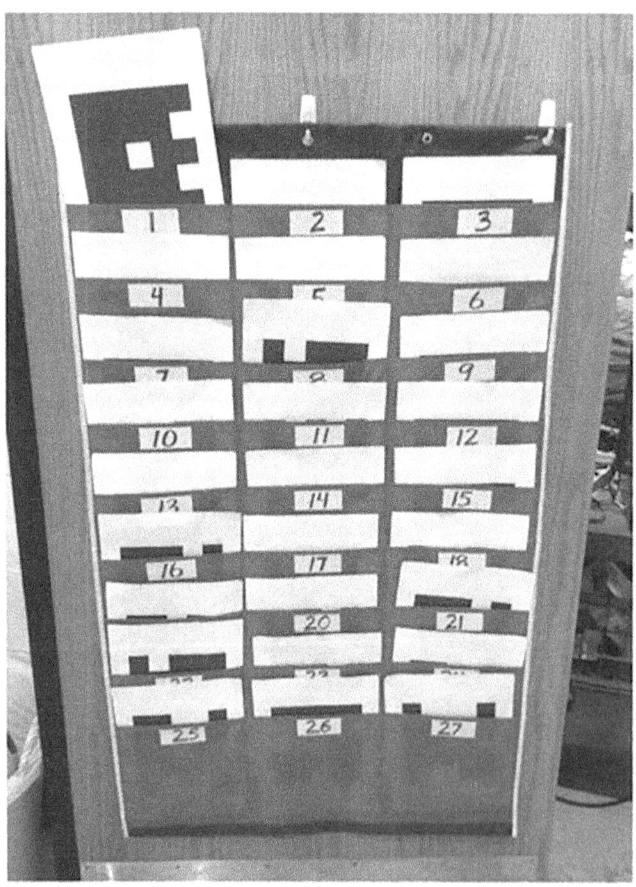

FIGURE 12.8 A way to organize cards.

FIGURE 12.9 Interface showing how to project questions on the screen.

and thereby reduce the time to distribute the cards. Before starting the class, each instructor plans the work, which helps to work for their specific classes.

12.2.2.7 Step 7: Implementing Real-Time Assessment

After teaching or presenting the course topic, the instructor starts the quiz or survey by projecting each question on the screen, as shown in Figure 12.9.

Students read the questions and are ready with their responses by holding the Plickers card to project the correct answers. Small letter markings on the card help to place the card in hand correctly to indicate the responses. The instructor taps the camera at the same time using a digital device and by using Plickers app as shown in Figure 12.10, and the participant's responses are recorded and displayed in real time.

Once the participants' responses are recorded, they can place their cards down. The Plickers app helps the instructor to know participants whose responses are not captured. This information is used for updating attendance. It takes approximately ten seconds to capture 60 responses (Chng & Gurvitch, 2018). The best method recommended is that the instructor stands in front of the class to see all the students within a small angle range to enhance the speed of capturing the feedback. The application provides a graphical representation to show the responses and how many are correct so that instructors do not need to grade. The answers are recorded, and students receive immediate feedback.

12.2.2.8 Step 8: View Results

When initiated by the instructor, the "Live View" tab helps to display the result to participants, as shown in Figure 12.11.

Plickers supports real-time response and feedback so that participants can see that the answers are correct or incorrect. Instructors can go through the answers instantaneously to correct any fallacies. The Plickers program allows the instructor to immediately know the participants' level of understanding about the topic, and thus plan the remaining issues and the evaluation mode.

FIGURE 12.10 Capturing the responses of participants by the instructor.

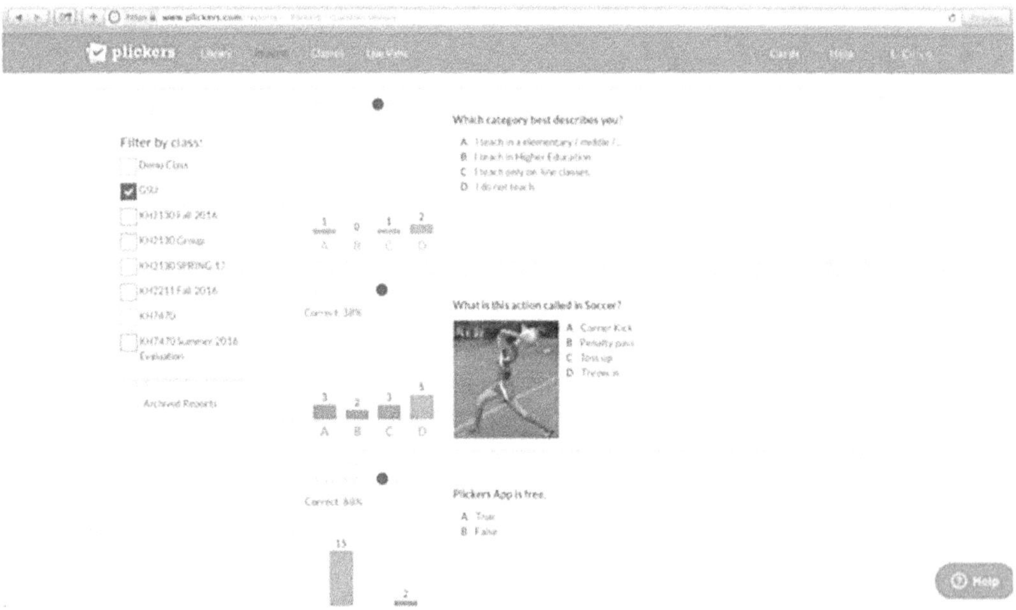

FIGURE 12.11 Real-time interface to show the results.

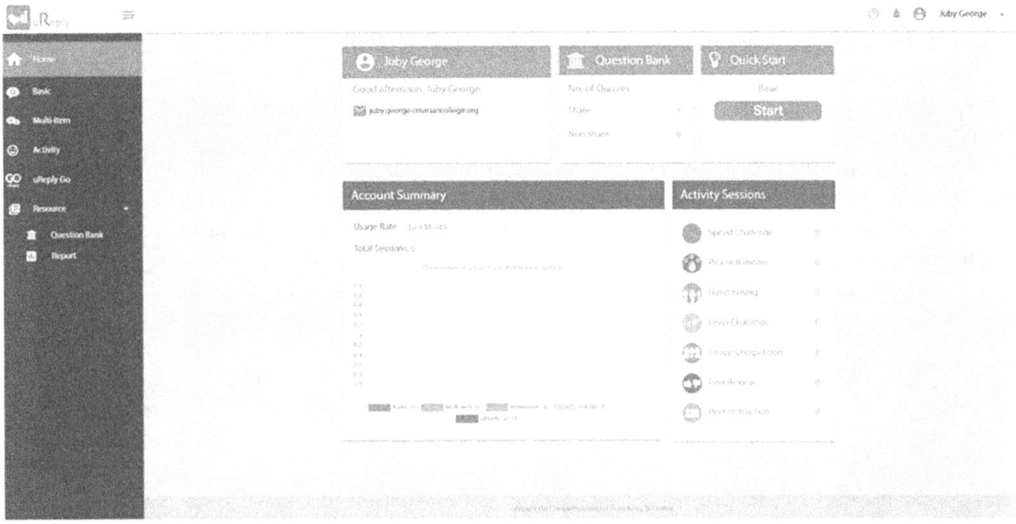

FIGURE 12.12 The uReply interface.

12.2.3 uReply

The web-based uReply student response system can be accessed by students directly from their mobile phones, iPads, iPods, and tablets. It was developed by City University, Hong Kong, to promote active learning and enhance student interaction. The response time is much faster than Clickers (City University of Hong Kong, 2020).

12.2.3.1 Distributing Homework to Students Using uReply

Instructors always assign homework to students after class to revise and understand the knowledge that they gained. To assign homework to participants, the question bank of uReply is used by selecting the "Multi-item" option, using the following steps. Using login as an instructor, the interface looks like as shown in Figure 12.12.

12.2.3.2 uReply Interface

Basic: Basic options help the instructors to preset different types of questions and store them in the Question Bank for later usage. This option also can be used to ask an instant question through simple steps.

Multi-item: The "Multi-item" option can be used for creating exercises and invite participants for active responses. It helps the students to see all questions at once, and participants can do their work at their own pace.

Activity: Activity options help the participants perform Game-like activities such as speed challenges and peer-reviewed exercises to make the class more engaging.

uReply Go: This option helps add action points onto an online map, and each point in the map will associate with a question so that a learning trail is easily created. Participants learn as they go.

Resource: Two Components under this option Question Bank and Report

Question Bank: Add Action points or pins onto an online map or create different types of questions for later usage. Students learn as they go.

Reports: The report option saves all responses of participants. Different types of reports are available to suit different purposes to assess the involvement of participants by instructors.

12.2.3.2.1 Using the uReply Interface

Step A: From the question bank, a quiz is created. Different types of questions are there in the question bank, as shown in Figure 12.13.

Step B: Start a multi-item session as shown in Figure 12.14. The created homework was selected as a quiz.

Step C: To make the homework session live, select the pencil icon from the bottom of the page, and the session continues to be live even if the browser is closed, as shown in Figure 12.15. The instructors can view the "Keep open" option that will insist the instructor's close the session instead of automatically closing the session.

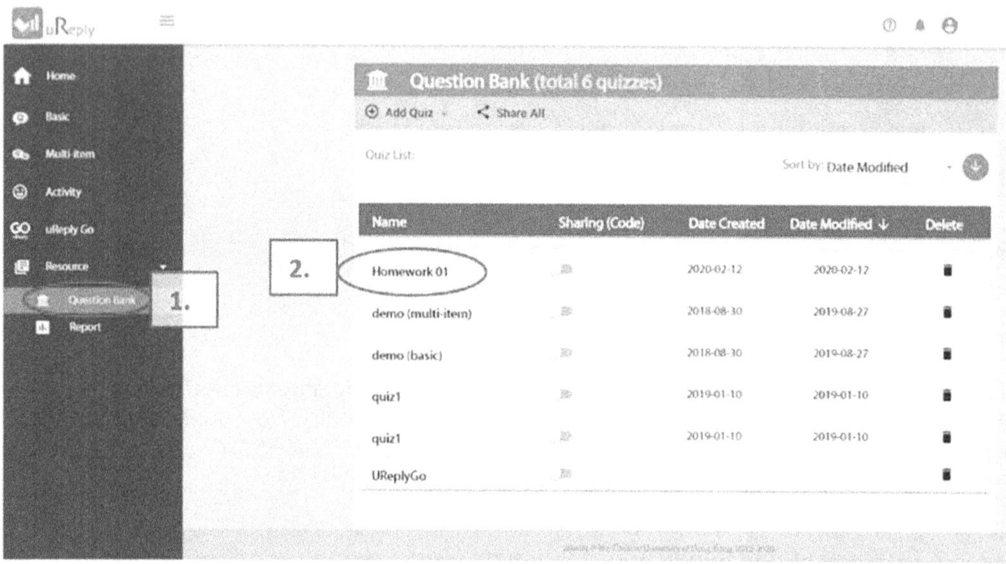

FIGURE 12.13 The interface of uReply showing different types of questions.

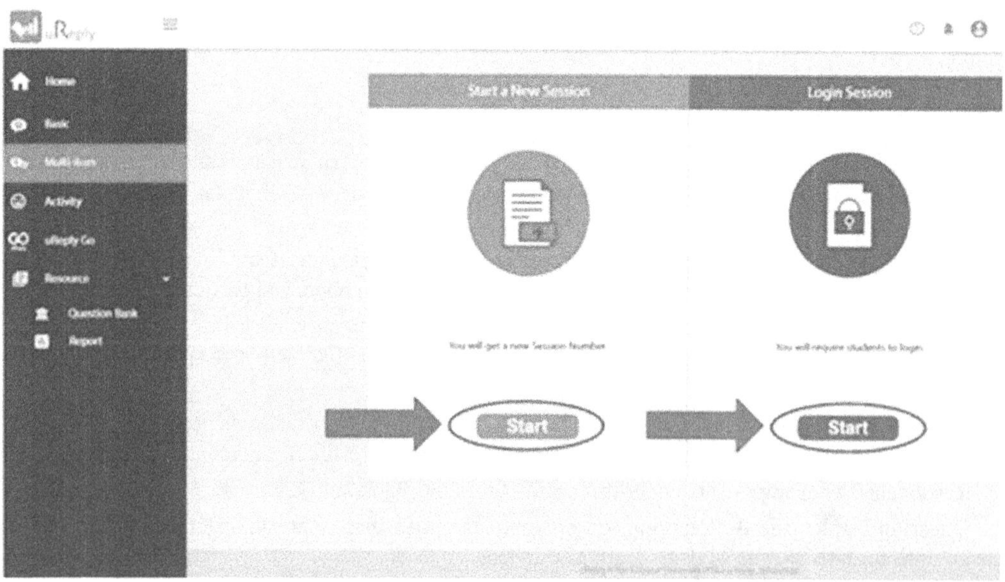

FIGURE 12.14 Interface to show a multi-item session.

FIGURE 12.15 Showing the live session.

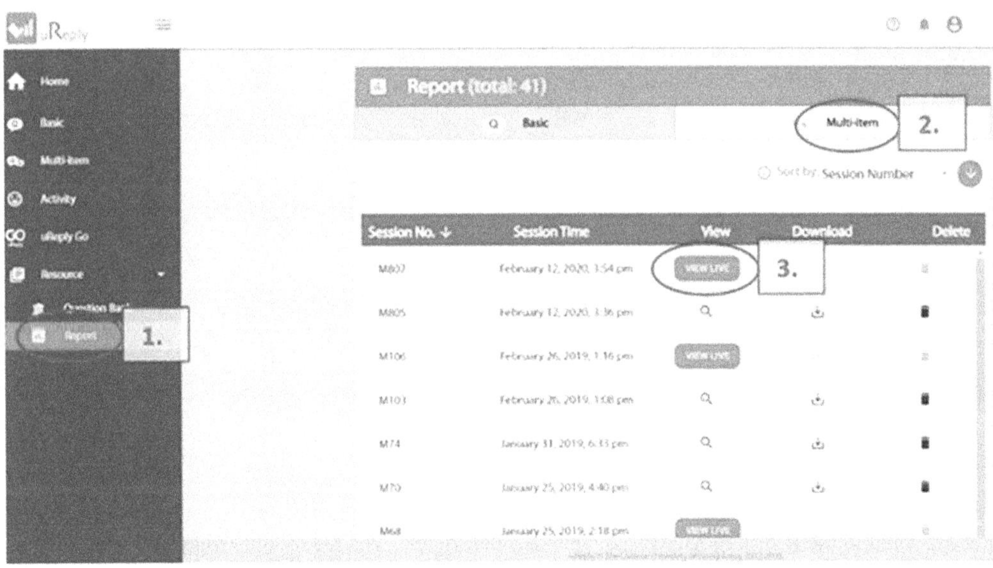

FIGURE 12.16 Interface to display the reports and re-enter the session.

Step D: Selecting the "Report" button from the left pane, the instructors can initiate the session again, as shown in Figure 12.16. Select the "Multi-item" option from the left pane to view the homework session. To re-enter the session, select "View live."

Step E: Select the "End" button as shown in Figure 12.17 to finish the session. The instructor from the report session can evaluate the performance of students.

FIGURE 12.17 Interface for ending the session

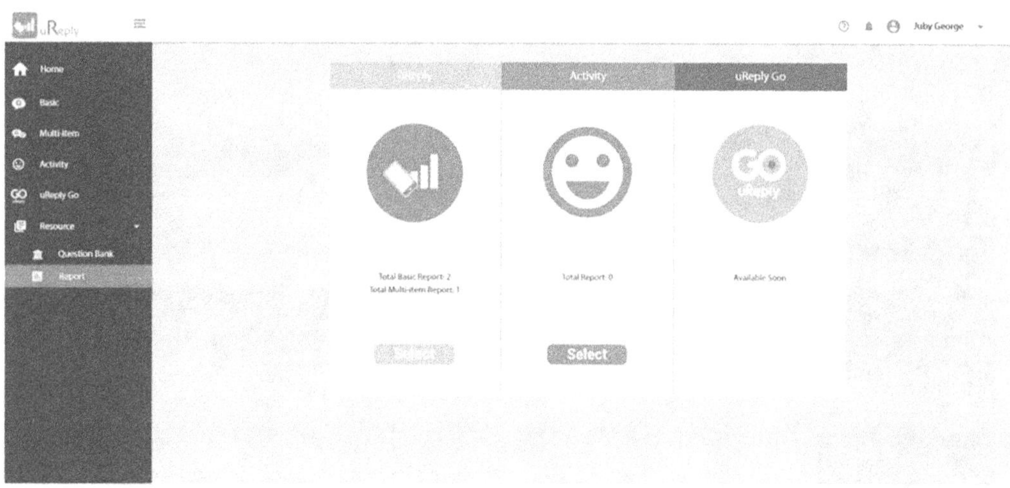

FIGURE 12.18 Interface for showing the detailed report.

Step F: uReply can be repeatedly accessed even if the class section ended, and by selecting the "Report" button, the instructors can analyze a detailed report. The tabs will display at first as shown in Figure 12.18. Instructors can view the detailed report of basic and multi-item by selecting the first tab, or detailed report of activity by selecting the "Activity" option.

Step G: If the instructor adds several questions and wants to view each answer, they can go for the detailed report option. The "Participation details" option under the View menu helps to view the detailed information regarding the participation, as shown in Figure 12.19.

12.2.3.3 Taking Students' Attendance Using uReply

By instructors asking a question, attendance taking can be enabled. Sign-up ensures the accurate recording of attendance. The steps are as follows.

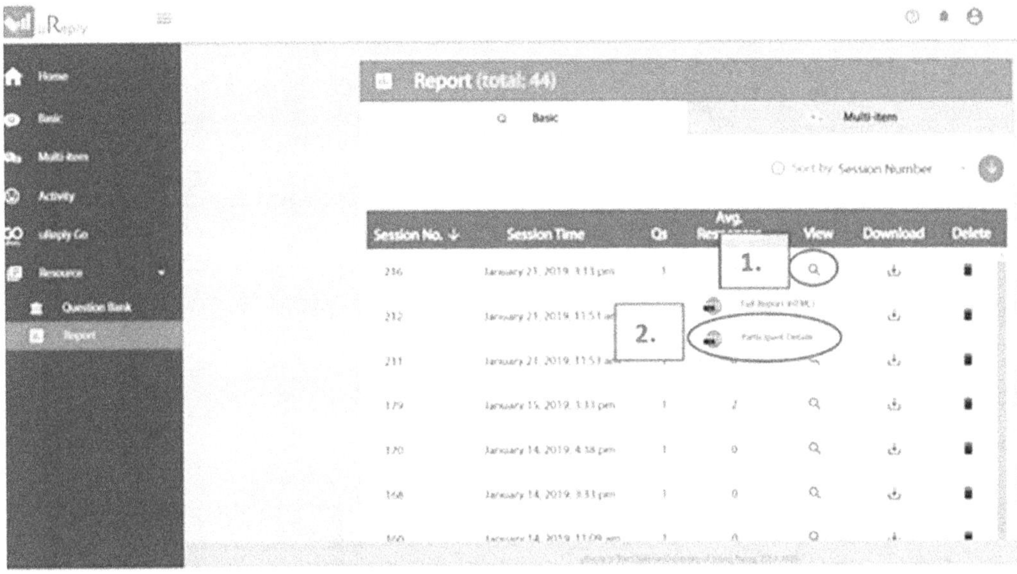

FIGURE 12.19 Interface showing participants' details from a report.

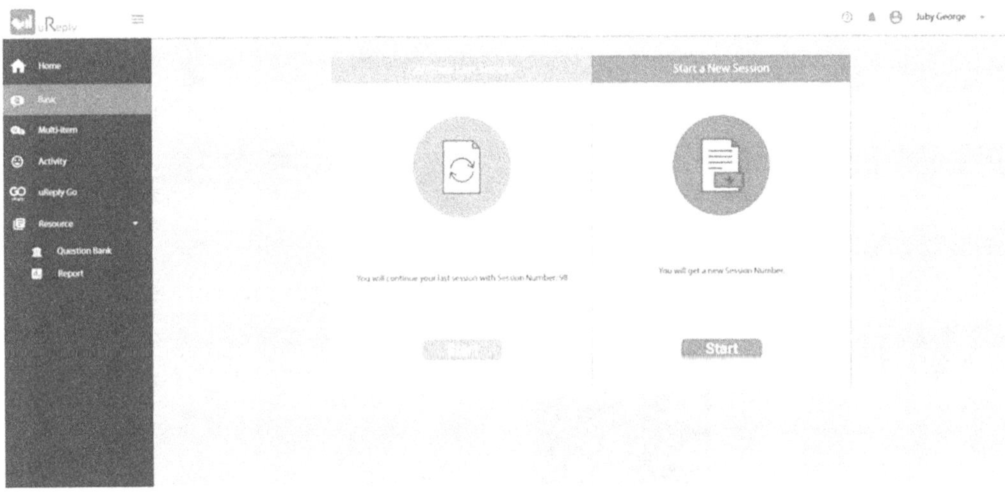

FIGURE 12.20 Interface showing the "Basic" tab.

Step A: Select the Basic tab after sign in to uReply, as shown in Figure 12.20.

Step B: Insist students use "Login session" to log in.

Step C: Either select a question from the question bank or set up a question to start, as shown in Figure 12.21.

Step D: Instruct participants to join the class. Participants need to join uReply on a browser, as shown in Figure 12.22, or the uReply app. They can even use Zoom (City University of Hong Kong, 2020).

Step E: All participants' responses are automatically saved once the instructor receives enough responses and ends the session using the "End" option, as shown in Figure 12.23.

Step F: The participants' involvement in all sessions is tracked, and the instructors may continue using the uReply activity by asking more questions.

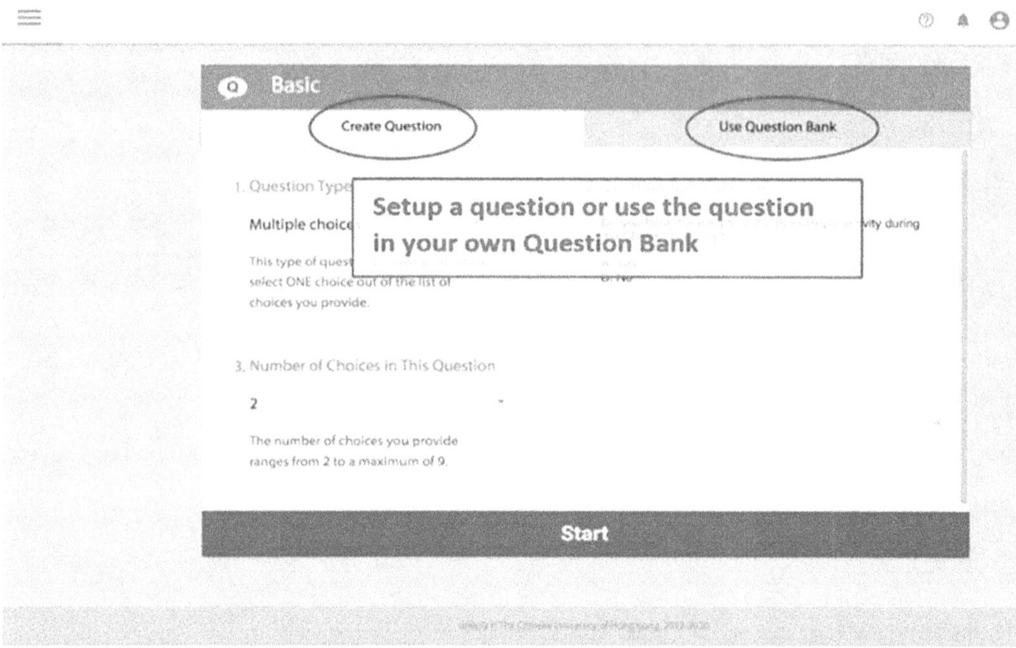

FIGURE 12.21 An interface for selecting a question.

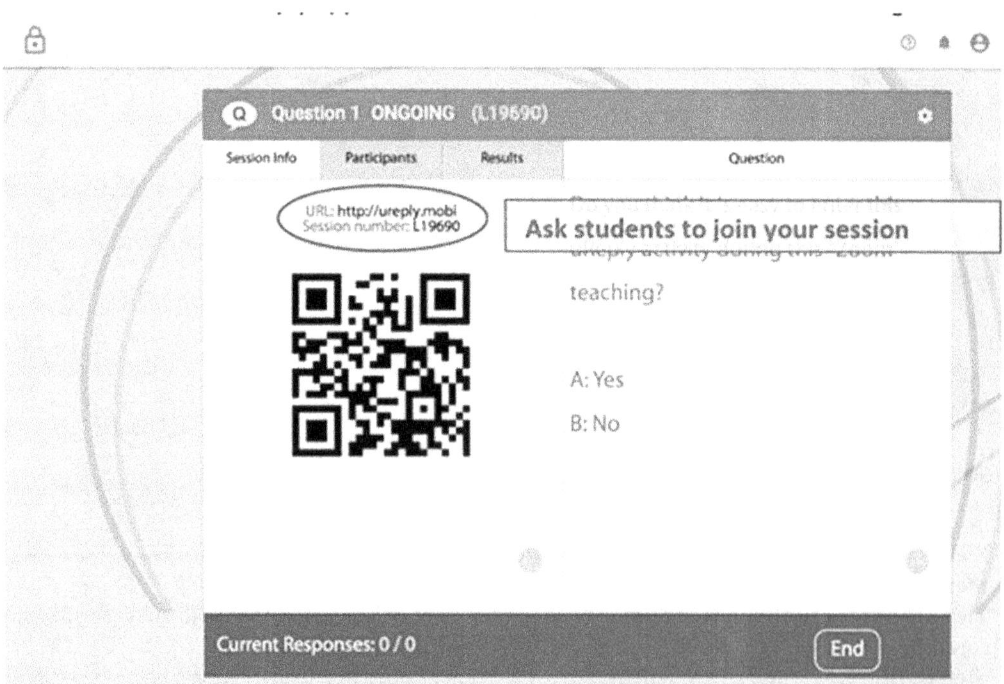

FIGURE 12.22 Interface asking students to join.

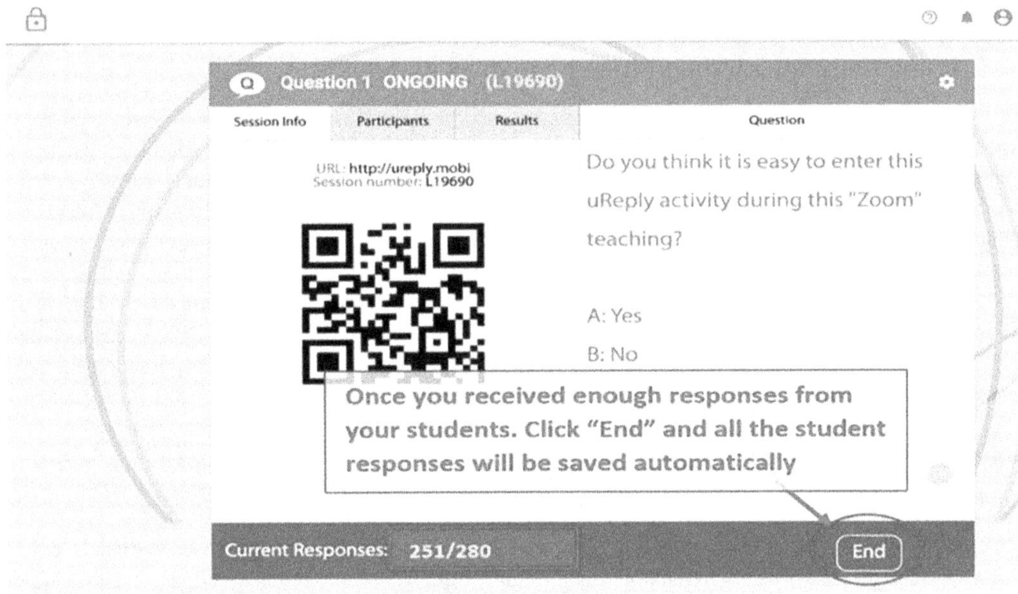

FIGURE 12.23 Interface showing enough responses.

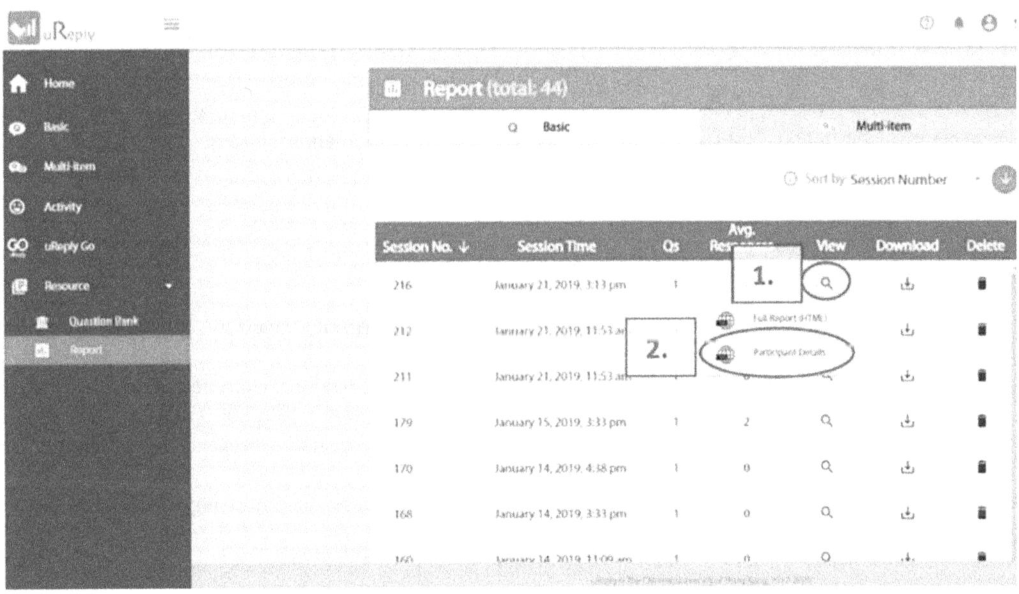

FIGURE 12.24 Interface showing the tab to show details.

Step G: After completing the uReply session/Zoom, the instructors can access uReply again by selecting the "Report" option to show the detailed report, as shown in Figure 12.24.

Step H: If the instructor asked more questions, the "Participation details" option shows the status of participants, and the instructor knows if the participants answered the question. Select the "View button" and select "Participation details" to see the session details, as shown in Figure 12.24.

Step I (optional): The report can be downloaded, and the downloaded files can be opened in Microsoft Excel, which is suitable for instructors to further analyze the student's participation and performance.

12.3 Psychological Impact and Learning Experience Using Online Learning Management Tools

Access to online educational platforms and focused outcome-based learning continue to spread across all types of learning environments, in universities, hospitals, colleges, etc. Studies revealed that instructor-student interaction—as well as students themselves—interact effectively and focus on learning outcomes (Mironov & Borzea, 2013; Keller &Cernerud, 2002). The learners are more innovative using the learning management tools, and they interact effectively. The studies' findings also reveal that online instruction using learning management tools leverages the psychological affordances of the remote and personalized learning platform rather than attempting to replicate the traditional classroom approach (Lam et al., 2011). To boost student engagement in active learning, the outcome-based content, delivery of the content to motivate students to actively involve in innovation, and further learning is made possible to a great extent using various learning management tools (Rogers, 2003).

12.4 Conclusion

Mentimeter allows instructors to use live polling in the class, where students can use either a laptop, tablet, or smartphone to engage in the poll. It is fast and straightforward, and is excellent for asking questions to a larger group of participants. Instructors can choose to have the results and reports appear live or hide them until the end of the voting period. The charts or responses are visually clear and attractive, too, so they look relatively good. Different subjects like mathematics, science, etc., can use Plickers cards. Documentation of the analysis and performance of participants is possible using Plickers. Instructors use the repository of data collected for analysis and reviewing their instructional process and can provide feedback to students, which is a critical element in teaching and learning. By using uReply, instructors have the option of instantaneous feedback to class to enhance learning. Monitoring and reporting of class activities are also retrievable from the repository by instructors for a later time to analyze performance. The time invested in learning and preparing these learning management tools should benefit instructors in the long run. These tools help instructors the opportunities to communicate the expectations to participants so that learning becomes effective.

REFERENCES

Bruff, D. (2017). *Class response systems ("Clickers")*. Center for Teaching, Vanderbilt University. Retrieved from https://cft.vanderbilt.edu/guidessub-pages/clickers/

Chng, L., & Gurvitch, R. (2018). Using plickers as an assessment tool in health and physical education settings. *Journal of Physical Education, Recreation & Dance*, 89(2), 19–25. DOI: 10.1080/07303084.2017.1404510

City University of Hong Kong. (2020). www.cityu.edu.hk/elearn/pdf/instructionUReply-onlinelearning.pdf [Accessed March 22, 2020].

Imwold, C., Rider, R., & Johnson, D. (1982). The use of evaluation in public school physical education programs. *Journal of Teaching in Physical Education*, 2, 13–18.

Keller, C., &Cernerud, L. (2002). Students' perception of e-learning in university education. *Journal of Educational Media*, 27(1–2), 55–65.

Lam, P., Lee, J., Chan, M., & McNaught, C. (2011) Students' use of eLearning strategies and their perception of eLearning usefulness. In *Global Learn, Association for the Advancement of Computing in Education (AACE)*, pp. 1379–1388.

Mironov, C., & Borzea, A. (2013). An emigrant teachers' excursion in the world of digital native students. In *Proceedings of the Education and Psychology Challenges—Teachers for the Knowledge Society—2nd edition EPC—TKS 2013*, Vol. 128, pp. 262–268. www.marcprensky.com/writing/Prensky%20-%20Digital%20Natives,%20Digital%20Immigrants%20-%20Part1.pdf

Rogers, E. M. (2003). *Diffusion of innovations* (5th ed.). New York: The Free Press.

Tech de Monterrey, Mexico. (2020). https://innovacioneducativa.tec.mx/wp-content/modelo_flexible/documentos/, mentimeter_1.pdf [Accessed March 22, 2020].

13

Industry 4.0 and Jobs 2030

Italia Joseph Maria, T. Devi, and P. Kaliraj

CONTENTS

Objectives

This chapter provides an introduction to Industry 4.0 with a perspective on the jobs in light of the Fourth Industrial Revolution. The chapter gives a description of the mission of universities for 2030 and discusses what is meant by Education 4.0 and Curriculum 4.0. The chapter elaborates how the faculty can be trained to match themselves with Education 4.0 and Curriculum 4.0 with continuous faculty development programmes and online content development training, and how they can be effective facilitators to the students of this digital age. The chapter further discusses the various skills required for students in the future, and also discusses the challenges of Mission 2030 and briefs on the nature of jobs in 2030.

13.1 Introduction

A new term in the industrial world, Industry 4.0, stands for the Fourth Industrial Revolution. The World Economic Forum explains it logically, referring the first three industrial evolutions, since this builds on the Third Industrial Revolution, which was nothing but the revolution brought about by digital technology. The third was built on the second, which was the introduction of electricity, and the second in turn was built upon the first one, which was the introduction of mechanisation. In the fourth stage, the digital, biological, and physical aspects do not differ much. Here you can see automation in every aspect, artificial intelligence (AI) in almost all domains, robots in most of the places, and thus limitless scope for technology (The Duke Perspective, 2019).

DOI: 10.1201/9781003318378-13

13.1.1 Industry 4.0

The Fourth Industrial Revolution is bringing transformation worldwide. This revolution is propelled by cyber-physical systems (CPS) and AI, and all of those exposed to technology can see themselves being in the midst of this. This can be explained in simple terms as follows. Currently it is the age of the Fourth Industrial Revolution and just looking back one can see that the first revolution was powered when Isaac Newton described the laws of motion, and thereafter, mechanisation started with steam engines in the forefront. The second revolution gained momentum when Michael Faraday and James Maxwell unified the forces of electricity and magnetism, which in turn produced electricity and electric motor magnetic and electric forces, leading to electricity generation and the electric motor, which were instrumental in the assembly lines that have come to dominate many industries. The Third Industrial Revolution was catalysed by the discovery of the transistor, which ushered the age of electronics that gave us transistors, computers, and the internet. This fourth wave of industrial revolution will revolutionise industries so substantially that much of the work that exists today will not exist in 50 years (Xing and Marwala, 2017).

Industry 4.0 involves a combination of innovative practices and approaches in terms of processes, services, applications, and products. AI and machine learning, automation and robotics, Big Data, the Internet of Things (IoT), augmented reality (AR), and virtual reality (VR) are some of its new tools (Kupper, 2020). It will certainly transform education ecosystem in a major way. Due to Industry 4.0, the employees of the future will have to utilise their knowledge and skills in new ways and keep upgrading and improving their knowledge to be successful. Industry 4.0 certainly would revolutionise the education sector, as automation—which is its most important feature—is going to affect the career options as early as 2020 (Akash, 2018).

13.1.1.1 The Nine Technologies Driving Industry 4.0

The nine technologies driving Industry 4.0 are: additive manufacturing, AR, autonomous robots, Big Data and analytics, cloud computing, cybersecurity, system integration, IoT, and simulation (Boston Consulting Group, 2020).

- **Additive manufacturing:** The classic example of additive manufacturing is three-dimensional (3D) printing. Instead of prototyping individual components, companies can now produce small batches of customised products. The resulting advantages include the speedy manufacturing of complex, lightweight designs.
- **Augmented reality:** AR systems support a variety of services, such as selecting parts in a warehouse and sending repair instructions over mobile devices. With AR, companies can provide workers with real-time information that improves decision making and work procedures.
- **Autonomous robots:** Autonomous robots can interact with one another and work safely side by side with humans. These robots will cost less and have an increasing range of capabilities over time.
- **Big Data and analytics:** In an Industry 4.0 context, the collection and comprehensive evaluation of data from many different sources—production equipment and systems, as well as enterprise- and customer-management systems—will become table stakes.
- **The cloud:** The more production-related initiatives a company undertakes, the more it needs to share data across sites. Meanwhile, cloud technologies continue to get faster and more powerful. Companies will increasingly deploy machine data and analytics to the cloud, thus enabling more data-driven services for production systems.
- **Cybersecurity:** It is no surprise that Industry 4.0 boosts increased connectivity and the use of standard communications protocols. As a result, the need to protect critical industrial systems and manufacturing lines from cybersecurity threats rises dramatically. For this reason, secure, reliable communications are essential, together with sophisticated access management for machines and identity verification of users.

- **Horizontal and vertical system integration:** Industry 4.0 allows companies, departments, functions, and capabilities to become much more cohesive. Cross-company, universal data-integration networks evolve and enable truly automated value chains.
- **The Industrial IoT (IIoT):** Industry 4.0 means that more devices are enriched with embedded computing. This process allows devices to communicate and interact both with one another and with more centralised controllers. It also decentralises analytics and decision making, thus enabling responses in real time.
- **Simulation:** Simulations are a cornerstone of Industry 4.0. They are used extensively in plant operations to leverage real-time data and to mirror the physical world. Done correctly, these models allow operators to test and optimise settings in numerous variations, thereby driving down machine setup times and increasing quality.

13.1.2 Mission 2030

The mission each university should have is to:

1. Be an inclusive, innovative, and international university.
2. Be devoted to excellence in teaching, research, and in the transfer of knowledge and to serve the social, economic, and cultural needs of the country.
3. Be innovative and promise high quality educational programmes in all disciplines possible with synergetic interaction with the society and industry.
4. Impart skills and knowledge of international competence to our learners and inculcate global vision among them.
5. Contribute to knowledge acquisition and advance through applied research, facilitating more new products and processes by collaborating with other academic and research institutions and industries of global standards.
6. Promote the uptake of innovative results and contribute to the emergence of start-ups and incubators.

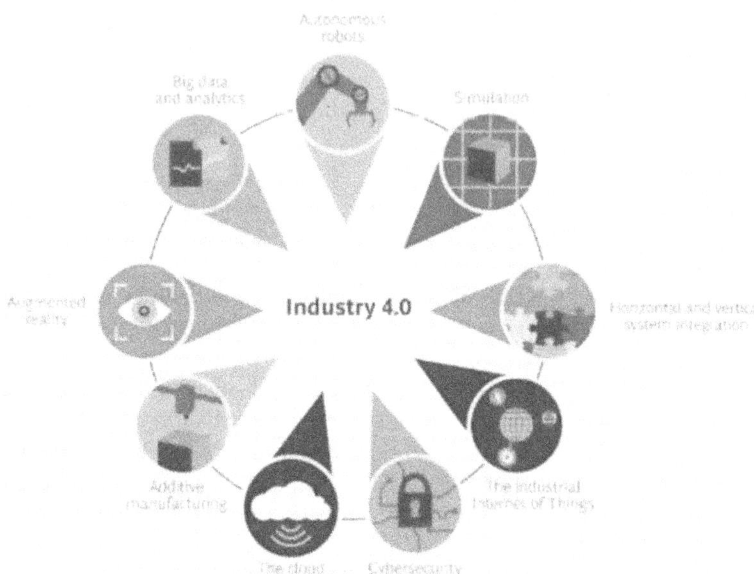

FIGURE 13.1 The different tools of Industry 4.0.

7. Focus on understanding and contributing to solving environmental issues that challenge the integrity and sustainability of the ecosystem.
8. Offer extension services to address the problems of society in the areas of education, health, poverty, inequality, climate, and peace through the knowledge available to us.

13.2 Education 4.0

In the era of the Fourth Industrial Revolution, the scenario of Higher Education (HE) 4.0 is an exciting, dialectical, and complex opportunity which can surely renovate society for better causes. Since this revolution is driven by AI, it is expected to change the work atmosphere from task-based characteristics to human-centred characteristics—and due to the convergence that may happen between humans and machines, the distance between the subjects of social science and humanities, and also between science and technology, may ne lessened. This substantially calls for more interdisciplinary teaching, research, and innovation (Xing and Marwala, 2017).

Today, all graduates encounter a world revolutionised by technological advancements whereby social media, cloud computing, and the internet open up various opportunities and challenges for formal systems of education. Driven by AI, these technologies revolutionise the world so much that social concepts like "post-work" are defining the current era more and more (Suganya, 2017). This time period requires some particular skills that are not at all the skills that were needed in the third wave of digital revolution, when the key driver was the internet and computers. These skills are emotional intelligence, people management, critical thinking, cognitive flexibility, judgement, negotiation, knowledge production and management and crisis management (Akash, 2018).

The future of education and learning is said to be Education 4.0, which really is an outcome of the integration of technology in the educational sector, and it aims to convert students to be future ready (Thomas, 2019). Both students and teachers should be assured of the maximum possible experience of teaching and learning. Here comes the need for Education 4.0, which will be an experience for students and teachers to address the requirements of the world around us, which is developing very fast (Jain, 2020). With the aim of imparting knowledge and developing the skills of students through experiential learning and practical exposure, Education 4.0 exploits technologies like flipped classrooms and blended learning. It places its focus on making students ready for training, projects, and jobs of tomorrow by including in the curriculum various methods like learning outside the classroom and undertaking field work (Thomas, 2019).

13.3 Curriculum 4.0

> We have to develop a globally shared and comprehensive view of how technology is influencing our lives and redefining our human, cultural, social, and economic environments. Never was there a time of greater peril, or greater promise.
>
> **Klaus Schwab, executive and chairman founder of the World Economic Forum (Automation Alley, 2019)**

The McKinsey Global Institute provides an analysis which reports that "51% of job activities are highly susceptible to automation", which is a fact influenced by the needs of Industry 4.0 (Jain, 2020). Industries are now ready to associate with educational institutes for Industry 4.0, and to help in making ready future generations to cope with this evolving scenario—and hence, academic institutions would need to build up collaborations with industries. Government agencies, corporations, universities, colleges, and research centres need to unanimously embark on this process.

For Education 4.0 to be a reality, the back force will be Curriculum 4.0. The end result of Curriculum 4.0 should be industry-ready students. Rigorous re-training of teachers and cautious coordination and groundwork of students will be backbone for this. If delivery of academic content is not modernised, learning also will not become modern. Curriculum 4.0 should be the tool of choice for Faculty 4.0.

Technological applications should be in the tool set of teachers for carrying out cognitive learning. Adaptive learning techniques which are personalised should be the foundation for learning outcomes. Teaching concepts should be powered by intelligent and smart digital assets. The whole experience of teaching and learning should be made more interesting and engaging by active teacher-student interactions (Jain, 2020).

Curriculum 4.0 calls for more *industry exposure*, which emphasises the involvement of more industrial experts as special invitees in the boards of studies of each programme. These experts can be research and development managers, product development managers, or industrial experts. The quality and relevance of Curriculum 4.0 should promote and encourage more strong cooperation between education, research, industry and training organisations, and it should be capable of aligning advanced education and training envisioning the requirements of the new industrial era (Skills for Industry, Inc., 2019).

Students need to have *international exposure*, which is essential for local students to acquire global thinking and global outlook. There are a variety of learning pathways for this, including experiential learning, case-study based approaches, problem-solving approaches, practicals and team-based project work. Use of information and communication technology (ICT), e-learning resources, self-learning courses, digital and online learning options for students like study webs of active learning for young aspiring minds (SWAYAM) and massive open online courses (MOOCs) are to be promoted. Blended learning should be a part of the curriculum. Moreover, field-based training, internships, visits to industries, and undertaking projects should also come under the umbrella of Curriculum 4.0. Ample space should be provided for promoting multiple approaches of learning, and these should be listed in the syllabus with reference to which approach will be used for mastering each part of the course.

When more than two academic disciplines are combined into one activity, this can be termed *interdisciplinary studies*. It can mean a science student acquiring skills and knowledge from several other domains like psychology, anthropology, sociology, and economics. It is nothing but thinking beyond boundaries (Wikipedia, 2020b). Interdisciplinary programmes should be made mandatory whereby students will have the freedom of choosing the courses they are interested in apart from the required core courses. Another important matter of concern should be the preservation of knowledge by building a repository of curricular materials and learning resources—both print and digital media—for easy access by students, faculty, and researchers. Digital content development must happen in such a way that it is easy to use so that it provides one step access to knowledge which students seek.

13.4 Faculty Development

Continuous *professional development programmes* for all faculty is a need of the day, since no teacher can be an expert on everything—even in the teacher's own area of interest. This shows the need for support units for learning technology so that teaching in this digital age is more effective and efficient. Student feedback, peer assessments, and online student satisfaction surveys continue to serve as important motivators to teachers in improving themselves. They can update their teaching methods based on student feedback and incorporate more innovative techniques in their curriculum for content delivery.

Digital content creation is the contribution of information to digital media for students in specific courses. Typical forms of content creation related to academics can include creating and uploading YouTube videos; uploading course materials to the cloud, which may serve as a single rich repository of correlated information; maintaining blogs and updating them; creating forums and responding to queries; and editing and distribution of digital media. *Training on digital content development* is essential, since most teachers may not be experts in these areas. Therefore, digital content development should be given sufficient priority in faculty development.

Moreover, with the increasing use of technology in education today, teachers are to be facilitators where they have to provide an initial learning environment and atmosphere. This will bring the students together and help them to build their own personal learning environments. This will enable learners to connect to "successful" student networks, with the presumption that learning will happen automatically. For this to happen, digital content must be readily available, and teachers must be trained for flipped classroom teaching and blended teaching experiences.

13.5 Skills Required in the Future

The main factors that will transform the work atmosphere and will identify the major job skills needed for the future will be emotional intelligence, people management, critical thinking, communication skills, cognitive flexibility, critical judgement, negotiation, and knowledge production and management. *Communication skills* include the traditional skills of speaking, reading, and writing clearly and coherently, with added communication skills needed for social media, which comprise the ability to extend one's ideas via the internet to a wide variety of people, skills required to create small YouTube videos, skills needed to receive and incorporate feedback, and the ability to share information correctly and to identify ideas and trends (Bates, 2015). *Critical thinking skills* include open-mindedness, self-regulation, problem-solving, analysis, interpretation, inference, and explanation. It is means by which one is capable of thinking in a rational and organised way in order to understand relationships between facts and/or ideas. It aids one in deciding what the right information is and whether to believe it. This is a process of identifying one's thinking and analysing it and correcting the mistakes or in other words; it is "thinking about thinking" (Tomaszewski, 2020).

The ability to think about two subjects simultaneously and switch between them, at times, and being able to think about multiple concepts at the same time is termed *cognitive flexibility* (Wikipedia, 2020a). Quick learning, providing creative solutions for problems, adapting to new situations, and effectively responding to issues are some of the signs that a person is cognitively flexible, and this is considered to be a very important skill for students (Stengar, 2017). *People management skills* consist of training, motivation, delegation, leadership, communication, and even performance feedback (Suttle, 2020). For a student, it can also mean getting connected with others, having empathy towards others, listening to others, empowering others, and finding one's own space—and at the same time, allowing others to grow in their respective personal spaces. Relationship management, social awareness, self-management, and self-awareness are the skills that come under *emotional intelligence*, whereas *crisis management skills* include awareness of situational reality, creativity, and adaptability. *Knowledge management* is considered to be a very important skill in a society that is knowledge based, not only because knowledge is quickly changing, but also because information sources are increasing (Bates, 2015). This means that the knowledge that a student acquires from university studies can quickly become obsolete, so they should know how to find, assess, examine, apply and distribute information within specific contexts.

13.6 Contributions of Retired Teachers

Any higher educational institution (HEI) will have a network of eminent retired professors, scientists, and industry experts who are willing to provide their academic services voluntarily to HEIs in nearby geographical vicinities. With experience and the desire to continue to make contributions, the retired teachers are valuable resources in colleges, and they can play irreplaceable roles in the cultural heritage and cultural education which will benefit students in their cultural education. Moreover, it will have positive effects on retirement management and the construction of a harmonious campus. Their services can also be employed as advisers or mentors to not only students, but to faculty and even administrations. Another area where their expertise can be employed is in sharing the subject knowledge for e-learning development using AR, AI, and "technology for education" development.

13.7 Challenges of Mission 2030

1. Mindset of stakeholders to adapt to Industry 4.0, digital revolution for intelligent systems—self driving cars, automated systems.
2. Attracting international students to raise the standards and quality of education in India.
3. Identifying experts (who have blended knowledge in both education and Industry 4.0) for faculty development.

4. Motivating teachers to attend the professional development programmes.
5. Motivating teachers to make use of ICT tools in the process of teaching and learning.
6. Infusing the technology to non-technical teachers (or) developing technology-based support systems to help the teachers.
7. Grants for students and faculty exchanges.
8. To inculcate creativity, problem solving, good decision making in complex and uncertain situations, innovation into curriculum, and faculty development programmes, and make students ready for Industry 4.0.
9. Publicity of good Indian educational institutions across the globe.

13.8 Jobs in 2030

Today, we are in a scenario whereby both normal white-collar and blue-collar jobs can easily be automated by algorithms and robots. Many existing jobs may be decreasing in demand, while the demand for highly paid digital skills in the upcoming industries will increase. This novel digital economy, which is powered by innovation, needs workers who are highly creative and curious, who can adopt new technologies, and who can constantly improve their social, technical, and creative skills (Pearce, 2019). With Industry 4.0, five of the major skills for employment in the future will be human skills such as creativity, people skills and interdisciplinary knowledge, mental elasticity, complex problem solving, and critical thinking (Crimson Education, 2020).

To face the challenges in society and industry, India requires young graduates who design and manufacture new products, and programmes to mould learners who grow up to the expectations of government, incubation, and innovation centres must be started by every educational institution. This may help small industries to access high-end technologies, professors with high profiles, well trained students, and sophisticated infrastructure facilities. For the institution, this will be an opportunity to build links with local bodies and also to improve the scope of student employability. This can happen when students are equipped with cognitive learning skills and every institution is furnished with sophisticated gadgets that are in use in industry (Prasad, 2020). Students should take the responsibility to solve the challenges faced by the world. Thus, incubation and innovation should be a hallmark of every institution. In other words, classroom learning needs to be linked to the aspirations of the country.

Prominent sectors that will have *more jobs* are healthcare, education, information technology, digital marketing, automation, manufacturing, logistics, and the like. The demand for doctors, nurses, pharmacists, and drug developers will be ever increasing, and so will be the demand for better medicine and treatments. Though digital transformation will happen in Education 4.0, the demand for teachers as facilitators and mentors will never decrease. As Industry 4.0 will take over our daily workspace, and AI, IoT, data analytics, and AR will be the driving forces, specialists in these areas will ever more be needed. Digital marketing will be another area where experts will be required for marketing and promotion of online businesses and firms. Any business without an online platform will struggle to thrive in this digital era, and hence, digital marketing experts will be ever in need. Automation specialists like drone pilots, data specialists, and informatics specialists will be in high demand due to advancements in technology. The manufacturing filed will require specialists when robots and AI will take over most of the jobs. Global trade will take new forms which will create more jobs in logistics. Moreover, digital careers like 3D printing, user experience designing, mobile application development, cybersecurity, and data analysts also will be in high demand in industry. At a time when robotics is gaining more roots, skills needed to design, build, and service robots will be difficult to master, and so, robotics engineers will be in high demand.

13.8.1 Artificial Intelligence Jobs in 2030

By 2030, automation and AI will drive the world. Automation is already manifested by driverless cars and machines that are able to read X-rays and algorithms that are able to react to customer-service queries (Pavan, 2019).

Automation Can be Applied in the Following Sectors Worldwide

1. Pharmaceuticals (research and development)—96%
2. Marketing (consumer marketing/digital marketing)—90%
3. Automotive (redesign and new development)—86%
4. Oil and Gas—85%

In 2030, Prominent Sectors That Will Have More Jobs

1. **Healthcare/medical:** Doctors, nurses, pharmacists, drug developers—demand for better medicine and treatments is ever increasing.
2. **Education:** Teachers (school, college), other education professionals, education support workers.
3. **Information Technology Specialists:** IoT, AI, data analytics, AR computer specialists.
4. **Digital Marketing**.
5. **Automation Specialists:** Drone pilots.
6. **Manufacturing:** Automation using robots and AI.
7. **Logistics:** As globalisation will lead to more global trade.
8. **Restaurant Cooks**.

13.8.1.1 Jobs 2030

As per the latest report of McKinsey Global Institute entitled *Jobs Lost, Jobs Gained: Workforce Transitions in a Time of Automation* (2017), when Jobs in 2030 are looked at, it is estimated that about 250–280 million fresh jobs can be created from the effect of rising incomes on consumer goods alone (Figure 13.2), with an additional 50–85 million jobs generated from increased expenditure in education and health (McKinsey & Company, 2017).

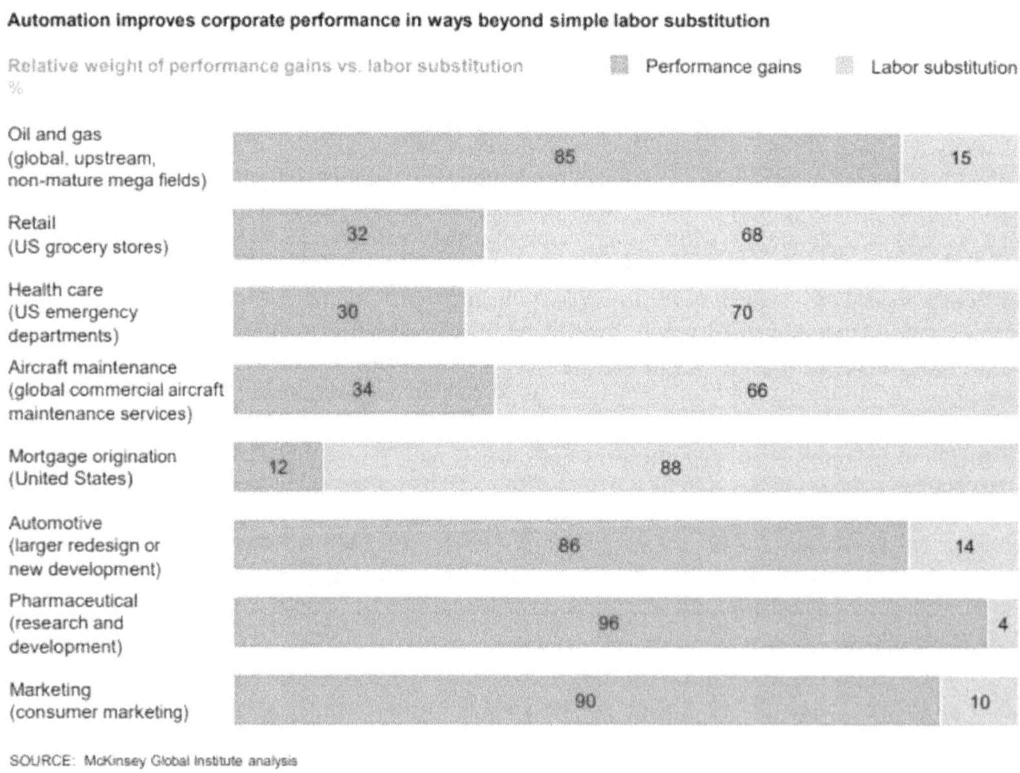

FIGURE 13.2 Impact of automation: performance gains vs. labour substitution.

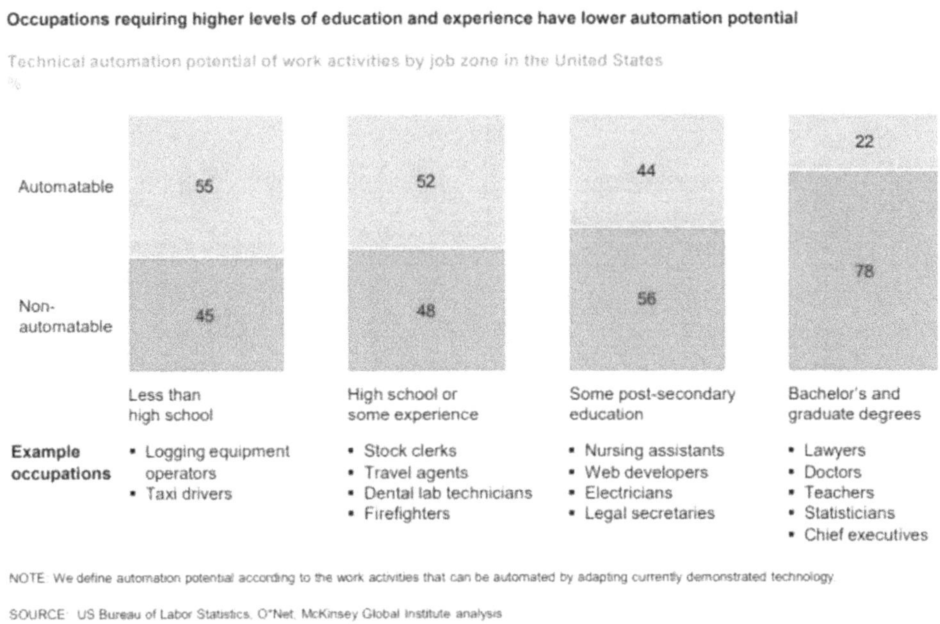

FIGURE 13.3 Education level vs. automation potential.

The requirements for the current status of occupations involved with education is related to the chance that activities could be brought under automation. The technical automation potential for occupations needing less than a high school diploma is 55%, whereas for those with a college degree, that is far lower, at just 22% (McKinsey Digital, 2016). For those with education higher than secondary education, the occupations that can be automated are fewer, and for those with high school education and some practical knowhow, occupations that can be automated are greater, as depicted in Figure 13.3 and Figure 13.4 (McKinsey Global Institute, 2017).

Some Jobs That Will Be Available in 2030

1. Postsecondary teachers.
2. School teachers.
3. Other education professionals.
4. Education support workers.
5. Computer engineers/specialists.
6. Construction workers.
7. Doctors.
8. Nurses, physician assistants, and pharmacists.
9. Health aides and health support.
10. Therapists.
11. Health technicians.
12. Childcare workers.

Depending on the occupation and the sector, how the employment opportunities will be influenced by automation will vary. Jobs vulnerable to automation include physical jobs such as fast food preparation and operating machinery. Two other categories that can be faster and better automated include the collection and processing of data. This, in turn, will replace a big number of jobs; for example, in back-office transaction processing, accounting, paralegal work, and mortgage origination (McKinsey & Company, 2017). Again, it should be remembered that even while there are some jobs automated, there may not be a decline in employment, but instead, employees mat have to acquire new skills and perform new jobs.

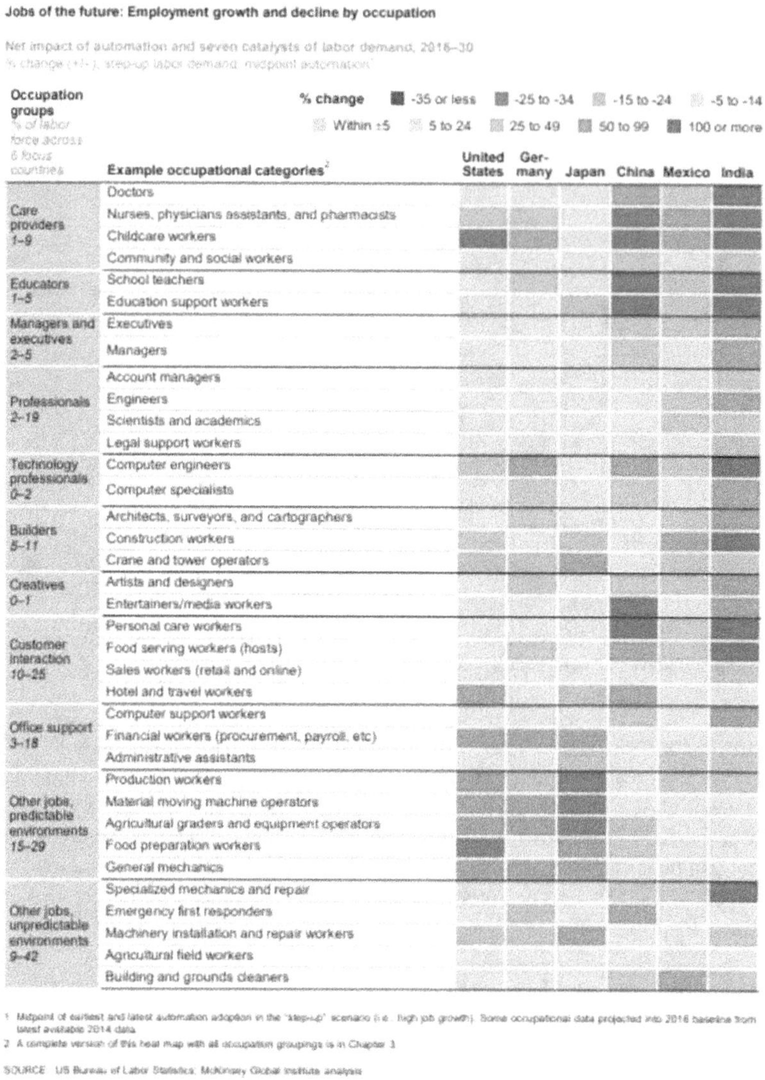

FIGURE 13.4 Jobs of the future: employment growth and decline by occupation.

Moreover, in some occupations, employment may increase if the overall demand for that particular occupation overwhelms the rates of automation (McKinsey Global Institute, 2017).

In jobs whereby machines cannot match human performance, such as social interactions, applying expertise, and managing people, automation will have little influence. Again, some other jobs that are technically difficult to automate and require low wages such as providers of child care, employees of old age homes, plumbers, or gardeners will normally be less automated by 2030 (McKinsey & Company, 2017).

13.9 Summary

The fourth digital wave of industrial revolution will significantly change the way people communicate with one another, live, work, and educate. This is possible due to smart and intelligent technologies like the Internet of Things, augmented reality, Big Data, blockchain, artificial intelligence, and automation.

Today, it is these technologies that are disrupting every industry around the globe at unmatched speed. Industry 4.0 thus inevitably implies Education 4.0, Curriculum 4.0, and Research 4.0, which requires Faculty 4.0. This technology will transform universities where education is provided as a service, which eventually turns out to be Service 4.0, which may benefit the whole world by making the prospective employees—i.e., current students—ready to face the volatile, uncertain, complex and ambiguous (VUCA) world of 2030 through acquiring the proper skill sets necessary for Industry 4.0.

REFERENCES

Akash, 2018. Is Indian education sector ready for industrial revolution 4.0? https://digitallearning.eletsonline.com/2018/12/is-indian-education-sector-ready-for-industrial-revolution-4–0/, [Accessed March 5, 2020]

Automation Alley, 2019. 7 Inspirational quotes on industry 4.0, https://automationalley.com/Blog/2019/August-2019/7-Inspirational-Quotes-on-Industry-4–0.aspx, [Accessed April 24, 2020]

Bates, A. W., 2015, Teaching in a digital age, https://opentextbc.ca/teachinginadigitalage/, [Accessed April 23, 2020]

Boston Consulting Group, Industry 4.0, www.bcg.com/en-in/capabilities/manufacturing/industry-4.0 [Accessed April 23, 2020]

Crimson Education, 2020. Top 10 jobs in 2030: Skills you should be developing! www.crimsoneducation.org/ru/blog/campus-life-more/jobs-of-the-future/, [Accessed April 23, 2020]

The Duke Perspective, 2019. Impact of industry 4.0 on education, https://sites.duke.edu/perspective/2019/03/21/impact-of-industry-4-0-on-education/, [Accessed March 6, 2020]

Jain, S., 2020. Why do students need curriculum 4.0 and faculty 4.0? www.asmaindia.in/blog/why-students-need-curriculum-4-0-and-faculty-4-0/, [Accessed April 23, 2020]

Kupper, D., 2020. Embracing industry 4.0 and rediscovering growth, https://www.my-mooc.com/en/article/embracing-industry-40-and-rediscovering-growth/, [Accessed March 18, 2020]

McKinsey Digital, 2016. Where machines could replace humans—and where they can't (yet), www.mckinsey.com/business-functions/mckinsey-digital/our-insights/where-machines-could-replace-humans-and-where-they-cant-yet, [Accessed March 20, 2020]

McKinsey & Company, 2017. Jobs lost, jobs gained: What the future of work will mean for jobs, skills, and wages, www.mckinsey.com/featured-insights/future-of-work/jobs-lost-jobs-gained-what-the-future-of-work-will-mean-for-jobs-skills-and-wages, [Accessed March 19, 2020]

McKinsey Global Institute, 2017. Jobs lost, jobs gained: Workforce transitions in a time of automation, https://www.mckinsey.com/~/media/mckinsey/industries/public%20and%20social%20sector/our%20insights/what%20the%20future%20of%20work%20will%20mean%20for%20jobs%20skills%20and%20wages/mgi-jobs-lost-jobs-gained-executive-summary-december-6-2017.pdf, 160pp., [Accessed March 24, 2020]

Pavan, C. H., 2019. Jobs lost, jobs gained: What the future of work will mean for jobs, skills, and wages, https://humanengineers.com/jobs-lost-jobs-gained-what-the-future-of-work-will-mean-for-jobs-skills-and-wages/, [Accessed April 24, 2020]

Pearce, K., 2019. The new professions: 10 High-paying careers of the future, www.diygenius.com/high-paying-careers-of-the-future/, [Accessed April 28, 2020]

Prasad, A. V. R., 2020. Importance of innovation and incubation in higher educational institutes in India, www.thehighereducationreview.com/opinion/last-word/importance-of-innovation-and-incubation-in-higher-educational-institutes-in-india-fid-41.html, [Accessed April 23, 2020]

Skills for Industry Inc., 2019, Skills for industry: Curriculum guidelines 4.0, http://skills4industry.eu/skills-industry-curriculum-guidelines-40, [Accessed April 28, 2020]

Stengar, M., 2017. 7 Ways to develop cognitive flexibility, www.opencolleges.edu.au/informed/features/7-ways-develop-cognitive-flexibility/, [Accessed April 21, 2020]

Suganya, G., 2017. A study on challenges before higher education in the emerging fourth industrial revolution, *International Journal on Engineering Technology Science and Research*, 4(10).

Suttle, R., 2020. About people management skills, https://smallbusiness.chron.com/people-management-skills-2985.html, [Accessed April 21, 2020]

Tomaszewski, M., 2020. Critical thinking skills: Definition, examples & how to improve, https://zety.com/blog/critical-thinking-skills, [Accessed April 29, 2020]

Thomas, A., 2019. How technology is shaping the future of education education 4.0, www.futurereadyedu.com/how-technology-is-shaping-the-future-of-education/, [Accessed April 24, 2020]

Wikipedia Inc., 2020a, Cognitive flexibility, https://en.wikipedia.org/wiki/Cognitive_flexibility, [Accessed April 29, 2020]

Wikipedia Inc., 2020b, Interdisciplinarity, https://en.wikipedia.org/wiki/Interdisciplinarity, [Accessed April 29, 2020]

Xing, B., and Marwala, T., 2017. Implications of the fourth industrial age on higher education, https://arxiv.org/ftp/arxiv/papers/1703/1703.09643.pdf, [Accessed March 6, 2020]

14

Gamification: A Boon for Higher Education

G. Singaravelu, and P. Janardhanakumar Reddy

CONTENTS

Objectives

1. To enrich knowledge of gamification.
2. To understand the purpose and concept of gamification.
3. To implement gamification in higher education.
4. To ensure the need for gamified curriculum.
5. To understand activities of gamification in classroom transactions.
6. To implement online learning of gamification.
7. To learn gamification blogs for teaching and learning for higher education.

DOI: 10.1201/9781003318378-14

14.1 Introduction

Gamification is applying game mechanics in non-game conditions, similar to a site, online local area, learning the executive's framework to expand more interest and contribution of the understudies. Gamification of education is an encouraging approach for increasing learners' motivation and engagement by incorporating game design elements in the environment of teaching and learning in the classroom. Gamification aims to engage the students in learning continuously and to inspire the students to be attentive with collaboration, sharing, and interaction with teachers. Gamification can eliminate the problems of the students in the hard spot of the curricula. It motivates the learners to accelerate the learning more in a limited time. The Kenan Institute effected the gamification approach in implementing courses in higher education. After the implementation of gamification elements in the teaching and learning process, many institutions of higher education written out in the classroom transactions. Outcome-based gamification is the need of the hour for Industry 4.0 and Education 4.0. Techniques of gamification are intended to leverage learners' natural desires for socializing, learning, mastery, competition, achievement, status, self-expression, altruism, or closure, or simply their response to the framing of a situation as a game or play.

14.2 Concept of Gamification

Gamification is a strategy that consists of different activities, awards, and rewards to promote and create the involvement of the students in learning. It is a contemporary educational strategy that systematically influences the various rudiments and physiognomies of gaming culture. It can be called a motivational framework of experiential learning; elements of common gamification include points, timers, badges, and leader boards. Games are communitarian or serious exercises played by a set of rules and have an ultimate objective or win-state. Learning by gamification is an instructive technique to urge understudies to learn by utilizing computer game plans, game components in e-learning conditions, and online conditions. Happiness, commitment, and edutainment through catching the premium of students and moving them to keep learning are the fundamental idea of gamification in schooling. It builds commitment by giving motivation to students to focus and finish exercises. The additional prize, regardless of whether it is theoretical, can energize better tuning in and perception. At the point when the student is engaged, they are bound to ingest the data introduced to them. The elements of gamification are shown in Figure 14.1.

14.3 Purpose of Gamification

Gamification is adding game mechanics into non-game conditions, similar to a site or online local area learning the executive's framework to expand investment. The motivation behind gamification is to draw

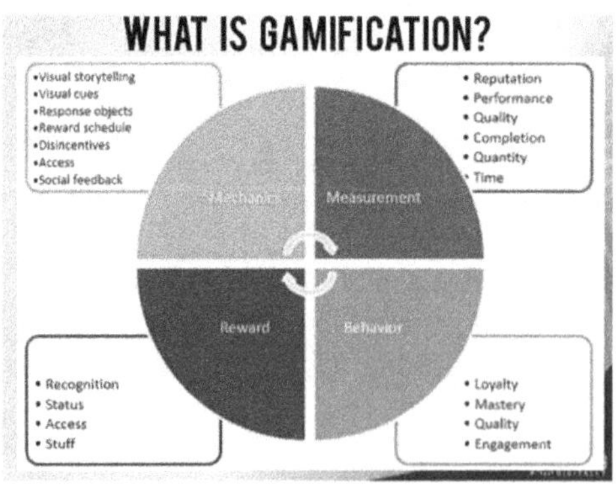

FIGURE 14.1 Gamification.

in with understudies to move cooperation, sharing and association in learning and understanding the idea. Gamification in training is the use of stylish game components into non-gaming settings (like figuring out how to improve an understudy's commitment, energy, learning, and critical thinking abilities). Gamification is the technology mingled and simplifying the teaching and learning in the classroom environment. The purpose of gamification is not the creation of the technology itself. Rather, it is the development of learning environments, motivation systems, and engagement systems; all created through meaningful decision-making, rewards, and feedback. Muntean (2011) describes it best in writing that "gamification does not mean creating a game. It means making education more fun and engaging, without undermining its credibility" (p. 32). Industry 4.0 and Education 4.0 can be enhanced in the teaching and learning process in the classroom transactions.

14.4 Gamification Theory and Learning

The gamification hypothesis in training is that students get familiar with the best when they are likewise having a good time. Not just this—they likewise learn best when they have objectives, targets, and accomplishments to go after, obviously in a way the student sees as fun. In view of the habit-forming highlights of computer games that interest kids (and grown-ups) and get them snared, it is just normal that it seemed comparable commitment results when these game-based components are applied to learning materials (Biro G., 2014).

Learning by gamification includes utilizing game-based components, such as point-scoring, peer contests, and collaboration, and score tables to drive commitment, assist understudies with acclimatizing data, and test their insight. It can apply to class-based subjects and school-based trains, but on the other hand is utilized generally in self-educating applications and courses, showing that the impacts of gamification do not stop for grown-ups. Innovation penetrates many everyday routines—it has changed the best approaches to experience, shop, work, play, eat, meet individuals, and mingle. Strategy creators are beginning to investigate the expected advantages of utilizing innovation in instructing and learning.

14.5 Gamification Eliminates Hurdles in Learning

Gamification is the need of the hour to free learners from stress and learn the content in an unpretentious way and learn at their own pace and learn with absurdity.

> Unfortunately, these days a large part of the substance that should be learned by understudies isn't straightforwardly propelling to them and the word "exhausting", or one of its socially sensitive equivalents, for example, "dry" and "specialized" regularly crosses their lips—regardless of whether the students be in school, school, companies, callings, or even the military.
>
> (Prensky, 2003, pg. 1)

14.6 Benefits of Gamification

The following benefits are enriched by gamification.

- Goal-oriented learning.
- Amusement-based learning.
- Inspire mediated learning.
- Curiosity elevated learning.
- Problem solving.
- Opportunity to design and create (coding).
- Creating friendly competition.

- Inducements and incentives.
- Brooch (A brooch is a decorative pin that fastens onto a piece of clothing. The garment you pin the brooch to supports the weight of the brooch) for achievement.
- Environmentally supporting in learning.
- Affording timely feedback.
- Community-based learning.
- Scaffolding learning as progress through a game.
- Learning is supported with audio and visuals.
- Develops learner for higher information technology (IT) skills.
- Tracking and analytics in learning.
- Flexible learning.
- Creating intrinsic motivation.
- Creating competitiveness in learning.
- Learning becomes faster.
- A feeling of students having ownership over their learning.
- Exploring different identities through different avatars or characters.
- Providing immediate feedback.
- Encouragements to become more technologically literate.
- Increasing online learning.
- Online taking in implies understudies can gain from any place and whenever.
- Introducing innovations.
- Building up student self-confidence.
- Boosting information retention of the students.
- Encouraging Continuous learning.

14.6.1 Gamification in Higher Education

In a study conducted at the University of Limerick, the students who performed best in a gamified version of their undergraduate accounting curriculum were not the top academic students but were students who were less bookish (Patrick Buckley, Elaine Doyal, 2017). This confirms that the classic learning model—lectures, final exams, and research essays—suits one group of learners, while gamification broadens the learning field by engaging the less bookish students. Further, the students who participated in the gamified accounting class reported that the new learning method better prepared them for realistic problem solving. Rather than rote memorization for an upcoming test, these students engaged with true-to-life situations and better developed the ability to approach related problems in the future. Gamification has been shown to increase engagement among adult learners in MOOCs.

14.6.2 Importance of Gamified Curriculum

More students desire to join in higher studies but opportunities to acknowledge to regular stream are very few. The nature of higher education is quickly changing due to pandemic situations that increase the number of students joining online courses. Earning while learning concepts is prevailing in the minds of adult students. This leads to massification when more individuals are pursuing higher levels of education than are necessary to replace the graduating students and fill job openings. In simpler terms, when the most recent incoming generation of college students graduate, there will likely be fewer jobs that require higher education than there are highly educated applicants. As a result of overcrowding and the pandemic situation, more students endeavour and prefer to get admission in online courses, which encourages gamified curriculum in higher education. Gamified curriculum can motivate the students

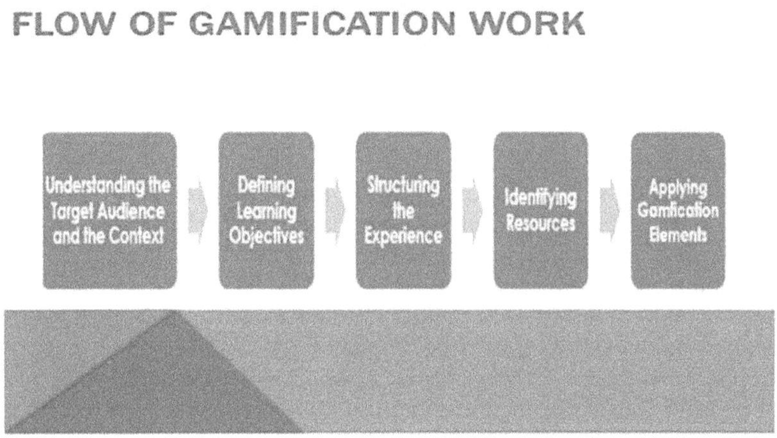

FIGURE 14.2 Flow of gamification

and eliminate the learning problems by using different gamified software. A study conducted at National Taiwan University, researchers found that among adult learners, the most motivating elements of the gamified curriculum include the ability to earn virtual goods, earn points, and appear on a leader board (Chang and Wei, 2016). In other words, elements that appeal to a learner's desire for visible and quantifiable achievement create the most engagement in a learning environment. These findings suggest that even though games at first thought may seem juvenile, our desire for measurable success—as gamification can create—is not outgrown.

14.7 Impact of Gamification in Higher Education

Following are some of the ways how gamification positively affects learning in classrooms.

1. **Accelerating and Motivating Students**
   Numerous persuasive strategies are utilized in gamification; for example, experiences and rewards that help understudies to remain enthused during the time spent learning.
2. **Encouraging Self-Regulated Learning**
   Utilizing gaming components helps in intelligently beating homework challenges and changes the customary assessment technique using an award framework.
3. **Increasing Span of Attention**
   Gamifying learning ideas in an intriguing manner (acquiring identification, giving input) makes understudies give significantly more consideration to what in particular is being taught to them.

Gamification is part of persuasive system design, and it commonly employs game design elements to improve user engagement, organizational productivity, flow, learning, crowdsourcing, knowledge retention, employee recruitment and evaluation, ease of use, the usefulness of systems, physical exercise, traffic violations, voter apathy, public attitudes about alternative energy, etc. (Figure 14.2).

14.8 Gamification in the Classroom

Fostering the procedures of gamification is fundamental in higher education with definite arranging and rebuilding of existing showing strategies by instructors. The educational programme must be patched up to coordinate the gamification in the centre papers. This strategy must be fruitful, on the off chance that it is incorporated into the educational program comprehensively. The following represents a portion of the manners by which advanced education establishments can effectively utilize gamification in their homerooms.

1. Discussing academic objectives.
2. Integrating non-academic objectives.
3. Finding barriers of the syllabus and arranging challengeable activities.
4. Creation of academic competitions among the students in the classroom.
5. Comparing and reflecting on performance in nuanced ways personalized for each student.
6. Creating rewards and awards for unique students.
7. Grading the progress of the students and providing immediate feedback.
8. Finding solutions to solve problems by using technology-based effort.
9. Permitting students to learn at their own pace by using e-learning.
10. Activating mobile learning to improve interactive learning and homework.
11. Initiating learner-centred gamification activities in the classroom.
12. Helping students assume specific perspectives in learning—as a judge, designer, etc.
13. Encouraging gadget-based learning to learn English syllables.
14. Boosting augmented reality in lab-oriented activities.
15. Accelerating video-mediated teaching drama in the classroom.
16. Cheering game-based digital learning for data analytics.
17. Entertaining teamwork.
18. Implementing gamification in grading.
19. Introducing point-based reward system.
20. Exciting game-based online courses.
21. Getting instant feedback.
22. Creating a gamified study environment.
23. Increasing participation in learning.
24. Inspiring the grasping power of late bloomers and moderate learners.

14.8.1 Gamification in MOOCs

Gamification has been exploited to play a major role in the growth and efficacy of massive open online courses (MOOCs). In these courses, which are generally free and open to anyone, retention and completion are difficult. Gamification is introduced to keep learners engaged through the completion of the material by creating learner–learner, learner–instructor, and learner–content game elements.Game elements have been shown to increase the otherwise low, 5–10% on average, completion rate of MOOCs.

Gamification categories for teaching and learning consist of courses without online support, MOOCs, blended/flipped learning courses, e-learning sites, gamified platforms/systems, and mobile learning (Figure 14.3).

14.9 Gamification Software and Apps

Gamification programming is any apparatus or stage utilized for applying game mechanics to non-game settings to support commitment and fruitful results. Gamification programming advances client commitment, persuades clients, and improves execution with fun exercises and accomplishments. An expert is a gamification instrument for educators.

1. Engagement—learning platform for mobile devices.
2. Quizizz—interactive learning platform.
3. Playbooks—incorporating artificial intelligence.

The utilization of gamification methodologies in instruction can empower and draw in the understudies of advanced education with course content, which are the fundamental contentions supporting

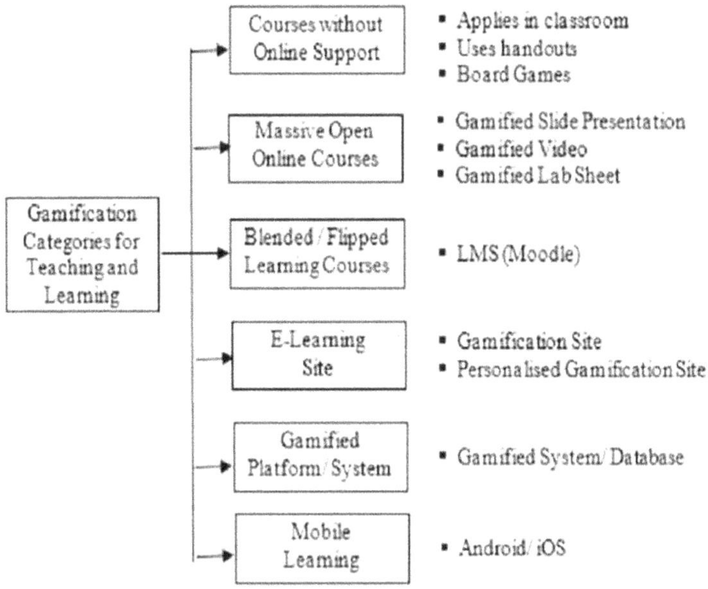

FIGURE 14.3 Categories of gamification.

their reception. In other words, they can make learning more appealing and fun, and hence—eventually—more viable. Gamification applications include Gimkit, ClassDojo, Book widgets, TETED, Khan Academy, Coursera, Udemy, Blinkist, Memrise, Solo Learn, Duolingo, etc.

Gamification is the application of game elements and digital game design techniques to non-game problems, such as business and social impact challenges. This content will teach the mechanisms of gamification (Figure 14.4).

14.10 Implementing Gamification in Online Learning

14.10.1 Inducing Out-of-the Box Thinking

A well-planned gamified course is something beyond rules and constructions. It centres on the learning measurements as opposed to the diversion esteem. Gamified exercises and activities energize inside-and-out reasoning. Distinctive game components and rewards—for example, pioneer sheets, identifications, and so forth—support joint effort and out-of-the-box thinking.

14.10.2 Elaborating Span of Attention

Game-based online courses keep understudies spurred and increase their ability to focus to keep replacements with more limited abilities to focus captured for long. The objectives, challenges at various levels, and rewards make the learning cycle seriously intriguing. These exercises rebuild the perspective and increment cerebrum work.

14.10.3 Encouraging Accomplishment

Any movement or undertaking gets exhausting if there is no feeling of achievement. The equivalent applies to instruction. When there's no sense of achievements in understudies, learning can get exhausting. Gamification can assist with keeping understudies propelled for a more extended timeframe.

FIGURE 14.4 Perspectives and effects of gamification.

Components like focuses, rewards, and endowments urge students to contend and try sincerely after each level.

14.10.4 Creating a Healthy Competition

Gamification can make a bunch of objectives for the understudies to select them in a collecting contest. Joining bunch rewards, focuses, may encourage solid rivalry between understudy gatherings.

14.11 Gamification Blogs for Teaching and Learning

14.11.1 Games and Learning

Games and Learning is a lively site that aggregates statistical surveying, investigation, and the most recent reports on the gamification of instruction. Through representing the advantages, just as snags are confronted, the site helps illustrate what it will take to get games additionally coordinated into innovation (ResearchGate, 2022).

14.11.2 TeachThought

Instruct Thought has target materials for improving your showing style and talks about gamification in the study hall, alongside flipped homerooms and their advantages and downsides (TeachThought, 2022).

14.11.3 Game Learn

Game Learn comprehends the gigantic potential for improving instructive norms through gamification and plans natural games to improve things; for example, using time effectively and exchange abilities. The ways for making gamification interesting to the audience and examples for gamification are given by Zicherman G (2010).

14.12 McDonald's Gamification Features

The McDonald's Monopoly game is a sales promotion run by fast food restaurant chain McDonald's, with a theme based on the Hasbro board game Monopoly. The game first ran in the U.S. in 1987 and has since been used worldwide.

- **Realistic game mechanics:** stories were created for emotional engagement; setting (restaurant), characters (customers), and narrative (orders) were created.
- **Gaming elements:** like lifelines, bonuses, and challenges were incorporated to engage the learner. Sound effects and voice modulations helped in creating a gaming feel.
- **Instant feedback:** learner's choices were analysed in real time, and instant feedback was provided.
- **Stop the clock:** learners could stop the clock and answer questions.
- **Time machine:** they used the term "time machine" innovatively in business training; what it meant is that if you fail a question, you could go back and try again.
- **Different levels:** there were different levels that an employee would have to go through to earn rewards.

REFERENCES

Biro, G. (2014). Didactics 2.0: A Pedagogical Analysis of Gamification Theory from a Comparative Perspective with a Special View to the Components of Learning. *Procedia—Social and Behavioral Sciences*, 141, 148–151.

Chang, J. W., & Wei, H. Y. (2016). Exploring engaging gamification mechanics in massive online open courses. *Journal of Educational Technology & Society*, 19(2), 177–203. https://eric.ed.gov/?id=EJ1097207.

Muntean, C. (2011). Raising Engagement in E learning through Gammification. Proceedings of the 6th International Conference on Virtual Learning/Cluj-Napoca, Romana.

Patrick Buckley, Elaine Doyal, (2017). Game on student' perceptions of gamified learning. *Educational Technology & Society*, 20(3), 1–10.

Prensky, M. (2003). Digital Game-Based Learning. *Computers in Entertainment (CIE)*, 1(1), 21–21.

ResearchGate, 2022, https://www.researchgate.net/publication/343341464_Gamification_in_Education, 16 Nov 2022.

TeachThought, 2022, https://www.teachthought.com/the-future-of-learning/examples-gamification/ 16 Nov 2022.

Zicherman. G., (2010). Fun is the Future: Mastering Gamification [Video file]. https://files.eric.ed.gov/fulltext/EJ1143830.pdf

15

Curriculum 4.0 for Incorporating Industry 4.0 Tools in Higher Education

P. Kaliraj, T. Devi, V. Bhuvaneswari, T. Amudha, R. Rajeswari, J. Satheeshkumar, M. Punithavalli, and S. Sarala

CONTENTS

DOI: 10.1201/9781003318378-15

Objectives

As an outcome of reading this chapter, the learner will gain knowledge on the following.

1. New higher education degree programmes.
2. Courses and the corresponding syllabi relevant to Industry 4.0 in education to realise the vision for the next ten years.
3. Guidelines for incorporating Industry 4.0 tools across various disciplines of arts and science education.
4. Guidance for framing curriculum.

15.1 Introduction

The Fifth Industrial Revolution, Industry 5.0, is changing the world around us. Industry 5.0 is a future but already penetrating trend of change processes directed towards closer cooperation between humans and machines, and systematic prevention of waste and wasting including industrial upcycling. There are two common themes in each phase of industrial evolution: speed and energy. From the start, the race in technological revolution is always about achieving speed by exploiting energy sources—speed from mechanical automation to mass-scale cognitive automation, and energy exploitation from steam power to, nowadays, nuclear power. Growing clamour about sustainability and the environment will push leaders towards looking for alternative means for achieving both speed and energy. It is believed that new innovations will be about industrial transformation in the face of even faster and scalable production in a sustainable manner. Technology-wise, evolution of 5G (fifth-generation broadband networks) and quantum computing will play significant roles in achieving the speed factor, along with industrial innovations in energy production, distribution, and consumption.

The modern world is already moving on in the age of Industry 4.0, a term that stands for the Fourth Industrial Revolution characterized by automation of all kinds of processes, artificial intelligence (AI) in all spheres of life, robotics, and endless possibilities that technology opens up (Kaliraj and Devi, 2022a). Education imparted should always align with the contemporary advancements of modern world. The problem of what knowledge to impart to make the students ready for Industry 4.0 will be addressed in this chapter. The details of courses in this chapter can be used for framing the curriculum of higher education programmes. This chapter will be a great boon as a guide, as it will guide the educationists to design courses and to use the materials given in this book for framing syllabi and curricula, and for teaching and learning. By teaching the courses with the syllabi mentioned in this chapter, students will gain exposure to Industry 4.0 tools, case studies, and applications of Industry 4.0 tools in various verticals. Also, it gives the fundamental knowledge on Industry 4.0 tools and their linkages with higher education, Industries such as Insurance, Healthcare, agriculture through use cases and case studies.

15.2 Tools of Industry 4.0

AI and machine learning, automation and robotics, Big Data, Internet of Things (IoT), augmented reality (AR) and virtual reality (VR), and creativity are the tools of Industry 4.0. The Fourth and Fifth Industrial

Revolutions are affecting the roles that Indian universities and colleges prepare students for, and educational institutions are ideally placed to help produce the workforce for this new world and the student experience to match it. It is necessary to align higher education with Industry 4.0 and 5.0 through education on the tools of Industry 4.0 and 5.0. It is also very essential to impart the skills that are necessary to develop the students to face the volatile, uncertain, complex, and ambiguous (VUCA) world around us. Thus, awareness and practice on Industry 4.0 and 5.0 tools and skill development to face a VUCA world and technological advanced infrastructure become the keys for successful development of future pillars of our globe. Linking Industry 4.0 and 5.0 with arts and science education is the need of the hour.

Today, the rate at which the transformation happening is very disruptive in nature, and exponential changes are being witnessed. We have already witnessed how many conventional business models and technologies got disrupted in the last few years. Technologies such as AI, machine learning, robotic learning, AR, and VR are mutating very quickly. Industry 4.0 is getting fast forwarded due to some of these drivers. Educational institutions have to be way ahead of the requirement and prepare their students to meet the new challenges to be created by Industry 5.0. Currently, educational institutions are at a crossroads and do not know how to interweave the Industry 4.0 tools into the arts, science, social science, and teacher education programme in universities. This chapter gives them a direction.

The administrators of the higher education system are looking for ways and means to align the education with Industry 4.0 and Industry 5.0 to make their students understand developments such as process automation, intelligent systems through AI and Big Data, and IoT in the industrial sector. There is not enough literature on how to design the programmes and courses for their interdisciplinary nature; i.e., process automation in healthcare, machine learning for economy and policy decision making, IoT in education, and AI and IoT in insurance knowledge are to be imparted to the students, scholars, and teaching community.

15.2.1 Big Data and Data Analytics

Big Data analytics has gained attention after the advent of social networking in 2010 and evolved as an important technology for analyzing huge volumes of data. Data has tremendously increased in large volumes generated by business and individual users through social networking platforms accumulated as data silos in structured and unstructured formats. Traditional computing environments faced the limitation in analyzing this complex huge volume of datasets and require high computational resources with huge investments. Big Data analytics platforms provide solutions by analyzing the huge data using commodity hardware without high investment. Google and Yahoo are the pioneers in devising the Big Data processing architecture Hadoop, which overcome the limitations of the traditional computing environment. Big Data analytics is as well used as tool to gather understanding based on the patterns from the data silos which are used in various business domains to gain deep insights about their customers and past operational data, and to augment the data warehouses. Big Data analytics is used by e-commerce organizations as a marketing tool by identifying the customers' requirements based on click streams and recommend products. Big Data analytics using AI in the aviation industry has enormous insights as streaming data from various sources such as weather, aircraft engine data, flight data, and customer data integrated to provide insights on fuel efficiency, aircraft maintenance, cargo maintenance, and ticket prediction.

15.2.2 Artificial Intelligence (AI)

AI is a quite inevitable and essential technology in today's world. AI is everywhere and it plays a significant role in various aspects of life. AI can be seen as a part of robotic automation, self-driving cars, health care and medical support, defence, online shopping, and many other technologies (Kaliraj and Devi, 2022a). This course will enable readers to gain a systematic understanding of AI from the history and fundamentals to the future applications and tools. It also emphasizes the challenges of AI faced by the technology developers and practitioners. This course will serve as a great starting point for beginners to learn and understand AI, regardless of their diverse domains.

15.2.3 Automation

Automation is a buzzword in the technological arena which leads to massive transformation in the manufacturing sector, with enabling technologies such as AI, robotic processes, machine learning and data analytics. Automation reduces the workload of humans by employing machines to perform repetitive, time-consuming, and complex tasks. Nowadays, smart machines are capable of analyzing and learning from their assigned tasks, expand their knowledge base and are even more capable of applying the acquired knowledge rationally in decision making, thereby reducing human intervention. The fundamental aspects to be identified by every industry before shifting to automation are: (i) potential areas of automation; (ii) feasibility and scalability factors of automation; and (iii) the extent to which automation can be made in order to reap the benefits without significantly affecting the existing industrial ecosystem. Process automation can be adopted to any type of business, based on the organizational requirements, availability of resources, and constraints. Today, many enterprise solutions are readily available for automation, which can provide high level of integration efficiency with minimal disruption to the existing organizational setup.

15.2.4 Robotic Process Automation

Robotic process automation (RPA) is used to design software robots that can automate the tasks of interacting with digital systems (Javed et al., 2021). Examples of tasks that are performed by software robots include extraction of data from web pages, filling forms, preparing reports, managing files, interpretation of texts, chat and conversations with customers, and decision making. These tasks can be categorized as repetitive and voluminous tasks, as well as tasks which require critical thinking. The software robots are intended to carry out both categories of tasks and hence help in improving the productivity and efficiency in companies. There are a number of tools used for RPA; UiPath is one of the most popular tools.

15.2.5 Internet of Things (IoT)

IoT is a collection of physical objects with sensors, software, and other technologies which have the capability to communicate with each other via the internet. These objects include smartphones, computers, laptops, smart watches, cars, televisions, refrigerators, and washing machines. The characteristics of these IoT devices are that they are based on different types of platforms. It has been estimated by Statista Research Department (2016) that the number of IoT devices in the world will be approximately 75.44 billion by 2025. IoT is one of the key players to enhance the quality of manufacturing process and products in industries. The usage of IoT for industries is known as Industrial IoT (IIoT). With IIoT, machines have the capability to monitor themselves, which in turn increases their efficiency. IIoT also helps in managing inventory, which in turn decreases the wastage and in ensuring that necessary goods are always available. IIoT will help in automatically understanding the consumers' interests and in making appropriate changes in the marketing strategies of retail stores (Kaliraj and Devi, 2022c).

The world has already moved to Industry 4.0. Students graduating from higher education institutions should be equipped with skills so that they can take up a career in Industry 5.0. It is essential to integrate all the key technologies including AI, AR/VR (Kaliraj and Devi, 2022b), Big Data analytics, cloud computing, IoT, and robotics in the curriculum of higher education. IoT can be integrated into the curriculum of higher education depending on the programmes that they have enrolled. All graduates should be made aware of the basic concepts of IoT, so that they become aware of the IoT devices around them. The graduates who would take up active careers in Industry 5.0 should be given hands-on experience also so that they themselves can create and use IoT systems.

15.3 Learning

The three domains of learning, according to Bloom's Taxonomy, also known as KSA—knowledge, skills, and attitude (Kaur, 2019) are: (i) cognitive domain, focused on **k**nowledge; (ii) psychomotor domain, focused on **s**kills; and (iii) affective domain, focused on **a**ttitude.

Cognitive domain focuses on knowledge and comprises six sub-categories: knowledge, comprehension, application, analysis, synthesis, and evaluation. The first three—knowledge, comprehension, and application—involve low-order thinking skills; analysis, synthesis, and evaluation involve high-order thinking skills. The new version of learning is classified as remembering, understanding, applying, analyzing, evaluating, and creating.

Psychomotor domain is also called kinaesthetic domain, and relates to natural, autonomic responses or reflexes. There are models of psychomotor domain: perception set, guided response, mechanism, and complex overt response—to know what will be the result immediately after performance, adaptation, and origination.

Affective domain was proposed by Krathwohl et al. (1973). It is concerned with feelings and emotions, which can be arranged as receiving, responding, valuing, organization, and characterization.

The levels of learning are classified as listening, reading, reflecting, assimilating, and implementing.

15.3.1 Lecture Listening

An oral presentation of the lesson by the teacher is known as lecture, it is considered as the most ancient method of instruction. It is used for addressing larger groups, and it is economical, as more information can be provided to students in a short span of time. Students listen and learn through the flow of information given by the teachers (Kaur, 2019).

15.3.2 Demonstration Learning

Demonstration means explaining or showing students the practical working of any procedure or object. It is most commonly used in teaching different subjects where demonstration is needed to help boost the interest of students, which enhances understanding of the topic. Students remain more active while watching demonstrations (Kaur, 2019).

15.3.3 Heuristic Learning

This type of learning was proposed by Armstrong (1902); the word heuristic means "to find". This makes students to learn curiously by discovery, instead of receiving information. Students should try to explore, explain, describe it gives purposeful experience, self-thinking, self-study, etc. The teacher gives a topic or problem to students and they have to find the solution using a library, a laboratory, online resources, seminars, or workshops (Kaur, 2019).

15.3.4 Flipped Classroom

In this modern concept, teachers record their lectures and share them with students, so it has been named "flipped classroom" since 2007. Students can study video lectures and handouts at their own pace. There can be better discussions on assignments in the classroom (Kaur, 2019).

15.3.5 Kinaesthetic Learning

Hands-on learning, or tactile learning, places more emphasis on physical activities instead of lectures or demonstration. Students learn by experiences, role playing, drama, sports, drawing, etc. It helps students to retain what they have learnt so that students learn with greater interest and curiosity (Kaur, 2019).

15.3.6 Discussion

Discussion acts as a better source of learning than lecturing or explaining, as discussion involves two-way communication and lecture involves only one-way communication. Discussions can enhance confidence of students if they are encouraged to speak. There is a tendency of high student participation in discussions. It also improves communication skills, critical thinking, creative thinking, etc., of students.

15.3.7 Team Teaching

In team teaching, not only one teacher plans the class activity; rather, two or more teachers plan the activities, aids, and evaluation strategies for the same set of students. It encourages friendship among teachers, which will bring positivity in the learning environment. This process is helpful for interdisciplinary approach to teaching and learning.

15.3.8 Open Learning

Open learning is a form of learning in which there are no barriers of age, place, time, etc. Students can learn wherever and whenever they wish to. Learning is the responsibility of students. Open learning is a student-centred approach to learning. It is helpful for those students who cannot attend regular classes. There are no restrictions on learning; it has greater flexibility.

15.3.9 Project/Activity-Based Learning

This is also a part of many degree programmes. Students conduct research, carry out surveys, and then present the findings of research in the form of a report. It helps students to learn and prepare the projects on their own.

15.3.10 Panel Discussion

Subject experts are invited for panel discussion where students will get to learn from experts in the field. By observing the discussion, students will learn how to communicate their ideas and viewpoints.

15.3.11 Brainstorming

This is marked by spontaneity—students have to share their opinion or idea about the topic. The views presented by the students during the session are not subject to criticism. It has greater scope for participation with large groups, and as such boosts creativity, confidence, and innovation whereby learning happens from the group.

15.3.12 Programmed Instruction

This addresses individual differences by providing immediate feedback to students on correct answers to the solved questions. Learning by doing principle is used in this type of learning, which can also be used in the absence of the teacher.

15.3.13 Role Playing

Students are assigned with different roles and made aware of different perople and their perspectives. This helps in sharpening the critical thinking, creative thinking, debating, negotiating, and reasoning ability of students. Role playing can be used effectively to shape the attitude of students.

15.3.14 Simulation

Simulation is also a form of role playing, but it is based on experimental learning whereby students learn in an environment similar to real-life situations. It develops problem-solving abilities in students, mainly focused on skill development.

15.3.15 Computer-Assisted Learning

With the use of technology, learning has become much faster as compared to when using traditional techniques. It makes learning active, efficient, easier, and more convenient by the use of modern technology.

15.3.16 Game-Based Learning

Learning is imparted with the use of games, which increases student participation and also boosts their interests. There are gaming applications for building vocabulary and practising typing, and also, great technologies like AR offer students game-based platforms for simulation learning.

15.3.17 Seminars

In almost all educational institutes, seminars are organized every year. It is a great source of information, as the experts of a particular field present the topics and the information received is authentic. Students participating in seminars get to know about research activities and improve the presentation skills.

15.3.18 Tutorials

The student presents and the teacher supervises the presentation, which is followed by a question-and-answer session, when other students can ask queries; if the presenter is not able to resolve the queries, the teacher can help. This sharpens the communication skills of students.

15.3.19 Assignments

This classroom activity which helps in self-learning as an extension of classroom learning. Students learn time management skills by working with deadlines. Students have flexibility in completing it at their own convenience—but before the deadline.

15.3.20 Case Studies

Case studies based on real-life situations are assigned to the students, defined by actual situations—usually involving a decision, a challenge, an opportunity, a problem, an issue, or a controversy affecting a company or person. This boosts creativity, critical thinking, communication, interpersonal relations, and time management skills in students. These bridge the gap between the theoretic and the practical—that is, students learn to apply theory to tackle real-life situations.

15.4 Digital Classroom and E-Learning Tools

The advent of information and communication technology (ICT) has transformed traditional classroom into digital classrooms (Kaur, 2019). A digital classroom improves teaching and learning processes by providing a conducive environment for interaction between teachers and students. Digital classrooms will play a crucial role in the forthcoming years in the teaching learning process of higher education. There are a number of tools used for e-learning (Ekaran, 2018). These tools help in creation and management of course content, content delivery, assessment of students, and tracking the progress of courses undertaken by students. The tools for e-learning include Socrative, Scratch, Prezi, SelfCAD, Quizlet, Google Classroom, Adobe Spark Video, Khan Academy, SeeSaw, ClassDojo, MOOCs, SWAYAM, SWAYAM PRABHA, CEC, ePathshala, NPTEL, ICT-based tools, and audio-visual aids.

15.4.1 Socrative

Socrative is a cloud-based student response system, allowing teachers to immediately test student understanding by way of mini-quizzes assigned to them on class laptops or tablets (Ekaran, 2018).

15.4.2 Scratch

Scratch users can combine music, graphics, and photos to create interactive games, animations, and slideshows. All of their creations are shareable with others in a student's online community (Ekaran, 2018).

15.4.3 Prezi

Prezi is a cloud-based presentation software used for creating, giving, and tracking interactive presentations. Prezi presentations are nothing like traditional presentations, instead zooming in and out and moving side to side across one single, very attractive and modern canvas, focusing in on images and videos inputted by the user (Ekaran, 2018).

15.4.4 SelfCAD

SelfCAD is free and a cloud-based three-dimensional (3D) computer-assisted design (CAD) software package for students. It is incredibly easy to use, yet provides an authentic, "real world" 3D design experience and also provides a database of already completed 3D printable designs, making thousands of 3D objects available for immediate 3D printing (Ekaran, 2018).

15.4.5 Quizlet

Quizlet provides a platform for students and teachers to create and share their own learning materials, including flashcards and diagrams. It also provides interactive games, and students must all contribute, stay focused, and communicate well to win (Ekaran, 2018).

15.4.6 Google Classroom

Google Classroom is a powerful community-based social tool for learning. It allows students to post questions and receive answers from their teachers and fellow students. Furthermore, teachers can post intriguing questions and lesson materials for review at home (Ekaran, 2018).

15.4.7 Adobe Spark Video

This application enables students to produce short animated, narrated explainer videos. Students can easily add photos, video clips, icons, and voice, as well as professional-quality soundtracks and cinematic motion to their video creations. Video and vlog making is a great way to engage students creatively, and an "out of the box" approach to class projects or reviewing learning materials (Ekaran, 2018).

15.4.8 Khan Academy

Lessons are presented by way of videos, interactive activities, and challenges. Learners also earn badges in line with their achievements and can save their progress to their own profile. Khan Academy is a great way to supplement your teaching, provide extra work to your gifted and talented students, or help those who are struggling with certain content (Ekaran, 2018).

15.4.9 SeeSaw

SeeSaw is an easy-to-use learning portfolio application, enabling students to document, showcase, and reflect on what they are learning at school. Work can be made accessible to parents, as well (Ekaran, 2018).

15.4.10 ClassDojo

ClassDojo is a free classroom communication, community building, and behaviour management application. A well-behaved student body is associated with better learning for everyone in the class, as it minimizes distractions and improves student focus. ClassDojo enables teachers to not only track behaviour and share this with parents, but also assign students tasks which build positive behavioural skills and traits (Ekaran, 2018).

15.4.11 MOOCs

Massive open online courses (MOOCs) are online courses that available free of cost. Such courses are taught by prestigious Indian and foreign institutes on platforms such as MOT OCW, SWAYAM, edX, Udacity, and Coursera. Anyone can enrol in a course of their choice without any restrictions on the qualifications. Online courses comprise videos, course handouts, suggested readings, and online tests.

15.4.12 SWAYAM

Study webs of active learning for young aspiring minds (SWAYAM) is a MOOC-based initiative by the Indian government, whereby courses from prestigious institutes are available online. Students can enrol in these courses free of cost.

15.4.13 SWAYAM PRABHA

SWYAM PRABHA is a set of 34 DTH channels which telecast high-quality educational programmes using the GSAT-15 satellite. The website of SWAYAM PRABHA https://www.swayamprabha.gov.in/ is maintained by INFLIBNET Centre. New content is telecast everyday for at least four hours and it is then repeated five times—totalling 24 hours—so that students can learn at a time of their convenience that day.

15.4.14 CEC

The Consortium for Educational Communication (CEC) was set up in 1993 by the University Grants Commission (UGC). It is an inter-university centre and the nodal agency to coordinate, guide, and facilitate the production of educational content at the national level through its network. It streams live as well as recorded sessions available on YouTube. Students can interact with teachers through text mode, over the telephone, or through videoconferencing.

15.4.15 ePathshala

This is a platform which supports a collection of a wide range of educational e-resources including textbooks, audio, video, periodicals, and other materials. It can be used by teachers, researchers, educators, and students.

15.4.16 NPTEL

National Programme on Technology Enhanced Learning (NPTEL), a joint initiative by the Indian Institutes of Technology (IITs) and Indian Institute of Science (IISc) for improving the quality of teaching by providing online content which can be used by teachers and students. It helps to use courses to plan the classroom lectures.

15.4.17 ICT-Based tools

Online solutions like Google Classroom make it possible to share online content with students, have discussions, receive assignments, and conduct online tests.

15.4.18 Audio-Visual Aids

These include recordings, slides, charts, posters, pictures, graphs, maps, mind maps, diagrams, display boards, summary cards, and projectors.

TABLE 15.1

New Degree Programmes in Industry 4.0

Undergraduate Programmes	Postgraduate Programmes
B.Sc. Data Analytics	M.Sc. Data Analytics
B.Sc. Artificial Intelligence	M.Sc. Artificial Intelligence
B.Sc. Cybersecurity	M.Sc. Cybersecurity
B.B.M. Learning Management	M.B.A. Learning Management
B.B.A. Learning Management	M.B.A. Industry 5.0
B.Com. Finance Analytics	M.Com. Finance Analytics
B.Com. Business Analytics	M.Com. Business Analytics

15.5 New Degree Programmes and Courses

In order to meet the challenges of aligning education with Industry 4.0, it becomes necessary to create specialized knowledge pools. Hence, undergraduate and post graduate programmes for digital transformation as below become very essential. Table 15.1 shows the new undergraduate and postgraduate programmes in Industry 4.0 that can be offered in higher education institutions. The programmes will offer specific courses related to the concepts and tools of Industry 4.0.

15.5.1 New Courses

It is necessary to introduce new courses for Industry 4.0 technologies as specified in Table 15.1. Industry 4.0 transforms all domains and sectors into smart factories through automation. Automation replaces the repetitive tasks, which generate boredom for the job aspirants, but will not take away the opportunities but replace their skills as technology based. It is important to equip learners with the basic operating technological skills required for Industry 4.0. All the technologies run using the fuel of data which is an important components to drive the insights, solutions, and challenges. The new courses for Industry 4.0 skills set are presented in Table 15.2. A mapping of the digital transformation technology, i.e., Industry 4.0, components onto the various subject areas or departments of science, social science, humanities, and arts is shown in Table 15.2.

15.5.1.1 General Courses on Industry 4.0

- Introduction to Industry 4.0
- Advancements in Industry 4.0

TABLE 15.2

Tools of Industry 4.0 as Courses in the Departments

Name of the Industry 4.0 tool	Name of the Departments
Big Data and Data Analytics	Commerce, Social Science, Management, Social Work, Economics, Applied Maths, Women's Studies, Bio-informatics, Environment Science, Biotechnology, Extension and Career Guidance, Physical Education, Human Genetics, Statistics, Maths, Psychology, Computer Science
Internet of Things (IoT)	Environment Science, Physics, Medical Physics, Nanotechnology, Electronics and Instrumentation, Computer Science
Augmented Reality	Chemistry, Textiles, Communication and Media Studies, Education Technology, Education, Computer Science
Artificial Intelligence	All Departments
Robotic Process Automation	All Departments

15.5.1.2 Big Data and Data Analytics Courses

- Programming Essentials—Basics
- Data Management Using SQL
- Introduction to SQL Programming
- R Programming for Social Science
- R Programming for Text Analytics
- Python Programming
- Big Data Analytics using SPARK
- Advanced Data Analytics Using R
- Web scrapping Using Python
- Data Visualization Using R and Python
- Basics of Machine Learning
- Machine Learning Applications
- Statistics for Data Analytics and Machine Learning
- Data Analytics for Social Sciences
- Principles of Data Science
- Data Analytics for Health Care
- Machine Learning Using Python
- Data Analytics for Education
- Behavioural Analytics Using Sentiment Analysis
- Opinion Mining for Marketing
- Clinical Data Analytics
- Introduction to Data Integration Basics
- Sports Analytics
- Python Programming for Bio-Informatics
- Big Data Analytics Biological Databases
- Business Analytics
- Advanced Business Analytics using R

15.5.1.3 Artificial Intelligence Courses

- Artificial Intelligence
- Basics of Machine Learning
- Machine Learning Applications
- Artificial Intelligence Using TensorFlow
- Python for Artificial Intelligence
- Natural Language Processing
- Speech Processing
- Reinforcement Learning
- AI in Healthcare
- AI in Finance and Economics
- AI in Automobiles
- Knowledge Management
- Human Computer Interaction
- Bio-Inspired Computing

- Agent-Based Computing
- Evolutionary Computing
- Deep Learning
- Fundamentals of Robotics (actual robots, not soft bots, similar to using Lego Mindstorms, EV3 core set)

15.5.1.4 Robotic Process Automation (RPA) Courses

- Process Automation Using UiPath
- Artificial Intelligence and Robotic Process Automation for Biological Sciences
- Robotic Process Automation
- Robotic Process Automation Design and Development
- Robotic Process Automation for Business

15.5.1.5 Internet of Things (IoT) Courses

- Basics of Electronics
- Introduction to the Internet of Things
- Arduino Platform and C Programming
- Raspberry Pi and Python Programming
- Developing Java-Embedded Applications using Raspberry Pi
- Programming with Cloud IoT Platforms
- Internet of Things: Sensing and Actuation from Devices
- Internet of Things: Networks and Protocols
- Internet of Things and Smart Cities
- Internet of Things for Executives
- Cybersecurity and Internet of Things
- Internet of Things in Healthcare
- Industrial Internet of Things
- Big Data Analytics and Internet of Things

15.5.1.6 Creativity, Design Thinking, and Problem Solving Courses

- Design Thinking
- Creativity and Design Thinking for Problem Solving
- Human to Machine Interaction

15.6 Learning Path—Industry 4.0 Skill Sets—Scheme

Industry 4.0 has been adopted by almost all industries and is changing the skill sets required by students for jobs in the near future. It is very essential to equip students with the knowledge of various Industry 4.0 tools. Various courses are designed by Bharathiar University for undergraduate and postgraduate programmes to incorporate the knowledge of Industry 4.0 tools such as AI, Big Data, AI, and IoT among students. The schemes and syllabi of these courses are given in this section. The abbreviation "UG" means undergraduate and "PG" means post-graduate; "T" represents theory and "P" represents practicals. Table 15.3 enumerates the courses that can be offered at the undergraduate level in the commerce and management streams. Table 15.4 enumerates the courses that can be offered at the postgraduate level in the commerce and management streams. Table 15.5 presents the courses that can be offered at the postgraduate level in the Social Science, Sociology, Social Work, Psychology and Women's Studies streams.

15.6.1 UG—Commerce and Management

TABLE 15.3

Course for UG—Commerce and Management

S.No	Subject	Credits	T/P	Semester
1	Industry 4.0	4	T	1 or 2
2	Introduction to Databases	4	T	1
3	Data Manipulation Using SQL		P	2
4	Big Data Analytics		T	2
5	Data Analytics Using R	4	P	3
6	Artificial Intelligence	4	T	3
Electives				
1	AI—Robotic Process Automation (UIPATH)—E	4	P	4
2	Advanced Data Analytics Using R	4	P	
3	Sentiment Analysis	4	P	
4	Android Programming	4	P	

15.6.2 PG—Commerce and Management

TABLE 15.4

Course for PG—Commerce and Management

S.No	Subject	Credits	T/P	Semester
1	Industry 4.0	4	T	1 or 2
2	Big Data Analytics	4	T	1
3	Programming Essentials for Data Analytics	4	P	2
4	Artificial Intelligence	4	T	2
5	Data Analytics Using R	4	P	3
6	Robotic Process Automation (UIPATH)	4	P	3
7	Elective			
Electives				
1	Advanced Data Analytics Using R	4	P	
2	Sentiment Analysis	4	P	

15.6.3 PG—Social Science, Sociology, Social Work, Psychology, Women's Studies

TABLE 15.5

Course for PG—Social Science, Sociology, Social Work, Psychology and Women's Studies

S.No	Subject	Credits	T/P	Semester
1	Industry 4.0	4	T	1 or 2
2	Database Management Systems	4	T	1
3	Big Data Analytics	4	T	2
4	Data Manipulation Using SQL	4	P	2
5	Artificial Intelligence	4	T	3

S.No	Subject	Credits	T/P	Semester
6	Data Analytics Using R	4	P	3
7	Text Analytics	4	P	
8	Elective			
Electives				
1	Advanced Data Analytics Using R (unstructured Data)	4	P	
2	Sentiment Analysis	4	P	
3	Robotic Process Automation (UIPATH)	4	P	

15.6.4 Linguistics, English

Table 15.6 shows the courses that can be offered in the Linguistics and English streams. Table 15.7 enumerates the courses that can be offered in the Physics and Chemistry streams. Table 15.8 presents the courses that can be offered in the Life Sciences streams, including Botany, Zoology, and Textiles. Table 15.9 lists the courses that can be offered in the Biotechnology, Environmental Sciences, Human Genetics, and Bio-Informatics streams. Table 15.10 enumerates the courses that can be offered in the Physical Education stream. Table 15.11 presents the courses that can be offered in the Mathematics, Applied Mathematics, and Statistics streams. These courses will make the students aware of the digital transformations that are being made in their respective streams. They can also use the Industry 4.0 tools they have learnt to drive the changes of Industry 4.0.

TABLE 15.6

Courses—Linguistics and English

S.No	Subject	Credits	T/P	Semester
1	Industry 4.0	4	T	1 or 2
2	Database Management Systems	4	T	1
3	Text Analytics	4	T	2
4	Artificial Intelligence	4	T	2
5	Electives			
Elective				
1	Sentiment Analysis	4	P	
2	Robotic Process Automation (UIPATH)	4	P	

15.6.5 Physics, Chemistry

TABLE 15.7

Courses—Physics and Chemistry

S.No	Subject	Credits	T/P	Semester
1	Industry 4.0	4	T	1 or 2
2	Introduction to Data Science	4	T	1
3	Python Programming	4	P	2
4	Artificial Intelligence	4	T	2
5	Internet of Things	4	P	
6	Elective			
Electives				
1	Applied Machine Learning	4	P	
2	Robotic Process Automation (UIPATH)	4	P	

15.6.6 Life Sciences: Botany, Zoology, Textiles

TABLE 15.8

Courses—Life Sciences

S.No	Subject	Credits	T/P	Semester
1	Industry 4.0	4	T	1 or 2
2	Introduction to Databases SQL Programming	4	P	1
3	Artificial Intelligence	4	T	2
4	Data Analytics Using R	4	P	2
Electives				
1	Genomic Data Analytics Using R Programming	4	P	3
2	Robotic Process Automation (UIPATH)	4	P	
For Textiles (in Addition to the Above)				
3	Augmented Reality	4	P	

15.6.7 Biotechnology, Environmental Sciences, Human Genetics, Bio-Informatics

TABLE 15.9

Courses—Biotechnology, Environmental Sciences, Human Genetics, Bio-Informatics

S.No	Subject	Credits	T/P	Semester
1	Industry 4.0	4	T	1 or 2
2	Python Programming	4	T	1
3	Artificial Intelligence	4	P	2
4	Big Data Analytics	4	T	2
5	Genomic Data Analytics Using R Programming	4	P	3
6	Internet of Things	4	T	3
7	Data Analytics Using R	4	P	3
8	Programming Essentials for Data Analytics	4	P	2
Electives				
1	Applied Machine Learning Using Python	4	P	
2	IoT LAB	4	P	

15.6.8 Physical Education

TABLE 15.10

Courses—Physical Education

S.No	Subject	Credits	T/P	Semester
1	Industry 4.0	4	T	1 or 2
2	Introduction to Data Analytics	4	T	1
2	Internet of Things	4	T	2
3	Data Analytics Using R Programming	4	T	2
4	Artificial Intelligence	4	P	3
5	Elective			
Electives				
1	Sports Data Analytics Using R (unstructured Data)	4	P	
2	IoT LAB	4	P	
3	Robotic Process Automation (UIPATH)	4	P	

15.6.9 Mathematics, Applied Mathematics, Statistics

TABLE 15.11

Courses—Mathematics, Applied Mathematics, and Statistics

S.No	Subject	Credits	T/P	Semester
1	Industry 4.0	4	T	1 or 2
2	Python Programming	4	T	1
3	Artificial Intelligence	4	P	2
4	Big Data Analytics	4	T	2
5	Data Analytics Using R Programming	4	P	3
8	Programming Essentials for Data Analytics	4	P	2
Electives				
1	Applied Machine Learning using Python	4	P	

15.7 Syllabi for New Courses—Syllabi 4.0

Various courses that deal with Industry 4.0 tools are: Introduction to Industry 4.0, Advancements in Industry 4.0, Big Data Analytics, R Programming for Social Science, Data Analytics Using R, Advanced Data Analysis Using R, Python for Data Analytics, Artificial Intelligence, Robotic Process Automation, Robotic Process Automation Design and Development, Robotic Process Automation for Business, Internet of Things, Critical Thinking, Design Thinking and Problem Solving, Quantum Computing, Cybersecurity, and Ethical Hacking. The syllabi for these courses are given in Appendix A.

15.7.1 Introduction to Industry 4.0

15.7.1.1 Objectives

At the end of completing this course, students will have knowledge on Industry 4.0, the need for digital transformation, and the following Industry 4.0 tools.

1. Artificial Intelligence
2. Big Data and Data Analytics
3. Internet of Things

15.7.1.2 Syllabus

15.7.1.2.1 Unit I: Industry 4.0

Need—Reason for Adopting Industry 4.0: Definition—Goals and Design Principles—Technologies of Industry 4.0—Big Data—Artificial Intelligence (AI)—Industrial Internet of Things—Cybersecurity—Cloud—Augmented Reality

15.7.1.2.2 Unit II: Artificial Intelligence

Artificial Intelligence (AI): What and Why?—History of AI—Foundations of AI: The AI Environment—Societal Influences of AI—Application Domains and Tools—Associated Technologies of AI—Future Prospects of AI—Challenges of AI

15.7.1.2.3 Unit III: Big Data and IoT

Big Data: Evolution—Data Evolution—Data: Terminologies—Big Data Definitions—Essential of Big Data in Industry 4.0: Big Data Merits and Advantages—Big Data Components: Big Data Characteristics—Big Data Processing Frameworks—Big Data Applications—Big Data Tools—Big Data Domain Stack: Big Data in Data Science—Big Data in IoT—Big Data in Machine Learning—Big

Data in Databases—Big Data Use Cases: Big Data in Social Causes—Big Data for Industry -Big Data Roles and Skills: Big Data Roles—Learning Platforms; Internet of Things (IoT): Introduction to IoT—Architecture of IoT—Technologies for IoT—Developing IoT Applications—Applications of IoT—Security in IoT

15.7.1.2.4 Unit IV: Applications and Tools of Industry 4.0

Applications of IoT: Manufacturing, Health Care, Education, Aerospace and Defence, Agriculture, Transportation and Logistics—Impact of Industry 4.0 on Society: Impact on Business, Government, People—Tools for Artificial Intelligence: Big Data and Data Analytics, Virtual Reality, Augmented Reality, IoT, Robotics

15.7.1.2.5 Unit V: Jobs 2030

Industry 4.0—Education 4.0—Curriculum 4.0—Faculty 4.0—Skills required for Future—Tools for Education—Artificial Intelligence Jobs in 2030—Jobs 2030: Framework for Aligning Education with Industry 4.0—Framework for Achieving Next Ten Years Vision: Challenges

Books

1. P. Kaliraj, T. Devi, Artificial Intelligence Theory, models and Applications, 2022, ISBN 9781032008097, Boca Raton, CRC Press, Taylor & Francis Group.
2. P. Kaliraj, T. Devi, Securing IoT in Industry 4.0 Applications with Blockchain, 2022, ISBN 9781032008103, CRC Press, Taylor & Francis Group, New York.
   P. Kaliraj, T. Devi, Industry 4.0 Technologies for Education, Transformative Technologies and Applications, 2022, ISBN 9781032139142, CRC Press, Taylor & Francis Group, New York.
3. P. Kaliraj, T. Devi, Big Data Applications in Industry 4.0, 2022, ISBN 9781032008110, Boca Raton, CRC Press, Taylor & Francis Group.

15.7.2 Advancements in Industry 4.0

(Choose any five units out of the following)

15.7.2.1 Unit I: Machine Learning

Machine Learning—Introduction—Definition—Types of Machine Learning—Supervised, Unsupervised, Reinforcement Learning—Algorithms for Machine Learning—Problems Solved by Machine Learning—Tools for Machine Learning—Applications Areas of Machine Learning

15.7.2.2 Unit II: Robotic Process Automation (RPA)

Robotic Process Automation (RPA): Introduction to RPA—Need for Automation—Programming Constructs in RPA—Robots and Softbots—RPA Architecture and Process Methodologies—Industries Best Suited for RPA—Risks and Challenges with RPA

15.7.2.3 Unit III: Cloud Computing

Cloud Computing: Need, Definition—Types of Cloud—Types of Services—SaaS, PaaS, IaaS

15.7.2.4 Unit IV: Cybersecurity

Cybersecurity: Cyber Crime and Information Security—Classification of Cyber Crimes—Types of Cyber Attacks—Cyber Crime and Indian IT Act 2000—Security Methods

15.7.2.5 Unit V: Virtual Reality

Virtual Reality: Definition—Types of Head-Mounted Displays—Tools for Virtual Reality—Applications of VR in Education, Industries—Difference between VR and Augmented Reality (AR)

15.7.2.6 Unit VI: Augmented Reality

Augmented Reality: Definition—Tools for Augmented Reality—Hololens—Advantages and Challenges of AR—Applications of AR in Education, Industries—Mixed Reality

References

1. P. Kaliraj, T. Devi, *Industry 4.0 Technologies for Education, Transformative Technologies and Applications*, 2022, ISBN 9781032139142, Boca Raton, CRC Press, Taylor & Francis Group
2. P. Kaliraj, T. Devi, *Artificial Intelligence Theory, Models and Applications*, 2022, ISBN 9781032008097, Boca Raton, CRC Press, Taylor & Francis Group
3. P. Kaliraj, T. Devi, *Innovating with Augmented Reality: Applications in Education and Industry*, 2022, ISBN 9781032008127, Boca Raton, CRC Press, Taylor & Francis Group
4. P. Kaliraj, T. Devi, *Securing IoT in Industry 4.0 Applications with Blockchain*, 2022, ISBN 9781032008103, Boca Raton, CRC Press, Taylor & Francis Group
5. UiPath Inc., www.uipath.com/rpa/robotic-process-automation
6. UiPath Inc., www.uipath.com/rpa/academy

15.7.3 R Programming for Social Science

15.7.3.1 Unit I: Introduction to R Language

Understanding R Features—Installing R and RStudio—Packages and Library—R Basic Data Types—R Data Formats—Basic Operators—R Objects: Vectors, Lists, Arrays, Matrix—Factors—DataFrame—R File Formats—Importing and Exporting Files: CSV File—JSON File—txt File—Command Line vs. Scripts

15.7.3.2 Unit II: Data Wrangling

Data Understanding—Data Structure—Data Summarization—Viewing Data—Converting Objects—Generating Data: Regular Sequence—Random Sequence—Built-In Functions—Loop Structure: for–while–repeat—Loop Avoidance: ifelse—Switch—sapply()—lapply()—Pre-Processing: Omitting NA

15.7.3.3 Unit III: Data Manipulation

Slicing—Subscripts and Indices—Data Subsets—Dplyr Package: Select Function—Filter Function—Mutate Function—Arrange Function—String Function: tolower()—toupper()—strsplit()—gsub()—grep()- regexpr()

15.7.3.4 Unit IV: Data Visualization

Introduction—Exploratory Data Analytics—MASS Package—Lattice Package—Datasets—Graphical Parameters—Histogram—Box Plot—Scatter Plot—Categorical Variable—Wordcloud—Bar Charts

15.7.3.5 Unit V: Reporting Tool

Analyzing Gathering Information—Story Telling—R Markdown—R Markdown Framework—rmarkdown Package—Knit for Embedded Code: knitr Package—Convert File: HTML, PDF,

MS Word—Markdown Formatted Text—ShinyApp—Shiny Package: Built Shiny App—Control Widgets—Customize Reactions—Reactive Expressions—Customize Appearance—Deploy Shiny App

Books

1. V. Bhuvaneswari, "Data Analytics with R Step by Step", India, Scitech Publisher, ISBN—978-81-929131-2-4, Edition 2016.
2. Roger D.Peng, "R Programming for Data Science", India, Lean Publishing, 2014.
3. Vignesh Prajapati, "Big Data Analytics with R and Hadoop", India, Packt Publishing, ISBN-978-1-78216-328-2, 2013.
4. Sholom Weiss, et.al, "The Text Mining Handbook: Advanced Approaches in Analyzing Unstructured Data", New York, Springer, Paperback 2010.
5. Emmanuel Paradis, "R for Beginners", France, 2005.

15.7.4 Artificial Intelligence and Robotic Process Automation for Biological Sciences

15.7.4.1 Objectives

The objectives of the course are as follow.

1. To introduce artificial intelligence and machine learning for biology students
2. To facilitate students to learn and apply AI tools for solving research issues in biology
3. To understand the basics of robotic process automation
4. To develop automated solutions for research problems in biology

15.7.4.2 Syllabus

15.7.4.2.1 Unit I: Artificial Intelligence (AI)

Introduction to AI—Fundamentals—Need for AI—Foundations of AI—AI Environment—Application Domains of AI—AI Tools—Challenges and Future of AI

15.7.4.2.2 Unit II: Machine Learning (ML) and Deep Learning (DL)

Fundamentals of ML and DL—ML Algorithms to Find Associations across Biological Data, Cellular Image Classification and Identification of Genetic Variations—AI in Biology Research—AI in Drug Design—AI in Phylogeny—AI in Next Generation Sequencing—AI in Protein Structure Prediction—AI in Protein Folding Analysis

15.7.4.2.3 Unit III: Python Programming

Introduction to Python Language—Python, Machine Learning, and AI—Data Types, Variables, and Operators—Conditions and Loops—Structure of a Python Programme—Packages and Function—Writing Simple Python Codes

15.7.4.2.4 Unit IV: Robotic Process Automation (RPA)

Fundamentals of RPA—Programming Basics from RPA Perspective—Applying RPA—RPA Development Methodology—Architecture of RPA—RPA and Emerging Ecosystems

15.7.4.2.5 Unit V: UiPath Studio

Introduction—Automation Debugging—Automation Library—Activities Packages—Basic Automation Tasks—Text and Image Automation—Data Tables in RPA—Extracting Data from Data Tables and PDFs—Building Simple Automation Projects

References

1. P. Kaliraj, Devi Thirupathi, "Artificial Intelligence Theory, Models, and Applications", Auerbach Publications, Boca Raton, CRC Press, Taylor and Francis group, 2021.

2. Ethem Alpaydin, "Introduction to Machine Learning", Third Edition, MIT Press, 2014.
3. Martin C. Brown, "Python: The Complete Reference", McGraw Hill Education, 2018.
4. www.uipath.com/landing/academic-studio-download
5. www.uipath.com/rpa/robotic-process-automation
6. https://www.uipath.com/rpa/academy

Unit II of the preceding syllabus shall be redefined for every department—say, for botany, zoology, biotechnology, micro-biology, and bio-informatics—separately after discussing with the respective department experts who will have a vision for the next ten years. Units IV and V RPA topics can be offered uniformly to all the departments except MBA, M.Com. and related disciplines, as there is another course offered by UiPath Inc., Romania for Business managers, which could be adopted for these disciplines. The rest of the units given in the syllabus can be made common.

15.8 Guidelines for Framing New Courses in Industry 4.0

Industry 4,0 tools cut across various domains such as health care, manufacturing, agriculture, tourism, entertainment, and agriculture. The guidelines for framing new courses are devised and the steps that are to be followed to invent or frame new courses in your discipline are as follow.

- Choose any of the Industry 4.0 and 5.0 tools. Say the tool is "T"
- Analyse how this tool will be useful in your discipline
- Choose the area in your discipline where this tool will be applicable. Say the area is "A"
- Search for the following:
  - Knowledge on tool "T"
  - Methods of applying the tool "T" in area "A"
  - Case studies or use cases for the tool "T" in area "A"
  - Industries who are the fore runners in "T"
  - Industries who are the fore runners in "A"
  - User-friendly software tools for "T"
  - Recent developments in "T" + "A"
- Carry out the following:
  - Attend good training programmes on "T"
  - Network with industrial experts with expertise on "T"
  - Network with Industries using "T" in area "A"
  - Tie up with research organizations or experts in "T" + "A"
- Frame the syllabus for "T" + "A" as follows:
  - Unit I on the area "A" of your discipline
  - Unit II on the "Introduction to the tool 'T' "
  - Unit III on the methods of applying the tool "T" in area "A"
  - Unit IV on "How to use the software tool for "T""
  - Unit V Case studies or use cases for the tool "T" in area "A"

15.9 Skill Development

Critical thinking, people management, emotional intelligence, critical judgement, negotiation, cognitive flexibility, knowledge production, and management are the various skill sets that are required to be possessed by the modern student. The education process needs to adopt each individual student to achieve 5 Cs: communication, collaboration, competence, creativity, and critical thinking (Pinnamaneni, 2020).

Students should equip themselves with critical thinking, creativity, and problem solving in order to fetch jobs in Industry 4.0. These skills are essential for developing intelligent and creative solutions for various complex problems. Critical thinking and judgement are the skills which help the students to interpret things correctly and take proper decision in any workplace. Similarly, teamwork and collaboration also help in advancing the technological processes in a company. Cognitive science plays a crucial role in enabling the machines to think like humans. Knowledge management in Industry 4.0 is essential for proper machine–human interaction.

15.9.1 Design Thinking

15.9.1.1 Course Objectives

To impart knowledge on adopting principles of design thinking to bring innovations by transforming organizations culture and to solve complex problems which are difficult to decipher

For students to mainly understand on the core concepts of design thinking, which includes: (i) empathy; (ii) brainstorming; (iii) prototyping; and (iv) storytelling

15.9.1.2 Unit I: Definition and the Perspective on Design Thinking Process

Introduction: Definition—The Role of Design Thinking and Designers—The Modes of Thinking—Design Process (Double Diamond)—Design Principles and Other Methods

15.9.1.3 Unit II: Formation of Complexities and Building Strategy for Organizations

Challenges: A Powerful Way to Use Data (Data Collection)—Frame Design and Generate Design—Thinking Strategy to Reframe the Complexities with Capability: Formation of the Problem for the Organizations—Creation of Design Thinking Strategy and Capability (Structure, Culture, Skills, Process)—To Reduce Risk and Enable Performance

15.9.1.4 Unit III: Problem Solving by Exploring Tools

Explore: Discover Challenges—Interpret through Empathy Study—Empathy Study Tools—Perform Risk Assessment

15.9.1.5 Unit IV: Idea Generation and Development of Concepts

Ideate: Generate Ideas—Shortlist a Workable Solution—Perform Risk Assessment. Create: Develop Prototypes of a Big Idea—Get Feedback—Perform Financial Analysis of the Solution and Risk Assessment

15.9.1.6 Unit V: Design Thinking Setup within Firm and Development Service

Evolve: Design Thinking Integration in Organizations—Success Factors and Measuring the Solution—Design for Effective Services: Developed Product vs. Development Services—Service Development—Experience Lifecycle

Books

1. Vianna, M., Vianna, Y., K. Adler, I., Lucena, B. and Russo, B., 2012. Design Thinking Business Innovation. 1st ed. Rio de Janeiro: MJV Press, pp. 1–85.
2. Ling, D., 2015. Complete Design Thinking Guide For Successful Professionals. 1st ed. Singapore: CreateSpace Independent Publishing Platform, pp. 1–183.

15.10 Conclusions

The Fourth Industrial Revolution, Industry 4.0, is changing the world around us. It is necessary to align higher education with Industry 4.0 through the education on the tools of Industry 4.0. Introduction of various courses on Industry 4.0 tools would ensure upgrading of students' skills and their knowledge to match the newly created jobs of Industry 4.0. Bharathiar University has taken steps to impart the knowledge of Industry 4.0 tools by introduction of various undergraduate and postgraduate programmes. This chapter provided an extensive review of various tools of Industry 4.0. It also provided the scheme and syllabi of various undergraduate and postgraduate programmes introduced by Bharathiar University to teach Industry 4.0 tools.

REFERENCES

Ekaran, Sammy, 2018. Top 10 tools for the digital classroom, elearning industry, https://elearningindustry.com/tools-for-the-digital-classroom-top-10.

Henry E. Armstrong, 1902. The Heuristic Method of Teaching, School Science, 1(8), https://doi.org/10.1111/j.1949-8594.1902.tb00110.x

Javed, A., Sundrani, A., Malik, N. and Prescott, S. A., 2021. *Robotic Process Automation using UiPath StudioX*. Apress.

Kaliraj, P. and Devi, T., 2022a. *Artificial Intelligence Theory, Models and Applications*, ISBN 9781032008097, Boca Raton, CRC Press, Taylor & Francis Group.

Kaliraj, P. and Devi, T., 2022b. *Innovating with Augmented Reality: Applications in Education and Industry*, ISBN 9781032008127, Boca Raton, CRC Press, Taylor & Francis Group.

Kaliraj, P. and Devi, T., 2022c. *Securing IoT in Industry 4.0 Applications with Blockchain*, ISBN 9781032008103, CRC Press, Taylor & Francis Group.

Kaur, H., 2019. *Teaching & Research Aptitude*. 1st ed. Boca Raton, Oxford University Press, pp. 1.10–1.22.

Krathwohl, D. R., Bloom, B. S., & Masia, B. B., 1973. *Taxonomy of Educational Objectives, the Classification of Educational Goals. Handbook II: Affective Domain*, New York: David McKay Co., Inc.

Pinnamaneni Bhanu Prasad, Discussions on Industry 4.0 and 5.0, Bharathiar University, 2020.

Statista Research Department, 27 November 2016, Internet of Things—number of connected devices worldwide 2015–2025, www.statista.com/statistics/471264/iot-number-of-connected-devices-worldwide/ [Accessed 28 April 2020].

16

Curriculum for Education 4.0: A Design Thinking Approach

V. Saravanan, M. Daniel and K. Prem Nazeer

CONTENTS

16.1 Introduction

Tertiary education is a complex educational system driven by the curriculum that constitutes knowledge, skills, professionalism, and entrepreneurship. A good curriculum promotes tertiary education with choice and flexibility for vertical and horizontal mobilities. The outcome of education based on a

DOI: 10.1201/9781003318378-16

good curriculum meets the needs of society, industry, and higher learning institutions, and contributes to the growth of the knowledge economy. A recent survey conducted by the *Economic Times* reveals that 80% of Indian engineers are not fit for any job in the knowledge economy [1]. The survey also reveals that only 2.5% of Indian graduates have the relevant skills to make a career out of emerging technologies. The *Indian Skills Report 2019* [2] recommends revalidating the curriculum to meet the industry demands and then work with the companies to put them into use. Thus, this is the right time for higher educational institutions to take up the issue seriously and design, build, and develop the right kind of curriculum for the future to bridge the existing gap between academia and industry. This chapter proposes using the design thinking approach for the curriculum framework in higher educational institutions.

16.2 Design Thinking

Design thinking is a design methodology that provides a solution-based approach to solving problems [3]. It is an iterative process that seeks to understand the users, namely the learners and employers, redefine problems, and create innovative solutions. This chapter proposes the revision of curriculum by designing, structuring, and developing the same using the design thinking approach to fulfill the needs of the learners and employers. The design thinking process usually involves the following five stages.

16.2.1 Empathize

The first stage of the design thinking process is to gain an empathetic understanding of the problem affecting the efficiency of the curriculum in terms of job prospects by consulting the main stakeholders, namely students, faculty, peer, and industries.

16.2.2 Definition

During this stage, the information gathered from the stakeholders during the empathetic phase is put together. The definition stage helps define the core problems identified up to this point, related to the mismatch between job prospects and the curriculum of discipline-centric courses.

16.2.3 Ideate

During the third stage, new ideas are generated by "thinking outside the box" to find new solutions. In this stage, for the specific problem identified in the curriculum, the scope and breadth for each program are defined, and new tracks are determined based upon the need of learners and employers.

16.2.4 Prototype

This is an experimental phase aiming to identify the best possible solution for each of the problems identified during the three stages. Here, a model is developed by mapping the tracks appropriately to the breadth, scope, and identifying courses for each track to address knowledge, skill, and professionalism.

16.2.5 Test

In the final stage, the best solution identified as a quality curriculum is arranged to deliver after proper validation. Figure 16.1 presents the five steps of the design thinking approach used for curriculum design.

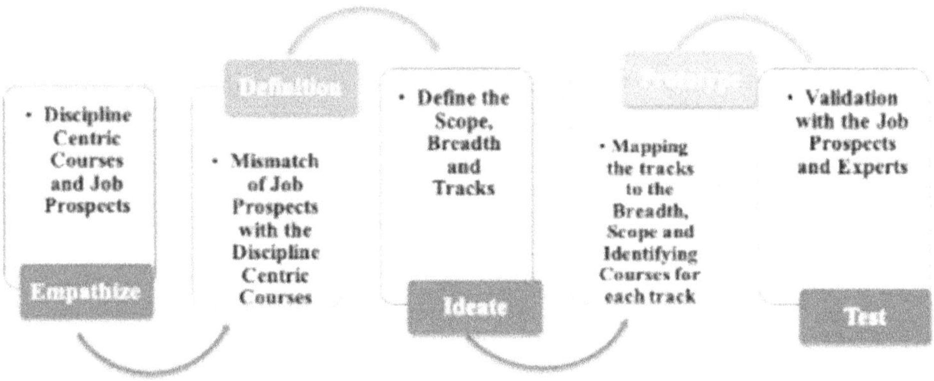

FIGURE 16.1 Design thinking approach

16.3 An Institution Moving toward World-Class Curriculum under Education 4.0

16.3.1 Overall Structure of the Curriculum

Dr. SNS Rajalakshmi College of Arts and Science (Autonomous), Coimbatore, is a leading zutonomous institution serving society for the past two decades. It is a trend setter in higher education and has been recognized well at the national level through ranking and accreditation. The institution offers programs at different levels, viz. undergraduate, postgraduate, and research. While the undergraduate curriculum is tailored for three academic years with six semesters, the postgraduate curriculum is designed for two academic years with four semesters. The institution has the practice of introducing innovations regularly in the different domains of education and research on the campus. An attempt to develop a novel model curriculum for the undergraduate and postgraduate programs based on the design thinking approach under a choice-based credit system with well-defined outcomes for the courses and programs is one such innovative approach toward developing curriculum for the future under Education 4.0. In the following, we present a gist of how a world-class curriculum for undergraduate and postgraduate programs has been designed, structured, and developed, based on the design thinking approach for implementation and delivery at Dr. SNS Rajalakshmi College of Arts and Science (Autonomous), Coimbatore [4].

The program's curriculum is built to inculcate knowledge; research aptitude; soft, technical, and professional skills; creativity; innovation; critical thinking; employability and entrepreneurial skills; personality development; capacity building, etc. The curriculum and various courses are designed to embody facts and information, concepts, skills, problems, case studies, applications, training modules, and employability and entrepreneurial spirit.

The curriculum of the programs is built on a precise scope. While the undergraduate programs are driven by employment, the postgraduate programs are driven by research. The curriculum is designed and structured under semester pattern in a choice-based credit system (CBCS) tailored with course outcomes (COs), program-specific outcomes (PSOs), program outcomes (POs), and program educational objectives (PEOs). The curriculum helps to make a holistic development on the learners to make them globally competent graduates, post-graduates, and researchers. The curriculum features cultivation of knowledge, skills, entrepreneurship, languages, and a foundation for values and ethics, sports and

TABLE 16.1
Distribution of Credits for Undergraduate Curriculum

Part	Type of Course	Total Credits
I	Language	8
II	English	8
III	Supportive/Allied (compulsory)	16
	Core (compulsory)	73
	Elective (optional)	19
	Ability enhancement	6
IV	Foundation	8
V	Extension	2
Total credits		**140**

TABLE 16.2
Distribution of Credits for Postgraduate Curriculum

Type of Course	Total Credits
Core—theory and laboratory	44
Research review	2
Article publications	2
Application development	2
Internship and project	14
Elective	24
Ability enhancement	2
Total Credits	**90**

entertainment, and social responsibility. Thus, for the undergraduate programs the curriculum is divided into five parts as mentioned in Table 16.1, with appropriate credits for the courses under each category.

Table 16.2 represents the design and structure of the postgraduate curriculum.

16.3.2 Discipline-Based Core Curriculum

The undergraduate programs running into three academic years and six semesters under the choice-based credit system are specifically structured into a discipline-specific, cluster-based, and interdisciplinary program to promote flexibility and interdisciplinary learning and provision for vertical and horizontal mobility. The undergraduate programs under Part III of the curriculum offer a variety of courses under different components that include compulsory core (cluster and discipline-centric), optional elective (cluster, discipline-centric), supportive (allied), laboratory, project, courses for ability enhancement (soft and quantitative skills, value-added technical skills, professional skills, discipline-centric practices), and open/interdisciplinary elective courses cutting across disciplines. Information and communication technology (ICT)-enabled and Web-based learning and using the library is an integral part of the program. Internship, field and industrial visits, and entrepreneurship training are included in the curriculum to enhance understanding. Students are encouraged to participate in seminars, hands-on training, quizzes, competitions, and summer research projects. Participation in co-curricular, extra-curricular, and extension activities is also a requirement. There is also scope to learn additional elective courses and register for national/international certification programs (online) beyond the regular curriculum. The postgraduate curriculum includes courses on core, elective, research review, research publications, and self-learning apart from skill development.

The overall curriculum is evolved from the core values of the National Assessment and Accreditation Council (NAAC) for sustaining the quality and the institution's core values to correctly map to the

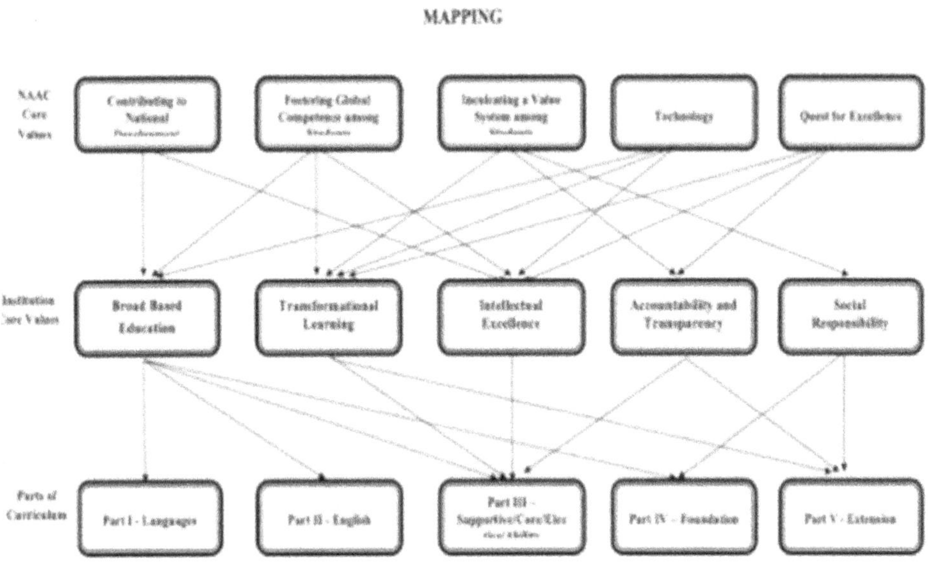

FIGURE 16.2 Mapping of core values and parts of the curriculum.

graduate attributes and mapped to the different parts of the curriculum. Figure 16.2 represents the mapping of the NAAC, the core values of Dr. SNS Rajalakshmi College of Arts and Science (Autonomous), Coimbatore, and the various parts of the curriculum.

16.4 Outcome-Based Curriculum

Outcome-based education (OBE) is an educational theory that maps the different parts of the educational system through goals and outcomes. Under this system, each learner should have achieved the goal. In recent times, outcome-based methods have been adopted in the education system at different levels across the globe. The development of an effective outcome-based curriculum for a program involves defining the correct graduate attributes (GAs) and good programme educational objectives (PEOs), program outcomes (POs), program-specific outcomes (PSOs), and course outcomes (COs), with exact mapping among them and evaluating the level of attainment. In the following, after defining the graduate attributes of the institution, the program educational objectives, the program outcomes, and the program outcomes are defined and mapped approximately in the case of the B.Sc. (information technology [IT]) program.

16.4.1 Graduate Attributes (GAs)

Graduate attributes are the qualities, skills, and understandings a university community agrees its students should develop during their time with the institution. The institution uses the following 12 graduate attributes.

1. Knowledge and skill
2. Design and development
3. Modern tools
4. Problem analysis and solution
5. Communication
6. Teamwork

7. Project management
8. Creativity and innovation
9. Entrepreneurship
10. Sensitivity to multi-ethnic cultural environment
11. Professional ethics
12. Life-long learning

16.4.2 Program Educational Objectives (PEOs)

Program educational objectives (PEOs) are broad statements describing the achievable skills expected by the graduates of a particular program. The PEOs of the BSc (IT) program follow.

The program will produce graduates who:

1. Practice as computing professionals in IT areas with an appropriate combination of theoretical knowledge and hands-on skills.
2. Enhance their skills in new computing technologies through self-directed professional development.
3. Engage in life-long learning to remain current in their profession by enhancing analytical and design skills and/or pursue postgraduate studies to improve their career positions in IT industries.

16.4.3 Program Outcomes (POs)

The program has documented measurable program outcomes that are based on the needs of the program's constituencies. The BSc (IT) program enables students to achieve, by the time of graduation, the following outcomes.

Graduates of the program will have the ability to:

1. Analyze a complex computing problem and apply principles of computing and other relevant disciplines to identify solutions.
2. Design, implement, and evaluate a computing-based solution to meet a given set of computing requirements in the context of the program's discipline.
3. Communicate effectively in a variety of professional contexts.
4. Recognize professional responsibilities and make informed judgments in computing practice based on legal and ethical principles.
5. Function effectively as a member or leader of a team engaged in activities appropriate to the program's discipline.

16.4.4 Program-Specific Outcomes (PSOs)

The program has documented measurable program-specific outcomes based on the needs of the program's constituencies. The BSc (IT) program enables students to achieve, by the time of graduation, the following program-specific outcomes:

1. Identify and analyze user needs and consider them in the selection, creation, integration, evaluation, and administration of computing-based systems.
2. An ability to use and apply current technical concepts and practices in the core information technologies of human-computer interaction, information management, programming, networking, and web systems and technologies.
3. Design and develop computer programs/computer-based systems in the areas related to networks, communication systems, visual analytics, and cybersecurity of varying complexities.

Table 16.3 presents the mapping of graduate attributes with the program outcomes/program specific outcomes.

Table 16.4 presents the mapping of program educational objectives with the program outcomes and program-specific outcomes of the BSc (IT) program.

TABLE 16.3
Graduate Attributes vs. POs/PSOs Mapping

	Knowledge and Skill	Design and Development	Modern tools	Problem Analysis and Solution	Communication	Teamwork	Project Management	Creativity and Innovation	Entrepreneurship	Sensitivity to Multi-Ethnic Cultural Environment	Professional Ethics	Life-long Learning
PO 1	✓		✓	✓				✓		✓		
PO 2		✓	✓			✓	✓				✓	
PO 3					✓	✓	✓					✓
PO 4	✓				✓					✓	✓	✓
PO 5						✓	✓		✓			
PSO 1		✓	✓				✓				✓	✓
PSO 2			✓	✓		✓			✓		✓	✓
PSO 3		✓	✓			✓	✓		✓	✓		✓

TABLE 16.4
PEO/PO/PSO Mapping

	BSc (IT) Program		
	PEO 1	**PEO 2**	**PEO 3**
PO 1	✓		
PO 2	✓		
PO 3		✓	✓
PO 4			✓
PO 5		✓	
PSO 1	✓	✓	
PSO 2	✓	✓	
PSO 3		✓	✓

16.5 Course Outcomes and Attainment

Course outcomes are statements clearly describing the meaningful, observable, and measurable knowledge, skills, and/or dispositions students will learn in this course. All the courses are defined with five-course outcomes. Four levels of outcome achievement at section or course level have been determined. For a section or whole course, the final judgment of the attainment of the student outcomes by all students enrolled in a course or a section is evaluated as provided in Table 16.5.

TABLE 16.5
Assessment of Attainment Levels

Exceeds Expectations (EE)	Meets Expectations (ME)	Progressing toward Expectations (PE)	Does Not Meet Expectations (DNME)
80% or more of students are achieving the satisfactory level or above	≥ 70% and < 80% of students are achieving the satisfactory level or above	≥ 60% and < 70% of students are achieving the satisfactory level or above	< 60% of students are not achieving the satisfactory level or above

16.6 Designing Curriculum Based on Design Thinking Approach for the Core and Elective Domains

Having made a layout, the foundation, and the general constitution of the curriculum, we now proceed to develop the curriculum for undergraduate and postgraduate programs based on the various steps of design thinking found in Section 16.2. Before designing as a first step, the scope for each program is defined. The list of possible scopes of different programs at the undergraduate and postgraduate levels is given in the next section. Toward ideating and defining a world-class curriculum, based on the scope, the relevant industries are identified across the globe. The job prospects connected to these industries are then listed and the domain skills required in the curriculum corresponding to these listed prospective jobs are marked as the elective tracks sfor the chosen program. The core tracks which serve as pre-requisite for the elective tracks are defined. Each elective track will have three courses in it on three different levels. While the first course contains knowledge and information, the second course provides the necessary skills, and the third course leads to professionalism. Internships and projects in the respective industries are infused into the curriculum as mandatory, leading to the right kind of employment. Figure 16.3 depicts this linkage and network model for the BSc (IT) curriculum as an example.

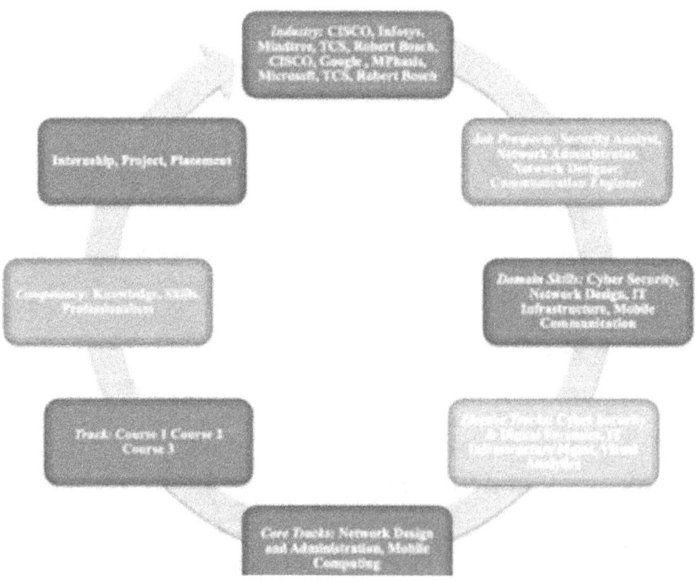

FIGURE 16.3 A typical flow chart connecting the curriculum, industries, job prospects, and elective tracks for the BSc (IT) program.

16.7 Scope of the Programs

The scope of the different undergraduate programs is defined based on the industry needs and emerging trends. However, the scope is determined for the postgraduate programs based on current research trends and employment. Table 16.6 presents the defined scope for all undergraduate and postgraduate programs offered in the autonomous institution, Dr. SNS Rajalakshmi College of Arts and Science (Autonomous), Coimbatore.

TABLE 16.6

Scopes for a Set of Sample Programs Offered at Dr. SNS Rajalakshmi College of Arts and Science (Autonomous), Coimbatore.

Program	Scope
Computer Studies: Traditional Computer Science and Contemporary IT Tools	
BSc (CS)	Mathematical and theoretical foundations of computing
BCA	Application of computer science at the interface of business and technology
BSc (CT)	Integration of computer-related hardware, software, and networked communication tools
BSc (IT)	Administering software, networks, and database systems
MSc (CS)	Traditional computer science and its applications through research
MCA	Latest computer applications and skills to design, develop, and evaluate computer-based systems
Commerce Studies: Conventional Commerce and Management Thoughts with Modern IT Applications	
BCom	Economics and financial matters along with managerial skills
BCom (CA)	Bridging commerce concepts with computer applications
BCom (IT)	Study of information technology and its applications in the commercial domain
BCom (PA)	Essential accounting knowledge and business skills in law and auditing
BCom (Finance)	Principles of capital and investment in a commercial setting
MCom	Financial matters and managerial skills through research
MCom (CA)	Advanced commerce concepts with computer applications through research
Management	
BBA	Fundamental education in business and management principles
BBA (CA)	Fundamental education in business and management principles with computer applications
MBA	Critical acumen and leadership
Sciences	
BSc (Mathematics)	Understanding of mathematical problems and approaches
BSc (Mathematics–CA)	Using mathematical and scientific expressions, notations, and computational techniques
MSc (Mathematics)	Advanced mathematics and its forefront research usage
BSc (Physics)	Physical laws, structure of matter, and principles that govern the nature of universe
BSc (Chemistry)	Composition, matter, fundamental properties of chemicals and the way they Interact
BSc (CDF)	Innovative garment designing in textiles and fashion
BSc (CS&HM)	Culinary expert and management professionalism in the hospitality industry
English	
BA (English Literature)	Nuances of novelty in literary characters
MA (English Literature)	Nuances of aesthetic pleasure and research capability

Notes: CS: Computer Science; CT: Computer Technology; IT: Information Technology; CA: Computer Applications; PA: Professional Accounting; CDF: Costume Design and Fashion; CS&HM: Catering Science and Hotel Management

16.8 Distribution of Courses and Credits across Breadths

The main advantage of the choice-based credit system is its flexibility with provisions for vertical mobility and horizontal mobility within the cluster, across the cluster, and across disciplines. However, there should be a well-defined boundary between breadths (domains) and programs within the cluster. To promote this idea, breadths have been defined based on the defined scope and nature of the program, which will act as the vertical pillars for each program. Even though there is a substantial overlap of breadths across different disciplines within the cluster, the percentage of credits and the number of core and elective courses will vary from program to program. Table 16.7 gives the details of breadths defined and the

TABLE 16.7

Distribution of Credits and Courses of Core and Elective Classes of the Undergraduate and Postgraduate Curriculum under the Breadth

	Breadth 1	Breadth 2	Breadth 3	Breadth 4	Breadth 5
Program	(Values in Percentage)				
BSc (CS)	Theory 46	System 11	Software 35	Applications 8	-
BCA	4	12	38	46	-
BSc (CT)	4	35	54	7	
BSc (IT)	4	53	35	7	-
MSc (CS)	40	16	24	20	
MCA	5	7	44	44	-
BCom	Commerce 35	Finance 17	Regulations 17	Business management 22	Technology 9
BCom (IT)	39	7	7	8	39
BCom (CA)	32	12	12	12	32
BCom (PA)	24	8	40	4	24
BCom (Finance)	32	12	12	12	32
MCom	48	16	4	24	8
MCom (CA)	38	5	10	14	33
BBA	Business 39	Administration 32	Finance 19	Ethics 3	Technology 7
BBA (CA)	27	21	18	3	30
MBA	Business 33	Management 26	Regulations 13	Ethics and values 26	Technology 2
BSc (Mathematics)	Theoretical mathematics 50	Applied mathematics 30	Applicable mathematics 10	Computational mathematics 10	-
BSc (Mathematics–CA)	28	32	12	28	-
MSc (Mathematics)	45	30	10	15	
BSc (Physics)	Classical physics 35	Modern physics 35	Applied physics 20	Technological physics 10	-
BSc (Chemistry)	Organic chemistry 29	Inorganic chemistry 21	Physical chemistry 16	Analytical chemistry 16	Applied chemistry 20
BSc (CDF)	Textiles 40	Design 30	Fashion 20	Entrepreneurship 10	-
BSc (CS and HM)	Culinary 40	Hotel Mgmt 60	-	-	-

Program	Breadth 1	Breadth 2	Breadth 3	Breadth 4	Breadth 5
	(Values in Percentage)				
BA (English Lit.)	Language and literature 60	Culture 20	Criticism 10	Technology 10	-
MA (English Lit.)	65	15	10	10	-

Notes: CS: Computer Science; CA: Computer Applications; CT: Computer Technology; IT: Information Technology; PA: Professional Accounting; CDF: Costume Design and Fashion; CS and HM: Catering Science and Hotel Management

percentage of credits allocated for core and elective courses of the curriculum for various undergraduate and postgraduate programs conducted over six and four semesters, respectively.

16.9 Distribution of Tracks under Breadths

To promote flexibility in learning knowledge across clusters and disciplines, gain skills, add values toward capacity building, and reduce the gap between industry and academia, tracks have fixed for each curriculum under the breadth to suit the emerging trends, needs of the industry and the interest of the learners [5, 6]. Table 16.8 represents the tracks for the different undergraduate and postgraduate programs offered at Dr. SNS Rajalakshmi College of Arts and Science (Autonomous), Coimbatore.

TABLE 16.8

Tracks under Breadths for Different Undergraduate and Postgraduate Programs

Program	Tracks
BSc (CS)	Algorithms and theory, artificial intelligence, high-performance computing, software engineering, higher education, entrepreneurship, social analytics
BCA	Cloud computing and virtualization, data analytics, informatics, web development, higher education, entrepreneurship, Internet of Things (IoT)
BSc (CT)	Multimedia systems, computer hardware and network architecture, graphics and gaming technologies, robotics and applications, higher education, entrepreneurship, open-source standards
BSc (IT)	Network design and administration, mobile computing, IT infrastructure management, visual analytics, higher education, entrepreneurship, cybersecurity, and digital forensics
MSc (CS)	Cloud management, creative technologies, cybersecurity, data analytics, machine learning, scientific computing, computing systems, hardware design, interactive intelligence, IoT, intelligent robotics, mobile communication, civil services
MCA	Artificial intelligence and robotics, user experience/user interface (UX/UI) design and development, mobile application development, internet of thing programming, digital forensics, business intelligence, network infrastructure management
BCom	Essentials of accounting, industrial accounting and auditing, management of enterprise, banking and law, computing laboratory, financial planning, entrepreneurship, higher education, accounting for business
BCom (IT)	Essentials of accounting, contemporary accounting, composites of business computing laboratory, accounting for business decisions, human resource, entrepreneurship, higher education, IT in commerce
BCom (CA)	Essentials of accounting, business accounting, managing commercial activities, computing laboratory, computer applications in accounting, managing the organizations, higher education, entrepreneurship, computer applications in business
BCom (PA)	Essentials of accounting, law and economics, assessment of accounting books, computing laboratory, enterprise finance for business, banking and ethics, higher education, entrepreneurship, tax and accounting standards

(*Continued*)

TABLE 16.8 (Continued)

Program	Tracks
BCom (Finance)	Essentials of accounting, markets, and institutions, legal aspects of finance, computing laboratory, financial services, analysis and reporting, higher education, entrepreneurship, strategic and contemporary financial issues
MCom	Finance, banking and insurance, law and taxation, marketing, human resource management, entrepreneurship, civil services
MCom (CA)	Finance and investment, tax and regulations, business analytics, digital marketing, logistics, human resource management, civil services
BBA BBA (CA)	Strategy and general management, entrepreneurship and business planning, legal aspects of business, business environment, finance and accounting, production and operations management, business, government and society, marketing, human capital management, agri-business management, entrepreneurship, innovation and quality, e-operations
MBA	Marketing, human resources, finance, hospitality management, business analytics, logistics, and supply chain management, material management
BSc (Mathematics)	Algebra, numbers and analysis, calculus and equations, mathematical structures, mathematical iteration, mathematics for physics, education, entrepreneurship, mathematical models
BSc (Mathematics–CA)	Algebra, analysis, calculus and equations, computing applications, computing laboratory, mathematical iteration, mathematical structures, mathematical optimization, entrepreneurship, computational models
MSc (Mathematics)	Algebraic structures, groups, numbers, analysis, topology, differential equations, operators, dynamics, fluid mechanics, graph and fuzzy sets, civil services
BSc (Physics)	Microscopic physics, mesoscopic physics, earth and space physics, medical physics, theoretical physics, ionics and photonics, education, entrepreneurship, material physics
BSc (Chemistry)	Synthetic organic chemistry, chemistry of solids, physical methods in chemistry, spectroscopy, polymer chemistry, electrochemistry, agricultural chemistry, theory and simulation, dye chemistry, petroleum chemistry, education, entrepreneurship, trends in chemical biology
BSc (CDF)	Color and weave, fiber and fabric, art and trend, garment unit and documentations, merchandising and marketing, fashion forecast, entrepreneurship, style, and fads
BSc (CS and HM)	Production ideology, applied production, service ideology, applied food service, hotel management ideology, applied hotel management, contemporary culinary, contemporary food service, contemporary hotel management, entrepreneurship, trending adds
BA (English Lit.)	Genres, galaxy of creativity, customs and traditions, technology, flavor of literature, creative writing, contemporary writing, education, publishing
MA (English Lit.)	Theater, cultural heritage, literary canon, gender issues, civil services

Notes: CS: Computer Science; CA: Computer Applications; CT: Computer Technology; IT: Information Technology; PA: Professional Accounting; CDF: Costume Design and Fashion; CS and HM: Catering Science and Hotel Management

16.10 Selections of Types of Courses under Core and Elective to Fit in Tracks

The tracks for each program are further subdivided into core and elective tracks. Each track shall have three courses related to knowledge, skill, and professionalism. The job prospects connected to the industries are then listed, and the domain skills required in the curriculum corresponding to these listed prospective jobs are marked as the elective tracks for the chosen program. The core tracks which serve as pre-requisites for the elective tracks are defined. Each elective track will have three courses in it on three different levels; the first course contains knowledge and information, the second course provides the necessary skills, and the third course leads to professionalism. Internships and projects in the respective industries are infused into the curriculum as mandatory, leading to the right kind of employment.

16.11 Distribution of Courses with Knowledge, Skills, and Professionalism

The content of the courses under different breadths and tracks addresses knowledge skills and professionalism in varying percentages depending on the program's scope and nature. Table 16.9 and Figure 16.4 present the distribution of knowledge, skills, and professionalism in the content of the undergraduate and postgraduate programs.

From Table 16.9 and Figure 16.4, it is observed that while the curriculum of the program BSc(CS&HM) is dominating by professionalism, the remaining programs are dominated either by knowledge or by skills.

Programs dominated by knowledge: BSc (Mathematics), BSc (Mathematics–CA), MSc (Mathematics), BSc (Physics), BSc (Chemistry), BA (English Literature), MA (English Literature)

Programs dominated by skill: BSc (CS), BCA, BSc (IT), BSc (CT), MSc (CS), MCA, BCom, BCom (IT), BCom (CA), BCom (PA), BCom (Finance), MCom, MCom (CA), BBA, BBA (CA), MBA, BSc (CDF)

Programs dominated by professionalism: BSc (CS and HM)

TABLE 16.9

Distribution of Knowledge, Skills, and Professionalism in the Curricula of Different Undergraduate and Postgraduate Programs

	Knowledge	Skill	Professionalism
Program		**(Values in Percentage)**	
BSc (CS), BCA, BSc (CT), BSc (IT)	31	42	27
MSc (CS)	16	52	32
MCA	26	41	33
BCom	30	52	18
BCom (IT)	31	42	27
BCom (CA)	32	44	24
BCom (PA)	36	36	28
BCom (Finance)	32	44	24
MCom	20	60	20
MCom (CA)	23	50	27
BBA	35	39	26
BBA (CA)	24	42	33
MBA	30	47	23
BSc (Mathematics)	50	33	17
BSc (Mathematics–CA)	48	28	24
MSc (Mathematics)	50	20	30
BSc (Physics)	52	27	21
BSc (Chemistry)	40	45	15
BSc (CDF)	31	42	27
BSc (CS and HM)	30	30	40
BA (English Lit.)	45	40	15
MA (English Lit.)	35	55	10

CS: Computer Science; CA: Computer Applications; CT: Computer Technology; IT: Information Technology; PA: Professional Accounting; CDF: Costume Design and Fashion; CS&HM: Catering Science and Hotel Management

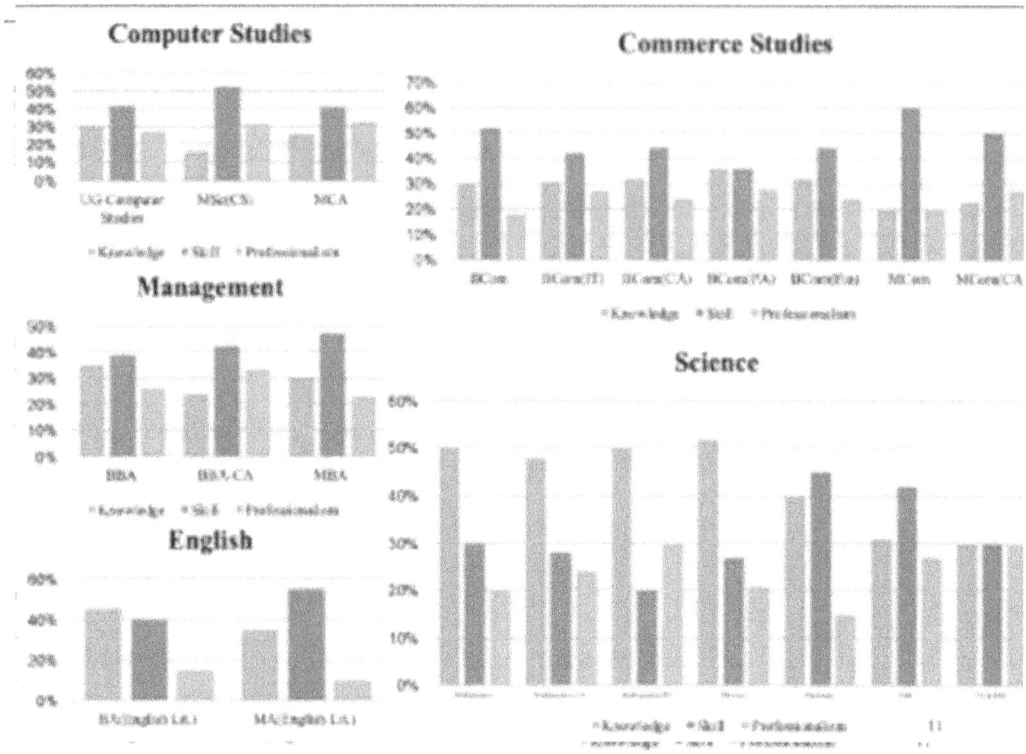

FIGURE 16.4 Distribution of knowledge, skills, and professionalism in the curriculum of different undergraduate and postgraduate programs.

16.12 Distribution of Courses with Opportunities in Employment, Entrepreneurship, and Higher Studies

As mentioned earlier, the undergraduate curriculum is mainly employment-driven, and hence the content of the courses is tailored to suit the job requirements through knowledge, skill, and professionalism apart from internships, projects, and value addition of the curriculum. Also, specific courses in the elective track indulge in progressing toward true entrepreneurship through training in incubation centers. Further, learners aspiring for higher studies, including research, are addressed through high-level courses in specific defined tracks. In Table 16.10 and Figure 16.5, we present the distribution of courses of various undergraduate and postgraduate programs toward employment, entrepreneurship, and higher studies.

From Table 16.10 and Figure 16.5, we observe the following.

Programs dominated by employment: BSc (CS), BCA, BSc (IT), BSc (CT), MCA, BCom, BCom (IT), BCom (CA), BCom (PA), BCom (Finance), BBA, BBA (CA), BSc (Mathematics), BSc (Mathematics–CA), BSc (Chemistry), BSc (CDF)

Programs dominated by entrepreneurship: BSc (CS and HM), MBA

Programs dominated by higher studies: BSc (Physics), MSc (CS), MCom, MCom (CA), MSc (Mathematics), BA (English Literature), MA (English Literature)

TABLE 16.10

Distribution of Content Related to Opportunities for Employment, Entrepreneurship and Higher Studies in the Curriculum

Program	Job	Entrepreneurship	Higher Studies
	(Values in Percentage)		
BSc (CS), BCA, BSc (CT), BSc (IT)	50	27	23
MSc (CS)	28	20	52
MCA	49	18	33
BCom	44	30	26
BCom (IT)	55	27	18
BCom (CA)	56	32	12
BCom (PA)	48	32	23
BCom (Finance)	56	32	12
MCom	24	32	44
MCom (CA)	23	31	46
BBA	64	26	10
BBA (CA)	66	24	10
MBA	42	40	18
BSc (Mathematics)	40	27	33
BSc (Mathematics–CA)	45	25	30
MSc (Mathematics)	20	15	65
BSc (Physics)	31	11	58
BSc (Chemistry)	40	32	28
BSc (CDF)	40	25	35
BSc (CS and HM)	40	40	20
BA (English Lit.)	25	15	60
MA (English Lit.)	10	15	75

CS: Computer Science; CA: Computer Applications; CT: Computer Technology; IT: Information Technology; PA: Professional Accounting; CDF: Costume Design and Fashion; CS&HM: Catering Science and Hotel Management

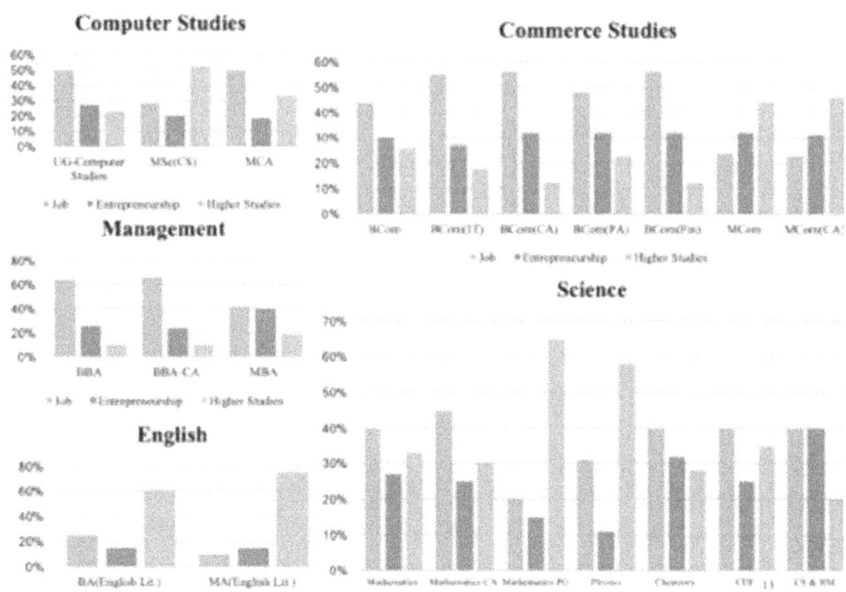

FIGURE 16.5 Distribution of content related to opportunities for employment, entrepreneurship and higher studies in the curriculum.

16.13 Distribution of Teaching Pedagogies and Learning Pattern for the Topics in Courses

Having developed the curriculum, the final stage of the design thinking process—namely, the test—can be carried out by implementing the deveined curriculum among the learners. The success of any curriculum depends on the effectiveness of the delivery of the same. One cannot follow the same delivery pattern for all the breadths, all the tracks, all the courses, and further for the undergraduate and postgraduate programs. This is because the curriculum courses contain knowledge, skills, and professionalism, leading to employment, entrepreneurship, and higher studies. Therefore, an effective curriculum delivery would blend traditional methods, learner-centric methods, activities, research, technology, experimentation, and experience. Table 16.11 and Figure 16.6 depict this.

The following are observations from Table 16.11 and Figure 16.6 related to the teaching methods and learning pattern

Programs dominated by traditional teaching methods and learning patterns: BCom, BCom (IT), MCom, BBA, BSc (Mathematics), BSc (Mathematics–CA), MSc (Mathematics), BSc (CDF), BA (English Literature), MA (English Literature)

Programs dominated by technology-supported teaching: BSc (CS), BCA, BSc (IT), BSc (CT), MSc (CS), MBA, BSc (Physics), BSc (Chemistry),

Programs dominated by experience and experiments: MCA, BCom (CA), BCom (PA), BCom (Finance), MCom (CA), BBA (CA), BSc (CS and HM)

TABLE 16.11
Distribution of Teaching Methods and Learning Patterns of the Undergraduate and Postgraduate Curricula

Program	Traditional	Technology Supported	Experience and Experiments
	(Values in Percentage)		
BSc (CS), BCA, BSc (CT), BSc (IT)	15	46	38
MSc (CS)	12	40	48
MCA	18	41	41
BCom	48	35	17
BCom (IT)	40	18	27
BCom (CA)	20	24	56
BCom (PA)	24	36	40
BCom (Finance)	20	24	56
MCom	44	28	28
MCom (CA)	19	23	58
BBA	48	10	42
BBA (CA)	42	10	48
MBA	24	46	31
BSc (Mathematics)	56	12	32
BSc (Mathematics–CA)	40	32	28
MSc (Mathematics)	60	30	10
BSc (Physics)	31	54	23
BSc (Chemistry)	28	40	32
BSc (CDF)	40	20	40
BSc(CS and HM)	20	10	70
BA (English Lit.)	40	25	35
MA (English Lit.)	35	35	30

CS: Computer Science; CA: Computer Applications; CT: Computer Technology; IT: Information Technology; PA: Professional Accounting; CDF: Costume Design and Fashion; CS&HM: Catering Science and Hotel Management

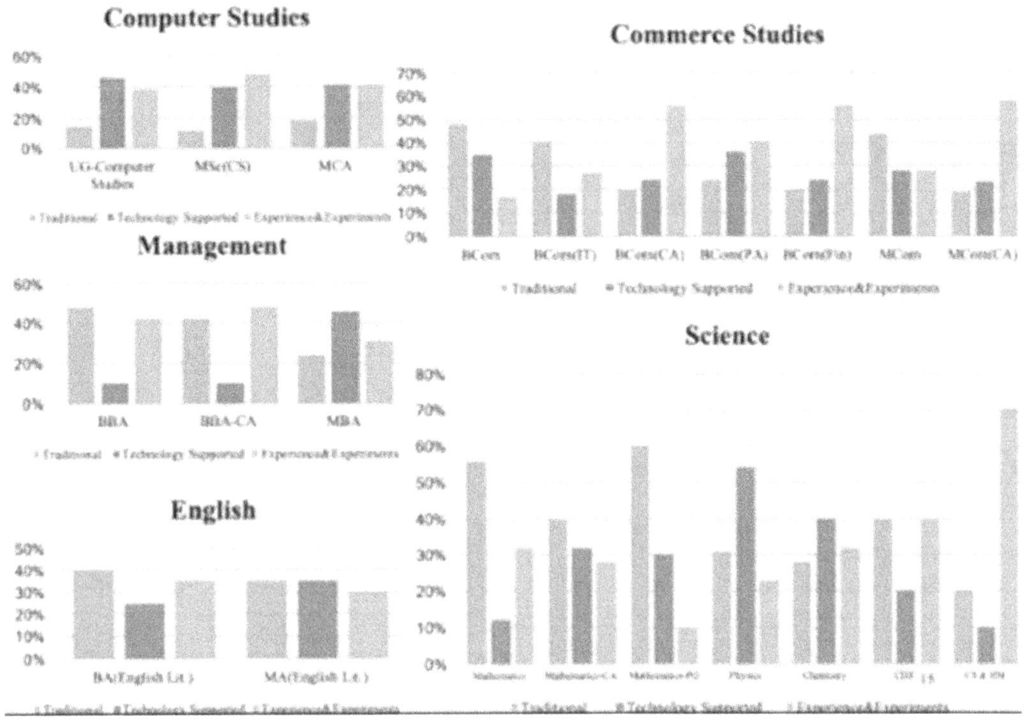

FIGURE 16.6 Distribution of teaching methods and learning pattern of the undergraduate and postgraduate curricula.

16.14 Conclusion

For the first time, the design thinking approach is used for designing undergraduate and postgraduate curricula for study programs in different domains in higher educational institutions. The curriculum structure presented in this chapter smoothly bridges the existing gap between academia and industry. The uniqueness of this presented curriculum is the holistic approach in connecting the various elements such as scope, breadth, tracks, and job prospects. All the required pre-requisites for the outcome-based education curriculum are well connected. The outcome is measured by calculating the attainment score for all the courses/programs, which undoubtedly helps the higher educational institutions identify issues in teaching and learning. Remedial measures are suggested, and appropriate actions are taken for the identified problems—thereby, the loop is closed for effective monitoring of teaching and learning. The authors are delighted to note that Dr. SNS Rajalakshmi College of Arts and Science (Autonomous), Coimbatore, is India's first institution to design the curriculum using the design thinking approach. This curriculum was implemented in the academic year 2020–2021 and will take two academic years' time frames for postgraduate programs and three academic years' time frames for undergraduate programs. This curriculum leads to more employability for the students as the requirements are originated from the recruiters. This chapter will serve as a guideline to other higher educational institutions for enhancing the quality of their curricula.

16.15 Acknowledgments

The authors grateful and kindly acknowledge the management of the college, in particular the Chairman Dr. S. N. Subramanian, the Correspondent Dr. S. Rajalakshmi, the Secretary Dr. V. S. Velusamy, and the Technical Director Dr. S. Nalin Vimal Kumar for providing the platform for designing and developing a curriculum based on design thinking and all the needed support and encouragement. Our special thanks are due to Dr. S. Nalin Vimal Kumar, the technical director, for introducing the concept of design thinking in every aspect of education in SNS institutions which paved the way for designing the curriculum.

REFERENCES

Internet

1. ETOnline, 2020, Employability Survey 2019: Jobs slip away from the ill-equipped Indian engineer, https://economictimes.indiatimes.com/jobs/employability-survey-2019-jobs-slip-away-from-the-ill-equipped-indian-engineer/articleshow/68559686.cms [accessed 25 Apr 2020]
2. AICTE, 2019, https://www.aicte-india.org/sites/default/files/India%20Skill%20Report-2019.pdf [accessed 20 Apr 2020]
3. Design, 2020, https://www.interaction-design.org/literature/topics/design-thinking [accessed 24 Apr 2020]
4. Dr. SNSRCAS, 2020, OBE Curriculum, Dr. SNS Rajalakshmi College of Arts and Science, Coimbatore, India, 2020.
5. Curriculum-India, 2020, Curriculum and Syllabi of the following Educational Institutions from India [accessed Oct-Dec 2020]
   a VIT Bhopal, Bhopal.
   b Andhra University, Hyderabad.
   c Indian Institute of Management, Bengaluru.
   d Indian Institute of Management, Ahmedabad.
   e Indian Institute of Science, Bengaluru.
   f Indian Statistical Institute, Chennai
6. Curriculum-Abroad, 2020, Curriculum and Syllabi of the following Educational Institutions from outside India [accessed Oct-Dec 2020]
   a Stanford University, USA.
   b Carnegie Mellon University, USA.
   c University of Michigan, USA.
   d Carnegie Mellon University, USA.
   e American Chemistry Society, USA
   f American Physical Society, USA

17

Education 4.0: Curriculum Development for the Educational Framework

D. Napoleon and V. Ramanujam

CONTENTS

DOI: 10.1201/9781003318378-17

Objective

The objective is to highlight the future strategy for curriculum development for the Education 4.0 revolution in Industry 4.0.

17.1 Introduction

The development of the steam engine by James Watts in 1780 changed labour permanently. Any unexpected physical hard work is becoming less popular as computers can complete jobs faster and more accurately. New technology was formed, and people moved from the environs to the city, from farming life to the industry's existence. This employment was looked at around 1900 and became conventional during Industry 2.0. In a while, labourers all had their assignments to complete in the assembly line, with expertise in one tiny territory, instead of knowing the complete cycle of a product. The ultimate target was to improve effectiveness, which results in the products selling in a resourceful manner. A long time after this, the Third Industrial Revolution brought computers to complete the revolution. This framework of utilizing the computers in Industry 3.0 established a creation line that spread all over the businesses, from horticulture to the finance sector, administration, and shipping. In 2000, the ubiquitous nature of the web ushered in the Fourth Industrial Revolution. Networking between systems has made remote working and participation plausible, allowing organizations to establish worldwide endeavours and retail to explode globally with the assistance of generation, transportation, and financial online enterprises. Society has balanced to become dynamically social and more knowledgeable, and many acknowledge that the world may be more of a distant smaller spot than at any other time. The Fourth Industrial Revolution brought the transformation in education, too. This is shown in Figure 17.1.

17.2 The Effect on Education

Education is the primary indicator of life, and has shown its outcome in employment, social status, financial income, attitudes, and well-being. Education has shaped people's social and economic identities to create a better understanding of relationships with others. During the First Industrial Revolution, education became a hazard for students who overcame so many hurdles. The public realized that trade and hands-on training were the only way to get into social life. They do not want to go schooling, and it was an extravagance for the rich. During the Second Industrial Revolution, there was a need for an education system with several factors of view still set up today. In this revolution, faculties are the masters. Students got their knowledge only from the educators, who each take care of unique subjects, and towards the end, the students were tested to verify that they recollected what they had been instructed. This proposed a strong framework for learning disciplines and creating knowledge about schooling values. Training experts took their hands-on teaching of science and re-established that teachers with computers can empower education, with students' mastery to be augmented by machines. Even during the internet revolution, the shape of our training structure has nevertheless been left unchallenged. The outcome of learning is still being examined utilizing the criteria framed in the Second Industrial Revolution. The existence of the Third Industrial Revolution has brought a built-in electronic utilization and data innovation to make it progressively mechanized. In this revolution, the outcome of education has led a way to educators and learners in a unique way.

17.2.1 Industry 4.0 and Its Burden on Education

Another influx of worldwide innovation will change global production. Pioneers in this new era will need to be masterminds and problem solvers, and have the option to interact across the globe. In short, they should be generously instructed. However, by what method should this education be imparted? The forthcoming employees have been trained. Future employees should be taught using the budding tools and the help of the latest innovations. Later on, we should not just have the ability to develop capacity

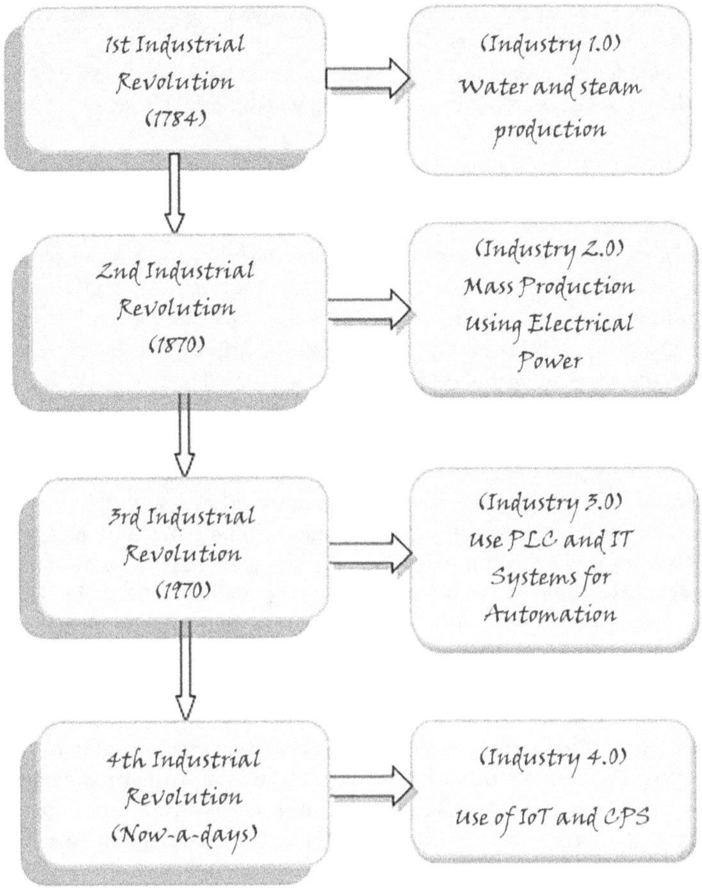

FIGURE 17.1 Overview of the industrial revolutions.

and to build up the innovation, but rather additionally know whether, when, and where to utilize that innovation. That sort of reasoning is both intelligent and interdisciplinary. As it were, Industry 4.0 will require the world to produce another kind of worker—an information specialist. Tomorrow's industry leaders and managers must have new ranges of abilities to adapt, oversee, and take advantage of Industry 4.0. They have the capability of clear thinking, are very good at communication, and possess strong knowledge of problem solving and assessment-based initiatives.

These people can view the technology, which is far beyond the techniques for the use of that technology. They ought to understand the novelty; yet another challenge is to solve the problems provoked by this technology. This has added a new dimension to the development of higher education. This advanced teaching in the Fourth Industrial Revolution is common to all—an intention and energetic entry which can revolutionize society's thoughts and promote the standard of living for day-to-day conciliation. The focus of the working place is forged and tainted in the Fourth Industrial Revolution, which gets ongoing properly; the confusion between humans and machine weakens the detachment between an individual, and the public, among knowledge and expertise.

17.2.2 Education 4.0 Requires a Move to Industry 4.0

Education 4.0 is the expectations of education, including the following qualities.

1. Responds to the necessities of "Industry 4.0", where machine and humans align to empower new developments.

2. Has the capability of incorporating computerized advancements, open-sourced content, and the new humanity of the universally associated world.
3. Establishes a plan for the eventual fate of students gained from adolescence through schooling, learning in the working environment, and playing a better role in society.

For the past 250 years, four industrial revolutions have been come across by society—this has changed the manufacturing industry's face, as is well known by all. This is the belief that modernization in the industry directly influences how the education model gives rise to today's pupils. Students can become precious members of the working environment, good administrators, and problem solvers. They act as superlative models to reconstruct a new rebellion in modern society. An Education 4.0 facility is one that permits the utilization of advanced technologies, including robotics, the Internet of Things (IoT), digitalization, automatization, and remotely coordination. Industry 4.0 is a term used in an industrial setting to depict the computerization and information trade utilized in manufacturing technologies. This includes existing ideas; for instance, distributed computing and artificial intelligence (AI). In total, these innovations are changing the essence of manufacturing.

Much like an assembling firm needs an adaptable production line to adjust the changes sought after and client inclinations, education must likewise be customized in a way that gets students ready for this evolving environment. To successfully execute Education 4.0, training needs to empower more support by students. Ten to 15 years previously, it was not unusual for a classroom of students to be sitting inconspicuously, tuning in to a teacher lecturing on a specific topic. Taking notes on that subject from a whiteboard or overhead projector, students were passive detached beneficiaries of information on which they were later tested. In an individual learning process, students are the passive recipient and dynamic contestants of communication in Education 4.0. Continuously guided by the teacher, students should develop their insight effectively instead of precisely ingesting knowledge from the teacher or other online resources. At once, an approach guaranteed that students ought to be given "basic knowledge" to fabricate extra knowledge. The issue is that the meaning of fundamental knowledge has never been refreshed and, as a result, it is now irrelevant. Education 4.0 involves coordinated efforts on the part of peers, guests, teachers, and administrators. This environment fosters conversation and collaboration.

By empowering elevated levels of collaboration, open communication, and solid associations among students, teachers can more viably prepare students for success in college, the workforce, and life. Nowadays, students are refurbishing the educational framework that is being flipped on their heads with many existing beliefs. Education 4.0 helps 99% of students fabricate an academic curriculum that brings out the subjects in modern technology such as robotics to go far beyond open learning. The instructor must impart knowledge to the students so that students can sit down tactfully and study without contact with their peers and different students or guests.

17.2.3 Education 4.0: The Sunrise of Digital Technology

In the epoch of smartphone classrooms, robotic home assistance, and online assessments, it is not generally hard to envisage what Education 4.0 holds for us. Tapped as the fate of education—ready to change the utilization of information sensationally—Education 4.0, in a way, finishes the marvel of consistent computerized infiltration into our lives.

Instruction 4.0 is the new buzzword, disturbing our conventional idea of tutoring, teaching, and learning. Today's students have never observed a world without the web, and along these lines, they cannot envision living without being online. They are the genuine model of digital natives. They live and inhale innovation. Growing up associated with the cyber world utilizing different gadgets empowers them to process and ingest vast amounts of data daily. They are social media addicts. Their brains are continually streaming and moving in different directions. They can flourish in four-dimensional simulated or augmented reality environments. We see digitalization approach by which the economy delivers and trades products and enterprises utilizing savvy and self-sufficient frameworks powered by information and machine learning between Industry 4.0 and Education 4.0. What we have in the Fourth Industrial Revolution is the extending human-machine association, bringing forth an innovative society.

17.2.4 Education 4.0 amid Industry 4.0

This is the right time in the 21st century to bring education into force. Students ought to have teachers who use a developed perfect curriculum for students. Tomorrow, some of the tools will help students become active learners whereby every individual identifies with their potency for education rather than knowledge.

17.3 The Divergence in Education 1.0, 2.0, and 3.0

The academic shift from Education 1.0 to Education 4.0 is one from education to people. Education institutions are doing well moving from Education 1.0 and subsequently to Education 2.0 and Education 3.0, to where they have to plan and implement Education 4.0. In this digital world, the internet has become a vital force all over the globe. This internet world is improving well-being for the individual, which has positively impacted the web. Today's internet has become a massive factor in human behaviour and thinking. At this point in time, the internet helps students to work, learn, and play a healthy way in society at large.

17.3.1 Education 1.0

Nowadays, most education organizations are still going with Education 1.0 which they are working through. Many institutions now refuse the utilization of Education 1.0 because of the focal point on curriculum-based teaching, which can be challenged in many ways: 1) as dictatorial; 2) as students are the passive beneficiaries; 3) as a teacher-centred system whereby teachers feed knowledge to the students; and 4) as technology can be outlawed inside the classroom (Figure 17.2)

Students sit in the classroom at their desks, and the teacher teaches the subject. It is a unidirectional process whereby students attend the educational institutions to get knowledge from their teachers, who can provide data as an outstanding schedule that may incorporate the utilization of class notes, course books, recordings, and lately the web.

17.3.2 Education 2.0

Education 2.0 has flourished using Web 2.0, which interacts with individuals and organizations and reveals better optimism or facilitation using the innovation. Here, the discussion happens lawfully using information and communication tool. This has hastily generated a new challenge for teachers and students to build a façade with online teaching. In an e-learning environment, teaching and learning take place differently than in the traditional classroom, giving the educators and learners new challenges in utilizing the online learning environment. In Education 2.0, communication and teamwork are growing now, in a results-based approach. Remember that by learning, many people taught that they stopped talking about teaching. They talk about knowledge and educational consequences, but they are still on documents. Still, schools are talking about the hours of teaching, but still learning about hours of learning. Development of the technological invasion (Education 2.0)—invasion of technology and social networking—means that they apply technology to the classroom as a trend indicator. The lesson still endures to have the same structure, students faced complete confusion, and learners distinguish that technology is better than teachers. There is no design for what is used and what is not; for many choices, there is no money for buying and applying them (Figure 17.3).

FIGURE 17.2 Education 1.0

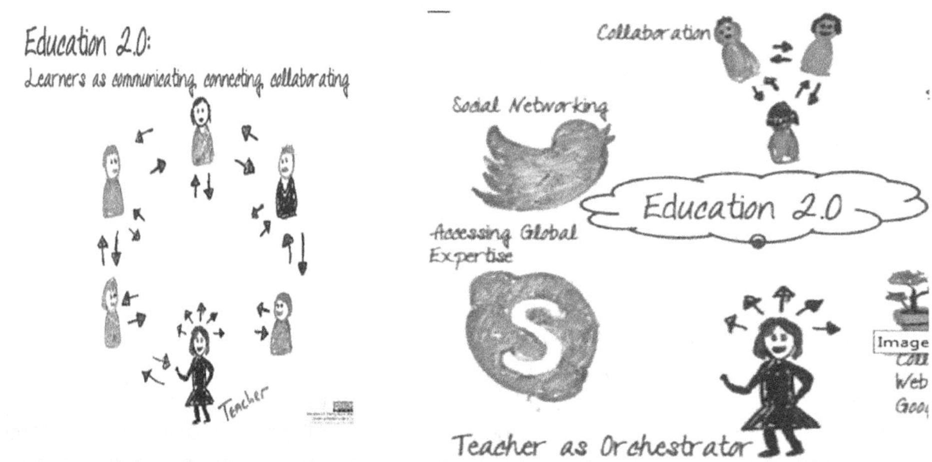

FIGURE 17.3 . Development of technological invasion (Education 2.0).

17.3.3 Education 3.0

Education 3.0 is grounded on the certainty that information is explicitly and rapidly accessible, and on internet-based scholarship whereby analytical thinking, novelty, and innovation compel the data. It is portrayed by rich, cross-institutional, multifaceted instructive open doors inside which the students participate in knowledge creation by collectively interacting personality to personality, which plays a substantial role in social building by: 1) a learner-centric approach; 2) educators being transformed as catalysts and mentors; 3) learners delving into research; 4) flip-class room methods are applied; 5) more dialogue—technology is everywhere; 6) students are self-learning and everywhere; 7) the classical style classroom no longer exists; and 8) lesson plans are now called learning plans (Figure 17.4).

Education 3.0 is a way of dealing with educating and learning. There is a prominence in learning and teaching methods with interest in the educational transformation to break the restrictions among mentors and learners in higher educational institutions. Mentors, students, and technological devices are one kind of substance that can gather individual learners, teachers, and enlightening needs.

FIGURE 17.4 Education 3.0.

17.4 Is Education 4.0 the Ultimate Vista of Learning?

Since Education 4.0 signifies changes, significant to Industry 4.0—and since it is in light of the global call for activity by the World Economic Forum—industry can expect a better-readied workforce, and students will have better employability and better grounding for the future with a superior return expectation for educational investment. Education 4.0 is planned for improving the profitability of a representative and improving the seriousness of the industry. It intends to strengthen the excellent and competitive capacity of the nation as a whole.

Such a framework whereby creativity and innovativeness of the human intellect are improved will make educated students progressively arranged for an uncertain and unstable future. In this way, with Education 4.0, the students, the industry, and the country will have the option to harvest the profits better amid the Fourth Industrial Revolution. Each child is a conceived virtuoso and is gifted with potential in specific regions and accompanies an option to acquire an effective life, and the education framework must empower each child to do so. The essential motivation behind education and training is to engage people to have fruitful existence and contribute best to themselves and their families, society, nation, and humanity.

17.4.1 How Do We Adapt to The Fourth Industrial Revolution?

With innovation quickly changing our economic and social realities, the subject of how to set up the more youthful—and even the current—generation for the Fourth Industrial Revolution has been a problem that is begging to be addressed by contemporary higher education. Are our education frameworks and programmes pertinent to the Fourth Industrial Revolution? Furthermore, if not, how would we remake our education systems with the goal that they are?

17.4.2 Embedding Industry 4.0 in Higher Education Institutions

The "21st-century skills" often involve competencies identified with learning and invention and alphanumeric literateness, as well as vocation and lifetime [1]. This testament expands on the conversation by critical investigative services for the Fourth Industrial Revolution—Industry 4.0. There are two fundamental methodologies that enlightening outlines may take near Industry 4.0: instruction followers or modification creators. Groups have the right skill sets and aptitudes for replying to the variations in their workplace, adapting their presentations, and figuring out how to adapt to technological development. Working with cyber-physical framework features is the significance of human communication: we are more interconnected than ever before. As digitalization, robotization, AI, and the modern web expand the level of irrelevant work, human abilities for idea sharing, basic reasoning, and underscoring with others are called for. While Industry 4.0 is as yet developing, and we probably will not have comprehensive sympathy for the right skills until we look back 30 years from now, forerunning organizations are embracing innovations to realize the potential embedded in Industry 4.0.

17.4.3 Education 4.0 for Teachers

Education 4.0 and technological innovations bring a new revolution to serve many stakeholders, including mentors and learners (Figure 17.5). Instructors believe that Education 4.0 is tailored wisdom that will base more work on knowledge. On the other hand, it is helpful for mentors and learners in educational organizations who are more likely to meet the requirements of learners. Through mentors are learners edified, not classes where instructional tools and techniques advance this personalized learning objective. This shows better learning and enlightening outcomes, which can bring a relay on mentors and instructors. Education 4.0 mentors and learners concur to find the best approach and scheme to ease

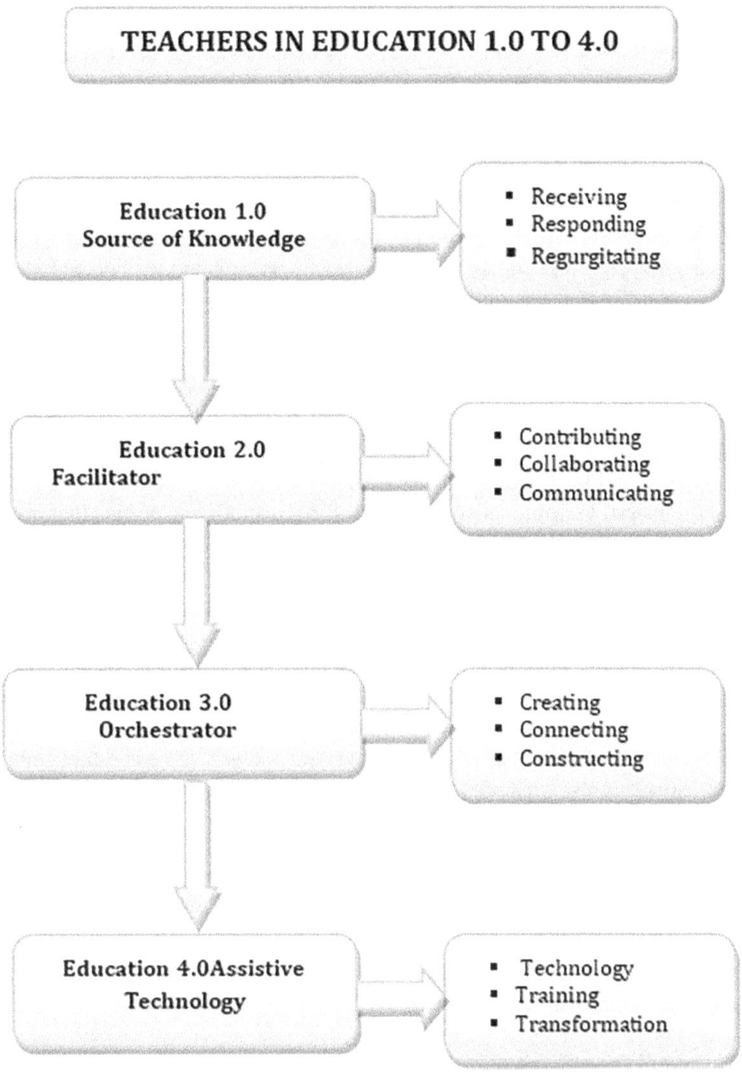

FIGURE 17.5 Teachers in Education 1.0 to Education 4.0.

energy [2]. Many automations and procedures reduce the burden of the top-level administrators while modernizing precise measures and teaching techniques—Education 4.0 plans to improve performance by improving teaching aptitudes and civilizing student knowledge outcomes.

17.4.4 Education 4.0 for Students

The most crucial objective of Education 4.0 is to persuade students and improve learner outcomes, since students play a predominant role in the educational ecology and produce learning outcomes as an output. In the history of education, ecology students are the dominant recipients of Education 4.0. Employing mentors, learners can join together more healthily with bountiful stakeholders in the framework by interacting with the parents, mentors, and administrators. In Education 4.0, the degree of implementation is the learners learning outcomes. Learning can be improved as a more significant part of tools and techniques that assist with learning more successfully than the traditional teaching methods. As part of curriculum development, Education 4.0 is a characteristic in teaching techniques, which makes students indulge in learning through different gears and stages when learners attach and study easy retrieving to education resources.

17.4.5 The Role of Qualitative Research in Education 4.0

In the progress of higher education, the pertinence of qualitative investigation in Education 4.0 is an excellent point of interest. Qualitative research is exceptionally pertinent in advanced education primarily because qualitative research develops and sustains abilities that are fundamental in the Fourth Industrial Revolution. These skills include sense-making, social insight, adaptive thinking, personal adaptability, cognitive flexibility, and knowledge management. Sense-making alludes to our underlying concepts and deeper meaning, and more profound significance of what is being communicated by the research participants. Social intelligence is best exhibited in qualitative research during interviews, focus group discussions, and the like. Social intelligence is a vital aptitude in the Fourth Industrial Revolution, as workers are essential to labour together besides constructing relationships with people across social and cultural settings.

Like sense-making, social knowledge is another advantage of humans over machines, which is pertinent in the Fourth Industrial Revolution. Adaptive thinking is another expertise that qualitative research works among scientists. Our ability to react to one-of-a-kind and unforeseen circumstances to figure out solutions is appropriate to emerging problems. Adaptive thinking relates to our ability to deal with conceptual variations, particularly in addressing discrepancies between generated knowledge and existing social assumptions and constructs [3].

The troublesome idea of the Fourth Industrial Revolution proffers vulnerabilities and haphazardness in all parts of life, making the versatile reasoning aptitude essential. Qualitative research additionally sustains intellectual adaptability. Qualitative research requires a conception of ideas across multiple perspectives simultaneously during data collection and data analysis. This is established as our knack to analyse data with transparency, particularly those data representing diverse epistemological and ontological groundings.

17.4.6 The Effects of Education 4.0 in Industry 4.0

Higher education needs to extend its innovation framework reforms in the fourth era of the current upheaval by breaking all hindrances to innovation. The speed of innovation should be increased to help economic and social development (Figure 17.6).

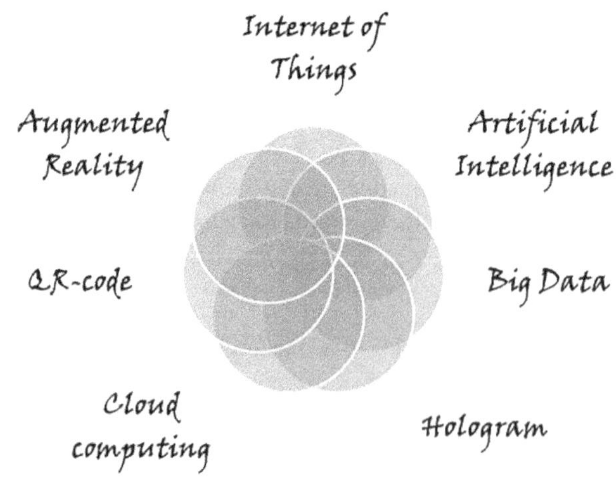

FIGURE 17.6 The effects of Education 4.0 in Industry 4.0.

17.5 Education 4.0: Is India Ready?

With the arrival of information and communication technology (ICT) in teaching, scalability and personalization of teaching and learning have become easier to accomplish. Nowadays, universities can spread out to engage yet unreached students over digital stages and subsequently scale up their support to the learners (Figure 17.7). Also, filings can be curated as per the level of beginners in these stages, which gives a trace of knowledge modified or tailored to them [4].

These existences, the mainstream knowledge fillings can be digitized and communal over knowledge portals which can be retrieved on any innovative strategies everywhere. The examination also articulates that the "new-fangled Millennial" beginners are massively tech-friendly and are armed to consume online knowledge. Amity University and other higher teaching institutions are currently overpowering these tests by leveraging the operational tools and digitizing study material for portable delivery of expertise to every corner of the world.

17.5.1 Education 4.0: A New Paradigm in Changing the Prospect of Education in India

The significant role of Education 4.0 in Industry 4.0 is use of new technological advancements by higher learning institutions. Fusing the latest technologies can raise the feasibility of the educating and learning processes. With new advances, students would have more attention towards learning, and they would require more. Following are examples of the most recent innovations headways in Education 4.0 (Figure 17.8).

17.5.1.1 Augmented Reality (AR)

This innovation can quicken the education and knowledge process, and also improve the student culture experience. It can decrease the unimportant work that teachers need to do, increasing the meaningful learning experience for the students [5].

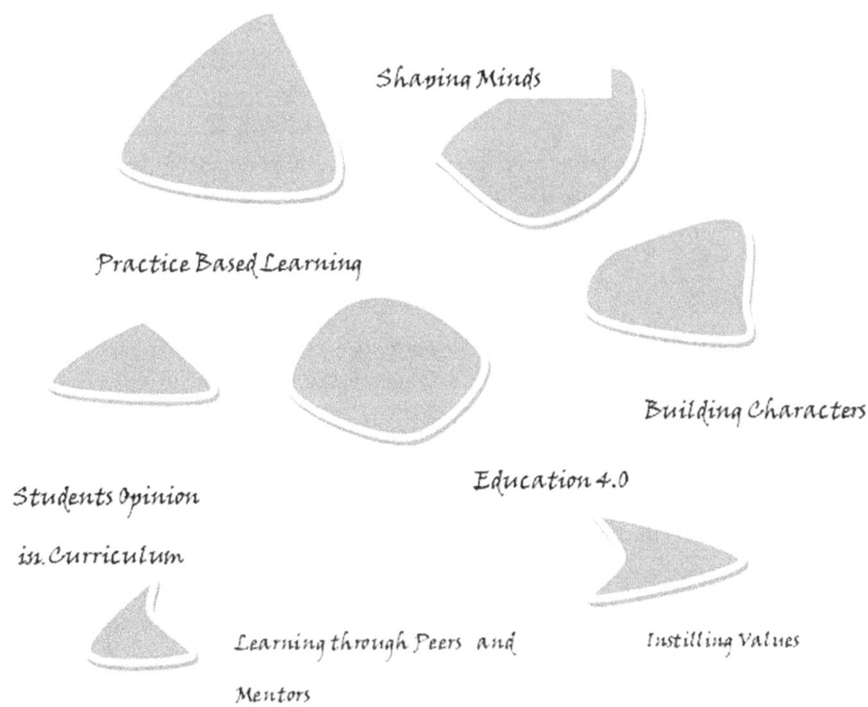

FIGURE 17.7 Trends for Education 4.0.

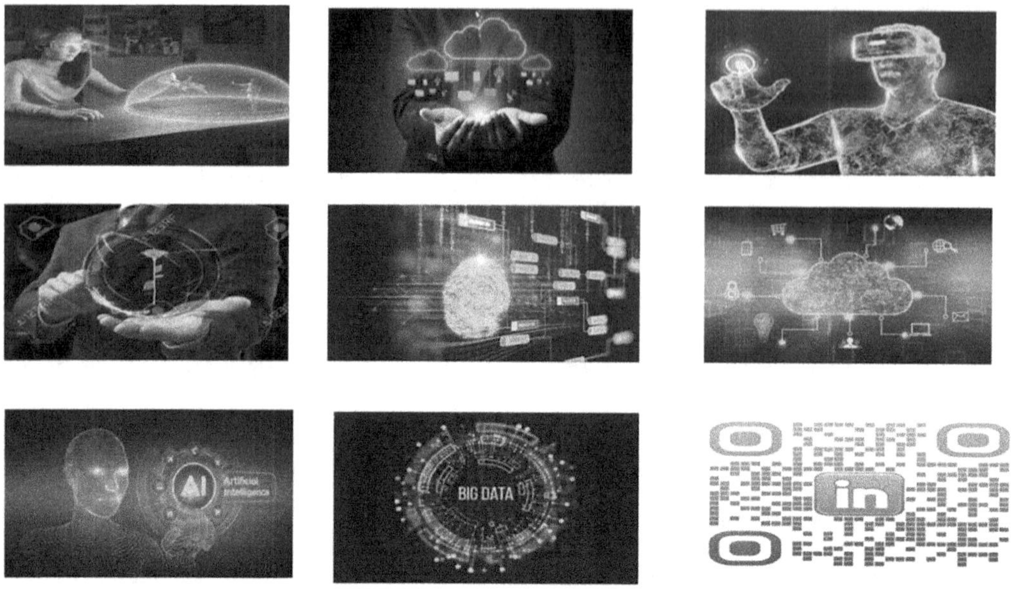

FIGURE 17.8 QR code: An easy access.

17.5.1.2 Cloud Computing

This trend-setting innovation helps students lessen their burden to convey their homework, substantial course readings, and assignments. With a web connection, they can access their work at home from their group at anytime and from anywhere.

17.5.1.3 Virtual Reality (VR)

This technology allows students to increase deeper engagement as compared with a traditional textbook. VR adds visual components and effectively improves the associations between learning ideas and information.

17.5.1.4 Holograms

This technology causes students to learn progressively, which can be incorporated into the natural environment. This innovation additionally offers a visual and intelligent learning experience.

17.5.1.5 Biometrics

Facial recognition, fingerprints, and eye-tracking are useful in class participation, which can spare time in the classroom for security purposes and make students' comprehension superior.

17.5.1.6 Internet of Things (IoT)

The IoT affects training explicitly with the ever-developing ubiquity of mobile and other web-connected devices. This innovation assists with building up fast collaboration between students and teachers in and out of the classroom.

17.5.1.7 *Artificial Intelligence (AI)*

This innovation can quicken the teaching and learning process and improve the student learning experience. It can decrease the unimportant work that teachers need to do, resulting in a more meaningful learning experience.

17.5.1.8 *Big Data*

This innovation helps oversee information that is conceivable to discover evidence, and can encourage exchange of information among institutions and students' academic performance related to attendance patterns.

17.5.1.9 *QR Codes*

A quick response (QR) code is an advanced digital image available from a free QR scanner that can be filtered using gadgets. Use in the classroom can decrease the dissatisfaction of long web addresses, which they can quickly scan the QR code.

17.5.2 University: The Prospect of an Open System

Educational institutions are able to widen interest in open scholastic frameworks among the neighbourhood networks and the social order everywhere, turning them into a vital piece of an institution of the higher education environment—a keen interchange among the institution of higher education, industry, and the public headed for developing a living platform with the dissemination of thoughts and information [6], with necessities on every individual being provided by others (Figure 17.9). Educational institutions could create healthy relations among the public and corporations by contributing the practical elucidation based on their confined questions. The prospective methods of carrying out learning and research will include Intensification of Multi-Disciplinary Research,

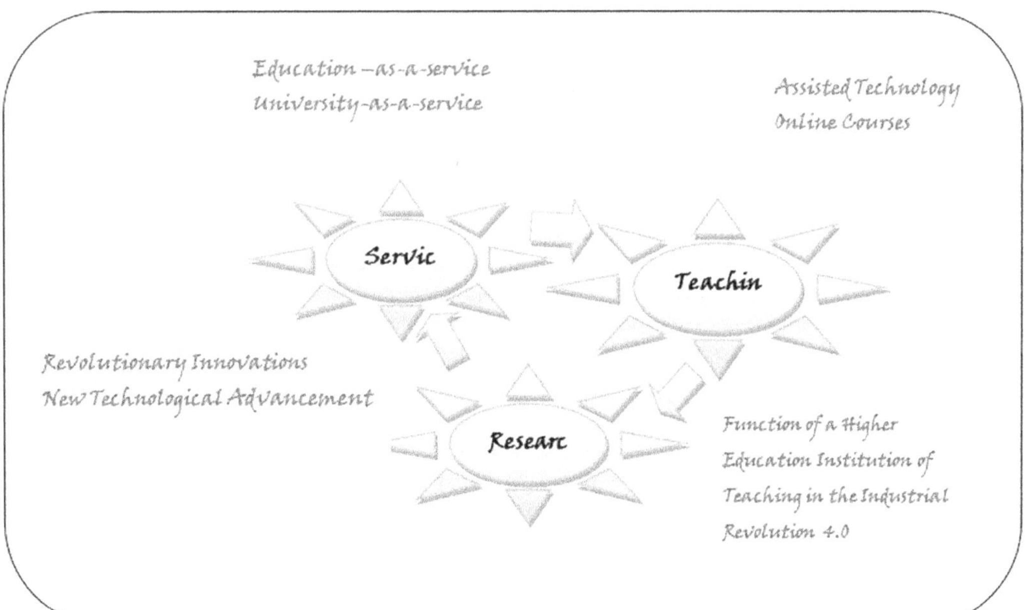

FIGURE 17.9 The prospect of an open system.

1. **Intensification of Multi-Disciplinary Research**

   Higher educational institutions like the universities require breaking the inmost steps of exploring and working collectively through the superlative of various departments surrounded by the institution and different institutions route for compelling the expertise potency. It is leased to collaborate in other research fields, which may prompt contemporary and the social order neighbourly follow a line of investigation.
2. **Experiential Learning for Better Knowledge Prospects**

   Instruction could move through erudition of responsibility, as the industry and the simulators attach consent to growing like the experimental learning systems. Among such organisms, learners are more likely to welcome the use of the information communicated, and furthermore, it is presently transmitting the global challenges. Technology utilization such as simulation and AR/VR might be developed for revelation of the practical world [7]. Educational institutions require pursuit of the model instances of utilizing the most recent innovations to get better throughout the experience by teaching students, providing equivalent significance to interchange guiding methods like data analytics, chatbots, and AI.
3. **Platform Approach to Learning**

   The educational institution's future would empower gaining from the facilitator of education, online learning system, experts from corporate, former students, and stakeholders of the student community. It would encourage a climate of a friendlier learning system, societal gathering, and advising by peer groups like alumni, faculty, peers, and industry experts [8]. The educational institutional should embrace the pioneering technology as guidance for lessons planned together with experimental learning, interactive learning, mobile learning, etc.

17.5.3 Application Intensification of Learning Analytics at the University Level

The chief object of this investigation is to hurry the expansion of Education 4.0 based on a holistic examination of the impressions of Industry 4.0 and current education policies and performs concerning digitalization and cohorts of significant quantities of information. The consequences comprise the description of the present nation of the art of manufacturing Revolution 4.0 and Education 4.0 to provide and improve requests of industry speaking to the short emergencies such as interoperability, information slide and trust, and occasions to implant education analytics inside Education 4.0 in advanced teaching administrations [9].

17.5.4 Strategy for Curriculum Development: A Simplified Framework

Extensive data collection and analysis relate a massive quantity of information for requests utilizing extrapolative analytics, information withdrawal, arithmetical examination, and other tools. Because of the students' exercises, their presentation can be anticipated by applying information, content, and web mining strategies—for example, deterioration, connotation rules detection, cataloguing, gathering, gratified and up-to-date examination, and data mining software (Rapid Miner, XLMiner, Data R) [10]. Prognostic analytics empowers the expectation of a student's conduct, aptitudes, and execution by examining various traces of their work while efficiently connecting with the virtual learning environment (VLE).

Learning analytics (LA) is concerned with the variety, inspection, valuation, and seeing through of material about beginners and teachers directing sympathetic and enhancing knowledge procedures and the connected secondary surroundings where imparting knowledge is execution. Academic analytics (AA) are recognized with the commercial vision and performs in higher education institutions. Business intellect is an organization of operations and inventions for a social affair, examining and granting admission to assist relations to construct a healthier employment conclusion.

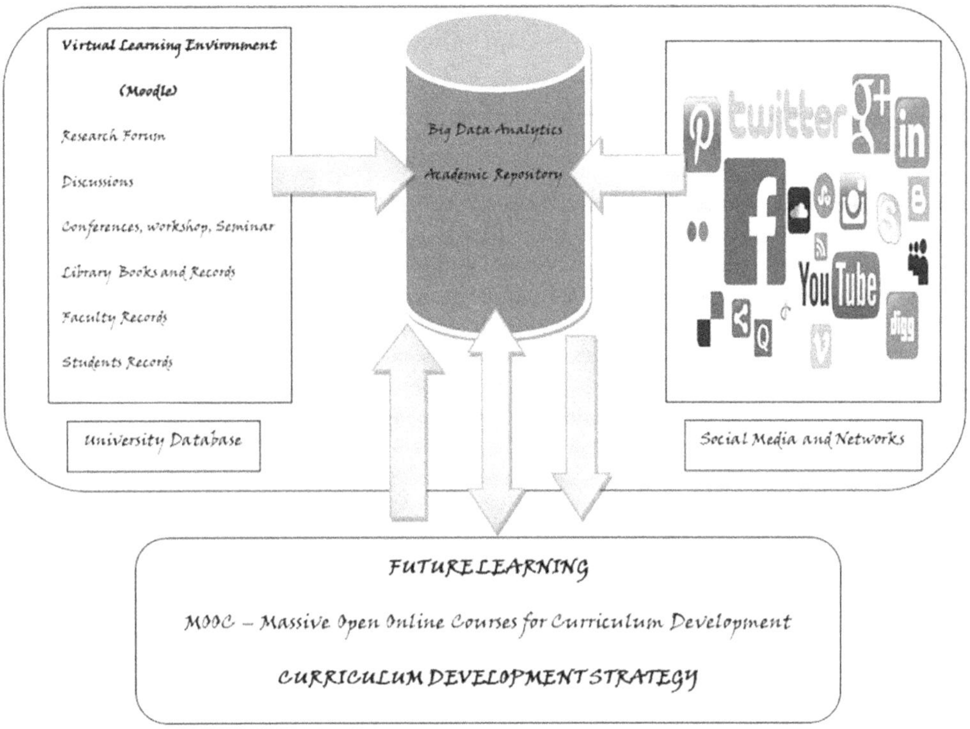

FIGURE: 17.10 Strategy for curriculum development in Education 4.0

Confront of Big Data Analytics

1. Information incorporation construction and organizations.
2. Assortment of appropriate data dispensation, examining schemes and gears.
3. Data confidentiality and moral matters of through discovering learner and staff information.

Flout of Big Data Analytics

1. Data reconciliation architecture and frameworks.
2. Determination of suitable information preparing and dissecting frameworks and tools.
3. Information security and ethical issues of utilizing/investigating student and staff data.

The Endorsements for Applying Knowledge Analytics

1. Integration of VLE (such as Moodle) with different frameworks (attendance monitoring, feedback tracker, etc.) and related databases.
2. Moodle ought to be incorporated as a part of the Moodle VLE to engage educators/instructors to deal with the learning journeys of their learners.

Broadening this conceptual framework will additionally bolster the application of Education 4.0 that is portrayed by educators and coaches utilizing Industry 4.0 innovations (IoT, Big Data, AI, virtual reality) which may boost the sensitivity of the studied material. Also, showing production lines 4.0 will plug into the recently initiated and can adopt latest technologies with hands-on exercise experience and workspaces which call all the pupil to utilize these advanced techniques which will recover the excellence and bestow feasibility of their tasks perhaps opening new capacities. These methods in the teaching labs will heighten their assimilation into a genuine industrial environment as new pioneers have familiarized themselves with the reliable perspective and the capabilities provided by Education 4.0.

17.6 Conclusion

One of the approaches to support our education system framework is utilizing advanced tools in the education and erudition processes, which will assist students in understanding the learning contents more successfully than using a conventional approach. The technological revolution as of late, known as Industry 4.0, is roused by the development of Big Data database innovations, distributed computing, machine learning, artificial intelligence, and the Internet of Things. Due to the advancements and development of the new scientific solutions referenced, the procedures of innovatively organized analyses of enormous data assortments gathered in Big Data database systems dynamically develop. Educators need to know how to utilize advanced technology to build up their abilities and competency.

17.7 Acknowledgement

I would like to express my most profound appreciation to all the people behind me in completing this chapter work. First and foremost, I proffer my sincere gratitude to the honourable vice-chancellor Prof. Dr. P. Kaliraj on his excellent leadership for instilling confidence in me during the pursuit of the chapter and even though he allowed me to work in my way and contribute the level of my work to encouragement in the book. I express gratitude to Dr. K. Murugan, former Registrar i/c, Bharathiar University, for the academic support provided to carry out the research work. I show appreciation to Prof. Dr. T. Devi, coordinator, and everyone involved in completing the book. I put forward my sincere thanks to Dr. E. Chandra, professor and head, Department of Computer Science, for providing the background designed for enrichment of this chapter towards the end of precious work in the province of Education 4.0 for curriculum development.

REFERENCES

[1] Priya Sharma, "Digital Revolution of Education 4.0", *International Journal of Engineering and Advanced Technology (IJEAT)*, Volume 9, Issue 2, December 2019.

[2] Anealka Aziz Hussin, "Education 4.0 Made Simple: Ideas For Teaching", *International Journal of Education and Literacy Studies*, Volume 6, Issue 3, July 2018, p. 92.

[3] Rasika Lawrence, Lim Fung Ching, Haslinda Abdullah, "Strengths and Weaknesses of Education 4.0 in the Higher Education Institution", *International Journal of Innovative Technology and Exploring Engineering (IJITEE)*, Volume 9, Issue 2, Series 3, December 2019.

[4] D. Mourtzisa, E. Vlachoua, G. Dimitrakopoulosa, V. Zogopoulos, "Cyber- Physical Systems and Education 4.0 – The Teaching Factory 4.0 Concept", *Procedia Manufacturing*, Volume 23, 2018, pp. 129–134.

[5] Tania Jezabel Lopez-Garcia et al., "Review of Trends in the Educational Model of Distance Education in Mexico, towards an Education 4.0", *Computer Reviews Journal*, Volume 3, 2019. ISSN: 2581–6640.

[6] A. Hariharasudan, Sebastian Kot, "A Scoping Review on Digital English and Education 4.0 for Industry 4.0", *Social Sciences*, Volume 7, 2018, p. 227.

[7] Aida Aryani Shahroom, Norhayati Hussin, "Industrial Revolution 4.0 and Education", *International Journal of Academic Research in Business and Social Sciences*, Volume 8, Issue 9, 2018, pp. 314–319.

[8] Dr Ruchi Tandon, Dr Sanjeev Tandon, "Education 4.0: A New Paradigm in Transforming the Future of Education in India", *International Journal of Innovative Science, Engineering & Technology*, Volume 7, Issue 2, February 2020.
[9] Anealka Aziz Hussin," Education 4.0 Made Simple: Ideas For Teaching", *International Journal of Education & Literacy Studies*, Volume 6, Issue 3, June 2019, pp. 92–98.
[10] Phan Kieu Linh, "Education in Industry 4.0", *International Journal of Engineering Science Invention (IJESI)*, Volume 8, Issue 6, Series I, June 2019, pp. 9–13.

18

Industry 4.0 for Service 4.0 through Research 4.0: A Framework for Higher Education Institutions

Italia Joseph Maria and T. Devi

CONTENTS

Objectives

The fourth wave of the industrial revolution, Industry 4.0, has already called upon Education 4.0. This chapter provides a framework for Education 4.0. It examines what Education 4.0 is and how faculty and students should be equipped for it, and discusses various means by which the curriculum of higher education institutions can be transformed to support Education 4.0. Another significant topic of discussion of this chapter is Research 4.0, which should be the backbone of all these processes. The chapter reiterates the fact that all these transformations should lead to Service 4.0, whereby education and its benefits reach the rural and urban population alike.

18.1 Introduction

Industry 4.0, the fourth important step made in the manufacturing process, was a technological approach envisioned for 2020. With 2020 having already arrived, most of the world's countries are in the streak of adopting this new technology to achieve an advanced level of automation and a more improved level of operational efficiency and productivity (Lu, 2017). This new revolution was proposed as an emerging concept for refurbishing the German economy in 2011 (Zhou et al., 2015). Though it was originally considered only for the manufacturing industry, with the fact that billions of people are connected by mobile devices with immense processing capability, access to knowledge, and storage capacity—and with the

DOI: 10.1201/9781003318378-18

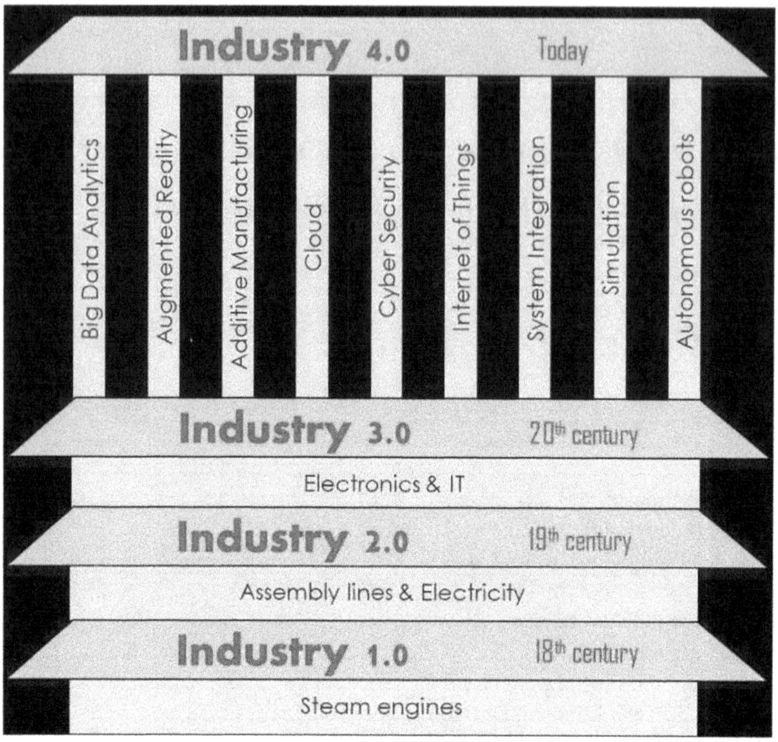

FIGURE 18.1 Industry 1.0 through Industry 4.0, and the nine pillars of I4.0.

powerful network established by the Internet of Things (IoT)—every walk of life is seeing the impacts of Industry 4.0. Professor Klaus Schwab, founder and executive chairman of the World Economic Forum, says in his book *The Fourth Industrial Revolution* that Industry 4.0, as he calls it, has started to change the way people relate to one another, live, work, educate, and grow (Schwab, 2017). Augmented reality (AR), the industrial IoT (IIoT), autonomous robots, additive manufacturing, cloud computing, horizontal and vertical system integration, cybersecurity, simulation, and Big Data analytics are said to be the *nine pillars* (Figure 18.1) of this fourth wave of technological advancement (Rüßmann et al., 2015). Enterprise resource planning (ERP), cloud-based manufacturing, radio frequency identification (RFID), and social product development are some of the technologies and paradigms associated with Industry 4.0.

Following with an introduction in Section 18.1, Section 18.2 discusses the progress from Industry 1.0 to Industry 4.0, Section 18.3 describes the core of Industry 4.0, Section 18.4 describes how Education 4.0 can be achieved by restructuring Curriculum 4.0 in the light of Industry 4.0, and Section 18.5 discusses the transformation needed by faculty and students to be ambassadors of Industry 4.0 as Faculty 4.0 and Student 4.0. Section 18.6 makes a discourse on how Research 4.0 can take Education 4.0 to the forefront and Section 18.7 addresses the big question of the future of jobs in the light of this industrial revolution. A framework for higher education institutions (HEIs) is proposed in Section 18.8, which shows Service 4.0 as an essential outcome of Research 4.0, and how it should benefit society. Section 18.9 provides the conclusion.

18.2 Industry 1.0 to Industry 4.0

To look back briefly into the short history of Industry 4.0, one has to date back to the 1760s, when steam and water-powered engines were developed to assist workers. This paved the way to the First Industrial Revolution, when a transition to new manufacturing processes involving steam and water was seen. It took almost two centuries until, by the advent of the 20th century, electricity emerged as the prime source of power, to have a transition to the Second Industrial Revolution. By the last decade of the 20th century, with the invention of transistors and integrated chips, the Third Industrial Revolution started and continued to progress even at the commencement of the 21st century with the use of electronics and information technology to support further automation of manufacturing (Liao et al., 2017) and the widespread use of the Internet. Thus, we can say that while the First Industrial Revolution introduced automation, the Second Industrial Revolution introduced production, whereas the third is characterized by the utilization of robots. The aim of the Fourth Industrial Revolution, as it was conceived in 2011, was the use of intelligent production robots (Gubán & Kovács, 2017).

18.3 The Core of Industry 4.0

Today, this Fourth Industrial Revolution wave is not just about industry, smart manufacturing, and the production of robots. Making exponential growth in terms of technical change and socioeconomic impact (Morrar et al., 2017), the heart of Industry 4.0 is the development and implementation of intelligent network-linked systems—or stated in another way, people, products, equipment, and machines that communicate with each other. Though envisaged for 2020, this new technological reform has already made an impact in many aspects of everyday life. Leveraging the usage of the Internet, machines can already be controlled using remote devices and mobile phone applications. Another attractive feature is 'smart factories', where thousands of identical parts can be simultaneously manufactured and a batch of one piece can be produced seamlessly on the same production line with no extra setup or cost. Communication, virtualization, and cyber-physical systems are some other significant areas where Industry 4.0 has brought breakthroughs. Whatever be the technological advancements, innovative and sustainable system solutions (Bassi, 2017) should be the by-product of this important transformation. Equally important is the fact that this is the first time when an industrial revolution has been predicted beforehand, instead of being observed after its inception (Drath, 2014).

18.4 Education 4.0 Using Curriculum 4.0

We are in an era characterized by intelligent technology where fast changes can be seen in the physical, digital, and the biological world (Xing & Marwala, 2017). Industry 4.0 involves a combination of innovative practices and approaches in terms of processes, services, applications, and products. It will surely remarkably renovate the education ecosystem. Education has already transformed from the traditional classroom modes to digital learning and e-learning. In India, the motto of the Department of Higher Education which comes under the Ministry of Human Resources Development is 'Quality at Scale' (GKToday, 2019). This can be achieved only through a large infusion of appropriate technology into the teaching and learning process. Education 4.0 when it aligns with Industry 4.0 should incorporate *digital platforms which include interactive learning, adaptive software, video games, conventional literature, simulation*, and *peer discussions*. Moreover, this is suitable in today's society due to the availability of new digital technologies, its wide reachability, the world being digitally networked, and also because it guarantees inclusion and equity of all people regardless of their ages, educational qualifications, and communal backgrounds. There are many innovative methods in which digital learning can be materialized, such as online learning, augmented learning, flipped classrooms, personalized learning, blended learning, innovative learning, and open and distributed learning (ODL) (Maria et al., 2019).

18.4.1 What is Curriculum 4.0?

When education is thus transformed in drastic manners, of course, it might be an after-effect of the transformation made in the underlying curriculum, which means Education 4.0 is the natural by-product of Curriculum 4.0. Universities have redefined the conventional means of content delivery with disruptive and innovative measures (Xu et al., 2018) so that *outcome-based programmes* are designed. This is to train our generations with up-to-date knowledge and skills to face the realities of the future (Ellahi et al., 2019) so that the result would be industry-ready students. Moreover, *innovative practices, social initiatives, domain expertise programs, and value-added courses* should also become an integral part of the curriculum. Outcome-based education (OBE) is an approach for nurturing the autonomous learning ability of students. It fosters innovation and practice, as well, in addition to aiding in developing personal skills such as independent innovation ability and systematic thinking. OBE can be delivered using simulated platforms, research projects, or by trying novel teaching methods in classrooms. These new teaching methods can be *project-based learning, problem-based learning*, or even *application-based learning*. The outcomes of this modality of learning might be surprising in the form of improved personality traits, higher personal motivation, and even increased cognition (Zhang et al., 2021).

All innovations in education benefit HEIs since these they are ranked today by many agencies nationally and internationally. These *accreditations for HEIs* are a boon in disguise which ensures quality education is imparted to students in all aspects. The need for accreditation comes from the fact that there is a multitude of new programs and courses designed to meet local requirements and foreign trends. Moreover, there are novel forms of partnerships signed between private/public and local/foreign bodies. Education providers are arising all the more, and the modes of delivery are diverse and innovative, which registers the fact that there should be some form of quality checking (Knight, 2005).

Curriculum 4.0 calls for extensive *industry exposure* which emphasizes the involvement of more industrial experts as special invitees in the boards of studies of each programme. These experts can be research and development managers, product development managers, or industrial experts. The quality and relevance of Curriculum 4.0 should promote stronger cooperation between industry, research, education, and training organizations, and should better align advanced manufacturing education and training with the needs of the new industrial age. Students and faculty should be encouraged to conduct industrial visits and also take up short-term internships in industries. Credits for these activities should be included in Curriculum 4.0.

International exposure is another important agenda that should be included within the curriculum. This enables local students to acquire global thinking and a global outlook. A multitude of methods is available for this, including faculty-student exchange programs, paper presentations in international conferences, case-based study approaches, experiential learning, problem-solving approaches, and team-based project work. Courses should be designed so that maximum use of e-learning resources, self-learning courses, digital and online courses, and information and communication technology (ICT) are promoted. Blended learning, field-based training, industrial visits, projects, and internships also should come under the umbrella of Curriculum 4.0, and these multiple approaches of learning should be enlisted in the syllabus with reference to which part will be used for mastering each part of the course.

Choosing a particular branch or domain should not restrict students from exploring other areas in which they are interested. Curriculum 4.0 should contain the provision for *interdisciplinary studies*, which involves combining two or more academic disciplines into one activity (Wikipedia Inc., 2020). Interdisciplinarity is about creating something by thinking across boundaries. It can mean a science student acquiring knowledge from other domains like psychology, sociology, arts, or economics. Apart from the core courses required of students, it should be mandatory for them to freely choose from other disciplines in which they are interested.

Preserving knowledge using *digital repositories* should be another area of concern while moving towards Curriculum 4.0. Students should be provided with an immensely rich repository of curricular materials and learning resources, both print and digital, in such a way that it is easy to use and provides one-step access to knowledge. Typical forms of content creation related to academics can include creating and uploading YouTube videos; uploading course materials to the cloud, which may serve as a one-stop repository of related information; maintaining and updating blogs; creating forums; and responding to queries and editing and distribution of digital media (Bates, 2015).

18.5 Faculty 4.0 for Student 4.0

Creation of a continuous *professional development programme* for all faculty is a need of the day, since no teacher can be an expert on everything, even in their area of interest. Hence, learning technology support units are necessary for the actual development of teaching in the current digital age. *Student feedback and peer assessment and online student satisfaction surveys* continue to serve as important motivators to teachers in improving themselves. They can update their teaching methods based on student feedback and incorporate more innovative techniques in their curriculum for content delivery. Since Curriculum 4.0 asks for digital content development, Faculty 4.0 should be equipped to contribute their knowledge and expertise so that they are transferred to digital media. *Digital content development* should be given sufficient priority in faculty development, since most teachers may not be experts in these areas. Moreover, teachers should use technological applications that augment cognitive learning abilities, and personalized adaptive learning techniques should be used for preparing learning outcomes.

18.5.1 Faculty 4.0 Profile

Today, with the increasing use of technology in education in the Fourth Industrial Revolution, the prime objective of a teacher will be to provide the initial learning environment and context. This will bring the learners together. It will also help them to develop their own learning environments that in turn will connect them to 'successful' networks. As a result, learning will automatically occur through exposure to the flow of information and the individual's autonomous reflection on its meaning. For this, the student will have to depend on digital repositories that are readily available, and the teachers will be facilitators who are trained for flipped classroom teaching and blended teaching experiences. The profile of Faculty 4.0 should include *expertise in digital tools, familiarity with open and free digital content, ability to deliver and manage proper content, collaborative learning skills, and proficiency in creating digital content* (Figure 18.2) (Maria et al., 2019). In short, Faculty 4.0 should go hand in hand with Curriculum 4.0 to transform a student into Student 4.0.

FIGURE 18.2 Profile for Faculty 4.0.

FIGURE 18.3 Student Standards set by ISTE.

18.5.2 Student 4.0 Profile

The ISTE (International Society for Technical Education), which empowers educators who use technology in education, in 2016 set standards for students (Figure 18.3) to enable them to thrive and engage in a digitally connected world. This is essential in transforming a student into Student 4.0 to cope up with Education 4.0. According to ISTE, the students who started to use technology in the late 1990s started to use it to learn by 2007, and now tin Education 4.0 have started using technology to transform learning. The ISTE standards for students ensure that learning is a student-driven process, and they accordingly envision a student as a *digital citizen*, a *global collaborator*, a *creative communicator*, a *computational thinker*, an *innovative designer*, a *knowledge constructor*, and an *empowered learner*. This profile will prepare a student to face the challenges of Education 4.0, and for this purpose, teaching and learning methods should go hand in hand with the skills of this new educational revolution. One simple method to cite as an example will be remote learning or flipped classrooms, whereby students gain theoretical knowledge by digital means, and practical skills are acquired by face-to-face interactions and involvement in workshops (International Society for Technology in Education, 2020).

18.6 Research 4.0: To Take Education 4.0 to the Forefront

The instinct to know and learn more is inherent in every human being. With Education 4.0 aligned with Industry 4.0 at the doorsteps of even rural areas, more and more research has to be carried out as to how digital technology like artificial intelligence (AI), cloud computing, industrial internet, and predictive analytics can be of more help to take knowledge creation to new levels. For sure, it is the extensive and in-depth research on the IoT, AI, cybersecurity, AR, cyber-physical systems, simulation, and the other pillars of the Fourth Industrial Revolution that resulted in the technological advancements the world experiences today. In other words, rapid advancements in technology are seen daily, which is an outcome of research on cutting-edge technology, but it makes research on emerging technologies a need of the hour. Scientists, researchers, and academics are responsible for giving increased research attention so that state-of-the-art outcomes are produced in line with Education 4.0, instead of making meagre numerical manipulations and claiming research results. Research should be improved with creative thinking and the adoption of out-of-the-box methodologies. Good research results will always be society-oriented and for the common people, as is evident in Industry 4.0, which is influencing the way one works, lives, and grows (Schwab, 2017). Thus, Education 4.0 must be augmented by Research 4.0, thus becoming all the more committed towards Service 4.0.

18.7 The Big Question: Jobs 4.0

Looking at the jobs scenario today, both routine blue-collar and white-collar jobs are easily automated by robots and algorithms. But drawing lessons from history, McKinsey & Company (2017) report that automation is not a new phenomenon, but rather is right from Industry 1.0—the First Industrial Revolution—when the panic about jobs and fears about the transformation of the workplace were active. Continuing the same trend, today at the verge of Industry 4.0, as well, many existing jobs may be decreasing in demand while the demand for highly-paid digital and creative skills in the emerging industries will increase. At a time when industry and the whole way of living are being transformed by this new wave of digital technology, McKinsey & Company concludes that about 400–800 million current occupations could be displaced by 2030, but only in the case of jobs involving physical labour, data collection and processing, manufacturing, and accommodation-cum-food services (McKinsey & Company, 2017). McKinsey researchers note that if history can be trusted, *about 10% of labour demand in 2030 will be for new types of jobs* that were previously nonexistent. This is rightly underlined by the World Economic Forum, which predicts *rapid growth of employment in emerging sectors like robotics, blockchain, and AI*, and in non-technical sectors like *customer service*, *sales*, *marketing*, and *skills development* (Leopold et al., 2018). The good news is that combined with expected employment growth in sectors of elderly care, green technology, and the like, there can be *overall 555–890 million new jobs created by 2030*, which is much more than the jobs lost due to automation (International Society for Technology in Education, 2020).

18.7.1 Skills Needed

With Industry 4.0, the key skills required for future employment will be the five human skills of *interdisciplinary knowledge, people skills, critical thinking, mental elasticity and complex problem solving, and creativity* (Gopalakrishnan, 2019). These human skills should enable students to manufacture new products thus meeting the expectations of government and society. Setting up *innovation and incubation centres* is needed to augment the creative minds of young graduates to meet the expectations of society, industry, and the government. Already, most of the HEIs have incubation centres with governments and agencies supporting them with funds and infrastructure. The opening of incubation centres provides young minds like highly trained students, professors, and small industries with open access to leading-edge technologies and infrastructure facilities (Prasad, 2017). Moreover, the host institutions benefit from building links with local bodies, which expands their aims regarding student employability.

18.7.2 Prominent Job Sectors

Prominent sectors that will have more jobs are *healthcare*, *education*, *information technology*, *digital marketing*, *automation*, *manufacturing*, *logistics* and the like. The demand for doctors, nurses, pharmacists, and drug developers will be ever-increasing, and so will be the demand for better medicine and treatments. Although the digital transformation will happen in Education 4.0, the demand for teachers as facilitators and mentors will never decrease. As Industry 4.0 will take over our daily workspace, and as AI, IoT, data analytics, AR will be the driving forces, specialists in these areas will ever more be needed.

Digital marketing will be another area where experts will be required for the marketing and promotion of online businesses and firms. Any business without an online platform will find it hard to thrive in this digital era, and hence, digital marketing experts will be ever in need. *Automation specialists* like drone pilots, data specialists, and informatics specialists will be in high demand due to the advancement in technology. The *manufacturing field* will require specialists when robots and AI will take over most of the jobs. Global trade will take new forms which will create more jobs in logistics. Moreover, *digital careers* like 3D printing, user experience designing, mobile application development, cybersecurity, and data analysis also will be in high demand in the industry. At a time when *robotics* is gaining more roots, skills needed to design, build, and service robots will be difficult to master, and robotics engineers will be in high demand. All these shed light on the fact that jobs will never be less for Student 4.0, rather he should be equipped for Jobs 4.0, in line with the Education 4.0 he received.

18.8 Service 4.0: The Framework for HEIs

The term service means the action of helping someone or doing work for someone. Every research should be for the good of society and the betterment of the lives of people. In that aspect, whatever research be done under the umbrella of Industry 4.0–cum–Education 4.0–cum–Research 4.0 should focus solely on Service 4.0. Services and integrated solutions resulting from research should bring a multitude of benefits in the economic, environmental, and biological domains (Paschoua et al., 2018). Sophisticated living ways are possible for humans in urban areas, whereas basic living conditions remain a dream for many, both in India and in the whole world. Klaus Schwab, the founder of the World Economic Forum, is right when he says that inequalities may grow and societies may fragment if organizations are unable to adapt to the new wave, and governments may fail to regulate new technologies in the light of Industry 4.0 (Schwab, 2017). But this should not happen. Service 4.0 is now a term in the literature that refers to meeting customer needs, service, digitization of services, services sector, and after-sales maintenance. *Service 4.0 should be for the benefit of the common man, the whole world, and the whole ecosystem in which humanity lives. Hence, Education 4.0 should lead to Service 4.0, whereby people of all walks of life are enjoying all benefits of Industry 4.0 and Research 4.0, regardless of the differences they may have* (Figure 18.4).

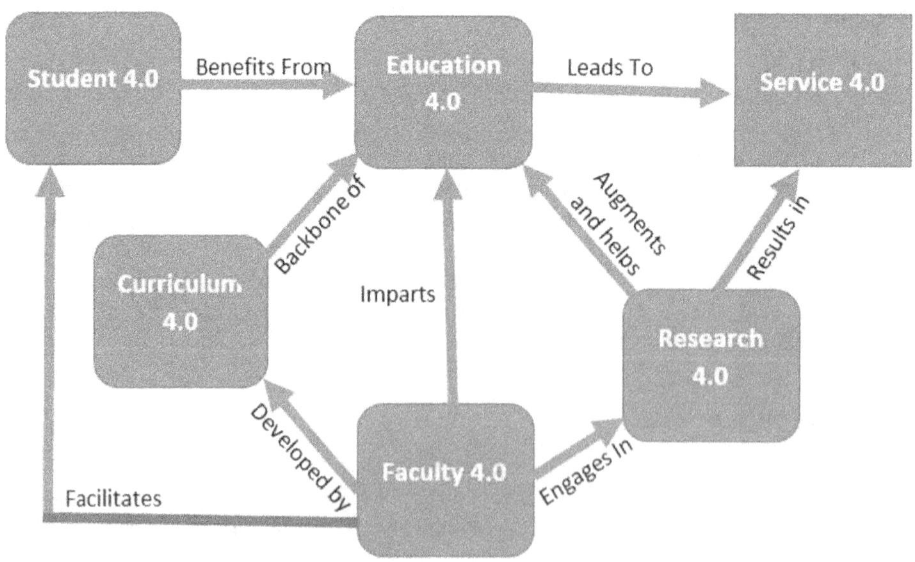

FIGURE 18.4 Framework: Education 4.0 for Service 4.0.

With industries working on Industry 4.0, youth becoming educated with Education 4.0, and research carried out in line with Research 4.0, it should be the responsibility and priority of industries and HEIs, in particular, to make Service 4.0 reach every human—regardless of caste, creed, colour, and income. Progress in AI, cybersecurity, and all the nine pillars of Industry 4.0 should reach and benefit people in all walks of life. Education 4.0, which makes students industry ready, should inspire them to become responsible citizens of the country, with rich ethical and social values. Research 4.0 should have the common people in mind and hence be focused on delivering innovative and quality products and services for the betterment of their lives. Unless this happens, the transformations of faculties to Faculty 4.0 and students to Student 4.0 will be of no worth. Faculty should be ready and skilled to impart quality and responsible education as envisaged by Curriculum 4.0 to the students going through this Fourth Industrial Revolution. This makes Industry 4.0 not just making revolution in terms of smart factories or smart manufacturing, but bringing transformations in all walks of life. Thus, *Industry 4.0 aimed at Service 4.0 should bring about Lifestyle 4.0.*

18.9 Conclusion

The Fourth Industrial Revolution is drastically changing the modes in which individuals relate to each another, live, work, and educate their children. These shifts are enabled by smart technologies, including artificial intelligence, Big Data, augmented reality, blockchain, the Internet of Things, and automation. These technologies are disrupting every industry across the world at an unprecedented speed. This chapter was an attempt to provide a framework to Education 4.0 in Higher education institutions in the light of Industry 4.0. Education 4.0 can be achieved only through revised Curriculum 4.0, which is made up to date by Research 4.0. Faculty 4.0 is required to develop this curriculum, conduct the necessary research, and deliver this to Student 4.0. Higher education institutions where education is provided as a service should eventually turn out to focus on Service 4.0, which may bring significant benefits to the whole world.

REFERENCES

Bassi L., 2017, "Industry 4.0: Hope, hype or revolution?" *IEEE 3rd International Forum on Research and Technologies for Society and Industry (RTSI)*

Bates A. W., 2015, *Teaching in a digital age: Guidelines for designing teaching and learning*, Vancouver, BC: Tony Bates Associates Ltd, ISBN: 978-0-9952692-0-0

Drath R., 2014, "Industrie 4.0—eine einführung", *Open Automation*, Vol. 3, pp. 2–7

Ellahi R. M., Khan M. U. A., Shah A., 2019, "Redesigning curriculum in line with industry 4.0", *Procedia Computer Science*, Vol. 151, pp. 699–708

GKToday, 2019, "EQUIP: 5-year vision plan on quality education by HRD ministry", www.gktoday.in/current-affairs/equip-5-year-vision-plan-quality-education-hrd-ministry/, [Accessed June 29, 2020]

Gopalakrishnan B., 2019, "Essential skills for future job—Skills for year 2030", https://community.nasscom.in/communities/talent/future-of-jobs/essential-skills-for-future-job-skills-for-year-2030.html, [Accessed February 29, 2020]

Gubán M., Kovács G., 2017, "Industry 4.0 conception", *Acta Technica Corviniensis—Bulletin of Engineering; Hunedoara*, Vol. 10, No. 1, pp. 111–114

International Society for Technology in Education, 2020, "ISTE tandards for students", www.iste.org/standards/for-students, [Accessed April 12, 2020]

Knight J., 2005, "The international race for accreditation", *International Higher Education*, Vol. 40

Leopold T. A., Ratcheva V. S., Zahidi S., 2018, "The future of jobs report 2018", *World Economic Forum*, https://www3.weforum.org/docs/WEF_Future_of_Jobs_2018.pdf, [Accessed March 20, 2020]

Liao Y., Deschamps F., Loures E. F. R., Ramos L. F. P., 2017, "Past, present and future of Industry 4.0—a systematic literature review and research agenda proposal", *International Journal of Production Research*, Vol. 55, No. 12, pp. 3609–3629

Lu Y., 2017, "Industry 4.0: A survey on technologies, applications and open research issues", *Journal of Industrial Information Integration*, Vol. 6, pp. 1–10

Maria I. J., Thirupathi D., Rajendran R., Velumani B., 2019, "Technologies, challenges and tools for digital learning," *2019 IEEE Tenth International Conference on Technology for Education (T4E)*, Goa, India, pp. 268–269

McKinsey & Company, 2017, "Jobs lost, jobs gained: Workforce transitions in a time of automation", [Accessed April 18, 2020]

Morrar R., Arman H., Mousa S., 2017, "The fourth industrial revolution (industry 4.0): A social innovation perspective", *Technology Innovation Management Review*, Vol. 7, No 11, pp. 12–20

Paschoua T., Adrodegaria F., Rapaccinib M., Saccania N., Peronaa M., 2018, "Towards service 4.0: a new framework and research priorities", *10th CIRP Conference on Industrial Product-Service Systems*, (IPS), Sweden

Prasad A.V. R., 2017, "Importance of innovation and incubation in higher educational institutes in India", *Higher Education Review,* https://www.thehighereducationreview.com/opinion/last-word/importance-of-innovation-and-incubation-in-higher-educational-institutes-in-india-fid-41.html, [Accessed March 26, 2020]

Rüßmann M., Lorenz M., Gerbert P., Waldner M., Justus J., Engel P., Harnisch M., 2015, *Industry 4.0: The future of productivity and growth in manufacturing industries*, Boston, MA: Boston Consulting Group

Schwab K., 2017, "The fourth industrial revolution: what it means, how to respond", *World Economic Forum*, www.weforum.org/agenda/2016/01/the-fourth-industrial-revolution-what-it-means-and-how-to-respond/, [Accessed March 20, 2020]

Wikipedia Inc., 2020, "Interdisciplinarity", *Wikipedia, the Free Encyclopedia,* https://en.wikipedia.org/wiki/Interdisciplinarity, [Accessed March 27, 2020]

Xing B., Marwala T., 2017, "Implications of the fourth industrial age for higher education", *The_Thinker__Issue_73__Third_Quarter_2017,* https://papers.ssrn.com/sol3/papers.cfm?abstract_id=3225331, [Accessed March 23, 2020]

Xu M., David J., Kim S. H., 2018, "The fourth industrial revolution: Opportunities and challenges", *International Journal of Financial Research*, Vol. 9, No. 2

Zhang X., Ma Y., Jiang Z., Chandrasekaran S., Wang Y., Fofou R. F., 2021, "Application of design-based learning and outcome-based education in basic industrial engineering teaching: A new teaching method", *Sustainability*, Vol. 13, No. 5, p. 2632

Zhou K., Liu T., Zhou L., 2015, "Industry 4.0: Towards future industrial opportunities and challenges", *12th International Conference on Fuzzy Systems and Knowledge Discovery*, Zhangjiajie, China, pp. 2147–2152

19

Electronics in 2030

S. R. Vijayalakshmi and S. Muruganand

CONTENTS

Objectives

Technology development takes place in many important electronic subfields such as a microcontrollers, communication, web technology, semiconductors, etc. Technology innovation will be of two different kinds, known as supporting and disruptive. If the existing market evolves with better value, then it is supporting innovation. An example of supporting innovation is a higher speed microchip improving the performance of the personal computer. Disruptive innovation creates a new market, which hugely alters the existing one. Automatic cars, digital media, and downloadable new software are a few examples of disruptive innovation. New smart products will penetrate the market by 2030.

DOI: 10.1201/9781003318378-19

19.1 Introduction

Technology distribution enables new online business models. It ultimately eases the business to develop economic growth. Mobile phones are used for digital payments. They facilitate price-fixing for the crop market between farmers and sellers remotely, which improves transparency in fixing prices and delivers the product in real time. Online digital payments can be processed in a real-time developing financial transaction [1]. The distance between innovators and adapters is much reduced. Digitalization reduces communication obstacles and enables a stronger exchange of information worldwide.

A hospital doctor network is possible with innovative medical technologies. By 2030, India will require 12 times as many doctors as currently available, but this gap will be narrowed by the technologies such as remote medical analysis, Internet treatment advice, new biological methods to address diseases, virtual counseling by doctors, e-records, telemedicine, and online medicine/drug delivery. Genetically modified mosquitos crash malaria disease-carrying species. Genetically modified crops help to diminish natural deficiencies. By 2030, chronic diseases will increase due to aging and changing living habits. Technology innovations help to increase the lifetime. Artificial organs, 3D printed implants, induced pluripotent stem cells (IPSs), and neuro-scientific progress for early diagnosis are some of the medical developments. IPSs heal harmed cells and cure tumors.

The speed of innovation in the Internet of Things (IoT) is difficult to predict. Trillions of devices will be connected to the Internet in 2030. Smart cities are built in which all objects are connected for communication with the human through the Internet. Mobile augmented reality (AR) and virtual reality (VR) are big computing platforms. By 2030, open-system hardware and sensors will be incorporated into cloth, glass cars, etc. There are many changes to come in different fields.

Meta-materials are composite structure artificial materials. They have properties that do not exist in nature. They attain desired effects and allow flexibility in many applications. These materials will be manufactured and used in the future. Smart fabrics are wearable and can perform electronic functions. Smart fabrics have components such as biomedical sensors, microcontrollers (MCUs), wearable antenna, and anything required. Wearers get increased safety and added value such as sensing medical vital data which can react to environmental radiation and are quick to send out alerts in emergency cases. Sportsmen use these to monitor physiological parameters.

Open-source development boards such as Raspberry, Panda, and Arduino have modified this decade's electronics. In the future, such new development boards will arise for new applications. Network-on-chip microprocessors will be available for better artificial intelligence (AI) integration. MCUs with networking on-chip communication, multi-processor system-on-chip, chip-microprocessor, and many other new MCUs are developed based on user requirements. A single chip contains hundreds or thousands of processors. Customer demand will increase and be the reason for the development of electronics in the future.

Fifth-generation (5G) capability has started now and will be the major mobile technology until 2025; 6G might appear afterward. IoT, inter-vehicle communication, and terahertz (THz) communication are 6G elements [2]. The high-frequency spectrum between gigahertz (GHz) and THz is the operating frequency for 6G. Technologies incorporated into 6G include millimeter-wave technologies, multiple input/multiple output (MIMO), dense networks, universal filtered multicarrier frequency division multiplexing, and flexible duplex and time division duplex (FDD and TDD). It plays an important role in the retail market, augmenting products to evolve the marketplace. New technologies such as new field communication, AR, smart drones, data mining with predictive analysis, thermal imaging cameras, smart shopping, and the sixth sense are used rapidly in the retail market to meet the rapid speed and challenges of retailers.

19.2 Semiconductors

AI and quantum computing need compound semiconductors to attain full commercialization. New emerging technologies demand improvement. Silicon alone is not sufficient. Next-generation chip needs

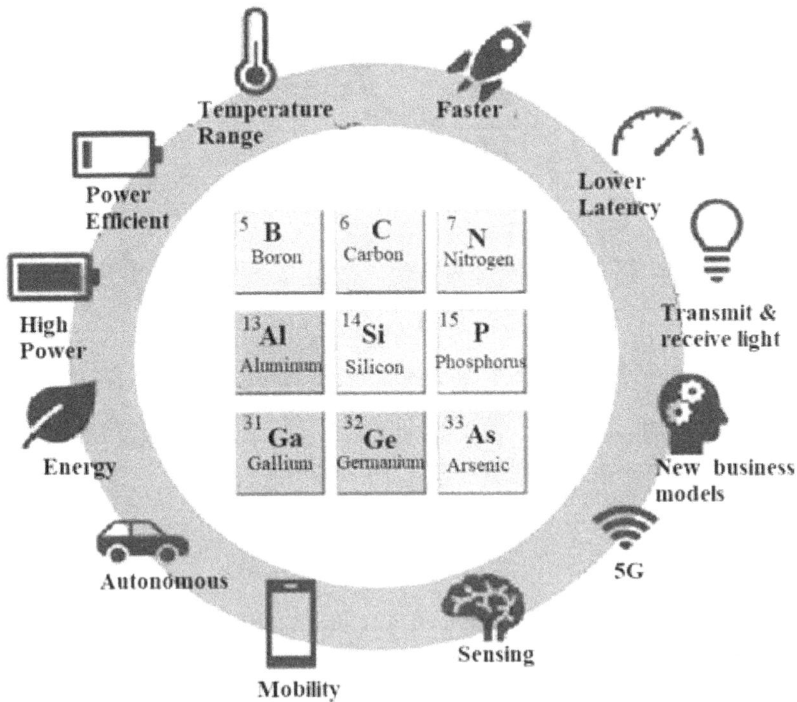

FIGURE 19.1 Table of elements for next-gen electronics by compound semiconductors.

compound semiconductors, which combine two or more elements to create new compounds such as gallium nitride (GaN) and indium phosphide (InP).

Speed, light, and power are three application areas in which silicon has drawbacks, as mentioned. Compound semiconductors outperform in these areas. Compound semiconductors operate at higher frequencies than silicon. They are useful in high-speed data transfer over 5G networks. Compound semiconductors emit and detect light efficiently, and they are suitable for 3D sensors which are used in health diagnostics and facial recognition. Silicon cannot emit light, and light detection efficiency is also limited. Compared with silicon, compound semiconductors can handle higher power levels with lower losses, which extends the range of electric vehicles. Figure 19.1 shows a table of elements for next-generation electronics powered by compound semiconductors.

The low utilization rate of compound semiconductors compared with silicon is due to their performance and cost ratio in the supply chain. Hence, compound semiconductors have not been used for high-volume applications of silicon. The supply chain contains five stages, as shown in Figure 19.2: wafer, die, chip, system, and final product. The compound semiconductor supply chain is also the same as the silicon supply chain. The lithography process etches transistors from the wafer and created an array of chips on the die. The chips are cut from the die then individually packaged as chips. After that, they are integrated into the system and then finally are assembled into the product. The value increases by 5–10 times from one stage to another in the case of compound semiconductors.

The wafer is created in a compound semiconductor using a process known as epitaxial growth. This process is complex and more difficult, producing wafers not more than 100mm in diameter. Compound semiconductor die is more difficult to handle than silicon. The compound semiconductor needs a special packaging process, but a silicon wafer is a single crystalline growth with high-level purity. The high volume of silicon chips is created from 450mm diameter silicon wafers. This scalability maintains a high performance and low cost ratio for silicon chips.

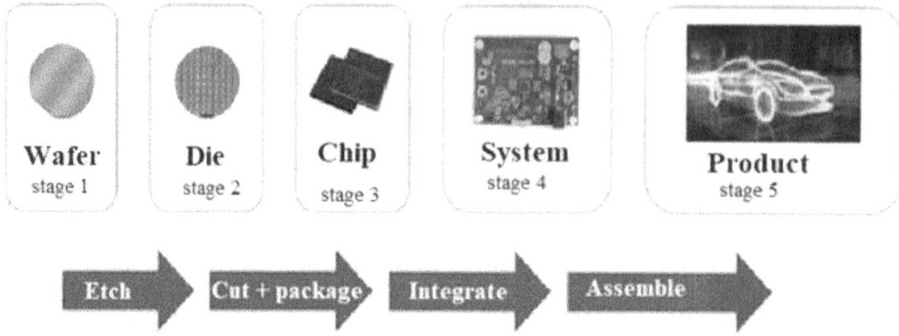

FIGURE 19.2 Stages in the supply chain.

Quantum computing and quantum cryptography need precise lasers to freeze atoms. They operate at absolute zero. Such operation is possible only with compound semiconductor lasers. By 2030, it is expected that chips housing quantum systems will be created.

19.2.1 Chip Resistors

Chip resistors or surface-mounted devices are small and mostly available in square chip packages. They do not have leads. They have superior heat dissipation and stable resistance value. The length and width determine their power ratings. The commonly used resistor codes are three-digit and four-digit systems. Surface mount technology is a method for producing electronic components in which components are mounted directly on the printed circuit board surface.

19.2.2 Light-Emitting Diodes (LEDs)

LEDs are not only used for lighting applications, but also in the health sector. LED surgical light helps for high-intensity white light with high color production during surgery. It reduces eye strain and mental fatigue of the surgeons. It never radiates heat, thus reduces cooling requirements. High-powered white LEDs are used as the source of fiber optic devices in endoscopic lighting. It gives high luminous output, high light wavelength control, high quality, and superior energy efficiency. Flexible micro-LED arrays are used as wearable light sources and high-tech surgical gloves.

Phototherapy provides specific color ranges using light wavelength and duration of exposure to treat a variety of medical health issues. Red light penetrates the deepest tissue and could help to stimulate the natural biological process. It helps damaged and weakened cell healing. Blue light is used to treat new-born neonatal jaundice disease. Bright white light helps to give treatment for sleep disorders. The retina of the eye is exposed to timed bright white light for a specific period. The light triggers a biochemical reaction in the brain, preventing melatonin production which determines the sleep cycle.

Photodynamic therapy uses LED light to treat skin conditions and cancer cells. Skin wounds and severe skin spots are cured by the LED light. LED light can emit at a consistent, uniform narrow-band wavelength. By 2030, new technologies and new developments will be taking place in LED. A new ultra-thin elastic micro-LED display fits comfortably on the skin. The integrated biomedical sensor system is composed of an elastic display, lightweight sensor, nano-mesh electrode, and wireless communication module. This flexible skin electronics measure medical data through sensors and display it on the screen. It also transmits the data to the cloud and memory devices.

The vertical micro-LED wearable device stimulates treatment for re-growing hair without generating heat and without causing thermal skin damage. The glucose level in the tear is monitored by the smart contact lens. Sensors to measure glucose, wireless transfer information circuits, and LEDs are in-built in a smart contact lens. The sensed level is displayed on an embedded LED display in real time. The lenses also provide drug delivery for eye treatment when lenses are integrated with transducers for diagnosing and treating visual diseases, as shown in Figure 19.3.

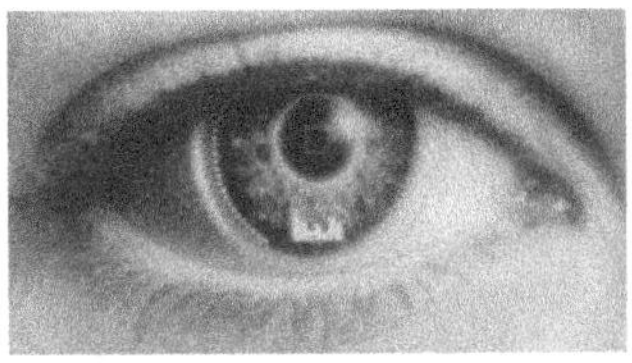

FIGURE 19.3 Contact lens to treat visual diseases.

FIGURE 19.4 OLED to monitor oxygen.

A flexible OLED (organic light-emitting diode) sensor could detect the blood oxygen levels of humans. OLED sensors assembled on printed sheets of photodetectors on top and organic red and infrared (IR) LED on the bottom can detect oxygen levels and be placed anywhere on the skin as shown in Figure 19.4. LED IR therapy helps in reducing pain in the neck and back caused by muscle tension, irritated joints, and strains.

19.2.3 Transistors

New transistor types—2nm and 1nm nodes—are scheduled to come after 10–15 years; 2.5nm and 1.5nm nodes are scheduled to come in 2027 and 2030, respectively. But, 3nm and beyond are predicted not to happen because of Moore's law and chip scaling. Today's leading-edge transistor technology, finFET type, could not provide beyond 5nm. Next-generation transistor technology called gate-all-around field-effect transistors (FETs) are replaced by finFET to provide beyond 4nm. In this gate-all-around FET, finFET is placed on the side, and the gate is wrapped around it.

High-performance computing, AI, machine learning, autonomous driving, 6G, mobile, and servers will require more horsepower in the future. Several technologies are working for 2.5nm and 1.5nm nodes. Hence, industry is going to extend gate-all-around FETs, complementary FETs, negative-capacitance FETs, and vertical nanowire FETs, integrating devices into an advanced package.

FinFETs will have the next generation. Beyond that, material changes to germanium or channels III–V and gate-all-around. Moore's law states that transistor [3] density will double every 18 months. At each node of the process, the cost and complexity hit the roof. Now applications require advanced processes like self-driving cars. Hence, for 2.5nm 1.5 nm nodes, some gap is available in the fabrication industry. To overcome this, new technologies will be implemented in the industry. Extreme ultraviolet (EUV) lithography is required for beyond 7nm. Beyond 5nm, high numerical aperture EUV lithography is

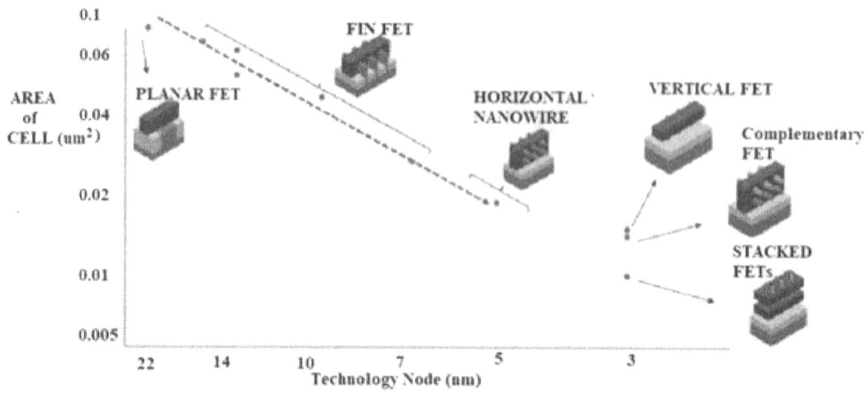

FIGURE 19.5 Next-gen transistor architectures.

required. The fabricator requires an array of selective deposition and etching technologies. It will enable the vendor to deposit and remove materials in precise locations. The wiring scheme in the chip needs new materials to avoid congestion. Figure 19.5 shows next-generation transistor architecture.

The gate-all-around FET uses tiny wires and sheet-like materials for channels in the case of nanowire FET and nanosheet FET, respectively. It improves performance and reduces leakage. Complementary FET stacks both n-type and p-type FET on each other for area scaling. It helps in power and performance, but it is difficult to make a taller structure in the fabrication. Vertical FET stacks the wire vertically, and it gains area. Source, drain, and gate are stacked on top of each other. This technology is also difficult to make in fabrication. 3D nanofabrics will also be possible in the future to meet new field requirements.

19.2.4 Integrated Circuits

Silicon MOSFET for integrated circuits (ICs) are expected to run out of shrink benefits by 2030. The extreme UV (EUV) lithography switched from lenses to mirrors because of such small wavelengths of light. These mirrors need very precise coatings with zero tolerances, but with a precise mirror, only 70% of light can be reflected—so getting enough light requires a very bright source of light such as a laser. Laser EUV tools need to push 30 million worth of information onto each wafer in coming years.

Beyond 2024, high numerical aperture (NA) EUV is expected to upgrade fabrication. Higher NA means bigger mirrors. Multi-color lithography, e-beam patterning, nanoimprinting technology, 3D transistor stacking, and physics of new materials will affect IC fabrication by 2030. Table 19.1 shows the developments in IC fabrication.

TABLE 19.1

Development in IC Fabrication.

Year	Technology
Until 2010	Dry technology, scaling and strain limitation, Wavelength λ = 248nm
Up to 2020	Immersion technology, geometric confinement Wavelength λ = 193nm Numerical aperture = 0.85 NA
Plan 2025	Extreme ultraviolet (EUV) technology, 2D advancements Wavelength λ = 13.5nm Numerical aperture = 0.33 NA
Plan 2030	High numerical aperture EUV technology, 3D, new physics, new material advancements Wavelength λ =13.5nm Numerical aperture = 0.55 NA

19.2.4.1 Disruptive Technologies in ICs

If materials like nanotubes, diamond, or graphene are used for ICs instead of silicon transistors, then processor logic could be different. All materials have high thermal conductivity. CMOS (complementary metal oxide semiconductor) technology has limitations such as heat dissipation and limited clock rates. It could integrate with the latest technologies to overcome these limitations.

Silicon can be replaced with diamond. Diamond-based transistors have excellent electrical characteristics. High electrical conductivity is a property of graphene and nanotubes. Because of lower dissipation power, heat generated by these is very much reduced, increasing energy efficiency. It allows high clock rates and high integrated packages.

Photons are used for communication in photonics technology. It is used for inter- and intra-chip bus communication. Die stacking is another technology that could result in 3D multiple-core microprocessors. This technology reduces intra-core wire length. It enables high bandwidth transfer, low latency, and low power consumption.

3D stacking will be used to scale flash memory. Flash memories by the 3D method are substituted by memristor or non-volatile memory technologies. These technologies have high structural density, low leakage power, and fast read and write access, and they are cost efficient and stronger. Using non-volatile technology, storage-class memory is the first machine. It has new data access models and protocols. This technology increases efficiency, with increased fault tolerance, increased capacity, and low latency.

Resistive computing, neuromorphic computing, and quantum computing are some other technologies for new hardware accelerators. Low power consumption and huge parallelism are advantages of resistive computing. Artificial neural network (ANN) applications need energy efficiency and space capability. Neuromorphic computing is well suited for ANN. Cryptography, searching, and specialized computer applications are solved by quantum computing technology.

Die stacking and 3D chip integration represent stacking ICs vertically in multiple layers. Processors and memories are stacked vertically in these technologies. It can be achieved by connecting separately manufacturer's wafers or dies vertically. The mechanical and electrical contacts package as system-in-package and package-on-package.

19.3 Microcontrollers

Microcontrollers will alter the IoT and human lives, with a supercomputer in every pocket and everywhere in the world. Smartphones usage keeps increasing, and there are as many phones as humans now. After the hardware revolution, the next comes to smartphones by 2030. There will be a hundred times more non-mobile phones interconnected devices in the world than the human population due to the IoT. This is shown in Figure 19.6. Technology growth is repetitive. Something comes big and changes our relationship with the world—smartphones, the Internet, television, and so on. All these things have a deep affect on the human relationship with the world. GPS directions change how we operate with our surroundings and with each other. In less than ten years, 2030 technology will have an unimaginable large effect upon our styles and species.

19.3.1 Microcontroller Generation

A microcontroller (MCU) is a standalone mini computing chip. An MCU has everything it needs to run. It includes memory for code and application storage, and random-access memory (RAM) to execute. These are built to control hardware and process the operation running on it. They play important roles in embedded hardware, so they have lots of general-purpose input/output (GPIO). Communication between MCUs and control hardware peripherals is done through GPIO. These include digital I/O, analog I/O for reading environmental parameters with connected sensors along with associated protocols such as I2C, serial, SPI, CAN, and other analog sources, and many more. MCUs have features such as JPEG hardware, and cryptography to control camera and security products. They also have display controllers and 2D graphics. They have drivers to drive displays and accept touch screen input.

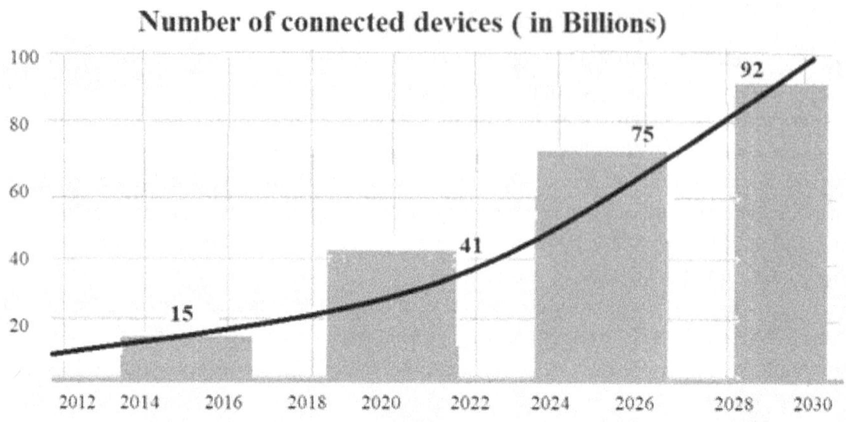

FIGURE 19.6 IoT-connected devices growth.

The smart home has 30 times as many microcontrollers as central processing units (CPUs). There are at least 30 microprocessors in new cars, and automatic cars may have more than that. Many home appliances are controlled by microcontrollers, which are also used in complex applications. They have built-in support for gateway connectivity such as ethernet, wi-fi, and other means. Their memory buses enable them to drive external flash, allowing them to be extended. They are designed to use little energy. They have built-in power-saving features such as sleep function. Machine vision and IoT run well on microcontroller. The IoT revolution keeps on increasing and will be powered by billions of tiny connected microcontrollers.

19.3.2 Open-Source Hardware and Software

Open source provides a path to develop hardware and software [4]. Thousands of contributors around the world created this to apply for new applications that can be ported to target boards. Target boards have various microcontroller and microprocessor families. On an open-source embedded hardware system, tremendous IoT and embedded vision application products are developed. Many designed single-board computers are available at low cost to develop our IoT application.

Open source is a free license. Software, as well as hardware, are available for free access. Users can modify the program and hardware. Users could add new features to the existing board, or easily fix a bug because of multiple contributors are working to identify a problem. Users can add more value to the product by fixing the bug quickly. Developers can take the software routine available and enhance it as per application. Open-source operating systems are available, such as Android for mobiles.

Open-source hardware is an open development hardware source for industrial, manufacturing, and educational fields. It allows the interaction of all developers in the world. Programmable logic devices can be affordable. Chip manufacturing is capable for every IC developer because of open source. The designer will be able to code modules in FPGA (field-programmable gate array). FPGA boards act as free computing and debugging machines.

Future Internet service will be called "hardware computing resource protocol". It will enable the design of the algorithms based on hardware core. Upload it into the machine to execute and implement it. Open source introduces innovation, new technologies, and applications in the future.

19.3.3 Internet of Things

Tiny high-quality, low-cost, low-energy connected components—along with new apps, new processes, and capacity to make lots of industrial things—are the mobile revolution. Controlling home appliances from a mobile phone is a standard feature. A lot of ubiquitous sensors and controls in the phone will alter industrial automation, smart buildings, and human interaction with the world around us. This interconnected ubiquitous hardware transformation is expected to be the biggest part of the revolution in IoT by 2030.

19.3.4 Sensors

Smart intelligent sensors—along with the evolution of wireless technology—are growing due to energy saving and digital health ecosystems. Microelectronics, microcontrollers, miniature circuits, wireless data transmission, telecommunications, data analysis, and sensor manufacturing techniques have now opened smart sensors in wearable technology and digital health monitoring systems. Smart sensors measure any required environmental, medical, and field parameters. They measure parameters like temperature, pressure, soil dryness, acceleration, heart rate, brightness, stiffness, material property, pulse rate, humidity, and many more. Smart sensors are incorporated in agricultural products, consumer electronics products, textile products, automotive products, wearable devices, and many more devices. Due to their miniaturization, flexibility, minimum cost, scalability, high reliability, and high performance, smart sensors are integrated with many products.

Oxidation-reduction potential sensors, temperature and humidity sensors, DO sensors, pressure sensors, touch and flow sensors, turbidity sensors, and pH sensors are some of the smart sensors based on type. Smart sensors have components such as sensors, analog-to-digital converters (ADCs), transceivers, microcontrollers, and digital-to-analog converters (DACs). MEMS (microelectromechanical systems), NEMS (nanoelectromechanical systems), and CMOS technology, optical spectroscopy, and embedded vision are some of the technologies used in smart sensors.

Printable and flexible sensors play a dynamic and vital role in printed electronics. They are used to measure electric or optical signals. They are applied in medical and consumer electronics, breath sensing, and devices like drug screening, electronics for the screen in TV, and smart packing. They are miniature, light, and affordable cost sensors. Piezoelectric, capacitive, piezo resist sensors, digital sensors, temperature sensors, photodetectors, and biosensors are types of categorized printed sensors. Inkjet, gravure, screen printing, and flexography are technology involved in flexible sensors.

Nanosensors are used in electronics access control system equipment, the healthcare electronics industry, and the IoT. They are the tiny, physical, chemical, biological and surgical sensory devices to sense and detect nanoparticles with sizes of 1–100 nm. In nanotechnology, these sensors are devices. They measure the physical and chemical properties of regions which are very hard to reach. They have the capability of monitoring properties of simple organisms to complex cell organisms. Physio-mechanical properties and electromagnetic properties also are detected by nanosensors. They are used in oil, gas, criminology, ecological protection, fiber optic nano-cameras, laboratory-on-chips, cancer recognition, robotics, total blood analysis, volume and pressure measurement, nanoelectronics, safety, armed services and security surveillance, foodstuffs, aeronautical, space science, automobiles, petrol products and many more. Many technologies are involved in nanosensors like carbon nanotubes (CNTs), solar fuel cells, etc.

Demand for ultrasonic sensors in 2030 will be for uses such as automation industries, detection of obstacles, the distance between objects, smart agriculture, and many more. Accelerometers, magnetometers, and gyroscopes are the major types of MEMS-based motion sensors. These MEMS are widely used in smart wearable devices, smartphones, and medical equipment. According to the [5] Institute of Electrical and Electronics (IEEE), in 2020, around 27 billion IoT devices were present globally, and this is projected to reach 125 billion units by 2030.

With IoT, along with rapid advancements in technologies such as embedded systems, AI, machine automation, Big Data analytics, fog computing, and Deep Learning, the demand for smart vision sensors is increasing; these can be used for detecting defects from the set of reference data pictures. Vision sensors are used for inspection of manufactured products in the automotive, electronics, and food and beverage industries, and garment production. Automation in manufacturing, industrial automation, is done by the image vision sensors used for making the products automatic and intelligent. 3D vision-sensing technology is suitable for vision sensors to identify the orientation and position of the target objects three-dimensionally. Using this technology, industrial robots would enable faster and more accurate assembly of the bulk parts by automating the human-rigorous process in assembly and inspection of the objects.

Light sensors are used in ambient light sensing, gesture recognition, RGB (red/green/blue) color sensing, proximity detection, and IR detection. In automobiles, this sensor is used for automatic dimming of headlamps and visibility maintenance. Ambient light sensors help save battery power through the automatic adjustment of backlight. Light sensors increase quality for mobile phones, digital displays, televisions, and tablets.

The position sensor can be used in transportation applications in determining articulation angle, steering angle, and boom arm detection for use in wind turbines or solar panels. The position sensor is used in clutch plates, sensing steering angle, pedal positioning, and various other applications. Based on type, the fiber laser is divided into IR, ultraviolet (UV), ultrafast, and visible fibers. The UV fiber lasers are highly suitable for micro machine drills and cleaning surfaces. They are also used in glass, plastic, ceramic, and metal stripping. UV is also well suited for thin film making and cleaning of surfaces.

Parking sensors are adopted in vehicles to produce accident-free travel. They are used to easily identify vacant parking areas. Parking sensors are classified into ultrasonic sensors, electromagnetic sensors, and infrared sensors. 3D printing helps in personalization of the purchased products, allowing for the quick and accurate building of a model that enables manufacturers to increase the efficiency and cost effectiveness of manufacturing processes. Various industries, such as aerospace and defense, consumer electronics, and automotive, are gradually using this technique to fulfill the demand of their customers.

CMOS (complementary metal oxide semiconductor) and CCD (charge-coupled device) are two different kinds of image sensors. CMOS-based image sensing devices are preferred because of their reduced size and lower power consumption. There are two-dimensional (2D) and three-dimensional (3D) image sensor processing types. These sensors are used in surveillance and security, fire fighting, medical imaging, and industrial diagnostics.

Global navigation satellite system (GNSS) chips are used in AR, surging demand for precise real-time data, and increasing development of smart cities across the globe. Image sensors, temperature sensors, level sensors, inertial measurement units (IMUs), humidity sensors, flow sensors, heart rate sensors, electrocardiogram (ECG) sensors, blood glucose sensors, ambient light sensors, pressure sensors, blood oxygen sensors, motion and position sensors, accelerometers, and chemical and gas sensors are increasingly used in IoT—denoting the internetworking of physical and virtual objects, which allows these devices to communicate with each other through cloud technology to share information and data.

Detecting various gases are done by infrared (IR) gas sensing technology. CO_2, benzene, acetylene, and many more gases are measured by this IR gas sensing technology. Wearable sensors are used for consumer, enterprise, and industrial health monitoring. Smart clothing incorporates sensors in clothing for measuring various health and fitness parameters. Such sensors are integrated into clothing and are capable of measuring the energy output of the user's muscles, respiratory rate, and heart rate.

Skin-like sensors are used in wearable electronics, personal healthcare, and robotics. It is made of hydrogel and is biocompatible. Skin generates ion movements when the skin undergoes strain and temperature change. These ion movements in the sensing area are measured as voltage or current electrical signals by skin-like sensors.

19.3.5 Wireless Sensor Network

A wireless sensor network (WSN) is a system of sensors working cooperatively to transfer real-time data. These are self-configured networks, which help collect data from the physical environment surroundings and then wirelessly transmit the information to a base station. The sensors sense physical, medical, and environmental conditions, such as temperature, pressure, humidity, sound, and many more parameters.

Software is an integral part of a WSN system, where it is the governing element for decision making. The software is responsible for data transfer, power management, self-configuration, and fault tolerance, and many more. The software category in WSN is estimated to witness the peak growth rate in the market during the forecast period (2020–2030).

The camera image sensors can be attributed to the growing demand for surveillance and monitoring industrial activities. Healthcare, industrial, automotive, retail, aerospace and defense, and banking, financial services, and insurance (BFSI) are some of the industries seen to be driving the growth of image sensors in the future. Building automation, the development of smart cities, healthcare facilities, wearable devices, and factory automation are the major application areas in the WSN.

WSNs are used in a smart city for many applications, including traffic monitoring, intelligent connected street lights, waste tracking, and pollution management. The smart city market is expected to reach its highest growth by 2025, with government initiatives being the major driver for its growth. For instance, in 2015, the government of India allocated resources for developing smart cities across our country. It includes smart meters to develop smart grids for better management in energy distribution during peak demand periods.

19.4 Artificial Intelligence

AI with machine learning can sense, think, and interact, deriving sensing ability through collecting and processing signals via sensors or any other methods, demonstrating "thinking" ability via classifying, reasoning, and predicting possible outcomes. Interaction is possible with people or other machines. The new field of AI now shifts toward building intelligent systems. Robots that can interact with people to teach are intelligent AI systems. Figure 19.7 shows all the abilities given to the intelligent system, and Table 19.2 gives examples of AI in different applications in the future.

AI is a step forward, to use a good search of technical legal issues. A lawyer can find similar paragraphs and parameters in other judgments using machine learning. AI uses a broader knowledge base and can review millions of documents that a human eye may miss. AI automates several high-volume, frequent tasks such as finding documents or filling certain forms. AI generates more work in less time. By 2030, AI will be used in many white-collar jobs. It is expected to be used in 30% of corporate audits. AI has been predicted to become part of the corporate board of directors by 2030.

AI-based electronic devices decode and interpret animal sounds such as barks into language that humans can understand. This technology comprises electroencephalography sensors, micro-computing, and special brain–computer interface software technologies. Sensors placed in the headset detect electrical signals in animal brainwaves. It analyzes signal patterns to communicate between animals and humans in the next ten years.

Surveying, planning, forecasting, and facility management for safety are applications in the oil and gas industry using AI. Drilling, automated inspection, improved efficiency of various operations, and

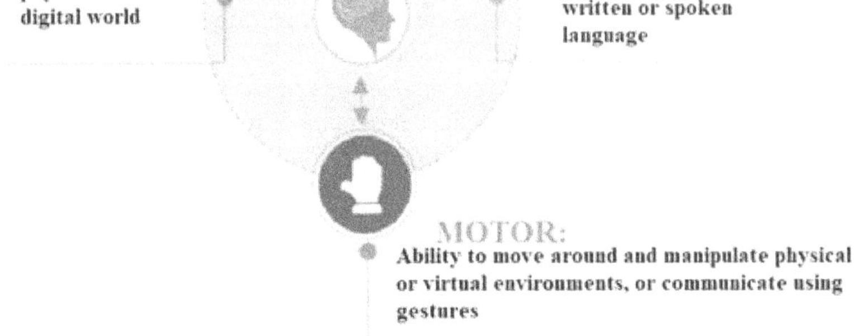

FIGURE 19.7 Intelligent AI system.

TABLE 19.2

Examples of Artificial Intelligence in Consumer and Business Applications

Products and Technologies	Potential Value	Relevant Industries
Driverless cars and drones	Transportation Delivery Quality assurance Security	Transportation and logistics Oil and gas Manufacturing Security and defense
Augmented and virtual reality	Cross-channel awareness Language translation 3D maps Computer shopping	Hospitality Travel Retail Gaming Entertainment Media Manufacturing Medicine
Chat bots and intelligent agents	Customer service and experiences Personal productivity Knowledge management	Consumer Sales Transport Retail Beauty shop Electronics Legal facilities
Machine learning algorithms	Forecasting Knowledge management Price/purchase prediction Virtual sales assistants	City planning Financial services Retail Food safety Healthcare Transportation Security
Imaging (computer vision)	Virtual diagnostics Brand management Quality assurance	Manufacturing Medicine Architecture Retail Food and beverage Security
Robots and robotics	Automating manual processes	Manufacturing Security Smart homes Precision medicine Transportation

decisions are made by AI. AI-based autonomous drones are used for power line inspection. The autopilot feature is expected to be executed in 2030. Unmanned combat aerial vehicles (UCAVs) have AI, along with the capability of flying to pre-determined locations.

AI-powered robots are taking the role of traditional writers in the publishing industry. In automated journalism, news articles are generated by computer programs. It reduces the human journalism workload. AI includes translation and customer interaction. It produces large quantities of information at a quick speed. Figure 19.8 shows an interpretation of AI in the media industry.

AI deploys a database of marine species for marine management. Machine learning, integrating cloud computing with AI, is now capable of identifying species with high accuracy in marine applications. AI programs can automatically identify marine organisms and can provide a clear picture of the world's oceans. Underwater AI colonies or ocean colonization is the expansion of the livable area. Accessing undersea resources, new recreational activities, and human settlement in the oceans may take in 2040 in an artificial island. As space stations in space, base stations in oceans are deployed by robots and AI machines. They help to study the hard-to-reach deep-sea ecosystem.

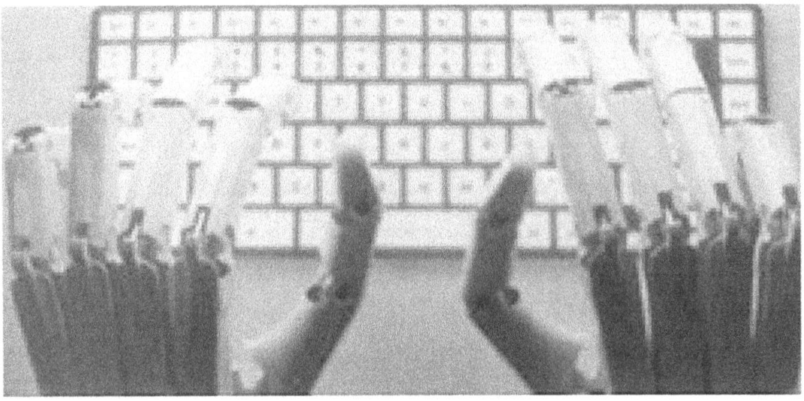

FIGURE 19.8 An interpretation of AI in the media industry.

AI is used in the aviation industry to assist customers in many ways, including check-in requests, providing accurate information about flights, and passenger identification safety management. Online check-in through mobile apps, security scanners, baggage screening, biometric identification, and ticketing kiosks are using AI. Aircraft manufacturers use cloud-based data storage to improve the reliability of aircraft maintenance. The process is easy and free of failure. Any malfunction, abnormality, or emergency is displayed and corrective action is automatically initiated to rectify the abnormality. A camera with AI is used to deliver a clear view of the airport to the traffic controller. UCAVs managed by remote pilots are intended to have full autonomy, with humans not piloting but authorizing the firing of weapons.

19.4.1 Web Technology 2030

Wireless communication and the World Wide Web enable us to connect people and objects anytime anywhere in the physical and virtual world. Through GPS, the car driver knows the best route from the current location to reach the destination by analyzing traffic patterns. This helps to avoid traffic jams, and determine the most efficient route to conserve fuel. It increases energy efficiency. By 2030, automatic driving cars will be driving themselves using the same methods to find efficient routes. Health monitors is possible remotely. The information from the objects is sent to the cloud. They are analyzed, filtered, and responded to when required. The growth of the web is shown in Figure 19.9.

Google Maps provides directions. The web is combined with virtual reality to find misplaced items. The user has the ability to Google the home to search for misplaced car keys or other items. *The web in 2030 will be an open, linked, intelligent, mobile, symbiotic and emotional web.* This web will be powerful and fully executing. The development of Web technology is shown in Figure 19.10.

The linked web connects all devices and communicates between real and virtual worlds in real time. Smart appliances connected with the Internet perform their task of their own without human participation. The radio frequency identification (RFID)-tagged refrigerator can sense the vegetables available and give a recipe to prepare using them, and can also sense the quantity of milk available in the refrigerator. It could contact a grocery store to order if the amount of milk is low. It sends the message to the user about collecting milk from the grocery store during return to home from the office. RFID tags in devices are used for the supply chain management. These RFID tags create lives connected to the web of the Internet.

The emotional web gives emotional interaction between humans and computers. This interaction is based on neuro-technology. With headphones, users interact and select content based on their emotions. It changes the song by facial recognition. It can respond according to the emotions of humans.

The intelligent or symbiotic web behaves like a virtual assistant. This assistant predicts the need from the behavior of the user. The web will interpret information on more complex levels. Emotionally as well as logically, the web interprets information. The web will do things that we do. AI enables computers

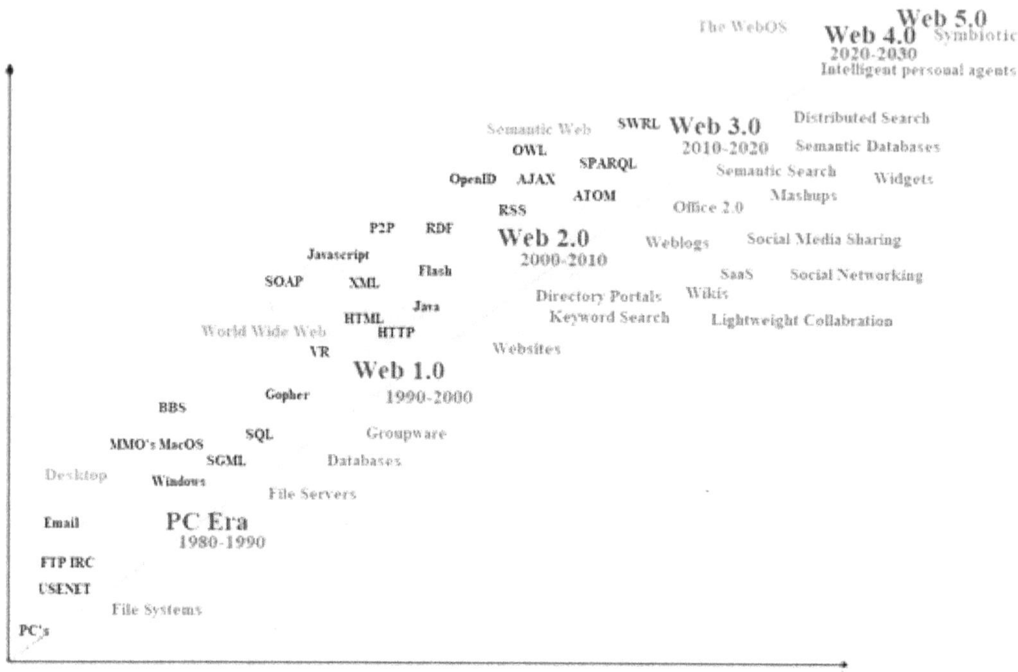

FIGURE 19.9 Growth of the web in computer applications.

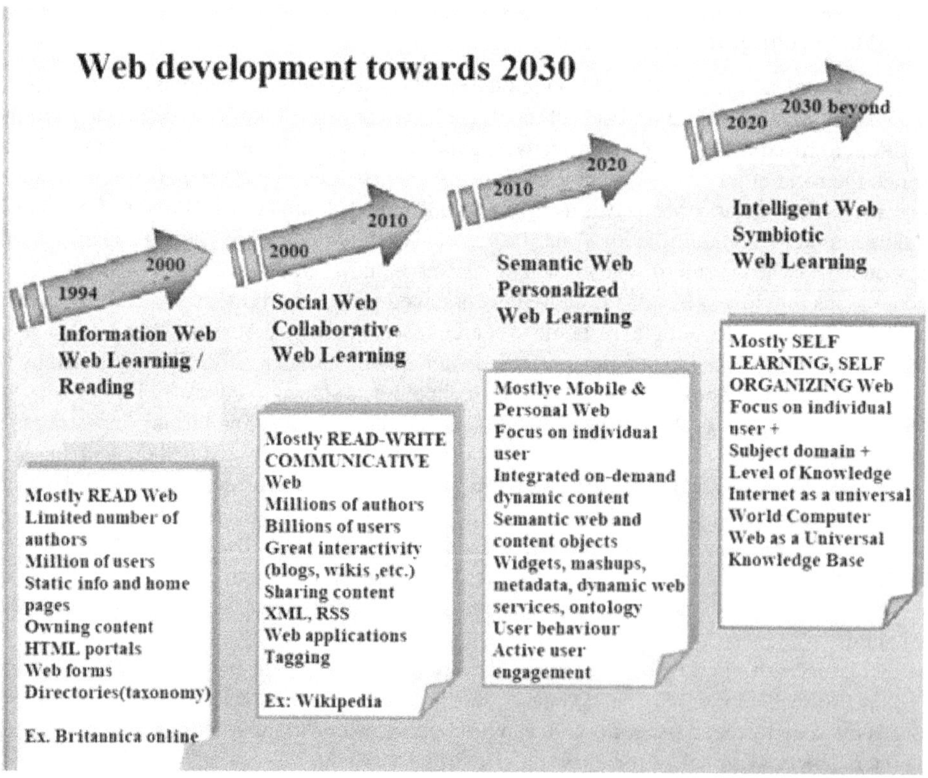

FIGURE 19.10 Evolution of the web.

to communicate like a person, but the intelligent web enables devices to think, reason, and respond like humans.

Web or intelligent web will be available after 2030, reaching up to the level of human intelligence and the human brain. Using virtual realities and holograms, computers will assist humans. Home appliances will be controlled through the IoT. Chips will be implanted into human brains. Intelligent interaction between machines and humans could be possible in 2030. After 2030, highly intelligent web or telepathic web will advance, AI is converted into the intelligent web, and brain implants will be highly common.

Brain implants communicate with the Internet through thoughts, giving power to a human. It is a complex web generation and is very advanced. Users think about a question and a web page related to that question will open. All devices are controlled by mobile apps or through the thinking ability of humans. Payments will be done through a microchip implanted in the brain. All devices are connected to the Internet. The Internet provides global transparency, governance, distribution, and participation. Collaboration with industry, political, social, and other communities through the online network are achieved. The human brain and webOS work in parallel and provide highly intelligent interactions.

19.5 Communication

The high-definition space telescope is operational in 2030 to observe new space with a diameter of 11.7m. This telescope is designed to locate dozens of Earth-like planets. It is more sensitive. It has a disk that blocks light, so that it makes dim planets more visible. Spectroscopy is analyzed to determine their atmosphere, confirming the presence of water and any other organic compounds like oxygen, methane, etc. It can locate objects at distances of more than 10 billion light-years. It can detect the nucleus of a small galaxy or gas cloud, and study faint objects. UV sensitivity is used to map the distribution of hot gases. These gases are available outside the perimeter of the galaxy. It will show chemically improved gases flow in and out of the galaxy. The cosmic web can be revealed by the UV sensitivity of the telescope. This can pick up the sun, which is 30 million light-years away. Solar system images with good resolution and detail features could be done by the telescope. Features like weather conditions on gas giants, a hidden member in the solar system, and icy plumes from the moon are traced using the telescope.

19.5.1 Space Tourism

Indian space research organization planned 2030 for Gaganyaan, a spacecraft mission to take humans to space. India planned for the best, cost low space journey. If space travel by humans is achieved, then colonizing the moon and later Mars will be achieved. Human space flight, national security, satellite communication, and image data analytics are the main work of space companies in 2030 [6]. A rocket for space tourists which is used to travel from one place to another on earth quickly. Point-to-point space travel will happen. A reusable rocket engine leads to fly cargo and people to the moon on a lunar lander. Mini satellites emerge to launch. Figure 19.11 shows spacecraft.

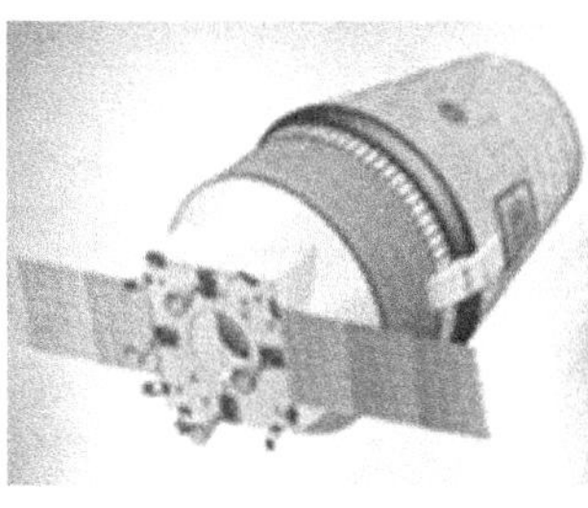

FIGURE 19.11 Spacecraft.

19.5.2 Optical Fiber for Future Data Centers

Big Data centers are for data processing, data routing, and data storage in the network. In the future, high-speed data accessing and compatibility in saving data will be required in data centers. Increasing the use of the Internet, the online platform will lead to increased efficiency. Not only efficiency but space, maintenance, and risk avoidance are also important aspects in designing a data center. Cabling in the data center is designed to move data quickly without latency. Big data centers want data rates to be as fast as possible.

Optical fibers are excellent in managing cloud computing resources. Multi-gigabit speed will be served by optical fiber at any location. Data centers may be located anywhere if they have optical fiber. An optical fiber cable delivers the fastest, most reliable connection for business. It is more reliable and less costly. Table 19.3 gives fiber types and their typical reaches. Figure 19.12 shows a fiber optic cable that is used to link a server and external data storage.

19.5.3 Wireless Power Transfer

Wireless power transfer is a technology to transfer electric power without wires. Electric, magnetic, or electromagnetic fields are capable of supplying power from alternating current (AC) sources to batteries. It utilizes the electromagnetic field generated by charged particles to transfer energy through the air; when received, energy is converted into usable direct current (DC). Exchange of energy between two

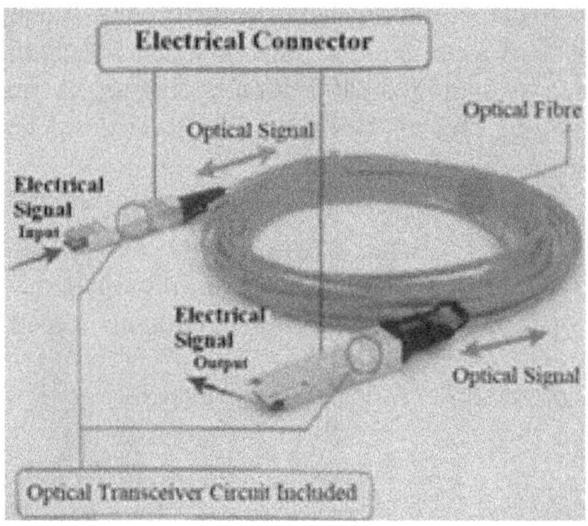

FIGURE 19.12 Optical cable structure.

TABLE 19.3
Fiber Types and Their Typical Reaches

Fiber types	Typical Reach
Active optical cables (AOCs)	≤100m
Duplex multimode fiber	≤100m–180m ≤220m–500m
Parallel multimode fiber	≤100m ≤400m
Duplex single-mode fiber	≤500m–2km ≤10km ≤20km–40km
Parallel single-mode fiber	≤500m–2km

FIGURE 19.13 Wireless power transfer.

objects is possible only when they have similar resonant frequencies. Figure 19.13 shows wireless power transfer.

Charging devices or power banks are not necessary to be carried by users. Magnetic resonance technology or inductive technology is the way for wireless power transmission. Wireless charging points for electric vehicles are possible by this way. Charging an electric vehicle may not be an obstacle in this case. Special roads can be constructed across utilities. These roads are maintained with inductive coupling to provide continuous charging for electric vehicles.

Wireless transmission is useful in recharging electrical products, transmitting the energy from the source to load wirelessly. This wireless charging is used in products such as smartphones, tablets, laptops drones, electric vehicles, and wearable electronic devices and transmitters. This wireless charging is used in many fields. Air conditioning, electronics, and engineering are a few fields for wireless charging.

Reliable, efficient, fast, continuous charging and low maintenance cost are advantages of wireless power transmission. It can also be used for long or short ranges. As it is galvanically isolated, there is no risk of electrical shock in this charging. In disaster-prone areas, quick recovery is possible with wireless. It stops equipment damage during a disaster. Simple design, lack of power cables, lower frequency operation, and remote area power transmission are some of the advantages of wireless. Charging anywhere without chargers is possible. Induction methods, microwave power transmission, and laser beam power transmission are the types of wireless power transmission.

19.5.3.1 Induction Method

Wireless charging for toothbrushes, mobiles, and portable devices use the method of induction charging, which features no direct connection between primary and secondary coils of transformer and wireless induction charging. Mutual induction causes energy transfer between primary and secondary coils. In this charging technique, the charger has an induction coil which acts as a primary coil. When power is supplied to the primary, an electromagnetic field is created. The device to be charged has a secondary coil. The portable device connected with the charger receives power from the primary electromagnetic field. The second coil of the portable device converts the electromagnetic field into an electrical current and charges the battery.

This method of charging is convenient and safe. There are no hazardous conductors exposed. There is no electrical shock risk. Resonant induction coupling is used for power transmission. It increases the transmission range. In this case, both primary and secondary resonate at the same frequency. Electricity has been given to the primary coil, which generates an oscillating magnetic field. The magnetic field is picked up by the secondary coil. The secondary coil converts this field into electricity for the load.

Capacitive coupling is another method of coupling used in wireless transmission. Its principle is electrostation induction. It involves capacitive coupling between two or more electrodes or plates. These plates have high frequency, high potential AC. Both methods are limited with small distances.

19.5.3.2 Microwave Power Transmission

This method is suitable for long distances. Directional power transmission is possible with a microwave transmitter. It utilizes an antenna that generates microwaves. The receiver converts the microwave into electricity. One drawback is that it needs very large-scale antennas.

19.5.3.3 Laser Beam Power Transmission

The photovoltaic effect converts light into electricity. This method uses a photovoltaic cell with the photovoltaic effect principle. Power is converted into a laser beam and transmitted from the source. The photovoltaic cell is used as a receiver. It converts laser beams into electricity. The laser beam has the advantage of transmitting over a considerable long distance. Its disadvantage is that laser beams are harmful to humans and animals. Highly directional cells are exposed to the transmitted laser beams to avoid loss of power. It is difficult to achieve, as atmospheric absorption, scattering effects, and weather will affect the efficiency of power transmission.

19.5.4 Seventh Sense in Communication

Seventh sense technology is used for communication between humans and electronics. It uses human hand gestures for control. Pranav Mistry, an inventor, introduced this futuristic technology. In science fiction movies, computer screen displays appear anyplace, like a wall. Screen display commands are set by hand gestures. The smart digital settings speak to a human to do the task. These will all be thinkable by 2030. The gesture control devices are based on a microcontroller unit using Zigbee, a suite of high-level communication protocols which can be used to control autonomous robots at distant places using a GSM module or Zigbee transceiver or satellite broadcasting. It is very easy to execute without much cost.

Microcontroller devices and robots are constructed for specific applications now, but seventh sense equipment is designed to do multidimensional tasks. Sensors and night vision cameras are used to control these products at any distance with human movements. It has the facility of the computer-generated keyboard for providing activities to devices from distance.

This technology is a wearable gesture interface. It enriches and improves communication of the physical world surrounding us with digital information. AR is the basic concept for the seventh sense technology. The seventh sense technology consists of hardware components connected wirelessly to the computing device. It uses surfaces, walls, and physical objects as interface devices. Technologies such as hand gesture recognition, speech recognition software, touch recognition, image capturing, image processing, and image manipulation are associated with seventh sense technology.

Wear Ur World (WUW) seventh sense technology device consists of a camera, projector, and mobile with the computing device and colored sensors to wear on the fingers of a human. These are shown in Figure 19.14.

The camera is a digital eye for the seventh sense system. It captures the scene when the user makes framing gestures and hand movements. The projector projects visual images on the surface of a wall, table, book, or human hand. The user moves their hands with colored markers on fingers to form different movements. The camera captures and is connected with a projector using a mobile connecting device. Computer vision helps in recognition, and software processes movements into gestures. These hand signals can do input in place of keys to the application which is projected by the projector. The mirror reflects the picture to the front formed by the projector. The microphone is used only when paper is an interface. It senses sound signals touching the paper. It is combined with tracking information about user fingers computing device. Hence, a touch interface is created. The work is shown in Figure 19.15.

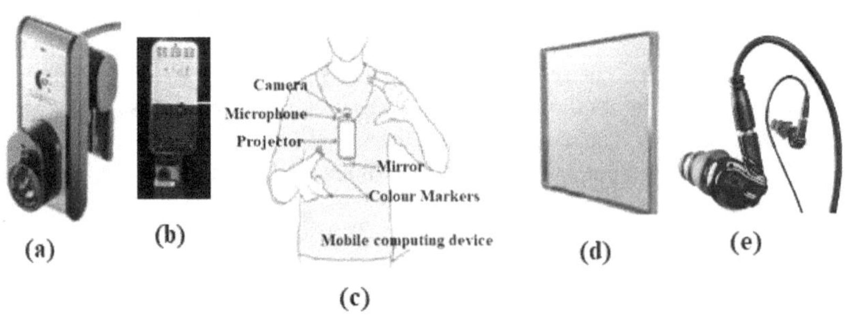

FIGURE 19.14 Wear Ur World: (a) camera; (b) projector; (c) mobile computing device; (d) mirror; (e) microphone.

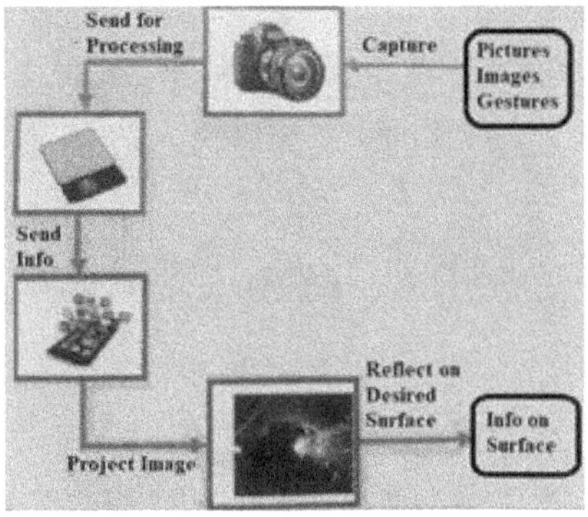

FIGURE 19.15 Working of the seventh sense device.

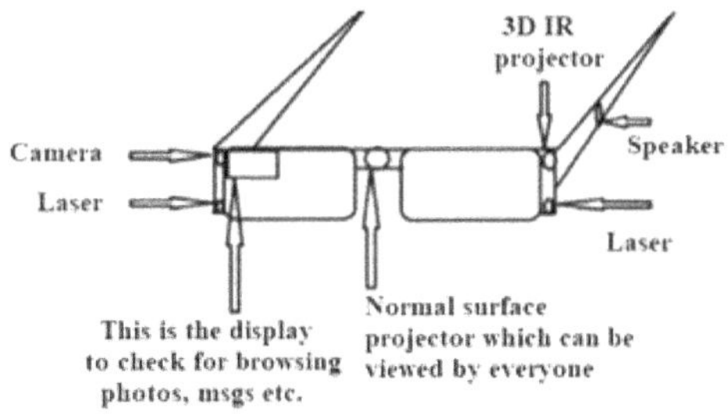

FIGURE 19.16 Sensing glass

FIGURE 19.17 Applications of seventh sense technology.

The mobile computing device used as a processing device with the user. All of the depicted components are connected to this device by either wired or wireless connections. The software validates all features run on this computing device, which is connected to wireless. Gesture recognition is software for interpreting human gestures via a mathematical algorithm with a pointing device cursor. It replaces the keyboard and mouse.

Sensing glass, a gesture recognition device, uses laser filter glass. It is shown in Figure 19.16. It has a camera 3D laser projector, two lasers at both ends, a small display, and a projector at the center. The display is made up of optical glass. It also has a microphone for recording sound using voice. It works on battery power. This glass is used to click photos, record video, browse data, check directions, send a message, or dial a call. It is shown in Figure 19.17.

19.5.5 Flying Electric Taxis

The electrically powered personal air vehicle will be available with a capacity of four passengers on the trip. It can fly in the air during traffic and riding on-road as well as water. It has a driving speed of 97km up to 290km. Electric vehicles (EVs) may be self-dependent on batteries, solar panels, or electric

FIGURE 19.18 Electric vehicle.

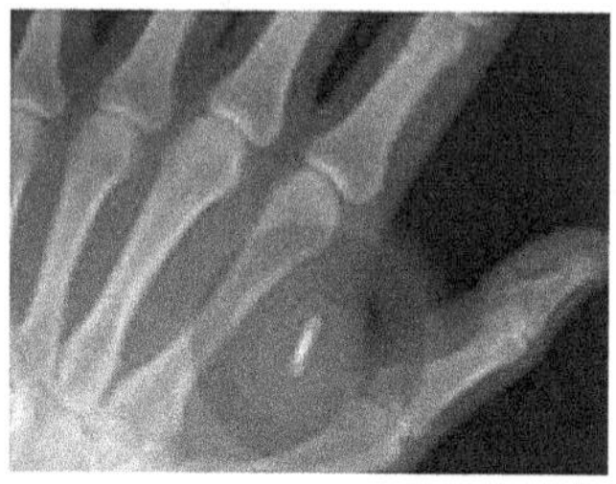

FIGURE 19.19 Mobile implant.

generators. These panels convert fuel into electricity, using renewable-based electricity. It reduces carbon pollution emissions. EVs receive electricity by being plugged into the grid and storing it in batteries. Figure 19.18 shows electric taxis.

19.5.6 Implantable and Edible Electronics

The implantable mobile phone are expected to be available in 2025 to track a person's health more accurately. Pacemakers and cochlear implants are health devices already available. More implantable technologies are expected to emerge and lead to more implantable products by 2030. This attached mobile phone will communicate the traced health information through a signal to the caretaker. Figure 19.19 shows implantable mobile phones. Implantable and edible electronics devices stay inside the body for diagnosis and treatment of diseases. Ingestible cameras help doctors to see the patient's small intestine and colon [7].

19.5.7 Network

Ubiquitous connectivity will be possible with network technologies, which means that everything will be available every time and everywhere. Network 2030 validates capabilities as a dynamic attribute with time and holograms. Hologram are new media objects. Time engineering is the capability to identify information at a specific period. It is the capability to schedule to expect the data to arrive. Time characteristics are concerned with the precise time of an event data.

IIoT devices such as programmable logic controllers (PLCs) and autonomous driverless vehicles should have to be designed with accurate time. New verticals in the different fields need a new type of media such as video voice and text in the future network, all working independently with different types of users in the different connected systems. Network 2030 will identify a new set of network technologies both in hardware and software required to deliver many real-time applications and communication needs of the world and space. Figure 19.20 shows network characteristics.

The first characteristic of Network 2030 is new verticals, or autonomously operating machinery in industry enabling new fundamental media objects such as holograms. The second characteristic is new communication services that enable more intelligent and high-precision networks. Network time needs to be taken into account, as well as new verticals which depend on data arrival times. The third characteristic is network infrastructure, which is concerned with constraints or opportunities needed to retrieve information terrestrially, over the air, and via space technologies.

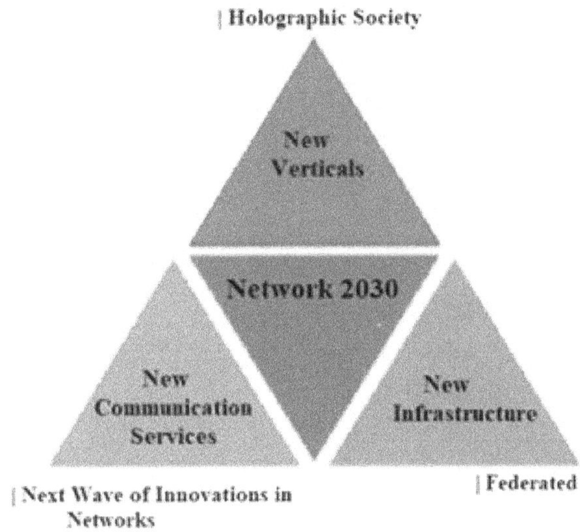

FIGURE 19.20 Network 2030 characteristics.

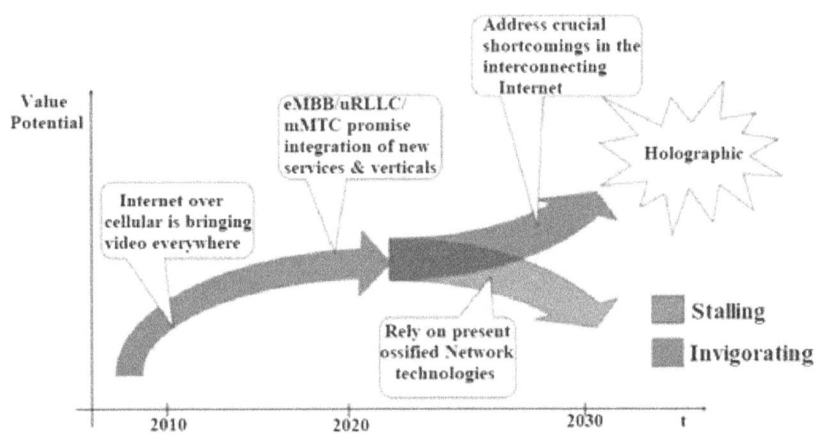

FIGURE 19.21 Opportunities in Network 2030.

Cloud computing, multimedia, mobile network, sensor technologies facilitate a new set of applications and innovations in the industry. Holographic applications have the special capability to transmit holographic data and stream it from a distant location. Holographic telepresence will allow members who are distant to be projected as holographic presence in the meeting chamber. Repair applications will permit the technician to cooperate with holographic interpretations of items at a distant place and difficult-to-reach situations like in space or on oil drilling platforms. It needs very high bandwidth, and it has to handle large data volumes.

Future network applications involve senses like optical (video, holograms), acoustic (audio) sense, touch (tactile), vision, hearing, smell, and taste. Multi-sense networks like a human will be created in the future. Many applications like the senses of smell and taste, etc., are developing and will be powerful the network for more volume and enlarged ability in the future. The separation in communication is shown in Figure 19.21 either stalling (delay) or being invigorated (strengthened). Network 2030 powerfully trusts holographic media, 3D digital projection with multi-senses, remote presence, and full-sensory capabilities to new application openings in new verticals.

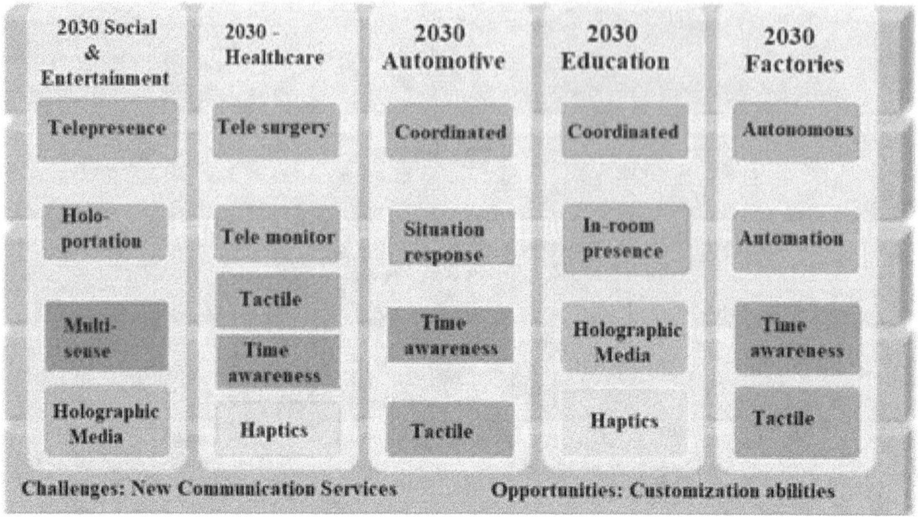

FIGURE 19.22 New verticals with Network 2030.

The connected digital society in the future will be on new verticals. Figure 19.22 illustrates opportunities in different verticals due to innovation in communication engineering. New services lead to holoportation, digital avatars, self-operating industries, digital food sampling, and fully automated factories. Holographic type facilities allow learners to be involved in their courses by being virtually present in the class.

Such customization extends storage resources, bandwidth requirement, zero latency, and other factors to fulfill the necessities of the new verticals across the communication. Through this, the network industry will receive a tremendous boost from Network 2030 by broadening the application areas across many vertical and new communication services. Several new initiatives such as 5G, 6G, or 7G mobile technologies will develop.

19.6 Conclusion

The beginning of autonomous vehicles, the era of sensors, the Internet of Things, the web, artificial intelligence, and immersive media of today will importantly change the future. People attempt to achieve the promises of high-resolution multimedia over the Internet, the industrial IoT, mIoT (m refers medical or mobile), automation, and autonomous vehicles to become existent. A lot of automation and intelligent industries will be expected in the forthcoming years. Application developers use these technologies in as many fields as possible. They may be used by human beings or by physical, digital, or virtual objects. The concepts explained in these chapters are based on developing technologies. A new concept will also arrive that we could not be able to predict now.

REFERENCES

[1] www.businessinsider.com/
[2] www.electronics-notes.com/articles/connectivity/
[3] https://semiengineering.com/transistor-options-beyond-3nm/
[4] www.eetimes.com/an-introduction-to-open-source-hardware-development/#
[5] https://blog.usejournal.com/the-future-is-tiny-44dea02e4517
[6] www.futuretimeline.net/21stcentury/2030.htm
[7] www.electronicsforu.com

20

Framework for Academic Writing and Product Naming through Software Assistance

V. M. Subramanian

CONTENTS

DOI: 10.1201/9781003318378-20

20.1 Introduction

Writing is one of the important expressive skills through which academic activities are conveyed from one to another. Employing computer technologies in writing activities will be more helpful to the writers as well as the readers. The present chapter has two major objectives the first one is to provide an innovative idea for writing manuscripts of various research by making use of the software techniques.

The proposed software will guide the writers to complete the manuscript without missing the core elements of research writing. The second objective is to introduce a model for new software that can handle finding new names for the research products and methods. The linguistic resources will be best employed in the proposed software for naming the newer scientific products. It can suggest reasonable name combinations in which the suitable one can be selected by the researcher. This software is named as 'Product Name Generator', and is aimined at helping the researchers and scientists to name their product in a unique manner.

Writing is a productive activity that helps human beings to express and explore their ideas, achievements, predictions, etc., to others. The writing habit of human beings started 3,000 years ago, and it has undergone tremendous changes in the evolution process. Due to the abundant development of science and technology, the art of writing is refined through the process such as improving the script forms, script modifications, and consolidations. Present writing form and method helps in all teaching, learning, testing, presenting and administering activities of the global citizens. There are many definitions provided to writing activity based on the function, process and domain. Some of the important notions of the writing activity are discussed here so as to make the people understand the nuances of writing. Peter Elbow (1981), describes 'writing as a kind of magic' which takes place between abstract ideas and visual scripts. The art of transforming mental conceptions into visual cues as characters is a learned behavior of human beings that is followed for a prolonged period. If a writer really aims to convey some ideas or keep them permanent in the written form he needs considerations on things like meaning, aim and purpose, and target audience of his writing. The thought and message of particular writing are based on the writer's mood, intention, context, language style and method. The proficiency of a writer is based on his linguistic competence in that particular language in which he writes. Regardless of the topic and its interest, two characteristic features such as the writers' knowledge about the matter on which he is writing and his skill in employing the language control his writing. If a writer understands the techniques of writing, he can succeed even if his message is simple. At the same time, some writers prefer the concepts—which are very much liked by the readers—and they may create their writings to appeal to the audience; for example, proficient writers adopt different strategies in order to make their readers very clear about what they write. Experienced and proficient writers are able to bring out the global issues by making use of their knowledge and linguistic talents to the audience, whereas the writers of amateur groups cannot reach the audience due to their lack of proficiency and planning in writing. For fluent and coherent writing, the writer needs to consider the basic things such as plan, thought and knowledge of the message he wants to write.

In many cases writing fails due to the lack of skill in using the right words in the right context by the writer. Inappropriate word choices of the writer will lead to misconceptions and misunderstanding, and sometimes creates problems for the readers in catching the intended ideas of the writer. Unless the writer is careful in the use of words, it will lead to crisis. Writings on social, political and cultural matters many times create international issues. Writers of witty styles can touch upon the universal and sensitive issues by means of their rhetorical expertise and intellectual delights. Writing is more reliable and unshakable in nature endowed with permanency, aristocracy, authenticity and convenience.

20.2 Writing and Emotional Instinct

Writing is based on writers' linguistic expertise, mental thought, and emotional and intellectual instincts. In academic setups, learners are provided practices in structural forms rather than conceptual models. The grammatical and syntactical knowledge of the language is given priority in teaching and testing systems, whereas the ideology of teaching and testing concepts of the language are very much less emphasized. Language is also related to one's emotions and sense of application and appreciation of things. The description of a natural scene written by a student will be more interesting than his description about a machine or in the things in which he shows less interest. Writing is based on the writer's personal interest and emotional instincts. To conclude this discussion, we must agree that the thought or feeling about writing and the linguistic abilities of the writer plays a key role in the writing activity. Figure 20.1 shows the role of emotion and instincts in the writing activity.

Ideas and concepts are related to one's intellectual, emotional and physical instincts, and in most cases, the intellectual instinct plays a crucial role to get the writer into the thought. A writer who wants to write about nature, beauty and music prefers an extremely calm and beautiful place, whereas a news writer who writes about the severe disaster of bomb blast does not need that tranquil atmosphere; instead, he begins his writing from the spot he visits. Both of the writers generate thought and ideas from their emotional instincts by means of their visual perception. Every writer has his own intention, aim and target audience; for example, the writings and criticisms on a particular fashion show or its ideology may not be applicable for a student who is studying waste management systems. The importance and usefulness of writing are determined by the target audience, whereas the critic who assesses the writing pinpoints

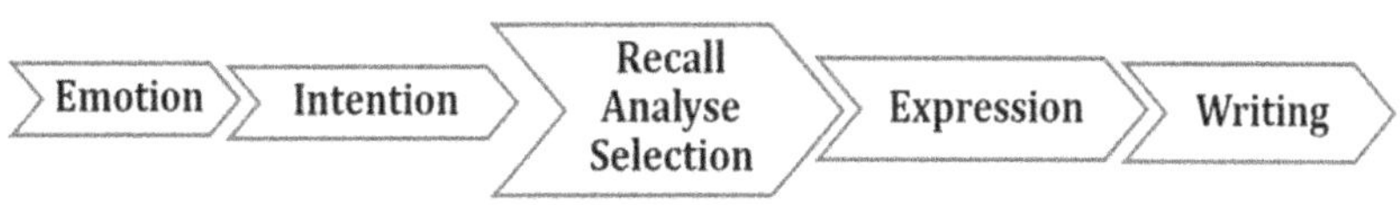

FIGURE 20.1 Process of Emotional Instinct in Writing.

the quality of writing. Target audience refers to the readers who read the book, as well as those who get benefit out of the knowledge explained in the book. For example, if a mechanical engineering professor writes, his target audience will be the students and researchers of the same field. The professor has to write the book with his theoretical and application of scientific talents, along with linguistic skills, so as to make the readers understand the newer knowledge introduced by him.

20.3 Aspects and Mechanics of Writing Skills

Writing activity involves various mechanics and aspects which are employed in concrete and abstract methods. Skillful employment of all these items considers the comprehensive value of the writing, while considering the mechanics and aspects of writing the components such as the following.

1. spelling
2. vocabulary
3. punctuation
4. grammar
5. word order (syntax)
6. meaning (semantics)
7. pragmatics
8. style
9. fluency

These are considered as core and integral part to make the process a complete one. The writer's performance is duly based on efficiency in the employment of these components. Various factors affect the language teaching, learning and testing processes at different levels. Among those factors, these nine important components play crucial roles in the testing and evaluation of the language of the learners (Figure 20.2).

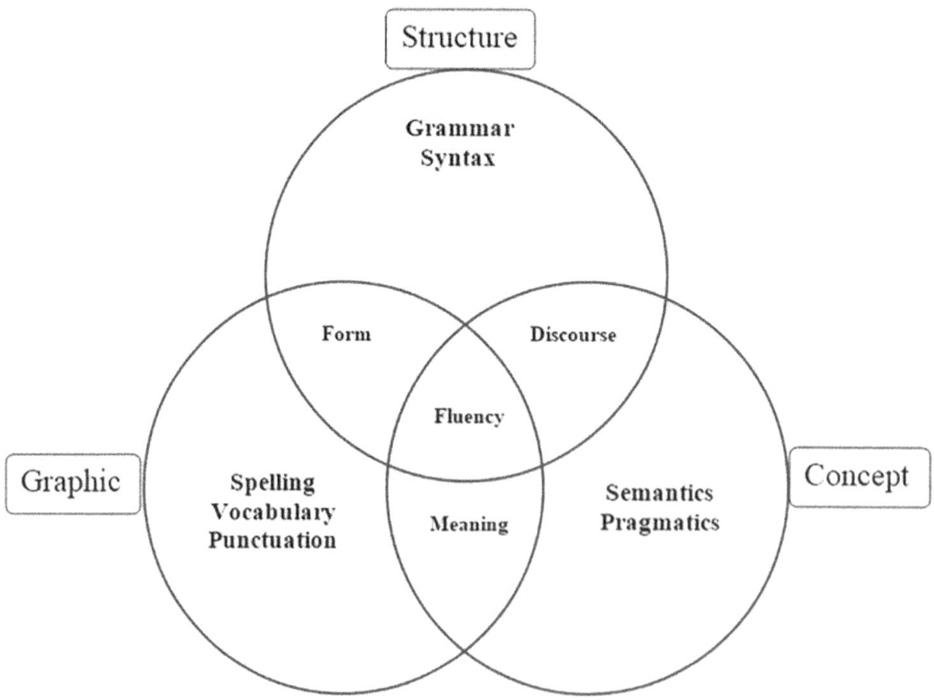

FIGURE 20.2 Components of writing

20.3.1 Spelling

The basic unit of writing is considered as characters. Characters are spelled in a pattern pertaining to language. The spelling pattern differs from language to language. The pattern of spelling determines the word; if the pattern follows the already established form, then the word is meaningful; otherwise, it is just a sequence of characters without meaning. Spelling plays a crucial role in writing because the characters employed in it are not always pronounced in a unique method. The irregular pattern of spelling and pronunciation combinations confuses the writer, thereby leading to spelling errors.

20.3.2 Vocabulary

Choice of vocabulary items employed by the writer decides his meaning, and a careful selection in this process is essential. A writer needs to identify and understand the choice of his vocabulary item in terms of its grammatical, linguistic and functional form and use. The writer has to understand the diversified and exploited use of the vocabulary items to use them in the proper sense, eliminating ambiguity and misunderstanding on the part of the reader.

20.3.3 Punctuation

Punctuation fulfills the writing with several salient features. Writers use punctuation marks in their writing such as pause, stop, emphasize, or question using a comma, a period, an exclamation point or a question mark to provide a special emphasis, style or extra meaning to their writing. Employment of correct punctuation marks and techniques adds clarity and precision to writing, and it helps the readers understand the gist of the writing in the true sense and intention of the writer. Punctuation such as hyphens, apostrophes, quotation marks, parentheses, colons, semicolon, commas, dashes, capitalization and full stops are explained in the following subsections.

20.3.3.1 Hyphens

Hyphens help the writers to frame compound words and join word units, prefixes and suffixes. It is used to join two nouns to make one complete word, to join an adjective and a noun to make a compound word (accident-prone), to join two words that, when linked, describe a noun (agreed-upon sum, two-dimensional object) and to join a prefix with a noun (ex-mayor). Hyphens can be used with compound phrases to describe the components such as ages, phrases, and adjectives; for example, 'the 30-days-old baby', 'father-in-law', 'day-to-day', etc.

20.3.3.2 Apostrophes

Apostrophes indicate contractions and possessives in sentences. Contraction is used to show the missing letters or the letters left out in the order for ex. doesn't = does not. Possession is to show that something belongs to someone or something. The apostrophe always comes directly after the name of the owner of the object, followed by what they own. General practice is to form the possessive of monosyllabic proper names ending in a sibilant sound (s, z, sh, zh, ch, j) by adding an apostrophe and another 's'.

20.3.3.3 Quotation Marks

Quotation marks in writing help to indicate the starting and endpoint of a quotation or title. They are also used to point out the exact words of speakers, writers and works.

20.3.3.4 Parentheses

Parentheses are used to provide additional information about the word, phrase or sentence. The information provided in the parentheses helps the readers understand the meaning of the phrase or sentence in a better way. In technical writing, they are also used for introducing tables or figures within a sentence and to indicate product manufacturer names.

20.3.3.5 Colons

Colons are used to introduce a list of items, introduce a quotation, expand an idea to a larger length, or add emphasis in the sentences. Colons occur before words, phrasal forms, sentences and quotes. Colons are employed after the independent clause in a sentence.

20.3.3.6 Semicolons

The semicolon has two major uses in sentences. The first one is to join two complete meaningful sentences of similar ideas, and the second one is listing the complex items in the running sentences that contain commas. Semicolons are also employed in sentences to join two independent clauses having a close connection in meaning and form.

20.3.3.7 Commas

The comma is used in sentences to show the individual ideas clearly for an easy meaning-making process. It is employed to join two sentences with a conjunction, to add extra information to the basic sentence, or to list a series of items and to introduce quotations.

20.3.3.8 Dashes

Dash symbols help to express the immediate idea or thought in a sentence. It helps to separate groups of words, phrases and clauses, e.g. *The Traitor*—a Hollywood crime thriller movie based on a biography. Hyphens are similar to dashes but smaller in size (-) used for adjective phrases for ex. e-learning. Dashes are also used to indicate the concluding idea of the sentences; for example: The teachers of the online courses need to check important points that the students should follow—timely login, on-screen response, follow-up instructions and interactions.

20.3.3.9 Capitalization

Capital letters are used in the initial position of the first word of sentences. Capital letters are also used to mention the pronoun 'I', to write the acronyms and to write proper nouns including the name of the titles, places and institutions. Capitals are also followed in writing the names of months and days.

20.3.3.10 Full Stops

Full stops help to identify the individual sentences and help the readers to make meaning in sentence levels. The initial letter of the word following a full stop is capitalized. Full stops help the writers to complete the sequence of meaning in a sentence and begin the next idea in the following sentence.

20.3.4 Grammar

Grammar is a rule-governed activity pertinent to the use of language that helps to maintain a systematic function among the users. Grammar contains a set of rules with regular and irregular patterns followed traditionally. Sometimes the arbitrary nature of the spoken form of language use is also followed as a systematic rule after the literacy features are created into it. Grammatical features of language differ from language to language, and are considered unique features of them. Several languages consider the irregular pattern of the language as a special feature of them and the writer has to consider carefully all the grammatical rules and use them while writing.

20.3.5 Syntax

Syntax in writing refers to the word order in sentences. The word order of languages differs from one to other, the same as that of grammar features of languages used worldwide. This feature determines writers' ability to convey the intended idea to the readers. This unique feature of arranging the words in sentences is influenced by the spoken form of the same language, and other languages lead to errors in writing. A similar meaningful expression can be written in a simple as well as complex manner by employing skillful syntactic techniques.

20.3.6 Semantics

Semantics deals with the meaning of writing. This feature is applied from word to structure levels. The writer needs to choose his words in the right intended meaning considering its grammatical, lexical and functional feature. Choice of words and selection of sentence structure with pragmatic implications are considerations in the sematic feature of sentences. Incorrect choice of words or sentence forms will lead to meaningless or ambiguous writing.

20.3.7 Pragmatics

Pragmatics deals with the writer's meaning, contextual meaning, extended meaning and relativity in expression. Pragmatics in writing provides special features and is often conditioned by the social and functional meaning of the expression. The writer needs to consider the socio-cultural, political and contextual implications of the words and expressions while writing. Unless the writer is particular in the contextual meaning of his writing, it may lead to misunderstanding by the readers and thereby end up with conflicts in opinions.

20.3.8 Style

Style is the way the writer writes, and it varies from writer to writer. It is often viewed as a technique or strategy of the writer. The style of a writer is controlled by choice of words, syntax, logic and expression. Styles are ranging in different levels; namely, conversational, expository, narrative, descriptive, persuasive, argumentative, critical, creative and technical. It is the choice of the writer in fixing the style to convey his meaning in accordance with his readers' needs.

20.3.9 Fluency

Writing fluency is the natural flow and organization of thought and form of written work. Fluency of writing has multidimensional variables related to form, rhythm and expression. It is conditioned by the ability of the writer to write with a natural flow, production, process variation, revision, pause behavior, rhythm and music. Fluent writers use grade-appropriate word patterns, vocabulary and content organized logically, making the overall message of the piece easier to understand. Writing fluency is an important skill that students need to develop through curriculum practices. Students should be trained to focus on attending to the higher-order writing activities such as organization, paragraph cohesion and cohesive features and flow of thought related to the writing item rather than overlooking the contents and recalling the related meaningful words too often during the process. Writing fluency is the ability to create text without relying too much on memory (Lenski & Verbruggen, 2010).

20.4 Planning an Essay

Writing is an encoding process in which the writer marks his mental concepts in a sequence in order to make his ideas permanent on paper. During the process of writing, the writers' mental thought on

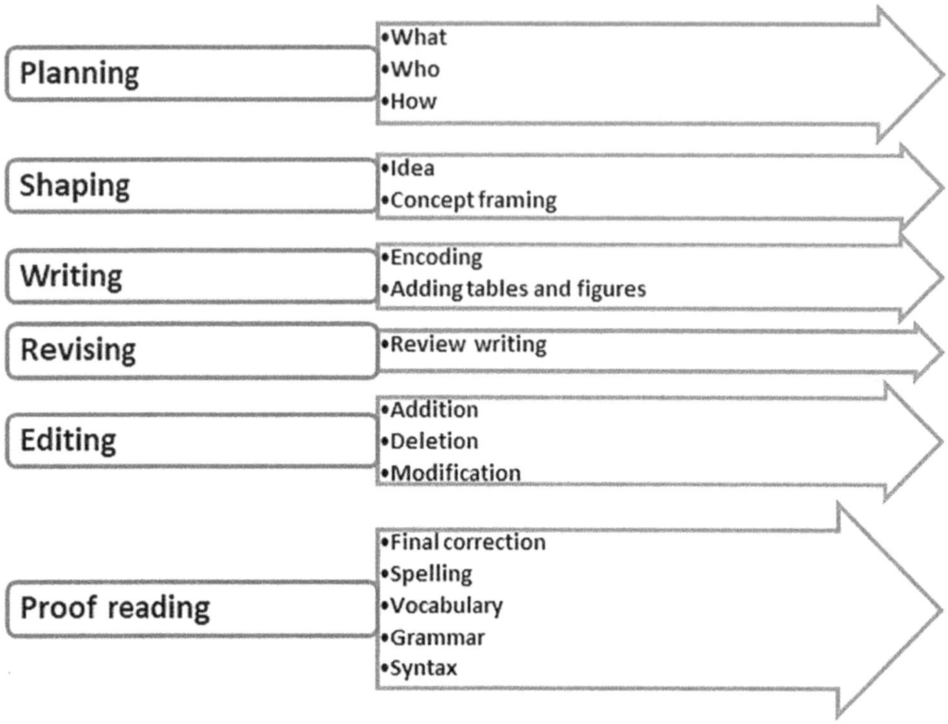

FIGURE 20.3 Writing Process

the writing of a particular topic undergoes several changes: first he thinks about the matter he wants to write, and then he transforms his ideas into verbal form then encodes them in the writing. Many times, the writer fails to convey his desired idea in writing due to reasons like lack of thought, lack of lexical power or lack of employing the proper style. In the writing process, the writer may create ideas, investigate concepts, criticize other models of writing and inform new methods. Writing is a constant process involving soft and hard skills like decision-making, selecting the idea, editing and rearranging materials. The writing process involves various skill-related and activities, among them six important activities that decide the characteristics of writing: planning the idea of writing, shaping the content, writing the intended idea, revising the written material, editing the content and proofreading for the final draft. These six skills of the writing process are listed in the following diagram with their form and function (Figure 20.3).

20.4.1 Planning

Planning is the primary activity of the writing, and this process takes up the purpose of writing, the rationale behind the selection of the topic and the audience who will benefit from it. Planning activity also involves the cognitive process of the writer's idea and intention.

20.4.2 Shaping

The shaping process helps the writer to arrange the materials to help him to write, refer, quote and read. There are several types of written sources available in print, electronic and online hypertext markup language (HTML) forms.

20.4.3 Writing

The writing or encoding process follows the two previous processes. Well-conceived ideas of the writer are given form in this process. The writer writes his pre-determined thoughts by making use of his linguistics and knowledge expertise.

20.4.4 Revising

The revising process in writing activity helps the writer to read and revise his own writing. This process involves the activities considering the commissions and omissions of the writing in form and conceptual levels. In this process, the writer can analyze the pros and cons of his writing by reviewing his script. The writing process related to addition, deletion and modification in conceptual levels can be done at this stage to make the writing exact.

20.4.5 Editing

Editing is an important process that helps the writing be more refined and polished. The correction process related to the linguistic elements such as grammar, spelling, vocabulary and syntax is done in this process. Employment of vocabulary items in terms of their semantic and functional implications, along with all other mechanics and aspects of writing, are considered in this process.

20.4.6 Proofreading

The final process of writing is proofreading, in which the graphological and syntactical errors and mistakes are corrected. The writer needs to read his script carefully to find any missing characters, words and fragments. Every writing should meet the desired and the intended idea of the writer—and in this stage, the writer has to make sure whether his writing fulfills the intention or not.

The above mentioned six stages of the writing process may help writers to carry out the writing activity in a comprehensive manner, regardless of the domain. Writing is a creative process and it requires a good knowledge of the intended topic, experience in reading and the ability to control the linguistic elements. The writer has to make his meaning exact and let his readers understand the idea without any missing or overstatement of the intended concept. Writing activity is considered as more valid, permanent and authentic for which the writer needs to employ the meaning and form of writing with more care and appropriateness.

20.5 Research in Social Sciences and Science

Research of academic interest, theoretical developments and applications of science, technology and engineering have wider focus and perspectives in the present scenario. They have several common principles and methods in their implications. Considering their approach, development and process, the following seven aspects play crucial roles.

20.5.1 Research Question

Developing a research question is important in scientific research which can be reached by means of converting rational views into working principles of large theories and models which are already proved and/or are in developmental stages. However, the problem or the question of the research topic needs to be explained clearly. The question or the proposed topic of the research needs to explain its social and scientific importance, and its approach to solving issues, and supplement sufficient factual evidence related to the research issue and the significance of the research problem.

20.5.2 Revisiting of Earlier Literature and Material Collections

Collecting information about the experiment, review and observation based on the topic is very much essential in developing the research work. Literature searches and preparatory laboratory experiments and field trials will gradually help the research progress.

20.5.3 Framing Hypothesis

A hypothesis is a specific, testable prediction about the researcher's expectations for what will happen in his research work. It helps in the testing of the theories and practices of the past and present. A hypothesis is scientific research which indicates that the tentative relationship between two or more variables may be simple or complex. The prediction of a hypothesis may be based on an educated guess or a formal theory; at the same time, it may be proved as well as disproved. The hypothesis is framed based on the research gap and observation, and should be empirically testable, whether it is right or wrong.

20.5.4 Data Collection

Data collection is an important process of collecting and measuring information on variables. It has two methods: namely, qualitative and quantitative. Qualitative data deals with the quality of the data descriptively and is not measurable. These data are collected through observation and narrative techniques. Quantitative data are the measurable values or numbers identified through a numerical form such as length, size, amount, time and duration. Quantitative data are more reliable and objective, and thus have greater creditability.

20.5.5 Data Analysis

Data analysis is a process of manipulating and analyzing the data in order to find information that can be used in the decision-making of the collected data. Data analysis is the process of systematically applying statistical tools and logical techniques in the scientific method to explain, compare, contrast and value the data. Data analysis needs to consider the necessary skills to analyze, applying unbiased inference and eliciting statistical values.

20.5.6 Conclusion

Applying logic and science in concluding the research project is very important. The discussions of the research analysis help the research project get summarized, and this summary will lead to understanding the findings of the project. This part includes key facts from the background of the research to help to explain significant results in a logical sequence. It is important to explain whether the results of the research support or nullify the intended hypothesis. The form, nature, process, function and relationship of the variables also need to be explained for better understanding. The conclusion should provide suggestions and recommendations for future research.

20.5.7 Writing and Publication

The scientific method of writing is meant to convey the technical and factual information to the reader in a direct presentation and discussion for which the paragraphs and sentences should be simply constructed. Writing of research work should define a research question, which results in a well-designed research procedure that plans the overall approach meticulously. This structural method of writing should lead to a set of documents from which the manuscript can be constructed. The manuscripts submitted to journals for publication should consist of the headings such as title page, abstract, introduction, research methods, results, discussion, findings, conclusions, acknowledgments, references, tables and figures.

20.6 The Framework of Writing Research Papers through Software Support

Writing research papers concerns the outcome of the research and the presentation abilities of the researcher. The ability of the researcher to present his research work with all nuances of his research to the readers is controlled by his knowledge and writing skills. As discussed in previous sections, manuscripts should carry all the components to covey the original outcome of the research to others. Extending or shortening the manuscript on the components of the research writing will lead to misunderstanding or confusion on the part of the reader. In order to avoid the shortcoming in writing manuscripts, this section tries to introduce software, which will help the writers in writing all the needful information of the research coherently. This software takes up the key features of manuscript writing and is made mandatory to complete writing. This software has dedicated sections for each and every component of writing with all structural limitations. Further, this software will help the writers not to miss any of the components to be included in their writing.

20.7 Writing Style of the Research Paper

The style of the writing can be opted based on the APA (American Psychological Association) writing format, which is used for writing research papers on science, psychology and other related subjects. Another option is MLA (Modern Language Association) style writing format, which is preferable for writing materials in social sciences and humanities. Any type of writing style can be preferred by the writer under the writing style option of the software (Figure 20.4).

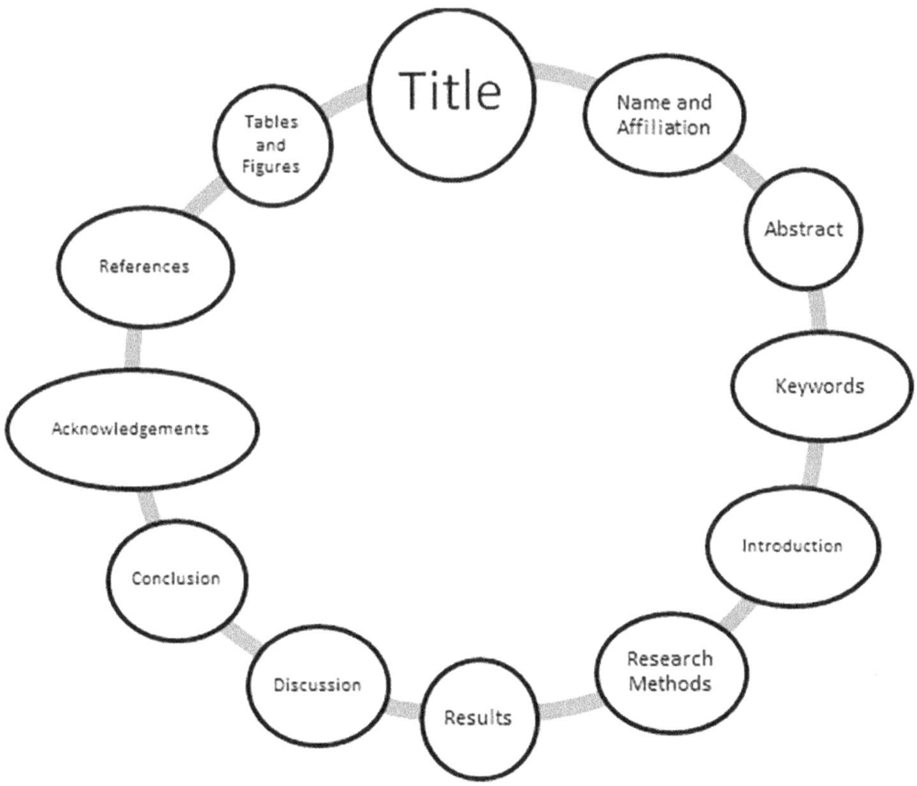

FIGURE 20.4 Components of Research paper

20.7.1 Title

The title of the research work should be typed in the given box. The writer needs to observe the number of vocabulary items he employs for the title and its relevance to the research. The software will have the functions of spell check, capitalization and word counts.

20.7.2 Name and Address Details

The writer needs to provide the required information related to him for reference and future contacts. All the mandatory fields of the writer such as name, institution, address and email address should be filled appropriately.

20.7.3 Abstract

The abstract of the research paper should aim to convey the gist or essence of the research paper swiftly so as to help the reader decide whether to read the full paper or not. The abstract should supplement the details of the analysis, research arguments and findings of the research in a way that helps the readers remember the key points of the paper. This section of the software will control the word counts and format of the writing.

20.7.4 Key Words

Writers can provide key words in this section that are discussed and employed in the research work. While writing the key words, the software will not accept words which are not used in the writing.

20.7.5 Introduction

The introductory part of the writing should introduce the topic and present the background and context of the research. The purpose of the research, its approach and its hypothesis also need to be explained. The importance of the research, rationale and plan of the research are also to be provided in this section. Limitations of words and format of the writing are controlled by the software in this section.

20.7.6 Research Methods

In this part, the writer has to explain the research techniques and research methods adopted in the research. Apart from writing on the research methods and process in running style, the researcher has to highlight the specific research method chosen for the research that is mandatory in this section. Word counts and limitations are also followed in it.

20.7.7 Results

The result part of the paper is a comparatively larger section among others. In this section, the writer provides all the supporting points of the research paper/project and constructs valid arguments. The data analysis and observation result can be presented in table, graph and text forms. Research findings should be provided in text with illustrations, as well as with figures and tables. All the relevant citations and analysis need to be provided in this section. This part of the paper should focus on the rational developments of the research with valid reasoning and solid argumentations at all aspects touched upon the research. The software will control the word limits, tables and citations employed and noted in the reference section.

20.7.8 Discussion

The writer should provide the discussion and interpretation and describe the significance of the research findings. This is an important section of writing in which the selected research problem and findings are compared, contrasted and discussed vividly so as to supplement any new understanding or fresh insights arrived due to the research. The discussion should connect to the introduction of the research questions/problem or hypotheses selected for the research, and the discussion should explain how research perused to arrive at the results. The discussion part should clearly state the potential limitations, validity and weaknesses of the research and comment on the relative importance in relation to the overall findings. Finally, suggestions and recommendations for further research should be provided.

20.7.9 Conclusions

The conclusion part of the research should be clear and written in simple language so as to help the readers understand the research in a better way. The conclusion part does not just reiterate the results and summary; rather, it should provide a synthesis of key points. It should supplement the opportunities and suggestions for future research of the same line or with similar implications of relative fields.

20.7.10 Acknowledgments

Acknowledgments enable the researcher to thank all those who have helped in carrying out the research. A careful selection of people and bodies to be mentioned is essential in the acknowledgments. Mostly the affiliated institution, funding bodies and those who offer help by providing materials, instruments, data collection, sampling and laboratory facilities, research ideas and discussion are to be acknowledged.

20.7.11 References

All the referred articles, research projects, reports, books, web pages, online sources, maps and pictures employed in the research paper should be provided under this section. The software takes up the key role and the writer can fill in the details of the reference of authors such as the name, title, year, publication, place, etc., and the software will suggest them one by one. The writer needs to key in the details as suggested by the software.

20.7.12 Tables and Figures

Tables, figures and display items are very useful tools to present large amounts of complex data simply and easily. Employment of these items improves the quality of the manuscripts. It reduces the verbal expression and comment to a large extent, and instantly provides a worthy glimpse of the research findings. The tables and figures are self-explanatory, through which various numerical and statistical information can be expressed without too much stress or strain on the part of the reader. The numerical and characters used in the tables should be written clearly without ambiguous nature. Numbers and titles of the tables and figures should be selected relevant to the content and referred to in the manuscript. The software will have control over the fixation of the table and its size, number, title, color and space limitations.

20.8 Naming the New Products

The newer and modern research of humanities, sciences, technology and engineering in theoretical—as well as practical—applications leave a great number of unique outcomes in the form of methods, processes and products. These newer products/results are to be named appropriately for reference of the current research, as well as future applications. There are several strategies and methods applied to name the products, and some of them are discussed here.

20.8.1 Descriptive Method

In this method, the name of the new product, method and procedure, etc., are explained in a literal way. The new products of methods are described by means of their form, function and use.

20.8.2 Associative Forms

This technique is used to create a new name by combining an existing word with another one and thereby arriving at a non-word for the new product. Examples: Walmart, Instagram.

20.8.3 Irregular Selection

This is an idea of choosing a word that is completely not related to the product based on the choice or interest of the producer or developer. Examples: Apple, Amazon.

20.8.4 New Coinage

Selection of a non-word that has no lexical or semantic connection to the product. It is just invented specifically for the purpose of the naming product without prior rationale. Examples: Revertron, Infinix.

20.8.5 Compounds

This is a simple technique to combine two words together which are closely related to the product. The first word expresses the nature and the second one the activity of the product for easy understanding. Examples: Pinterest, Shareit.

20.8.6 Affixes

In this technique, a new combination is created by the addition of a free or bound morpheme. Adding the morphemes in the prefix or suffix position of a word or on either position to coin a non-word is the strategy to name new products. Example: Coolify.

20.8.7 Metaphorical Forms

Selecting a metaphorical name based on the product's shape, size, form, color, superiority, importance or function is another strategy for making the users understand the product easily. Examples: Dove, Killer, SuperFresh, Timewear.

20.8.8 Phonic Choice

People like names with familiar and prospective phonemes for clear utterance among fellow beings. The same strategy is also applied to name a new product for reaching the people with the right pronunciation. Sometimes people prefer the names with auspicious sounds of their language and culture. Example: Crackz.

20.8.9 Acronyms

Selecting an acronym is an easy way of reducing a long descriptive product name into a short name. Acronyms of two or three characters are a good idea to make the users remember it for a long. Examples: PPE, NATO.

20.8.10 Name of the Inventor

Naming the new product after the inventor's name is another strategy and will help the users to remember the product—as well as the inventor. Example John Deere.

20.9 The Framework for Developing 'Product Name Generator' through Software Support

Researchers prefer their choice in selecting names for their products mostly based on the root names of the product components and by their function. Since the global scenario in research and development is growing faster, there will be possibilities of fixing similar names for a different product. To avoid confusion in selecting names and creating unique names for the new products, this software may provide solutions. The proposed software tries to provide suggestions for the new names of the products through the amalgamation of components related to the product's use, form, process, function, field, type and creator name. All these components are variables of the software and the anagrammatic forms of the lexical items will be displayed when the words are entered. It is the choice of the writer to choose among the anagrammatic forms which will be suitable to the product or of his personal interest (Figure 20.5).

In Table 20.1, Column 1: The name of the researcher, institution or product developer can be typed in, and this box will show the anagram of the name. Based on the number of characters used in the name, the number of entries will be displayed. The researcher can choose his favorite among the options shown in the dropdown section, or he may opt for it in the sequence along with other word forms from other columns. Names of any category can be used in this section.

Column 2: The name related to the product or its root name or the basic name is to be typed in this box, and the dropdown section will show all the anagrammatic forms of the word. This section will show the lexicons as well as an anagram of the word.

Column 3: In this section, the verb category will probably be used because it has to explain the use of the product. All the grammatical and lexical forms of the words, as well as the anagrammatic forms, will be shown for options. The primary part of the optional words is ranging in all meaningful forms of lexical categories. Word forms in terms of number, tense, degree, meaningful inflection and grammatical transformations will be provided in the primary options.

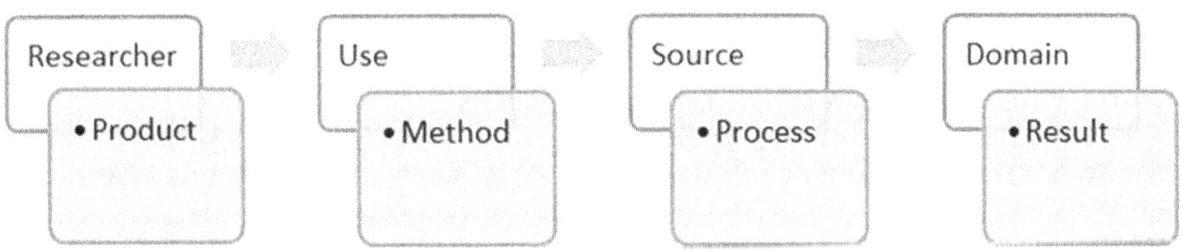

FIGURE 20.5 Steps in product name generator

TABLE 20.1
Product Name Generator

1	2	3	4	5	6	7
Researcher's/ Company's Name	Product's root name	Use/implications	Form/Method	Source/Medium	Process	Field/domain
Bharathiar	Language	Learn	Artificial intelligence	Online	control	linguistics
Bharathi	Langue	Learning	Art intel	One	Controls	Linguistic
Bharath	Lane	Learner	Article intelligence	On	Controlled	Lingus
Bharathar		Learned			Controller	List
		Learned	Art intelligent		Control	Ling
		Lean				Lint
		Len				
		Le				

Column 4: The product's form—such as color, shape, nature, or the method of its use—will be typed here. Single words or phrases also can be selected in this category. The selected word or phrase will be shown with all lexicons and non-word categories for selection.

Column 5: In this section, the source or medium of the product can be typed to get all the meaningful and non-word forms. Users can select single words or phrases to type in the box.

Column 6: This box is for keying in the word related to the process or activity of the product. A single word or compound word can be employed in this category. The dropdown section will show all the possible meaningful words and non-words for selection.

Column 7: The final box dedicated for key in the field or domain name with a single word or compound words options. The entire possible meaningful lexicons and the shortened forms will be shown in the dropdown section for choice.

The seven columns provided in the software have priority and the user can opt for any numbers based on his choice. Once the required number of columns is filled with words, the dropdown column will show the lexicons and non-word forms for selection. The user can select them from each column, one by one, based on his choice. Once the choice is made, the display box will show the selected words in order. This option is individual manual selection based on the choice of the user. The automatic version will show all the possible phrasal forms like sentences starting from the minimal pair to a larger complex form.

20.10 Conclusion

The present chapter introduced the art of writing in general and academic writing skills in particular, with an explanation of the major components involved in it. It has introduced a new model through software technologies, which can be developed for the application of academic writing, especially among young researchers. The second model introduced in this chapter is the 'Product Name Generator' or a linguistics database supported by software to name new products in a unique style.

REFERENCES

Elbow, P. (1981). *Writing with Power.* New York, Oxford University Press.

Lenski, S., & Verbruggen, F. (2010). *Writing Instruction and Assessment for English Language Learners K-8.* New York, Guilford Press.

21

Perception of Industry 4.0 and Education in Teaching and Learning

P. Janardhanakumar Reddy and G. Singaravelu

CONTENTS

DOI: 10.1201/9781003318378-21

Objectives

1. To enable personalized learning for students depending on their capabilities.
2. To increment dynamic movement in lessening gaps in abilities.
3. To foster abilities that will make the understudies ready to fulfill work markets.
4. To support the self-propelled and business-related learning measures.
5. To remember for the exploration cycle of professional learning instruction to meet the necessary assumptions with regards to Industry 4.0.
6. To carry out the educational program according to ventures needed.
7. To beat the unsure reasons in employability.
8. To empower instructors to improve their instructing abilities to grow expertly.
9. To assist understudies with picking their intriguing field where they are suited.
10. To receive an adaptable learning structure as opposed to embracing an unbending design.
11. To track down the genuine impact on employability after the execution of instruction model 4.0 in schools and higher training.
12. To replace clumsy old procedures of conventional education.
13. To transform the future of education using advanced technology and automation.
14. To choose the tools and techniques through which students want to acquire knowledge in flipped learning, blended learning, etc.
15. To create a more multifaceted society whereby everyone plays their best role, adding to a self-sustainable model of education in both school education and higher education.
16. To provide 24/7 virtual learning platforms to offer personalized learning.
17. To foster lifelong learning.

21.1 Introduction

Presently, the business world is changing to a completely digitized production framework, and we are confronting the fourth mechanical unrest, Industry 4.0. With this new modern transformation, the labor force and the preparation and instructive frameworks will be affected. This drove academics to investigate the potential changes that may emerge in the instruction and abilities of things to come in the labor force. The future labor force—whose members are the present understudies—will experience a more globalized, robotized, virtualized, and organized world. As the work environment changes quickly, new capabilities will surface, soon delivering them fundamental abilities for understudy intensity and employability. Considering this unique circumstance, the creators chose to start this investigation, whereby those new capabilities and abilities will be explored, and suggestions are offered with regards to the necessary changes in the advanced education framework.

21.2 Industry 4.0

Improvements in both innovation and advancement are the fundamental variables influencing mechanical upheavals, and these upsets have achieved critical changes in our methods of working and living. Since the beginning, there have been three mechanical unrests and we are right now going through a change towards the fourth modern unrest. Industry 1.0 traded human force with the force of steam. At

FIGURE 21.1 Industry 4.0 components.

the point when James Watt presented the steam motor in the eighteenth century, the automation, creation, and transportation frameworks changed.

Therefore, there was a significant expansion in efficiency. Industry 2.0 was brought about by electrical energy and large-scale manufacturing around 100 years after the fact. At the point when Henry Ford presented the sequential construction system, with large-scale manufacturing and the utilization of electrical energy, there was a huge decline in costs and a further expansion in usefulness. Industry 3.0 was during the 1960s and accompanied the presentation and utilization of personal computers (PCs), which acquainted the world with a quicker and more skilled type of preparing ability. This denoted the start of the data innovation time for business. Industry 4.0 alludes to the following formative stage in the assembling business and was first presented by the drive made by scholastics, industrials, and the German government (Leah Gourley, 2020; Rana, A.K. et al., 2021; Industrie 4.0 project official website, 2022). Its point is "to strengthen the seriousness of the assembling business in the country by computerization".

Industry 4.0 has been defined as a name for the current trend of automation and data exchange in manufacturing technologies, including cyber-physical systems, the Internet of Things, cloud computing and cognitive computing and creating the smart factory (Figure 21.1).

21.3 Artificial Intelligence

Artificial intelligence (AI) is a recent addition to the list of issues that have plagued employees in the past, such as mechanization and computerization. Machines that hijacked human physical labor have now begun to occupy the human brain with the help of computer technology. We have started consuming applications of AI from mobile to automated transport. The basic role of AI is to make a satisfactory model for human arrangement and these models can be set up with the thoughts and techniques from different parts of Science.

21.4 Artificial Intelligence in Education

Central Board of Secondary Education (CBSE) schools have decided to add AI to the curriculum from the eighth grade onwards. Students in higher education—including mathematics, physics, computer science, and engineering—can develop their skills by directly targeting the field of AI. The Finance Commission of the central government has recommended the introduction of AI in education, medicine, infrastructure, transport, and agriculture. AI already exists in the private sector, such as automotive manufacturing, software, and financial consulting. Since everything is in its infancy, one can explore the next stage of development of AI and multiply capabilities accordingly.

21.5 Application of AI in Higher Education

Numerous scholastic organizations are working intimately with ventures to fill ability gaps in the AI space. Continuous up skilling is not just for tech talent or those currently affected by AI. AI and emerging technologies require multidisciplinary thinking and creative ideas from every corner of an organization, to move beyond just technical possibilities. Since the rise of human-made reasoning, it has encountered over 50 years of investigation and change, showing enthusiastic essentialness. Science and technology promote industrial revolution and industrial revolutions promote educational reform. With the constant improvement of human-made brainpower innovation, conforming to the real necessities of schools and colleges to prepare imaginative abilities and show understudies as per their fitness, it will undoubtedly be the overall pattern to apply computerized reasoning to advanced education. The primary examinations are that the current circumstance of AI improvement plans the general structure of AI innovation mix in the field of advanced education, and calls attention to the future advancement course of AI in blend with advanced education—for example, upgrading the use of computer-generated reality innovation, customized learning, collaborator instruction, building astute cloud schools, and so forth, which gives another perspective for the data development of advanced education.

21.5.1 Deep Learning Applications in AI

- Fraud detection
- Autonomous cars
- Virtual assistants
- Supercomputing
- Customer relationship management (CRM) systems
- Investment modeling
- Facial recognition systems

21.6 Merits of AI in Education

- Ability to detect weakness
- Deep involvement in the education process
- Create curriculum automatically with recent updates
- Chance to find the best teacher

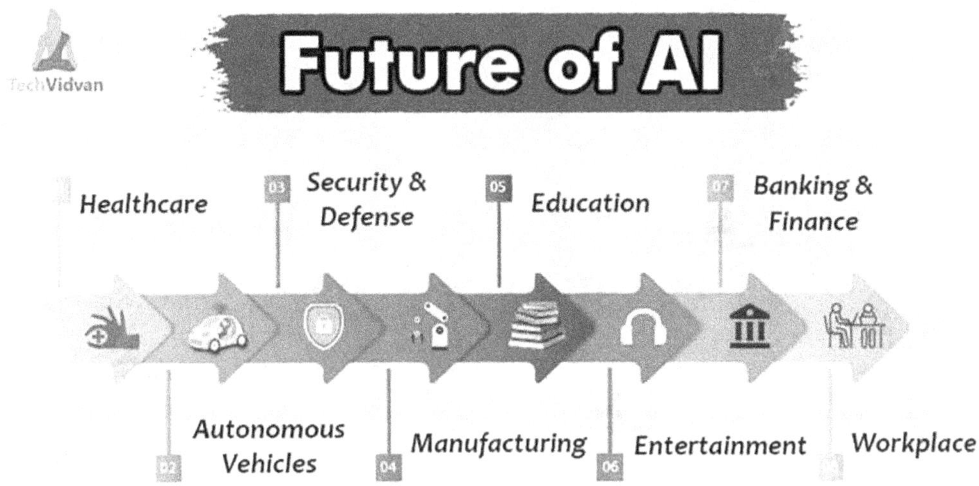

FIGURE 21.2 The future of artificial intelligence.

Source: https://techvidvan.com/tutorials/artificial-intelligence-future/

- Allow teachers to act as learning motivators
- Catering to the needs of all sorts of students
- Smart content
- Intelligent tutoring system
- Virtual facilitators

Computer-based intelligence has impacted our lives from multiple points of view that nobody has at any point seen or expected previously. AI is not enchantment—it is simply loaded with mathematics. The thoughts behind reasoning machines and the likelihood to mirror human conduct are finished. Analytical thinking skills play a vital in AI. AI would certainly help the students to explore more real-world complex problems and obtain accurate solutions in no matter of time.

AI is the most fascinating and universally accepted field of computer science which has a significant scope in the future. AI can be inclined to have a machine to work as a human. In simple words, AI is when machines think, learn, and make decisions similar to those of humans (Figure 21.2).

21.7 Augmented Reality

We live in a world of sophisticated technology. New discoveries are being made every day. That is to say, these AI-based technologies have achieved tremendous growth. In that sense, the future of augmented reality (AR) technology may have taken this modern world to the next level. AR is the act of putting together a layer of artificial software that we need in a real environment (around us). In short, it is about mixing our imagination with reality. The highlight of this is that it looks like it is real, even though it is imaginary. By overlaying computer-generated information on the real world, AR amplifies human perception and cognition in remarkable ways (Figure 21.3).

The first documented reality technology was invented in 1968. However, this AR technology became the talk of the town after the popularity of Pokemon Go a few years ago. Gradually, it became popular after this, and today, it is growing into a huge technology. This imaginary AR software is created on the computer with the help of graphics technology. AR gadgets—designed to be worn as glasses—help with this.

FIGURE 21.3 Augmented reality in practice.

Source: https://edtechmagazine.com/k12/article/2019/02/k-12-teachers-use-virtual-and-augmented-reality-platforms-teach-coding-perfcon

21.8 Augmented Reality in Education

AR in tutoring will in a little while paffect the customary learning measure. AR can change the region and timing of inspecting, to introduce new and additional ways and procedures. Limits of AR development may make classes genuinely enrapturing and information more conceivable. Teachers realize that the learning cycle ought to be about innovation and communication. While instructors do not have to enroll all understudies into science, they will likely get them keen regarding a matter. That is the place where AR could prove to be useful.

These days, youngsters own cell phones. Many of them are dynamic cell phone clients who utilize these devices to get to social stages, mess around, and regarding companions and family members. Meanwhile, fewer youthful grown-ups utilizes telephones for considering purposes, doing schoolwork, burrowing into data about a subject, and so on.

The capability of joining cell phones and AR for schooling is critical, however, it actually must be completely found. AR, in an unexpected way, could yield understudies extra and more advanced information about any subject, and make complex information more self-evident. An example of the use of mobiles for teaching and learning for school students was seen during the COVID-19 period.

Online classes through virtual technology are being welcomed at a kindergarten in Kerala. Bangalore has created aerodynamic images of planes, planets, and astronauts realistically with AR for children to easily understand. This method is said to increase the learning ability of students. This type of online class, which has been very popular, is to be extended to schools in other parts of the state. The arrival of new technology, as is the case of AR devices, captures the teachers' attention. It creates the expectation that its uses may provide students with new ways to interact, new possibilities of collaboration between students and between students and teachers and potentially an increase in the motivation for learning (Figure 21.4).

Integration of AR or virtual reality (VR) or mixed reality is shaping pedagogy. Learning will become more fruitful when you can show a three-dimensional object or process rather than a two-dimension one. Simulations give learners a chance to take risks and experiment with ideas. Virtual laboratories will play an essential role in teaching and learning.

21.8.1 Merits of Augmented Reality in Education

- Increased content agreement
- Learning spatial construction and capacity
- Learning language affiliations

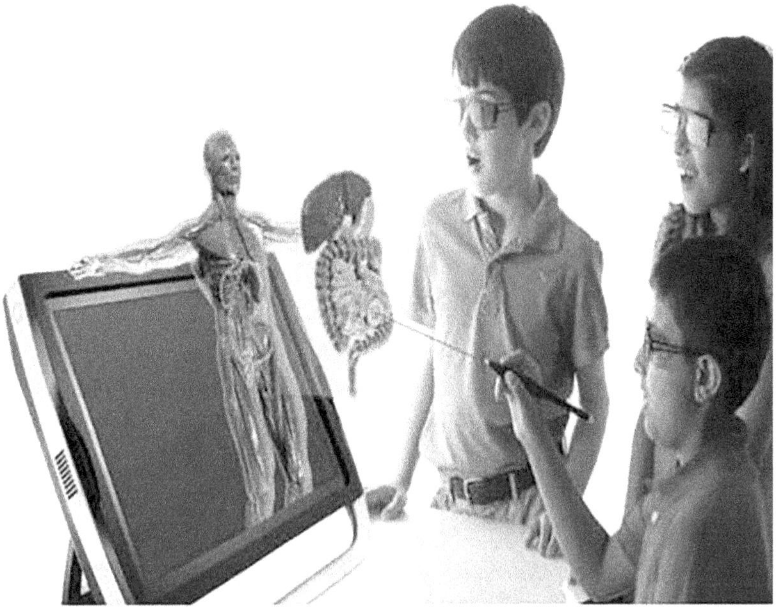

FIGURE 21.4 Augmented reality in pedagogy.

- Long-term memory maintenance
- Improved actual errand execution
- Improved collaboration
- Increased student inspiration

Perhaps the most empowering advantage is understudies' energy about using AR when learning. High energy to attract with AR experiences is noted in numerous investigations about where customers report feeling higher satisfaction, making great memories, and being more ready to go as a result of the AR experience. Peculiarly, customer motivation remains essentially higher for AR structures.

This technology is used to remove the boundaries between real and virtual connections. Of course, we can hope that this AR will become our future technology throughout and will be of great help in many different applications.

21.9 Cloud Computing

Suppose we build a wind farm or a system in our house that can generate electricity which we need for our home. The cost of building and maintaining that system will be much, much higher than the cost of obtaining the electricity we use if we buy it from outside organizations, including the government. This idea is the main reason for the development of cloud computing. Big companies like Google are developing a system called cloud computing. They provide high-performance servers, storage, databases, networking, and software applications. If you want to use these, you can use them with the help of the Internet for very little money.

Cloud computing is a term used to describe the advanced technology of computers and applications that we are currently using. Any cloud computing that is connected to the Internet can be used for storage, including applications. The largest companies are integrating and maintaining billions of electronic devices in the largest locations for cloud computing technology. Cloud computing is turning into a top C-suite plan strategy as organizations are changing from a piecemeal way to deal with a more

FIGURE 21.5 Cloud providers.

comprehensive start to finish advanced change with the cloud at its center. Cloud service providers are software infrastructure that stores data on remote servers. This data can be accessed through the Internet (Figure 21.5).

21.9.1 Cloud Computing in Education

Appropriate figuring in preparing helps understudies, instructors, and administrators, and appropriate registering grants understudies permission to do homework anywhere there is a web connection, helps teachers to quickly move learning materials, and helps managers to conveniently cooperate and get a decent arrangement on amassing data. Building a cloud-prepared labor force is a vital aspect for empowering innovation drove development in India that will drive advancement at speed and make sway at scale.

Incorporating cloud educational plans as a feature of standard advanced degrees addresses a change in the manner in which the business and scholarly communities can meet up to assemble the up-and-coming age of profoundly talented cloud experts. We are regarded to work with licensed instructive foundations in India to drive this change.

The fundamental reason for distributed computing is to establish a learning climate where understudies, guardians, and instructors can sign in from any place, any time.

21.9.1.1 Cloud Computing Applications in the Education Sector

Over the long term, the schooling business has made considerable progress. Educating and learning is not, at this point, limited to course books and homerooms and now arrives via PCs and cell phones. Today, students are constantly connected—regardless of whether they are on or off school grounds. Simultaneously, correct innovations enable them with the genuine world and vocation-prepared abilities. Innovation assumes an enormous part in this problematic change.

Disseminated registering suggests a course of action of figuring resources that can be shared wherever, paying little heed to the space of the customers. Via circulated processing, it becomes possible to

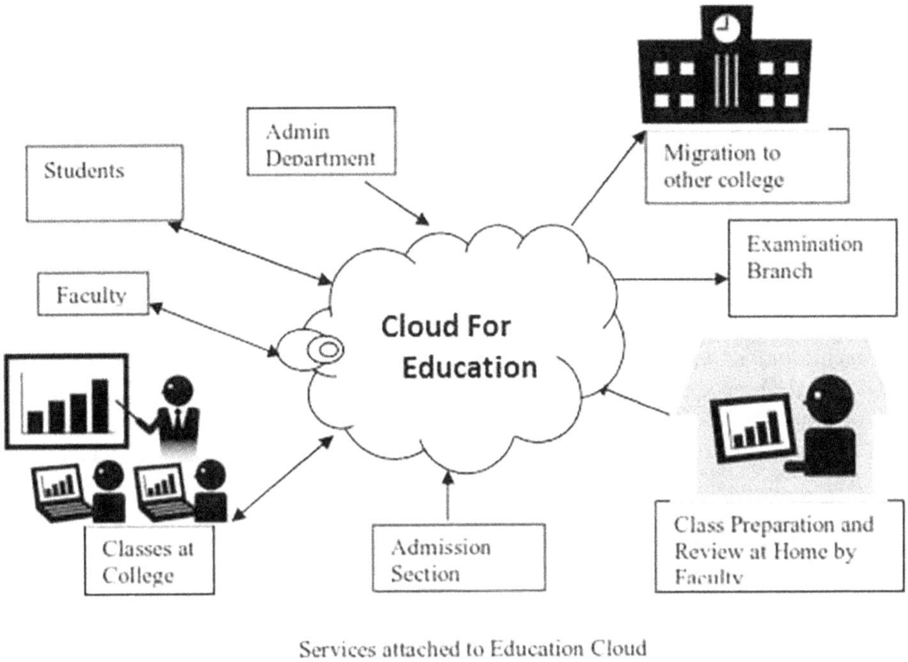

FIGURE 21.6 Cloud-based services for education.

join teachers and understudies on a single, bound-together stage. Educational affiliations like schools, colleges, and universities need not tolerate, own, and keep up their specialists and data-centric focus. Maybe, they can utilize dispersed processing to profit register power, informational indexes, amassing, and various organizations when they need them. Likewise, they can by and large make sure that their resources are secure on the cloud. Permit us to elucidate the expansive benefits of appropriate registering in the field of guidance. Some of the available learning apps in cloud computing are:

- Learn Cloud Computing
- Cloud Academy
- A Cloud Guru

Cloud computing in education helps students, teachers, and administrators alike. Cloud computing allows students access to homework wherever there is an Internet connection, teachers to instantly upload learning materials, and administrators to easily collaborate and save money on data storage (Figure 21.6).

21.9.1.2 Merits of Cloud Computing in Education

- Learning materials are updated
- Easy access
- Data security
- No need to buy expensive textbooks
- Reaching out to a diverse range of students
- No need to carry around devices

The cloud has offered huge potential in changing how instruction as an industry functions from the point of view of offering programs on the web to adjust the customary working environment.

21.9.2 Cyber security

The web has expanded into each aspect of life for the present age, from talking using texts and messages to banking, voyaging, and shopping. Individuals' expanded utilization of the web has required the assurance of delicate data. A PC with deficient security insurances can be contaminated by malicious attacks, permitting admittance to any kind of data very quickly. Online protection is characterized as securing networks, information, programs, and other data from unlawful access, change, or obliteration. The Internet is the interconnected organization of data innovation foundations, which incorporates the media communications organizations, PC frameworks, and installed processors and regulators. Many companies create software to protect their data. The data is safeguarded by these programs. Cyber security is critical since it not only protects information but also protects systems from viral attacks. India has the most Internet users after the United States and China.

Education institutions need to focus on network protection. In spite of the area confronting significant difficulties like an absence of staffing and an absence of subsidies and assets, digital assaults are no less incessant or less extreme in instruction. Indeed, they appear to be becoming more prevalent year after year as examples of penetrations into systems of schools and advanced education are generally revealed.

21.9.2.1 Cyber security in Education

The higher education area is progressively investigating the utilization of data frameworks and innovation to address the issues and assumptions for different students who request something beyond conventional study hall–based encounters. New course movement models attempt to stir very close segments with webinars, e-learning, and other online mechanized methods. Building trust and enabling responsibility among customers of web learning structures are huge, because there are openings for both facilitated and strange associations with the system. Facilitated learning happens dynamically, with all individuals teaming up at the same time, while no simultaneous learning is independent and licenses individuals to take an interest in the exchanging of contemplations or information without the dependence on different members' affiliation at the same time.

The creating use of e-learning systems has been accounted for by different assessments and with a massive turn of events; regardless, little thought has been given to the issue of security of e-learning structures, both in investigation and guidance. Since e-learning frameworks are open, dispersed, and interconnected, security at that point turns into a barren test to guarantee that intrigued entertainers just approach the correct data at the proper time and proposes various suggestions for higher education.

Advanced education institutions face many online protection challenges. In spite of the facts that the online protection challenges confronting advanced education are incredible, and the expense of addressing them is steep, the potential financial and reputational chances that accompany inadequate guards are likely much higher. Establishments across the advanced education scene may come to the conclusion that powerful network safety arrangements can at last pay for themselves.

21.9.2.2 Cybersecurity in the Education Sector

Network safety should be an essential piece of each instruction association's order. Understudies, educators, and administrators all need admittance to the learning devices important to comprehend, recognize, and keep away from digital dangers they may experience in their day-to-day exercises. Breaking down information obtained from years past is critical to seeing how schools are focusing on limiting data security hazard factors and how they can be dealt with. Instructive conditions present new learning openings for everybody enlisted and on staff. In any case, large numbers of these establishments are powerless against digital assaults.

With the worldwide pandemic giving programmers plentiful chances to foster new tricks and unsafe programming, instruction is the way to tend to the quick danger scene. To ensure your information, security mindfulness preparing should be at the front line of your safeguard procedure. Proactive security mindfulness preparing will give the members the heads-up on the techniques that cybercriminals are utilizing now and instruct them on prescribed procedures to ensure their data and frameworks.

21.9.2.3 Cyber security Tips for Students and Teachers

- Keep software updated
- Install anti-malware and anti-virus software
- Choose strong passwords
- Undergo security awareness program
- Appoint internal cyber security ambassadors
- Abstain from tapping or clicking on emailed connections or opening connections.

21.9.2.4 Some Cyber security Apps in Education

- Wireshark
- Nmap
- Metasploit
- Entersoft Apps
- Web security
- Aircrack-ng

21.10 Big Data Analysis

Big data analysis is the technology that integrates more information into the results that we need or want to know in the future. Big Data analytics is the use of advanced analytic techniques against very large, diverse data sets that include structured, semi-structured, and unstructured data, from different sources and in different sizes from terabytes to zettabytes (Figure 21.7).

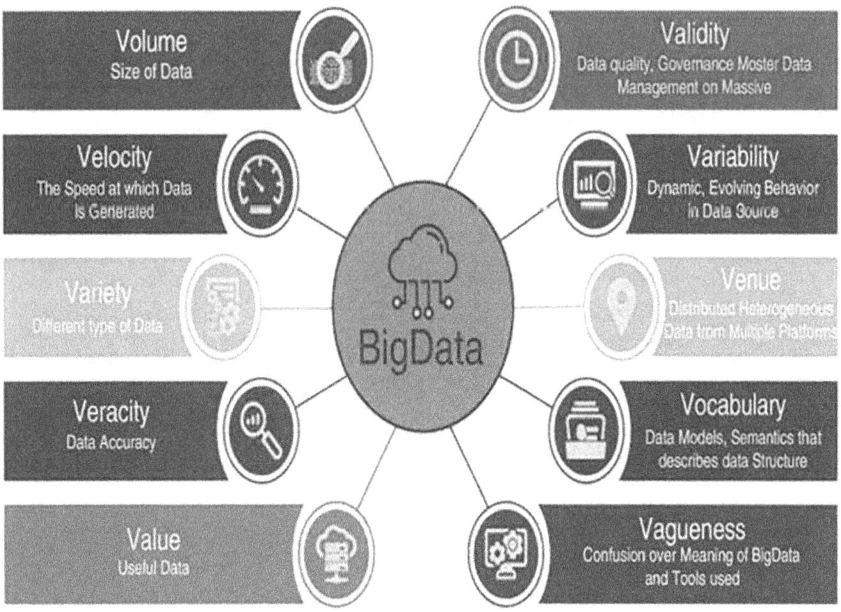

FIGURE 21.7 Big Data.

Source: https://manifoldcomputers.com/big-data/

Big Data *means* "excess information". Big Data technology is the process of collecting excess information and then extracting information from it and then integrating it to obtain the required statistics. Gathering large amounts of data in Big Data, storing it securely (storage and security), extracting information from it, and making final statistics with little error is seen as a challenge.

21.11 Data Science in Education

Today, we are becoming familiar with the different utilizations of data science in education. Information science is a field that includes various strategies and methods to gather information from various sources. At that point, we can remove some significant bits of knowledge from it to take care of true issues. Information science is a multidisciplinary field that requires the abilities of math, software engineering, measurements, and so on. The utilization of data science has in the previous few years filled quickly in pretty much every field, including education.

The accessibility of a lot of instructive information has created various freedoms for data scientists to find some inventive uses of data science in education. Likewise, the examination of Big Data may help those in the instruction area take care of their issues by understanding the various sorts of understudies. Schools, universities, and colleges have a colossal measure of understudy information like scholastic records, results, grades, individual interests, social interests, and so on to deal with. Early warning signs can help teachers reach out to students and offer interventions. Further, data analytics makes it possible to track every student's activity to understand where they are most and least engaged. Based on this, teachers can create personalized learning plans to move away from the one-size-fits-all paradigm. A feedback system is thus created to help instructors to discover solutions to the most common problems in online learning (Figure 21.8).

The examination of this information can help instructors in discovering progressed techniques for upgrading understudy learning. Current data science instruments can help in the instruction area. Different machine learning calculations—for example, random backwoods, strategic relapse, choice trees, support vector machines, and so on—are utilized for this reason. However, there are as yet numerous neglected use instances of data science that may bring about accomplishments in the education field.

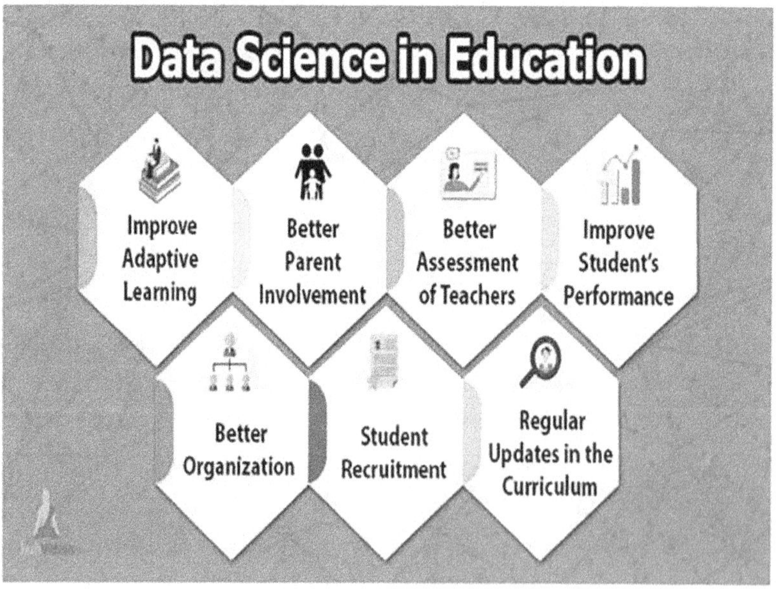

FIGURE 21.8 Advantages of data science in education.

Source: https://techvidvan.com/tutorials/data-science-in-education/

For each space contacted by large information examination, "better" can be included front of it: that is, better security, better preparation, better instruction, better business, and so forth. That is the capability of the innovation.

21.12 Big Data Analysis in the Education Sector

21.12.1 Studying and Research

Microsoft Excel is perhaps the most broadly utilized software in the investigation of large information and is likewise accessible on numerous understudies' home and school PCs. Something beyond a bookkeeping page device, Excel permits educators and understudies to dissect information they have gathered utilizing the product's inward program capacities. For an understudy who is attempting to investigate certain measurements in a math or science class, Excel can be especially helpful.

The Ardunio Science Journal application permits STEM (science, technology, engineering and mathematics) understudies to gather and store information about their external world, similar to how noisy a vehicle horn is, or how brilliant it is outside during specific times. Accessible on Android and iOS gadgets, the application additionally permits clients to dissect and decipher the information they gather, assisting with honing their investigation abilities.

21.12.2 In the Classroom

Illustrative, indicative, prescient, and prescriptive examination are the four primary kinds of investigation which are a crucial part of training understudies' instruments and philosophies when deciphering information. They are utilized to investigate information to figure out what is going on, why it is occurring, what may occur, and possible answers for addressing future results.

Visual arrangements are quite possibly the best employments of examination, as they empower people to introduce discoveries in straightforward pictures, diagrams, and charts. Showing STEM understudies fun approaches to construct diagrams can help them in their present examinations and all through their future training and profession. Academic records include a few exercises that can empower children to gather and examine the information and assemble resulting outlines. For instance, one of the exercises is reviewing different understudies at school about what their favorite Thanksgiving dish is, investigating the information, and afterward creating a pie chart that mirrors those experiences.

Google's Analytics Academy can help more established or further developed understudies acquire proficient information investigation apparatuses and abilities. The foundation begins with a fledgling course that digs into the essentials of computerized investigation, reports, and mission following. Understudies who are especially intrigued can proceed into the more progressed parts of the institute.

21.12.3 Advantages of Big Data in Education

- Enhancing student results
- A better reviewing framework
- Gaining attention
- Customized programs
- Reducing the number of dropouts

21.13 Mobile Learning

Our current period is described by steady change and quick improvement in different parts of life, including logical information and realities that develop quickly. Versatile learning (m-learning) has become pertinent in the current situation. Due to the blast of information, new progressive disclosures, and development of cutting edge innovations alongside the appearance of compact PCs and numerous electronic contraptions, people can acquire the ideal information from numerous data sets and their data by utilizing a web office whenever and from anywhere. Since the early 2000s, many started using mobile phones in information searches and to learn many new facts taking place all around the world.

People of different ages learn and collect information using mobile phones, whereby the information is also available as per the age of the user. As people are less able to use public in-person sources of learning in this pandemic period, people prefer to collect information online via smartphones. Things that cannot be seen but only can be imagined—such as atoms, molecules, space, etc.—can be seen through advanced animated videos and images using many browsers. Smart people update themselves from their homes rather than searching for a tutor and spending money.

21.13.1 Importance of M-Learning in Education

One of the most important reasons we choose to have more technologies mainly in the field of teaching is to speed up the process of learning and enable students to understand the concepts and make the process more efficient rather than mucking it up. Many coding classes have been developed for children to create apps at young ages. Choosing an online virtual classroom that is browser-based is a start to avoid students being blocked from a lesson. Informative platforms are constantly being developed starting from video players to editing icons that allow all-around accessibility.

Professors, trainers, and teachers show students visually these concepts for their betterment. Online learning has given space for self-learning. Preparation for any entrance exams or government exams has become much easier by means of e-learning. Downloading texts, pictures, documents, etc., for the purpose of projects and assignments has become common practice everywhere. Mainly, mobile learning allows for flexibility by eliminating the need for learning to happen at a particular place and time.

Many jobs and career opportunities can be brought up to date, which has changed the lives of many people. Even many educational apps have been developed and are available online, which has helped many people with career guidance. Online quizzes and puzzles are presented in such a way that they attract the students and help them to expand their knowledge in interesting ways. Highly experienced people all around the world started to share their views on their areas of interest, whereby this online has changed into a common forum. Also, huge numberrs of people from different corners of the world can access these for discussions on different topics or related to different subjects.

21.13.2 Mobile Learning in Education

Cell phones are ubiquitous with college understudies these days, empowering them to concentrate autonomously on spot, time, and authority. With an expanding number of individuals utilizing cell phones, there will be expanded revenue in mobiles, and realizing this will bring about more versatile learning drives, including for advanced education. Most understudies use m-learning for their examinations to finish an absence of data from their in-person classes, to re-examine study materials before doing an assignment or a test, or just to find out about their investigation results. Sixty percent of them utilize their cell phones for their investigations a few times each week, yet primarily at home; albeit half of them conceded utilizing the cell phone additionally while voyaging or being at school. The primary justification for utilizing it at home is, by all accounts, the great Internet connection.

M-learning expects students to engage in an assortment of undertakings, for example, to fundamentally assess the data they access with the assistance of their cell phones, to define objectives for the fruitful passing of their investigations, and to engage as a team with their friends and instructors to build up the learning content. For the most part, they need to take on obligations regarding their own investigations. Furthermore, such learning requests qualified and experienced instructors who help their understudies by working with their portable examinations through steady consolation, nonstop input, utilizing the web specialized devices, or planning suitable intuitive learning exercises. Mobile learning, also known as m-learning, is defined as the need and ability to learn through virtual media, such

FIGURE 21.9 Mobile learning.

Source: www.hurix.com/top-mobile-learning-platforms-elearning/

as personal electronic gadgets, social interactions, and content. Devices that can be used for m-learning include smartphones, tablets, laptops, and digital notebooks. It focuses on the learners' freedom of movement and their interaction with technology. In this case, simplifying learning by using mobile tools is what constitutes this informal learning setup (Figure 21.9).

21.13.2.1 Mobile Learning Apps for Education

- BoostHQ
- Evernote
- Skill Pill
- Udemy
- WordPress

21.13.3 Benefits of M-Learning in Education

M-learning is a characteristic augmentation of e-learning. The primary advantage of m-learning is that the understudy can improve by making information and learning accessible whenever and anywhere autonomously. M-learning oversees distinctive learning prerequisites, whereby it is unmistakably designed for permitting understudies to get information at their own speed. It is self-motivated and self-disciplined, possessing the following additional advantages.

- Content can be accessed at any time and from anywhere
- It supports distance learning
- Enhances student-centric approach
- It very well may be utilized successfully for them in unexpected ways
- It can upgrade collaboration between understudies, students, and educators
- It can reduce social and correspondence boundaries among workforce and understudies by utilizing correspondence channels as understudies wish

Thus, we survive in a world where technologies grow faster for all our needs. Learning online leads to many innovative ideas and helps us to grow in our field of interest. Rather than carrying loads of books, having an electronic gadget to browse is more than enough for a person to gain more knowledge.

21.14 Internet of Things (IoT)

To manifest the Internet of Things (IoT), workers will be able to reduce demand in large numbers. One can get information about something before it happens. IoT is not just a technology for home use. Its uses in offices, factories, and hospitals will continue to grow. The IoT is a system of interrelated computing devices, mechanical and digital machines, objects, animals, and people who are provided data from them (Figure 21.10).

IoT is a system that exchanges information between your computer, digital devices such as mobiles, and mechanical items such as doors, microwave ovens, etc., in your home through a specific unique identifier (identification number) without the help of any human or computer. All of the tools and systems are connected to the IoT platform via sensors. These involve the exchange of information over the Internet. It also integrates information from various tools and systems, and automatically draws conclusions from it.

21.14.1 IoT in Education

IoT in schools suggests an unrivaled related and more communitarian future for guidance. IoT devices give understudies better induction to everything from learning materials to correspondence channels, and they empower teachers to check understudies' learning progress consistently. It is not about the development; it is connected to sharing data and information, passing on capably, building learning organizations, and making a culture of cleaning ability in schools. These are the essential obligations of every enlightening pioneer. Chalkboard gives an associated learning experience and encourages a group of people in an assortment of fields, including K–12 and advanced education. A computerized learning climate customizes the instructive experience, the virtual study hall innovation builds cooperation, and marked sites keep guardians, understudies, and others refreshed with the most recent evaluations, participation, occasions, and news.

21.14.2 IoT Applications in Education

The applications of IoT in the education sector are the following.

FIGURE 21.10 Internet of Things (IoT).

21.14.2.1 Interactive Learning

Today, learning is not limited unmistakably to the blend of pictures and messages, yet is rather considerably more than that. Various course books are joined to electronic areas that merge additional accounts, materials, developments, assessments, and various materials to help the learning cycle. This gives a more broad perspective to the understudies in procuring data on new things with an unrivaled game plan and joint effort with their associates and teachers. These current reality issues are inspected in homeroom by the informational specialists and understudies are made to find the reactions for these issues.

21.14.2.2 Security

As there will be various understudies present in a class of any educational foundation, checking the whereabouts and activities of every understudy is positively not a simple task. Additionally, the understudies in an informative foundation are more introduced to possibilities and require advanced security when differentiated from the general population at some other workplace. IoT can add significant worth to the extent of overhauling the security of schools, colleges, and some other learning natural surroundings. With the help of developments like 3D arranging, understudies can be noticed the entire day and their quality can be represented at some arbitrary point on the timetable. For checking understudy lead, WYZE camera vision can be used close by. Lately, PC vision advancements have improved an unbelievable arrangement and can screen any imprint advancements. This development can normally keep any astonishing events from happening.

21.14.2.3 Increasing Efficiency

In various schools and colleges, a lot of time is spent on practices that do not expand the worth. For instance, the collaboration of the understudies ought to be taken a couple of times every day. Moreover, this data should be dispatched off the central office for different purposes. The IoT can stop this inefficient structure. With the help of IoT end devices, this data can be accumulated and sent off to the central office specialist, thus taking out the necessity for any human intervention. On account of this reformist shift toward the IoT, dreary tasks of instructors and understudies can be restricted. This licenses them to zero in on additional on teaching and knowledge, which is the middle of any point of convergence of learning.

21.14.2.4 Smart Boards

- Attention to attendance
- Significant safety
- Adjusting disability
- Mobile applications and tablets

21.14.3 Merits of IoT in Education

- Protecting students with programmable security protocols
- Attendance and automation
- Custom temperature controls in a school setting
- Monitoring device usage
- Providing accommodations for students with disabilities and special needs
- Augmented reality applications in classrooms
- Conference room and study room scheduling
- IoT asset tracking in higher education
- Engaging students with IoT learning opportunities

The school is moreover equipped with release distinguishing advancement, and IoT-related devices, for instance, shaded lights and electronic shows thus preparing understudies, staff, and police nearby if there should arise an occurrence of an intruder. The security structure is furthermore changed with shows for various emergencies, similar to outrageous environment perils. Different settings trigger different alerts all through the school, yet the overall outcome is a safer learning environment for understudies and teachers.

REFERENCES

1. I. Bandara, F. Ioras, K. Maher, "Cyber Security Concerns in E-Learning Education", Proceedings of ICERI2014 Conference, 2014. ISBN: 978-84-617-2484-0.
2. Industrie 4.0 project official web page, https:// www.bmbf.de/de/zukunftsprojekt-industrie-4-0-848.html, Accessed on 12 Sep 2022. www.toppr.com/guides/essays/cyber-security-essay/
3. www.drishtiias.com/to-the-points/paper3/cyber-security
4. www.dissertationhomework.com/essays/security/the-importance-of-cyber-security-in-modern-internet-age
5. www.aplustopper.com/essay-on-cyber-security/
6. Youssra Riahi, Sara Riahi, "Big Data and Big Data Analytics: Concepts, Types and Technologies", *International Journal of Research and Engineering.* ISSN: 2348–7860 (O) | 2348–7852 (P) | Vol. 5, No. 9 | September–October 2018 | PP. 524–528.
7. R. Silva, J. C. Oliveira, G. A. Giraldi, "Introduction to Augmented Reality", www.researchgate.net/publication/277287908
8. Keyur K. Patel, Sunil M. Patel, "Internet of Things-IOT: Definition, Characteristics, Architecture, Enabling Technologies, Application & Future Challenges", *International Journal of Engineering Science and Computing*, ISSN 2321 3361, Vol. 6, No. 5, May 2016, PP. 6122–6131.
9. V.V. Subrahmanyam, K. Swathi, "Artificial Intelligence and its Implications in Education", International Conference on Improved Access to Distance Higher Education Focus on Underserved Communities and Uncovered Regions, Kakatiya University, Warangal, Telangana, India 11–12 August 2018.
10. Rana, A.K., Sharma, S, Industry 4.0 Manufacturing Based on IoT, Cloud Computing, and Big Data: Manufacturing Purpose Scenario, 2021, In: Hura, G., Singh, A., Siong Hoe, L. (eds) *Advances in Communication and Computational Technology. Lecture Notes in Electrical Engineering*, vol 668. Springer, Singapore. https://doi.org/10.1007/978-981-15-5341-7_84 Lijia Chen, Pingping Chen, Zhijian Lin, "Artificial Intelligence in Education: A Review", IEEE Access, Digital Object Identifier. Doi: 10.1109/ACCESS.2020.2988510 Leah Gourley, What is Industry 4.0? A Guide to the Fourth Industrial Revolution, 2020, https://www.ptc.com/en/blogs/iiot/what-is-industry-4-0.
11. https://www.i-scoop.eu/industry-4-0/
12. https://raccoongang.com/blog/what-mobile-learning/

22

Education 4.0: Revisiting Contemporary Paradigms in Social Work Education

F.X. Lovelina Little Flower and J. Tresa Sugirtha

CONTENTS

22.1 Introduction

We live in an era of digital revolution when technological advancements permeate all activities of our society, from our personal lives to our work environments. In addition to transforming the daily life of individuals, it has also overhauled industries and transformed jobs and skills (Mühleisen, 2018). The complexity, scope and rate of transformation are unlike anything that humankind has experienced in the past (Schwab, 2016). Contemporary technologies such as artificial intelligence (AI), Big Data analytics and the Internet of Things (IoT) have facilitated innovations in business and industry. The exponential growth of technology has greatly influenced industries, leading to a new industrial revolution much distinct from the others. The Fourth Industrial Revolution encompasses the fusion of various technologies that conceal and blur lines between the biological, physical and digital spheres. Industry 4.0 is a subset of the Fourth Industrial Revolution, though both terms are often used interchangeably. Though it is ambiguous in what way the Fourth Industrial Revolution will unfold, the response to it should be integrated, encompassing all stakeholders of politics, industries, academia and the larger society. Implications for education might involve dramatic modifications in the requirements for knowledge and skills, as well as growing possibilities for teaching and learning (OECD, 2018).

22.2 Correlation between the Industry 4.0 Technological Revolution and Education 4.0

The Fourth Industrial Revolution has transformed industries from traditional labor-intensive operations to completely digitalized ecosystems. The proliferation of technology in industries demands a highly

DOI: 10.1201/9781003318378-22

skilled and competent workforce. Traditional education—with the primary goal of imparting knowledge in a particular discipline and obtaining graduation—is now becoming obsolete. Today, the axes of education have shifted such that skill development is regarded as the foundation of education. While empirical studies on the correlation between Industry 4.0 and Education 4.0 are scarce, the preliminary observations unveil the proposition that higher education needs to upgrade its programs to outfit students for the highly digitized and automated environment of Industry 4.0. As industries transform, there should also be a parallel evolution of education to adapt to the changes—not only of technology but also changing jobs, people, culture and particularly the changing attitudes of students toward learning. To this end, higher education should encompass innovative strategies and transform itself from providing tailor-made education to offering customized services to the student population with the active use of emerging technologies.

22.3 Recent Trends in Social Work

Social work is a multi-branched profession that seeks to deal with the myriad and most complicated interactions between persons and their environments (IFSW 2000). In the present-day world, described by accelerating social problems ascending from innumerable global forces such as changing socioeconomic and political structures, disasters, oppression, genocide and pandemics, social workers are challenged by contemporary problems that amplify their responsibilities (Ponnuswami & Sugirtha, 2018). Taking heed of the emerging global trends, the conventional paradigms of social work policy and practice need to be amended to turn out to be globally and socially sensitive (Faruque & Ahammed, 2013). Ever-increasing global interdependence has persuaded the social work profession to reorient and globalize itself to adeptly deal with the diverse social problems arising worldwide. Social work is not the only profession exploring and resolving issues such as "internationalization" and "global engagement"; these terms are commonplace in most institutions of higher learning (Lyngstad, 2013; Bourn, 2011; Svensson & Wihlborg, 2010). In addition, fluctuating socioeconomic conditions worldwide have a profound impact on many professions, including social work. The contemporary challenges amplified by the emerging economic policies have presented a plethora of challenges for the profession to deal with. Further, the development of technology and its implication on social work practice has also brought substantial changes in social work education, such as increasing the digitalization of social work education in many Western and developed countries. The rapidity of technology integration in social work practice and education has paved way for the development of uniform technology standards for social workers guiding their practice by the National Association of Social Workers (NASW) partnered by the Association of Social Work Boards (ASWB), the Council on Social Work Education (CSWE) and the Clinical Social Work Association (CSWA). Over the past few years, there have been several initiatives by various stakeholders to include technology in social work policy, practice and education which have become inevitable in the COVID-19 era.

22.4 Technology in Social Work Education

> Technology is ubiquitous in the contemporary society.
>
> **Anne C. Deepak, Ph.D., associate professor at Monmouth University School of Social Work**

From production and consumption, information and communication, and networking through social media to organizing digital campaigns, social technologies have reshaped our milieu and created both opportunities and obstacles to individual, social and community growth and wellbeing (Coyle, 2017). Extensive progress of technology has led to remarkable changes in the way modern society connects, learns and socializes (Altbach et al., 2009). Simultaneously, educational practices worldwide have undergone immense transformation. As a result, many institutions of higher learning are currently using technology-oriented pedagogical methods as sustainable alternatives that might possibly match, or surpass, the competencies of traditional lecture-based classroom instruction. Social work is no exception, as many institutions offering social work courses globally have swiftly yet systematically implemented technology in their classrooms and curricula (Regan & Youn, 2008). The application of technology by social workers has been proliferating in recent years. It has overhauled the nature of social work practice, enhancing skills and competencies of social workers to assist their clients (NASW, 2017). Today, social workers are capable of providing professional services to their clients through online counseling, cloud meetings, telephone counseling, mobile applications, internet-based interventions and many other ways using technology. Technology has enabled social workers to interact and interconnect with clients through innovative modes modifying the outlook of the conservative worker–client relationship. Further, the helping profession applies newly emerged technology to gather, organize, store and access data pertaining to their clients in a protected manner on their smartphones and in the "cloud", and have the knowledge and skills to use the internet and search for client-related information. (NASW, 2017).

Technology has brought dramatic changes in social work education, widening its scope. Students pursuing social work education in the present generation have the opportunity to take courses online, view recorded lectures uploaded on various websites, participate in online discussions and social work practice simulations in the virtual environment, interact with fellow students pursuing social work from distant locations across the globe, and listen to podcasts. Technology helps in the engagement of students who are millennials and digital natives. It has also provided opportunities for social workers to gratify their desire for continuing education by enrolling themselves in live sessions and online courses, and attending lectures delivered by experts from remote locations with the help of web-based technology. They may deliver essential services and acquire training, supervision and consultation from distant places through live conferences using various applications (NASW, 2017). However, there is a perpetual debate about the incorporation of technology in social work education, with supporters arguing the importance of adopting new technology in order to improve opportunities for students whereas skeptics are concerned with its implications on traditional social work practice. Despite the disinclination of many to incorporate technology in social work education, technology seems to have permeated into various levels of social work practice (Vernon et al., 2009).

22.5 Technological Advancements and Their Application in Social Work

The world today is undergoing rapid transformation, particularly in the industrial sector as an outcome of Industry 4.0. The key tools of Industry 4.0 include AI and machine learning, automation and robotics, Big Data, IoT, augmented reality (AR) and virtual reality (VR). These new tools have not only transformed industries but have also heralded the need for redesigning higher education so as to provide a competent workforce for future roles in diverse fields—and social work is no exception. Technological advancements have indeed altered the traditional patterns of service delivery to clients though slow-paced. The stakeholders themselves being governed by the evolution of technology and electronic gadgets are ready to adapt to changes in service delivery, which for them becomes simple. The application of the key tools of Industry 4.0 in social work practice is described in the following subsections.

22.5.1 Big Data and Data Analytics

Big Data has become the buzzword in today's data-driven society. The term Big Data refers to the large volumes of data pouring in from various sources in different formats. Big Data—when used responsibly and analyzed carefully—promises new insights, leading to better decisions and strategic interventions, and also helps to address various complex social problems (Gillingham & Graham 2016). Though Big Data is used extensively in business and allied fields, the social sector still lags in its application of data-driven strategies. Claudia J. Coulton et al. (2015) have rightly pointed out that Big Data will change the way government agencies and non-profit organizations make decisions, and can shift the curve on the rate of knowledge development and impact by incorporating data science into the social sphere. With the growing importance of evidence-based policy and practices in social work, Big Data provides social workers opportunities for evidence-based research and practice, and will help to create evidence on the achievement of positive outcomes. Non-governmental organizations need to demonstrate pieces of evidence of their success in order to establish their credibility and pool funds from funding agencies and donors. Big Data allows social workers to effectively use the information that is readily available in the various databases rather than collecting data which increases the spending.

Jeffrey Zetino and Natasha Mendoza (2019) have stated that:

> the capacity to combine huge public databases and develop actionable information that defines, analyze, predict and recommend newfangled interventions to social problems are inevitable skills that social workers need to develop and utilize for the common good. The merged databases enable utilization of various computerized records in social care such as criminal records, childcare records, medical records, etc. The electronic records thus accessed would enable service providers to assess larger populations, measure the impact of various social phenomena and suggest interventions. It will also help in better diagnoses of mental health disorders, improved understanding of dysfunctional behaviors giving rise to new integrated models of social functioning. It will further enable development and implementation of evidence-based practices.

Big Data is used by social workers in various developed nations in myriad fields including healthcare, child welfare services, domestic violence, etc. Big Data has proved useful in mapping the spread of diseases such as malaria, identifying high-risk groups, modeling the patterns of human behavior, arriving at predictions, etc. A very recent example of the utility of Big Data and data analytics in healthcare is the COVID-19 pandemic that has affected countries across the globe. The analysis of data from the countries where the infection first spread led to understanding the pattern of spread of the disease and also formulate effective measures to control the global contagion proving to be effective in various countries. The World Economic Forum (WEC, 2020) has highlighted how various states in India have used data to prevent the spread of the pandemic. The Indian states of Kerala and Maharashtra have been recognized by the WEC for effectively using data analytics to analyze the travel history of national and international passengers, and trace their contacts thoroughly to prevent the spread of the disease. Further, the Indian government has also created a mobile application to spread awareness and track the movement of individuals and alert them if they have come into contact with infected patients. The government of Kerala and few other state governments also developed their own application to generate awareness of the disease

The significance of Big Data has been realized in various other crises. The importance of disaster management from the perspective of Big Data and technology is evident from the 2013 *World Disasters Report* focusing on the rapid spread of technology and the way it has influenced humanitarian action through humanitarian information and communication technologies (ICTs). Big Data has proved useful for identifying victims and providing relief during natural disasters such as the earthquakes in Haiti in 2010 and Nepal in 2015. The data we generate with our mobile phones, social media and satellites provide clues to respond in the best possible way to the disaster situation. In addition to natural disasters, Big Data can be used to address the impact of man-made disasters such as civil war, terrorist attacks and public violence, and provide relief.

Big Data has not just changed the patterns of social service delivery but has also created new career options for social workers such as Big Data professionals, data analysts and data scientists. Dr. Shonda Lawrence (2019), assistant professor at Clark Atlanta University, has stated that she believes that the approaches in data analytics would be beneficial for the future of the profession. She considers data science as a revolutionary approach that helps social workers understand human behavior more comprehensively through data-driven insights. Big Data will provide researchers the ability to interpret the impacts of micro-, mezzo- and macro-socioeconomic and political factors that influence the epidemiology of mental health, social functioning and adaptive behavior in a better manner. She also emphasizes that

> as we advance in the field of social work, it is indispensable to comprehend the prospect of data science in all fields of study and their interconnectivity while working together to

> address the needs of the communities we serve, irrespective of discipline but specifically for social work.

Though the field of data science does not seem relevant for social work, from a client-centered perspective, social workers need to enhance their knowledge in data science, bearing in mind the need for the ethical handling of data and prevention of bias leading to further marginalization of the marginalized. Debra Parker-Oliver and George Demiris (2006) have advocated for social work informaticians with a new specialization named social work informatics to help the organization of information and enhancement of knowledge to assist social work practice as technology influence in practice expands day by day. The authors define informatics as the integration of both computer and information science to social work to support the organization and processing of data, information and knowledge to support social work practice.

> These specialists might play a significant role in the future as the profession tries to adapt itself to the changes brought by technology and the demands of technology-driven clients. These informaticians may perhaps educate and counsel the profession on ethical and legal issues, and licensing concerns. It will also be necessary for the profession to develop competent systems to analyze whether technology initiatives are accomplishing their goals.

22.5.2 Internet of Things (IoT)

IoT refers to a set of systems, principles, applications and technologies related to Internet-connected objects. The term was primarily used to describe a world of unified connected devices that might reduce costs while saving time as well. IoT has been proved to be helpful for many industries with diverse requirements and conditions. With recent advances in technology, new possibilities have developed, improving the delivery of social welfare services and health care. Considering the favorable attitudes of patients toward health-related IoT, HIoT has the prospective to thrive in the forthcoming years. In health, social care and wellbeing, IoT can bring changes from the mere provision of treatments for illnesses to facilitating preventive care and wellbeing solutions (Laya, 2017). HIoT provides plentiful advantages to people and healthcare professionals, including social workers, ranging from testing of treatments and operation of medical devices to monitoring fitness and wellbeing, which is drawing consumers in the market with popular applications and wearables. The use of the HIoT through various applications has benefit social and medical care institutions. Devices used in health and social care IoT will gather information about clients and patients, and share it with clinical teams and social workers, about a range of various parts of the person's life to improve health outcomes and support members of the multidisciplinary team in health care. The IoT devices create large amounts of data that can be retrieved by professionals when required to make assessments of the daily living of individuals. This, in turn, can also help in monitoring clients in elderly care and mental disorders and disabilities, and further enable social workers to respond immediately to client needs.

Social work has transformed itself and has initiated the development and application of new web-based intervention strategies (Del Fresno García, 2015), leading to noteworthy changes in the delivery of interventions. An array of new digital procedures has spearheaded broader dimensions in research, therapeutic interventions and social networking in social work. A new area of specialization called e-social work is taking shape, which affects social work intervention paving way for e-therapies comprising web-based assessments, therapeutic games, psychological interventions and psycho-education.

22.5.3 Virtual Reality

VR refers to a simulated experience that can be either similar to or different from the real world. It refers to a computer-generated simulation of a three-dimensional image or environment that enables interaction with one another with the use of electronic equipment in a superficially real or physical way. In an evolving digital society, several virtual communities exist which as important to its participants as members of their primary group (Gonchar & Adams, 2000). The New Media Consortium has reported that "The social aspects of virtual worlds are beneficial for educational purposes. These man-made worlds provide students opportunities for role-playing and scenario building, allows learners to take up responsibilities briefly without suffering real-world consequences" (New Media Consortium, 2007). Virtual worlds, in addition to providing opportunities for recreation through gaming, can also be used in the field of education. With the advent of various online degree programs offered by various universities abroad, the virtual worlds serve as a learning platform for the students. Considering such developments, social work educators worldwide ought to identify options for delivering online courses, encouraging online discussions on virtual platforms. The enthralling graphic nature of virtual worlds may develop interest among students who will support online social work instruction. Vernon et al. (2009) have stated that they have used virtual technology (Second Life) in their classrooms and from their experience suggest that virtual worlds may be used for teaching, conducting exercises and role-plays, exploring client systems and examining practice competency issues.

As mentioned earlier, there are many virtual worlds designed and developed by developers. Second Life is one such online virtual world, developed and owned by the San Francisco-based firm Linden Lab. Launched on 23 June 2003, Second Life's rapid growth within a few years led to an estimated one million users by 2013. The virtual world is inhabited by residents called avatars. It consists of various communities for people of various interests and also has communities for educators students and researchers (Giffords, 2009). Second Life is used as a platform for imparting education by several institutions, including colleges, universities, libraries and government bodies. Many universities like Harvard, MIT, and Stanford have inhabited virtual property in Second Life. Drexel University has created its own e-campus called Drexel Island, where students can take practice quizzes, access lecture videos, look at three-dimensional molecular models and chat with students and faculty. The virtual world is suggested to be relevant for social work education, as it consists of many social service organizations. The virtual world also has independent counseling services, some provided by volunteers and others by credentialed professional institutions. Vernon et al. (2009) stated in their study "Virtual Worlds and Social Work Education: Potentials for 'Second Life'" that they have used the virtual platform in their classroom instructions for social work students. Lectures, virtual tours to social agencies, presentations and class discussions all take place in Second Life. This is only one example of how VR can help students acquire knowledge by effective and constructive use of technology, while several other virtual platforms exist. The accelerating need for cross-cultural competence in social work practice arising from various factors including globalization, migration, etc., can be achieved by the utilization of virtual platforms. The virtual worlds keep the students engaged and provide them a better understanding than classroom teaching.

22.6 Revisiting Social Work Education

Technology has entrenched itself into every sphere of life on earth, transforming almost everything around us. Adjustment to the emerging paradigm shift is a major challenge facing social work as both a scientific discipline and a helping profession (López Peláez & Marcuello-Servós, 2018). While most of our counterparts in various other domains have started exploring recent trends in learning powered by present-day technology, social workers cannot afford to remain idle and simply watch the transformations doing nothing to give the century-old profession a facelift (Wretman & Macy, 2016). Failure to adapt to the digital environment will render the social work profession obsolete. Therefore, it is indispensable to create new dynamics incorporating technology both in higher education and practice and strengthen the profession. Despite the skepticism, the profession needs to revolutionize existing paradigms and deal creatively with technological changes, bearing in mind the profession's ethics. Many of our academic counterparts in various countries have even now embraced the changes and have redesigned the social work curriculum. Sue Coyle (2017) states that social work educators in the United States and many other countries have combined digital and social technology into their curricula. In addition to teaching lessons, technology also enables them to guide discussion and prepare their students for the next step into the professional world. With the nature and practice of social work being influenced by technology, there is a need to shift the focus from what students need to be taught to what practitioners are expected to do (Jocelyn et al., 2017), which will help academicians to design the curriculum to suit the emerging job requirements. In order to inculcate technological competencies in social workers, higher education should effect change in both curricula and pedagogy.

The social work curriculum needs to be revamped to include courses that familiarize students with the emerging technological advancements and their implications in social work practice. Considering the career prospects of the students in a rapidly digitalizing society, universities and higher education institutions ought to focus on modifying the curriculum to outfit contemporary needs. Though the current generation of social work students belonging to the millennials and are familiar with the internet and social media, courses imparting knowledge of technology and its practical usage need to be integrated into the social work curricula. Therefore, the curriculum should be designed to include courses on data science, data analytics, cloud computing, Big Data and other technological advancements and their applications in social work practice. The curriculum also needs to include courses on the ethical use of technology complying with the prescribed standards.

In addition to revamping the curricula, higher education institutions also need to focus on pedagogical methods adopted by the faculty. This in fact is a challenge as it demands faculty to take time to master technology-based pedagogy. Sue Coyle (2017) in her article "Teaching with Technology in Social Work Education" has pictured how individual faculty members prefer the usage of different forms of technology in their classes such as live polls, podcasts, online chats, etc., which they are comfortable with and that which engages students. Universities and higher education institutions should make provision for ICT-enabled classrooms and encourage technology-enabled instructional strategies. The technology-enabled pedagogical methods keep the students engaged and also provides them a wider view of the subject matter.

Another major component of social work education is fieldwork, which ensures that social work skills and competencies are mastered by students. Traditional fieldwork involves the placement of students in various social care organizations, but today, virtual fieldwork placements are provided by various universities. The virtual fieldwork placements range from online meetings with actors who pretend to be clients to fieldwork placement in organizations in a virtual world like Second Life (Vernon et al., 2009). Virtual tours to different organizations in different parts of the globe will enable to students to understand and compare the patterns of social service delivery and enhance their cross-cultural competence and skills. The NASW Code of Ethics (2017) recognizes the use of social media as a tool to provide services to clients named as "technology-assisted social services", and such techniques can hence be incorporated into the social work curriculum. With the escalation of the global pandemic, almost all educational institutions have switched to online programs enabling distance learning. But there has been a suspension of fieldwork programs. The present situation has made us realize the importance of technology for social work education. To bridge this gap, simulated learning experiences can be created for the benefit of the students. A simulation refers to a pedagogical method whereby a real-time experience is offered through a mock situation. The various forms of simulations range from mannequin-based scenarios to VR simulators (Hitchcock, 2017). The virtual simulations help social work students to deal with crucial situations that they rarely face in real time. It also provides students to discuss with experts. With the mushrooming of social work institutions, many field agencies struggle to accommodate a large number of students due to various issues. To overcome this situation, virtual field placement can be introduced by institutions by partnering with several social organizations. Many universities abroad have adopted virtual placements for their distance and blended learning programs, and these efforts have proved successful.

22.7 SWOC

SWOC analysis is a technique used to analyze the strengths, weaknesses, opportunities and challenges in any particular area. It helps in gaining an overview by assessing the internal and external factors that affect a particular initiative. SWOC analysis can be used to assess and review the curriculum and to portray the status of education in India. Table 22.1 depicts the strengths, weaknesses, opportunities and challenges of Education 4.0 in social work education.

TABLE 22.1
SWOC Analysis of Education 4.0 in Social Work Education

Strengths	**Weaknesses**
• Prepares students for novel technology-driven careers • Provides students a more pluralistic world view • Encourages exchanges and ensures knowledge development • Develops cross-cultural competence and skills • Improves student engagement by using technology • International awareness develops the ability to deal with international issues. • Possibility for global mobility of social work students	• Inadequacy of resources in many institutions • Systematic and structural barriers • The ambiguities, tensions and contradictions and skepticism in implementing technology in social work education • Concerns on ethical practice • Inadequacy of budget in education institutions hindering incorporation of technology • Concerns about students from an underprivileged background in accessing technology. • Requirement of time and enormous efforts
Opportunities	**Threats**
• International collaborations and partnerships in support of university initiatives, and programs • Improved quality of education • Use of distance education, blended learning and adoption of latest ICT tools • Increased opportunities for student teachers exchanges with universities worldwide • Increased career prospects for social work students in the international job market • Competition with International Institutions	• Dangers of losing traditional identity and values of the profession • Unaffordability: increased costs of education can hamper the opportunities for poor students • The disparity in digital literacy in rural and urban areas • Trigger inequality of opportunities • Increased pressure on the local education systems • Increased pressure on faculty • The hostility of social work instructors to adopt new technology • Increasing ethical issues emerging from the use of technology

The table represents the strengths, weaknesses, opportunities and threats in the implementation of Education 4.0 in Social Work Education. It portrays the advantages and concerns to be considered while implementing education 4.0.

22.8 Conclusion

Education 4.0, a product of the Fourth Industrial Revolution, has created an obligation for education to come out of its shell and adopt emerging technologies in order to produce a new kind of workforce with competency and skill sets whose members can take advantage of Industry 4.0. The incorporation of technology in social work education might be challenging for academics, owing to a lack of knowledge, skepticism and ethical issues. Pedagogical concerns expressed by educators belonging to the pre-digital era and the reluctance of the academic disciplines to modernize themselves can hinder the integration of technology by universities and higher education institutions. Bearing in mind that resistance to change would render the profession obsolete, social work educators need to take steps to transform social work education to cater to the needs of the new-age learners. However such transformations should be applied responsibly and ethically. The professional organizations NASW, ASWB, CSWE and CSWA have together developed standards of social work practice using technology that maintains the profession's values and protects the clients. Based on these standards, social work educators should identify various possibilities and implications of integrating technology into education and practice of social work, and they should reform contemporary social work education to adapt to the digital era.

REFERENCES

Altbach, G. P., Reisberg, L. & Rumbley, L. (2009) Trends in global higher education: Tracking an academic revolution. A Report Prepared for the UNESCO 2009 World Conference on Higher Education.

Bourn (2011) From internationalization to global perspectives. *Higher Education Research and Development*, 30:5, 559–571.

Coulton, Claudia J., et al. (2015) *Harnessing Big Data for Social Good: A Grand Challenge for Social Work*, Working Paper No. 11. American Academy of Social Work and Social Welfare. Retrieved from https://grandchallengesforsocialwork.org/wp-content/uploads/2015/12/WP11-with-cover.pdf

Coyle, Sue (2017) Teaching with technology in social work education. *Social Work Today*, 17:2, 14.

Del Fresno García, M. (2015) Connecting the disconnected: Social work and social network analysis. A methodological approach to identifying network peer leaders. *Arbor*, 191:771, a209. DOI: 10.3989/arbor.2015.771n1011.

Faruque, C. J. & Ahammed, F. (2013) Development of social work education and practice in an era of international collaboration and cooperation. *Journal of International Social Issues*, 2:1, 61–70.

Giffords, E. (2009) The internet and social work: The next generation. *Families in Society: The Journal of Contemporary Social Services*, 90, 413–418. DOI: 10.1606/1044-3894.3920.

Gillingham, P. & Graham, T. (2016) "Big data" in social work: The development of a critical perspective on social work's latest "electronic turn". *Australian Social Work*. DOI: 10.1080/0312407X.2015.1134606.

Gonchar, N. & Adams, J. R. (2000) Living in cyberspace: Recognizing the importance of the virtual world in social work assessments. *Journal of Social Work Education*, 36, 587–596.

Hitchcock, I. L. (2017) Learning social work skills from simulations. *E-News Exclusive, Social Work Today*. Retrieved from www.socialworktoday.com/news/enews_0917_1.shtml

IFSW (Ed.) (2000) ifsw news 2/2000. Retrieved May 15, 2017, from cdn.ifsw.org/assets/ifsw_33158–4.pdf

Jocelyn, Clare R., et al. (2017) Curriculum redesign for competencybased education: Redesigning baccalaureate socialwork curriculum. Redesigning Our Majors Symposiumaugust 19, 2017, San Francisco State University

Lawrence, Shonda K. (2019) Data science: A promising field of study for social workers? Retrieved from www.socialworker.com/feature-articles/practice/data-science-a-promising-field-of-study-for-social-workers/

Laya, A. (2017) The internet of things in health, social care, and wellbeing. Doctoral Thesis in Information and Communication Technology, School of Information and Communication Technology, KTH Royal Institute of Technology,Stockholm. Retrieved from https://kth.diva-portal.org/smash/get/diva2:1135406/FULLTEXT01.pdf

López Peláez, Antonio & Marcuello-Servós, Chaime. (2018) e-Social work and digital society: Reconceptualizing approaches, practices and technologies. *European Journal of Social Work*, 21:6, 801–803. DOI: 10.1080/13691457.2018.1520475

Lyngstad, R. (2013) Contextual social work and internationalizing social work education: Two sides of the same story? *Journal of Social Work, Sage Journals*, 13:4, 400–418.

Mühleisen, M. (2018) The long and short of the digital revolution. *Finance and Development*, 55:4.

NASW (2017) *NASW,ASWB,CSWE &CSWA Standards for Technology in Social Work Practice*. NASW. Retrieved from https://www.socialworkers.org/includes/newincludes/homepage/PRA-BRO-33617.TechStandards_FINAL_POSTING.pdf

New Media Consortium (2007) 2007 Horizon report. Retrieved from www.nmc.org/pdf/2007_Horizon_Report.pdf.

OECD (2018) The future of education and skills education 2030.

Parker-Oliver, D., & Demiris, G. (2006) Social work informatics: A new specialty. *Social Work*, 51, 127–134.

Ponnuswami, I. & Sugirtha, T. J. (2018) International social work in the emerging global economic order—challenges and dilemmas. In: M. Pfaller-Rott, E. Gómez-Hernández, & H. Soundari (Eds.), *Soziale Vielfalt*. Wiesbaden: Springer VS.

Regan, Jo Ann & Youn, Eric (2008) Past, present, and future trends in teaching clinical skills through web-based learning environments. *Journal of Social Work Education—J SOC WORK EDUC*, 44, 95–116. DOI: 10.5175/JSWE.2008.200600592.

Schwab, K. (2016) *The Fourth Industrial Revolution*. Geneva: World Economic Forum. Svensson, L. & Wihlborg, M. (2010) Internationalizing the content of higher education: The need for a curriculum perspective. *Higher Education*, 60:6, 595–613.

Vernon, Robert, Lewis, Lisa & Lynch, Darlene (2009) Virtual worlds and social work education: Potentials for "second life". *Advances in Social Work*. DOI: 10.10.18060/236.

World Disaster Report (2013) Focus on technology and the future of humanitarian action. Retrieved from https://www.researchgate.net/publication/262069509_World_Disaster_Report_2013

World Economic Forum (2020) Why India has the upper hand against COVID-19. Retrieved from www.weforum.org/agenda/2020/04/india-covid19-coronavirus-response-kerala-uttar-pradesh/

Wretman, Christopher J. & Macy, Rebecca J. (2016) Technology in social work education: A systematic review. *Journal of Social Work Education*, 52:4, 409–421.

Zetino, Jeffrey & Mendoza, Natasha (2019) Big data and its utility in social work: Learning from the big data revolution in business and healthcare. *Social Work in Public Health*, 34:5, 409–417. DOI: 10.1080/19371918.2019.1614508

23

Fintech Application in Commerce

Sumathy Mohan

CONTENTS

DOI: 10.1201/9781003318378-23

Objectives

This chapter provides simple insight into financial technology. No doubt, technology and the internet have taken over all aspects of our lives. It began with computer connectivity via the web, then people connectivity via the internet, and eventually connectivity of every other part of our lives through the internet. Finance is one of the fields in which technology and the internet have expanded—and the impact on daily life is immense. This chapter includes understanding fintech and Industry 4.0; understanding fintech industry innovations; examining how competitive interests will affect fintech's reshaping of conventional banking; deciding how fintech companies shift the conventional currency regime; discovering who adopts and drives financial technologies using real-world examples to evaluate improvements, challenges, and modifications arising from the emergence of fintech solutions; and examining how fintech has altered funding through new means and models. This topic ends with a description of the various application areas where financial technology is used.

23.1 Introduction

Fintech (financial technology) is a word that refers to financial services that are largely determined by technology or that use technologies to optimize financial services. Access to technology has become extremely affordable because of the internet revolution and the widespread adoption of smart phones. This has resulted in the rapid rise of financial technology. Initially, technology was restricted to banks and trading organizations' back offices, where it was utilized exclusively for accounting and bookkeeping. This perception, however, has shifted dramatically in today's modern world. Fintech now comprises a broad spectrum of technological interventions in all aspects of finance, from personal to business.

Fintech now encompasses a broad range of financial services powered by technology, including instant money transfers, quick response (QR) code–based payments from smart phones, applying for loans without going through a bank, raising funds for a business startup, and managing your investments without human intervention.

Financial institutions (banks and insurance companies) ignored their customers for years. What fintech is seeking to do is tap into the holes where brick and mortar finance has struggled to find appropriate solutions. It has brought about what has been described by many as a financial sector "disruption."

23.2 Definition of Fintech

Fintech is a two-word portmanteau incorporating "finance" and "technology." In other words, it explains the integration of finance and technology—or how technology increases access to finance, from making payments, currencies, peer-to-peer lending, and even wealth management.

> Gartner [1] defines "Fintech" as startup technology providers that approach financial business in innovative (sometimes disruptive) ways through emerging technologies. Fintechs can fundamentally change the way in which a financial services institution's products and services are created, are distributed, and generate revenue. The term may also refer to the technologies these providers offer.

Arner, DW; Barberis, JN; Buckley, RP 2015 [2] defined "financial technology" or "fintech" as technology-enabled financial solutions. The term fintech is not confined to specific sectors (e.g., financing) or business models (e.g., peer-to-peer [P2P] lending), but instead covers the entire scope of services and products traditionally provided by the financial services industry.

Farha Hussain 2015 stated that fintech can be characterized as the act of developing and then popularizing new financial instruments, as well as new financial technologies, institutions, and markets. It includes the creativity of organizations, goods, and processes.

There is currently no widely accepted definition of the word "fintech." The preceding list was a brief overview of its usage within established scholarly literature. A definition is drawn up through a general overview of fintechs' characteristics and an enumeration of the individual segments that make up the fintech industry.

The Financial Stability Board (FSB), an international institution that evaluates and makes recommendations on the global financial system, has classified fintech into five broad categories: (i) payment processing, clearing, and settlement; (ii) deposits, lending, and raising of capital; (iii) insurance; (iv) investment management; and (v) market support;

Financial technology has made many pathways for payments. One example is electronic payment i.e., e-payment, like M-Pesa, which is being operated in various countries like Kenya and Tanzania. In India, e-payment services like Paytm, which is operated through mobile phone–enabled digital wallets, is made to enable everyone to make fund transfers and obtain points and cash back. This also simplified transactions for people.

23.3 Motives of Fintech Innovation

Innovation linked to monetary services is no new trend. Innovations allowed us the use of smart cards(credit/debit) in the 1960s, just a few decades ago. Cash distribution and distribution of terminals such as mobile banking and automated teller machines (ATMs) developed during the 1970s and 1980s. With the 1990s, in the beginning of capital markets and bonds reform, new financial products were developed. Internet banking came into being in the following decades, offering many advantages and the capacity to make banking transactions remotely. This strategy avoids face-to-face contact between the customer and the bank. With the advent of technology such as mobile networks and other related tools, new actors have emerged, including mobile telephony, internet-based businesses, and both hardware and software vendors. As a result of the former, we can anticipate that direct funding will supplant costly and inefficient indirect financing and monetary intermediation.

23.4 Digitization of Finance

The technological disturbance created a huge impact on various habits and behaviors of the current technical/professional world. This technology is integrated with mobile phones, and the speed of service delivers unlimited advantages to the users and financial institutions. The apps and systems have progressed and been created as a result of tougher laws and constantly changing consumer demand.

Following are a few key mechanisms of DTF (digital transformation of finance).

23.4.1 High Standardization

A high level of standardization is achieved by combining finance responsibilities with standardized processes and data management structures.

23.4.2 Highly Automated Functions

The adoption of new technology technologies results in increased automation of processes for services such as money transfer, "know your customer" (KYC) verification, and other similar services.

23.4.3 Insight-Driven Functions

As a result of digitalization, financial models have been altered to emphasize resources on knowledge creation rather than transactions.

23.4.4 Improved Customer Experience

Customer experience is improved through data quality, effective analytics, and lightweight payment interfaces.

23.4.5 Better Service Delivery

The legacy schemes incorporated into emerging technology have altered the financial operating model. The standardized processes enhanced the delivery of services.

23.5 Innovations in Financial Service Space

Business enterprises use innovative creativeness and technology to expand services, reconfigure delivery channels, integrate payments, and deliver proactive advice. Globally, financial technologies affect the whole service arena. Companies with the latest technology are getting into a new finance space. Examples are Amazon Pay, Phone Pay, Paytm, Apple Card, and Google Pay.[3]

On the other hand, fintechs have already experimented with new mobile apps and voice-enabled devices to optimize delivery and contextual customization processes. The fintech industry will continue to invest more in innovations and digital upgrades as technology improves. From KYC to online payment systems, bank reconciliation, and loan applications, fintech is working hard to improve its business transactions. Fintech is currently introducing a new concept of adopting personalized client policies based on lifestyles, attitudes, aspirations, and mindsets. Brokerages, insurance companies, and mortgage organizations are prepared to push beyond customization and build communication. Data availability has also enabled digital innovations. This acts as a segment thanks to the power of Big Data and Analytics.

Another side, API (application programming interface), which acts as a software intermediary and allows various applications to converse with each other, is raising innovation which leads to a huge fintech ecosystem. Which includes after-sales services, and which make the lifestyle of the consumer better? Fintech in the pace of the developing world provides the best consumer value proposition

Many more innovations take us to the evolution of chat bots to link with the customers, distributed ledger knowledge for debit and credit cards (digital currency), robotic process automation(RPA) to provide an automated workforce to complete complicated and frequent responsibilities to execute the assigned financial services.

23.6 What Is Industry 4.0?

The First Industrial Revolution benefited significantly from equipment powered by water and steam. Throughout the Second Industrial Revolution, manufacturing evolved to mass production and electrical systems. Throughout the Third Industrial Revolution, mechanical integration and mechanization expanded. The Fourth Industrial Revolution (Industry 4.0) is the most recent stage of the Industrial Revolution, focusing on connectivity, automation, machine learning, and real-time data. Machines and factories are currently moving to cyber-physical systems, or "digital factories," as a result of this shift.

The Fourth Industrial Revolution is a sea change in the way we live, work, and interact with one another. These advancements bring together the physical, interactive, and biological domains, creating enormous prospects for both. The speed, extent, and complexity of this shift requireus to rethink how businesses grow and produce value (Figures 23.1 and 23.2).

A term coined by the German government during its promotion of industrial computerization, Industry 4.0 refers to the following four principles.

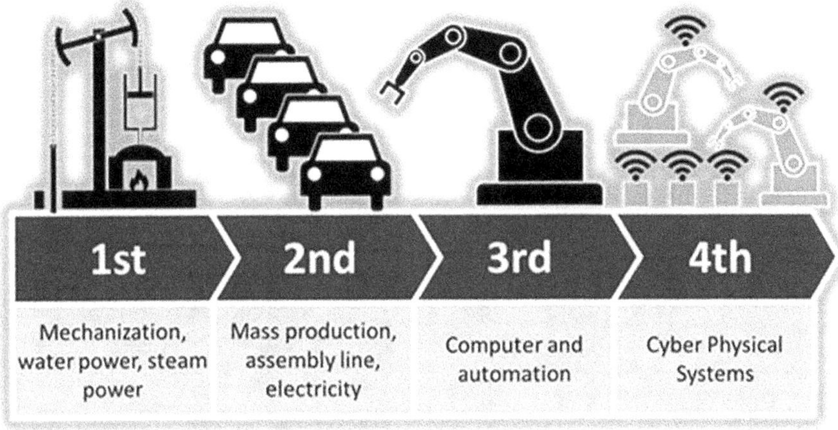

FIGURE 23.1 Four stages of industrial revolutions

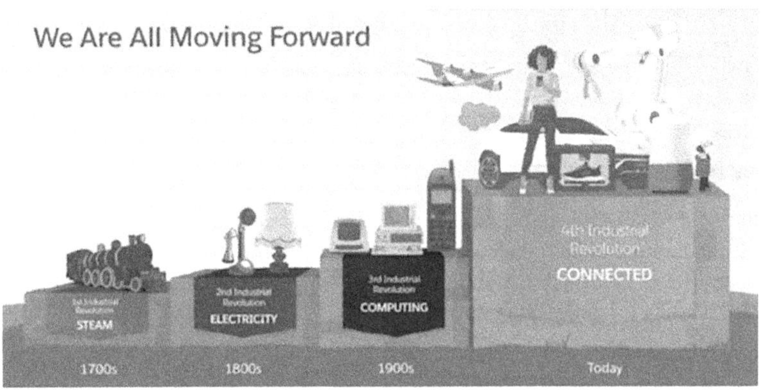

FIGURE 23.2 Inventions that came out of four stages of industrial revolutions

23.6.1 Compatibility

The capacity of machines to interact and communicate via the Internet of Things (IoT) (Figure 23.3) or the Internet of People (IoP).

23.6.2 Transparency of Information

The capacity of information technologies to create a virtual representation of the real environment through the use of sensor data and digital network models.

23.6.3 Assistance with Technical Matters

To begin with, assistance systems have the ability to assist humans through informed decision-making and rapid resolution of pressing problems, and second, the urge to assist people emotionally through a variety of activities that are unpleasant or harmful for their human coworkers.

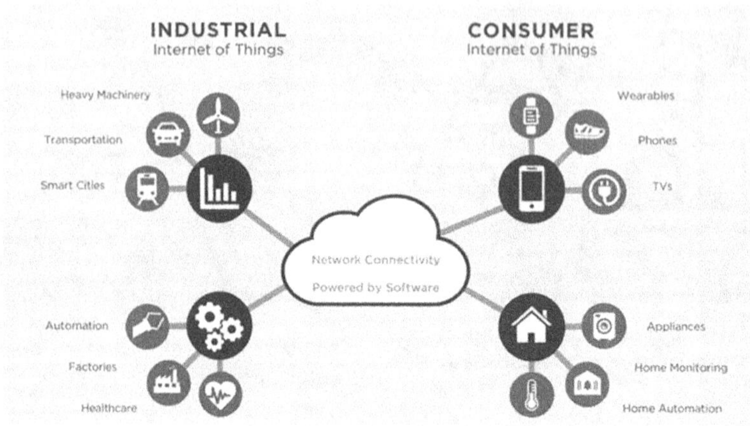

FIGURE 23.3 Industrial Internet of Things

23.6.4 Decentralized Alternatives

The ability to make independent decisions and conduct operations as independently as feasible.

23.7 Innovative Breakthroughs

The Fourth Industrial Revolution and technological advancements have altered the course of daily activities. Financiers must comprehend these technologies and their implications for finance. The following sections discuss artificial intelligence (AI), blockchain, cloud computing, cybersecurity, data analytics, the IoT, and RPA, among other developing concepts.

23.7.1 Computer-Aided Intelligence

AI is a branch of computer science that focuses on the development of intelligent machines that behave and act like humans. Any of the duties assigned to artificial intelligence machines are envisaged for the following.

- Interpretation of spoken language
- Education
- Preparation
- Problem-solving abilities

In other words, sophisticated computer systems are capable of replicating human abilities or the difficulty inherent in having computers and machines perform jobs that require knowledge when carried out by humans.

In finance, examples include pattern recognition in banking, computerized data entry, automated profiling, and credit scorecards (Figure 23.4).

23.7.2 Blockchain Technology

Through the use of public-key encryption and proof of work procedures, the open, frictionless, and publicly available ledger known as blockchain enables us to safely transfer ownership of value units.

FIGURE 23.4 Inside of a Bank

Collective action is used to manage the network, which implies that it is not consolidated and controlled by a single bank, corporation, or government. The more tightly controlled and widely distributed the network, the more efficient it gets.

At its most fundamental level, blockchain is essentially a chain of blocks, but not in the normal sense of those terms. In this context, the terms "block" and "chain" refer to digital data (the "block") that is kept in a public database (the "chain").

In finance, examples include the removal of payments and reconciliation, KYC authentication, and automated and real-time clearing and settlement.

23.7.3 Information Security

Cybersecurity or information systems protection refers to the techniques used to protect computers, networks, programs, and data from unauthorized access or exploitation assaults.

The following are the key areas covered.

Application protection—This refers to the procedures or remedies implemented throughout the software development life cycle to safeguard programs from threats caused by faults in their design, development, delivery, update, or maintenance.

Data Protection—To prevent identity theft and to assure security, data is safeguarded from unauthorized access. The most critical procedures are identification, authentication, and user authorization, followed by cryptography.

Catastrophe recovery planning—This is a process that entails risk assessment, goal formulation, and the development of disaster recovery solutions. Any organization should have a well-defined disaster recovery plan in place to quickly resume normal business operations following a calamity.

Network protection—This necessitates operations that ensure the network's accessibility, reliability, credibility, and security. Effective network protection addresses a variety of risks and stops them from entering or propagating over the network. Network security shall comprise use of the following components:(i) antivirus and antispyware software to locate and defend against malicious attacks; (ii) a firewall to prevent unauthorized access to your network; (iii) intrusion prevention systems (IPSs) to identify dangers that propagate rapidly, such as zero-day or zero-hour assaults; and (iv) virtual private networks (VPNs) provide a secure method of remote access.

23.7.4 Cloud Computing

- Cloud computing is "a business model for providing ubiquitous, convenient, on-demand network access to a shared pool of configurable computing resources (e.g., networks, servers, storage, software, and services) that can be easily distributed and released with little management or service provider engagement effort." (NIST Cloud Computing Standards Roadmap) [4]
- Cloud computing refers to the practice of utilizing computing resources as a service across networks such as the internet. This is the utilization of a variety of resources—such as web development systems, servers, storage, and applications—across a network of many networks collectively referred to as "the internet." Consider Google Apps.
- Cloud computing is a service that combines hardware and software processing resources and is supplied across a network. The enduser is unaware of the physical location of the server and associated equipment. Cloud computing software clients access to "what they require on the internet" and "pay only for what they use."
- Cloud computing finance applications include Zoho Books and Quicbooks.

23.7.5 Big Data Analytics and Data Mining

Data analytics is defined as the science of analyzing raw and unprocessed data in order to arrive at conclusions. It entails a collection of methods and strategies for taking raw data and cleaning it, removing any anomalous or distorting aspects, and transforming it into a format suitable for analysis to facilitate decision-making. Simply said, data analytics is the science of studying raw data in order to derive conclusions about it.

From an accountant's perspective, data analytics is a generic name for computer-assisted audit tools and procedures (CAATTs), which involve the selection of digital data access methods, techniques, and best practices for analysis. Software analytics enables auditors to leverage digital data auditing technology, granting access to all data and doing data analysis to obtain information insights. Data analytics enables auditors to maximize the audit's time and efficiency.

In finance, examples include credit modeling, fraud prevention, risk-based planning, consumer demand forecasting, and business model creation.

23.7.6 Internet of Things

The IoT is a network of networked computer devices, mechanical and digital machinery, artifacts, animals, and persons that all have unique identifiers (UIDs) and the ability to communicate data without human-computer interaction.

Finances encompass inventory and asset tracking, as well as fraud detection, optimization, and surveillance.

23.7.7 Automation of Robotic Processes

The term "robotic process automation" refers to an automated instrument that automates manual, rule-based, and repetitive human tasks. RPAs work by simulating human behavior and interacting with software programs to execute tasks such as data entry and standard transaction processing.

It is computer-coded software that does repetitive operations according to predefined criteria and is capable of operating across several functions and applications.

As the approach is systematic and fairly routine, it is possible to automate the process of reviewing the acceptable timesheet, raising the invoice in the enterprise resource planning (ERP) system to the relevant client, sending an email to the client, and tracking the invoice as part of receivable management.

Automated, repeatable transactions or activities are instances of finance that involve accounting software-assisted, self-reconciling, and so forth.

23.8 Pragmatic Evaluation of the Potential for Disruption in the Financial Services Sector

Beyond Fintech: A Comprehensive Assessment of Financial Technology's Disruptive Potential,[5] a World Economic Forum and Deloitte Global report, examines the transformative role of fintech and other disruptive factors in the financial services industry as a whole, as well as seven sectors, including payments, digital banking, loans, insurance, business infrastructure, crowd funding and investment management.

The report highlights the following three key takeaways.

23.8.1 The Rise of Platforms

Increased client demand would have a considerable impact on product design and delivery, and the duties of firms would almost certainly evolve as a result. Platforms that can communicate with a number of financial institutions via a single channel will eventually become the dominant manner of delivering financial services. The introduction of these networks, such as open banking, has the potential to alter financial services by making them interchangeable. This helps platform owners to manage ecosystems more effectively by balancing product producers' interests with user demand.

23.8.2 Financial Regionalization

Diverse regulatory agendas, technical capabilities, and consumer needs cast doubt on the narrative of expanding financial globalization and pave the way for regional financial services models that are locally conditioned. However, global firms require distinct tactics in order to maintain a regional competitive edge and adapt to local ecosystems. While fintechs are likely to confront significant regulatory restrictions in a number of countries, even as technology lowers entrance barriers, as fintechs chase chances for quick revenue growth, incumbents will become critical partners.

23.8.3 Critical Technologies for the System

Attempts by established financial institutions to replicate the fundamental competencies of giant technology organizations may result in increased reliance on the same massive technology enterprises.

Financial institutions, for example, are becoming increasingly reliant on massive cloud-based technology infrastructure to scale and deploy operations, as well as to leverage AI as a service to better consumer digital experiences and uncover customer product data and profits.

23.9 Disruptive Forces That May Alter the Competitive Environment of the Financial Ecosystem

23.9.1 Commoditization of Costs

Financial institutions are embracing innovative technologies to accelerate the commoditization of cost drivers.

23.9.2 Redistribution of Profits

The location of benefit pools within and between value chains is evolving as a result of new technologies.

23.9.3 Possess Ownership Experience

Distributors should use their strategic strength as customer service owners, while producers should become hyper-scaled and hyper-focused.

23.9.4 The Rise of Platforms

Financial institutions are increasingly turning to multi-provider networks as a means of regional distribution and exchange.

23.9.5 Monetization of Data

Financial institutions are beginning to leverage a variety of data methodologies in an attempt to catch up to technology enterprises' advantage in data monetization.

23.9.6 A Workforce That Is Bionic

Artificial intelligence-related advancements would have a significant impact on the workforce of financial institutions.

23.9.7 Critical Technologies for the System

Financial institutions of all sizes rely on the resources of the largest technology companies.

23.9.8 Financial Regionalization

Divergent regulatory expectations and consumer needs make way for tailor-made regional financial services models.

23.10 Why Fintech in Commerce?

In 2018, global investment in fintech companies exceeded $111.8 billion (KPMG 2018),[6] with deal sizes projected to rise rapidly in 2019 amid growing interest in artificial intelligence and blockchain. With this progress continuing to disrupt and revolutionize the delivery of financial services across sectors, more organizations would need to become familiar with the requisite regulatory structures and infrastructure.

In the financial industry, fintech has been called a disruptive force—one to plan for, or even protect against. However, its rapid adoption among financial institutions and across industries makes it essentially futile to fight fintech's rise. Therefore, the maturing world is changing from hazards to allies, with conventional financial institutions and startups adjusting to the changes and applying creative fintech concepts and strategies to their organizations. The industry is no longer characterized by the future effect of fintech but rather by who drives this disruption at the moment and how to interact strategically with financial technology. This requires a formal fintech course, combined with appropriate hands-on workshops. This will also ensure the millennials and future graduates are ready for business and equipped with current skills.

23.11 Fintech Course Description

A fintech course should provide realistic perspectives and information about the fintech industry and how technology affects the finance domains, and improve students' potential to do the same.

Following are the subjects that prospective students will be conscious of.

- Introduction to Fintech
- Industry 4.0 and Its Impact
- Fintech Transformation
- Fintech Evolution 1.0: Infrastructure
- Fintech Evolution 2.0: Banks
- Fintech Evolution3.0/3.5: Startups and Emerging Markets

- Collaboration between Financial Institutions and Startups
- E-Commerce and M-Commerce
- Digital Finance and Banking
- Data Regulation and Management
- Regulatory Landscape in Fintech
- Overview of the New Concepts of Technology
- Artificial Intelligence and Its impact on Finance
- Blockchain and Cryptocurrencies
- Legal and Regulatory Framework of Cryptocurrencies
- Digitization of Financial Services
- Cloud Computing
- Data Analytics and Tools

23.12 Opportunities for Students

Through this course, students will get the opportunity to work in the fintech companies that use advanced tools and algorithms to help businesses and customers more efficiently handle their financial operations and investments. A few possible opportunities through top fintech companies in India like Paytm, Bill Desk, Pine Labs, Incred, Mobikwik, Razor pay, Bank bazaar, Policy Bazaar, Phone Pe, etc., and few top fintech companies in the Indian state of Tamil Nadu like Bank Bazaar, Credit Mantri, Kaleidofin, Funds India, and FlexiLoans.com. In Tamil Nadu, which is known as India's "tech capital," the city of Chennai successfully embraces the wave of financial technology and helps consumers overcome their financial needs.

23.13 Teaching Methodology

In these sessions, the teaching approach will extend outside the classroom. The teaching approach is widely recommended to consist of:

- Online and video-based lectures
- Self-paced: students progress at their own speed
- Live project–based
- Industry specialist speakers
- Case studies
- Online application-oriented testing
- Credits and acknowledgment:
    - Introduction of Fintech from the University of Hong Kong
    - Fintech by Harvard University
    - World Economic Forum and Deloitte Global's latest report
    - Data Security Council—Future of Banking

23.14 Learning Objectives and Outcomes

- To familiarize basic concepts of accounting and finance
- To introduce the students to understand the basics of financial technology
- To provide an overview of the Indian Industrial environment

- To provide aprelude to the institutional technological environment for industrial finance
- To introduce the students to understand the basics of financial technology
- To impart the necessary skills to manage various functions of banking and financial organizations
- To understand the role of information technology in the process of preparing accounts
- To introduce the Indian banking and financial system
- To expose the developments taking place in the banking industry in recent times in India
- To teach techniques and approaches to students so that they may analyze and develop businesses

23.15 Learning Outcomes

- Helps the students to deal with complex management decision-making processes relating to finance
- Helps the students to find the appropriate solutions for business problems by using financial technology
- Students who complete this course can understand and prepare financial statements
- Helps the students to develop the business systems using financial
- Technologies including computing, storage, networking, desktop, and application virtualization
- Helps the students to gain knowledge in data center management
- Understanding of banking channels and payments gateways
- Helps the student to build a solution for banking systems
- On successful completion of the course, the students will be able to use current techniques, skills, and tools necessary for business intelligence to make suitable decisions.

23.16 Conclusion

Fintech is expected to transform how people access financial solutions and finance. The digital revolution is true, and everybody at least can attest to having interacted with one type of fintech nowadays. It remains to be seen, however, where banks lead or if they will be pulled right into the revolt.

We are keen to continue to extend and refine the principle of disruptive innovation, and there is much work ahead. Universally successful solutions to disruptive threats, for example, remain elusive. Our current view is that organizations will create a dedicated division to develop and leverage an innovation paradigm, which operates under the security of senior leadership.

REFERENCES

1. https://www.gartner.com/en/information-technology/glossary/fintech
2. Arner Douglas, W., Barberis Janos, N., & Buckley Ross, P. (2015, October 1). The Evolution of Fintech: A New Post-Crisis Paradigm? University of Hong Kong Faculty of Law Research Paper No. 2015/047, UNSW Law Research Paper No. 2016-62, Available at SSRN: https://ssrn.com/abstract=2676553 or http://dx.doi.org/10.2139/ssrn.2676553
3. www.easyleadz.com/blog/fintech-companies-in-india/
4. https://www.lawinsider.com/dictionary/cloud-computing
5. https://www2.deloitte.com/mk/en/pages/financial-services/articles/beyond-fintech-pragmatic-assessment-disruptive-potential-financial-services.html
6. https://assets.kpmg/content/dam/kpmg/xx/pdf/2019/02/the-pulse-of-fintech-2018.pdf

24

Mobile Cloud Computing in Healthcare

Varshini Neethi Mohan and Thomas Alexander

CONTENTS

24.1 Introduction

It was not all that long ago when all electronic devices were giant unwieldy boxes with tangles of wires dangling out of them which had to be plugged into a fixed source of electricity to work.

Today, there's probably a mobile phone in your pocket that is a telephone, a phone book, a camera, a navigation system, an alarm clock, a calculator, and a music player all rolled into one compact portable package. Your watch is what the sci-fi movies in the 1980s predicted—you can answer calls with it, and set a timer for your toast and change your thermostat. What is more, nearly every single person of your acquaintance, from your professors to your grandparents, most likely owns a mobile device.

The applications of this omnipresence in healthcare are limitless.

Imagine a patient too sick or too injured to travel to a doctor's office—a few decades ago, the doctor would have had to visit this patient at their home, making the whole enterprise costly and time consuming. Today, the patient can call for an ambulance service, and when they reach the hospital, take their place in the queue. This is still not optimal for patients, especially for those in rural areas who usually must travel long distances while suffering from illness or physical trauma.[1]

The advent of mobile cloud computing is set to change the whole system of healthcare delivery—it has already made vast inroads into how we approach healthcare today. Patients can now be monitored, diagnosed, and treated wherever they are, by doctors and specialists who need not even be on the same continent.

DOI: 10.1201/9781003318378-24

We begin our chapter on the applications of this technology in healthcare with a brief introduction to the history of cloud computing.

24.2 The History of Cloud Computing

Cloud computing seems like a modern phenomenon, but it has been around for more than 60 years. In the 1950s, mainframe computers could occupy between 2,000 and 10,000 square feet. They consumed a lot of power, and were prohibitively expensive besides. In 1955, John McCarthy introduced "time-sharing", whereby several organizations would get together to share resources on these mainframe computers so that they could each use them from linked stations. This was the birth of the cloud.

In 1969, J.C.R. Licklider laid the foundation for the world as we know it today. Licklider imagined a "Galactic Network", a system of interconnected computers, leading to the development of the Advanced Research Projects Agency Network (ARPANET), a precursor to the modern Internet.

The following couple of decades saw the invention of technologies that enabled the implementation of cloud computing, the most notable of which are IBM's Virtual Machine (VM) operating system and telecom companies' offerings of virtualized private network (VPN) connections.

In 1999, salesforce.com pioneered the idea of website access for enterprise applications. With the launch of Amazon's Azure in 2008, Google's Cloud Storage in 2010, IBM's SmartCloud in 2011 and Oracle Cloud in 2012, cloud computing was by then being used by organizations and individuals alike to create and explore new opportunities.

24.3 Mobile Cloud Computing

The *cloud* is a computing paradigm—it is a pool of abstracted, virtualized, dynamically scalable, and managed computing power, storage platforms, and services that are available for on-demand delivery over the Internet.[2]

We define *mobile cloud computing* as a technology that integrates cloud computing with mobile devices, using the former to overcome the resource limitations of the latter in terms of computational power, memory capacity, and context awareness.[3]

FIGURE 24.1 J.C.R. Licklider (1915–1990).

Viewed one way, mobile cloud computing is mobile computing that has evolved by transferring to the cloud all the intensive data processing, storage, and computing.[4] This drastically reduces the computing capability and processing requirements of mobile devices and gives applications far more scope and functionality.

Viewed another way, the set of terminals that people use to access cloud services have expanded from just personal computers (PCs) and laptops to include mobile devices such as smartphones and tablets, bringing the flexibility and access-from-anywhere features of mobile devices to cloud computing.

Mobile cloud computing can effectively utilize distributed cloud server resources such as central processing units (CPUs), memory, network, and ports to execute mobile healthcare applications. Mobile devices can offload these applications to a cloud server for faster execution, allowing for real-time query processing.[5] These mobile devices can interact with cloud services by using either a web browser or native applications. Applications, or apps, are programmes developed specifically for mobile devices.

As a combined set of two powerful technologies—mobile computing and cloud computing—mobile cloud computing allows for easy access and much shorter response times for both task execution and real-time communication,[6] and has extensive prospects for applications in healthcare.

24.4 Applications of Mobile Cloud Computing in Healthcare

The applications of mobile cloud computing in healthcare can be broadly classified under the following four areas.

1. Bio-signal monitoring
2. Teleconsultations
3. Electronic health records
4. Systems of care

24.4.1 Bio-Signal Monitoring

Continuous—or real-time—telemonitoring of bio-signals and vitals is possible with appropriate mobile devices, and cloud computing enables fast processing of this large quantity of incoming data.

Small wearable devices that include smartwatches, activity trackers, embedded patches, and other mobile medical devices can collect a wide set of data, from blood pressure and insulin levels to sleep patterns and exercise routines. Data is collected in the following two ways.

1. Actively, whereby patients themselves enter data (such as medication adherence, menstruation cycles, weight, or moods) into apps
2. Passively, whereby sensors in devices that patients wear gather data (such as oxygen levels in the blood, heart rates, and gait patterns) and share them with apps via application programming interfaces (APIs)

The data that is gathered from various health apps can then be compiled through aggregators.[6]

With cloud computing, these bio-signals collected and pooled together can be used for the following.

- Prevention of disease and maintenance of health
  - By providing regular feedback to users on fitness and vitals, and advocating personalized diet and exercise regimes
  - By giving suggestions for lifestyle changes and alerting on risk factors using predictive algorithms with inputs evaluated from multiple devices
- Disease management
  - By delivering medication through smart drug delivery systems (for example, wearable microneedle patches that monitor glucose levels and autonomously administer insulin directly into the blood), an accurate and reliable way of ensuring medication adherence

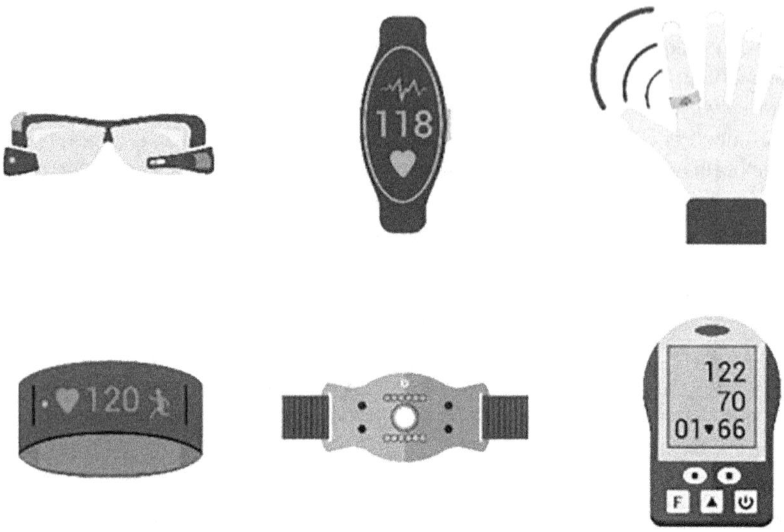

FIGURE 24.2 Examples of bio-signal monitors.

FIGURE 24.3 Teleconsultation.

- Early detection of possible adverse events
    - By detecting patterns and triggering alarms when pre-set thresholds are crossed (for example, accelerometer bracelets or sensorized insoles to detect walking patterns that could lead to disruptive events, such as falling and seizure onset)[7]

24.4.2 Teleconsultations

Healthcare resources—such as trained doctors, hospital staff, infrastructure, and readily available medicine—are unevenly distributed, with less developed and rural areas often facing severe shortages of these. Combined with a disproportionate share of the disease burden, this places an enormous strain on the healthcare systems in low- and middle-income countries. By some estimates, Africa has only 3% of the healthcare resources available globally and only 1% of the world's healthcare workers, but 25% of the world's burden of disease. North America, on the other end of the spectrum, has a quarter of the world's healthcare resources and a third of its healthcare workers, but only 3% of the disease burden.[8]

Mobile cloud computing could bring about more equity—it could provide a cost-effective and universally accessible telemedicine solution to this imbalance of healthcare services.

Cloud-based multimedia teleconsultation systems have already been tested across the world and adopted for applications such as:

- Primary care
  - Virtual consultations with doctors are possible with a variety of apps already available to video-link patients directly with doctors, without the need to visit a hospital or a clinic.
- Specialist consultations
  - Multiple healthcare professionals, such as doctors representing different specialties, nurses, and other advisers, may collectively give inputs and collaborate with each other virtually to consult with patients.[9] Multi-disciplinary virtual tumour boards, for example, could provide cancer patients with access to high-quality care.[10]
- Tele-ICUs
  - Telemedicine for intensive care units (tele-ICU) from a remote location can address the increasing complexity of patients and the insufficient supply of intensivists. Mobile platforms provide on-demand, two-way, audio-visual (AV) communication between ICUs and the tele-ICU centre. Further infrastructure provides access to electronic health records, telemetry, and imaging systems for data retrieval and documentation, risk stratification, and decision support.[11]

24.4.3 Electronic Health Records

Electronic health records (EHRs) provide several benefits over paper-based records—they are easier to access, more efficient, and potentially more secure. Cloud computing possesses the added advantages of transferability, scalability, and agility, with elastic storage-based pricing allowing further cost benefits when compared to using local servers within hospitals to store EHRs. This makes the cloud ideally suited for healthcare applications.[12]

FIGURE 24.4 Electronic health records.

With mobile cloud computing, a mobile- or web-based application lets authorized personnel access, edit, and share patient records depending on authentication level, without the need for additional specialized infrastructure. Various types of patient information—such as basic demographic details, medical history, lifestyle behaviours, laboratory reports, diagnostic test results, treatment strategies, prescriptions, clinical outcomes, discharge details, and follow-up remarks—can all be maintained in one comprehensive record and easily retrieved, even across different hospitals and locations, if there is appropriate standardization.

Medical practitioners increasingly rely on medical imaging for diagnosis. Images from instruments and techniques such as endoscopy, mammograms, ultrasound, positron emission tomography (PET), and computed tomography (CT) scans, magnetic resonance imaging (MRI), and computed radiography (CR), is used to diagnose and provide care to patients. These kinds of medical equipment usually generate a vast amount of large-sized data.

In order to economically store and conveniently access this enormous volume of medical images from multiple source machines, picture archiving and communication systems (PACSs) can be used. Images generated by these devices can be recorded and transmitted in the digital imaging and communications in medicine (DICOM) format, and non-image files might be in other standard formats such as portable document format (PDF).[12] With cloud computing and PACSs, the increasing demands on the healthcare infrastructure in terms of computation and storage on image-assisted medical procedures and diagnostics can easily be met.

A note of caution: EHR applications will have to ensure that patient privacy is maintained, that data is encrypted during transfers, and that all points of access are strictly monitored for any security breaches.

24.4.4 Systems of Care

Consensus-based guidelines and standardized protocols for systems of care have been developed and published for nearly all areas of medical care over the past few decades. Despite years of striving for standardized quality healthcare, systems performance remains inadequate. Only between 50% and 60% of care adheres to consensus-based guidelines. Medical expenditures could be reduced by about a third, and there are several instances when adverse events can be prevented merely by implementing better care.[13] This is due mainly to challenges in three main areas—initiating adoption, disseminating knowledge of benefits, and ensuring sustained implementation. Systems fail because "knowledge is unevenly distributed, poorly understood, and always contested" (pp. 444–483).[14]

Using mobile applications encourages adoption by enabling easier capture of metrics. This allows field staff to record data quickly and effortlessly, eliminating the need for paper reports to track outcomes.

Real-time analysis of data and feedback regarding the benefits of the system will encourage continued adoption. In addition, gaps in implementation can easily be identified and appropriate action can be taken.

Access to systems metrics in real time gives both the field staff and policymakers the ability to monitor and audit systems, and customize them for local conditions while allowing for broad standardization and adherence to quality metrics.

In this way, a large, decentralized set of stakeholders—from emergency service providers and hospitals to insurance agencies and pharmacies—can all be connected to ensure that the entire patient journey is streamlined, and a unified system of care is in place using mobile applications and cloud computing.

24.5 Case Study—The STEMI India Model

Ischaemic heart disease is the leading cause of death in India—12% of all premature deaths are attributed to heart disease. With over 60 million patients affected by heart disease annually, India has the highest burden of cardiovascular disease in the world.[15] More than three million of these suffer from ST-elevation myocardial infarction (STEMI), the deadliest form of a heart attack. A STEMI patient needs to be treated within 60 minutes of symptom onset. Every 30 minutes of delay thereafter results in a 50% loss of heart muscle.

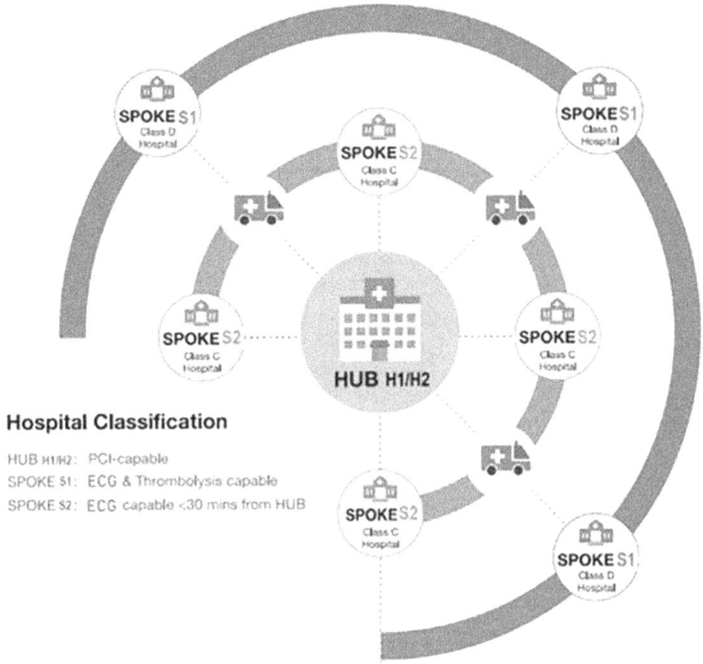

FIGURE 24.5 STEMI India's hub-and-spoke model.

The STEMI India Model is a system of care that uses mobile cloud computing as its technological core to address the issues in diagnosing and treating this killer disease.

The STEMI India Charitable Trust, in association with the Tamil Nadu state government and the Indian Council of Medical Research, implemented this protocol in four regions of Tamil Nadu. The model sets up a hub-and-spoke cluster—tertiary hospitals equipped with catheterization laboratoris ("cath labs") function as hubs, and peripheral hospitals operate as spokes.

24.5.1 Measurement of ECG and Vitals

A multifunctional 12-lead electrocardiogram (ECG) integrated multi-parameter monitoring unit with data entry capability (the STEMI kit) is installed in each hospital and the ambulances transferring patients between these. All patients reporting chest pain have their ECG, blood pressure, and oxygen saturation recorded on the STEMI kit. As these are all wirelessly connected, they are portable and compact. Basic patient details and other risk factors are also entered onto an application on the tablet that is a part of the STEMI kit.

24.5.2 Tele-ECG and Tele-CCU

The STEMI application installed on the STEMI kit has an "Ask Cardiologist" feature. This allows hospital staff at a remote spoke to send the ECG and other vitals recorded on the STEMI kit to be uploaded to the cloud and diagnosed by a cardiologist—either in the hub hospital or in a central control station. A turnaround time of five minutes is maintained. Evidence-based algorithms advocate the appropriate treatment strategy for the patient depending on risk factors, location, and other parameters.

In case the spoke requires further handholding for management of the patient, a tele-CCU (critical care unit) could be set up with specialists at the control centre guiding the hospital staff via access to all patient monitors and a two-way AV communication system.

FIGURE 24.6 STEMI kit schematic.

In this way, two primary barriers to optimum care in STEMI—delay in diagnosis and effective treatment strategy—are overcome using mobile cloud computing.

24.5.3 STEMI Patient Records

Once the patient is diagnosed with STEMI, every step of the patient journey and all relevant data are captured by the nurses, technicians, and doctors in the hospitals and ambulances on the STEMI kit, including treatment given, medication prescribed, outcomes, timelines, test reports, ECGs, etc. These are stored securely on the cloud.

24.5.4 Analytics and Audit for the System of Care

Real-time analysis of the efficacy of the system is possible through a dashboard whereby anonymized metrics can be viewed by administrators. Automated, periodic reports are sent to hospital administrators for an overview of patient numbers, treatment strategies, and outcomes. Patient outcomes are time-dependent for STEMI. As all data captured is automatically timestamped, a detailed review of relevant timelines such as symptom onset-to-arrival, door-to-needle or door-to-balloon, and assessment of how much they diverge from guidelines allows for hospitals to streamline their systems and to plan for implementable changes.

The STEMI India Model thus uses mobile computing to record and transmit vitals, telediagnose ECGs, remotely handhold field staff, maintain EHRs, and audit the entire system of care. Post-implementation of the model in Tamil Nadu, one-year mortality reduced by 19% relative to the base case.[16] This demonstrates that the use of mobile cloud computing in healthcare is feasible and effective, resulting in direct benefits to patients.

24.6 Challenges

While mobile cloud computing has opened up avenues to bring about ever more accessible and effective systems of care, some challenges remain in adopting this technology for healthcare applications. The primary ones are the following.

1. Data interoperability
2. Privacy and authentication
3. Security

24.6.1 Data Interoperability

Mobile- and cloud-based healthcare systems need to use inputs from several sources, including wearables, medical devices, mobile phones, vitals-monitoring equipment, and computer systems, all connected through multiple connection modalities in an intricate network to provide the best possible care to patients.

Usually, multiple suppliers—often from across the world—design and manufacture each of these components, each following different protocols and standards, resulting in costly and redundant work every time it is required to integrate health data from different devices. New universal standards that provide plug-and-play interoperability across medical equipment, communication devices and networks would enable healthcare providers to harness the vast potential of mobile cloud computing.

Although there are no such universal standards in the industry, mobile cloud computing in healthcare has benefited from the use of existing standards such as DICOM and HL7, which allow storage of EHRs as well as images using PACSs on the cloud. The latest in communication standards such as 4G LTE (and in many countries, 5G), at the time of this writing, enable healthcare providers to use high-speed mobile technologies and cutting-edge communication infrastructure to deliver cloud-based telediagnosis and telemedicine.[12]

There is, however, much scope for improvement. Universal interoperability between applications—such as in-home telehealth and remote telemonitoring for ageing or chronically ill patients, and for people with special needs—would bring about vast improvements in their access to healthcare. Creating such universal technical standards will go a long way towards streamlining several applications in healthcare.

24.6.2 Privacy and Authentication

One of the most fundamental requirements in e-healthcare is privacy.[17] When health records are maintained on the cloud, there is a loss of physical control of individual patient records; the non-locality of the server and the multiple applications accessing these patient records make maintaining patient confidentiality and privacy even more difficult. Encrypting the data at every point of transfer is usually undertaken, but this is sometimes insufficient.

The biggest challenge is the conflict that arises between privacy and usability. To quickly be able to diagnose remote patients, for example, medical practitioners from typically far away need fast and unhindered access to patient data. Patient records need to be accessed across various devices and on multiple networks. Unauthorized access needs to be strictly restricted, while at the same time, authorized access must be timely and complete for meaningful inputs to be provided.

In addition, accurate patient location information is sometimes necessary, particularly in emergency situations when it might be called for to send emergency medical services; however, access to this information can violate patient privacy and inadvertently allow unauthorized monitoring of patients' routines.

Authentication is another issue closely linked to privacy. In order to receive medical services, patients must usually be authenticated by proving their identities with technologies that recognize personal attributes—biometric, face recognition or the like. Misuse of such technology can seriously jeopardize privacy and could have far-reaching adverse consequences.

A balance must be made between patient privacy and easy access for authorized medical professionals, and between authentication and preservation of identity privacy.

24.6.3 Security

Another major concern when data and computing are outsourced to the cloud is system security.[18] Given the sensitive nature of medical data, health applications must necessarily meet stricter and more stringent security standards.

Smart mobile devices are becoming increasingly ubiquitous. Sensors and monitors are being attached to—and even implanted within—the human body. These are necessarily small in size and therefore have limited computing power, so there may be computational constraints in developing watertight security solutions.

Although there are standalone techniques for the individual problems discussed so far in healthcare applications for mobile cloud computing[12]—such as enabling universal access and interoperability, maintaining confidentiality, creating impenetrable security features, and anticipating and defending against attacks—there is a need for a systematic approach that holistically evaluates the trade-offs among cost, complexity, usability, and security.

24.7 Conclusion

Mobile cloud computing, with its ease of access, flexibilityn and nearly limitless computing power, opens up endless possibilities in healthcare—especially in the areas of continuous monitoring, telemedicine, EHRs, and improving systems of care. A patient's entire health record can be made available at the touch of a button by the appropriate healthcare provider, and medication adherence and patient outcomes can be closely tracked and monitored. Systems of care can also be streamlined, ensuring that ambulances, hospitals, and insurance agencies all follow standardized guidelines, and real-time feedback can allow for local customization.

It does, however, bring some challenges, the major ones being interoperability, privacy, and security. Addressing these will ensure that the seamless integration of these powerful technologies will eventually lead to better-quality, more affordable, more accessible, and—above all—more equitable health services.

REFERENCES

1. **Gilchrist, Alasdair.** *Industry 4.0 — The Industrial Internet of Things.* s.l. Apress, 2016.
2. **Foster, Ian, et al.** *Cloud Computing and Grid Computing 360-Degree Compared.* Grid Computing Environments Workshop, 2008, pp. 1–10.
3. **Khan, Atta Ur Rehman, et al.** A Survey of Mobile Cloud Computing Application Models. *IEEE Communications Surveys & Tutorials*, Vol. 16, 2014, pp. 393–413.
4. **Kumari, R., Kaushal, S., and Roopali.** *Application Offloading Using Data Aggregation in Mobile Cloud Computing Environment.* Leadership, Innovation and Entrepreneurship as Driving Forces of the Global Economy, 2017.
5. **Chun, Byung-Gon, et al.** *CloneCloud: Elastic Execution between Mobile Device and Cloud.* EuroSys'11: Proceedings of the Sixth Conference on Computer Systems, 2011, pp. 301–314.
6. **Dinh-Le, Catherine, et al**. Wearable Health Technology and Electronic Health Record Integration: Scoping Review and Future Directions. *JMIR Mhealth Uhealth*, Vol. 7, 2019, p. 9.
7. **González, I., Fontecha, J., Hervás, R., and Bravo, J.** An Ambulatory System for Gait Monitoring Based on Wireless Sensorized Insoles. *Sensors*, 2015.
8. **Bolt, Barbara J., Lehany-Trese, Anne Marie, and Williams, Timothy P.** Continuous Quality Improvement at Work: The First Team—Part I. 6. *Journal for Healthcare Quality*, Vol. 16, 1994, pp. 30–34.
9. **Wang, Xiaoliang and Jin, Zhanpeng.** An Overview of Mobile Cloud Computing for Pervasive Healthcare. *IEEE Access*, Vol. 7, 2019, pp. 66774–66791.
10. **Marshall, C.L., et al.** Implementation of a Regional Virtual Tumor Board: A Prospective Study Evaluating Feasibility and Provider Acceptance. *Telemedicine Journal and E-health*, Vol. 20, 2014, pp. 705–711.
11. **Udeh, Chiedozie, et al.** Telemedicine/Virtual ICU: Where Are We and Where Are We Going? *Methodist DeBakey Cardiovasc Journal*, Vol. 4, 2018, pp. 126–133.
12. **Jin, Zhanpeng and Chen, Yu.** Telemedicine in the Cloud Era: Prospects and Challenges. *IEEE Pervasive Computing*, 2015, pp. 54–61.
13. **Braithwaite, Jeffrey**. Changing How We Think about Healthcare Improvement. *BMJ*, 2018, p. 361.

14. **Contandriopoulos, D., et al.** Knowledge Exchange Processes in Organizations and Policy Arenas: A Narrative Systematic Review of the Literature. *The Milbank Quarterly*, Vol. 88, 2010, pp. 444–483.
15. **National Commission on Macroeconomics and Health, Government of India.** *NCMH Background Papers—Burden of Disease in India*. National Commission on Macroeconomics and Health, Government of India, September 2005.
16. **Alexander, Thomas, et al.** A System of Care for Patients With ST-Segment Elevation Myocardial Infarction in India: The Tamil Nadu—ST-Segment Elevation Myocardial Infarction Program. *JAMA Cardiology*, Vol. 2, 2017, pp. 498–505.
17. **Dong, Naipeng, Jonker, Hugo and Pang, Jun.** *Challenges in eHealth: From Enabling to Enforcing Privacy*. Foundations of Health Informatics Engineering and Systems, 2012 pp. 195–206.
18. **Xiao, Zhifeng and Xiao, Yang.** Security and Privacy in Cloud Computing. *IEEE Communications Surveys & Tutorials*, Vol. 15, 2013, pp. 843–859.

25

Eye-Tracking Technology for Education 4.0

Antony William Joseph and Ramaswamy Murugesh

CONTENTS

Objectives

Eye-tracking is a technique used for investigating eye activities where we look, what we look at and how long our point of gaze is on a specific area (Tobii Pro, 2020a). In our life, the eyes are considered one of the important means we utilize for making important decisions. Eye-tracking is a very commonly used technique by human–computer interaction (HCI) researchers and businesses to investigate human behaviour because it has great potential to measure visual attention accurately and objectively (Tobii Pro, 2020a). Research shows that eye-tracking has a long track record, and it has been used in cognitive psychology, medical, automotive and defence industries (Joseph and Murugesh, 2020). Domains like advertising, packaging, entertainment and interface design have benefited the most in recent times (Joseph and Murugesh, 2020). It is a recent phenomenon to use eye-tracking in educational research.

DOI: 10.1201/9781003318378-25

Industries worldwide are gearing up for the Fourth Industrial Revolution, and the pressure is growing to adapt to modern technology. The modern approach demands the development of skills for critical thinking and gaining of knowledge appropriate for problem-solving. In the context of developing critical thinking and Industry 4.0, there is a growing need to adopt modern technology-based teaching, learning and research in Indian universities. Education 4.0 is the future of education that brings together humans and machines to create new possibilities. In this context, this chapter explains what eye-tracking is, its history, eye-tracking in HCI, review of eye-tracking in educational research, cognitive load in learning, eye-based techniques for Education 4.0, types of eye-trackers available today, and eye-tracking metrics and indicators (Joseph and Murugesh, 2020), eye-tracking for Industry 4.0 and the application of eye-tracking technology in Education 4.0.

25.1 Introduction

We constantly explore our environment and make meaning through our eyes. We explore the place quickly with little purpose, but with respect to the clearly defined task, the research shows that our gaze goes to the most attracted and our eyes do not move aimlessly. Eye-tracking research can provide valuable information about what users are using, how frequently they are sampled and in what way they influence decision making. The eye is the main doorway to the brain (Brigham et al., 2001; Ellis et al., 1998; Joseph and Murugesh, 2020). Gaze events indicate cognitive activity and present information regarding the mental process (Land and Furneaux, 1997; Joseph and Murugesh, 2020). The eye-based technique is beneficial to many fields of research such as psychology, medicine and usability (Joseph and Murugesh, 2020).

The development of eye-based technology, the invention of modest camera-based techniques (Morimoto and Mimica, 2005; Joseph and Murugesh, 2020) and the proliferation of computing capability best utilized eye-based evidence. Eye-tracking systems measure the position of the eye, movement of eye and pupil size to identify areas in which the user has a particular interest at a specific time. This has paved the way for extending the use of eye-tracking methods over several research domains. It is widely used in several fields like neuroscience, neuromarketing, cognitive psychology, functional magnetic resonance imaging (fMRI), clinical research, immersive virtual reality, user experience (UX), sport and performance, formal training/safety, computer vision, vision-related research, human factors, HCI and education (Gaze Intelligence, 2020).

In the context of Education 4.0, the study of eye movements can provide insightful thoughts to researchers regarding how visual information is processed and the elements influencing the user's attention and cognitive load in relation to teaching and learning. It can also help the HCI researchers to comprehend the issues affecting the usability of systems or applications that are designed for Education 4.0. The following sections holistically explain eye-tracking technology, the relevance of eye-tracking for Education 4.0 and its application.

25.2 Defining Eye-Tracking

Eye-tracking is a technology used for measuring eye activities (Joseph and Murugesh, 2020). Where do we look? What is overlooked? When do we blink? How does our pupil respond to various stimuli? The concept appears to be effortless, but the process and interpretation might be complex (Eye Tracking, 2020; Joseph and Murugesh, 2020). Eye-tracking is the technique for evaluating eye activities applied to determine where we look, what we look at and how long our gaze is on a particular area of study (Tobii Pro, 2020a). Our eyes are considered as one of the important mechanisms we use in our daily life for decision making (Tobii Pro, 2020a). Eye-tracking is largely explored in HCI study and business to investigate human behaviour because it provides an opportunity to measure visual attention accurately and objectively (Tobii Pro, 2020a).

Many of today's eye-tracking systems contain two specific components: a light source and a camera (Eye Tracking, 2020; Joseph and Murugesh, 2020). The infrared (IR) light source is aimed at the eye.

For example, the pupil is monitored by the eye-tracking camera, reflecting the source of light as well as visible eye features (Eye Tracking, 2020). Many of today's eye-trackers assess the point of view by means of the "corneal reflection/pupil center" technique (Goldberg and Wichansky, 2003). Cutting-edge procedures are used for measuring the eye position and determining precisely where it is centered (Tobii Pro, 2020a). This assists HCI researchers in assessing visual behaviour. Eye movements offer insightful information regarding human cognition, and it is a well-accepted method in HCI and allied fields of scientific study (Joseph and Murugesh, 2020). HCI and UX researchers employ this method for evaluating interfaces.

Most importantly, one can trace the fine eye movements several times a second. How swiftly an eye-tracker can capture certain images is known as its frequency (Tobii Pro, 2020a). Eye-tracking systems create a dataset by capturing coordinates several times per second. The data can be used to evaluate the eye rotation, and eventually the gaze direction. Eye information such as blink duration, pupil diameter, and other data to eye activities can also be captured and interpreted to explain users' invisible actions when performing tasks. Every data point of eye information is translated into a set of coordinates of pixels (Eye Tracking, 2020). This type of study can provide information regarding attentional features, the pattern of eye movements and less focused area of content (Joseph and Murugesh, 2020). Visualizing techniques like heat maps and gaze plots (Joseph and Murugesh, 2020) are generated for envisioning the findings. Apart from the focus area on a screen, eye information is very valuable in estimating mental workload (Joseph and Murugesh, 2020). The cognitive activity index (CAI) is among the most used metrics (Joseph and Murugesh, 2020). Modern eye-tracking technology has the capability to track everything that has a visual component and its relevance is significantly felt in design research (Joseph and Murugesh, 2020). Eye-tracking technology is used in automotive, medical and defence industries to make us safer. Eye-tracking technology has brought a huge advantage to areas like entertainment, advertising, interface design and packaging in studying user behaviour (Joseph and Murugesh, 2020). Currently, eye-tracking technology has numerous prospects for integrating biometric techniques like electroencephalograms (EEG), galvanic skin response (GSR) and electrocardiograms (EKG) as an additional facility and making conclusions more scientific (Joseph and Murugesh, 2020). The eye-tracking analysis can lead to discoveries that would be significantly more difficulty with other testing methods available today. The causes of behaviour can be identified without relying on the fallible human memory.

25.3 History of Eye-Tracking

Research shows that, 100 years ago, different techniques were widely used to capture eye movements (Javal, 1878). The research findings reported that users do not read smoothly across a page but stop at some words while moving rapidly to others (Javal, 1878). Dodge and Cline (1901) first recognized the unintrusive eye-tracking method by means of light reflection from the cornea and recorded horizontal eye position on a photographic plate while keeping the subject's head motionless. Judd et al. (1905) later employed moving picture photography methods to obtain the two-dimensional (2D) eye movements. Scientists made significant progress in tracking eye movements in the early 20th century by integrating techniques of corneal reflection with the techniques of motion pictures (Mackworth and Mackworth, 1958; Joseph and Murugesh, 2020). In 1930, Tinker (1963) began utilizing photographic techniques to examine eye activities in reading and investigated the reading pattern and speed of the eye movement. In 1947, a motion picture camera was employed to examine a pilot's eye movement in the cockpit regarding airplane landing (Fitts et al., 1950). Later, Hartridge and Thompson (1948) developed an eye-tracker that was mounted on the head and provided flexibility to participants to move their heads freely. Later it was improved by Shackel (1960) and made more user-friendly by Mackworth and Thomas (1962).

Macworth and Mackworth (1958) developed a method in 1958 to observe eye movements on the participant's view of the evolving visual system which contributed to the study of the interaction between man and machine. Eye-tracking technology was improved further in the 1970s and helped the theory of psychology to find the missing link to cognitive processes (Joseph and Murugesh, 2020; Fisher et al., 1981; Senders et al., 1978; Monty and Senders, 1976). Further in the 1970s, considerable attempts were made to improve technical aspects in order to increase accuracy in eye-tracking methods. Later, minicomputers brought in quick data handling techniques in real time (Joseph and Murugesh, 2020; Anliker, 1976). In 1970, eye activities and fixations were investigated by psychologists but avoided problems like memory, attention and workload (Kowler, 1990; Joseph and Murugesh, 2020; Monty & Senders, 1976). This situation gradually improved due to the improvement of eye-tracking devices and experts in psychology began to study the relationship between cognitive workload and fixations (Just and Carpenter, 1976; Joseph and Murugesh, 2020). In every phase of evolution, eye-tracking technology has answered many questions and resolved many issues faced in the past (Senders, 2000; Joseph and Murugesh, 2020). Eventually, the availability of personal computers in daily life paved the way for eye-tracking to examine how users navigate and provide solutions (Card, 1984; Hendrickson, 1989; Aaltonen et al., 1998; Byrne et al., 1999; Joseph and Murugesh, 2020). The field of user-computer interaction was born in the 1980s, and eye-tracking methods enhanced the process (Joseph and Murugesh, 2020; Ware and Mikaelian, 1987; Glenn et al., 1986; Levine, 1984; Bolt, 1981, 1982).

In the beginning, invasive approaches were followed where participants were directly exposed to the eye to observe eye activities (Joseph and Murugesh, 2020). Later, bigger contact lenses were developed, covering the cornea and sclera using a metal coil rooted through for assessing differences in an electromagnetic area by moving the metal coil along with eyes (Duchowski, 2003; Joseph and Murugesh, 2020). In HCI studies today, the greatest number of eye-tracking techniques have seen considerable progress in evaluating usability aspects of computer interfaces (Joseph and Murugesh, 2020). In the current scenario, the usage of eye-tracking is increasing due to the arrival of new technologies and the development of numerous web-based applications (Joseph and Murugesh, 2020). Subsequently, it has gained importance in the field to find factors affecting HCI (Joseph and Murugesh, 2020).

25.4 Eye-Tracking in HCI

Eye-tracking technology is evolving, and it is being explored scientifically in the HCI domain to determine the gaze direction and position of a user on the screen. Eye-tracking is a significant means to estimate and analyze mental workload (Joseph and Murugesh, 2020). Eye-tracking has many possibilities and has the potential to deliver promising results (Joseph and Murugesh, 2020). Eye movements have become the basis for usability research. Eye-tracking basically begins with the point-of-regard and its analysis. In eye-tracking, the point-of-regard is interpreted as a fixation and eye movement and stresses on a specific area for a specific amount of time. Loftus and Mackworth (1978) discussed important areas that are studied naturally by using the fixations of the eye. Taking forward from this, Goldberg and Kotval (1999) found that when using a computer interface, the user's eye movements generally signify the user's spatial focus of attention on display. The concept of attention allocation clarified many important aspects of point-of-regard. If one's eye does not fixate on an element of interest for a specific period, the perception of that element becomes irrelevant. Hayhoe and Ballard (2005) report in their study that attention is not paid to irrelevant information subsequently they say the series of fixations are directly linked to the current task for obtaining specific information.

Saccadic eye movements that take place between fixations are very significant, and they can be used to explore scan paths (Poole and Ball, 2005). In visual scanning, more demanding tasks are hypothesized to require a sequential attention scanning of elements (Treisman and Gelade, 1980). Eye activity information can be used to measure cognitive processes while performing tasks. Poole and Ball (2005) suggest that saccade-derived measuring methods in the contexts of interface design and usability testing include backtracking. This means regressive saccades that suggest difficulty in information processing. Pupil size is apparently gaining more significance in cognitive research, both psychological and human factors, to assess cognitive load (Ahlstrom and Friedman-Berg, 2006; Marshall, 2002; Muldner et al., 2009; Pomplun and Sunkara, 2003; Stone et al., 2004). Pupil dilation analysis shows systematic changes in pupil size while the user is engaged with learning tasks. Sibley et al. (2011) state that pupil size would increase at the beginning of each difficult task and then decrease as the individual learned the task. Therefore, eye metrics explored in the HCI domain can be used effectively to make an adaptive learning system for education.

25.5 Eye-Tracking in Educational Research

Eye-tracking is a technique used to collect eye information regarding human perception, cognition, and behaviour. Basically, eye-tracking technology has been established to examine where we look. In the past and even now, researchers are investigating how the eyes move, trying to distinguish from a neurological perspective and develop tools to identify such eye movements were in focus. Though eye-tracking–based methods are evolving with newer challenges and demands, it has gained greater attention from other areas of study to apply them to answer research questions. Initially, eye-tracking techniques began with allowing people to view artwork (Yarbus, 1967). Later, eye-tracking has become a powerful research tool and has found its way into linguistics studies and resulted in new insights and challenges in this field (Rayner, 1998, 2009). Subsequently, usability and HCI researchers found the importance of eye-movement techniques in their research (Jacob and Karn, 2003).

Over the years, eye-tracking technology has evolved and advanced from a huge head-mounted device to the present wearable mobile devices. This enables researchers not only to research laboratory-based settings, but also in field settings such as examining a consumer's perceptual behaviour in a supermarket. Though eye-tracking methods have been largely applied in cognitive psychology for several years (Rayner, 1998, 2009), they have gained importance recently in educational research. For example, it was used to examine the performance of students in physics and mathematics (Hegarty and Just, 1993; Hegarty et al., 1992; Landy et al., 2008; Suppes, 1990), reading and understanding (Paulson and Henry, 2002; Rayner et al., 2006), and multimedia-based learning (van Gog and Jarodzka, 2013; van Gog and Scheiter, 2010). By understanding gaze data regarding students' attentional area of study, eye-tracking can enhance micro-level analyses of learning (Was et al., 2016). Eye-tracking in educational science is one of the youngest fields where it has begun to be applied, and so interest has been growing steadily among researchers. Educational science examines in what way learners gain knowledge and by what method learning could be enhanced. At this juncture, is very important to understand what is learning. It is an act of acquiring knowledge and skills. Acquiring knowledge is an active process more than a result. Hence, researchers in educational sciences examine this learning procedure to comprehend in what way learning is represented and in what manner it can be enhanced.

The eye-tracking method (Holmqvist et al., 2011) has been established as an important research technique to examine the knowledge acquisition process over the past. This is because we receive most information through our eyes, and learning has no exception. For example, scientific illustrations have existed for hundreds of years. It is not only experts who had to learn and understand illustrations, but also students who had to learn the subject matter. These days, visual-based learning approaches have proliferated in many educational and professional domains such as complex computer-generated simulations whereby learners often have to integrate information from many sources. In this situation, eye-tracking can become an aid to improving learning and remove complexity in the learning mind. The traditional learning environments with the blackboard as the platform is gradually moving towards electronic classrooms due to the innovation of digital products and applications like the internet, multimedia, and mobile devices. The inclusion of technologies into teaching and learning has created new learning models including multimedia learning, web-based inquiry learning, computer-based collaborative learning, e-learning, mobile learning, and game-based learning, and so on (Mayer and Fiorella, 2014; Slotta and Linn, 2009; Lai et al., 2016).

Currently, technologies function as tools to support knowledge creation, as a medium to explore knowledge and support learning-by-doing, as social media to help collaborative knowledge creation and as knowledge creators to assist learning by supporting (Jonassen et al., 1999; Goodyear and Retalis, 2010; Hwang and Wang, 2016). The adaptation of current technologies to conventional teaching and learning methods will improve the quality of teaching and learning, and incorporate different areas in education with effectiveness. Current new technologies like three-dimensional (3D) printing, virtual reality and eye-tracking have been found more education-related applications. By analyzing the learner's eye-movement data, a new framework can be developed for better teaching and learning. The eye-tracking technology has numerous applications in Education 4.0 and has several possibilities to improve educational standards.

25.6 Cognitive Load in Learning

Cognitive load is perceived as a result of task difficulty. Everyone realizes that task information is to be processed outside our cognitive ability. Thus, mental workload is increased trying to overcome the perceived cognitive load. There are many definitions given in the literature for a cognitive load. To add value to cognitive load, there is processing load (Beatty, 1982), mental load (Chen and Vertegaal, 2004), workload (Veltman and Gaillard, 1998; Brookings et al., 1996; Stern and Skelly, 1984), cognitive workload (Boehm-Davis et al., 2000; Ahlstrom and Friedman-Berg, 2006), cognitive task load (Neerincx et al., 2009) and cognitive effort (Piquado et al., 2010). All these terms were neither clearly defined nor differentiated from each other. As per the Multiple Resource Theory (MRT), the mental workload is hypothesized as the workload inflicted by tasks on the limited mental resources of humans (Wickens, 2008). Likewise, an explanation for cognitive workload could be identified in Cognitive Load Theory (CLT) (Chen and Epps, 2014), which is conceived as a multifaceted theory indicating the workload that carrying out a specific task enforces on the learner's mental ability (Paas et al., 2003). Though the research is underway on how the load is caused, it requires further clarification (Oviatt, 2006), especially with regard to task demands and mental effort (Chen, 2014).

Despite the fact, many definitions were used to explain the load on humans while a task is carried out; there is no difference in the procedure of enforcing load levels through cognitive tasks in earlier studies. From this viewpoint, these definitions are exchangeable with respect to causing workload and estimating it. The main variation here is what kind of cognitive task was used to cause the load and in what context the cognitive task was conducted. This can be reflected as external forces enforced on the human cognitive system and mental effort generated internally. The term cognitive load is derived from CLT, and it is used in this chapter to explain the perceived load on humans. Cognitive load is illustrated as the load required for human mental effort through cognitive activity and releasing the same. It looks from the receiver's viewpoint as if the load is being perceived while applying mental effort. The source of the load imposed on the human cognitive system in CLT is task specific. It becomes the base for measuring the load at various age groups and records the changes.

A cognitive load involves the demands of specific tasks and mental resources available for someone to meet those demands (Wickens, 2008). This can be also interpreted as slowness in processing information when a significant level of workload is used by a particular person (Rozado and Dunser, 2015; Debie et al., 2019). Cognitive load can be described as the interaction between the structure of systems and tasks with the capabilities, motivation and state of the human operator (Kramer, 1990). Thus, cognitive load explains the demands of tasks that necessitate the limited information processing ability of the brain (Wickens et al., 2013).

Working memory is very important for a person's learning process. However, there is a limitation to the ability to hold information. It can become helpless, especially when complex information is processed. In such a situation, the learner must make an additional attempt to manage the information. Here, mental workload denotes the complete activity of the mind forced upon the short-term memory. It is influenced by a number of factors that act together with working memory. It is believed that one can hold only a limited amount of information. If more information is presented to a person at once, it is difficult to retain it all. Therefore, it is important to understand cognitive load proficiently for effective learning.

CLT distinguishes mental workload under three categories: intrinsic, extraneous and germane (De Jong, 2010). Intrinsic cognitive load is defined as the effort associated with a specific topic, extraneous cognitive load denotes how information or tasks are given to a learner and germane cognitive load indicates the effort applied to constructing a long-lasting body of knowledge or a schema (De Jong, 2010). Intrinsic cognitive load signifies the imminent difficulty within specified tasks (De Jong, 2010). Some actions or information are much more difficult to process, and, in such a situation, this causes an intrinsic cognitive load. For example, solving complex mathematical calculations is harder than basic calculations (De Jong, 2010). It is very much associated with the nature and subject matter of the problem itself that the learner realizes mental taxation (De Jong, 2010). There are many factors that contribute to intrinsic cognitive load that is processed together and thus makes the task more complex. If a person needs to attend to many elements simultaneously, the intrinsic load will be greater in comparison to a smaller number of elements. It is not possible to change the inherent difficulty of the content; however, it can be achieved based on the learner's previous exposure regarding material, aptitude and capacity for learning.

Extraneous cognitive load is perceived based on how information is given to an individual (De Jong, 2010). The mental workload is the outcome of insignificant information that is presented to the person. Here, the nonessential information hinders the learning process and causes extraneous load. Thus, the unproductive method makes the learner unreasonably confusing and completed. This leads to the extra cognitive effort required by the learner and hinders learning. The extraneous load is also the result of background noise, and this makes the task difficult and believed as extraneous load. It is very difficult to decrease the extraneous cognitive load completely to enable learning.

Germane cognitive load is the outcome of the constructive method of managing information that fairly supports the learning (De Jong, 2010). Hence, germane load denotes effort applied to create an enduring repository of knowledge or schema (De Jong, 2010). This substantially quickens the learning method; for example, making a flowchart in a presentation to explain complex concepts. This organized means of presenting information facilitates the learner to learn easily and remember efficiently. The germane load consists of thoughts patterns or behaviour to classify categories of information (De Jong, 2010). Additionally, use of such behavioural schemas in different kinds of scenarios make the learner learn efficiently with less effort. It helps the learner to over multiple solutions and finally constructs and carried out systematically. To summarize, for an optimal learning method, the cognitive load requires to administer intrinsic load, enhance extraneous load and encourage germane load (De Jong, 2010). As learners become more familiar with content and skills, schemas change, so that information can be handled more efficiently by working memory.

25.7 Eye-Based Techniques for Education 4.0

In the past, numerous methods were followed to record eye movements. There are three eye-based techniques developed as major techniques and largely applied in research studies and commercial applications: a) videooculography (VOG); b) video-based infrared pupil-corneal reflection (IR-PCR); and c) electrooculography (EOG) (Majaranta and Bulling, 2014). Apart from its usage and applications in different areas, each of them has advantages and disadvantages. The video-based technique may be applied for attentive user interfaces (Majaranta and Bulling, 2014), which does not necessitate an exact spot of gaze tracking (Hansen and Pece, 2005). Additional information collected from IR-PCR gives the most precise gaze spot measurements of visual angle, and so it has become the choice for several scientists in the field of gaze-based interaction, usability studies and marketing research (Majaranta and Bulling, 2014). The EOG technique has been used for several years in the past to study the relative eye movements with high-level temporal accurateness (Majaranta and Bulling, 2014).

25.7.1 Videooculography (VOG)

VOG is a video-based technique with a distant noticeable small video camera mounted on the head (Majaranta and Bulling, 2014). Generally, the system includes a video camera that captures eye movements and a computer unit that stores eye information. The remote system consists of an eye-tracking camera placed beneath the monitor screen, and in the head-mounted unit, the camera is fixed to the eyeglasses frame or on the head unit (Majaranta and Bulling, 2014). It also includes a scene camera for recording user behaviours that may be utilized later to chart out participant's gaze information to the viewing scenario (Majaranta and Bulling, 2014). The video camera's resolution and frame rate are very important because they influence the quality of data. Since the eye-based study is dependent on video images, it is preferred to have a camera with a high configuration and a higher sampling rate (Tobii Pro, 2020b). Many issues can influence the quality of tracking like light conditions, reflections, drooping eyelids, and squinting eyes (Goldberg and Wichansky, 2003; Majaranta and Bulling, 2014). The video data captured are essential for evaluating the position of gaze on a screen. Typically, in video-based eye-tracking, variations in the position are captured, plotted to gaze coordinates and examined (Hansen

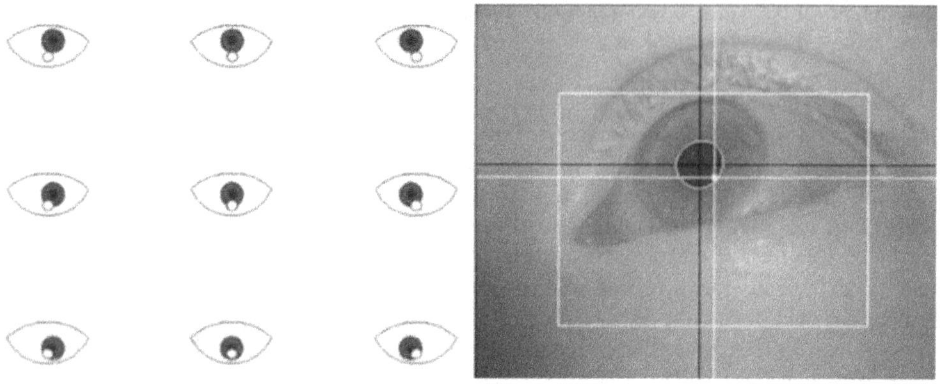

FIGURE 25.1 Association of pupil centre and the corneal reflection on the viewing screen.

Source: Adapted from Majaranta et al. (2009)

and Ji, 2009). The user must stay still for calculating the gaze vector accurately. Figure 25.1 shows the association of pupil centre and corneal reflection.

25.7.2 Video-Based Infrared Pupil-Corneal Reflection (IR-PCR)

In IR-PCR, the observable light and pupil centre appear to be imperfect and responsive to the movement of the head (Majaranta and Bulling, 2014). To overcome this issue, a reference point called corneal reflection may be included through artificial IR light targeted on- or off-axis in the eye (Majaranta and Bulling, 2014). A bright pupil effect results due to an on-axis light source, enhancing easy analysis and identifying the pupil in the scene (Majaranta and Bulling, 2014). This effect is the same as the red-eye effect generated through photography light. The outcome of dark pupil images is caused by off-axis light (Majaranta and Bulling, 2014). These will enable to keep the eye area bright and don't interrupt scene because to the human eye, IR light is invisible (Duchowski, 2003). The corneal reflection is measured accurately from the source of IR in relation to the centre of the pupil with accuracy. Gaze direction is estimated through computing varying relation between the movement of the pupil in the centre of an eye and corneal reflection (Majaranta and Bulling, 2014) as illustrated in Figure 25.1. The corneal reflection position continues to be stable throughout eye movement, and reflection will continue to be still (Majaranta and Bulling, 2014). Additionally, it provides information regarding an easy point of reference to compare moving pupils, and as a result, it supports measurement of eye gaze vector (Duchowski and Vertegaal, 2000). The IR has the disadvantage of changing ambient light and it does not work well in ambient light, such as in outdoor settings. But HCI researchers are constantly trying to solve this problem (Bengoechea et al., 2012; Kinsman and Pelz, 2012).

25.7.3 Electrooculography (EOG)

An eye of a human can be demonstrated as a dipole by placing its negative pole at the retina and positive pole at the cornea (Majaranta and Bulling, 2014; Tobii Pro, 2020b). The eye is the source of a stable electric field and the signal which may be calculated is called the electrooculogram (Majaranta and Bulling, 2014). Two sets of external electrodes are positioned in periorbital position over the and the signal is measured concerning an electrode positioned on the forehead (Majaranta and Bulling, 2014). Due to eye movement from the centre point in the direction of electrodes, the retina moves toward this electrode, whereas the cornea moves toward the opposite one (Majaranta and Bulling, 2014). The changes that occur in dipole orientation initiate alternation in the main electric field, which can be calculated for tracking eye movement. Though EOG is the best suitable technique for capturing respective eye movements (Majaranta and Bulling, 2014), it has a drawback that electrodes are required to be fixed to the skin near the eyes.

EOG indicators are conditional upon the noise of the signal and are susceptible to moving away, especially in the case of a mobile setting (Majaranta and Bulling, 2014). One positive aspect of EOG is that varying lighting circumstances have a minor effect on EOG signals and are convenient for conducting studies in the field (Majaranta and Bulling, 2014). EOG can be also recorded in less lighting or eyes-closed condition, and therefore, it is a well-accepted method for capturing eye activities occurring in sleep (Smith et al., 1971). The second advantage is that data processing is lightweight, and it does not necessitate any complicated image processing technique (Majaranta and Bulling, 2014).

The first two techniques possess many similar characters and all of them have relevance in many areas. IR and PCR give correct gaze point calculations of up to 0.5^0 of visual angle and hence it received attention in the scientific field, such as usability studies and commercial applications (Majaranta and Bulling, 2014). Finally, EOG has been applied in ophthalmological research for several years because it supports calculating relative eye movements with high-level temporal perfection (Majaranta and Bulling, 2014).

Each of the techniques described in this section has some specific advantages and disadvantages, yet all are useful in various contexts of Education 4.0.

25.8 Types of Eye-Trackers

There are varieties of eye-tracking devices available, but in principle, they all function similarly. Three important types of eye-trackers are found today: screen-based, which are stand-alone or individual devices; wearable, which consist of eye-tracking glasses and virtual reality (VR) headsets blended with eye-tracking; and webcam, which are comprised of webcam system fixed or hardwired to a computer system but without sensors or cameras (Tobii Pro, 2020b). Though there are different types of eye-trackers, the right kind of eye-tracker for researchers may be based on the nature of the research. Currently, eye-tracking devices are used for attention-based studies in the field of neuroscience and psychology, clinical research, marketing research, UX, education and professional performance, helping them make better business-critical decisions.

25.8.1 Screen-Based Eye-Trackers

Screen-based eye-trackers are stand-alone devices available both as an individual component and a separate panel that can be fixed to a screen, and they vary in setup, usage, performance and sample frequency (Tobii Pro, 2020b). Screen-based eye-trackers are generally explorers for studies in which participants interact or where the participants are subjected to stimuli on a screen or interaction (Tobii Pro, 2020b). In particular, such devices come with a wide-ranging sampling rate, and high-frequency trackers can offer huge data with complete detailed information about eye movement (Tobii Pro, 2020b). It allows the researcher to collect and analyze data in a controlled lab environment. Screen-based eye-tracking technology is a system that records eye information for a deeper understanding of user behaviour and eye activities based on eye fixation studies (Joseph and Murugesh, 2020; Tobii Pro, 2020b).

Figure 25.2 illustrates different components of screen-based eye-trackers such as cameras, illuminators and the processing unit that contains a 3D eye model, image detection and gaze mapping algorithms (Tobii Pro, 2020b). Most of the contemporary devices use techniques of near-IR together with a high-definition camera to record gaze direction. The fundamental idea behind eye-tracking is pupil centre corneal reflection (PCCR). The near-IR light is pointed toward the middle of the eyes producing reflections in the cornea that are captured by the camera (Joseph and Murugesh, 2020). The correctness of the eye-movement measurement deeply depends on the detection of corneal reflection and clear differentiation of the pupil.

25.8.2 Wearable Eye-Trackers

A wearable eye-tracking device is a system that records typical viewing behaviour in a real-world setting (Joseph and Murugesh, 2020). This helps to comprehend looking behaviours of a person while navigating

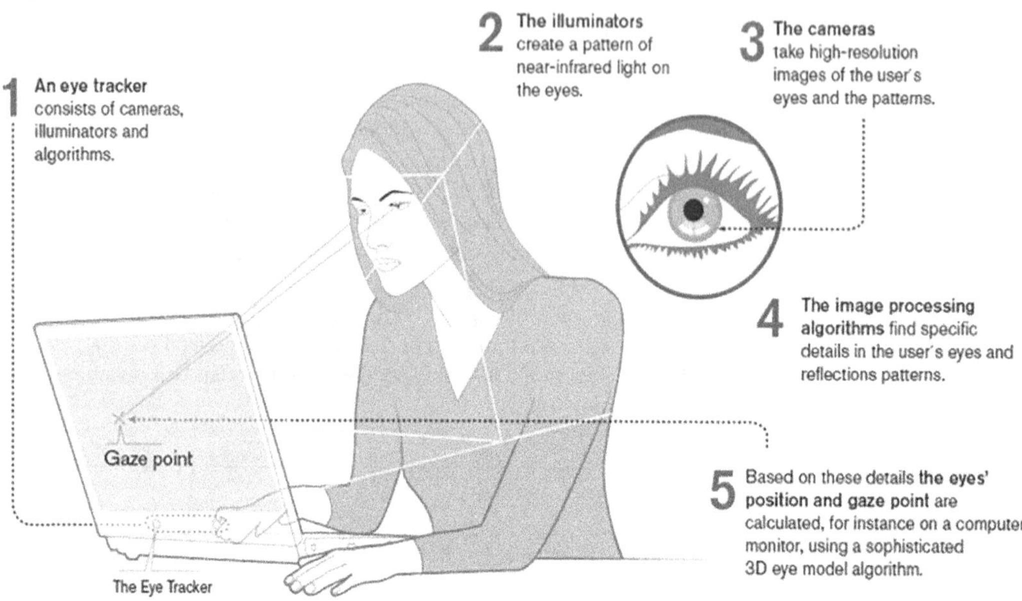

FIGURE 25.2 Components of screen-based eye-tracking System.

Source: www. tobiipro.com [accessed April 2020]

smoothly in a real-world situations and interaction behaviours with the real environment (Joseph and Murugesh, 2020). A wearable eye-tracking system gives numerous opportunities in understanding user behaviours (Joseph and Murugesh, 2020). The device allows other devices such as EEG or other biometrics to get deeper insights into human behaviour. Eye-tracking glasses are used for conducting research studies in real-life situations that allow natural eye movements and are unobtrusive (Tobii Pro, 2020b). It consists of an in-built camera for recording scenes and a microphone to record the surroundings (Tobii Pro, 2020b). As we have seen with screen-based eye-trackers, wearable eye-trackers have the same basic components and gaze mapping algorithms. During the study, even if the head unit slides a little, participants will remain calibrated and the quality of data will not be deteriorated (Tobii Pro, 2020b). The device includes gyroscope sensors and an accelerometer which enable scientists to distinguish between the head and eye movements that eliminate the influence of head movements on eye-tracking information (Tobii Pro, 2020a). There is little chance of human error due to a reliable and consistent automated calibration process (Tobii Pro, 2020a). Portability is a key feature of the wearable eye-tracking system which allows, for example, eye-tracking glasses allowing HCI researchers to conduct eye-tracking studies outside a studio environment. The insights gained from the eye-tracking study are extremely useful in many fields, including commercial applications as well as in academic research. Figure 25.3 illustrates different components of wearable eye-tracking glasses.

In general, it is noted that wearable eye-trackers are more promising for cognitive load measurement applications because of mobility, flexibility and lack of restrictions on user behaviours. Besides, eye-tracking has a lot of potential in more research domains. In the last few years, eye-trackers have advanced from heavy and inconvenient equipment to lightweight and mobile devices. The usage of eye-tracking devices and metrics for measuring cognitive load seems more scientific and authentic in the HCI domain.

A wearable eye-tracking system integrated with a VR headset enhances situational interactions to investigate multiple environments, and the environment not necessary to be present (Tobii Pro, 2020a). It is a valuable device for skills and health training, and is very dangerous to be in or very hard to set up

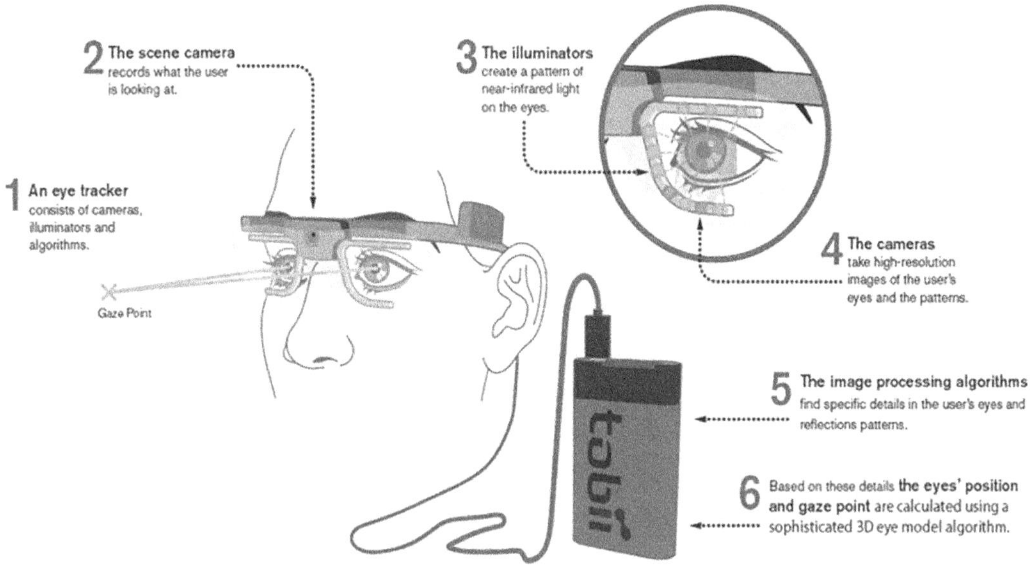

FIGURE 25.3 Components of wearable eye-tracking glasses.

Source: www. tobiipro.com (April 2020)

FIGURE 25.4 VR headset with an integrated wearable eye-tracking system.

Sources: www. tobiipro.com [accessed April 2020]; Barry Levine (2017)

(Tobii Pro, 2020a). The opportunities for testing inside the VR are really large. It can contribute to conduct employee professional training and assessment, and even it can be employed to treat social or situational phobias within a safe environment. The gaze data effectively enhance the training and improve skill sets. Current research on VR to train new hires and educate them is very promising. Training and market analysis are therefore some of the most common uses. Figure 25.4 displays the VR headsets with built-in eye-tracking device, and their use.

25.8.3 Webcam Eye-Trackers

In general, a webcam eye-tracker consists of an in-built or exterior camera fixed to a laptop or screen to gather eye data about the wearer's looking behaviours (Tobii Pro, 2020a), as shown in Figure 25.5. This tracker does not have IR light rays; rather, it depends on the image produced by the webcam (Tobii Pro, 2020b). To approximate the position of the head and eyes, an algorithm is used to compare the orientation

FIGURE 25.5 Webcam eye-tracker.

Source: McManus (2017)

of the eyes with an image on the display (Tobi Pro, 2020b). The intensity and precision of the obtained knowledge from this approach are not as reliable as the methods described previously.

This approach is ideally suited for large-scale experiments which are suitable for quantitative investigation. Webcam-based research is conducted in the early phase of the design process. Eye-tracking truly takes to the next level, providing a deep understanding of user interaction and visual attention information that enhances researchers to understand the cognitive processes and subconscious behaviours while teaching and learning.

25.9 Eye-Tracking Metrics and Indicators

For different aspects of oculomotor activity, eye monitoring metrics can be used according to the type of research involved (Bylinskii and Borkin, 2015). Generally, eye-tracking measurements are established on fixations and saccades, scan paths, pupil dilation, and eye blinking. These tests must be applied to the task when the individual is operating to assess cognitive load. The pupil size is the most widely used eye measure for assessing cognitive workload of both psychological and human factors (Ahlstrom and Friedman-Berg, 2006; Marshall, 2002; Muldner et al., 2009; Pomplun and Sunkara, 2003; Stone et al., 2004).

Eye-tracking is a technique used to capture eye activities indicating to the point of the user's visual gaze fixated on the screen (Joseph and Murugesh, 2020). This technology is a valuable tool to calculate and examine workload in the HCI and visual computing areas, and seems to be a very good area of work (Joseph and Murugesh, 2020). Eye-tracking gives convincing information that describes human behaviour to solve usability issues. Modern eye-tracking technology—both remote and mobile eye-trackers—provide ample opportunities to integrate additional biometric devices to find concrete ideas and insights in the HCI field. Its usage is hugely extended to most of the sectors for innovative and compelling solutions to solve usability problems. As the technology is advancing to newer interfaces and interaction, UX is gaining great momentum in the HCI field.

25.9.1 Eye-Tracking Visualization

There are many methods existing for visualizing eye-tracking data such as plotting of pupils' horizontal and vertical coordinates against time, plotting raw eye movements in 2D with the stimulus

FIGURE 25.6 Eye-tracking visualization on a mobile phone interface.

images as the background, and fixation maps. A modern visualization technique available in current eye-tracking systems is heat map and gaze diagram. The heat map is a graphical demonstration of the grouped data and their colour values (Joseph and Murugesh, 2020). Heat mapping gathers visual information regarding the most and the least attention of a visual scene. A heat map is determined as shown in Figure 25.6(a) by fixation duration and fixation numbers (Joseph and Murugesh, 2020), which are then plotted in the form of an eye-tracking heat map. It can substantially uncover the visual attention for many participants at a time, and it is a powerful communication medium to discover visual behaviour.

A gaze plot is a diagram showing the motion series of fixations on a display in the sequence as they occur (Joseph and Murugesh, 2020), as shown in Figure 25.6(b). This is essentially tracking the eye's path movement signified by rings as fixations, and the rings are relative to the fixation length (Joseph and Murugesh, 2020). An important aspect of the gaze plot is to show a sequence of looking time or where and when we look there. The duration spent looking on a scene is called fixation duration, which is highlighted by the size of the fixation rings. If the attention is longer, then the circle the larger. These two visualization metrics will assist researchers to appreciate how the mind of the user works while carrying out a task (Joseph and Murugesh, 2020). Table 25.1 contains visualization metrics and their indicators.

TABLE 25.1
Metrics of Heat Map and Gaze Plot (Joseph and Murugesh, 2020)

Metrics	Indicators
Heat map	Reveals the frequency of focus area to a specific spot on a display (Joseph and Murugesh, 2020)
Gaze plot	User's eye path; many steps to do a task denote an increase in cognitive load (Joseph and Murugesh, 2020)

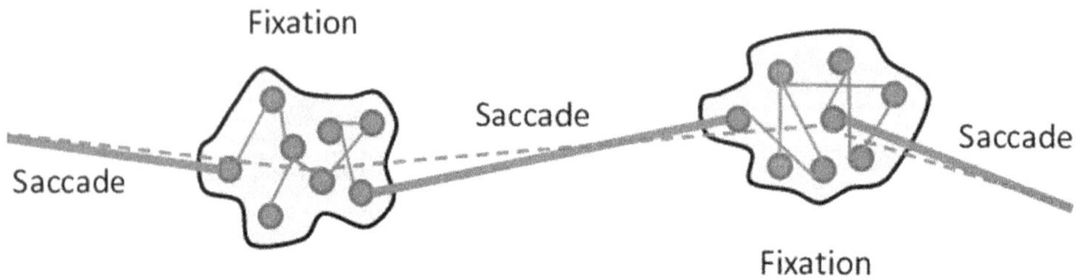

FIGURE 25.7 Eye-tracking paths consisting of fixations and saccades.

Source: Krueger et al. (2016)

25.9.2 Fixation

In eye-tracking, fixation is the most significant factor that researchers examine to make interpretations regarding the cognitive process (Joseph and Murugesh, 2020). It is the time during which the eye effectively stops at the scene and fixes to the centre of foveal vision (Joseph and Murugesh, 2020); hence, the visual system can concentrate on what is in focus. Gaze spots are explicit spatial marks on the line of sight, and they include (x, y) coordinates corresponding to measurement (Joseph and Murugesh, 2020), which is the result of an eye-tracking system. If an eye-tracking is functioning at 60 Hz, a gaze spot will be produced every 16.7 milliseconds (Joseph and Murugesh, 2020), likewise, at 300 Hz, gaze spots are spread out to a mere 3 milliseconds separately (Joseph and Murugesh, 2020). The fixation number shows how many times a specific area is looked at (Joseph and Murugesh, 2020), as shown in Figure 25.7. Gaze spots show what the eyes are focused on, and gaze spots are gathered based on the sampling rate of the eye-tracker per second (Joseph and Murugesh, 2020). If gaze spots are in proximity to space or time, it indicates focus on the visual scene and gaze direction is the suggestion to the aspect of interface for the current mental activity (Darrell et al., 2003).

Fixations consist of two features from gaze spots (Joseph and Murugesh, 2020). The first is in supplement to spatial (x, y) location and timestamps of start and end (Joseph and Murugesh, 2020). Second, fixations are assessable by means of fixation filters (Joseph and Murugesh, 2020). It is an attempt to rebuild these considerable eye activities as more significant regarding visibility, attention, understanding and cognitive operation (Joseph and Murugesh, 2020). Table 25.2 describes the fixation metrics and their indicators.

25.9.3 Saccade

A saccade is one of the valuable metrics in the HCI research—a rapid eye movement, when both eyes move together in the same direction from one point of interest to another (Joseph and Murugesh, 2020), as shown in Figure 25.7. The rationale behind this is to bring images of particular areas of the visual scene to fall onto the fovea. This signifies a switch within two fixations and is possibly activated by choice or spontaneously (Joseph and Murugesh, 2020). The eye fixates on a position only a short moment before quickly jumping to the next, and the distance of a saccade and its amplitude are associated linearly (Joseph and Murugesh, 2020). When the eye moves on its own from one spot to another, it takes 30–80 milliseconds to finish (Joseph and Murugesh, 2020). The velocity and distance of saccades can be used to examine the workload (Joseph and Murugesh, 2020). Longer saccades indicate a higher cognitive process (Victor Manuel et al., 2004). No encoding occurs during saccades, and hence, they cannot indicate

TABLE 25.2

Fixation Metrics and Indicators (Joseph and Murugesh, 2020)

Metrics	Indicators
Duration of fixation	Extended fixation duration shows difficulties associated with processing information or a more appealing element (Just and Carpenter, 1976; Joseph and Murugesh, 2020)
Fixation count	The effectiveness of information search is indicated through a number of fixations on media (Joseph and Murugesh, 2020)
Total number of fixations	The effectiveness of information search is indicated through a total number of fixations on media (Joseph and Murugesh, 2020)
Fixation spatial density	Fixations focused on a small area describe dedicated and effective searching (Cowen et al., 2002; Joseph and Murugesh, 2020)
Fixations per area of interest	More fixations on a specific region denote more meaningful to the user than other areas (Poole et al., 2004; Joseph and Murugesh, 2020)
On-target fixation	On-target fixations are divided by a number of total fixations; it shows an inefficient search (Joseph and Murugesh, 2020)
Time to first fixation on-target	The time takes to the first fixation for every area of interest (AOI) on all media (Joseph and Murugesh, 2020) shows that the target has an insightful property (Byrne et al., 1999; Joseph and Murugesh, 2020)
Average fixation count/ duration	The average length of fixations in each AOI on whole media describes the total duration of the average fixation continued (Joseph and Murugesh, 2020)
Fixation density	Fixation density is multiple gaze spots within a fixation occurred divided by small areas to capture all gaze occurrences (Brookings et al., 1996; Joseph and Murugesh, 2020); this indicates a higher level of attention.
Fixation rate	The frequentness of gazing at some element per second, representing attentiveness (Joseph and Murugesh, 2020)
Dwell time	Time consumed by the same position and area which denotes evaluating duration the participant stays at a result page (Joseph and Murugesh, 2020)
Gaze	The total duration of fixation in a particular area is used to analyze attention allocated between targets (Mello-Thoms et al., 2004; Hauland, 2003; Joseph and Murugesh, 2020).
Gaze samples	A sequence of gaze spots or a group of gaze spots in time and space shows a phase when the eyes are fixed on an object (Joseph and Murugesh, 2020)
Attention switching frequency	The dynamics of visual attention are measured by analyzing the entire changes among a set of AOI per minute (Joseph and Murugesh, 2020)

issues related to an interface on a screen (Joseph and Murugesh, 2020). However, progressive saccades could give evidence for calculating processing issues (Rayner and Pollatsek, 1989; Joseph and Murugesh, 2020). Table 25.3 gives detailed saccade metrics and their indicators.

25.9.4 Scan Path

Scan path is another eye-tracking metric that denotes the spatial sequence of eye activities performed by a user during a task. Eye-tracking scan paths include information regarding how people see. It clarifies visual attention signifying visual context attended (Joseph and Murugesh, 2020), and provides information about how users in interact with the visual scene. A continuous eye movement during visual scene exploration, the visual scan path consists of a series of saccades and fixations. There is no robust technology available to find the mean value of the scan path because of temporal and spatial conditions (Joseph and Murugesh, 2020). The most common method followed for scan path visualization is a gaze plot, which amounts to saccades and fixations with rings and straight lines corresponding to each other (Joseph and Murugesh, 2020). In general, analyzing scan path patterns is complex and consists of an arbitrary number of fixations. Although there are several procedures to determine patterns in multiple scan paths, scan path trend analysis (STA) discovers the maximum representative path of several participants on a visual display (Joseph and Murugesh, 2020). Table 25.4 describes metrics and indicators of scan path.

TABLE 25.3
Saccade Metrics and Indicators (Joseph and Murugesh, 2020)

Metrics	Indicators
Length of saccade	Time length of shifting the point of fixation; shows visual attention and perceptual importance (Joseph and Murugesh, 2020)
Number of saccades	A number of instinctive, sudden, fast, small eye movements continuously shifting the point of fixation; denotes a high-level visual search. (Goldberg and Kotval, 1999; Joseph and Murugesh, 2020).
Saccadic amplitude	Distance covered by a saccade from start to offset; greater saccades denote additional significant clues (Goldberg et al., 2002; Joseph and Murugesh, 2020)
Saccadic regression	Events that go in a reverse position to the text; regressions show the existence of lesser important cues. (Sibert et al., 2000; Joseph and Murugesh, 2020)
Saccade duration	The time taken for a quick eye movement amid two fixation spots; longer saccade period shows more time spent on searching (Joseph and Murugesh, 2020)

TABLE 25.4
Scan Path Metrics and Indicators (Joseph and Murugesh, 2020)

Metrics	Shows Indicators
Scan path duration	Time to complete a sequence of fixations and connecting saccades (Joseph and Murugesh, 2020); a long-lasting scan path shows less efficient scanning (Goldberg and Kotval, 1999)
Scan path length	Lengthier scan path shows less efficient searching (Goldberg et al., 2002; Joseph and Murugesh, 2020)
Spatial density	Less spatial denseness shows relevant direct search (Goldberg and Kotval, 1999; Joseph and Murugesh, 2020)
Scan path direction	The path on which the entire sequence of fixations and interconnected saccades take place (Joseph and Murugesh, 2020); this shows the user's search strategy (Aaltonen et al., 1998; Joseph and Murugesh, 2020)
Scan path regularity	Divergence from a regular scan path shows search problems linked to user interaction (Goldberg and Kotval, 1999; Joseph and Murugesh, 2020)
Saccade/fixation ratio	It is differentiation amid time taken for searching (saccade) and time taken for processing (fixations) (Joseph and Murugesh, 2020); a high value indicates better processing or inefficient searching behaviour (Joseph and Murugesh, 2020)

25.9.5 Pupil Dilation

Researchers have been using pupil dilation as an important eye metric to investigate cognitive load, information processing and human performance. Pupil dilation is an automatic response, and pupil dilation can differ in width from 1/16 inch to more than 1/3 inch (Joseph and Murugesh, 2020). Psychologists have recognized that a change in pupil dilation signifies difficult cognitive processing (Joseph and Murugesh, 2020). Earlier research studies confirm that the pupils widen during task difficulty and their cognitive effort to solve it intensifies (Joseph and Murugesh, 2020). The eye-tracking technology uses an IR light source and video cameras to capture the eye position, cornea reflections and pupil size (Joseph and Murugesh, 2020). Eye-tracking technology can be employed to examine pupil dilation responses with regard to the information on the screen and behavioural aspects during the study (Joseph and Murugesh, 2020).

Human pupil size increases due to various causes, including cognitive effort, memory load, arousal, pain, and so on (Beatty, 1982; Joseph and Murugesh, 2020). When a complex task is carried out by a user, pupils widen 1–2 seconds in reaction to the cognitive load of the task (Beatty, 1982; Joseph and Murugesh, 2020) and shrink gradually once the task is finished (Kahneman and Beatty, 1966; Hess, 1972; Joseph and Murugesh, 2020). To calculate variations in cognitive load under various tasks, the average variation in pupil size can be examined (Joseph and Murugesh, 2020). It is essential to have a baseline value that contains non-cognitive variables to estimate cognitive load levels with cognitive

TABLE 25.5
Pupil Dilation–Related Metrics and Indicators (Joseph and Murugesh, 2020)

Metrics	Indicators
Pupil size	The pupil size with respect to the media; the dimension of the pupil can be applied for indicating cognitive load (Marshall, 2000; Pomplun and Sunkara, 2003; Joseph and Murugesh, 2020)
Pupil dilation	Dilation is an automatic response, and diameter may vary from 1/16 inch (1.5mm) to 1/3 (8mm) (Joseph and Murugesh, 2020); variations in pupil diameter convey a considerable amount of cognitive processes (Joseph and Murugesh, 2020)

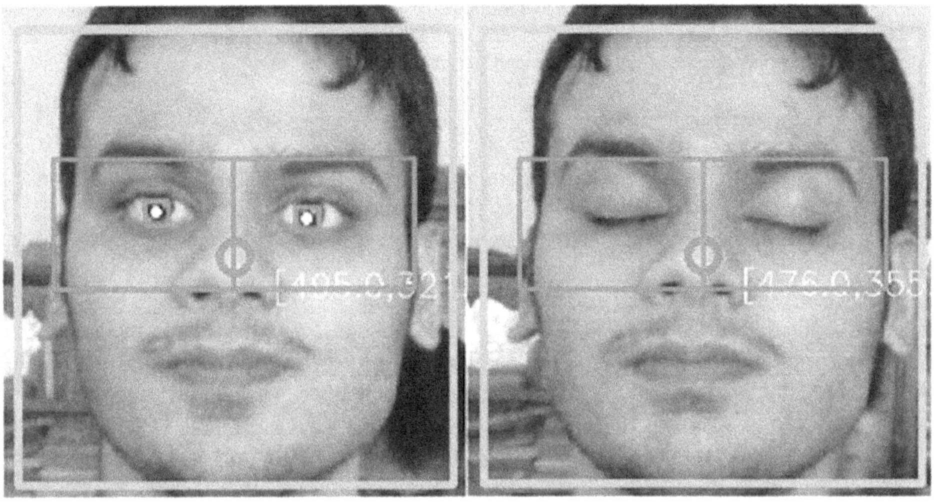

FIGURE 25.8 Eye blink detection: open and closed eyes.

Source: Noman et al. (2018)

variables. The cognitive load levels are determined based on the comparison between the baseline value and other values measured during the experiment. One must be very cautious to differentiate the actual source of the problem that triggered the pupil reaction, and this is linked to several causes (Joseph and Murugesh, 2020), such as alternations in illuminous, light reflex and error owing to gaze angles (Joseph and Murugesh, 2020). Table 25.5 explains pupil dilation–related metrics and indicators.

25.9.6 Blinking

Blinking behaviour is another eye-tracking metric considered for measuring cognitive load to a specific layer of information. Blinking is often an unconscious gesture in which the eyelid blocks the illuminator's pupil and cornea causing a lack of details in unprocessed data point (x, y) coordinate (Joseph and Murugesh, 2020). A fixation filter may be employed for analysis to take off the missing elements and to accurately deduce the information into fixations (Joseph and Murugesh, 2020). Blink rate and latency will give valid insights for better thoughtfulness regarding the attention status of participants (Joseph and Murugesh, 2020). High and low blink rates have been discovered to show high cognitive effort (Schleicher et al., 2008; Siyuan et al., 2011; Joseph and Murugesh, 2020). Likewise, research indicates that a decrease and increase in blinking velocity (Joseph and Murugesh, 2020) and a reducing degree of the eyelids' openings are signs of growing fatigue (Vicor Manuel et al., 2004; Joseph and Murugesh, 2020).

To detect blink in the eye, the investigator must observe the pupil's middle point, as illustrated in Figure 25.8 (Joseph and Murugesh, 2020). White pixels will appear on the image when the eye is open and will help to measure the pupil's centre point easily. If the eye is closed, the pupil's white pixels do not

TABLE 25.6

Blinking Metrics and Indicators (Joseph and Murugesh, 2020)

Metrics	Indicators
Blink rate	Blink frequency per minute (Joseph and Murugesh, 2020); pupil size and blink rate could be reflected as an indication of mental workload (Bruneau et al., 2002; Brookings et al., 1996; Marshall, 2000; Pomplun and Sunkara, 2003; Joseph and Murugesh, 2020)
Blink duration	Closure duration time of a blink in milliseconds; gives insights regarding mental workload and area of focus (Joseph and Murugesh, 2020)
Velocity of blinking	Velocity is achieved through closing and opening of eyelid; gives insights regarding mental workload and area of focus (Joseph and Murugesh, 2020)
Blink latency	In the saccadic system, about 200 milliseconds is the blink latency and relates to the time period from the start of the stimulus to the beginning of the eye movement; provides insights about mental workload and area of focus (Joseph and Murugesh, 2020)

appear on the image. Calculating the centre point is generated with a count variable. The variable is 1 when the eye is open and 0 when the eye is closed (Joseph and Murugesh, 2020). Both variables can help track measurements of the eye blink and their signifiers, as shown in Table 25.6 (Joseph and Murugesh, 2020).

Regarding the eye-movement measurement, there are three well-known measures: temporal, spatial and count (Joseph and Murugesh, 2020). The temporal measure shows that the eye movement is calculated in a dimension of time (Lai et al., 2013; Joseph and Murugesh, 2020); for instance, time duration take for some specific area or AOI. Temporal measures can address when and how long queries about cognitive processing (Liversedge et al., 1998). Spatial scale calculates eye movements with respect to a spatial dimension that includes directions locations, distances, sequences and relations of saccades or fixations (Lai et al., 2013; Joseph and Murugesh, 2020). Spatial events may address how and where queries with respect to mental processes. Scanning and saccadic behaviours are very significant because visual perceptions indicate the control of selective processes (Liversedge and Findlay, 2000). The counting scale calculates eye activities on a frequent basis and reveals the significance of visual information or materials (Lai et al., 2013). This indicates that various eye-movement measures might perhaps indicate the same cognitive process (Lai et al., 2013). The most commonly applied eye-tracking measures were temporal (Lai et al., 2013), then count and spatial measures though the selection of measures (Lai et al., 2013) depends on the specific research question.

In general, the previously discussed outline gives a fundamental principle towards understanding several kinds and attributes of eye-movement measures (Lai et al., 2013). Nevertheless, it must be noted that research in various fields might emphasize on distinct eye metrics based on the context of study and interpreted accordingly (Lai et al., 2013). In addition to this, measures like, pupil dilation and blinks are also discussed. To conclude, the eye-tracking method is an interesting and dominant tool (Lai et al., 2013) to study the cognitive processes of teaching and student learning. On the other hand, it is a big task for researchers and educators to incorporate eye-tracking methods into Education 4.0. Researchers in the educational domain need to understand how to use these eye measures as methodology, as well as how to apply and interpret them in different contexts of study so that student learning processes in the different learning environments can be understood.

25.10 Eye-Tracking for Industry 4.0

Industries worldwide are gearing up for the Fourth Industrial Revolution, which is called Industry 4.0, and many are facing trouble to continue with its demands and growing tension to retain workers with additional skills while maintaining quality and efficiency (Tobii Pro, 2020a). Digitization of manufacturing transformed the manufacturing process. Knowing how employees accomplish tasks and their work environment interaction are very vital to giving valuable directions and training as workers worldwide experience their responsibilities being rewritten (Tobii Pro, 2020b). We notice that tasks are more and more automated, and online interaction is increasing exponentially with the process shifting towards cyber-physical systems (Tobii Pro, 2020a). In the perspective of Industry 4.0, smart factories are increasing around the world and people in industry need to adapt to modern technology and the higher demands of their jobs. Technology is constantly changing, and adaptation is very much essential today. Industry 4.0 is changing the world around us. Global connectivity, smart machines and new media are some of the areas redesigning how we think about work, what constitutes work and how we learn and develop required skills to work in the future. Robotics, Big Data, artificial intelligence (AI) and the internet of things (IoT) (Wisskirchen et al., 2017) will together have a greater influence on jobs and industry. It is also to be noted that the 21st century's intellectually demanding jobs will be affected just like the First Industrial Revolution of the 19th century (Preparing for Education 4.0, 2020). This revolution has a direct influence on the roles of schools, universities and colleges to produce a workforce for this new era and student expertise to match it (Preparing for Education 4.0, 2020).

Eye-tracking has several applications in this change towards Industry 4.0 which can be employed to assist with skills transfer and training, streamline processes, enhance safety and bring out more contextual awareness (Tobii Pro, 2020a). Eye-tracking information can help to understand the subconscious processes, provide a visual representation of best practices, help to understand performance in critical situations, provide evidence of attention patterns linked to accident or injury, reveal information on cognitive load and understand behaviours of workers while doing tasks and highlight areas for further investigation. Roadblocks that delay processes or lower the quality can be identified, and insights can be applied to the training. Eye-tracking allows to see where users focus their attention, and this information can reveal cognitive load and barriers that can be addressed. Eye-tracking also provides very detailed information and a clear explanation of how certain tasks are performed, and makes it possible to incorporate these insights into training materials and resources. Technology that brings efficiency and increased productivity unluckily becomes counterproductive if the operator is not well equipped. Training takes time and consumes a lot of resources and in this situation; eye-tracking technology provides promising results. The biggest benefit of the eye-tracking–based approach is that it establishes the missing link between humans and machines.

Today, there is a huge demand to adapt modern technologies like eye-tracking and provide modern research tools in the labs to prepare students for Industry 4.0. This will be an opportunity for students in the Indian educational institutes/organizations to understand how visual attention can be analyzed and applied in many research fields.

25.11 Application of Eye-Tracking in Education 4.0

The application of eye-based methods in the education domain has increased in recent years. Lai et al. (2013) report that before 2009, the usage of eye-tracking techniques was much less due to the lack of communication between the fields of education and psychology, and the cost factor of devices. The review study by Lai and his team found two major problems identified by the educational researchers who applied eye-tracking techniques in their studies. In their review (Lai et al., 2013), it is interesting to know that only a few studies were explored concerning education and learning, and that eye-based technologies in learning have not been systematically analyzed. Currently, students' mental workloads are changing because of the shift from a traditional approach to a modern technology-based approach. The modern approach demands the development of skills for critical thinking and gaining of knowledge appropriate for problem solving. In the context of developing critical thinking and Industry 4.0, there is a growing need to adopt modern technology-based teaching, learning and research in Indian universities.

Education 4.0 is the future of education that allows humans and machines together to create new possibilities. The ability of digital technologies and open-source content can bring a substantial change in the global scenario. Education 4.0 establishes an outline for the future of teaching and learning. In this context, employing eye-based technologies in education and educational research can add significant value to the learning process. People acquire knowledge through their eyes, and such knowledge often becomes the "window to the observers' visual and cognitive processes" (Salvucci and Goldberg, 2000,

p. 71). This processes information from the external environment and determines how the processed knowledge is used (Ormrod, 2008). As the demand for Education 4.0 is increasing, it is essential to focus on the learning process incorporating modern technologies to make education more robust and relevant to the future. In this context, eye-tracking provides numerous opportunities for Education 4.0.

Eye-tracking is one of the modern tools with great potential that can be used to examine the education and learning process. It is also becoming a practice to use them in classrooms and labs, and teach young professionals who are tomorrow's workforce to explore possibilities of eye-tracking in different fields. Eye-tracking is a promising tool to investigate visual attention and social interaction in all learning environments (Tobii Pro, 2020a). The insight gained by understanding various aspects of the knowledge process has the potential to bring substantial change in educational outcomes. Currently, researchers in the educational domain are empowered to design experiments scientifically and bring changes in the teaching and learning methodology.

Eye-tracking is a modern-day tool used in educational research to examine the knowledge process, cognitive load and teaching and learning methods. Eye-tracking provides numerous possibilities to capture interesting insights regarding student learning behaviour and teaching methods in different educational contexts. The information collected from an eye-tracker system can show distinctive learning approaches for researchers to understand student cognitive load, and this can be also extended to evaluate teacher performance and instructional methods. By gaining a deeper understanding of classroom dynamics, researchers can suggest techniques to improve the quality of education. The eye-tracking technique can help Education 4.0 to determine the following:

- Differences in information gathering (Tobii Pro, 2020a)
- Differences in problem-solving skills (Tobii Pro, 2020b)
- Differences in teaching and learning strategies (Tobii Pro, 2020b)
- Social interaction of students reinforce the learning process (Tobii Pro, 2020b)
- How different educational materials work (Tobii Pro, 2020b)
- Usability aspect of educational systems and applications

25.12 Summary

Eye-tracking methods are employed to measure the position of the eye, movement of eye and pupil size to identify areas in which the learner has a particular interest at a specific time. This has greatly motivated researchers to apply eye-tracking techniques over several research domains (Joseph and Murugesh, 2020). Eye-tracking technology has evolved to a great extent, and today, everything that has a visual component can be eye captured (Joseph and Murugesh, 2020), and this has paved the way for educational research. Literature shows that eye-tracking technology in HCI has researched several aspects of usability and computer interfaces. As technology has entered everyday life, eye-tracking has become very important to examine the aspects influencing human interaction and calculate mental workload while performing tasks (Joseph and Murugesh, 2020). Though eye-tracking in the education domain is a very young field, it has shown promising results and so gained significant attention in this research community. By analyzing learning teaching and learning processes, a new framework can be developed to meet the future challenges of Industry 4.0. It is a new scientific tool that can become an aid to improve learning and remove complexity in the learner's mind. For a successful knowledge process, the cognitive load requires handling the intrinsic load, enhancing the extraneous load and encouraging the germane load (De Jong, 2010). As learners become more familiar with content and skills, schemas change so that the information can be handled more competently through working memory. The ability of digital technologies and open-source content can add significant value to Education 4.0. There are various eye-based techniques available today to track eye movements, but three eye-tracking techniques have gained the attention of researchers: Videooculography, video-based infrared pupil-corneal reflection and electrooculography. Typically, eye-tracking measurements are based on fixations, saccades, scan path, pupil dilation and eye blinking. These metrics may be applied in various aspects of oculomotor behaviour, subject to the type of research study involved (Bylinskii and Borkin, 2015). Industries worldwide are gearing up for the Fourth Industrial Revolution, which has a greater challenge in retaining skilled workers while maintaining quality and productivity. Global connectivity, smart machines and new media are some of the noted areas redesigning the future workforce. This revolution invites educational institutes and organizations to strategize and bring a new frame for Education 4.0. Eye-tracking is the one of the modern tools needed today to provide exposure to students and teachers in terms of teaching strategy, research and innovation.

25.13 Acknowledgements

The authors are sincerely thankful to Computer Application Department, Madurai Kamaraj University, as well as National Institute of Design for supporting and motivating us.

REFERENCES

Aaltonen, A., Hyrskykari, A. and Räihä, K., 1998. 101 spots, or how do users read menus? In *Proceedings of CHI 98 Human Factors in Computing Systems* (pp. 132–139). Los Angeles, CA: ACM.

Ahlstrom, U. and Friedman-Berg, F.J., 2006. Using eye movement activity as a correlate of cognitive workload. *International Journal of Industrial Ergonomics*, *36*(7), pp. 623–636.

Anliker, J., 1976. Eye movements: On-line measurement, analysis, and control. In R.S. Monty and J.W. Senders (Eds.), *Eye Movements and Psychological Processes* (pp. 185–199). Hillsdale, NJ: Lawrence Erlbaum Associates.

Barry Levine., 2017. Tobii Pro now invisibly tracks users' eyes in VR. Accessed from https://martechtoday.com/tobii-pro-now-invisibly-tracks-users-eyes-vr-199850. [Accessed on April 12, 2020].

Beatty, J., 1982. Task-evoked pupillary responses, processing load, and the structure of processing resources. *Psychological Bulletin*, *91*(2), p. 276.

Bengoechea, J.J., Villanueva, A. and Cabeza, R., 2012. Hybrid eye detection algorithm for outdoor environments. In *Proceedings of the 2012 ACM Conference on Ubiquitous Computing, UbiComp'12* (pp. 685–688). New York: ACM.

Boehm-Davis, D.A., Gray, W.D. and Schoelles, M.J., 2000, July. The eye blink as a physiological indicator of cognitive workload. In *Proceedings of the Human Factors and Ergonomics Society Annual Meeting* (Vol. 44, No. 33, pp. 6–116). Los Angeles, CA: SAGE Publications.

Bolt, R.A., 1981. Gaze-orchestrated dynamic windows. *ACM SIGGRAPH Computer Graphics*, *15*(3), pp. 109–119.

Bolt, R.A., 1982. March. Eyes at the interface. In *Proceedings of the 1982 Conference on Human Factors in Computing Systems* (pp. 360–362). Gaithersburg, Maryland: ACM Press.

Brigham, F.J., Zaimi, E., Matkins, J.J., Shields, J., McDonnouugh, J. and Jakubecy, J.J., 2001. The eyes may have it: Reconsidering eye movement research in human cognition. *Advances in Learning and Behavioral Disabilities*, *15*, pp. 39–60.

Brookings, J.B., Wilson, G.F. and Swain, C.R., 1996. Psychophysiological responses to changes in workload during simulated air traffic control. *Biological Psychology*, *42*(3), pp. 361–377.

Bruneau, D., Sasse, M.A. and McCarthy, J.D., 2002. *The Eyes Never Lie: The Use of Eyetracking Data in HCI Research*. New York: ACM Press.

Bylinskii, Z., and Borkin, M.A., 2015. *Eye Fixation Metrics for Large Scale Analysis of Information Visualizations*. ETVIS Work. Eye Track. Vis.

Byrne, M.D., Anderson, J.R., Douglass, S. and Matessa, M., 1999, May. Eye tracking the visual search of click-down menus. In *Proceedings of the SIGCHI conference on Human Factors in Computing Systems* (pp. 402–409). Mahwah, NJ: Erlbaum.

Card, S.K., 1984. Visual search of computer command menus. In H. Bouma and D. G. Bouwhuis (Eds.), *Attention and Performance X, Control of Language Processes*. Hillsdale, NJ: Lawrence Erlbaum Associates.

Chen, D. and Vertegaal, R., 2004, April. Using mental load for managing interruptions in physiologically attentive user interfaces. In *CHI'04 Extended Abstracts on Human Factors in Computing Systems* (pp. 1513–1516). Vienna, Austria: ACM Press.

Chen, S., 2014. *Cognitive Load Measurement from Eye Activity: Acquisition, Efficacy, and Real-time System Design*. Sydney, Australia: University of New South Wales.

Chen, S. and Epps, J., 2014. Using task-induced pupil diameter and blink rate to infer cognitive load. *Human—Computer Interaction*, *29*(4), pp. 390–413. Taylor & Francis Group, LLC. Online publication.

Cowen, L., Ball, L.J. and Delin, J., 2002. An eye movement analysis of web page usability. In *People and Computers XVI-Memorable Yet Invisible* (pp. 317–335). London: Springer.

Darrell S. Rudmann, George W. McConkie and Xianjun Sam Zheng, 2003. Eye tracking in cognitive state dedection for HCI. In *Proceedings of the 5th International Conference on Multimodal Interfaces* (pp. 159–163). British Columbia, Canada: Vancouver.

De Jong, T., 2010. Cognitive load theory, educational research, and instructional design: some food for thought. *Instructional Science*, *38*(2), pp. 105–134.

Debie, E., Rojas, R.F., Fidock, J., Barlow, M., Kasmarik, K., Anavatti, S., Garratt, M. and Abbass, H.A., 2019. Multimodal fusion for objective assessment of cognitive workload: a review. *IEEE Transactions on Cybernetics*.

Dodge, R. and Cline, T.S., 1901. The angle velocity of eye movements. *Psychological Review*, *8*(2), p. 145.

Duchowski, A.T., 2003. Visual attention. In *Eye Tracking Methodology: Theory and Practice* (pp. 3–15). GB: Springer-Verlag London Ltd.

Duchowski, A.T. and Vertegaal, R., 2000. Eye-based interaction in graphical systems: Theory and practice. *ACM SIGGRAPH 2000 Course Notes*, *5*.

Ellis, S., Candrea, R., Misner, J., Craig, C.S., Lankford, C.P. and Hutchinson, T.E., 1998, June. Windows to the soul? What eye movements tell us about software usability. In *Proceedings of the Usability Professionals' Association Conference* (pp. 151–178). Washington D.C: Usability Professionals Association.

Eye tracking. Accessed from www.eyetracking.com/. [Accessed on May 2020].

Fisher, D.F., Monty, R.A., and Senders, J.W., 1981. *Eye Movements: Cognition and Visual Perception*. Hillsdale, NJ: Lawrence Erlbaum.

Fitts, P.M., Jones, R.E. and Milton, J.L., 1950. Eye movements of aircraft pilots during instrument-landing approaches. *Aeronautical Engineering Review*.

Gaze Intelligence: Eye tracking study. Accessed from https://gazeintelligence.com/eye-tracking-study. [Accessed on April 2020].

Glenn III, F.A., Iavecchia, H.P., Ross, L.V., Stokes, J.M., Weiland, W.J., Weiss, D. and Zaklad, A.L., 1986, September. Eye-voice-controlled interface. In *Proceedings of the Human Factors Society Annual Meeting* (Vol. 30, No. 4, pp. 322–326). Los Angeles, CA: SAGE Publications.

Goldberg, J.H. and Kotval, X.P., 1999. Computer interface evaluation using eye movements: methods and constructs. *International Journal of Industrial Ergonomics*, *24*(6), pp. 631–645.

Goldberg, J.H., Stimson, M.J., Lewenstein, M., Scott, N. and Wichansky, A.M., 2002, March. Eye tracking in web search tasks: Design implications. In *Proceedings of the 2002 Symposium on Eye Tracking Research & Applications* (pp. 51–58). New Orleans, Louisiana, USA: ACM.

Goldberg, J.H. and Wichansky, A.M., 2003. Eye tracking in usability evaluation: A practitioner's guide. In *The Mind's Eye* (pp. 493–516). North-Holland: Elsevier.

Goodyear, P. and Retalis, S., 2010. *Technology-Enhanced Learning*. Rotterdam: Sense Publishers.

Hansen, D.W. and Ji, Q., 2009. In the eye of the beholder: A survey of models for eyes and gaze. *IEEE Transactions on Pattern Analysis and Machine Intelligence*, *32*(3), pp. 478–500.

Hansen, D.W. and Pece, A.E., 2005. Eye tracking in the wild. *Computer Vision and Image Understanding*, *98*(1), pp. 155–181.

Hartridge, H. and Thomson, L.C., 1948. Methods of investigating eye movements. *The British Journal of Ophthalmology*, *32*(9), p. 581.

Hauland, G., 2003. Measuring team situation awareness by means of eye movement data. In *Proceedings of HCI International 2003* (Vol. 3, pp. 230–234). Mahwah, NJ: Lawrence Erlbaum Associates.

Hayhoe, M. and Ballard, D., 2005. Eye movements in natural behavior. *Trends in Cognitive Sciences*, *9*(4), pp. 188–194.

Hegarty, M. and Just, M.A., 1993. Constructing mental models of machines from text and diagrams. *Journal of Memory and Language*, *32*(6), pp. 717–742.

Hegarty, M., Mayer, R.E. and Green, C.E., 1992. Comprehension of arithmetic word problems: Evidence from students' eye fixations. *Journal of Educational Psychology*, *84*(1), p. 76.

Hendrickson, J.J., 1989, March. Performance, preference, and visual scan patterns on a menu-based system: Implications for interface design. In *Proceedings of the SIGCHI Conference on Human Factors in Computing Systems* (pp. 217–222). New York: ACM.

Hess, E.H., 1972. Pupillometrics. In N. S. Greenfield & R. A. Sternbach (Eds.), *Handbook of Psychophysiology* (pp. 491–531) New York: Holt, Rinehart & Winston.

Holmqvist, K., Nyström, M., Andersson, R., Dewhurst, R., Jarodzka, H. and Van de Weijer, J., 2011. *Eye Tracking: A Comprehensive Guide to Methods and Measures.* Oxford: Oxford University Press.

Hwang, G.J. and Wang, S.Y., 2016. Single loop or double loop learning: English vocabulary learning performance and behavior of students in situated computer games with different guiding strategies. *Computers & Education, 102*, pp. 188–201.

Jacob, R.J. and Karn, K.S., 2003. Eye tracking in human-computer interaction and usability research: Ready to deliver the promises. In *The Mind's Eye* (pp. 573–605). Amsterdam: Elsevier Science.

Javal, E., 1878. Essai sur la physiologie de la lecture. *Annales d'Ocilistique, 80*, pp. 97–117.

Jonassen, D.H., Peck, K.L. and Wilson, B.G., 1999. *Learning with Technology: A Constructivist Perspective.* Upper Saddle River, NJ: Merrill.

Joseph, Antony William and Murugesh, Ramaswamy, 2020. Potential eye tracking metrics and indicators to measure cognitive load in human-computer interaction research. *Journal of Scientific Research, 64*(1).

Judd, C.H., McAllister, C.N. and Steele, W.M., 1905. General introduction to a series of studies of eye movements by means of kinetoscopic photographs. *Psychological Review Monographs, 7*(1), pp. 1–16.

Just, M.A. and Carpenter, P.A., 1976. The role of eye-fixation research in cognitive psychology. *Behavior Research Methods & Instrumentation, 8*(2), pp. 139–143.

Kahneman, D. and Beatty, J., 1966. Pupil diameter and load on memory. *Science, 154*(3756), pp. 1583–1585.

Kinsman, T.B. and Pelz, J.B., 2012, September. Location by parts: model generation and feature fusion for mobile eye pupil tracking under challenging lighting. In *Proceedings of the 2012 ACM Conference on Ubiquitous Computing* (pp. 695–700). New York: ACM.

Kramer, A.F., 1990. *Physiological Metrics of Mental Workload: A Review of Recent Progress.* Navy Personnel Research and Development Center.

Krueger, R., Koch, S. and Ertl, T., 2016, October. Saccadelenses: Interactive exploratory filtering of eye tracking trajectories. In *2016 IEEE Second Workshop on Eye Tracking and Visualization (ETVIS)* (pp. 31–34). IEEE.

Lai, C.L., Hwang, G.J., Liang, J.C. and Tsai, C.C., 2016. Differences between mobile learning environmental preferences of high school teachers and students in Taiwan: A structural equation model analysis. *Educational Technology Research and Development, 64*(3), pp. 533–554.

Lai, M.L., Tsai, M.J., Yang, F.Y., Hsu, C.Y., Liu, T.C., Lee, S.W.Y., Lee, M.H., Chiou, G.L., Liang, J.C. and Tsai, C.C., 2013. A review of using eye-tracking technology in exploring learning from 2000 to 2012. *Educational Research Review, 10*, pp. 90–115.

Land, M.F. and Furneaux, S., 1997. The knowledge base of the oculomotor system. *Philosophical Transactions of the Royal Society of London. Series B: Biological Sciences, 352*(1358), pp. 1231–1239.

Landy, D.H., Jones, M.N. and Goldstone, R.L., 2008. How the appearance of an operator affects its formal precedence. In *Proceedings of the Thirtieth Annual Conference of the Cognitive Science Society* (pp. 2109–2114). Washington, DC: Cognitive Science Society.

Levine, J.L., 1984. Performance of an eyetracker for office use. *Computers in Biology and Medicine, 14*(1), pp. 77–89.

Liu, W., Djamasbi, S., Trapp, A.C. and Shojaeizadeh, M., 2018, July. Measuring focused attention using fixation inner-density. In *International Conference on Augmented Cognition* (pp. 105–116). Cham: Springer.

Liversedge, S.P. and Findlay, J.M., 2000. Saccadic eye movements and cognition. *Trends in Cognitive Sciences, 4*(1), pp. 6–14.

Liversedge, S.P., Paterson, K.B. and Pickering, M.J., 1998. Eye movements and measures of reading time. In *Eye Guidance in Reading and Scene Perception* (pp. 55–75). Oxford, UK: Elsevier.

Loftus, G.R. and Mackworth, N.H., 1978. Cognitive determinants of fixation location during picture viewing. *Journal of Experimental Psychology: Human Perception and Performance, 4*(4), p. 565.

Mackworth, J.F. and Mackworth, N.H., 1958. Eye fixations recorded on changing visual scenes by the television eye-marker. *JOSA, 48*(7), pp. 439–445.

Mackworth, N.H. and Thomas, E.L., 1962. Head-mounted eye-marker camera. *JOSA, 52*(6), pp. 713–716.

Majaranta, P., Bates, R., and Donegan, M., 2009. Eye tracking. In C. Stephanidis (Ed.), *The Universal Access Handbook* (p. 20, Chapter 36). Boca Raton: CRC Press.

Majaranta, P. and Bulling, A., 2014. Eye tracking and eye-based human—computer interaction. In *Advances in Physiological Computing* (pp. 39–65). London: Springer.

Marshall, S., 2000. Method and apparatus for eye tracking and monitoring pupil dilation to evaluate cognitive activity. U.S. Patent 6,090,051, July 2000.

Marshall, S.P., 2002, September. The index of cognitive activity: Measuring cognitive workload. In *Proceedings of the IEEE 7th Conference on Human Factors and Power Plants* (pp. 7–7). IEEE.

Marshall, S.P., San Diego State University Research Foundation, 2000. *Method and Apparatus for Eye Tracking and Monitoring Pupil Dilation to Evaluate Cognitive Activity*. U.S. Patent 6,090,051.

Mayer, R.E. and Fiorella, L., 2014. 12 principles for reducing extraneous processing in multimedia learning: Coherence, signaling, redundancy, spatial contiguity, and temporal contiguity principles. In *The Cambridge Handbook of Multimedia Learning* (p. 279). Cambridge: Cambridge University Press.

McManus, A., 2017. Eyes as windows to the soul: How to gather emotional ad responses with eye tracking. Accessed from https://blog.affectiva.com/eyes-as-windows-to-the-soul-how-to-gather-emotional-ad-responses-with-eye-tracking. [Accessed on April 2020].

Mello-Thoms, C., Nodine, C.F. and Kundel, H.L., 2004. What attracts the eye to the location of missed and reported breast cancers? In *Proceedings of the Eye Tracking Research and Applications Symposium 2002* (pp. 111–117). NY: ACM Press.

Monty, R.A. and Senders, J.W., 1976. *Eye Movements and Psychological Processes*. Hillsdale, NJ: Lawrence Erlbaum.

Morimoto, C.H. and Mimica, M.R., 2005. Eye gaze tracking techniques for interactive applications. *Computer Vision and Image Understanding*, *98*(1), pp. 4–24.

Muldner, K., Christopherson, R., Atkinson, R. and Burleson, W., 2009, June. Investigating the utility of eye-tracking information on affect and reasoning for user modeling. In *International Conference on User Modeling, Adaptation, and Personalization* (pp. 138–149). Berlin, Heidelberg: Springer.

Neerincx, M.A., Kennedie, S., Grootjen, M. and Grootjen, F., 2009, July. Modeling the cognitive task load and performance of naval operators. In *International Conference on Foundations of Augmented Cognition* (pp. 260–269). Berlin, Heidelberg: Springer.

Noman, M., Bin, T., Ahad, M. and Rahman, A., 2018. Mobile-based Eye-Blink Detection Performance Analysis on Android Platform. *Frontiers in ICT*, *5*, p. 4.

Ormrod, J.E., 2008. *Human learning* (5th ed.). Upper Saddle River, NJ: Pearson Prentice Hall.

Oviatt, S., 2006, October. Human-centered design meets cognitive load theory: Designing interfaces that help people think. In *Proceedings of the 14th ACM International Conference on Multimedia* (pp. 871–880). California, USA: ACM.

Paas, F., Tuovinen, J.E., Tabbers, H. and Van Gerven, P.W., 2003. Cognitive load measurement as a means to advance cognitive load theory. *Educational Psychologist*, *38*(1), pp. 63–71.

Paulson, E.J. and Henry, J., 2002. Does the degrees of reading power assessment reflect the reading process? An eye-movement examination. *Journal of Adolescent & Adult Literacy*, *46*(3), pp. 234–244.

Piquado, T., Isaacowitz, D. and Wingfield, A., 2010. Pupillometry as a measure of cognitive effort in younger and older adults. *Psychophysiology*, *47*(3), pp. 560–569.

Pomplun, M. and Sunkara, S., 2003, June. Pupil dilation as an indicator of cognitive workload in human-computer interaction. In *Proceedings of the International Conference on HCI* (Vol. 273).

Poole, A. and Ball, L.J., 2005. Eye tracking in human-computer interaction and usability research: Current status and future. Prospects. In C. Ghaoui (Ed.), *Encyclopedia of Human-Computer Interaction*. Pennsylvania: Idea Group. Inc.

Poole, A., Ball, L.J. and Phillips, P., 2004. In search of salience: A response time and eye movement analysis of bookmark recognition. In S. Fincher, P. Markopolous, D. Moore, & R. Ruddle (Eds.), *People and Computers XVIII-Design for Life: Proceedings of HCI 2004*. London: Springer-Verlag Ltd.

Preparing for Education 4.0. Accessed from www.timeshighereducation.com/hub/jisc/p/preparing-education-40. [Accessed on May 2020].

Rayner, K., 1998. Eye movements in reading and information processing: 20 years of research. *Psychological Bulletin*, *124*(3), p. 372.

Rayner, K., 2009. Eye movements and attention in reading, scene perception, and visual search. *The Quarterly Journal of Experimental Psychology*, *62*(8), pp. 1457–1506.

Rayner, K., Chace, K.H., Slattery, T.J. and Ashby, J., 2006. Eye movements as reflections of comprehension processes in reading. *Scientific Studies of Reading*, *10*(3), pp. 241–255.

Rayner, K. and Pollatsek, A., 1989. *The Psychology of Reading*. Englewood Cliffs, NJ: Prentice Hall.

Rozado, D. and Dunser, A., 2015. Combining EEG with pupillometry to improve cognitive workload detection. *Computer*, *48*(10), pp. 18–25.

Salvucci, D.D. and Goldberg, J.H., 2000, November. Identifying fixations and saccades in eye-tracking protocols. In *Proceedings of the 2000 Symposium on Eye Tracking Research & Applications* (pp. 71–78). FL, USA: ACM.

Schleicher, R., Galley, N., Briest, S., & Galley, L. (2008). Blinks and saccades as indicators of fatigue in sleepiness warnings: looking tired? *Ergonomics*, *51*(7), 982–1010.

Senders, J.W., 2000. Four theoretical and practical questions. Keynote address presented at the Eye Tracking Research and Applications Symposium 2000. Abstract in. In *Proceedings of the Eye Tracking Research and Applications Symposium 2000* (p. 8).

Senders, J.W., Fisher, D.F. and Monty, R.A., 1978. *Eye Movements and the Higher Psychological Functions*. Hillsdale, NJ: Lawrence Erlbaum.

Shackel, B., 1960. Note on mobile eye viewpoint recording. *JOSA*, *50*(8), pp. 763–768.

Sibert, J.L., Gokturk, M. and Lavine, R.A., 2000, November. The reading assistant: eye gaze triggered auditory prompting for reading remediation. In *Proceedings of the 13th Annual ACM Symposium on User Interface Software and Technology* (pp. 101–107). San Diego, CA USA: ACM.

Sibley, C., Coyne, J. and Baldwin, C., 2011, September. Pupil dilation as an index of learning. In *Proceedings of the Human Factors and Ergonomics Society Annual Meeting* (Vol. 55, No. 1, pp. 237–241). Los Angeles, CA: SAGE Publications.

Slotta, J.D., and Linn, M.C., 2009. *WISE Science: Web-based Inquiry in the Classroom. Technology, Education--Connections*. New York, NY: Teachers College Press.

Smith, J.R., Cronin, M.J. and Karacan, I., 1971. A multichannel hybrid system for rapid eye movement detection (REM detection). *Computers and Biomedical Research*, *4*(3), pp. 275–290.

Stern, J.A. and Skelly, J.J., 1984, October. The eye blink and workload considerations. In *Proceedings of the Human Factors Society Annual Meeting* (Vol. 28, No. 11, pp. 942–944). Los Angeles, CA: SAGE Publications.

Stone, B., Lee, M., Dennis, S. and Nettelbeck, T., 2004. Pupil size and mental load. In *1st Adelaide Mental Life Conference*.

Suppes, P., 1990. Eye-movement models for arithmetic and reading performance. *Eye Movements and Their Role in Visual and Cognitive Processes*, *4*, pp. 455–477.

Tinker, M.A., 1963. *Legibility of Print*. Ames, Iowa: Iowa State University Press.

Tobii Pro, 2020a. Education. Accessed from www.tobiipro.com/fields-of-use/education/. [Accessed on April 2020].

Tobii Pro, 2020b. Tools to deal with the shift to industry 4.0. Accessed from www.tobiipro.com/blog/tools-deal-with-shift-to-industry-4–0/. [Accessed on April 2020].

Treisman, A.M. and Gelade, G., 1980. A feature-integration theory of attention. *Cognitive Psychology*, *12*(1), pp. 97–136.

van Gog, T. and Jarodzka, H., 2013. Eye tracking as a tool to study and enhance cognitive and metacognitive processes in computer-based learning environments. In *International Handbook of Metacognition and Learning Technologies* (pp. 143–156). New York, NY: Springer.

Van Gog, T. and Scheiter, K., 2010. Eye tracking as a tool to study and enhance multimedia learning. *Learning and instruction*, *20*(2), pp.95–99.

Veltman, J.A. and Gaillard, A.W.K., 1998. Physiological workload reactions to increasing levels of task difficulty. *Ergonomics*, *41*(5), pp. 656–669.

ςιχτορ Μανυελ, ςιχτορ Μ. Γαρχ⬋α–Βαρριοσ, Χηριστιαν Γ✓τλ, Αλεξανδρα Πρεισ, Κειτη Ανδρεωσ, Μαφα Πιϖεχ, Φελιξ Μ⬀δριτσχηερ ανδ Χηριστιαν Τρυμμερ, 2004. ΑδΕΛΕ: Α φραμεωορκ φορ αδαπτιϖε ε–λεαρνινγ τηρουγη εψε τραχκινγ. Ιν *Προχεεδινγσ οφ ΙΚΝΟΩ 2004* (ππ. 609∝616).

Ware, C. and Mikaelian, H.T., 1987. An evaluation of an eye tracker as a device for computer input. In: *Proceedings of the ACM CHI+GI'87 Human Factors in Computing Systems Conference* (pp. 183–188).

Was, C., Sansosti, F. and Morris, B. (Eds.), 2016. *Eye-Tracking Technology Applications in Educational Research*. IGI Global.

Wickens, C.D., 2008. Multiple resources and mental workload. *Human Factors*, *50*(3), pp. 449–455.

Wickens, C.D., Hollands, J.G., Banbury, S., and Parasuraman, R., 2013. *Engineering Psychology and Human Performance* (4th ed.). Boston, MA: Pearson Education, Inc.

Wisskirchen, G., Biacabe, B.T., Bormann, U., Muntz, A., Niehaus, G., Soler, G.J. and von Brauchitsch, B., 2017. Artificial intelligence and robotics and their impact on the workplace. *IBA Global Employment Institute*, pp. 2012–2017.

Yarbus, A.L., 1967. *Eye Movements and Vision*. New York: Plenum Press.

26

Mobile Applications for Industrial Use

Devaraj Sambandan and T. Devi

CONTENTS

26.1 Mobile Communication in Industry 4.0

Industry 4.0 (i-scoope.eu, 2020) is powered by digital technologies such as artificial intelligence (AI), augmented reality, the Internet of Things (IoT), and smart factories that drive the gathering of tremendous amounts of real-time data to enable Big Data analytics/machine learning/AI processes to make informed decisions in real time. Using information technologies, the systems, humans, machines, and resources can communicate with one another by bridging the physical and digital worlds that blur the lines between them. Mobile communication technologies play a critical role in implementing Industry 4.0 concepts and form the backbone of all smart factories that allow communication with machines,

DOI: 10.1201/9781003318378-26

systems, and human resources in remote locations without the use of any physical connection wires or cables. Mobile communication technologies also enable real-time integration of people, processes, and systems, enabling higher operational efficiencies at a reduced cost, and industries who deploy these digital tools achieve enormous benefits including the following.

1. More efficient workflows enable substantial increases in resource efficiency and productivity.
2. Predicting the possibility of failure in machine/parts and performing proactive servicing and replacement results in manufacturing continuity.
3. Near zero-touch factory operations and streamlined decision-making processes.
4. Controlled supply chains, inventory, and warehousing results in significant annual savings with higher profit margins.

Industry 4.0 demands greater communication and real-time interactions with machines and processes, that can be enabled only by Mobile Communications. Mobile communications bring in the following advantages compared to traditional wired technology for Industry 4.0 (Nekovee, 2019):

1. Mobility: The ease of carrying a mobile phone/tablet has a great advantage when compared to traditional laptop/personal computers used in industry, as mobile communication technology enables seamless communication between the people, machines, systems, and resources.
2. Cost-benefit: Cost is reduced in mobile communication, as it reuses existing technology than building a dedicated communication interface.
3. Remote access: Mobile communication technology and internal sensors of cell phones gives the ability to measure anything in the remote work field.
4. Network connectivity: Mobile network connectivity ensures that people can be reached by anybody or any internal or external system rapidly.

Mobile communication technologies are realized by mobile device platforms such as mobile phones and tablets; they have already been an indispensable part of everyone's daily lives. Mobile applications (Wikipedia, 2020) are kinds of application software that are designed and developed to run on a mobile device platform such as a smartphone or tablet. Mobile applications are characterized by a small software image footprint; the ability to run in less powerful processors, consuming low battery power; and a user interface designed to be simpler and more intuitive considering the wider categories of end users (Figure 26.1). Mobile apps undeniably have become an indispensable part of everyday life and their usage scenarios are unlimited and

FIGURE 26.1 Mobile applications.

unending cutting across all parts of personal life. Manufacturing industries are also realizing the scope of what mobility solutions and industrial mobile applications can do for their business and how it could play an essential role to empower the Industry 4.0 communication, as mobile applications are cost-effective, are easy to roll out to end users' mobile devices, and can be made more intuitive for simplified operations.

26.2 Mobile Communication Technology

As mobile applications are used for more and more complex use cases, the need for high speed and network bandwidth in mobile communication technology becomes very important. Mobile communications technology (Mobile Communications, European Telecom Standards Institute [ETSI]) has evolved through multiple generations starting from 1G (first generation) based on analog technology to digital technology 2G (second generation) to the most advanced 5G (fifth generation) technology. As mobile applications and smartphones become more sophisticated supporting wider use cases, the need for increased network bandwidth becomes more and more important resulting in developing next-generation technology 4G (fourth generation) and 5G.

26.2.1 4G LTE

4G Long Term Evolution (LTE) technology (4G Specifications, ETSI) offers increased speed and capacity based on Internet Protocol (IP)-based mobile network architecture which enabled most sophisticated mobile devices and mobile applications to become part of everyone's life. 4G LTE supports 300 Mbit/s peak downlink rate with support for peak download speed of 150 Mbps and 75 Mbps peak uplink rate with support for peak upload speed of 50 Mpbs. 4G LTE specification also provides data transfer latency of less than 50 ms, which enables real-time mobile applications usage such as video conferencing, gaming, and high definition video streaming.

26.2.2 5G

5G technology (5G Specifications, ETSI) is proposed to deliver higher performance in terms of higher upload and download data rates/speeds, ultra-low latency, increased spectral capacity, high reliability and availability, and a superior and more uniform user experience like a fixed network. With these features, 5G shall empower the manufacturing industries to leverage more and more mobile applications based on mobile phones/tablets for realizing its use cases covering factories, plant floors, supply chains, and warehouses, and to have a whole new user experience for staff by connecting them to new industries (Figure 26.2). 5G shall become de facto technology for realizing Industry 4.0 use cases by interconnecting everyone and everything to the internet. 5G deployment use cases are grouped into three different classes which will empower Industry 4.0 adoptions, along with other use cases. The industry working group of the 3GPP (Third Generation Partnership Project) is developing standards for radio technology components that will accelerate Industry 4.0 connectivity requirements for manufacturing industry elements such as sensors, robots to support massive connectivity, ultra-low latency, and ultra-reliability. 5G standards are currently under development as interim solutions 5G shall be deployed along with 4G LTE technology to form NSA (non-standalone) deployment; once the 5G technology matures, it will be deployed in SA (standalone) configuration. 5G use cases are grouped into three different classes (Samsung, 2018) which will empower Industry 4.0 adoptions.

5G use cases for massive machine-type communications within a factory with around one million connected devices per square kilometer, ultra-reliable and low-latency use cases for automated cars and machinery with 1 ms latency and 10^{-9} error rate, enhanced broadband connectivity for 8K videos with a peak speed of 20 Gbps.

26.2.2.1 Enhanced Mobile Broadband

5G supports enhanced mobile broadband with a peak download rate of 20 Gb/s and 2,560 MB/s, and peak upload rate of 10 Gb/s and 1280 MB/s, thereby enabling rich experience virtual reality (VR) and

FIGURE 26.2 5G Use cases.

augmented reality (AR). This enhanced speed and upload/download throughput shall enable mobile applications supporting VR/AR to be made available in various Industry 4.0 use cases.

26.2.2.2 Massive Machine-Type Communications

Industrial devices such as industrial sensors, actuators, and machines could be connected to the internet using wireless technology forming IoT. 5G architecture shall enable the deployment of massive machine-type communications of autonomous devices and other types of machinery that are not directly controlled by humans, thereby empowering Industry 4.0 adaptations such as mobile applications for real-time monitoring of machines, optimization of their performance to suit the requirements, workplace safety monitoring, and industrial automation.

26.2.2.3 Ultra-Reliable and Low-Latency Communications (URLLC)

URLLC is the main driving technology for enabling the Industry 4.0 revolution. Industrial automation processes and machinery require an end-to-end network communication latency from mobile applications deployed in factory remote locations to centralized cloud applications to be lower than 1 ms and also must provide high reliability for data communications.

26.2.2.4 Private LTE/5G Deployments

The main challenge for realizing Industry 4.0 use cases by using mobile operator-owned 4G LTE and 5G networks is concerns about reliability, low latency, service quality, security, and compliance (Christine Jorgensen, 2019). This could be solved by industries by using a local 4G LTE/5G network in an organization by deploying private radio access network (RAN) equipment to service a bigger factory with custom mobile sims and LTE/5G core applications.

The use of dedicated RAN equipment (Hill, 2018) in factories allows it to be independent of traffic congestion when compared to the mobile operator-owned shared RAN. A private LTE network can be deployed in shared and unlicensed spectra, as well as locally dedicated licensed spectra, e.g., citizen broadband radio service (CBRS) priority access license (PAL) to empower the Industry 4.0 use cases which require low latency in very dense deployments with robotics, sensors, and other types of machinery supporting IoT applications and services; the private LTE network can be tailored for more optimized performance such as low latency (Figure 26.3).

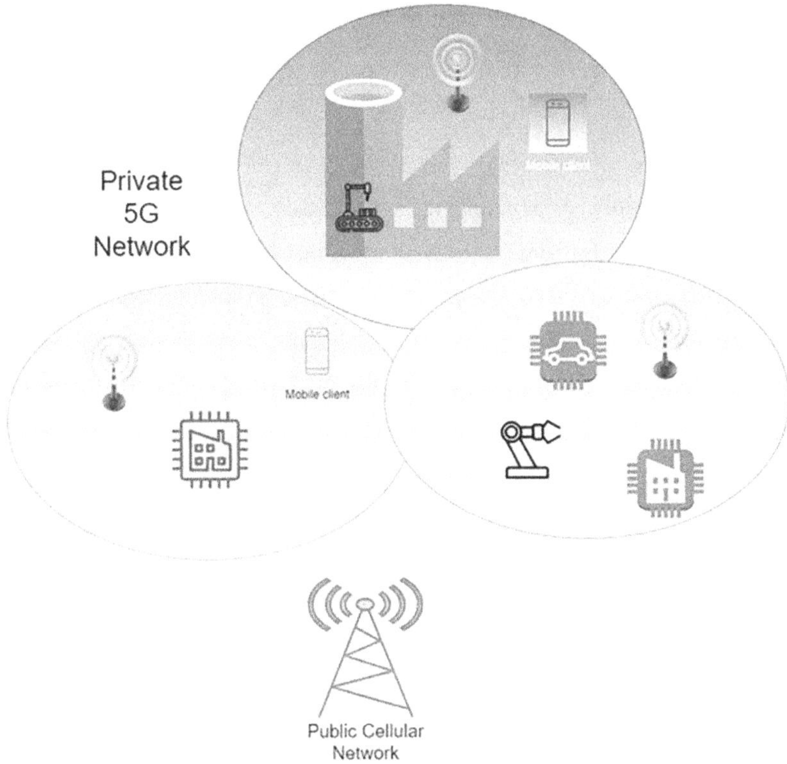

FIGURE 26.3 Private 5G network.

26.3 Mobile Application Development Platform

Over a decade, multiple mobile operating systems and application development platforms have been introduced by different mobile manufacturing vendors, and unpopular or propriety application development platforms eventually got diminished and were consolidated into the following two major mobile operating systems and application development platforms.

26.3.1 iOS

Apple Inc. developed an operating system called iOS (Apple Inc., 2020) and also published a mobile application software development kit called iOS SDK to support application developers to develop various mobile applications that could run on any mobile devices/tablets that support the iOS operating system. iOS SDK provides tools/APIs to interface with mobile device/tablet hardware elements such as touch screen, fingerprint scanner, video camera, the digital assistant platform Siri, etc., which enables developers to build sophisticated applications and also to enable ease of mobile application development for Industry 4.0 use cases with Apple providing the application development platform in partnership with multiple hardware manufacturing vendors to control the sensors, robotic devices, and other manufacturing equipment.

26.3.2 Android

Another popular (Google Inc., 2020) and the most widely used mobile operating system is Android, developed by Google, Inc.; its Linux-based open-source mobile operating system is installed on multiple vendor mobile devices. The Android mobile application SDK is based on Java programming language and provides tools/APIs for developers to build generic mobile applications that could run on any mobile device that supports the Android operating system. Multiple developers are building SDKs that support Industry 4.0 use cases leveraging AR- and VR-based mobile applications.

26.4 Mobile Application for Industrial Use Cases

There are unlimited use cases that could be realized using mobile applications in the industrial domain. Following are some of the use cases (Lu, 2017) that derive enormous benefits if mobile applications are used for automation and communications between systems, machines, humans, and resources.

26.4.1 Electronic Documentation/Paperwork Elimination

In the industrial world, almost everything must be documented and reported daily. The human workforce typically uses notebooks or forms, kanban cards, etc., for documenting all the activities. These manual paper documents burden the manufacturing workflows with countless manual tasks like hand-delivering forms to be typed again on a computer and saved into the database, filing documents, and so on. These manual, tedious tasks often result in detrimental delays and managers must wait until the end of the day to view the reports, making it difficult to run a lean operation. More than 80% of small to mid-sized manufacturing plants are still using paper forms and manual keyboard data entry to track their inventory and manufacturing operations (Green, 2019).

By using mobile applications to replace manufacturing forms, industry can more expediently gather critical manufacturing data, resulting in improved efficiencies, more timely insights, and increased communication. Mobile applications could be used to replace all paper forms that are used in industrial use cases such as creating quotes, filling timesheets, processing work orders, documenting inspection points, collecting briefings notes, quality assurance checklists, production/incident/accident reports, equipment maintenance/monitoring logs, inventory details, etc.

26.4.2 Employee Tracking

Over the decades, organizations evaluated the performance of their staffs by collecting data related to their work such as working hours, quality of the deliverables, wastages created, number of units manufactured, etc., using the traditional approach of paper-based worksheets and then feeding those collected data at the end of the day to centralized computer systems. Achieving the organization goal of an employee performance evaluation using a traditional mode of paper-based timesheet tracking is inefficient and does not support all flexibility that mobile application–based employee tracking systems provide. Employee-tracking mobile applications could provide multiple features such as GPS tracking of the location of the employee, mobile attendance, geofencing, routing location-based services ticketing, etc. GPS tracking apps enable tracking the physical locations of employees to ensure that the right employee is at the right place to work by support tracking using remote locations. Mobile attendance apps enable employees to clock in and out from anywhere using their mobile and also with built-in face recognition technology to check and verify the employee face as an extended feature. Geofencing enables tracking employees and raising alerts if they enter specific geographical areas and which could be used for workplace safety management and security.

26.4.3 Inventory/Asset and Supply Chain Management

By using mobile applications for inventory and supply chain management, manufacturers would be able to simplify the supply chain process and ensure that vendors have more control and accessibility over the inventory to better manage supply and operations planning, better optimize logistics and inventory management, and better provide actionable business intelligence that improves decision making.

Traditionally, these were done using computers, along with additional scanning devices, but using applications running on smartphones or tablets with support for barcode/QR (quick response) code scan enables an easy and more portable way to track the inventories in the remote locations or the stores wherever they are, rather than moving those inventories to a central location for scanning. Mobile applications provide greater benefit and are better suited when the supply management tasks are performed outside of the office (in the field, in the warehouse, on the factory floor) as mobile phones or tablets can be easily carried along.

26.4.4 Mobile Work Order Management

Mobile applications for work order management provide all the details for maintenance tasks directly on a mobile phone or tablet, to help technicians in the factory enter data, communicate, and complete work efficiently without having to wait until the end of the day to update all the tasks into centralized systems. Traditional paperwork orders or email work orders are inefficient and filled with errors, while work order mobile apps enable organizations to know where the field workers are and what they are doing in real time. The board and automated alerts keep the back office updated on job status whether they are on the way, on a factory floor, or finished. The mobile application could interface directly with the centralized order management system and enable field technicians to organize work orders and update their status whenever they are resolved. Map integration shows at a glance where the technicians are without having to make several calls, resulting in real-time visibility and accurate data, helping the industrial organizations become more efficient and grow.

26.4.5 Quality Assurance and Quality Control

Traditionally, quality assurance and quality control are managed using a paper-based checklist with technicians filling them for every batch of production orders. Using mobile applications for quality assurance and quality control processes makes it easy to manage every step of the quality assurance process to make continuous improvements in efficiency and product quality. Quality technicians can conduct in-process inspections of items in real time as they flow down the production line to ensure that any variation is within the limit of quality specifications of product requirements, and collect crucial data needed for audit reports which can automatically be emailed or to be stored in the cloud systems. Engineers could routinely monitor the product design, detect problems, and identify where quality improvement through corrective measures are advised and where corrective action is needed using real-time data, thereby enabling lean manufacturing practices at different locations.

26.4.6 Remote Monitoring and Diagnosis

With industries equipped with smartphones and having mobile applications for remote monitoring and diagnosis, the workforce can access anything everything from anywhere and at any time, and can maximize manufacturing time by having intelligent mobile workloads for remote monitoring. Remote monitoring enables mobile workflows, digitization of information, and knowledge capture, which can help improve a manufacturing facility's uptime by as much as 30%. A field service technician and the mobile worker could walk around and connect a mobile phone via Bluetooth to a particular sensor to retrieve diagnostic information and review the status of the equipment to check whether it is functioning appropriately and proactively transfer all the pieces of information to the centralized system to enable predictive maintenance.

26.4.7 Employee Health and Workplace Safety

Employee health and safety mobile apps will enable workers and supervisors to calculate weather conditions and optimal temperature of the work area, identify the symptoms and make educated decisions on health risk levels. Mobile apps could display warnings of possible threats for workers using AR or VR to enable workers to classify hazardous equipment or chemicals and the precautionary measures that workers must take in using or handling the equipment or chemicals. The app could also provide a simplified user interface to indicate information in a concise form rather than a bulky and lengthy physical manual, and could help first responders to provide aid in a timely fashion. The employee and workplace safety app could also track workers' activities and movements, and provide indications at constant intervals requesting them to take a short rest, perform breathing exercises, etc. The employee health safety mobile applications could also help workers during travels, providing location-aware services such as local environmental changes, nearby hospitals/insurance agent details, etc., Mobile safety apps are expected to become commonplace in the workplace, and the number of safety incidents across the country will likely decline as a result. Mobile safety applications open the door to improved coordination and a more proactive approach to risk management.

26.4.8 Automation of Company Processes

Business process automation mobile apps are essential for the success of organizations that are following Industry 4.0 tools and processes mainly to accelerate workforce activities/processes, increase overall productivity, reduce quality concerns or issues, increase communication between different business units within/across the organization, and overall increase customer satisfaction with the product/services offered.

Mobile applications can enable companies to automate nearly almost all their business processes and workflows which are more related to document management covering order processing, supply chain and warehousing, purchase orders and invoice management, payments, credits, and more, reducing the manual and error-prone processes.

26.5 Advantages of Mobile Applications in Industry 4.0

Following are the major advantages of using mobile applications in Industry 4.0 (Innovapptive, 2020):

26.5.1 Mobility

Mobile applications eliminate the need to use fixed desktop computers for updating the status of a task or retrieve any information/notifications; instead, they enable the staff to use the mobile application whenever they are on the factory floor.

26.5.2 Instantaneous Access to Information and Processes

Mobile apps enable end users to instantly access information and processes from anywhere on the factory floor, and they allow the central office team to be alerted instantly of issues in real time that enable them to act instantly instead of reacting after the event, thereby improving overall quality and customer relationships.

26.5.3 Workforce Productivity

Mobile applications can lead to better productivity as mobile applications are easy to understand and use for business process applications, eliminating the need for training the workforce on any new systems/processes using traditional desktop-based applications.

26.5.4 Precision Monitoring

Mobile applications support real-time GPS location monitoring from centralized systems where the mobile application could constantly update the location of the mobile device holder, thereby providing precision details on when the goods are arriving at a warehouse, etc.

26.5.5 Operational Benefits

Using mobile applications enables organizations to increase operational benefits such as reduced capital expenditures on centralized systems or workstations and increase return on investments in developing the mobile applications.

26.6 Summary

Mobile applications play an essential role in Industry 4.0 to ensure a seamless way to connect and communicate with machines using cloud applications, creating an agile, responsive, and truly collaborative environment. Mobile applications can be employed to unlimited use cases of Industry 4.0—since mobile applications have already become part of everyone's daily lives, they are cost-effective and easy to adapt. To enable ease of mobile application development for Industry 4.0 use cases, complete ecosystems are developed covering 5G technology, application development platforms in partnership with multiple mobile hardware manufacturing vendors. Mobile applications leveraging this new technology shall enable the adoption of Industry 4.0 use cases rapidly, and thereby bring enormous benefits to the manufacturing sector.

REFERENCES

Apple Inc., 2020. Apple IOS, Application developer documentation, https://developer.apple.com/documentation/ [Accessed 16 April 2020]

Christine Jorgensen, 2019. Private LTE/5G networks: A primer for developers, https://developer.qualcomm.com/blog/private-lte5g-networks-primer-developers [Accessed 20 April 2020]

ETSI. 4G Specifications, www.etsi.org/technologies/mobile/4g, [Accessed 16 April 2020]

ETSI. 5G Specifications, www.etsi.org/technologies/mobile/5g, [Accessed 16 April 2020]

ETSI. Mobile Communications, www.etsi.org/technologies/mobile [Access 16 April 2020]

Google Inc., 2020. Android, Application developer guide, https://developer.android.com/guide [Accessed 16 April 2020]

Green, Dr. Peter, 2019. Economics of replacing paper forms with barcode scanning for tracking manufacturing operations [Accessed 20 April 2020]

Hill, Kelly, 2018. Private LTE: Making the enterprise future-ready, RCR-Wireless-Report-July-2018

Innovapptive, 2020. Main benefits of mobility in manufacturing, www.innovapptive.com/blog/industry-4-0-mobility-in-manufacturing

i-scoope.eu, 2020. Industry 4.0 guide: The fourth industrial revolution guide to Industrie 4.0, www.i-scoop.eu/industry-4-0/, [Accessed 16 April 2020]

Lu, Yang, 2017. Industry 4.0: A survey on technologies, applications and open research issues

Nekovee, Maziar, 2019. What is 5G and how will it accelerate industry 4.0? www.thefuturefactory.com/blog/19 [Accessed 16 April 2020]

Samsung, 2018. 5G Is now, part 1: 2018, the year of 5G, www.samsung.com/global/business/networks/insights/news/5g-is-now-part-1-2018-the-year-of-5g/ [Accessed 18 April 2020]

Wikipedia, 2020. Mobile app, https://en.wikipedia.org/wiki/Mobile_app [Accessed 16 April 2020]

27

Cognitive Flexibility: Know-How

Sadhasivam Subramaniam

CONTENTS

Objectives

The term "cognitive flexibility" was invented by psychologists in 1960, and is used frequently in literature. During the conventional era, cognitive or mental flexibility was considered to be the person's ability to adjust oneself to a different task or environment. With further explorations in cognitive science and brain research, the concept of cognitive flexibility has considerably evolved over time. This chapter is intended to summarize the definition of cognitive flexibility, related theories, characteristics, neuronal perspectives, and different ways to improve cognitive flexibility for educational applications.

27.1 Definition and Overview of Cognitive Flexibility

Cognitive flexibility (CF) is a specialized skill that denotes the neural capacity of a person to focus on different tasks or understand concepts simultaneously. It is also defined as a proven ability to perform more than one task, engaging two different concepts at the same time. CF is defined as one's ability to shift between different tasks or strategies (Miyake and Friedman 2012). In other words, it is also explained by the characteristics of the stimulus, responses, perspectives, or strategies during the ability to shift attention between a pair of tasks (Zelazo 2015). In this process, the shift in cognitive thinking is

DOI: 10.1201/9781003318378-27

possibly mediated by stimuli demands; hence, CF is generally regarded as the prime executive function. The reason for its description as an executive function is explained by its unique way of adjusting our behavior to the given situation with improved results.

Based on the nature of changes that occurred in CF with respect to conscious and unconscious conditions, it is further sub-classified into task switching and cognitive shifting. From the neuroscience perspective, it is also called by different names, viz., cognitive shifting, mental flexibility, attention switching, etc. CF has a considerable role in regular tasks and everyday learning. It is often found that those who are not attentive also had problems with cognitive flexibility. From the synthetic point of research, CF can be seen from different frameworks, and it will significantly vary during the developmental stages or the lifespan of an individual. Based on theoretical conceptualization, the characteristic feature of CF is how effectively one can apply their prior perceived response, knowledge, or beliefs into the new situation, or applying things learned, while undertaking new tasks. In the simplest terms, it could be considered as an instantaneous approach to an idea or objective, to derive multiple aspects of a single problem.

After a detailed review of the prior research, different dimensions of CF are stated in the present chapter. It could be either dealing with multiple aspects of a specific objective or analyzing a complex situation. Some examples are given below to better visualize the concept of CF. Assume watching programs on TV, and if one is often stuck with a particular program or a channel, it is considered as mental inflexibility or cognitive rigidness. On the other hand, if one is capable of switching between different programs or channels and makes random choices, the person could be regarded as "cognitively flexible". Even among two individuals with different levels of CF, the one who can complete the assigned task in a shorter time would be determined with a high level of CF. Though both are cognitively fit, an individual's brain that could respond and adapt to the new stimuli is the finest. Specific laboratory tests are carried out to understand CF using task-switching paradigms. The method is to prove the cognitive cost in between the multiple tasks, and it is quantified by the phenomena called "switch cost". It explains the difference in performance among the individuals while switching tasks with respect to reaction time or error rate.

27.2 Cognitive Flexibility Theory

Few theories explain how they approached or framed the knowledge structures behind the formulation of cognitive flexibility theories. Cognitive Flexibility Theory (CFT) is an important one among many cognitive theories, as it deals with complex and ill-structured knowledge domains, in contrast to the well-structured domains in the form of linear or hierarchical formats (Spiro et al. 1988). There is another famous theory known as progressive transformation procedure that explains the condition of structural flexibility by forcing the learner to differentiate the similarities, as well as differences, during problem-solving (Steiner and Stoecklin 1997). It is further said that preserving structural flexibility is crucial during the learning process, and the learners have to understand the concepts or rules by themselves, rather than being instructed by the mentor or teacher (Spiro and Jehng 1990; Spiro et al. 1989), "By cognitive flexibility, we mean the ability to spontaneously restructure one's knowledge, in many ways, in the adaptive response to radically changing situational demands". The theory keenly demonstrates the use of acquired knowledge and skills in multiple perspectives with different examples. This theory also stated the effective use of learner's ideas and thoughts for a better learning experience.

There is another exciting theory, formulated by Spiro et al. (1989). The basis of this theory is to understand the concepts through different contexts, purposes, times, and roles. Hence, it opposes the concept of oversimplification, assuming that the learning in multiple perspectives would deliver the knowledge in a more transferable way. For example, certain ill-structured domains such as complex concepts, irregularity, and cases with large variability play a vital role in advanced knowledge acquisition. In such conditions, if one applies multiple perspectives in understanding the concepts, one could better explore the conceptual map in multiple ways. That is one easy way to improve expert flexibility. When students deals with such domains, the instructional design should force them to adapt critical analysis, perspective thinking, and problem framing for a better and flexible representation of a crisis. The theory implies that every teaching practice should engage a certain level of complexity in knowledge transmission, application, decision-making, and the responding time. It will help the learners to practice decision-making and deal with the uncertainty of day-to-day events.

27.2.1 Cognitive Flexibility Theory—Application and Case Study

When applying CFT, the following principles need to be considered: (a) the learning content should be offered in multiple formats; (b) instruction material should be minimal information without affecting the knowledge context; (c) it should not be merely information-oriented, but rather, case-oriented; and (d) knowledge source must be interlinked, rather than being singular. The main application of CFT is mostly used in history, literature, biology, and medicine by using interactive technology tools like videos and hypertext. The implementation of CFT was applied in transfusion medicine using a hypertext program (Jonassen et al. 1992). The program offers different clinical cases to the students to diagnose and report, using various sources of information. However, the learning setting has to be involved and designed with a particular difficulty level, which in turn forces the learners to decode the complexity of the learning process.

The impact of CFT was tested in 21 select trainee teachers from the University of Haifa, Israel, who taught literature for high school and junior high school students (Eilam and Poyas 2006). The objective of this study was to understand the role of CF in messy classroom situations. For that, the study has introduced a new internet-based training course for one semester, and the trainees were assessed before and after the intervention. The online course included five video cases, which were taken in real literature classrooms, and consisted of all the necessary information about the school, teacher, students, and curriculum, and the materials. The participants were also permitted to explore the university library, teacher intervention, external expertise, and access to web forums. In the end, the teachers were requested to provide a response describing the involvement of various contextual factors, their inter-relation, and interactions on the teaching and learning process in the said conditions. After the intervention, it was found that novice teachers demonstrated better control over complex classroom situations.

27.3 Factors Influencing Cognitive Flexibility

Based on CF theories, mental transition ability is the key tactic, but one mostly unattainable because of several biological and psychological factors. Even though many of them have multi-faceted abilities, they fail to apply knowledge in utterly discrete concepts. The list of possible elements that influence CF is discussed in the subsections which follow, to better understand the various dimensions of cognitive performance.

27.3.1 Stream of Consciousness and Multi-Perspective Analysis

According to William James, the 'stream of consciousness' is a description of the continuous delivery of an uninterrupted flow of ideas or thoughts in a more logical way (James 1884). "Consciousness is not merely transmitting the information, but also producing, assembling and processing information through self, attention and working memory". The stream of consciousness is "individuated", i.e., the person who experiences the consciousness can be cognitively flexible, whereas the other who just passively indulges in the process may not be so. In this context, CF could be regarded as the ability to observe various elements of the environment, and effectively present them in complex situations. Mental flexibility is dependent on the various executive function of the brain—viz., set-shifting or shift-task, working memory, inhibition and conflict monitoring, and manifesting the multitude of information sources from the point of stressor experience—as a coping strategy is a well-productive sign of cognitive performance.

27.3.2 Rigid Thinking and Deconstruction

Rigid thinking is a state of mind that implies unwillingness to act upon the new situation with respect to perceived thoughts and beliefs. Such personalities are less emphatic because they have difficulty in understanding other's perspectives and emotions. It is believed that mental inflexibility is the core reason, and it obstinately blocks the appropriate behavioral changes to adapt to a new or challenging situation. The term "deconstruction" can be viewed from different perspectives, but in the context of CF, it is to simplify the complex problem or thought and to visualize how the fragmented piece of information can be used to form intricate concepts. In other words, it also aims to identify the special element in the complex concept, and further explore it with other existing concepts, or develop new concepts.

27.3.3 Cognitive Domains

There are several cognitive domains such as memory, reasoning, attention, and flexibility that can influence the degree of CF. Memory is designated to secure and retrieve the information when needed safely. The term "reasoning" can be defined as the adjustment of the neural capacity in a new situation in flexible ways. This is also termed as "fluid intelligence". If the individual is showing the ability to reason fluidly, they are more likely to be cognitively flexible. The third important domain, attention, is used to regulate one's behavior during the process of distraction and putting oneself on track. Finally, flexibility can be defined as the ability of cognition, timely effortless shift between the dual concepts and thinking multiple concepts concurrently. Hence, CF is not just the single thing that governs the executing function of the brain and regulates the thinking process. Overall, it is the administration of the sum of mental abilities like inhibition, planning, organization, emotional stability, and working memory. The cognitively flexible individual can either use or inhibit the particular domain for the successful completion of tasks. CF represents not only the executive function, but also influences the other aspects of cognition, like reading fluency and comprehension. The cognitively flexible individual can simultaneously think about the sounds and meanings to improve reading fluency and comprehension. CF focuses mainly on the situations, rather than the stressors that will define the person's ability to cope-up with the specific condition.

27.3.4 Genetic Basis of Cognitive Flexibility

The salience network (SN) and fronto-parietal network (FPN) contribute the majority of functional intrinsic brain networks and thought to have greater control over goal-oriented behavior. The neurological basis of limited cognition is well demonstrated in an individual with autism, autism spectrum disorder (ASD) and obsessive-compulsive disorder (OCD). Further, exploring the genetic basis of an individual with limited CF may fetch more in-depth information and identify the role of neurobiological connection. Age is an essential element that can either positively or negatively influence CF, and it will continue to change throughout the individual's lifespan. The other neural defects, such as OCD or other cognitive disorders, can have severe implications for CF.

27.3.5 Latent Inhibition

Latent inhibition explains our brain's reaction to a familiar stimulus like preconceived images, sounds, and smells. For example, when hearing an ambulance siren, a driver would naturally slow down their vehicle, and leave the way for the ambulance. In such a context, one may not give serious attention to the type of vehicle. These types of events are classified under "familiar stimuli", and do not require any additional or constant neural processing; whereas, if one is exposed to a new place, or watch a new movie, the brain processes its full details and seizes the attention. Such events are termed as "new stimuli". In the case of low latent inhibition (LLI), the person treats both the familiar stimuli and new stimuli in the same way. It does not mean that they take extra time to even process the usual things; instead, they try to understand the stimulus better and look for more logical connections. Hence, an individual with LLI is naturally gifted, and also possesses a high IQ that helps to process the stimuli continuously. At the same time, LLI without sufficient IQ may result in poor cognitive conditions like autism. Hence, LLI individuals are rapid learners, with increased awareness of their surroundings, and can better adapt to any situation without fussing about it. Similarly, they also suffer from some drawbacks like being easily frustrated, facing difficulty in sleeping (because of constant processing) and losing interest in very linear instructions.

27.4 Neural Mechanism of Cognitive Flexibility

It is strongly believed that specific brain regions are actively engaged in CF tasks and mediate the different aspects of neural processing, i.e., working memory, attention, inhibition, response selection, and goal maintenance. Hence, neuroscientists are eager to understand the activity/role of specific brain regions, during the CF tasks by functional magnetic resonance imaging (fMRI) scans. It is said that the brain regions or neural networks such as basal ganglia, prefrontal cortex (PFC), anterior cingulate cortex (ACC), and posterior parietal cortex (PPC) have played central roles in the demonstration of CF. However, brain changes are significantly varied, depending on the age of the person and the degree of neural functionality. Children also show enhanced CF and increased regional gray matter and myelination, as was observed in adults. In contrast, elders are often cognitively deficient, because of the changes in brain anatomy, viz., loss of white matter integrity and brain volume. People with neurological disorders—viz., attention-deficit hyperactivity disorder (ADHD), autism, OCD, and schizophrenia—have shown reduced CF because of the declined brain functionality.

Various research has shown the neural network complexity in task-switching paradigms and the involvement of specific cognitive domains during a specific task, meaning that the activation of specific regions of the PFC is depended on the nature of the task and the test used. Some research has documented that the dorsolateral PFC modulates interference. Most experts believe that the PFC is the driving force behind CF. The basal ganglia are known to become active during the selection of responses, whereas the PPC is active as we update pre-existing information about how to perform a task. It may be too simplistic to assume that the mentioned areas are solely responsible for CF. If the person is having some repair in these brain regions, then it may significantly affect their CF.

An interesting laboratory-based CF test has proved that rats can exhibit better CF than mice, and can perform complex learning tasks with ease and productivity (Cressant et al. 2007). These results are not surprising if we can weigh the superior power of brain anatomy. It is explained because of thicker skulls with large surface areas in the rat (0.8–1.2 mm) as compared to skull thickness in mice (0.1–0.3 mm). Another reason is justified by the inherent feature (predator nature) of the rat, as it helps them to display novel stimuli in the new environments, whereas mice are prey in nature and displayed hatred to the obscure environment. The reduced motivation in mice is regulated by proximal cues, wherein the rat uses both proximal and distal cues flexibly for improved cognition. Besides, the rats displayed better spatial representation and long-term stability of place-cell firing and hippocampus place fields, which in turn help to achieve an effective spatial task performance. The rats are even superior to guinea pigs, rabbits, hedgehogs, and chickens, and can demonstrate a significant spatial learning ability because they use complex spatial strategies. Hence, rats can be used as an ideal model system to understand the cellular and synaptic mechanism in the exploration of CF.

In humans, the variations in temporal dynamics of neuronal activity will have a significant influence on the developmental differences in CF. To substantiate this claim, fMRI scans are taken to understand the response of temporal dynamics of neural activity in task switching (Wendelken et al. 2012). The study involves the understanding of neural activity between the two different rules: (a) remembering the rules or rule representation (repeat); and (b) rule switching between trails (switch) for the children (8–13 years) and adults (20–27 years). The fundamental role of the CF test is that the participants have to remember the cues (i.e., colors and shapes) and correctly remember both trials after a particular time interval. The behavioral analysis by fMRI has shown that adults are much faster and more precise than kids. The research further revealed that there is no difference between adults and kids in terms of using the brain regions, such as the dorsolateral PFC, left PPC, and left premotor cortex to perform both trails. However, the children take more time to complete the tasks because of their carryover neural activity from the previous task that had slowed down their neural activity. Although the children have displayed better developments in resolving conflict, the overall cognitive control will be gradually enhanced upon aging.

27.5 Improving Cognitive Flexibility—Implications and Suggestions

27.5.1 Revise or Alter Your Day-to-Day Routine

In the light of stated reviews and the series of analyses undertaken, the author proposes specific implications to improvise the CF of an individual in the following order. In routine circumstances, habitual behavior induces automatic responses which in fact result in limited CF (Zhou et al. 2020). One of the easy ways to alter the CF is by merely changing the daily routines, i.e., adjust your gym timing from morning to evening, take different commutes to reach your workplace and cook your meal alternatively, etc. It will result in better stimuli of neuronal pathways. Similarly, one can also add new aspects to routines to promote mental flexibility.

27.5.2 Do Things Innovatively and Practice Knowledge Transfer

Most of us are often comfortable and tend to think in practical ways. As a result, the psychologist Dr. Robert Sternberg (2003) has claimed that the students who do things in both practical and creative ways are not only efficient in academics but are also capable of applying their learning divergently. Henceforth, an innovative way of doing things will set the person free from the limited set of possibilities. Practice applying the knowledge that you have learned from one domain to another. It will establish new cognitive connections and thereby improve productivity. It is also suggested that citing different practical examples from a previously learned concept in one's way would also improve CF.

27.5.3 Engage in New Activities and Socialize More

CF will naturally improve when an individual is exposed to new stimuli. For instance, a few examples are visiting another country, deliberately incorporating an unfamiliar change in the work schedule, and revising the order of routine. To keep up the brain function for enhanced cognitive performance, the research suggests doing new things like learning a new language, playing a musical instrument, etc. As a result of such mental stimulation, the brain will develop a condition called "neuro-plasticity" whereby it undergoes the optimization of neural networks or remodeling of the neuro-synaptic organization for improved cognition and motor response. Neurogenesis is another scientific phenomenon that explains the growth of new neurons when exploring and completing new tasks. When we meet new people in different environments and listen to their perspectives, it will help the individual to reconstruct the rigid pattern of thinking. Further, the brain will secrete certain neuro-modulators like dopamine that will further activate a different set of genes that take part in learning and memory. Hence, the social connections outside your usual circle will have a positive impact on brain function and connectivity.

27.5.4 Videogames

It is believed that playing games will boost CF or performance as it presents several events, viz., learning from mistakes, divided attention, real-time processing of information and concise response time (Anderson and Bavelier 2011). Although games like Minecraft and Smartick Brain are not relevant to discuss here, as they are mainly for children. But if the adult has previously played such games, it will eventually help to show better math skills and overall academic performance. Studies have revealed that video games are a well-thought-out method to improve "mental flexibility", and the gamers who play the Total War, Call of Duty, and Battlefield franchises have shown greater CF than non-gamers (Colzato et al. 2013). However, there are certain severe limitations associated with video games, i.e., graphic content, excessive usage of eyes and fingers, long periods of sitting while playing, etc. For adults and elders, many online/offline "brain-fitness" games are available to sharpen their cognitive performance.

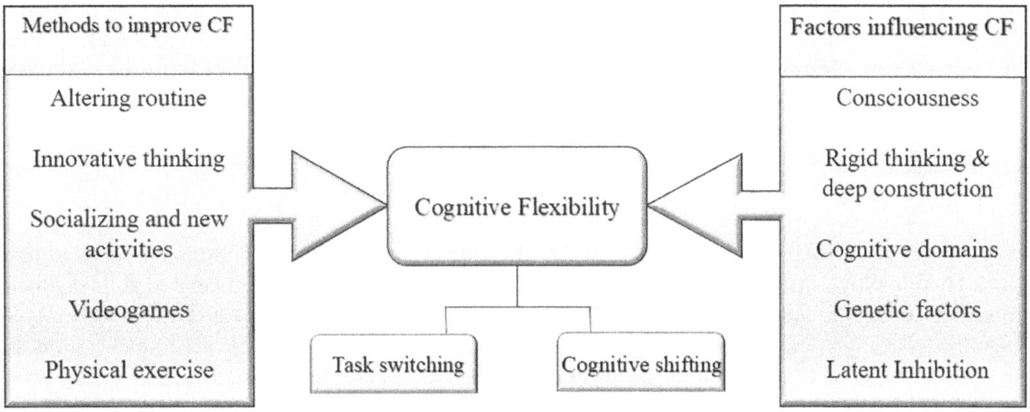

FIGURE 27.1 The conceptual framework of cognitive flexibility (CF). Cognitive flexibility can be divided into two types: task switching and cognitive shifting. The major factors influencing CF are consciousness, rapid thinking and deep construction, cognitive domains, genetic factors, and latent inhibition. The widely recommended methods which can improve CF are altering routines, engaging in innovative thinking, socializing in new activities, playing videogames, and practicing physical exercise.

27.5.5 Physical Exercise

It is apparent that any form of physical exercise (PE) will significantly improve the overall well-being of the human body. Similarly, more pieces of evidence suggest that even regular PE benefits executive functions like working memory, CF, and inhibitory control through the alteration of the structural, cellular, and molecular mechanisms (Mandolesi et al. 2018; Chen et al. 2020). The cellular changes include neurogenesis, glycogenesis, synaptogenesis, molecular variations comprised of a shift in the neurotransmission system, and increased neurotrophic factors. These studies have indicated the positive effects of PE, viz., enhanced cognitive, behavioral, and psychological abilities.

These elements that improve the CF are represented as a conceptual framework in Figure 27.1.

27.6 Significance of Cognitive Flexibility in Academia

CF will soon become the most important and must-have skill in academic platforms. The main principle of the educational policy is to prepare students to apply their learning process in simple daily living, as well as in complex scenarios. When CF practices are integrated into their curriculum, it will help students to be more attentive and to be a good thinkers. It is reported that preschool children who are subjected to such cognitive intervention demonstrated better inhibitory control and working memory. They scored the overall cognitive score of 85%, as compared to those children who had not undergone any intervention, and were subjected only to the school curriculum, with a score of 65%. When CF practices are followed early, their cognitive structures are significantly improved and allow them to be readily deliverable. Studies suggest that reflective thinking had a positive correlation for CF as an increase in reflective thinking increased CF. This positive effect will have a greater influence on autonomous learning which can be supported for development among students (Orakci 2021).

To improve the CF, "common core state standards initiative" has developed certain practices for high school students that demand a deep conceptual understanding of content knowledge, and application of skills in new situations. The teaching faculty should establish this sort of practice in such disciplines where the information is complex and non-linear. Cognitive flexibility hypertext (CFH) is an excellent type of instructional tool that offers the students to use their acquired knowledge in various environments because of its three-dimensional and "open-ended" material representations. In addition to CFH, adding problem-solving activities in the learning process will enhance brain power significantly. During such activities, the tutor should raise a question and look for multiple answers from the students by using their existing knowledge. Such discussion will open up a new way of foreseeing the situation from multiple perspectives. The cognitively flexible individual is highly desirable in academics and the workplace, as they can demonstrate excellent problem-solving skills in any critical situation.

27.7 Summary

Cognitive flexibility (CF) refers to our ability to disengage from one task and respond to another, or to think about multiple concepts at the same time. The person with lower CF is unable to shift the focus from one concept to another and is often described as being "stuck"; such persons have difficulty in adapting to changes and respond to the stimuli. By understanding the efficacy of CF, one can master sharpening attention to deal with the needs or demands of unforeseen circumstances. The higher a peron's CF, the better they are able to shift their attention or thoughts swiftly. Swift response to the shuttle between the concepts helps the person to get more new information. CF not only predicts the individual's adaptation rate toward the novel stimuli, but also helps to improve overall functioning of the brain. It helps in better comprehension, consciousness, and fluid intelligence. Employers highly prefer the person showing creativity and adaptability for future jobs. Hence, improving CF will maximize one's professional credibility and make them a better fit in the dynamics of the work environment.

REFERENCES

Anderson, A. and Bavelier, D. *Action game play as a tool to enhance perception, attention and cognition.* Charlotte, NC: IAP Information Age Publishing, 307–329.2011.

Chen, F.T., Etnier, J.L., Chan, K.H., Chiu, P.K., Hung, T.M. and Chang, Y.K. Effects of exercise training interventions on executive function in older adults: A systematic review and meta-analysis. *Sports Medicine*, 50, 1451–1467.2020.

Colzato, L.S., van den Wildenberg, W.P., Zmigrod, S. and Hommel, B. Action video gaming and cognitive control: Playing first person shooter games is associated with improvement in working memory but not action inhibition. *Psychological Research*, 77(2), 234–239.2013.

Cressant, A., Besson, M., Suarez, S., Cormier, A. and Granon, S. Spatial learning in long-evans hooded rats and C57BL/6J mice: Different strategies for different performance. *Behavioural Brain Research*, 177(1), 22–29.2007.

Eilam, B. and Poyas, Y. Promoting awareness of the characteristics of classrooms' complexity: A course curriculum in teacher education. *Teaching and Teacher Education*, 22(3), 337–351.2006.

James, W. On some omissions of introspective psychology. *Mind*, 9, 1–26.1884.

Jonassen, D., Ambruso, D. and Olesen, J. Designing hypertext on transfusion medicine using cognitive flexibility theory. *Journal of Educational Multimedia and Hypermedia*, 1(3), 309–322.1992.

Mandolesi, L., Polverino, A., Montuori, S., Foti, F., Ferraioli, G., Sorrentino, P. and Sorrentino, G. Effects of physical exercise on cognitive functioning and well-being: Biological and psychological benefits. *Frontiers in Psychology*, 9, 509.2018.

Miyake, A. and Friedman, N.P. The nature and organisation of individual differences in executive functions: Four general conclusions. *Current Directions in Psychological Science*, 21(1), 8–14.2012.

Orakci, Ş. Exploring the relationships between cognitive flexibility, learner autonomy, and reflective thinking tendency. *Thinking Skills and Creativity*, 100838.2021.

Spiro, R.J., Coulson, R.L., Feltovich, P.J. and Anderson, D. *Cognitive flexibility theory: Advanced knowledge acquisition in ill-structured domains.* Hillsdale, NJ: Erlbaum, 1988.

Spiro, R.J., Feltovich, P., Coulson, R.L. and Anderson, D.K. *Multiple analogies for complex concepts: Antidotes for analogy-induced misconception in advanced knowledge acquisition.* Cambridge, England: Cambridge University Press, pp. 498–531.1989.

Spiro, R.J. and Jehng, J. *Cognitive flexibility and hypertext: Theory and technology for the non-linear and multidimensional traversal of complex subject matter.* Hillsdale, NJ: Erlbaum, pp. 177–200.1990.

Steiner, G. F. and Stoecklin, M. Fraction calculation—A didactic approach to constructing mathematical networks. *Learning and Instruction*, 7(3), 211–233.1997.

Sternberg, R.J. What is an "expert student?". *Educational Researcher*, 32(8), 5–9.2003.

Wendelken, C., Munakata, Y., Baym, C., Souza, M. and Bunge, S.A. Flexible rule use: Common neural substrates in children and adults. *Developmental Cognitive Neuroscience*, 2(3), 329–339.2012.

Zelazo, P.D. Executive function: Reflection, iterative reprocessing, complexity, and the developing brain. *Developmental Review*, 38, 55–68.2015.

Zhou, X., Meng, Y., Schmitt, H. S., Montag, C., Kendrick, K.M. and Becker, B. Cognitive flexibility mediates the association between early life stress and habitual behavior. *Personality and Individual Differences*, 167, 110231.2020.

28

Education 4.0: Cognitive Flexibility

N. P. Komala Raveendra and R. K. Gowthami

CONTENTS

28.1 Introduction

The phrase "cognitive flexibility" (CF) was coined in the 1960s by psychologists,[1] and it became one of the most popular essential skills in recent modern times as we are quickly moving into a constantly changing dynamic world with rapid technological innovative disruptions in every domain. Initially, it was defined in terms of how well an individual can adopt another perspective, change one's thinking, or mentally adapt to one's environment.

Undoubtedly, it is a key life skill required for everyone who wishes to succeed in this complex volatile world, and it is a critical executive function used daily by all of us consciously or unconsciously. CF is a

DOI: 10.1201/9781003318378-28

core skill required for everyone to develop 21st-century skills like creativity, critical thinking, collaboration, and communication. It is impossible to dream of developing problem-solving skills and innovative or critical thinking patterns among individual students without CF skills. Hence, the top priority should be given to the *cognitive flexibility to rebuild today's educational echo system to suit the future global needs.*

28.2 What Does "Cognitive Flexibility" Mean?

CF means being flexible with one's thought process, thought patterns, and decisions, and the ability to see alternative ideas and perspectives by being able to modify and adjust one's thinking when presented with unexpected variables. It also means the mind's ability to switch between thinking about two different concepts and to think about multiple concepts simultaneously.

28.3 Definition

CF is defined as the ability to switch one's thinking (cognition, or train of thought) as an adaptation to the demands of stimuli. In neuroscience, the term is sometimes referred to as "attention switching," "cognitive shifting," "mental flexibility," "set-shifting," and "task switching."

The capability to be objectively flexible in action, to adapt to new situations and challenges, and to change strategies to encounter obstacles in everyday life effectively—and the ability to think creatively, critically, and innovatively—depends on the levels of CF skills one possesses.

28.4 What Is Cognitive Flexibility?

CF is the ability to think flexibly and shift mindsets easily. It refers to the brain's ability or capacity to think about two or more ideas or concepts simultaneously, and to switch (transition) from one to another appropriately when the situation demands. It is the ability to shift one's perspective and not to get stuck to a single perspective or a point of view. It is also the ability to perceive something in front of you in a new way.

It can be described as the mental ability to adjust to changing priorities and framing new perspectives by being able to shift from one perspective to another and one task to another task, without a lot of mental stress.

It can be described as one's mental ability to review one's plans and strategies, and move ahead when faced with new information, setbacks, mistakes, and unforeseen challenges. You can adapt when the circumstances change in your personal life, as well as your professional life. In a nutshell, it is the innate natural ability of an individual that enables them to adjust and change themselves to the ever-changing multiple needs at different stages in life.

This ability gets naturally developed in an individual during the course of life as one faces a series of various experiences—expected, as well as unexpected—from womb to tomb. Sometimes, like any other ability or skill, it can be consciously sharpened or developed very well to the extent one requires to meet the demands. Though this ability is present in all normal human individuals, the levels vary from person to person, depending on one's life's unique experiences and situations for which many factors are responsible.

28.5 Neural Mechanisms of Cognitive Flexibility

It is super amazing to think about the remarkable structural design and the architecture of our brain with countless neurons, neural connections, and neural pathways that are responsible for strengthening our

CF. Neurons make connections, connect different areas of the brain, and form neural pathways which are like roads. When more neural pathways are formed, more neural connections are made, and the brain creates multisensory experiences and sensations, becomes capable of processing the information with increased speed resulting in quick decision-making and CF.

The increase or decrease in the levels of CF always varies, depending on the activation of the specific brain region when particular tasks are performed. Research proves that brain damage in any form can result in causing low CF levels. The results of functional magnetic resonance imaging (fMRI) scans show that a variety of cortical networks are activated to facilitate CF.

These networks include the following.

- Anterior cingulate cortex
- Basal ganglia
- Posterior parietal cortex
- Prefrontal cortex

When a person's CF is measured through standardized tests, it is found that the basal ganglia region functions actively in the process of selecting responses and the posterior parietal cortex becomes active when updating information that is pre-existing in memory, indicating how a task is to be performed. The majority of expert researchers think that the prefrontal cortex is the actual force driving CF. Depending on the nature of the task, specific regions of the prefrontal cortex get activated during CF. Specific regions in the brain that become activated when a Stroop Test (Section 28.8.5) is administered do not become active during the administration of some other different CF tests, and they are subjected to variations based on the specific tasks that are being used.

28.6 Cognitive Flexibility Theory

In 2011, Dr. Spiro and his team [2] developed Cognitive Flexibility Theory (CFT). According to this theory, CF is the ability to spontaneously restructure one's knowledge in many ways, an adaptive response to radically changing situational demands. This theory emphasizes the whole (big picture) or multidimensional nature of real-life experiences. It includes the following two ways.

1. The way knowledge is represented
2. The processes that operate on the mental representations

New knowledge is built based on existing knowledge, and knowledge acquisition happens in complex domains through multiple perspectives. Hence, knowledge is made more transferable in hypermedia learning environments, particularly multimedia case-based methods used in professional education. Students need to be exposed to multiple concepts to deal with, rather than single conceptual dimensions. Most of their research work deals with trying to find ways to avoid oversimplifying instructions while designing them. CFT, concerning information and communications technology (ICT), is very important as it is based upon hypertext and hypermedia. We learn to transfer our knowledge from case to case depending on our previous experiences as we are provided a link to multiple resources.

28.7 Aspects of Cognitive Flexibility (List of Possibilities)

Many psychologists and research experts believe that CF is the ability to switch or shift (transition) between multiple ideas, concepts, and thoughts. It also covers models such as reprogramming and updating old beliefs, divergent thinking, and recognizing the similarities between totally unrelated patterns, ideas, and concepts. CF is inclusive of the following key elements that need to be clearly understood by all of us for a smooth and successful living.

28.7.1 Switch/Shift Attention/Transition "Stream-of-Thoughts"

CF is the ability to switch or shift (transition) between multiple ideas, concepts, and series of thoughts. For instance, when you are seriously talking with your father about your academic plans and career goals, suddenly your mother interferes and starts her discussion about your sister's marriage. In this situation, your ability to shift your attention (transition) between the two different issues (concepts) without any sign of irritation is your CF.

28.7.2 Reprogramming/Updating Beliefs and Cognition

It is very important to understand that CF enables us to re-program our conditioned thoughts and adapt to novel situations wherein we have to process the new information and respond to new stimuli, and it is essential for an innovative process. Some people are so conditioned to specific rigid patterns of thinking and old beliefs that it is difficult for them to accept anything new. They suffer from cognitive inflexibility, which in turn hampers their development and experience with various kinds of social and psychological problems.

28.7.3 Divergent Thinking/Observation in Multiple Facets

An individual with flexible cognition can easily involve in divergent thinking that helps them to arrive at two or more solutions for the same problem, and allows creative abilities to flourish naturally. This capability also empowers one with keen observational skills that are useful in critical scientific researches, evaluation systems, and decision-making with strong analytical abilities and skills.

28.7.4 Deconstruction of Thoughts

Sometimes, when we confront a critical problem, we tend to worry about the complexity of the problem and become skeptical about the possibility of arriving at a solution. An individual with a higher degree of CF will generally be proactive and perceives it differently. The problem will be studied carefully. This person understands the dilemma in detail, thinks of different possible ways of solving it and deconstructs it into smaller steps, and constantly works on it until the solution is found.

28.7.5 Extension or Expansion in Awareness

Generally, people with low CF seem to be narrow-minded and rigid in their day-to-day operations. They are unable to extend their imagination and think quickly about various possible choices or alternative available methods of doing a particular thing in the given situation. Contrary to this, people with better or high flexibility in cognition can quickly stretch or expand their imagination and think beyond or out of the box. For instance, some teachers who have high levels of CF will have a clear understanding and expanded awareness about every student's specific skills, abilities, and the problems they come across in their learning. This enables them to offer their guidance, services, and solutions for the better development of the student community.

28.8 A Few Available Testing Tools to Measure and Monitor Flexibility in Cognition

Most of the tests that are designed to measure one's flexibility in cognition are age-appropriate and age-specific. Some standardized simple tests are used to assess a child's abilities to identify the color and quickly shift focus on shape. They measure the levels of CF of individuals at different stages.

28.8.1 Piaget's A–Not–B Task

This test measures the flexibility levels in cognition of infants and children in their early childhood. A box-like structure with two different specific locations for hiding the object, generally within arm's reach, is visually presented to children when the test is administered. First, an object is given to the child. Then it is taken and hidden in location A initially, where the child sees it and finds it. The task is repeated three to four times and the child easily focuses and identifies location A every time where the object is hidden. Next, the same object is hidden in location B and presented visually. Infants younger than 1 year typically would look for the object in location A again. Children above 1 year of age show flexibility and can shift their attention to location B easily and find the hidden object.

28.8.2 Dimensional Change Card Sorting Task

The dimensional change card sorting task (DCCS) is a widely used method to assess executive function in children. In the standard version, children are asked to sort a series of bivalent test cards, first according to one dimension (color), and then according to the other (shape or size). During the process of sorting, the instructor asks them to shift sorting the cards by another dimension. Most 3-year-olds persevere during the post switch phase, exhibiting a pattern of cognitive inflexibility similar to that seen in patients with prefrontal cortical damage. By 5 years of age, most children can switch when instructed to do so. Performance on the DCCS provides an index showing the development of an executive function. It is impaired in children with disorders like ADHD (attention-deficit hyperactivity disorder) and autism.

28.8.3 Multiple Classification Card Sorting Task

Multiple classification card sorting (MCCST) is a popular research flexible tool used widely across many of the subfields of psychology. It also measures the CF of children. In this test, participants are shown various cards with multiple characteristics (shape, size, color, etc.) and are instructed to sort them into piles distinctively based on the specifications mentioned. Results have shown that this is relatively a difficult task for children in early childhood and becomes easy as they advance with their age. The ability to become flexible in cognition improves all through the developmental stages. As children grow, they demonstrate better CF in performing tasks of this kind in later childhood years, i.e., between ages 6 and 12. Significant development in CF is observed in this age.

28.8.4 Wisconsin Card Sorting Task

The Wisconsin Card Sorting Task (WCST) is a test of cognitive reasoning with a long tradition in psychology. During this test, children have to figure out classification rules to sort the cards based on different criteria. There are four different ways to classify each card, and the only feedback is if the classification is correct or not. One can classify cards according to the color of their symbols, the shape of the symbols, or the number of shapes on each card. The classification rule changes every ten cards. This test measures how well people can adapt to the changing rules. This cognitive test is also used to assess a patient's level of brain damage to the prefrontal cortex.

28.8.5 Stroop Color-Word Test

The Stroop Color-Word Test (SCWT) is a neuropsychological test designed by Stroop in 1935 [3] to measure selective attention, processing speed, and CF of individuals more than 11 years of age and also to assess their ability to inhibit cognitive interference. SCWT is also used to measure multiple cognitive functions. Participants are asked to read the following three different types of cards as rapidly as possible.

Type 1—color card (CC) that shows segments of different colors. Participants are required to identify and read the names of colors as fast as possible.

Type 2—word card (WC) has the names of colors printed in black ink and white. Participants are asked to read the names of these colors as fast as possible.

Type 3—color word card (CWC) has words printed in an inconsistent color ink (for instance the word green is printed in red).In this incongruent condition, participants are required to name the color of the ink instead of reading the word.

28.8.6 Age and Cognitive Flexibility

Higher levels of flexibility in cognition positively associate with adapting to changes during aging. Some children with low levels of CF usually have difficulty in shifting from one agenda to another when compared to adults. Students with higher levels of CF can easily shift from their agenda to your agenda. Children with cognitive inflexibility will have a deficit in executive function and have a tough time switching from one task to the other. They become stuck. CF in adolescence develops rapidly and adolescents are faster at learning and performing as far as certain skill set is concerned. The brain's capacity to be flexible fully develops by the mid-20s, and it continues to enhance further in multiple dimensions for a considerable period (Figure 28.1). Normal adults have enough cognitively potential to execute flexibility to a great extent by age 25. From later adulthood to later old age, a gradual transition takes place, showing the decline in CF—and slowly, neurodegeneration starts. People in their later old age seem to possess a lesser degree of CF when compared to youngsters.

28.8.7 Cognitive Flexibility Blocks

28.8.7.1 Biased Conformity

The majority of the population is habituated and conditioned to conformity. Due to this, we always seek out and look for the information and news with which we agree. We also view the information in front of us by shaping it in such a way to match our ideas and worldview. This is a big hindrance to our progress in real life.

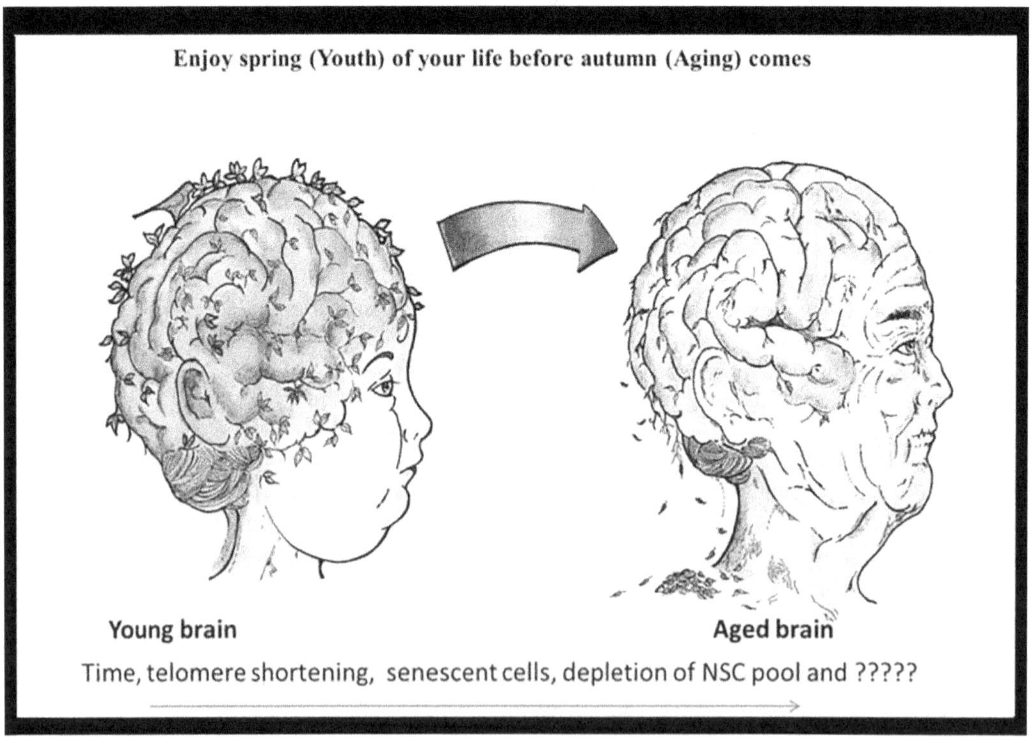

FIGURE 28.1 Age and cognition.

28.8.7.2 Flooded Information/Bottleneck

We are living in the technology-driven, over-flooded information era in which we encounter massive amounts of data. As we are unable to process this overflooded information in the right way, we have less clarity, resulting in indecisiveness and poor decision-making abilities.

28.8.7.3 Stay in Comfort Zone/Reinforcement

As we are very familiar with our past, we get stuck with similar past thought patterns that reinforce us to live in our comfort zone without trying for something new. Most of us fear the unknown, and hence, we re-live our past happily without aspiring to progress further and achieving nothing considerable indeed. We can overcome our CF blocks by being aware of them. We need to consciously use our energy, knowledge, skills, and other resources to contribute to our development by contributing to everyone's development—which brings the nation's development.

28.9 Why Is Cognitive Flexibility Important for Everyone?

Possessing CF is essential to be able to adjust and move forward by adapting to challenges that pop up in different situations all through life. It affects an individual's thought patterns, emotions, attitude, decision-making ability, behavioral aspects, and entire personality to a large extent—either positively or negatively, depending on the situation. The practical utilization of this ability/skill by an individual starts very early in childhood and continues constantly in every growth and developmental stage of life as and when required.

People with high CF are generally good at language acquisition abilities, comprehension, creativity, critical thinking, and problem-solving skills. Life becomes complex and gets complicated without this particular ability in almost all of the domains of life in general, such as physical, emotional, intellectual, social, psychological, etc. (Figure 28.2).

The opposite of CF is *cognitive inflexibility*, which is inclusive of rigid thinking and a fixed mindset which will not allow a person to learn from a new perspective and progress with different leanings

FIGURE 28.2 Important particular ability domains: flexibility.

that are required for every small or big accomplishment in life. Students with low levels of CF or high levels of cognitive inflexibility are said to have more academic problems resulting in various kinds of challenges. Cognitively inflexible people will have multiple problems like maladaptations, inferiority complexes, conflicts, adjustment problems, relationship problems, behavior disorders, and many other psychological problems. Life will not be smooth for them, their family members, and all their associates in any way. People with cognitive inflexibility are stuck in their ways, do not like to accept anything new, and are very rigid and unable to adapt to change in terms of learning, technological disruptions, business models, and behavior.

When we do not develop CF skills and utilize them, we may encounter some real-life serious complications. Without CF skills, we become stagnant, disillusioned, despondent, discouraged, and depressed. We also run the risk of sacrificing our hopes and dreams. CF is very important for living our best lives. Cognitive inflexibility in children, as well as in adults at different stages, causes anxiety disorders and psychological problems that turn to medical problems at a later age.

Therefore, it is strongly believed that the CF skill serves as the foundational skill in enabling any individual to acquire a 21st-century skill set that is crucial for successful living in this fast-changing, dynamic, disruptive world.

To reiterate how important CF is in one's life, an inspiring journey of a woman who is living amidst us is presented in what follows, in her own words.

My Journey

From a small-town girl to heading an industry vertical at an MNC (multinational corporation), here is my journey in a snapshot. I always believe in deciding your destiny and life is all about many "T" junctions we will come across throughout our life. You are the architects and designers of your own life.

I did my schooling and college in a tier 2 city in Andhra, and always aspired to be a doctor until my 12th grade, when I realized that it is not easy. After 12th [grade, I] joined home science just to keep me busy before I start my long-term coaching [for the] medical entrance exam. After few months into the course, I just fell in love with the subjects and that is when I hit my first "T" junction that I am consciously aware of: to continue home science or to go for my medicine. I took some time and did evaluate my pro[s] and cons, and made a choice to stick to home science. I did exceptionally well in my graduation, maybe because that was my choice and I am responsible for my own decisions. Then came my marriage. I was not ready for it, but like typical Indian middle-class families [who] wanted their daughters to be married at the earliest, I also succumbed to those pressures and I left that choice to my parents, keeping aside my aspirations of pursuing my Master's [degree] ahead. When the same marriage after a child turned out to be an abusive one mentally, physically, and emotionally, where I was left to myself in the USA at the age of 22 years, I hit my second "T" junction [and] had to choose if I [would] give in to a bad marriage where I do not know mine and my child's future, or pull myself up from the rags and rise to live a meaningful life that is in the interest of my son and self. I chose the latter. Initially for survival, [I] worked in dry cleaners and I did not miss any opportunity during that time to learn and improve myself. That was my first job in the US where I learned to communicate with confidence, I learned how to deal with customers and ensure customer satisfaction, [and] I learned the art of body language and gestures to build strong relationships with customers and partners.

After some time, I realized that it was not what I want[ed] in life to be successful and I need[ed] to do something different and better. [I] decided to work in a computer assembling unit in RMA (return merchandise authorization) team. I was inclined toward sales during that time, and when an opportunity came the way, I just grabbed it. Again, [I] made the best use of that role to learn computers, hardware, and above all, the best part that is still a very integral part of my career: "selling."

[A] few months down the lane I got a call from my cousin in Detroit regarding some Siebel training. I just packed my bags, pulled all the money from the bank, and left for Detroit for training.

Later, I realized that I was the only woman in the training room of 70–80 men who were all experienced in their fields. I had to shiver in my knees and my entire body was sweating as it is standing in the middle of the road on a hot summer day in Rama Gundam while the temperature in Detroit at that time was as its peak winter in December and knee-[high] snow everywhere. I ran from the training room, sat in the cafeteria, and was crying out of fear. After a couple of hours of tears rolling down, my mind and body came to senses and hit my next "T" junction again. Should I return to Dallas and work for dry cleaners or computer store, or gain courage and make it to training for a better future both personally and professionally? I chose to go back to the training—and from then [until now, I] never looked back.

It is almost 23 years into this journey and I have encountered multiple situations in life both personally and professionally. I take every such situation as the "T" junction principle and evaluate pros and cons, and identif[y] opportunities out of such situations. I never missed any such opportunities and harped on them to challenge myself and push my boundaries. These are all steps toward a better you and an improved version of you every time.

With regards to my career, success was never an option, it was a must. I should say that I was fortunate enough to realize some of the basic recipes to success earlier on, such as:

- Understanding customer needs
- Being passionate and believing in what you say and what you do
- Commitment to deliver
- Clear communications
- Adaptability
- Networking

Almost everyone gets opportunities to grow or succeed. What is important is how one capitalizes on those opportunities that come their way. From CRM [customer relationship management] functional consultant, technical architect, leading sales, solution, and delivery organization driving strategic consulting and transformational implementations in the airlines, leisure and hospitality, healthcare, insurance, automotive, retail/FMCG, [and] e-commerce. Further building on my experience, I ensured that even with the shortest interaction, the brand recall of myself and the organization was quite high. I believe this had enabled the customers to call me or reach out to the organization even after a break of a couple of years when the project interests were revived.

Finally, I was not just keen on growing; rather, I set hard deadlines to grow rapidly and make an impactful global presence. To achieve it, I have never hesitated to work across even four different major time zones—Australia, India, Europe, and the USA. The fire to succeed and exceed also kept my energy levels and enthusiasm high all the time. Further, I took up challenges, which many would prefer to walk away from. Delivering what I took up, on time and with quality, helped me to gain respect from all stakeholders.

After traveling to 30+ countries learned and experience in business development, sales strategy planning/execution and client management led me to win numerous accounts and also helped penetrate new markets like Canada, Australia, Mexico, Chile, and Russia.

Traveling taught me one thing for sure: "appreciating and adapting to cultures" and the wonderful experiences. [I] learned so much from global leaders, and thoroughly love my job—every bit of it—for that reason. I am also a prolific speaker at various industry events. All through these years, I have only learned one thing: there is no magic to achievement. It's really about determination, choices, hard work, and persistence.

(2018, in Bangalore)

This case study is the best example that shows what a person with CF skills can achieve in life. The sky is the limit for anyone who develops CF.

28.10 The Various Approaches and Methods of Developing Cognitive Flexibility

The cognitive flexibility of every normal individual can be very well developed right from early childhood to later stages of life through the following different activities and therapies (Figure 28.3).

1. *Play language and number games*

   There are many language games like word building, sentence building, crossword puzzles, Simon says, language cricket, and many other games that help individuals naturally develop their linguistic abilities that boost the improvement of CF. Number games include skip counting, ten more or ten less, making trains with number blocks, number hunts, paint by number art, connect-the-dots number puzzles, match playing cards, etc. Difficulty levels can be increased as individuals advance with the age. Regardless of age, at different stages of life, playing games can keep everyone cognitively flexible.
2. *Keep alternative plans always*

   Having a back-up plan is a must. Life is nothing but series of experiences and encounters. To accomplish anything in life, whether it is a small task like learning a skill, completing an

FIGURE 28.3 Methods of developing cognitive flexibility.

assignment, or succeeding in an interview, or a big task like setting up a business enterprise, constructing a big building, or aiming for high professional performance, we need to have plan A, plan B; sometimes, even plan C would be better. Commonly, sometimes we would be stuck in the process when we execute a plan and move accordingly. In such cases, it is always good to have alternative plans so that without anxiety and wasting much time worrying about the next step, we can immediately implement plan B and progress forward with our work until we succeed.

3. *Practice deliberate flexible daily routines consciously*

   No doubt, daily routines play an important role in maintaining consistency and discipline in getting things done systematically. If you allow yourself to make simple changes in your daily routines, new neural pathways will be built and strengthened, which in turn would enhance your CF. Small daily incremental changes implemented consciously can result in producing huge differences and help you in achieving massive success.

4. *Big deal/little deal*

   Most of the time, when we are stuck and encounter an unexpected situation, an obstacle, or a challenge, we get disturbed and tend to stop our work. Instead, we can develop a habit of questioning ourselves, whether it is a major deal or a minor deal every time we are stuck. Small and minor setbacks do not matter much. If one obtains a poor score in one subject, there is always a scope for improvement in the same subject with proper preparation. We have to cultivate a growth mindset and move forward progressively. Cognitively flexible people only can withstand adverse results and try again without disappointment and depression.

5. *Don't always join the easy crowd and resort to easy ways*

   We are blessed with scientific and technological advancements that very much allow us to live always in our comfort zone. We are just a click away from getting answers or information. We usually do not put our brains to work and resolve to go for easy ways in day-to-day operations that make us cognitively slow and lazy. Our smartphones have become our bosses, dictating and controlling us in many ways. Spend some time using your brain for thinking and calculations to sharpen your CF. We should be wise in using them to our advantage and development in multiple ways without getting addicted. Always be conscious of the overusage of electronic devices, and avoid health hazards.

6. *Welcome new experiences and look for changes*

   Whenever we learn something new and experience the joy of knowing what was not known to us, our brain makes new connections and forms more neural pathways that enhance our CF naturally. If we cultivate a habit of learning a new skill, a new language, a new art, cooking a new dish, or learning a new programming language, we become more strong and flexible cognitively. This is very much similar to practicing deliberate flexible daily routines.

7. *Be enthusiastic to meet new people*

   When we meet new people from different socio-economic and educational or professional backgrounds, we tend to be exposed to new perspectives and understand various viewpoints. We also experience the different possible ways of doing things. We learn to respect others, even though they differ from our points of view. Meeting new people and interacting with them helps develop our social skills. When our beliefs are questioned and challenged, our CF increases in the process.

8. *Play indoor or outdoor games and exercise*

   Playing indoor games like table tennis or chess, and any outdoor game, regularly increases neural pathways in the brain. Aerobic exercise enhances CF. Doing regular physical exercises, yoga, dance, etc., requires a higher degree of CF and coordination, which will help us develop sports spirit and team spirit that are very much essential to adapt to unfamiliar and unexpected situations in life.

9. *Make a habit of transferring your knowledge and learning*

   The core purpose of learning anything and acquiring knowledge or skill is to be able to apply it in real-life situations and solve problems. Some students cling to one method, even when it is not working for them; they should be always encouraged to inter-create different perspectives and to shift between problem-solving strategies by transferring their previous learning in different domains. Sometimes, we should be able to abandon previous successful methods when needed and see the value of different approaches.

28.11 Conclusion

We live in the internet era of enormously floods of information, self-driving cars, rapid scientific advancements, and innovative technological disruptions led by the automotive and artificial intelligence revolution, whereby computer-adaptive technologies and future technologies dominate every area of human life, allowing us to experience unprecedented changes. We cannot predict our future, but can affect and influence it to a large extent. To be able to do so, we need to redefine the educational echo system with a new curriculum with more scope for developing cognitive flexibility skills right from elementary education through university education, so that we can combat climate change, face bigger disruptions in the job market, and reinvent ourselves again and again as we evolve experiencing life, relationships, the economy, and politics. Unless we are highly flexible in cognitive abilities, we cannot develop emotional intelligence, mental stability, management skills, and psychological strength to keep learning and changing every day throughout life and master all the 21st-century skills required to succeed in this ever-changing world.

28.12 Acknowledgments

We extend our sincere gratitude to the authors from whose work we have extracted ideas and bits of content to develop this chapter. We also express our special thanks to the image creators and their associated websites.

REFERENCES

[1] https://www.opencolleges.edu.au/informed/features/10-keys-cognitive-flexibility/
[2] https://www.bu.edu/sph/profile/avron-spiro/
[3] https://www.ncbi.nlm.nih.gov/pmc/articles/PMC5388755/#:~:text=The%20Stroop%20Color%20and%20Word%20Test%20(SCWT)%20is%20a%20neuropsychological,known%20as%20the%20Stroop%20Effect

29

Tone of Cognition and Metacognition in Digital Learning Environments

N. Subramanian

CONTENTS

DOI: 10.1201/9781003318378-29

29.1 Introduction

In today's postmodern era, under the influence of digital technologies, our planet becomes figuratively smaller, bringing together peoples, states, and their cultures, and creating a cosmopolitan way of life in an educated society, and thus cosmopolitan citizens are formed. Digital technology represents an important and indispensable part of the learning process for teachers and learners in this world (Prodromou, 2020). Educational technologies have the capacity to monitor and assess cognitive, self-regulatory, and metacognitive behaviours, as well as to model and respond to learner effect. Technology-enhanced learning (TEL) environments that adapt to the learner do so through modelling, adaptation, and personalization techniques that are grounded in computational processes and underlying pedagogical and psychological theories. TEL environments initially aimed to deliver content that was personalized for better understanding or to suggest tasks or problems to better encode new strategies or skills. This uptake is mediated by learners' prior knowledge or cognitive competencies, as well as their metacognition, emotion, and the interplay between them. Cognitive strategies are activated to solve a problem or complete a task. Metacognition is a vital component of successful self-regulation. While not sufficient on its own, it drives the control, monitoring, and regulation of strategies in order to meet the goals of the learner. Metacognition encompasses a learner's knowledge about themselves for control. Metacognitive regulatory strategies include the awareness, monitoring, and subsequent regulation of cognitive processes. This includes awareness and control of behaviours such as planning, comprehension, and information management strategies. Metacognition and self-regulated learning abilities are difficult higher-order skills that are often lacking in both young and adult learners. This is because greater metacognitive knowledge results in a more flexible cognitive strategy repertoire. Consequently, one can more strategic and perform better. Ku and Ho (2010) pointed out that the importance of metacognitive knowledge is an important indicator of positive self-regulation and critical thinking. Self-regulated learning (SRL) and critical thinking are both associated with the application of appropriate skills and strategies to best suit a situation. Successful learners need to be aware, not only of their cognitive strategies, but also of their metacognitive processes (Jovanovic & Chiong, 2013), so the tone of cognition and metacognition cooperate a foremost role in the digital learning environment.

29.2 Digital Learning Environment

In an online, digital environment, the digital elements enable a high level of fidelity in replication of resources, while also enabling easy repurposing; the online element enables global networking to link learners with scholars and other students. The potential mixture of approaches to learning in the medium of online digital communications is immense. Combining audio recordings, video clips, discussion boards, live webinars, online libraries, image banks, and many other digital resources offers almost limitless opportunities to provide an educational experience. The evolving research base for digital learning has also expanded in recent years to establish our current understanding of digital literacies and capabilities, supporting a more critical exploration of the specific affordances of different educational technologies, and to provide evidence relating to digitally supported collaborative learning, learning in virtual worlds, adaptive learning environments, SRL and digital divides (Rennie & Smyth, 2020). By digital discussion environments, we mean Internet environments designed for conversation and collaboration. The explosion of social media and the popular use of Web 2.0 tools have made online discussions more popular than ever before. Virtual environments offer a multimedia experience and the opportunity to build a virtual discussion environment. Along similar lines, gaming environments offer yet another tool for digital discussions that incorporates visual as well as verbal elements. These environments may vary in terms of purpose, number of participants, software, and design, but they have several common elements: they are highly interactive, they require writing, and they encourage student-centred learning (Beach et al., 2014).

29.2.1 Metacognitive Knowledge in E-Learning Environments

Metacognitive regulation is the monitoring of one's cognition and contains sketching activities, awareness of conception and duty performance, and estimate of the efficiency of monitoring processes and strategies. Much of the research in this area focuses on metacognitive strategy instruction and inventions and details specific strategies to be implemented before, during and after a learning episode. John Hattie's (2009) meta-analysis pertaining to metacognition considered this dimension of metacognition, addressing metacognitive strategies, study skills, and self-verbalizing and self-questioning. Metacognitive knowledge, regulation, and monitoring prove especially important in e-learning environments, where students must be self-regulated and able to take accountability for their own knowledge, such as in the case of asynchronous environments in which there is no one else immediately present to help monitor and regulate the learning process. Garrison (2013) considers metacognition and SRL are two sides of the same coin that make up the notion of cognitive presence, a critical component of his conception of successful e-learning. In this, metacognitive knowledge and regulation comprise the building blocks that make possible higher-order metacognitive functioning (Cope & Kalantzis, 2017).

29.3 Cognition

Cognition refers to all the processes by which the sensory effort is altered, condensed, elaborated, stored, improved, and used. Cognition is a thinking process. It is also a finite sense, and the capability to process, store, recover, and preserve information by the brain is called cognition. We understand cognition through the performance of remembering in three ways: attention refers to the capability to centre on a particular spur without being diverted, orientation refers to the capability to be conscious of self and firm realities and facts while using the information which utters the capability of a person to react to stimuli and line up with daily life experiences, and decision-making and problem-solving refers to the capability to comprehend a problem, create resolutions, and evaluate these. These three areas of cognition move from and between levels of complexity. Through the degree of thinking, we have to separate cognition from metacognition. On an everyday basis, the devolution from and between lower-array and higher-array thinking, going from and amid cognition and metacognition, happens thousands of times, so the advanced level of thinking is metacognition (Schiering et al., 2011).

29.4 Metacognition

Metacognition is the ability to monitor, evaluate, and plan one's learning. The process of metacognition may be divided into three mechanisms: knowledge about metacognition, monitoring of learning progression, and control of those progressions; that is, self-regulation. Metacognition may be a hierarchical process in which monitoring of prior learning is a prerequisite for a more complex metacognitive control process. If students cannot differentiate between what they know or do not know, they can engage in more complex metacognitive activities that control learning directly (O'Neil & Perez, 2006). Metacognitive knowledge is defined as what we know about ourselves as a thinker and learner. It is important in education because such self-knowledge can be used not only to inform and support action, but also because it underpins our concept and identity as a thinker and a learner (Tarrant & Holt, 2016). There is not a division in metacognitive and cognitive reality, however a bonding of performing and being, an instantaneous of thinking and sensing for the generation of grasping/comprehension. Through metacognition and metacognition, comprehension is achieved (Schiering et al., 2011, 45).

29.5 Cognition and Metacognition in Comprehension

Memory, cognition, and metacognition are the elements of comprehension. Memory is the process of store accumulating, recollecting, and recovering emotions and thoughts. Cognition and metacognition are called lower-arrayed and higher-arrayed thinking, respectively. Comprehension is the application of a learner's memory and lower and higher levels of thinking, i.e., cognition and metacognition with the ability to realize or have knowledge about something. So for creating understanding, cognition is identified through comprehension. Comprehension may or may not be expressed, but the behaviours and actions are revealed by comprehension in three applications: i.e., 1) *literal:* reality-supported proof of comprehension; 2) *applied:* through learners' experience, comparison and dissimilarity comprehension may arrive; and 3) *implied:* the instructive substance is accessed through the visual, oral, kinaesthetic, or tactile arrangements. As a result, inferential comprehension is formed. Through these three submissions, comprehension is associated with cognition and the arrays of thinking, because in generating a verdict and cracking trouble, there's an amenable, meaning-making, and vigorous direction. As a result of the vigorous direction, learning is formed. It absorbs theoretical alteration that means a modification of learners' preceding comprehension of ideas so that they become more and more multifaceted and suitable (Schiering, 2011, 10).

29.6 Strategic Knowledge Metacognition for Teachers

Metacognitive knowledge involves a kind of self-knowing that refers to facts about one's cognitive abilities and constraints (Cope & Kalantzis, 2017). Most of the teachers do not have exact information about the teaching and learning processes. Generally, teacher education teaches various kinds of teaching methods to teachers, but it does not make sure that the teachers comprehend how, when, and why to utilize them for all at all times. Due to that kind of lack of knowledge, the learning of teachers in teacher education may remain immobile. Three necessary categories (declarative knowledge, contextual or conditional knowledge, and procedural knowledge) of strategic knowledge metacognition are required for teachers to efficiently keep in mind and apply the instructional principles and methods they have (Hartman, 2001).

1. *Declarative knowledge* includes knowledge about oneself as a student and knowledge about an aspect that might manipulate a concept (Cope & Kalantzis, 2017). It is also called truths, definitions, or concepts in a particular subject part. Declarative information can be drawn out by a "what" question.
2. *Contextual or conditional knowledge* is information regarding the cause and/or condition in which knowledge or methods are used. This kind of information is often required by a "when" or "why" question. This kind of knowledge is used for teachers to identify environments or atmospheres which are specific to use particular teaching methods, approaches, and laws. (Hartman, 2001).
3. *Procedural knowledge* is knowledge about strategies (Cope & Kalantzis, 2017); also, it knows how to use knowledge or methods teachers have studied and it comprises a course of actions and methods.

Strategic metacognitive knowledge about teaching strategies is used for teachers to compare assorted teaching methods, which leads to the achievement of specific objectives, and also it might be used to evaluate the benefits and weaknesses of each. While sketching a lesson, it can help instructors choose the most excellent method for the condition, as well as consider different methods that might be used as endorsements if–when observing a lesson–it emerges that modification is needed. To teach sharply, teachers would reflect metacognitively about their teaching, which leads to effective management of their teaching and excellent usage of teaching methods deliberately (Hartman, 2001).

29.7 Metateaching for Teachers

Metateaching is a teaching process whereby teachers execute metacognitive monitoring of their teaching progression by generating mindful efforts to sketch, observe, and evaluate the accomplishment of their teaching. As an outcome, the teachers will perk up their teaching and metacognition, as well as the learning outcome of their students including metacognitive learning effects. If the teachers used the student-centred teaching method and also used appropriate teaching methods in the classroom, the metacognition can be improved. If the learners have actively participated in the classroom learning and also they have the independence to sketch, observe, and assess their thinking process with teachers' direction and support, mechanically the metacognition is developed. Therefore, the teacher should be well-informed and dexterous in the effective methods and strategies for supporting metacognition—a teaching method called metateaching.

The educational science and educational practices are notably influenced by digital learning environments, and also, these kinds of environments are progressively becoming an indispensable constituent of the life and actions or behaviours of teachers—and teacher educators, as well. Nowadays, digitally skilled teachers and teacher educators are needed for the Department of Education and teacher education at all levels. They should be mastered in manipulating the digital learning environment. A mixture of digital technology—i.e., electronic tools, systems, devices and resources—and e-content—i.e., text, images, graphics, animation, audio, and video—and teaching methods to bear teaching and learning activities and assignments is called digital teaching and learning. Academics, teacher educators, and researchers in teacher education are more and more recognizing the significance of metacognition for learning. The process of generating consequential depictions of information through an internally intervened process including self-awareness, self-questioning, self-monitoring, and self-regulation is called learning (Railean et al., 2017).

29.8 Cognitive Presence in Online Communities

Cognitive presence involves students connecting in the significant discussion of course content and analyzing allocated material to assemble understanding and meaning, it relates to thinking, and it also involves the capacity of the learners to establish, generate, and authenticate meaning through manifestation and discussion in the online background. Social presence relates to affective aspects (emotional connection to the group) and the overall organization of the classroom community. Here, the learners express themselves socially and emotionally—but cognitive presence focuses on the critical thinking process with which learners must connect to learn in an online community. Practical inquiry is a construct whereby students cycle through phases of commencement, investigation, integration, and resolution to assimilate the "private and public globes of the learner". In online courses, cognitive presence has been associated with learner satisfaction and learning outcomes (Hartman, 2001, 23).

29.9 Metaliteracy, Multiliteracies, and Digital Metaliteracies

Metaliteracies recommend a way of thinking about one's own literacy. If the learners understand their strengths of present literacy and parts for enhancement and formulate resolutions concern to their learning, they will become metaliterates. Metaliteracy is the ability to recognize one's requirement for incorporated literacies and also critically self-assess different competencies in today's digital environment. This metacognitive approach confronts a dependence on instruction regarding skills-based information literacy and transfers the focal point to knowledge attainment in teamwork further. The learners who can adjust to shifting technologies and learning environments while merging and comprehending relationships among associated literacies are called metaliterate learners. To become a metacognitive learner, the learner should have a high level of investigative and critical thinking behaviours; and also for metacognitive learners in the open and social media environment, the self-conception of information literacy plays a main role. When the focal point is on communication with knowledge regardless of intermediates, information literacy itself might be seen as a metaliteracy that in the networked surrounding holds a variety of other literacies. Media literacy, visual literacy, computer literacy, and other network literacies are embedded in information literacy. (Mackey & Jacobson, 2014).

Teachers have the responsibility of preparing students with *multiliteracies* for a digital age, because today's most rewarding job opportunities require multiliteracies—and also, today's students will be employees, parents, and citizens. In those positions, they may also need multiliteracies. The field of educational research on information and communication technology has seen a burgeoning of new technologies, so defining the multiliteracies within the specific context is complex. Year by year, even month by month, technology may change. Nowadays, communication is enabled by digital technologies such as personal computers/laptops, smartphones, and the Internet, which are rapidly connected from the local milieu to the international level. Students with technological literacy which leads to the formation of creativity may improve their economic opportunities in the digital era. The collaboration and communication skills, functional skills (the use of digital technologies, the capacity to find and choose information, cultural and social consciousness, and comprehension), and critical thinking are digital literacies, which are closely interlinked. (Jovanovic & Chiong, 2013)

Educators should know how the complicated digital metaliteracies are an essential requirement of today's communication, and they must also think about the position of computer games on games. There is also a link between metaliteracy and multiliteracies, that is: "How children ratify digital literacies and how they mingle modern and postmodern literacies which require an organization and orientation of complicated knowledge: a metaliteracy to access multi-literacies" (Mackey & Jacobson, 2014, 47).

The methods of entering the chaos of postmodern texts and navigating digitalized knowledge programmed into changeable platforms are called *digital metaliteracies*. The researchers define an obvious connection among related literacies and recognize technology-mediated influences on information literacy. The "meta-literacy revolution" is a division of a superior communications revolt that contains alterations in language, literacy, and telepresence (McDonald, John D., & Levine-Clark Michael, 2017, 42). While this definition predates the influence of computer-mediated communications, the speedy growth of social media and hypertext updates a comprehension of metaliteracy based on noteworthy alters in communications "in all possible forms—symbolic, oral, and telepresence". In a digital age, collaboration and critical thinking are promoted by metaliteracy, which leads to the formation of a comprehensive framework. That framework is very useful for the learners to effectively contribute and interact in social media and online communities. It is an integrated establishment that holds this production, procurement, and allocation of information in shared or collaborative online communities. The conventional skills-supported techniques to information literacy by identifying related literacy kinds and assimilating developing technologies are challenged by metaliteracy (Mackey & Jacobson, 2014, 138).

29.9.1 Metacognition and Information Literacy

Metacognition is influenced by the acquisition, comprehension, retention, and application of what is learned, and that metacognition is also influenced by critical thinking, problem-solving, and learning efficacy. The mentors belonging to information literacy have the same kind of behaviours in how the learners attain, understand, maintain, and use what is learned about the information environment efficiently. In information literacy education, both problem-solving and critical thinking are noteworthy learning results, so the metacognitive approach is utilized for receiving information literacy which constructs on these constituents and confronts us to prepare our students to think about their learning. This is particularly appropriate to how students self-appraise their contribution in extremely social information atmospheres. From that, collaborative and interdisciplinary strategies are developed which lead to the formation of metacognitive opportunities that build on basic skills instruction (Mackey & Jacobson, 2014).

29.9.2 Metacognition and Metaliteracy

As metaliteracy developed as a pedagogical model, it emphasized metacognition with four domains of learning that also included affective, behavioural, and cognitive dimensions in support of a comprehensive set of goals and learning objectives. Metaliteracy integrates metacognition. Due to that, the students are allowed to move ahead of basic skill development which leads to the preparation of students to dig profoundly and appraise their learning. Reflective thinking and self-regulation are sustained by metacognition and challenge the skills-based approach of traditional information literacy definitions and practices. Metacognition is recognized as thinking about one's own thinking, and also it has a constitutive association to self-regulation, which is essential to metaliteracy.

Self-regulating learners have an improved consciousness of their own powers and flaws, and they are also more flexible in acclimatizing new strategies for problem-solving and are more proficient at avoiding the obstacles. This leads to the formation of metaliteracy, which is also called the integrated approach to metacognition. The formation of metaliteracy promotes learner organization and empowerment.

The metacognitive aspect of metaliteracy is both reflective and self-regulating. As part of this dynamic, metaliteracy shifts the emphasis from teacher to learner by envisioning the learner as both. Metacognition supports this expanded role for learners:

> Metaliterate students will be prepared to fill the gaps in learning and develop strategies for understanding more than we, as teachers; present or discuss. Through this process, the learner is also a teacher and each individual is a collaborative partner in the learning experience. If learners gain new insights about their knowledge in these areas, they will be better prepared to critically evaluate information and technology systems common today and in the future.
>
> (Mackey & Jacobson, 2019, 14)

29.9.3 Metacognition and Metaliteracy in Social Learning Environments

Imagining the learner as a teacher recognizes the pedagogical role we all play in social spaces by sharing this commitment in an equal way that promotes empowered learning and active participation with others. Metacognition provides an opening for individuals to consider their own strengths and areas for improvement, and to check those strongly held beliefs and biases that may prevent the objective evaluation of information in any setting. In collaborative social environments, individuals have a responsibility to participate ethically and to contribute in meaningful ways, but they are often swayed by their own predetermined mindsets. Within a variety of actual and virtual spaces, metaliteracy recognizes how learners gravely assess and comprehend their knowledge as individuals and contributors in social learning environments. Through this cognitive process, metaliteracy prepares learners to effectively participate by integrating critical thinking and evaluation, production and sharing of information, adaptation to new technologies, teaching, learning, and ultimately the acquisition of new knowledge (Mackey & Jacobson, 2019).

29.10 Self-Directed Learning

Self-directed learning is illustrated as learners taking hands-on administration of their own learning in the ralms of cognition and motivation. Online learning is generally understood to involve three categories of interaction, i.e., student-to-instructor, student-to-content, and student-to-student, which are identified to have a major impact on student accomplishment in online learning. The study skills of the students can be strengthened by self-regulation, which leads to the creation of better learning habits, the application of supportive learning strategies, observation of students' own performance, and evaluation of their scholastic accomplishments. In the virtual classroom, the teachers have to be knowledgeable with the identification and promotion of SRL.

29.10.1 Self-Regulation and Metacognition

Self-regulation is a more universal concept, whereas metacognition is a foremost aspect of it. Particularly, metacognition is learners' mindful control over their cognitive processes—namely, edging on a given input, discussing it, scrutinizing learners' preconceptions and consequent struggle to fresh inputs, and analyzing and echoing on an experience.

Metacognition is the awareness and knowledge about one's own thinking, and also thinking about how a learner performs a skill. Metacognition engages self-feedback on learners' learning; the component of consequential learning and dispatch is metacognition. In contrast, observing and administering learners' cognitive processes, as well as the awareness of and manage over ones' motivations emotions, environment, and behaviour as related to learning, are the components of self-regulation.

Utilization of technology, task administration (solo tasking vs. multitasking), and sensory contributions—namely, background sounds, temperature place, and physical position—are the constituents of the environment. Each learner should realize the kind of environment suitable for their learning. The process begins with self-monitoring and task-based self-talk, as in talking one's way through a novel mission. The student should analyze and monitor the outcomes of diverse emotions, motivations, behaviours, cognitive processes, and environments, and choose which ones enhance or obstruct learning. Those with optimistic/positive effects lead to reduce the cognitive load while the student is engaged in learning. Finally, the learner must work out self-control in generating the most favourable cognitive, affective, and physical surroundings, and the most excellent agenda for their learning (Nilson, 2013).

29.10.2 Challenge with Social Models of Self-Regulated Learning

Historically, there is a profound association between metacognition and self-regulation, which is essential to the control of cognition. In socially shared or collaborative thinking and learning activities, the problem is that "self" generates complexities. Despite the significance of social sharing and collaboration in comprehending and sustaining metacognition is recognized by the research on metacognition, the conceptual inconsistencies are created by the study of metacognition subsuming collaborative aspects of regulation within the self-regulation construct. There has been a recent movement in metacognition assumption away from the self and individualistic models to an acceptance of metacognition as socially situated and socially constructed to emphasize the process of thinking and learning collaboratively.

For this reason, metacognition is seen as arising from the interaction among individuals and their environments rather than largely an individual process. Therefore, cognitive sharing and collaboration is a significant action in the development of metacognitive consciousness. The perspective here is that the cognitively and motivationally engaged learners include individual and shared cognition, which leads to the development of metacognitive awareness. In this regard, metacognition is essential to elucidate and validate one's thinking to self as well as to others.

The significant system is the capacity to monitor and pay attention to other viewpoints and is best recognized through discussion. However, the obstacle with social models of SRL is that there is enormous variety in where social is located in the [self-regulated] model. Noteworthy queries remain about the concocts and dynamics that necessitate being comprised in a definition of socially shared metacognition. The avenue to developing possible metacognition constructs for collaborative learning environments is to include self- and shared regulatory tasks within metacognition construct. (Garrison, 2017, 14).

Developing metacognitive awareness and ability is core to becoming an effective inquirer, since it is essential that regulation of the learning process address monitoring and managing how well the inquiry process is transpiring. Observing regulatory tasks within the metacognitive concoct has the possibility to include room for both self- and shared regulatory processes. Furthermore, metacognition has been generally accepted as consisting of two components: awareness and implementation strategies. Awareness follows the learner to monitor the learning process and then to actively manage the inquiry process. In short, metacognition awareness and implementation ability provide the knowledge and strategies to monitor and manage effective inquiry (Garrison, 2017).

29.10.3 Development of Shared Metacognition Construct

A metacognition construct must have room for thinking and learning in a collaborative environment. This is called a coherent metacognition construct which is reliable with the hypotheses of a collaborative constructivist community of investigation. The challenge is that the SRL construct has an individual orientation that does not explicitly address the collaborative environment of the directive in a community of investigation. As such, new research on regulation has focused on self- and socially shared regulation. This also precipitated the development of shared metacognition construct that proposed two bidirectional aspects—co-regulation (distributed cognition) and self-regulation (individual) particular to thinking and learning collaboratively in a community of investigation (Garrison, 2017).

29.11 Shared Metacognition

The work on self-directed learning became a jumping-off point for our recent work on shared metacognition as manifested in a community of investigation. Shared metacognition is essential for thinking and learning collaboratively. Shared metacognition is a comprehensive understanding of thinking and learning that explicitly recognizes social influences and the importance of collaboration (Garrison, 2016, 32). The shared metacognition construct hypothesized that the dynamic self- and co-regulation aspects each exhibited an observing (consciousness) and a directing (planned action) task. The monitoring function is associated with the awareness of cognition and is a process of rection on thinking and learning in a community of investigation. Alternatively, the management function represents reflection in action. This is the strategic ratification and control of the investigation process that includes setting goals, exploring and questioning ideas, considering alternate hypotheses, and ensuring timely progress. Consistent with the shared metacognition construct, monitoring and management functions reflect the integration of the private and shared worlds of thinking and learning and the fusion of self- and co-regulation (Garrison, 2017, 43).

The monitoring function is associated with the awareness of cognition and is a process of reflection on thinking and learning in a community of investigation. Alternatively, the management function represents reflection in action. This is the strategic ratification and control of the investigation process that includes setting goals, exploring and questioning ideas, considering alternate hypotheses, and ensuring timely progress. Consistent with the shared metacognition construct, monitoring and management functions reflect the integration of the private and shared worlds of thinking and learning and the fusion of self- and co-regulation (Garrison, 2017) (Figure 29.1).

29.12 Digital Learning Technologies

Digital learning technologies can help students to grasp concepts more rapidly and completely, to retain a hypothetical set of facts, principles, or circumstances and applications more skilfully and to keep in learning more willingly, while also progressing instructional techniques, aiding the prevalent sharing of

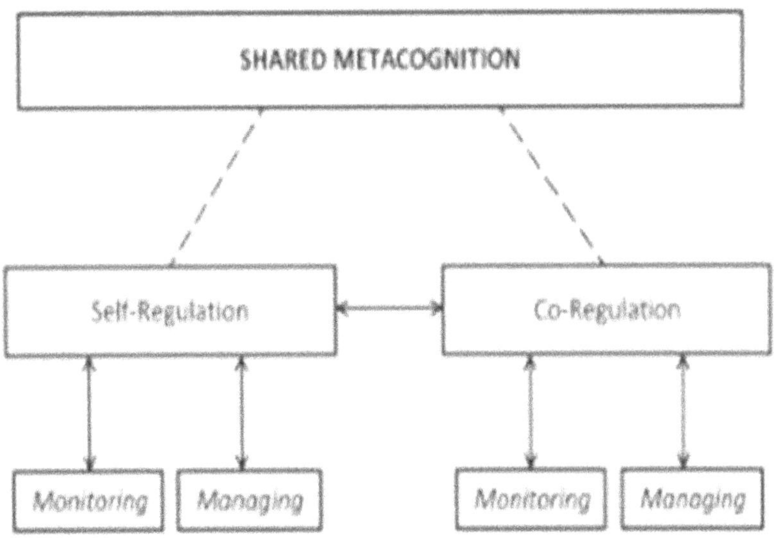

FIGURE 29.1 Shared metacognition construct.

knowledge, and leveraging teacher time. Digital technologies will facilitate these tasks in novel and superior ways, and also generate opportunities ahead of the edges of our current thoughts (Zheng, 2018). A huge diversity of learning technologies are flattering generals at a very speedy pace, such as peer review systems, tutorial dialogue systems, virtual worlds, games, open online repositories of educational materials, distributed online or hybrid courses, simulations, intelligent tutoring systems (ITSs), hypermedia environments, and electronic portfolios. As we must comprehend how students learn with these technologies and what obstacles they come across, the instructional designers and developers of technology-improved learning will generate learning backgrounds that promote learners and aid them to learn via superior methods, in place of being just an economical deliverance vehicle for "traditional" instructional methods.

These digital learning environments will not only aid students in obtaining profound conceptual information, multifaceted topics, or healthy cognitive skill, but will also aid them to turn into superior students across fields by permitting them to obtain, embody, allocate (with other human and non-human agents), and practice key self-regulatory skills and metacognitive skills. The study of metacognition and self-regulation in digital learning environments is timely and imperative, for several motives. It is becoming more and more clear that the way learners keep an eye on and regulate their learning in computer-based learning environments (CBLEs) has a major impact on their learning upshots (Azevedo & Aleven, 2013). In this chapter, the author covers every aspect of cognition and metacognition. Then, the author lists and briefly explains the various digital learning environments: namely, web-based learning environment/online learning environment, blended learning environment, massive open online course (MOOC) learning environment, gamification, mobile learning environment, personalized e-learning environment, augmented learning environment, and artificial intelligence (AI) with the tone of cognition and metacognition on each of these digital learning environments.

29.12.1 Cognitive and Metacognitive Processes in Digital Content

Concepts in the construct of the *cognitive process* include Utilizing digital technology to enhance students cognitive information processes, student's capabilities to process learning content with digital technology, utilizing multiple sensory methods to alter student's mode of learning and thinking, etc. The individual differences in digital learning significantly influenced personalized learning and cognitive Process. Research has additionally established that individual aptitude in learning may importantly interrelate with treatment—aptitude effect in digital learning where different technologies (e.g., auditory, haptic, visual, etc.). (Zheng, 2018, 16).

Self-knowledge, goal setting, strategic planning of learning path, etc., are the concepts included in the concoct of *metacognitive process*. The literature reviews have shown that there is a noteworthy relationship between digital learning and the metacognitive process. Supplementary outcomes showed that there is a significant correlation between learner performance in personalized and digital learning and metacognitive skills such as setting goals, observing learning lanes and processes (Zheng, 2018, 233).

29.13 Web-Based Learning Environments (WBLE)

Web-based learning environments (WBLEs) are computer-based devices composed of joints of information unified using hyperlinks, Such backgrounds include numerous depictions of information including animations, texts, diagrams, audio, and video (Azevedo & Aleven, 2013). When "web-based learning" is used, a range of environments may come to mind. There are nine types of web-based learning.

- ***Formal course or module of distance learning:*** It has a goal-focused background and is wholly provided through a distributed network. Place and time of instruction is partially unconstrained, because students may learn the course anywhere through the website.
- ***Blended courses:*** It has a goal-focused environment, core instructional delivery, and discussion is shared by live and computer-supported instruction. Some synchronous instruction is required. Blended courses have a changeable degree of instruction delivered online with an important component of individual, instructor, classroom, or peer support.

- ***Technology-supported courses:*** Course materials, assignments, chat, and other features are available to augment a traditional live teacher, but the balance is on live instruction. In this environment, most of the instruction is taking part in face-to-face environments.
- ***Technology-enriched environments:*** In this learning environment, the websites are provided practice chances or simulations, particularly for subtasks. Most of the instructions are in the live session.
- ***Discretionary web activity:*** This type of learning environment may also happen in a formal environment similar to the school setting, possessing additional spread goals. This learning environment is generally used for the enrichment of supporting computer literacy skills.
- ***Tool use:*** This type of learning environment happens with the use of devices that may provide equally formal and informal goals. In this learning environment, the students may be motivated by giving assignments that are accomplished through the use of word processing, spreadsheets, and browsers. It may also deliver practice in the smoothness of utilizing the software.
- ***Focused games and simulations:*** This type of web-based approach comes under the budding use of games and simulations to provide multifaceted practice backgrounds or to teach particular sketched targets. This kind of game generated for commercial purposes may engage strategic planning and execution, role-playing, and collaboration with others.
- ***Exploratory games and simulations:*** This kind of web-based environment engages a lesser amount of goal-oriented games and simulations. In this kind of learning, unpredictable learning happens because the learner is repeatedly persuaded to discover the effects of changeable variables, i.e., under this background, the simulations give learners greater occasion to design the situations in which they are engrossed.
- ***Domain-specific incidental learning:*** This type of web-based learning environment is related to learning regulations and remunerations of using (regularly) commercial sites. This type of learning happens in the practice of using systems proposed to complete ends other than learning (e.g., buy a smart television). Here, the evaluation comes under self-assessment (e.g., did I pay more than others?)

Understanding learning, especially in WBLE, probably also requires consideration of the effects of students' prior knowledge, in addition to motivation and metacognition (O'Neil & Perez, 2006).

29.13.1 WBLE and Self-Regulated Learning

For advancing consequential conceptual learning, web-based learning environments suggest numerous exceptional benefits. Their connected structure gives opportunities to search for rather than to conform, to test rather than to recognize, to assess rather than to accrue, [and] to interpret rather than to adopt (Azevedo & Aleven, 2013, 36). That means the group members co-operatively affect each other in forum conversations. Virtual communities are generated by forums. In forums, opinions with others in the group, sharing of knowledge, and argument about members' opinions are possible. Consequently, the learners illustrate their own thinking to other group members and also acclimate their own thinking to others' recommended solutions, which leads to the formation of more complicated conceptual comprehension. Unluckily, alongside these advantages, research has designated that learners also often practice cognitive overload and incomprehension in such surroundings, thus preventing comprehension of WBLE's full possibility for efficient learning. To counterbalance this overload, researchers recommended the necessity to promote SRL skills in WBLEs (Azevedo & Aleven, 2013).

Research findings point out that students with undirected learning strategies learn poorly from WBL. Those results suggest that such students have ineffective metacognitive processes such as monitoring of learning, evaluating it, and selecting appropriate learning strategies. Clearly, such a metacognitive process may be critical for success in WBL (O'Neil & Perez, 2006). Research has centred on the significance of SRL in academic achievement in current years. Self-regulation refers to self-generated feelings, thoughts, and actions that are sketched and cyclically acclimatized to the attainment of personal goals.

Commonly, self-regulated learners are proactive learners in progressing academic skills such as locating goals, choosing and organizing strategies, and self-monitoring one's effectiveness, rather than merely countering reactively to events that occur due to uncongenial forces.

Zimmerman's cyclical model of self-regulation features the following three cyclical stages within the environmental background (Azevedo & Aleven, 2013, 635).

1. Forethought (e.g., planning).
2. Action and performance (e.g., monitoring).
3. Self-reflection (e.g., evaluation).

Shared reciprocal regulation is a process in which individual team associates influence each other through co-regulation, so researchers have also begun to control accelerating attention to individual self-regulation at the social level. Researchers highlighted that co-regulation should be regarded as an indispensable part of a group's work when peers or other group participants act as peripheral regulators. Students learn to observe their own thinking through critically investigating others' ways of thinking and performing in determining divergences, which leads to the improvement of reasoning (Azevedo & Aleven, 2013, 635).

Frequently, most of the learners do not recognize that they must control their thoughts and do not identify how to regulate efficiently (e.g., locating goals). As a result, the learners are not impulsively free to distributing guidelines with other team constituents. Considering these complexities, Zimmerman (2008) proposed that multifaceted-constituent instruction is essential to aid students better understand the SRL stages in a learning environment context (Azevedo & Aleven, 2013). (Azevedo & Aleven, 2013, 635).

29.13.2 Metacognition in Online Learning Experiences

It is possible support the growth of students' metacognitive capital especially if the support is embedded within content matter(connectivity), a smooth and maintained application, and made explicit. It is therefore desirable to embed within online learning environments instructional support specific to fostering the development of academic metacognition. Before presenting a metacognitive sensitive for the design of online learning experiences, it is necessary to consider the concept - scaffolding, and to gain a basic understanding of the characteristics of common instructional design models. In Vygotsky's Zone of Proximal Development (ZPD), the complexion of reinforcement for enlarging metacognition can be finely conceptualized about scaffolding as comprehension. To operationalize Vygotsky's concept, the term scaffolding was used by Wells in 1999 (Information Sciences Management Association, USA, 2019, 40).

Vygotsky (1978) proposed the following two elements to learner development (Information Sciences Management Association, USA, 2019, 40).

1. The "actual" development level.
2. The "potential" developmental level.

The space amid the level of actual development as established by autonomous problem-solving and the level of potential development as established through problem-solving under matured persons' direction, or in teamwork with more talented peers, is called the ZPD. The word "scaffolding" is comprehended through Vygotsky's ZPD. It elucidates the position of the teacher in presenting reinforcement for the progress of metacognition among students.

Primarily, the teacher must establish the metacognitive abilities of the learners (i.e., what the students were capable of performing previously without help) and what metacognitive proficiencies are required to be enlarged to afford metacognitively. Then, the teacher executes techniques that leisurely reduce the space between what the student can do autonomously and what they can perform with reinforcement. In providing metacognitive scaffolds, this kind of "narrowing the gap" approach is a significant notion. The instructional strategies should amalgamate "fading" scaffolds to narrow the gap. It means that, as students increasingly acquire metacognitive abilities, scaffolds are withdrawn and decreased, permitting students to execute strategies autonomously (Information Sciences Management Association, USA, 2019).

29.14 Blended Learning

The optimal integration of the thoughtful synthesis of head-to-head verbal communication and online written/printed communication such that the powers of each are blended into a distinctive learning experience and harmonious with the context and proposed educational purpose is called blended learning. This type of learning simply constructs an additional luxurious educational stratum. It embodies a reshuffling of class contact hours with the ambition to improve engagement and to expand the right of entry to Internet-based learning chances. Most important, blended learning is a deep-seated redesign that renovates the arrangement of—and approach to—teaching and learning (Garrison & Vaughan, 2013, 7). Blended learning is defined as the utilization of two or more divergent methods of instruction. This kind of learning environment merges face-to-face instruction and computer-assisted instruction (Koc et al., 2009, 194).

29.14.1 Cognitive Presence in Blended Learning

The inquiry process is the basis of cognitive presence. Inquiry embraces the combination of interactive and reflective processes. Cognitive presence is a repeated process that includes the generation of notions, information swap, the bondage of thoughts, states of bewilderment, and the testing of the reliability of solutions. Cognitive presence plans the cyclical investigative pattern of learning from experience through conceptualization and reflection to action and on to further experience. In blended learning, the establishment and maintenance of cognitive presence are essential and supreme necessitate of research. Cognitive presences enter into the spirit of a group of people of curiosity. And also it has been disputed that the online community reinforces the cognitive progress of individuals. Recent research focused on the nature of prescribed, intentional online educational communities and their capability to support cognitive presence (Vaughan et al., 2013, 14).

Metacognitive awareness and action are enhanced by direct instruction only. The reflective processes and model discourse will be revealed by sharing the thought processes of a discipline expert. Originally, to enlarge the students' consciousness of the inquiry process and argue why it is significant to monitor and manage to learn, the students need to be introduced to the inquiry. Knowledge, monitoring, and regulation of cognition contextualized within the community of investigative framework are included in the metacognitive construct. Metacognitively mature students are generated through elucidating, questioning, clarifying, defending, or supplying methods, mutually within a community of investigation. Metacognition starts with the knowledge or consciousness of metacognition. The set of superior knowledge and capabilities to observe and regulate apparent cognitive procedures of self and others is called metacognition in an online learning community. Feedback and this responsibility must be allocated through discussion which is required by metacognition. This again points to the collaborative and shared environment of teaching presence, comprising direct instruction. The teachers must be stimulated and encourage their students to expain their thinking and, tactically, how it will make possible the accomplishment of resolution. Metacognitive abilities are improved by the practices such as peer appraisals, combined thoughts, and simulating metacognitive processes (Vaughan et al., 2013).

The asynchronous text-supported background reduces the cognitive load of students, and also, there is necessity for dependence on memory to practice large numbers of truths and thoughts. The online investigation would come into view to present learners a substantial benefit in processing information and creating meaning. Cognition and learning—above a certain degree of several truths and thoughts—is inversely proportional to the cognitive load. Online communities of the investigation were also exposed to be more comprehensive and less menacing. Researchers have also exposed that a sense of community is positively correlated to the insight of learning in an online environment. Nevertheless, little cognitive presence research has centred on blended learning environments and the powers of amalgamating spoken and written communication (Garrison & Vaughan, 2013). Teachers who construct metacognition into the plan of their lessons—which leads to the encouragement of the students to sketch, monitor, reflect on, and revise their efforts—will have more success associating with their students and sharing the workload in the classroom. The students necessitate taking an energetic role in the classroom partnering with teachers to formulate key resolutions about what, when, and how they learn, so that only the metacognitive skills of the students may be developed (Tucker, 2020).

29.15 Massive Open Online Courses (MOOCs)

MOOCs are a famous emerging new educational exemplar. The MOOC is an emerging instructional delivery model in education that delivers high-quality interactive free, open, online courses for a massive number of learners from around the world. All that is required is an easy and simple free sign-up with a web-based e-mail address. There are no specific academic qualification requirements and limitations to take participate in a MOOC. To sign up and complete an open online course, learners need to have a computer with an Internet connection and the latest web browser.

Massive: It allows a massive scale of learners to register and take participate in a course simultaneously.

Open: It provides free and open access to course materials to learners across the world.

Online: Effective learning and teaching will be conducted online (World Wide Web) using various advanced technologies and innovative pedagogical techniques.

Course: A course comes with all kinds of innovative learning objects such as video lectures, subtitles, audio illustrations, presentations, images, Wikis, quizzes, interactive exercises, collaborative tasks, project-based activities, weekly assignments, peer assessments, discussion forums, exams, and many other elements. The course may be instructed by one or more educators.

(Pethuraj, 2015)

29.15.1 Metacognition in MOOC

Cognition of association between learners' preceding experience and fresh knowledge and cognition of learning techniques and methods are the two main characteristics that are included in the metacognition of MOOC learners. If the learners have an elevated level of metacognition, they can normalize and progress their learning strategies continuously, regulate and sharpen their learning strategies, and utilize their preceding experience to rectify realistic problems. The majority of MOOCs accept peer review for non-objective questions of course appraisal, and this method is also utilized as a teaching approach to advance teaching efficacy. During a MOOC, there is a very useful learning strategy that is available for the learners to comprehend the learning state of other learners. Due to this, every MOOC learner can learn from others. More than 50% of MOOC learners trust peer appraisal and it is a procedure for them to discover novel thoughts and sharpen their comprehension, and over 90% of them believe in taking MOOC tests, which is supportive for them to advance their knowledge. This means that the greater part of MOOC learners are enthusiastic to adopt learning methods such as peer appraisal and taking tests to move forward in learning and to advance their learning results. In general, the learners support the MOOC teaching approaches and show positive comprehension toward peer appraisal, tests, and other learning approaches in terms of metacognition. Learners perceive that the teaching approaches and evaluation techniques engaged in MOOCS are helpful to their learning and similar to their forecast of the learning strategies (Zheng et al., 2018).

29.16 Gamification

Unbeaten gamification in e-learning is distinguished by: a centre on the learner, not games; a centre on learner behaviour, not knowledge; applying motivational approaches of games to learning that is pertinent to life; and communication of objectives and rapid criticism of progress. Gamification is not playing a game and utilizing game technicalities to amplify user commitment, happiness, and faithfulness. This means that gamification takes constituents from game design and the general principles and theories which drive gameplay and utilizes them to other circumstances.

Before utilizing gamification in education, the game developer, the instructor, and the learners are required to comprehend the situations whereby game constituents can influence learning behaviour. Educational gamification intends the utilization of game-like player experiences, rule systems, and cultural roles to outline learners' behaviour. Likewise, the games influencing learners in three chief areas: cognitive, emotional, and social.

The games in learning backgrounds can influence the cognitive development of the learners by initiating a diverse set of regulations to function towards goal particular knowledge and abilities through the achievement of assignments (such as when receiving badges for the accomplishment of a quest). Similarly, the utilization of games in educational practices can iaffect the emotional development of the learners through the variety of feelings or emotions stimulated by games, specifically accomplishment, such as when learners have an alternative of subtasks that offer numerous pathways to accomplish success at a superior task. The game also engages replicated trialling whereby the player goes through speedy sequences of disappointment, with low chances of success, so players can try until they accomplish a goal. This kind of gaming experience produces positive emotions such as joy and pride in place of the fear and anxiety raised in high-stakes testing. This experience provides noteworthy, learning that failure or disappointment becomes seen as fundamental to learning.

Social development in gamification happens through shared activities. This kind of shared or collaborative activities join the player to the content of the game and/or other players; in school surroundings, meeting social needs can be facilitated by permitting students to frankly recognize as scholars with the game offering "social trustworthiness and identification for academic accomplishments" (Information Resources Management Association, USA., 2018, 232).

29.16.1 Cognitive Engagement and Metacognition in Gamification

Gamification can boost a learner's behaviour or modify a learner's attitude. For instance, we previously recognized that learners take an instant to pause and think about their learning while studying (called metacognition), which leads to learning further, so a gamification endeavour aimed at amplifying metacognition is possible to progress learning. Morris et al. (2013) argued that there are three types of mechanisms through which video games can underpin scientific thinking. Initially, there are several motivational scaffolds, such as remunerations or rewards, feedback or criticism, and stream affirmations that keep students relative to traditional cultural learning devices. Second, there are several cognitive scaffolds, namely embedded reasoning skills and simulations that recompense for the limitations of the individual cognitive system. Third is metacognition. It is exclusively for the development of scientific thinking, and also, video games offer metacognitive scaffolding in the form of identity adoption and constrained learning.

Fredricks et al. (2004) recognized a multidimensional model of engagement, comprising behavioural engagement, emotional engagement, and cognitive engagement. (Information Resources Management Association, USA., 2018, 232). It offers a device to evaluate engagement, a skeleton for drawing game-based learning environments, and pedagogy to stimulate learners for academic achievement. Behavioural engagement is something we can monitor to interpret learners' effort, persistence, contribution, attention, and involvement. Emotional engagement can range from happiness to anxiety, from interest to boredom, and other ranges of affective conditions. At last, the cognitive engagement is depicted as being willing to employ in endeavoured tasks with purposiveness and approach use, construct cognitive speculation in learning, and employ in self-regulating learning and metacognition.

In the dimension of cognitive engagement, the game developers should think about a variety of approaches to connect learners—and simultaneously, when the learners do challenging tasks, they used the embedded cognitive and metacognitive strategies for scaffolding the learners. Some of the research scholars argued that gamification should lead to the identification and development of the learners' critical thinking, problem-solving, and metacognitive abilities. To this end, the game should be purposefully devised to sustain cognitive engagement, which certainly is expressed through learners' behavioural engagement (Information Resources Management Association, USA., 2018).

29.17 Mobile Learning

Mobile learning is an experience given a chance by the progress of educational technologies. It is anyplace, anytime learning allowed by instantaneous, on-demand admittance to a personalized world packed with the tools and resources we favour for generating our knowledge, satisfying our interests, sharing with others, and nurturing experiences otherwise unattainable (McQuiggan et al., 2015). Mobile technologies can be used to enhance 21st-century skills in the classroom. These skills, often known as the "four Cs" (creativity, critical thinking, communication, and collaboration), can all be developed in student-centred, dynamic, and motivating ways.

Creativity and critical thinking: There are many ways in which mobile learning can develop creativity. It is particularly suited to project work, since students can work anywhere and collaborate online outside the classroom, as well as face-to-face in class. They can research information on the Internet or call on expert advice via Twitter or another forum. Students can work together to create magazines, e-books, and videos in two dimensions (2D) or even three dimensions (3D), then use their mobile devices to present their ideas online or in person. Learning to deal with a wealth of information, and deciding what is correct—and what is not—helps students to develop their critical thinking skills. When they conduct online research, they build these skills—for example, through choosing effective search terms, evaluating materials, or deciding how to adapt and use the information they find.

Communication and collaboration: Mobile learning also helps students to focus on communication and collaboration. For example, students can connect through messaging outside the classroom. They can chat, ask questions, discuss ideas, and share work via the class website, all through their mobile devices. Messaging apps can be used for quickly sharing media, such as photos, during a lesson (assuming everyone is connected to the same network). WhatsApp is a trendy cross-platform mobile messaging application that permits people to send messages without having to compensate for an SMS (short message service, or text messaging).

Digital literacy: Digital literacy can be defined as the knowledge of digital tools, combined with the ability to evaluate information and socially engage with it. The skills needed on both individual and social levels to deal with these digital tools are known as digital literacies, which can be broken down into various categories. For example, information literacy engrosses identifying where and how to locate, use, and assess information, while media literacy is the ability to deal with different text types and genres. Remix literacy is about reusing audio, images, video, etc., to create something new. To effectively carry out online research, students need to be digitally literate. They need to be able to evaluate the information they find to determine how useful it is. This involves understanding the context of the source of information; for example, is it an academic paper, a newspaper article, an advert, or a text message? Students are required to be capable of construing the information and applying it to inform the effort they are undertaking, without simply copying and pasting the information openly from the source. It is also important to be aware that copying and pasting can infringe copyright laws in some circumstances (Wilden, 2017).

Mobile learning presents a fresh approach to reach students, and also it presents flexibility in when the learning takes place. Mobile learning offers personalized content and teachers relevant skills for the future. It has the prospective to create a generation of learners who observe the world as their classroom. Tablets and smartphones have dramatically modified the technology background and renovated the way we as a society converse and access information. These technologies have been integrated into the place of work and in homes, and utilized to transform and increase the efficacy of everyday activities—but traditional schools are still comparatively defiant about or unharmed by these iconoclastic technologies. Nowadays, in schools as well as in colleges, the usage of mobiles inside the school or campus is restricted. Due to such restrictions, school students and college students may be missing many opportunities for educational innovation through mobile learning (McQuiggan et al., 2015).

29.17.1 Metacognition in Mobile Learning

Metacognition is portrayed as the mission control of cognition which leads to the regulation of behaviours—namely, when and where we need to direct our concentration or appraisals of progress towards a goal. Metacognition plays an important role in the lifetime of learners, because students are less often learning in a formal or official setting and more frequently expected to take on the greater part of accountability for their learning. Metacognition and usage of best strategies are extremely impactful on the efficacy and effectiveness of learning, and they straightforwardly affect long-term academic accomplishment. The omnipresence of mobile technologies in contemporary or modern life aids independent learning, as learners are open to utilizing this pedagogical method any time, any place—so mobile technologies provide an exceptional setting for sustaining metacognition and strategies in the form of devices, as well as chances for performance. When integrating mobile technologies into pedagogy, the following instructions are to be followed by the teachers or instructors seriously.

1. Think about the role of mobile learning as a tool for sustaining the utilization of metacognitive skills and strategies (e.g., organization, note-taking, time management, and goal monitoring).
2. Concept mastery and progress monitoring are the metacognitive behaviours that are required to be scaffolded.
3. The teachers or instructors support the application of a variety of strategies for learning by offering chances for self-appraisal to stimulate the learners' comprehension of what the learner does and does not know.

A good mobile application aligns with and sustains the line of attack in which we build consequential knowledge by adhering to the cognitive, metacognitive, and motivational needs of the learner, which leads to the representation of exact comprehension, understanding, and mastery (McQuiggan et al., 2015).

A lack of highly sensitive metacognitive skills among the learners is one of the obstacles in the utilization of mobile learning. The capacity of learners to be conscious of and monitor their learning process is called metacognition. Adult education literature recommends that the more learners realize how they learn, the better able they are to evaluate how well they are learning and to be able to regulate their learning. The challenge in mobile learning is that learners have little practice with this delivery mode and the related instructional approaches. The lack of peripheral feedback can cause learners to query their goals and accomplishments. The use of mobile learning delivery tools and approaches for SRL compounds this challenge. Differentiation must be made between the students' capacity to self-monitor and their capacity to self-assess in metacognitive skills. The students can monitor their advancement without difficulty against a sketch that trails task completion, time on task, and quiz scores. Self-assessment is the more difficult metacognitive skill, i.e., the learners' capability to judge how well they have obtained new skills and knowledge (Guy, 2010).

29.18 Personalized E-Learning Environment (PELE)

In a personalized e-learning environment (PELE), to personalize the e-learning experiences, the instructional designer needs to personalize the learners, the environment, the content, the roles related to the utilization of pictures and photographs, learning objectives, learning sequences, conversation, navigation, and the media—and also, the instructional designer needs to recognize the individual competency of the learner. A PELE is an environment that is formulated to sustain the information reclamation, information manipulation, and learning support needs of the students The PELE system is extended as a mobile-based (via server, laptop, phone, flash drive, and organizer) website to reproduce as many of the learning resource centre functions as possible. These utilities can include study skills, learning support, information technology (IT) support (administrative), media services, IT support (academic), learning resources, and career services. The PELE should permit the learner to accumulate, recapture, and wield information from constitutional or internal sources (digital documents, hard drives, and images, and so on) and extraneous sources (World Wide Web, Internet, etc.). A PELE is also called a virtual learning environment, and it is performed as an interface to learning sources, as well as to other learning systems and atmospheres. The course of expanding the PELE is observed as a way of allowing students to develop as independent learners. It means that this kind of environment helps them to think about their own learning. Personalized electronic learning is significant because each student learns differently. Consequently, in order to the development of an effective learner, personalization should be taken into consideration on learning objectives, necessitates, prerequisites, skill level, and learning capabilities of each learner (Garcia Penalvo, 2008).

29.18.1 Metacognition in PELE

Metacognition is significant in supporting the learner in sketching and observing their learning task, as well as in comprehending their powers and flaws as learners and connecting in suitable and valuable help-seeking in personalized, self-paced electronic learning environments. Researchers have exploited the following two methods to hold up metacognition in instructional interferences.

1. Strategy teaching is used to aid the working of metacognition and self-directed learning.
2. Generating a supporting social environment to make possible long-term metacognition.

Self-regulation regulates the motivational, cognitive, and behavioural states of the learner. Metacognitive engagement in electronic learning environments can be underpinned through either software or human mediation (e.g., the teacher as a facilitator of learning). Software mediation can take a multiplicity of appearances, such as being implanted in the illustrations of the learning environment or built on the fly from computational agents who keep an eye on the user tasks and offer a suggestion as necessitated. However, technological or technical clarifications for active metacognitive support, hinting at the learners' progression, and offering on-demand support have only been probable in very limited problem-solving conditions, such as ITSs, while even in these conditions, there have been reports of ineffective use of the software. A lack of adaptive scaffolds (e.g., metacognitive prompts) have been used to support ongoing metacognition (Mourlas et al., 2009). The combination of student and PELE leads to the formulation of student learning system (SLSs) to construct a greater efficient e-learning system. A firm pairing between student and PELE is fabricated by this new system, and this permits an unfastened and stretchy coupling with the subjects as e-learning systems and added university/institutional e-learning and learning support systems. This is called a flexible student alignment. By improving each student's metacognitive abilities and self-regulatory consciousness, the locus of control is moved towards the student. The greater independent system that appears is better capable to manipulate the commands of dynamic and self-governed e-learning.

29.19 Augmented Reality (AR)

Augmented Reality (AR) is technology that overlays virtual objects (augmented components) onto digital representations of the real world, such that these virtual objects emerge to coexist in the same spaces as real-world objects. AR can renovate how we work together with nearly every industry today, and it will be evenly transformative both from consumer and enterprise viewpoints. It is already transmuting sectors like healthcare, education, and real estate. AR technology is used in educational backgrounds; it assists students to employ in reliable investigations in the real world. It assists the surveillance of occurrences that cannot easily be viewed with the bare eye by exhibiting virtual constituents alongside real objects, and it amplifies students' enthusiasm and aids them to develop exploration skills. The utilization of AR in education creates immersive mixed learning environments that mingle digital and physical objects, which leads to the development of processing skills (e.g., problem-solving, critical thinking, and communicating through mutually beneficial collaborative practices) (Prodromou, 2020).

AR is an undeviating or deviating live vision of a physical, real-world environment. Its constituents are augmented by computer-created sensory input such as graphics or global positioning system (GPS), video, sound, and other data. AR is the amalgamation of the real world with digital information about it. The principal dissimilarity between AR and virtual reality (VR) is that VR generates a completely simulated environment, while AR utilizes the current environment and intensifies new information on top of it. VR environments present various learning chances to learners such as: knowing and doing the learning, self-directed learning, learning by experience, learning by observing, sharing knowledge, and building knowledge (Guazzaroni & Pillai, 2020).

29.19.1 Metacognition in Augmented Reality

The objective of media constituents should not only be to create a programme that merely looks appealing, but also to distribute the instructional methods and content. Students understand where they are, what they are doing, and how things are arranged through the selection of visual design constituents. Dixson et al. (2016) reverberated this sentiment, highlighting that the visual appeal of online materials must be a consequence of fine instructional design. Devine (2015) reinforced this significance of visuals in educational substances stating, "Our lessons must be attention grasping, visual, exhilarating and instantaneous if they are to compete with all the visual devices our children have access to" (Kyei-Blankson et al., 2019, 139). We should be more child-led, discovering innate curiosity and maintaining the innovative spark alight. The reason may be that today's students grew up with digital gadgets and "are used to fast-moving computer games with amazing graphics". Slater (2010) described this conception as visual literacy. Visual literacy aggressively connects students and boosts the metacognition of students in the learning process. This concept is called metacognitive visual learning (MVL) tasks. It is a type of learning in which learners are presented with "visuals such as, figures, diagrams, images, graphs, or charts". (Kyei-Blankson et al., 2019, 139).

At present, this could also comprise visuals such as hyperdocs, GIFs, embedded videos, and more. Change is frequently happening, and Newman (2017) lists out these transmutation trends in education; amid these are visual tech comprising VR/AR/mixed reality, classroom sets of devices, and gamification (Kyei-Blankson et al., 2020, 139). AR affords various chances for teaching developers/designers and academicians to think and reflect more profoundly about students' backgrounds and status. Augmented learning could facilitate: 1) omnipresent, collaborated, and situated learning; 2) learning content in three-dimensional perspectives; 3) undetectable; 4) learners' sense of presence, instancy, and immersion; and 5) bonding formal and informal learning. The researchers found that constituents of AR can enhance the participation, inspiration, and fulfilment of learners while executing learning activities (Kyei-Blankson et al., 2020, 139).

AR technologies can take any, location, situation, experience, or environment to an entirely new level of understanding and meaning (Kurubacak & Altinpulluk, 2017). Azevedo et al. (2017) pointed out that emotions and metacognition play a significant responsibility in learners' capacity to monitor and control their learning about 21st-century proficiencies pertaining to STEM (science, technology, engineering, and mathematics) content while using ITSs, serious games, hypermedia, and AR, which are called advanced learning technologies (ALTs).

Ng et al. (2016) designed the ATTech system (augmented technology system) for educational rationale in learning Form 4 biology in Malaysian secondary schools utilizing makers as pointing devices, and also they said this ATTech system supplies an improved means to help students learn in an interactive learning environment and obtain the cognitive and metacognitive skills for enhanced "transfer" of learning (Pedaste, M.; Mitt, G. & Jürivete, T., 2020, 94). "Transfer" can be progressed by assisting students to become conscious of and aggressively monitor their performance in comprehension or understanding. The students are advanced the reflection of the metacognitive processes by generating a suitable representation of the learning process in a rich background using AR interfaces. Through the metacognitive processes, the students could see the real world with additional information (Ng et al., 2016). AR has many affordances for application in inquiry-based learning, which leads to the accomplishment of metacognitive, motivational, and emotional aspects of learning and cognitive learning outcomes (Pedaste et al., 2020).

29.20 Artificial Intelligence (AI)

AI was described in 1991 was "a modeling science, enlarging, utilizing and examining systematic models of salient features relating to learning and instruction, permitting reasoning and root of new facts, thereby giving the models in use an active flavor". But in 2009, the definition of AI was completely changed to "the science and engineering of making intelligent machines, particularly intellectual computer programs". Ten years later, the position of AI was in an unexpected level that "a discipline of study that handles with approaches to substantiate that human intelligence is simulated by the computer" (Habib, 2020, 61). In the past two decades, AI technology has been applied to the discipline of education.

ITS covers every main AI topic (e.g., machine learning, knowledge representation, planning, natural language, explanation, and reasoning), and the systems have figured an interesting test-bed to validate cognitive theories and to experiment with their operationalization. AI I used in diverse domains, including botany, zoology, chemistry, physics, programming, writing essays and reading, as well as the expansion of instructional systems. Intelligent tutoring, knowledge representation, autonomous agents, and natural language processing are the largest representation of distinctive AI applications in the educational field. The utilization of AI has generated influential learning environments and positive interactive practices for students over the decades (Habib, 2020).

In the late 1980s, the formal inception of the fields of AIED (artificial intelligence in education) and ITS have been openly located to accept the challenge of advanced personalized learning. The aim of both of these research areas is to obtain an intelligent software tutor for every learner. The adaptive learning distributes paced, modifiable instruction with real-time feedback that permits quicker learner succession, supports efficient skill advancement, and enhances better learner commitment with educational content by utilizing interactive software. Past research findings reported that intelligent cognitive tutors execute as well as human tutors when creating learning achievements in students. In reaching these findings, multiplicities of AI techniques have been generally used. As AI can resolve numerous of the previously mentioned problems, the position of AI in shaping education is significant.

The utilization of AI is stimulated by the advances in hardware, namely graphical processing units (GPUs), and extensive access to machine learning software libraries, specifically in profound learning research and the use of data analytics. A superior transmutation over the coming years is anticipated as robots and other new technologies come into the field at a rapid speed whereby AI is looking forward to nurturing by as much as 47.5% by 2021. One of the major difficulties being confronted, however, is that of transfer. Many of the intelligent systems and software tutors do not perform as well or as expected in learning environments that vary ethnically from the unique context of use (Knox et al., 2019).

29.20.1 Human Cognition in AI

The following two introductory theories may aid in the development of approaches in the use of AI to assist human cognition.

Foundational theory of the extended mind: It investigates how human cognitive progressions are expanded in the world. It affords a structure for comprehending how human decision-making is supported by AI because it contends that tools (even simple tools like writing utensils) outside of human biology can be considered as expansions of human cognitive conditions and processes.

AI-extenders: This is a budding approach that investigates how AI can be applied to supporting human cognition (comprising decision-making and other capabilities). There is a difference between human cognition with AI and the fully externalized utilization of AI. AI is not autonomous. It is an extension, rather than a self-governing representative. AI may be utilized to expand cognition and allow the enhancement of an AI -enhanced human intellectual edge. Al-extenders are utilized by the field of the military to enhance the excellence and receptiveness of decision-making by individuals and squads.

The extended mind thesis has gained traction during recent decades in cognitive science, the philosophy of mind, and epistemology. This thesis refutes the concept that cognition is limited to individual minds or brains. Numerous authors have argued that an individual's cognitive processes spread further than biological boundaries but the resource of the extended cognition thesis is generally tributed to Andy Clark and David Calmers, who are the author of the thesis "The Extended Mind" (1998) (Ryan, 2020, 11). Their thesis depicts how the devices that humans utilize to aid them to complete cognitive tasks can become flawlessly integrated into their biological abilities. The main thought is that the combination of tools and biological intelligence plays an essential role in bringing about human functions.

In solving multifaceted equations, for example, pen and paper are useful for a mathematician. Pen and paper are utilized as part of a process that—if it were done in the head—would be identified as a fraction of the cognitive process. Devices such as GPS and computers offer comparable functions for military personnel. These kinds of cognitive tools are more than just tools; they are integrated as element of the mind. Therefore, the extended mind thesis presents an uncomplicated, helpful, and understandable theory for enhancing human cognition. The utilization of technology could permit humans to broaden further than their biologically based cognitive capacities. This might authorize humans to be more competent and healthier at a range of different functions if this external technology is suitably and morally incorporated. "Appropriate integration", for Clark and Chalmers, requires that information in these peripheral technologies is extremely reachable, dependable, and frequently available. Meeting these circumstances, it is argued that external tools can supply humans with extended or even novel cognitive capacities. The assemble of AI-extenders administers this conception of cognitive extension to more complicated tools, and these kinds of tools are stimulated with AI capabilities (Ryan, 2020).

29.20.2 Metacognition in AI

Metacognition refers to cognition about cognition, and it is a cognitive process which is applied to cognitive processes. This does not engender a great deal of anticipation of we say we mean by cognition. The word "Cognition" is used in diverse limbs of cognitive science and AI as both wide and narrow utilities. Many authors differentiate cognition from perception and action. Nevertheless, Newell (1990) gave causes why perception and motor abilities should be comprised in "unified theories of cognition". If we wish to consider metacognition as generally as possible, then it creates intellect, to begin with a wide idea of cognition, including perception, reasoning, learning, and acting, as well as other cognitive capabilities Newwell identified, such as comprehending natural language, imagination, and consciousness (Jackson, 2019, 19). As cognitive processes may be broadly practical to other cognitive processes, we may consider several different forms of metacognition, such as reasoning about reasoning, reasoning about learning, and learning how to learn.

Others have centred on different features of metacognition, namely "knowing about knowing" or "knowing about memory". Cognitive capacities could be considered in elongated metacognitive mixtures—e.g., "imagining, how to learn about perception"—and the mixture could be instantiated to refer to a particular perception. These kinds of examples illustrate that natural language has syntax and semantics which can hold up, explaining dissimilar forms of metacognition. More importantly, "a natural language of thought" could assist an AI system to perform metacognition by holding an inner speech and by facilitating the look of specific thoughts about specific perceptions, etc. In terms of broad metacognition, inner speech corresponds to a perception of a silent speech action expressing thought in natural language. The thought that is expressed may be a phrase, statement, or question about anything, in any domain. The thought may refer to a perception of an external situation or event or an (actual or possible) action in the external environment, or it may refer to another thought, or an emotion, or oneself, or to a combination. So the thought expressed by an inner speech act may itself indicate further metacognition (Jackson, 2019).

29.21 Conclusion

With digital learning, as well, novel and apparently entirely unidentified opportunities are being opened up that are derived from web-based, online, blended, massive open online course, mobile, personalized, and augmented learning environments, gamification, and artificial intelligence (AI). All of these digital learning environments are the concentrated progression of sovereign learning as self-planned, selforganized, and self-assessed learning. According to Nickerson (1987), the astonishing dyad individual/digitized learning environment displays specification of interpersonal communication: "bidirectionality, diverse [mutual] initiative . . . shared situational background, peer [equal] status of contributors". It does not matter how significantly we regard these contrasts; people feel the specific allures of this learning environment every day (Schraw, 1998, 34).

It attracts because learners take pleasure in comprehending an obscure system, controlling and steering the processes, beginning the attainment of information themselves, and determining interrelationships. In doing this, the learners feel as if they are performers. This beginning situation itself appears to support, provoke, and even stimulate learners to self-learning. This oddity of the beginning situation emerges to be especially beneficial to independent learning. If we take a closer look, we can see other uniqueness of the digital learning environment which makes independent, self-planned, and self-regulated learning simpler. We say that students have all the information in the world at the tips of their fingers (Peters, 2000). To occur this character of the self-directed learner, learners must widen "executive functioning" abilities that permit them to take charge of their own thinking processes. The ultimate theory of learning in this sequence explains the consequence of metacognition in attaining this goal. Even though definitions fluctuate, metacognition at its root engages planning, monitoring, and evaluating one's own learning (Schraw, 1998).

Metacognition is fundamentally a part of self-directed learning and refers to the conscious planning, control, and evaluation of one's own cognitive processes, i.e., our own thoughts that connect in learning processes (Sternberg & Sternberg, 2012: 234). Self-directed learners are motivationally, metacognitively, and behaviourally energetic participants in their own learning processes. Metacognitively, self-directed learners are persons who sketch, systematize, self-instruct, self-monitor, and self-evaluate at a variety of stages during the learning process. Motivationally, self-regulated learners recognize themselves as proficient, self-efficient, and independent. Behaviourally, self-regulated learners choose, structure, and generate environments that optimize learning (Kaplan et al., 2013). Teaching students to become more metacognitive provides them with abilities to "drive their brains" and become self-regulated learners. Metacognition is noteworthy, but often ignored, a constituent of a 21st-century education that teaches learners how to learn. As the research demonstrates, we now realize that metacognitive and cognitive capacities are not endowed; however, they can—and should—be taught and learned. Additionally, offering this groundwork for learners through unambiguous instruction alongside core subject lessons will facilitate enlarging their capacities to become self-regulated learners who are superiorly capable to enhance their academic performance across the curriculum and efficiently reassign and utilize what they have learned. As Dunlosky emphasizes, "teaching learners how to learn is as teaching them content, because gaining both the right learning strategies and background knowledge—if not essential—for advancing lifelong learning" (Conyers & Wilson, 2016, 23).

Metacognition has been a focus of recent research into AI to offer mechanisms for more and more complex systems to identify and analyze failures. Given the "black box" characteristics of many AI systems (people do not know how AI comes up with decisions), the design of metacognition into next-generation AI also intends to offer greater declaration to human users (Ryan, 2020). The research on the application of metacognition in AI is still growing—in particular, the use of AI with the enrichment of metacognition in education is not fully developed. There is an urgent need for more research on the application of metacognition in digital learning environments, especially in AI. This chapter may stimulate the teachers, teacher educators, academics, and educational researchers to do more research on the applications of metacognition in digital learning environments.

REFERENCES

Allport, G.W. (1937). *Personality: A Psychological Interpretation.* New York: Rinehart and Winstons, 34.

Azevedo, Roger & Aleven, Vincent. (2013). *International Handbook of Metacognition and Learning Technologies.* New York: Springer Science + Business Media.

Azevedo, Roger; Mudrick, Nicholas; Taub, Michelle & Wortha, Franz. (2017). Coupling between metacognition and emotions during stem learning with advanced learning technologies: A critical analysis, implications for future research, and design of learning systems. *Teachers College Record, 119*(13).

Beach, Richard; Anson, Chris; Breuch, Kastman, Lee-Ann & Reynolds, Thomas. (2014). *Understanding and Creating Digital Texts.* Maryland: The Rowman & Littlefield Publishing Group.

Conyers, Marcus & Wilson, Donna. (2016). *Teaching Students to Drive Their Brains: Metacognitive, Strategies, Activities, and Lesson Ideas.* Alexandria, VA: Association for Supervision and Curriculum Development(ASCD).

Cope, Bill & Kalantzis, Mary. (2017). *E-learning Ecologies: Principles for New Learning and Assessment.* New York: Routledge Taylor & Francis group.

Costa, Jonathan. (2012). *Digital Learning for All Now: A School Leaders' Guide for 1:1 on a Budget.* Singapore: Sage Asia-Pacific Lte. Ltd, 54.

Garcia Penalvo, Francisco. (2008). *Advances in E-learning: Experiences and Methodologies.* Hershey: Information Science Reference.

Garrison, D. & Vaughan, N. (2013). *Blended Learning in Higher Education.* San Francisco, CA: Jossey-Bass.

Garrison, Randy. (2016). *Thinking Collaboratively: Learning in a Community of Inquiry.* New York: Routledge Taylor & Francis Group.

Garrison, Randy. (2017). *E-Learning in the 21st Century: A community of Inquiry Framework for Research and Practice.* New York: Routledge Taylor and Francis Group.

Giuseffi, Frank. (2018). *Emerging Self-Directed Learning Strategies in the Digital Age.* Hershey, PA: IGI Global, 45.

Guazzaroni, Guiliana & Pillai, Anitha. (2020). *Virtual and Augmented Reality in Education, Art, and Museums.* Hershey: IGI Global.

Guy, Reeta. (2010). *Mobile Learning: Pilot Projects and Initiatives.* California: Information Science Press.

Habib, Maki. (2020). *Revolutionizing Education in the Age of AI and Machine Learning.* Hershey, PA: IGI Global.

Hartman, Hope. (2001). *Metacognition in Learning Instruction: Theory, Research, and Practice.* Dordrecht: Springer Science + Business Media.

Information Resources Management Association, USA. (2018). *Gamification in Education: Breakthroughs in Research and Practice.* Hershey, PA: IGI Global.

Information Sciences Management Association, USA. (2019). *Multicultural Instructional Design: Concepts, Methodologies, Tools, and Applications: Concepts, Methodologies, Tools, and Applications.* Hershey, PA: IGI Global.

iry-Based Learning? *Education Sciences, 10*(4), 94. doi: 10.3390/educsci10040094

Jackson, Philip. (2019). *Introduction to Artificial Intelligence.* New York: Dover Publications Inc.

Jovanovic, Jelena & Chiong, Raymond. (2013). *Technological and Social Environments for Interactive Learning.* California: Information Science Press.

Kamarainen, Amy; Reilly, Joseph; Metcalf, Shari; Grotzer, Tina & Dede, Chris. (2018, April). Using mobile location-based augmented reality to support outdoor learning in undergraduate ecology and environmental science courses. *The Bulletin of the Ecological Society of America, 99*(2), 259–276. doi: 10.1002/bes2.1396.

Kaplan, Matthew et al. (2013). *New Pedagogies and Practices for Teaching in Higher Education: Using Reflection and Metacognition to Improve Student Learning Across the Discipline and Across the Academy.* Virginia: Stylus Publishing LLC.

Kinshuk, V. & Huang, Ronghuai. (2015). *Ubiquitous Learning Environments and Technologies.* New York: Springer Science + Business Media, 67.

Knox, Jeremy; Wang, Yuchen & Gallagher, Michael. (2019). *Artificial Intelligence and Inclusive Education: Perspectives on Rethinking and Reforming Education.* Singapore: Springer Nature Singapore Pte Ltd.

Koc, Selma et al. (2015). *Assessment in Online and Blended Learning Environments.* Charlotte: Information Age Publishing Inc. 194.

Ku & Ho (2010). Metacognitive strategies that enhance critical thinking. *Metacognition and Learning, 5*(3), 252–267.

Kurubacak, Gulsun & Altinpulluk, Anadolu. (2017). *Mobile Technologies and Augmented Reality in Open Education.* Hershey, PA: IGI Global.

Kyei-Blankson, Lydia; Ntuli, Esther & Nur-Awaleh, Mohamed. (2020). *Emerging Techniques and Applications for Blended Learning in K-20 Classrooms*. Hershey, PA: IGI Global.

Lai, E.R. (2011, April). *Metacogntion: A Literature Review: Research Report, Pearson's Research*. New York, 45. URL: https://images.pearsonassessments.com/images/tmrs/Metacognition_Literature_Review_Final.pdf(accessed on 24 April 2020) (Note: Digital Report)

Mackey, Thomas & Jacobson, Trudi. (2014). *Metaliteracy*. New York: American Library Association.

Mackey, Thomas & Jacobson, Trudi. (2019). *Metaliterate Learning: For the Post—Truth World*. Chicago: American Library Association.

Marcus-Quinn, Ann, et al. (2012). *The Digital Learning Revolution in Ireland: Case Studies from the National Learning Resources Service*. UK: Cambridge Scholars Publishing, 56.

McQuiggan, Scott, et al. (2015). *Mobile Learning: A Handbook for Developers, Educators, and Learners*. NJ: John Wiley & Sons Inc. 34.

Morris, B.; Croker, S.; Zimmerman, C.; Gill, D. & Romig, C. (2013). Gaming science: The "Gamification" of scientific thinking. *Frontiers in Psychology*, *4*.

Mourlas, Constantinos; Tsianos, Nikos & Germanakos. (2009). *Cognitive and Emotional Processes in Web-Based Education: Integrating Human Factors and Personalization*. Hershey: Information Science Reference.

Ng, Giap Weng et al. (2016). An augmented reality system for Biology Science Education in Malaysia. *International Journal of Innovative Computing*, *6*(2), 8–13.

Nilson, Linda. (2013). *Creating Self-Regulated Learners: Strategies to Strengthen Students' Self-Awareness and Learning Skills*. Virginia: Stylus Publishing, LLC.

O'Neil, Harold & Perez, Ray. (2006). *Web-based Learning: Theory, Research, and Practice*. New Jersey: Lawrence Erlbaum Associates, Inc., Publishers.

Pedaste, M.; Mitt, G. & Jürivete, T. (2020). What Is the Effect of Using Mobile Augmented Reality in K12 Inquiry? *Education Sciences*, *10*(4), 94.

Peters, Otto. (2000). Digital learning environments: New possibilities and opportunities. *International Review of Research in Open and Distance Learning*, *1*(1).

Pethuraj. (2015). *Massive Open Online Courses for Everyone: Kindle Edition*. New Delhi: Amazon Asia Pacific Private Limited.

Prodromou, Theodosia. (2020). *Augmented Reality in Educational Settings*. Leiden: Brill Sense.

Railean, Elena; Elci, Alev & Elci, Atilla. (2017). *Metacognition and Successful Learning Strategies in Higher Education*. Hershey, PA: IGI Global.

Rennie, Frank & Smyth, Keith. (2020). *Digital Learning: The Key Concepts*. Oxon: Routledge Taylor & Francis Group.

Schiering, Marjorie; Bogner, Drew & Buli-Holmberg, Jorun. (2011). *Teaching and Learning: A Model for Academic and Social Cognition*. London: Rowman & Littlefield Publishing Group.

Schraw, G. (1998). Promoting general metacognitive awareness. *Instructional Science*, *26*, 113–125.

Sternberg, R.J. & Sternberg, K. (2012). *Cognition*. 6th ed. Australia: Wadsworth, Cengage Learning.

Tarrant, Peter & Holt, Deborah. (2016). *Metacognition in the Primary Classroom: A Practical Guide to Helping Children Understand and How They Learn Best*. London: Routledge Taylor & Francis.

Tucker, Catlin. (2020). *Balance with Blended Learning: Partner with Your Students to Reimagine Learning and Reclaim Your Life*. United States: Corwin Press.

Vaughan, Norman; Cleveland-Innes, Martha & Garrison, Randy. (2013). *Creating and Sustaining Communities of Inquiry*. Edmonton: AU Press.

Wang, Victor. (2016). *Handbook of Research on Learning Outcomes and Opportunities in the Digital Age*. Hershey, Pennsylvania: Information Science Reference.

Wilden, Shaun. (2017). *Mobile Learning: Into the Classroom*. London: Oxford University Press.

Zheng, Quinhua; Chen, Li & Burgos, Daniel. (2018). *The Development of MOOCS in China: Lecture Notes in Educational Technology*. Singapore: Springer Nature Singapore Pte. Ltd.

Zheng, Robert. (2018). *Digital Technologies and Instructional Design for Personalized Learning*. Hershey, PA: IGI Global.

Zimmerman, B.J. (2000). Attaining self-regulation: A social cognitive perspective. In M. Boekaerts, P. R. Pintrich, & M. Zeidner (Eds.), *Handbook of Self-Regulation* (pp. 13–39). https://www.sciencedirect.com/science/article/pii/B9780121098902500317.

30

The Role of the IoT in Teaching and Learning: Challenges and Issues

S. Sharmila and S. Vijayarani

CONTENTS

Objectives

The main objectives of IoT in education are the following.

1. To make objects think intelligently and it generate real-time self-reports.
2. To provide a better collaborative and connected learning environment.
3. To facilitate students' effective access to everything from learning content to communication channels that make the real-time assessment easy for the teacher.
4. To measure the learning progress of students by teachers simply and effectively.

After an introductory Section 30.1, the remainder of the chapter is systematized as follows: IoT layered architecture is given in Section 30.2, characteristics of IoT are given in Section 30.3, IoT in education and interactive e-learning is given in Section 30.4, various IoT-based applications are explained in Section 30.5, challenges and issues in IoT-based education system is given in Section 30.6, the chapter is concluded in Section 30.7.

30.1 Introduction

The IoT—the Internet of Things—is a collection of physical things that are coupled through a network. These physical objects are described as "things" which are embedded with sensors, necessary technology, and software.[1] The connected objects are utilized to exchange and connect with other electronic devices that are connected over the internet.[2] "Things" in the term Internet of Things has emerged due to the confluence of several technologies—namely embedded systems, commodity sensors, ubiquitous

DOI: 10.1201/9781003318378-30

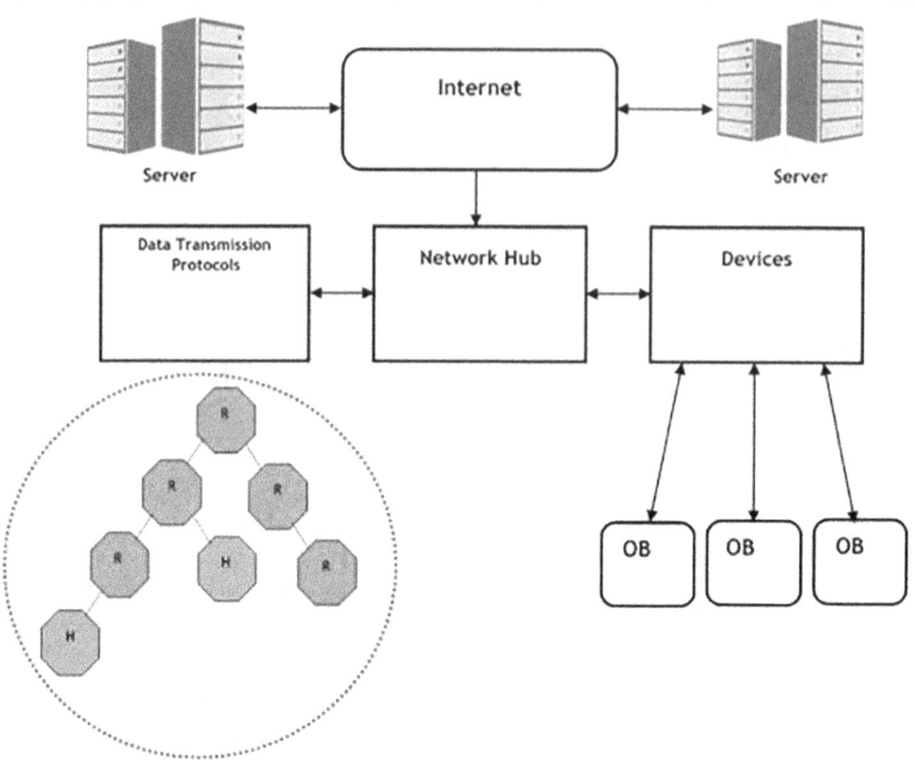

FIGURE 30.1 IoT framework, showing objects (OB), routers (R), and hubs (H).

computing, machine learning, Deep Learning, and real-time analytics. Conventional domains of automation, control system, wireless networks, sensor networks and more provide in enabling the functionalities of IoT.[3]

In the marketplace of clients, IoT knowledge is identical or familiar with goods concerned with the context of "smart education" encompassing appliances and devices (such as thermostats, cameras, fittings of lighting, and security systems in education) which assist one or more general ecosystems and are regulated through devices related to that ecosystem, namely smart speakers and smartphones. IoT is widely utilized in numerous economic sectors, namely education, healthcare, business, etc.[4] In the education system, IoT has a huge impact and also plays a prominent role.[5] An IoT framework is illustrated in Figure 30.1.

The IoT delivers an effective connection among all things virtually and physically. The smart education system permits students to be connected online with labs, smart libraries, didactic materials, educational messages, assessments, and administrative events effectively in a huge size of a virtual classroom.[6–7] The origin of e-learning was initiated in the 1980s, depicting incorporating electronic tools, hardware, and processes based on web- and software-based applications in the context of e-learning systems.[8] IoT delivers a massive platform for instructors and learners, with an exclusive variation of learning at distance with objects and devices. The IoT is utilized in numerous ways, including e-learnings.[9]

30.2 Internet of Things (IoT) Layered Architecture

In general, there are four layers in the architecture of IoT: The first layer is the sensing layer, the second layer is the network layer, the third layer is the management layer, and the fourth layer is the application layer [10] (Figure 30.2).

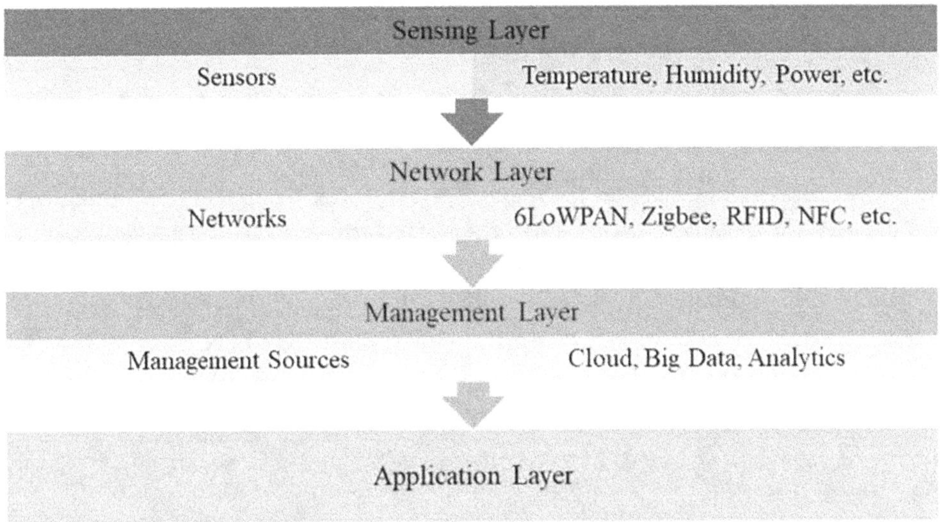

FIGURE 30.2 IoT layered architecture.

- ***Sensing layer:*** The sensing layer is composed of various smart objects embedded with vast sensors with diversified characteristics. The main function of these sensors is to make the interconnection between the digital and physical worlds. It also allows collection and sending of real-time information to higher layers. Radio frequency identification (RFID) tags, sensors, actuators, cameras, meters, etc., are some examples of this layer. Communication technologies in the sensing layer consist of IPv6 over Low-Power Wireless Personal Area Network (6LoWPAN), IEEE 802.15 PHY, Bluetooth Low Energy (BLE), Wi-Fi, NFC, 802.15.4 MAC, ZigBee, Cellular Networks (2G/3G/4G), Z-Wave, thread, etc.
- ***Network layer:*** The data sensed by the sensing layer are transmitted to the application layer through standard communication protocols. [11] Routing protocol for IPv6, Lossy Network (RPL), Next Generation (LOADng), User Datagram Protocol (UDP), Internet Communication Message Protocol (ICMPv6), and LLN On-Demand Ad Hoc Distance vector Routing Protocol operate at this layer.
- ***Management layer:*** The sensed data are transmitted through the network layer to the management layer. Since sensing devices are resource-constrained, they cannot save or process data. Hence, the management layer does the functions of saving, processing, analyzing, and creating actionable information. Cloud computing technologies, Big Data analytics, [12] and data processing methods are used to generate meaningful and actionable information in this layer.
- ***Application and service layer:*** The interaction between the user and the IoT system is possible with the help of this application layer formed by Constrained Application Protocol (CoAP), MQTT, HTTP, etc.

IoT layers address IoT application requirements. However, communication standards in IoT share some common properties such as communication range, data rate, power demand, and network topology support. [13]

30.3 Characteristics of IoT

IoT can be deployed anytime [14] and anywhere, regardless of the location and time. Figure 30.3 shows the characteristics that make IoT differ from other networks.

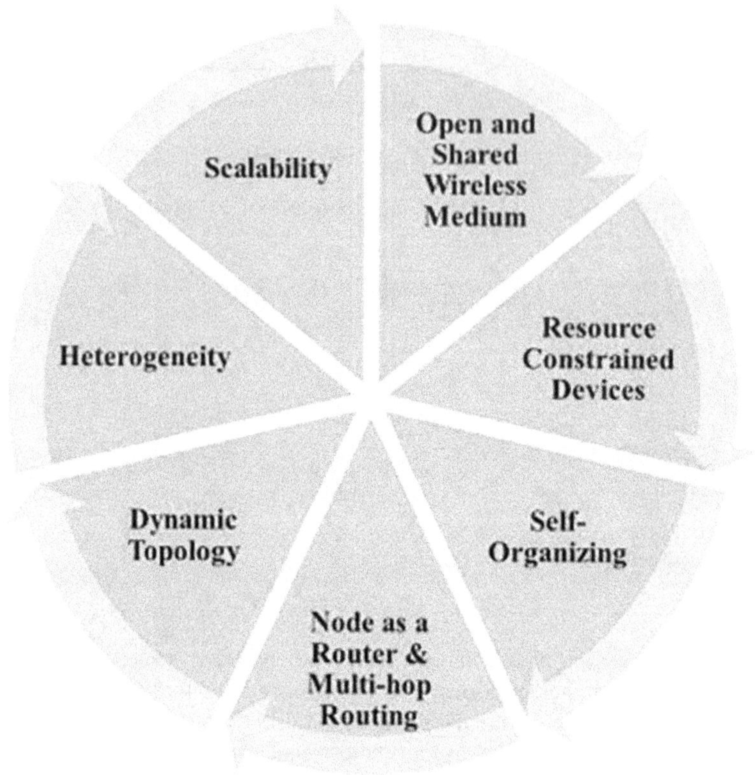

FIGURE 30.3 Characteristics of IoT.

- ***Resource-constrained devices:*** Things in IoT are small in size. They also have constrained resources: memory, power, processing capacity, low data rate, and lossy medium. To save energy, some nodes may be in sleep mode or do not involve in forwarding traffic. Moreover, the usage of complex algorithms to protect the network in terms of security can also drain the battery power.
- ***Self-organizing or self-healing devices:*** Nodes in IoT networks are self-configuring and self-organizing in nature. They only need minimal human intervention. Thus, nodes in the IoT network have the ability of autonomous decision making; therefore, each node makes decisions and they do not rely on any trusted third party or central administration.[15] In times of node failure or attack by malicious nodes, it can heal and self-organize from such untoward situations. This feature also avoids a single point of failure in the IoT environment.
- ***Dynamic topology:*** Nodes in IoT are designed to adapt dynamically to changing contexts. The primary activity is to collect and transmit data at periodic intervals. Therefore, nodes need to dynamically adapt to the changes that take place in the network. Devices can also easily join or leave a network. This does not hinder the network.
- ***Node as a router/actuator:*** In a wired network, there is a dedicated router to forward traffic, but in an IoT network, each node acts as a router to forward data and traffic. The nodes may not be expected to be in the same communication range as their neighbor all the time, so data or traffic is forwarded using multi-hop or intermediary nodes. [16]
- ***Heterogeneity:*** Heterogeneity is another characteristic of IoT networks. IoT networks consist of heterogeneous devices, communication protocols, hardware platforms, and service and application platforms. In a way, IoT is a convergence of various technologies to meet the demand of innumerable applications.

- ***Scalability:*** Generally, the number of devices in an IoT network ranges from a few to many thousands, i.e., 102–107 nodes in an urban environment. All these devices communicate with each other seamlessly, so device management for a large scalable network is a big challenge.
- ***Open and shared wireless medium:*** Wireless links in the IoT environment are mostly open and shared by all the participating devices. Consequently, adversaries can easily enter into the network and disturb normal operations.
- ***Multi-hop routing:*** Due to its wireless nature, nodes may be in different communication ranges. If nodes are in the same communication range, they communicate directly; otherwise, they depend on intermediate nodes [17] to reach the destination node—so it ultimately becomes multi-hop in nature. [18]

30.4 Impact and Role of IoT in Education

Nowadays, there are numerous tools available for improvement in the education system that makes the process in education better, smarter, and easier. IoT is one of the significant tools among them. IoT assists in education for training, monitoring, and assessing, which improves the educational lives of teachers and students—simple as well as smart. IoT unifies the academic atmosphere as a new one that assists the process of interaction of people virtually and physically. It is a prominent subject due to the advancement of technology that is vastly exciting for students; to explain the concept of every subject, IoT is an epitome in both teaching and learning. [19]

IoT supports students in utilizing information and communication technology (ICT) as a tool and learning paradigm to comprehend IoT's role in the real world. To construct the essential notion of programming language, IoT is utilized to explain information to the students.[20–24] As a teaching tool, IoT is utilized in teaching even complicated subjects with the support of a trained IoT-based model. The constructed model utilizes visual and voice sensors for acquiring knowledge from the experts, and the generated model can teach to the learners. Some other system utilizes objects with embedded tags and a learning management scheme to compile data and investigate students' learning schemes utilizing learning analytics methods. [25–27] The role of IoT in education is outlined in Figure 30.4.

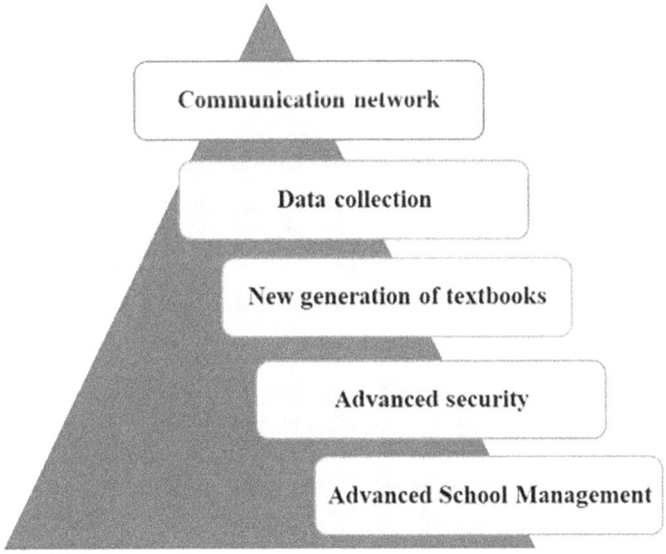

FIGURE 30.4 Impact and role of IoT.

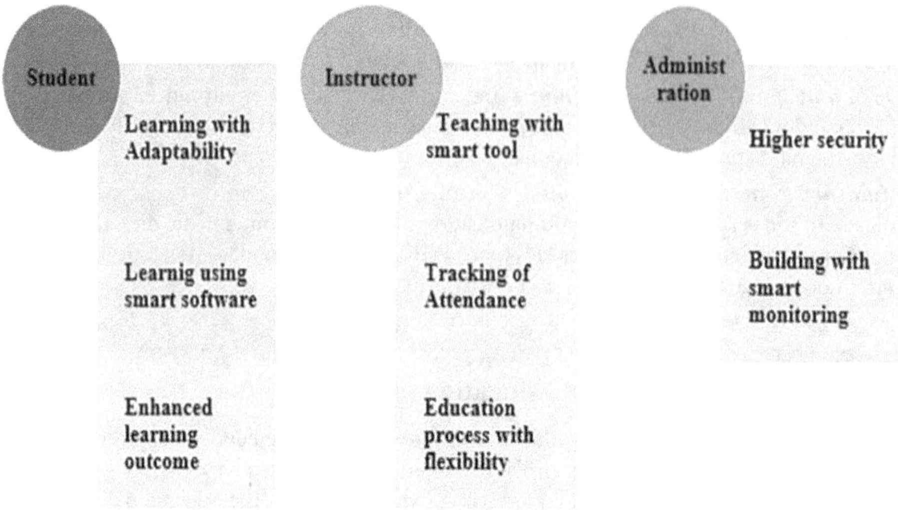

FIGURE 30.5 Advantages of IoT-based education.

IoT in educational institutions means a well-connected and more cooperative future for learning. IoT devices deliver to students' effective access to everything from the perspective of learning to the channels of communication. The teachers can estimate the progress of student learning in real time. The major advantages of education are shown in Figure 30.5 and described in the following subsections.

30.4.1 Students

In the education domain, students play a significant role. The definition of a student comprises scholar, pupil, and learner. College students and scholars should know about the use of IoT technology in higher education and utilize it effectively.

- Adaptive learning can be done based on the needs of the students. This is also called personalized learning.
- At present, students can learn from anywhere and they have accepted the "learn from everywhere" concept. This was happened because of the availability of required electronic gadgets and relevant software.
- The progress of the student's involvement in the learning process is continuously monitored and regulated.
- By learning, results are improved.

30.4.2 Instructors

Professors, lecturers, experts, and school teachers are also called instructors. The benefits obtained from the IoT domain for these instructors in the education field are to,

- Make use of modern IoT tools. It will assist them to explain the concepts in a better way.
- Tracking of students' attendance is improved.
- The IoT tools provide student assessments effectively.

30.4.3 Administration

Principals, deans, and department heads are administrators. These administrators are responsible for managing various education-related activities and processes, and providing facilities. From their perspective, the IoT capabilities are the following.

- Providing smart infrastructure: monitoring the building, lighting system, HVAC system, locks, etc.
- Provide an effective security mechanism.

The prominent solution brought by IoT in education is communication networks, a new generation of books, data collection, advanced security, and school management.

30.5 IoT-Based Applications for Education

Incorporating IoT technology is essential today in universities and schools. It will make the educational institutions to work smarter by providing promising solutions. IoT provides a great perspective to redefine how students, administrators, and teachers connect and interact with devices and technology in the circumstance of the classroom.[28–29] IoT-based classrooms enrich the experience of learning, enhance outcomes of education, and minimize costs. A few educational solutions for IoT follow.

- Interactive digital media and smart whiteboards can analyze and accumulate data for students and teachers for classroom utilization or anywhere else, and at any time. It also optimizes the instruction and improves the outcome of learning.
- Solutions—namely smart heating and temperature sensors, air conditioning, and ventilation-related equipment—can minimize the utilization of energy, and also management operation is automated.
- Smart attendance-tracking devices, tracking of school buses, parking management, and student ID cards can monitor the physical presence of every individual student when effectively maintained.
- Surveillance systems, door locks with wireless connectivity, recognition of a student using face detection and cameras can deliver effective security for staff, teachers, and students.
- Research programs have been enriched with the automated and more advanced in major areas of study, namely agriculture, engineering, and medicine. [30–31]

30.6 Challenges in the Deployment of IoT in Education

The self-organized nature, dynamic topology, and scalability of LLNs (low-power and lossy networks) provide plenty of applications in terms of portability, flexibility, efficiency, reliability,[42] and increased productivity. At the same time, distinct characteristics of LLN-based IoT face major challenges that one has to consider. The main tasks in IoT affect the design, performance, and deployment of LLN-based IoT applications. Challenges faced in the deployment of IoT in education are shown in Figure 30.6.

- ***Resource constraints:*** Traditional algorithm and optimization methods are not suitable for resource-constrained IoT networks. Limited battery, bandwidth, processing capacity, data rate, and memory in IoT necessitate lightweight computational mechanisms and algorithms to optimize the network resource and obtain efficient results.
- ***Self-organizing:*** Self-organizing capabilities of LLNs lead to difficulties in neighbor discovery, topology construction, and topology maintenance. A node can join and leave or detach from the network at any time, and hence, achieving such functionalities in IoT is a challenge.

TABLE 30.1
Applications of IoT-Based Education Systems

Application	Description	Implication	Year	Reference
Educational game	The process of teaching and learning is enriched by the game-based teaching method. Education is promoted with interactive games.	This system has a collection of web services that is integrated with Moodle learning and management system.	2017	[32]
Indoor environment monitoring system	The monitoring facility in the indoor is accomplished with IoT.	Development of an IoT-based environment monitoring system for indoor workplaces and configuration of the nodes and the networks.	2019	[33]
Gamification and educational tool	This approach focuses the high school students.	Cost-effective and long-term energy efficiency schemes or policies are utilized.	2019	[34]
Smart classroom	With this approach, students' automatic seat map is generated.	Indoor localization and smart objects are incorporated.	2016	[35]
Cloud-integrated Smart Classroom	Cloud-integrated smart classrooms help students to create new logical and innovative ideas for social issues.	Digitally interconnected campuses enrich the learning of students and the sustainability of the environment.	2019	[36]
Smart laboratory	An energy-efficient and comfortable, smart atmosphere is offered for students.	IoT-based smart kit and MQTT protocol are utilized.	2018	[37]
Smart bus monitoring system	Trustworthy and secure transportation service is established. Real-time transportation information is reported regularly.	The transportation information is accessed by students and parents. It uses RFID technology.	2017	[38]
Student monitoring system	Integrated electronic devices, smartphones, and cloud computing platforms with sensors for interaction among the devices monitor students in the school.	IP-based CCTV (closed-circuit television) cameras are utilized for monitoring the activity of the student. It uses the OpenFace method for comparing the face information of the student.	2020	[39]
Web learning	Web-based learning facilitates the students to learn from anywhere remote.	Through computational technology, students can learn via the web.	2020	[40]
Smart campus	Every activity is automated with the assistance of IoT technology.	IoT-integrated web service is utilized in the smart campus.	2013	[41]
Intelligent digital learning in laboratory	Academic activities are monitored and automated with the IoT.	An application program interface is integrated with IoT technology over an internet facility.	2021	[42]

- ***Standardization and interoperability:*** IoT networks are a convergence of many technologies. The devices, protocols, and techniques used to connect and optimize constrained resources need to be standardized.[43] IoT involves many vendors with a large number of products to meet the application demands. Therefore, standardization of devices, processes, protocols and security mechanisms are very crucial to the success of IoT vision.
- ***Scalability:*** The nodes in the IoT environment are not expected to be in the same communication range because each device's communication range may vary depending on its configuration. In a large network, effective communication of information to all nodes in the network is

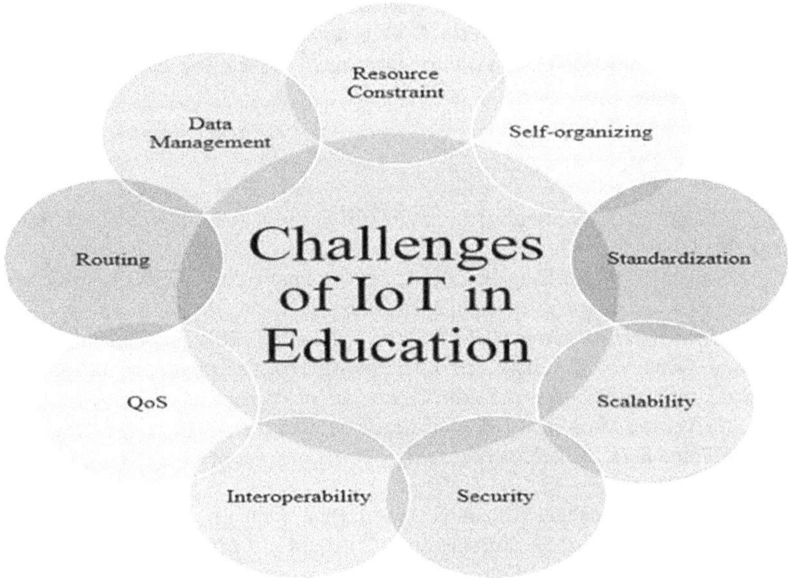

FIGURE 30.6 Challenges faced in deployment of IoT in education.

a challenge. In wired networks, the scalability issue can be easily addressed because of central administration, whereas in IoT, it is a challenge. [44]

- ***Security:*** A fundamental weakness of IoT arises from the open and shared wireless mediums. Both legitimate network users and adversaries access the wireless. The devices and components placed in an intimidating atmosphere with comparatively poor physical protection have a high probability of being compromised. [45] In addition, the lack of centralized control creates problems in distinguishing the legitimate users and adversaries. Security issues become complicated if the adversaries are inside the network.
- ***Quality of service:*** In a wireless sensor network, information must travel on the fly and destination nodes may be beyond the transmission range; hence, the signals may be affected because of factors like obstacles and natural climatic conditions. Dynamic topology and the movement of nodes lead to unpredictable routes, and the information may face difficulties in reaching the destination in time and without any loss. Due to frequent link failure, nodes may join and leave the network at any time; therefore, coordination among the nodes may also be affected and lead to poor quality of service (QoS). [46]
- ***Routing:*** Routing is an important functionality in IoT for many reasons. Routing in a dynamic topology is a challenge in itself, since routes are unpredictable and determining an optimized path is always a challenging task. [47] The wide range of IoT applications requires many routing demands. Efficient routing is a challenge when more than one requirement is to be met.
- ***Data management:*** The success of IoT applications depends on actionable information the system can provide to the user, so efficient sensing, transmission, processing, storing, and retrieval of data is essential. Devices deployed at various places, and the privacy and security of data that has personal or financial details of individuals, is a huge risk and challenge. [48]

30.7 Conclusion

IoT is a smart objects network which encompasses embedded technology to transmit and interact with or sense their external or internal environment. The society of the internet has articulated IoT as a context whereby computing ability and network connectivity that extends to smart objects, sensors, and everyday items are not generally considered as computers, which permit these devices to produce, receive, and send data with minimal intervention of humans. IoT has revolutionized numerous fields and also made a huge impact on the education system. The traditional education system is enhanced when becoming an IoT-based education system.

REFERENCES

1. Rayes, A., & Salam, S. (2019). Internet of things (IoT) overview. In *Internet of Things From Hype to Reality* (pp. 1–35). Springer, Cham.
2. Dudhe, P. V., Kadam, N. V., Hushangabade, R. M., & Deshmukh, M. S. (2017, August). Internet of things (IOT): An overview and its applications. In *2017 International Conference on Energy, Communication, Data Analytics and Soft Computing (ICECDS)* (pp. 2650–2653). IEEE, Chennai, India.
3. Gupta, B. B., & Quamara, M. (2020). An overview of internet of things (IoT): Architectural aspects, challenges, and protocols. *Concurrency and Computation: Practice and Experience*, 32(21), e4946.
4. Gardašević, G., Veletić, M., Maletić, N., Vasiljević, D., Radusinović, I., Tomović, S., & Radonjić, M. (2017). The IoT architectural framework, design issues and application domains. *Wireless Personal Communications*, 92(1), 127–148.
5. Hassija, V., Chamola, V., Saxena, V., Jain, D., Goyal, P., & Sikdar, B. (2019). A survey on IoT security: Application areas, security threats, and solution architectures. *IEEE Access*, 7, 82721–82743.
6. Al-Emran, M., Malik, S. I., & Al-Kabi, M. N. (2020). A survey of internet of things (IoT) in education: opportunities and challenges. *Toward Social Internet of Things (SIoT): Enabling Technologies, Architectures and Applications*, 197–209.
7. Bagheri, M., & Movahed, S. H. (2016, November). The effect of the internet of things (IoT) on education business model. In *2016 12th International Conference on Signal-Image Technology & Internet-Based Systems (SITIS)* (pp. 435–441). IEEE, Naples, Italy.
8. Marquez, J., Villanueva, J., Solarte, Z., & Garcia, A. (2016). IoT in education: Integration of objects with virtual academic communities. In *New Advances in Information Systems and Technologies* (pp. 201–212). Springer, Cham.
9. Ramlowat, D. D., & Pattanayak, B. K. (2019). Exploring the internet of things (IoT) in education: A review. *Information Systems Design and Intelligent Applications*, 245–255.
10. Sethi, P., & Sarangi, S. R. (2017). Internet of things: Architectures, protocols, and applications. *Journal of Electrical and Computer Engineering*, 2017, 9324035.
11. Jain, R. (2018). *Networking Layer Protocols for Internet of Things: 6LoWPAN and RPL*. Washington University in Saint Louis, Saint Louis.
12. Ahmed, E., Yaqoob, I., Hashem, I. A. T., Khan, I., Ahmed, A. I. A., Imran, M., & Vasilakos, A. V. (2017). The role of big data analytics in internet of things. *Computer Networks*, 129, 459–471.
13. Sharma, C., & Gondhi, N. K. (2018, February). Communication protocol stack for constrained IoT systems. In *2018 3rd International Conference on Internet of Things: Smart Innovation and Usages (IoT-SIU)* (pp. 1–6). IEEE, Bhimtal, India.
14. Atlam, H. F., Walters, R., & Wills, G. (2018). Internet of things: state-of-the-art, challenges, applications, and open issues. *International Journal of Intelligent Computing Research (IJICR)*, 9(3), 928–938.
15. Shahid, N., & Aneja, S. (2017, February). Internet of things: Vision, application areas and research challenges. In *2017 International Conference on I-SMAC (IoT in Social, Mobile, Analytics and Cloud) (I-SMAC)* (pp. 583–587). IEEE, Palladam, India.
16. Ray, P. P., Dash, D., & De, D. (2019). Edge computing for internet of things: A survey, e-healthcare case study and future direction. *Journal of Network and Computer Applications*, 140, 1–22.
17. Musaddiq, A., Zikria, Y. B., & Kim, S. W. (2020). Routing protocol for low-power and lossy networks for heterogeneous traffic network. *EURASIP Journal on Wireless Communications and Networking*, 2020(1), 1–23.
18. Tharini, V. J., & Vijayarani, S. (2020). IoT in healthcare: Ecosystem, pillars, design challenges, applications, vulnerabilities, privacy, and security concerns. In *Incorporating the Internet of Things in Healthcare Applications and Wearable Devices* (pp. 1–22). IGI Global, Hershey, Pennsylvania.
19. Marquez, J., Villanueva, J., Solarte, Z., & Garcia, A. (2016). IoT in education: Integration of objects with virtual academic communities. In *New Advances in Information Systems and Technologies* (pp. 201–212). Springer, Cham.

20. Chin, J., & Callaghan, V. (2013, July). Educational living labs: A novel internet-of-things based approach to teaching and research. In *2013 9th International Conference on Intelligent Environments* (pp. 92–99). IEEE, Athens, Greece.
21. Wang, Y. (2010, October). English interactive teaching model which based upon Internet of Things. In *2010 International Conference on Computer Application and System Modeling (ICCASM 2010)* (Vol. 13, pp. V13–587). IEEE, Taiyuan.
22. Cheng, H. C., & Liao, W. W. (2012, February). Establishing an lifelong learning environment using IOT and learning analytics. In *2012 14th International Conference on Advanced Communication Technology (ICACT)* (pp. 1178–1183). IEEE, PyeongChang, Korea (South).
23. Al-Sakran, H. (2006, April). Developing e-learning system using Mobile Agent Technology. In *2006 2nd International Conference on Information & Communication Technologies* (Vol. 1, pp. 647–652). IEEE, Science Alert, Dubai, UAE.
24. Sarker, K. U., Deraman, A. B., & Hasan, R. (2018, August). Descriptive logic for software engineering ontology: Aspect software quality control. In *2018 4th International Conference on Computer and Information Sciences (ICCOINS)* (pp. 1–5). IEEE, Bahrain.
25. Alessi, S. M. (2000). *Trollip SR Multimedia for Learning*. Alling & Bacon, Massachusetts.
26. Chen, L., Feng, G., Joe, J., Leong, C. W., Kitchen, C., & Lee, C. M. (2014, November). Towards automated assessment of public speaking skills using multimodal cues. In *Proceedings of the 16th International Conference on Multimodal Interaction* (pp. 200–203). Association of Computer Machinery, New York, United States.
27. Jabbar, S., Ullah, F., Khalid, S., Khan, M., & Han, K. (2017). Semantic interoperability in heterogeneous IoT infrastructure for healthcare. *Wireless Communications and Mobile Computing*, 2017, 9731806.
28. Farris, I., Militano, L., Nitti, M., Atzori, L., & Iera, A. (2017). MIFaaS: A mobile-IoT-federation-as-a-service model for dynamic cooperation of IoT cloud providers. *Future Generation Computer Systems*, 70, 126–137.
29. Dyckhoff, A. L., Zielke, D., Bültmann, M., Chatti, M. A., & Schroeder, U. (2012). Design and implementation of a learning analytics toolkit for teachers. *Journal of Educational Technology & Society*, 15(3), 58–76.
30. Wiley, E. W., Shavelson, R. J., & Kurpius, A. A. (2014). On the factorial structure of the SAT and implications for next-generation college readiness assessments. *Educational and Psychological Measurement*, 74(5), 859–874.
31. Van Borkulo, S. P., van Joolingen, W. R., Savelsbergh, E. R., & de Jong, T. (2012). What can be learned from computer modeling? Comparing expository and modeling approaches to teaching dynamic systems behavior. *Journal of Science Education and Technology*, 21(2), 267–275.
32. Petrović, L., Jezdović, I., Stojanović, D., Bogdanović, Z., & Despotović-Zrakić, M. (2017). Development of an educational game based on IoT. *International Journal of Electrical Engineering and Computing*, 1(1), 36–45.
33. Assante, D., & Fornaro, C. (2019, April). An educational iot-based indoor environment monitoring system. In *2019 IEEE Global Engineering Education Conference (EDUCON)* (pp. 1475–1479). IEEE, Dubai, UAE.
34. Paganelli, F., Mylonas, G., Cuffaro, G., & Nesi, I. (2019, November). Experiences from using gamification and IoT-based educational tools in high schools towards energy savings. In *European Conference on Ambient Intelligence* (pp. 75–91). Springer, Cham.
35. Atabekov, A. (2016, April). Internet of things-based smart classroom environment: Student research abstract. In *Proceedings of the 31st Annual ACM Symposium on Applied Computing* (pp. 746–747). New York, NY, United States.
36. Revathi, R., Suganya, M., & NR, G. M. (2020). IoT based cloud integrated smart classroom for smart and a sustainable campus. *Procedia Computer Science*, 172, 77–81.
37. Poongothai, M., Subramanian, P. M., & Rajeswari, A. (2018, April). Design and implementation of IoT based smart laboratory. In *2018 5th International Conference on Industrial Engineering and Applications (ICIEA)* (pp. 169–173). IEEE, Singapore.
38. Raj, J. T., & Sankar, J. (2017, December). IoT based smart school bus monitoring and notification system. In *2017 IEEE Region 10 Humanitarian Technology Conference (R10-HTC)* (pp. 89–92). IEEE, Dhaka, Bangladesh.
39. Herlianto, H. R., & Kusuma, G. P. (2020). IoT-based student monitoring system for smart school applications. *International Journal*, 8(9).

40. Rukmana, A. A., & Mulyanti, B. (2020, April). Internet of things (IoT): Web learning for smart school system. In *IOP Conference Series: Materials Science and Engineering* (Vol. 830, No. 3, p. 032042). IOP Publishing, Bristol, England.
41. Nie, X. (2013, March). Constructing smart campus based on the cloud computing platform and the internet of things. In *Proceedings of the 2nd International Conference on Computer Science and Electronics Engineering (ICCSEE 2013)* (pp. 1576–1578). Atlantis Press, París, Francia.
42. Gonizzi, P., Monica, R., & Ferrari, G. (2013, July). Design and evaluation of a delay-efficient RPL routing metric. In *2013 9th International Wireless Communications and Mobile Computing Conference (IWCMC)* (pp. 1573–1577). IEEE, Sardinia, Italy.
43. Ishaq, I., Carels, D., Teklemariam, G. K., Hoebeke, J., Abeele, F. V. D., Poorter, E. D., & Demeester, P. (2013). IETF standardization in the field of the internet of things (IoT): A survey. *Journal of Sensor and Actuator Networks*, 2(2), 235–287.
44. Evans, D. (2011). The internet of things: How the next evolution of the internet is changing everything. *CISCO White Paper*, 1(2011), 1–11.
45. Chaturvedi, K., Matheus, A., Nguyen, S. H., & Kolbe, T. H. (2019). Securing spatial data infrastructures for distributed smart city applications and services. *Future Generation Computer Systems*, 101, 723–736.
46. Rajalingham, G., Gao, Y., Ho, Q. D., & Le-Ngoc, T. (2014, September). Quality of service differentiation for smart grid neighbor area networks through multiple RPL instances. In *Proceedings of the 10th ACM Symposium on QoS and Security for Wireless and Mobile Networks* (pp. 17–24). Association for Computing Machinery, New York, NY, United States.
47. Zussman, G., & Segall, A. (2003, March). Energy efficient routing in ad hoc disaster recovery networks. In *IEEE INFOCOM 2003. Twenty-second Annual Joint Conference of the IEEE Computer and Communications Societies* (IEEE Cat. No. 03CH37428) (Vol. 1, pp. 682–691). IEEE, San Francisco, CA, USA.
48. Lee, I., & Lee, K. (2015). The internet of things (IoT): Applications, investments, and challenges for enterprises. *Business Horizons*, 58(4), 431–440.
49. Huda, Y. (2021). Intelligent digital learning services laboratory in smart classroom environment. *Turkish Journal of Computer and Mathematics Education (TURCOMAT)*, 12(11), 889–893.

31

Integrative Analysis of Host–Microbiota-Based Multi-Omics Data: A Novel Path toward Precision Medicine

Ganesan Velmurugan and Krishnan Swaminathan

CONTENTS

31.1 Introduction

During the past decade, the world has witnessed rapid advancements in communication and data analysis tools, including artificial intelligence (AI) and machine learning (ML). It has famously said that biology is at the receiving end of the developments in other fields of science. By adhering to it, AI and ML are being utilized exhaustively in biology and medicine to understand the biological mechanisms, disease patterns, prediction of events, and development of new diagnostic and therapeutic strategies.[1] Studies from human epidemiological studies result in Big Data, with several hundred variables and new computational techniques which have been helpful in deciphering the new pathways and mechanisms. Velocity, volume, and variety are the three popular features of Big Data. One of the biggest challenges in analyzing Big Data is the heterogeneous nature of the samples.[2] Today, the combination of different computational analytical techniques with Big Data provides a new avenue for the prediction of disease etiology and patterns, the development of new therapeutics, and novel precision medicine.[3]

31.2 Human Biology Can No Longer Concern Itself Only with Human Cells

The advancement of high-throughput screening methods, coupled with computational biology, has changed the way we perceive the biology of living organisms, including human beings. Historically, phenotypic variations and disease susceptibility and progression have been attributed to genetics and environmental factors (diet, physical activity, lifestyle habits, etc.). The cells are defined as the basic units of the organisms—but the multicellular organisms including the human body are not made up of only human cells. The human body acts as a habitat for ten-fold higher of microbial cells in comparison with human cells. In parallel, the genes harbored by these microbes are 150 times higher than the human genes in our body (Figure 31.1A).[4–5] These numbers indicate the importance of microbes, and they

DOI: 10.1201/9781003318378-31

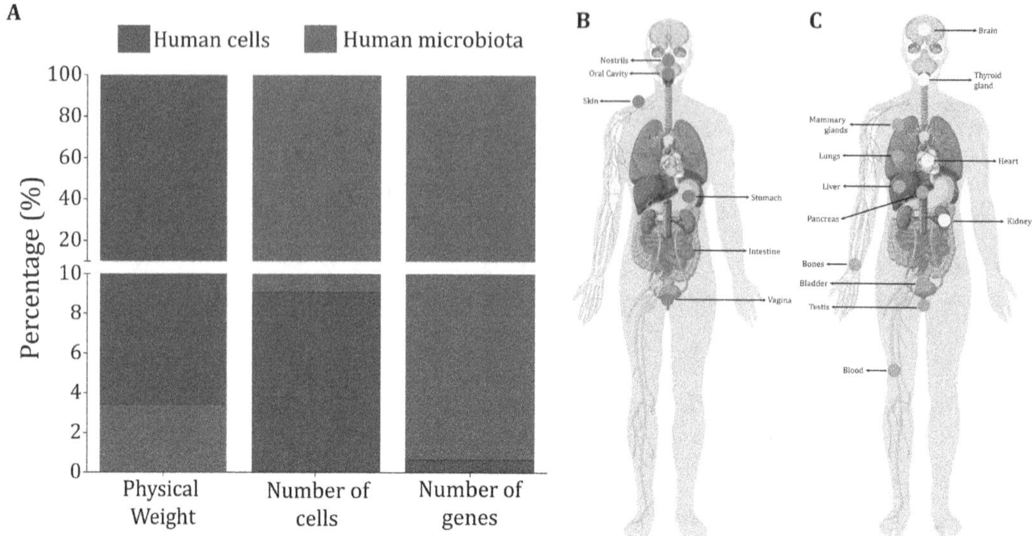

FIGURE 31.1 Microbiota and the human body. A. The proportion of human microbiota and human cells in terms of weight, number of cells, and genes. B. The well-studied and recognized niches of microbiota in human body (green circles). C. Newly explored sites of microbiota in human body (orange circles) and the sites that are influenced by the microbiota (yellow circles).

are not passive residents but functional units that drive different pathophysiological mechanisms—and hence, we are now termed as holobionts, i.e., organisms with associated living microorganisms.[6]

The microbiota comprise different microbial forms, including bacteria, archaea, fungi, viruses, and protozoans. The gut (complete digestive system), oral cavity, skin, nostrils, and vagina are considered the natural ecological niches of the human systems (Figure 31.1B). Particularly, the gut microbiota have been extensively studied as it relates to their role in digestion, immunity, development, physiology, metabolization of diet, drugs and other chemicals, and disease development. But recent studies have proven the presence of microbes in unexpected sites, which have been considered sterile for centuries. The newly explored microbial niches include blood, lungs, liver, pancreas, breast tissue, bones, bladder, and testes.[7–8] In addition, the products (proteins and metabolites) produced by the microbiota at one site—particularly the gut—travels all around the body *via* blood circulation and acts as a signaling molecule, and regulates several key physiological processes. Short chain fatty acids—particularly butyrate and propionate produced by the gut microbiota—are released into the systematic circulation and play a major role in gut–brain axis in the regulation of glucose homeostatsis.[9] Though the presence of microbes is not yet proven in certain organs like the brain, heart, kidneys; studies have proven the gut-microbiota-organ axis by communicating signals from the microbes.[10] Recent studies revealed the unique microbial signature in the tumor tissues in different organs, and these microbiota are proven to play an important role in determining the response to drugs and environmental pollutants.[11]

31.3 Host–Microbiota-Based Multi-Omics Data

Regardless of the number of cells, size, shape, habitat, and other characteristics, all organisms (microbes, plants, and animals) follow the central dogma of molecular biology (Figure 31.2).[12] All the living cells have double-stranded DNA (deoxyribonucleic acid) as the genetic material that encodes the functional genes, and depending on the situation, the required genes are converted into single-stranded RNA (ribonucleic acid) by the process termed transcription. Subsequently, the RNA is converted into the functional units—proteins—by the process termed translation. This process of mediation of codes in DNA into

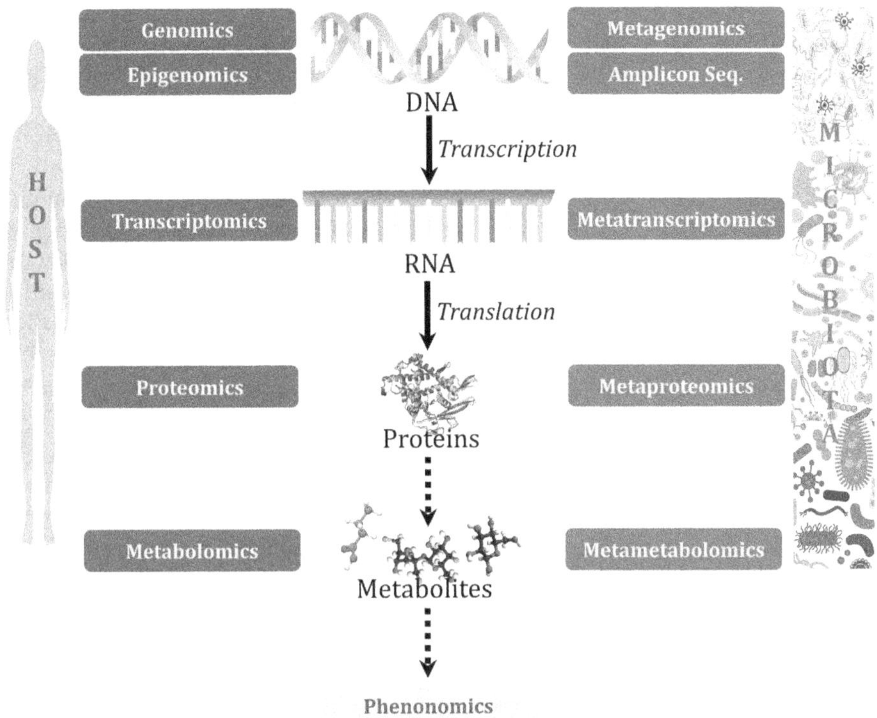

FIGURE 31.2 Different omics strategies in understanding host–microbiota interaction.

functional protein units is classically termed as central dogma and is universally present in all organisms. These proteins make changes on the molecular pathways of the small chemical molecules called metabolites and are collectively responsible for the phenotypic changes in living organisms.[13]

The advent of novel high-throughput technologies has enabled understanding the complete information at different stages of the central dogma. The complete profiling approaches have been entitled-omics strategies. The output of these experiments was compared with the existing library databases, and the differential expression between the healthy and diseased subjects were identified. The major omics strategies employed are described in the following list.[14–15] There is encapsulated hidden microbiota in the omics data available in the public databases, and its potential explorations are discussed in Box 31.1. [16–17]

BOX 31.1 THE ENCAPSULATED MICROBIOTA WITHIN HOST MULTI-OMICS DATA

In recent years, the exploration of omics technologies has been relatively extensive in human cells in comparison with microbiota. Trillions of omics data—particularly genomic and transcriptomics sequencing reads—are available publically deposited in databases like NCBI-SRA. As largely the focus is on understanding human genes and their interaction, the sequencing reads not matching with the human genome are generally considered as junk and discarded. In general, 5–10% of such reads remain unanalyzed. Now studies proven the presence of microbiota in traditionally considered sterile regions including human blood (Figure 31.1B).[16] Poore *et al.*[17] re-examined the entire genome and whole transcriptome sequencing data from 33 cancer types downloaded from *The Cancer Genome Atlas* (TCGA). The analysis using ML tools revealed unique cancer type-specific microbial signatures in the 18,116 sequence reads in TCGA. In a similar approach, our group has revealed the progressive dysbiosis of nasal microbiota during infection with SARS-CoV-2. Our study[18] showed the decline in beneficial bacteria and domination of pathogenic bacteria, and this dysbiosis remained unchanged even after the decline in viral counts. Thus, the viral infection leads to secondary bacterial and fungal infections, which is one of the leading causes of mortality due to COVID-19.

Genomics: Each organism has a unique genome with variations, which is encoded in its DNA. The complete sequencing of DNA is achieved by the evolution of DNA sequencers from Sanger sequencing, next-generation sequencing, and the third generation sequencers that enabled sequencing of long reads.[19] The genome information had helped understanding of the process of evolution and genetic variation, including polymorphisms and their association with different phenotypes.[20]

Epigenomics: Besides the content of the DNA, the changes in the organization of the DNA—including chromatin structures and DNA methylation—implicates the phenotypes. The field of understanding this DNA organization is called epigenetics, and complete profiling is termed as epigenomics.[21] This profiling is largely restricted to eukaryotes, as the prokaryotes—including bacteria—lack these epigenetic changes.

Metagenomics: The vast majority of microbes residing within us and in the universe are largely unculturable. The metagenomic approach enabled the isolation of complete DNA and sequencing. This strategy will provide the taxonomy of the microbial diversity and functional variations of the microbiota.[22] The amplicon sequencing focused on taxonomical biomarkers like 16S rDNA or ITS sequencing provides information on only the diversity of bacteria and fungi, respectively.[23]

Viromics: Viromics is a relatively unexplored field, whereby using sequencing technologies the diversity of viruses is explored. Viromics involves the isolation of viral-like particles as the first step.[24]

Transcriptomics and meta-transcriptomics (RNA-Seq): Messenger RNA (mRNA) acts as an intermediary between the information on the DNA and the functional proteins. The profiling of complete RNAs is termed as transcriptomics.[25] In general, transcriptomics is assumed to understanding the variation in functional genes. Similarly, metatranscriptomics[26] refers to the sequencing of microbial RNAs. In comparison to metagenomics, RNA sequencing provides the information of active functional units as metagenomics, including both active and passive genes. Besides mRNAs, there are several other functional sub-types of RNA—including small-noncoding RNAs, long non-coding RNAs, and circular RNAs—that are sequenced by employing selective elimination strategies.

Proteome and metaproteome: Advancements in mass spectrometry techniques enabled the sequencing of amino acid sequences of the peptide molecules for protein profiling.[27] Protein profiling is termed as proteome for the host and meta-proteome for microbes. The proteome at a particular organ provides the real functional insight, as the RNA and proteins produced at one place can be transported to different organs via blood circulation.

Metabolome and metametabolome: The profiling of small chemical entities called metabolites is termed as metabolomics. These metabolites act as signal transmitters and play a key role in physiology and pathology.[28] The profiling is achieved by mass spectrometry or nuclear magnetic resonance technologies. Metabolomics can be more specific by targeting different groups like lipids, ions, and carbohydrates, and termed as lipidomics, ionomics, glucomics, respectively.[29]

31.4 Integrated Multi-Omics Analysis

The independent analysis of individual omics data provides certain insights but not the holistic view, and hence, integration of different-omics data is mandatory. Dimensionality reduction, correlation, regression, and network-based methods are largely being employed for host–microbiome multi-omics analysis.

[30] The network-based approach is most suitable for biological systems. In particular, Bayesian network modeling provides better insight into the connecting nodes of the network between the host and microbiota. The interconnecting nodes in the network play a key role in this integrated analysis. For instance, the nodes with high degree and low betweenness of centrality are used to explore the keystone species within the microbiota that play major roles in linking with other mechanisms.[31]

Multivariate analysis tools like principal component analysis (PCA)[32] are used to reduce data dimensionality in omics analysis. In addition, correlation analysis—particularly canonical analysis—is used for exploring the association between different datasets.[33] Different tools have been developed to integrate data using pathway enrichment, biological network, or empirical correlation analysis. Some of the tools developed for pathway enrichment analysis[34–35] are IMPALA, iPEAP, and MetaboAnalyst, and the tools for biological network analysis include SAMNetWeb, pwOmics, MetaMapR, MetScape, and Grinin. For empirical correlation analysis, the following tools were developed: WGCNA, MixOmic, DiffCorr, qpgrap and huge. Most of these tools are based on R, Phyton and Java programming languages, which requires deep computational knowledge. Only very few user-friendly, web server-based tools (Galaxy, Paintomics, 3Omics)[36] have been developed for analysis, but these pose a risk of data piracy.

Case Study: Host–Microbiota Multi-Omics Reveals the Molecular Mechanism of Pesticide-Induced Diabetes

Our epidemiological studies revealed the higher prevalence of diabetes among the farming community in villages in Tamil Nadu. In comparison with the non-farming community in the same villages, we noticed a three-fold higher prevalence of diabetes in these communities (Figure 31.3A).[37]

Assessment of lifestyle characteristics and serum biochemistry revealed that the farming community has less or no prevalence of traditional risk factors of diabetes, including obesity, high fat diet, physical inactivity, etc. The only suspected risk factor here is their exposure to toxic pesticides during their farming occupation. Our survey and interaction with the farmers revealed that the organophosphate group of insecticides constitute nearly half of the pesticide usage. These organophosphates are toxic compounds that inhibit acetylcholine esterase (AChE), which are neurotransmitters. But surprisingly, we noticed no change in AChE level in this population that questioned the role of organophosphates in the etiology of diabetes in this population. To address this issue, we employed mice models; when they were exposed to these organophosphates at a small dose for a chronic period, the mice developed diabetes with no change in AChE, and the molecular mechanism is unclear.[37]

To unravel this mystery, we employed host–microbiota multi-omics strategy in the mice experiment. The rationale for the inclusion of microbiota is that these organophosphates have become the most-used pesticides primarily due to their biodegradable nature and studies from the soil community showed the degradation of these pesticides by microbes. We performed whole metatranscriptomics and metabolomics on the intestinal contents and intestine tissue, respectively. In addition, targeted host transcriptomics, host proteomics, metaproteomics, and metametabolomics were performed to validate the integrative analysis of metatranscriptomics and metabolomics data (Figure 31.3B). Our integrated analysis revealed that the organophosphate insecticide consumed via food is metabolized by the gut microbiota and gluconeogenic substrate primarily acetate is produced. The acetate is converted into glucose molecules by gluconeogenesis pathway in the intestine and liver that contributed to glucose intolerance (Figure 31.3C). Further fecal transplantation and culture transplantation studies in mice confirmed the role of microbiota in organophosphate-induced diabetes. Our network pathway was validated in human samples where we showed an association of serum organophosphate with fecal esterase activity and acetate levels.[37–38]

Implications on Clinical Practice and Precision Medicine

The implication of the knowledge generated from multi-omics technologies in clinical practice is termed as clinical trans-omics.[39] One of the important features of trans-omics is the integration of clinical

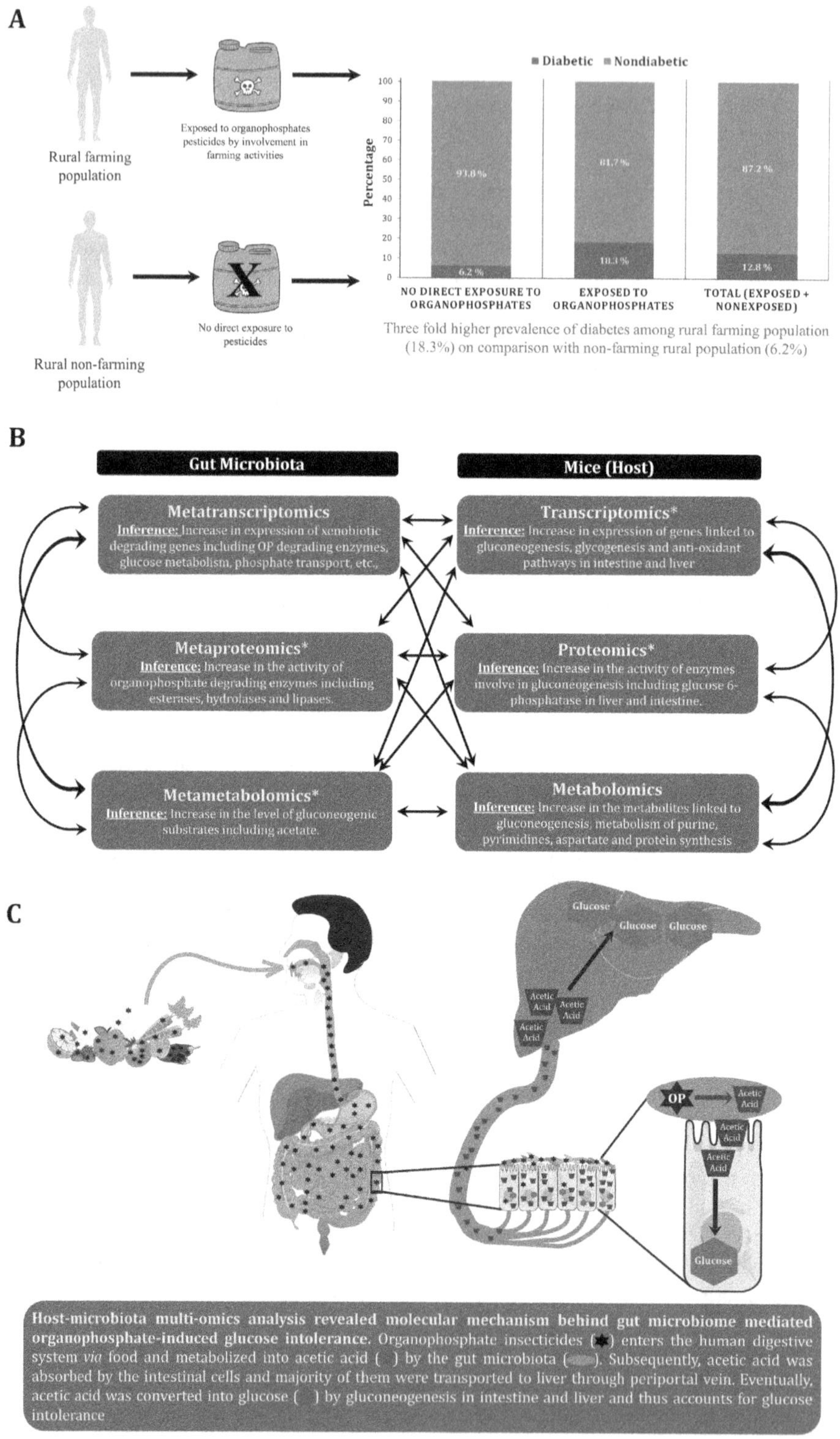

FIGURE 31.3 Case study for host–microbiota multi-omic analyses. A. Increased prevalence of diabetes among rural people exposed to pesticides. B. The experimental host–microbiota-based mulit-omics method employed in control and pesticide exposed mice models. The asterisk (*) indicates the targeted approach. C. Schematic representation of the inference of the molecular mechanism.

phenotype like disease status, serum biochemistry, response to drugs, etc., with the molecular data generated from omics studies. This approach will provide new avenues specifically for understanding the etiology of the diseases, which is largely omitted or ignored in modern medicine. This multi-omics approach can lead to the development of early diagnostic biomarkers and new therapeutic targets.[40] Yet another most important milestone that can be achieved *via* multi-omics analysis is health assessment and disease prediction based on the phenotype and molecular data. This is initiated by the integrated personal omics profiling (iPOM) project[41] executed by Stanford University. In this iPOM project, individuals were recruited for the study and they are longitudinally followed with an assessment of different health parameters and gut microbiome and host omics data. All the host–microbiota multi-omics data representing more than 1,080 different physiological states will be made publicly available, thereby enabling the researchers to further analyze the data. In the diabetes cohort, they have integrated wearable electronic gadgets, and the data acquired has been correlated with serum biochemistry and microbiome data. Based on this continuous glucose monitoring, a new sub-grouping called glucotypes has been proposed.[42] This resource will help in prediction of diseases and progression of diseases, and development of secondary complications.

There exists a huge variation in the efficacy of drugs among patients, and the negative side effects also have not been common. This indicates the need for precision medicine, which is defined as "the tailoring of medical treatment to the individual characteristics of each patient and classify individuals into subpopulations that differ in their susceptibility to a particular disease or their response to a specific treatment".[43] Currently, largely genetic markers are being used in precision medicine in clinical practice. The integrated network analysis of host–microbiota-based multi-omics data combined with clinical phenomics will lead to the clustering of patients into different groups (Figure 31.4).[16, 44] By analyzing the characteristics of the individual clusters, precision medicine can be practiced. Precision medicine could play a big role in organ transplantation (Box 31.2).[45–46] For instance, in the case of COVID-19 infection, precision medicines can be developed by clustering the infected population based on their host genetics (ethnicity), viral variants, respiratory tract microbiota, etc., and accordingly, different approaches can be employed for therapeutics by a combination of antiviral drugs with bacterial probiotics to prevent secondary infections.[47]

BOX 31.2 THE ROLE OF MICROBIOTA IN ORGAN TRANSPLANTATION

Organ transplantation is the only survival option for several end-stage diseases like kidney failure, liver cirrhosis, etc., Largely, the host genetic factors of the donors and recipients are taken into consideration during the planning of transplantation studies to ensure no rejection, and in addition, a large number of immunosuppressive drugs are also administered. The immunosuppressive drugs, on the other hand, make the recipients prone to microbial infections like COVID-19. Studies have shown the dysbiosis of gut microbiota of recipients upon organ transplantation plays a key role in the modulation of immunosuppression and organ rejection [45]. Fecal microbiota transplantation (FMT) has shown to have desirable effects in animal models and is currently under clinical trial for *Clostridium difficle* infection.[46] A combination of host–microbiota multi-omics analysis with FMT may be incorporated to establish safe transplantation and a better life for the recipients. In addition, the administration of probiotics and prebiotics may have desirable effects on organ transplantation.

31.5 Challenges and Limitations

The major challenge in host–microbiota-based multi-omics analysis is the lack of computational expertise among biologists and the lack of understanding of biological mechanisms among computation experts. A strong inter-disciplinary collaboration and establishment of a new generation of graduates with expertise in all fields of science are mandatory. In other words, viewing science as one core is essential rather than splitting it into different disciplines like physics, chemistry, mathematics, and biology.

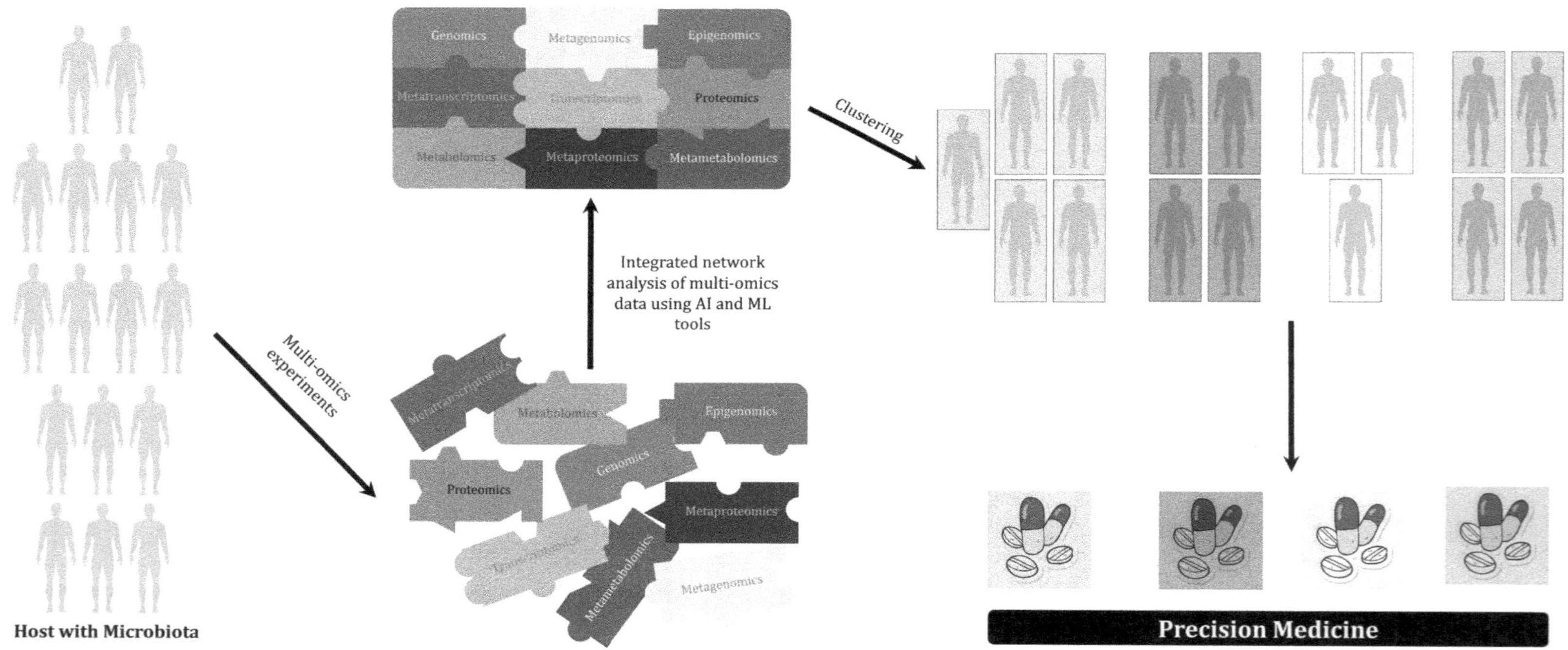

FIGURE 31.4 Translation of host–microbiota-based multi-omics data by networking and clustering to precision medicine.

The other potential limitations include uneven distribution of informatics resources, non–user-friendly analysis platforms, handling of error-prone and missing data, proper designing of studies with statistical knowledge, and so on. In addition, the ethical and social issues associated with access to human data related to healthcare—particularly data privacy and protection—also adds to limitations. The huge costs for multi-omics strategies also add to economic hurdles, as it may not be feasible to perform all omics experiments on all patients. In any event, the recent developments of novel handheld sequencers, mass spectrophotometers, and new low-cost technologies provide hope for overcoming this economic barrier.

31.6 Conclusion

We are hopeful that the limitations we have mentioned will be eliminated in the upcoming years, enabling the large-scale application of multi-omics strategies to understand the complex host–microbiota interaction. This holistic approach will enable comprehension of the etiology of diseases, and translation of molecular features and disease phenotypes will enable the identification of novel diagnostic markers for early prediction and prevention of diseases.[16] Primarily, the precision medicine approach will have profound implications on clinical practice, which will reduce mortality and morbidity due to diseases and the economic burden due to healthcare costs. Finally, this integrated host–microbiota-based multi-omics analysis is feasible only if there is an integration of scientists from different disciplines of science—specifically, computational science, experimental biology, and clinical medicine.

31.7 Acknowledgments

The authors acknowledge the Indo-French Centre for promotion of advanced research (CEFIPRA-6303–3) and SERB (SRG/2020/001867) for funding. We are thankful to the trustees of KMCH Research Foundation for their support and encouragement.

REFERENCES

1. Shah P, Kendall F, Khozin S, *et al.* (2019) Artificial intelligence and machine learning in clinical development: a translational perspective. *NPJ Digit. Med.* 2, 69.
2. Ehrenstein V, Nielsen H, Pedersen AB, *et al.* (2017) Clinical epidemiology in the era of big data: new opportunities, familiar challenges. *Clin. Epidemiol.* 9, 245–250.
3. Nicholas PT. (2019) Translational medicine in the age of big data. *Brief. Bioinform.* 20, 457–462.
4. Pflughoert KJ and Versalovic J. (2012) Human microbiome in health and disease. *Annu. Rev. Pathol. Mech. Dis.* 7, 99–122.
5. Qin J, *et al.* (2010) A human gut microbial gene catalogue established by metagenomic sequencing. *Nature* 464, 59–65.
6. Guchte M, Blottiere HM and Dore J. (2018) Humans as holobionts: implications for prevention and therapy. *Microbiome* 6, 81.
7. Castillo DJ, *et al.* (2019) The healthy human blood microbiome: fact or fiction. *Front. Cell. Infect. Microbiol.* 9, 148.
8. Nejman D, Liyatan I, Fuks G, Gavert N, *et al.* (2020) The human tumor microbiome is composed of tumor-type specific intracellular bacteria. *Science* 368, 973–980.
9. De Vadder, F. *et al.* (2014) Microbiota-generated metabolites promote metabolic benefits via gut-brain neural circuits. *Cell* 156, 84–96.
10. Cani PD and Knauf C. (2016) How gut microbes talk to organs: the role of endocrine and nervous routes. *Mol. Metab.* 5: 743–752.
11. Velmurugan G. (2018) Gut microbiota in toxicological risk assessment of drugs and chemicals: the need of hour. *Gut microbes* 9, 465–468.
12. Crick F. (1970) Central dogma of molecular biology. *Nature* 227, 561–563.
13. Lorenzo V. (2014) From the selfish gene to selfish metabolism: revisitng the central dogma. *Bioessays* 36, 226–235.

14. Wang Q, Wang K, Wu W, *et al.* (2019). Host and microbiome multi-omics integration: applications and methodologies. *Biophys. Rev.* 11, 55–65.
15. Whon TW, Shin N. Kim JY and Roh SW. (2021) Omics in gut microbiome analysis. *J. Microbiol.* 59, 292–297.
16. Velmurugan G, *et al.* (2020) Blood microbiota and circulating microbial metabolites in diabetes and cardiovascular disease. *Trends Endocrionol. Metab.* 11, 835–487.
17. Poore GD, *et al.* (2020) Microbiome analyses of blood and tissues suggest cancer diagnostic approach. *Nature* 579, 567–594.
18. Velmurugan G and Dinakaran V. (2021) Metagenomic analysis of RNA-sequencing data reveals SARS-CoV-2 mediated progressive dysbiosis of upper respiratory tract microbiota. *Biomed. J.* https://doi.org/10.1016/j.bj.2021.02.008.
19. McGuire LA, *et al.* (2020) The road ahead in genetics and genomics. *Nat. Rev. Gen.* 21, 581–596.
20. Imelfort M, *et al.* (2009) Discovering genetic polymorphisms in next generation sequencing data. *Plant Biotechnol. J.* 7, 312–317.
21. Tost J. (2020) 10 years of epigenomics: a journey with the epigenetic community through exciting times. *Epigenomics* 12, 81–85.
22. Martellacci L, *et al.* (2019) A literature review of metagenomics and culturomics of the peri-implant microbiome: Current evidence and future perspectives. *Materials* 12, 3010.
23. Liu Y, *et al.* (2021) A practical guide to amplicon and metagenomic analysis of microbiome data. *Protein Cell.* 12, 315–330.
24. Ramamurthy M, *et al.* (2017) Application of viromics: a new approach to the understanding of viral infection in humans. *Vir. Dis.* 28, 349–359.
25. Supplitt S, *et al.* (2021) Current achievements and applications of transcriptomics in personalized cancer medicine. *Int. J. Mol. Sci.* 22, 1422.
26. Shakya M, *et al.* (2019) Advances and challenges in metatranscriptomics analysis. *Front. Genet.* 10, 904.
27. Li L and Figeys D. (2020) Proteomics and metaproteomics add functional, taxonomic and biomass dimensions to modeling the ecosystem at the mucosal-luminal interface. *Mol. Cell. Proteomics* 19, 1409–1417.
28. Tang Z, *et al.* (2019) Multi-omic analysis of the microbiome and metabolome in healthy subjects reveals microbiome-dependent relationships between diet and metabolites. *Front. Genet.* 10, 454.
29. Smith R, *et al.* (2014) Proteomics, lipidomics, metabolomics: a mass spectrometry tutorial from a computer scientist's point of view. *BMC Bioinform.* 15, S9.
30. Liu A, *et al.* (2021) Network analysis in microbiome based on high-throughput multi-omics data. *Brief. Bioinform.* 22, 1639–1655.
31. Agler MT, Ruhe J, Kroll S, *et al.* (2016) Microbial hub taxa link host and abiotic factors to plant microbiome variation. *PLoS Biol* 14, e1002352.
32. Meng C, *et al.* (2016) Dimension reduction techniques for the integrative analysis of multi-omics data. *Brief. Bioinform.* 17, 628–641.
33. Parkhomenko E, Tritchler D and Beyene J (2009) Sparse canonical correlation analysis with application to genomic data integration. *Stat. Appl. Genet. Mol. Biol.* 8, 1–34.
34. Wanichthanarak K, Fahrmann JF and Grapov D. (2015) Genomic, proteomic, and metabolomic data integration strategies. *Biomark. Insights* 10, 1–6.
35. Misra BB, *et al.* (2019) Integrated omics: tools, advances and future approaches. *J. Mol. Endocrinol.* 62, R21–R45.
36. Fan J, Saha S, Barker G, *et al.* (2015) Galaxy Integrated Omics: web-based standards-compliant workflows for proteomics informed by transcriptomics. *Mol. Cell. Proteomics* 14, 3087–3093.
37. Velmurugan G, et al. (2017) Gut microbial degradation of organophosphate insecticides-induces glucose intolerance via gluconeogenesis. *Genome Biol.* 18, 8.
38. Velmurugan G, *et al.* (2017) Gut microbiota, endocrine disrupting chemicals and diabetes epidemic. *Trends Endocrinol. Metab.* 28, 612–625.
39. Wang X. (2018) Clinical trans-omics: an integration of clinical phenomes with molecular multiomics. *Cell Biol. Toxicol.* 34, 163–166.
40. Nyholm L, *et al.* (2020) Holo-omics: integrated host-microbiota multi-omics for basic and applied biological research. *iScience* 23, 101414.

41. Chen R, *et al.* (2012) Personal omics profiling reveals dynamic molecular and medical phenotypes. *Cell* 148, 1293–1307.
42. Hall H, *et al.* (2018) Glucotypes reveal new patterns of glucose dysregulation. *PLoS Biol.* 16, e2005143.
43. Ginsburg GS and Phillips KA. (2018) Precision medicine: from science to value. *Health Aff (Millwood).* 37, 694–701.
44. Ahmed Z. (2020) Practicing precision medicine with intelligently integrative clinical and multi-omics data analysis. *Human Gen.* 14, 35.
45. Dery KJ, Kadono K, Hirao H, *et al.* (2020) Microbiota in organ transplantation: an immunological and therapeutic conundrum? *Cell. Immunol.* 351, 104080.
46. Cheng Y, *et al.* (2018) Fecal microbiota transplantation for the treatment of recurrent and severe Clostridium difficile infection in solid organ transplant recipients: a multicenter experience. *Am. J. Tranplant.* 19, 501–511.
47. Singh R, *et al.* (2021) Multi-omics approach in the identification of potential therapeutic biomolecule for COVID-19. *Front. Pharmacol.* https://doi.org/10.3389/fphar.2021.652335.

32

Emotional Intelligence: The Complex Innate Traits of Humankind

Sadhasivam Subramaniam

CONTENTS

32.1 Introduction

Certain definitions tend to change with the span of time, and one such example is 'intelligence'. Until a few decades ago, the meaning of intelligence was referred to be 'being rational', but now it is a part of one component of total intelligence. With the expansion of cognitive research, controlling one's emotions is also playing a pivotal role in regulating and applying intelligence. Emotional intelligence (EI) is relatively a novel terminology—until 1990, the definition of EI was not lucidly explained or comprehended. A concrete conceptual framework was initially given by Payne (1986) and a comprehensive analysis was provided four years later by Salovey and Mayer, who defined "emotional intelligence" as "the ability to monitor one's own and others' feelings and emotions, to discriminate among them and to use this information to guide one's thinking and actions" (Salovey and Mayer, 1990). EI is a part of intelligence, and it is mainly related to the ability of one's competence to identify processes and to regulate and effectively apply them to where it matters the most. Further, it also aids to understand and respond to the emotions and feelings of others. EI is also relatively used with other terminologies like emotional quotient (EQ), emotional leadership (EL), and emotional intelligence quotient (EIQ). EI is also a part of cognition and it helps to maintain interpersonal behavior. If one is able to use and manage their emotions positively, it will help to build better communication, control stress and conflict, empathize with others, and build a

DOI: 10.1201/9781003318378-32

healthy relationship (Salovey and Mayer, 1990). EQ has been recently celebrated more for its essentiality in attaining success in life, academics, and career. While an individual would learn to understand and manage their emotions, they can also better adjust their behavior to any environment.

32.2 Origin and Developments of Emotional Intelligence

Renowned psychologist Edward Thorndike (1920) proposed the concept of "social intelligence" and elucidated it as the ability of an individual to communicate and connect with other people for improved human relations. Nearly two decades later, David Wechsler (1939) identified the different components of intelligence and how each element is essential for attaining success in one's life. In the early 1980s, Howard Gardner (1983) presented the term "multiple intelligence" which means intelligence is not a single thing, but it is rather a collective ability that denotes the person's capacity to apprehend the objectives, incentives, and requirements of other people. Though the phrase EI has existed in the usage for a longer time in theoretical or philosophical form, a proper construct framework was given in 1986 by Payne, who coined the term "emotional intelligence" in his Ph.D. dissertation. He was followed by Peter Salovey and John Mayer who had provided comprehensive theory and demonstration of EI and published their work "Emotional Intelligence" in 1990 (Salovey and Mayer, 1990). But the phrase EI was extensively popularized by Daniel Goleman (1995), a psychologist and a science writer who further disseminated the concept of EI through his book *Emotional Intelligence: Why It Can Matter More Than IQ*. After the publication of Goleman's book, a strong interest was created in the different dimensions of EI-like emotions and brain, gender differences in emotions, EQ tests, societal behavior, and the introduction of EI in academics, workplaces, leadership, etc.

32.3 Emotional Intelligence Framework

32.3.1 The Mayer–Salovey Model

The broad framework of "EI" was developed by the American psychologists Peter Salovey and John Mayer, and it was named the Mayer–Salovey model of emotional intelligence. They identified the four key domains involved in the regulation of EI in childhood and adults as: (i) perceiving emotions to identify, express, and discriminate the individual's feeling; (ii) using emotions to facilitate the emotions by selecting the problem, prioritizing the thought, and generating emotions; (iii) understanding emotions—the ability to label, interpret, understand, and recognize the transition between the emotions; and (iv) managing emotions to stay open to, engage and disengage with, and monitor and manage the emotions. The schematic representation of the Mayer–Salovey model of EI is represented in Figure 32.1. The Mayer–Salovey model of EI works in the order of basic to highest, explained as follows. The domains perceiving and using emotions are considered as the simplest of the EI; whereas the understanding and managing of emotions are considered as the complex nature of EI (Salovey and Mayer, 1990).

32.3.2 Attributes of EI: Daniel Goleman

Daniel Goleman (1995) has delineated the five main attributes of EI as self-awareness, self-regulation, motivation, empathy, and social skills. The attributes of EI proposed by Goleman are represented in Figure 32.2. The first three characteristics—self-awareness, self-regulation, and motivation—are classified as personal competency (how we manage ourselves), whereas empathy and social skills are demarcated as interpersonal skills (how we handle relationships with others). Self-awareness is the reflection and recognition of one's abilities, emotions, values, passion, strengths, and weaknesses, and it is one of the cores and essential components of EI. Self-awareness is classified into: (i) internal and (ii) external self-awareness; internal self-awareness is about the individual's inner feelings, and external self-awareness is about the acknowledgment and understanding of others. The development of self-awareness will make the students more productive, communicative, interactive, and happy. Self-regulation aids the

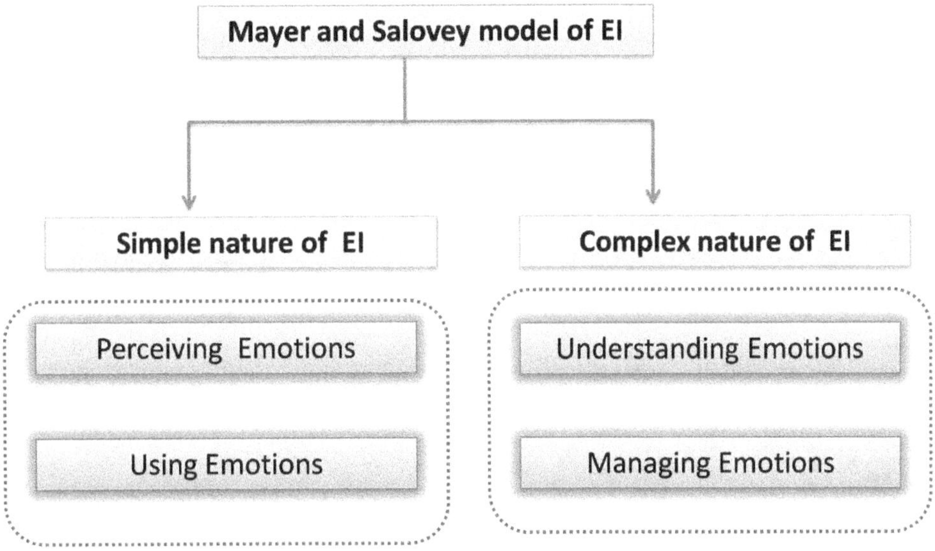

FIGURE 32.1 The Mayer–Salovey model of emotional intelligence. According to Mayer and Salovey, the EI exists in two natures: i.e., simple and complex. The simple nature of EI includes perceiving and using emotions, while the complex nature of EI includes understanding and managing emotions.

individual's ability to control and manage their emotions and impulses. Self-regulation can be attained by being conscious, self-restraint, trustworthy, and adaptable. Cognitive reappraisal is a self-regulation strategy that will help to lessen the emotional impact under the stressful situation by consciously reframing or re-patterning the thoughts. Its main application is the management of negative emotions like stress, anxiety, and depression.

Motivation is another personal skill or competency of an individual which is strongly linked to the EI construct. The elements such as drive for achievement, commitment, initiative, and optimism are considered as the personal drive to the concept of 'motivation'. Empathy is one's ability to comprehend one's own emotions and be sensitive to the feelings of others. It has been validated that an empathetic person can work with diverse people (leveraging diversity) and positively influences them. Another key component of EI is social skills, which are crucial to understand and empathize with others in varied academic or work communities. If the person is demonstrating good social skills, they are influential, possess leadership qualities, and are excellent communicators, relationship builders, collaborators, team players, conflict managers (Goleman, 1995). EI is a determinant tool for leaders and followers to achieve leadership effectiveness and social activeness. An individual with strong EI can create a working environment much more pleasurable and pleasant. The development of well-built EI is superior for all kinds of professionals who wish to enhance working environment qualities (Gragg, 2008).

In today's emerging world loaded with technology and data, work/life imbalance is a significant problem faced by many. It also implies accomplishment and delight in the other three domains of life (family, friends, and self). The association between EI and work/life balance is positively correlated. Individuals with high EI reported having a higher overall work/life balance compared to employees with low EI. The study also suggests that a healthy interpersonal relationship among team members will improve productivity (Shelar, 2016). A study among 120 social workers has revealed that work/life balance and compassion satisfaction can be attained through cultivating EI (Bae et al., 2020). A significant and positive relationship is established between EI and its components: self-awareness, self-management and relation control, and social awareness (Farahbakhsh, 2012).

The quality of EI can be determined by critical thinking, and especially individuals who are aware of their strengths, weakness, goals, and abilities can analyze and process all new information in their way and find the meaning. A longitudinal study conducted on nursing students established the correlation

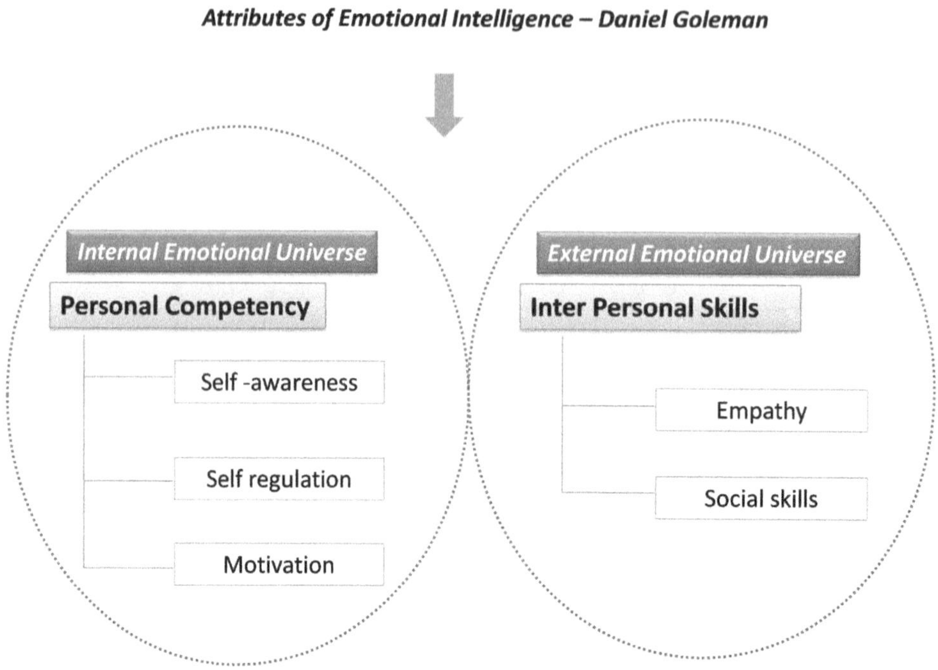

FIGURE 32.2 Daniel Goleman's attributes of emotional intelligence (EI). The major attributes of EI as proposed by Goleman include two types: personal competency that focuses on self-development—i.e., within ourself and hence termed internal emotional universe, consisting of the characteristics of self-awareness, self-regulation, and motivation—while the second type, interpersonal skill, deals with understanding emotions of other people, i.e., the external emotional universe, and includes the characteristics of empathy and social skills.

between EI and critical thinking (Kaya et al., 2017). Similarly, passion is another quality that is quite like EI and is required by an individual to be successful in life (Hernon and Rossiter, 2006). It is generally accepted that being passionate is one of the principal elements of the entrepreneurial process (Chin et al., 2012).

32.4 Tests to Measure EQ

Goleman and other scientists have insisted on the need for conducting an EQ test in addition to the conventional IQ tests for determining the ability of an individual to perform tasks. They advocated that the intelligence test should be inclusive of questions based on an individual's ability to deal with emotions (EQ) in conjunction with knowledge-based questions (IQ). EQ tests will identify the EI and explain the emotional strengths and weaknesses of the person subjected to the assessment. Different assessment tests or methods have emerged to quantify EI. Akansha and Dau (2005) categorized the measures of EI into three streams: (i) self-report tests; (ii) ability tests; and (iii) mixed model tests. Ability tests are cognitive in nature and employ performance tests to assess standard intelligence. It is a four-branch model, proposed by Mayer and Salovey (1997) and measured using multifactor emotional intelligence scale (MEIS), which was revised again in 2002 and published as the Mayer–Salovey–Caruso Emotional Intelligence Test (MSCEIT). While self-reports consider the non-cognitive nature of EI—also called trait models that are based on self-perception—the third stream comprises a mixed model in which emotional and other behavioral items are combined. Test measures such as the emotional quotient inventory (EQi) are of this nature (Bar-On, 1988; Ogurlu, 2021). Meta-analysis studies between EI and subjective wellbeing (SWB) among 8,420 participants (mean age: 21 years) by self-reported mixed EI instruments (third stream) showed a significant relationship (Sánchez-Álvarez et al., 2016). Some of the important test measures are described in the below subsections.

32.4.1 Mayer–Salovey–Caruso Emotional Intelligence Test (MSCEIT)

MSCEIT is an ability-based test and it measures the ability of an individual to perceive, identify, understand, and manage emotions. The scoring and reliability of MSCEIT to predict psychometric properties over MEIS are reported to be efficient (Palmer et al., 2005). The test score obtained in MSCEIT is based on experiential EIQ and strategic EIQ. Experiential EIQ explains the identification, comparison, and connection between the emotions, whereas strategic EIQ deals with the origin and applications of the emotions in a relationship. As this test provides a detailed analysis of different domains involved during emotional processing, it will bring to light the individual's ability to react in the given situations. MSCEIT was employed to study the interaction between EI abilities and work engagement on job and life satisfaction in secondary-school teachers. The results showed that emotion regulation ability (ERA) was significantly associated with work engagement, job satisfaction, and life satisfaction (Mérida-López and Extremera, 2020).

32.4.2 Bar-On's Emotional Quotient Inventory (EQ-i)

Reuven Bar-On (1988) is a renowned psychologist who introduced the EQ (conceptual and psychometric model) for the quantification of constructs related to EI, especially human behavior and performance. The Bar-On EQ-i is based on emotional and social intelligence conceptualization, and measures self-perception, self-expression, decision making, interpersonal relationships, and stress management by qualified persons. The EQ-i test falls under a self-report test which will be conducted for individuals who are 16 or more years old. The EQ-i measures mental ability rather than personality traits or cognitive ability that makes an individual aware of creating themselves to meet the environmental needs and pressures (Chopra and Kanji, 2010). A hypothetical study was conducted to find the association between ability, trait EI, and career decision making among 194 Italian high school students assessed by EQ-i and the Trait Emotional Intelligence Questionnaire (TEIQue). It showed that trait EI plays a more significant role in career decision-making self-efficacy than the ability model. It may be because the self-reported model incorporates various emotional experiences and thoughts which are interrelated with career issues and making an appropriate career decision (Di Fabio and Saklofske, 2014).

32.4.3 Emotional and Social Competency Inventory (ESCI) and Test of Emotional Intelligence (TIE)

ESCI works by evaluating the Self-Assessment Questionnaire, and it gauges the different emotional competence of the person. ESCI measures the social-EI of a person through a 360-question survey comprised of 12 different competencies based on the four distinct areas of self-awareness, social awareness, self-management, and relationship management (Boyatzis and Boyatzis, 2009). The conceptual measure of a test of emotional intelligence (TIE) is operative on an ability-based approach and it will be used to evaluate the set of emotional abilities of an individual or the group. In this method, respondents have to match the appropriate emotion according to the situation described, and their response is evaluated by the experts. This can be called one of the most dependable and accurate methods in the determination of EI in individuals. A study among 4,642 Polish people to test the psychometric properties and factorial structure of EI assessed by the newly designed TIE study indicated that the design was reliable, easy to use, and requires less time to perform, and showed a high internal consistency score (0.88) (Śmieja et al., 2014).

32.5 Personality Traits in Low EQ vs. High EQ

The significance of EQ has intensely gained momentum in the world of modern management and leadership. There are many pieces of evidence suggesting that a person's high IQ and an outstanding academic track record, on their own, failed to make them successful. The recent cognitive analysis has suggested that like IQ, an equal part of EQ will facilitate them to achieve more in academics, career, and life. This is substantiated by the fact that the individual with higher EQ can better understand and relate to the emotions of others, which in turn will facilitate the performance of the organization (Richardson and Norgate, 2015; Rockstuhl et al., 2011). There is a lot of science involved in the processing of EI, and it is chiefly mediated through the limbic system of the brain. There are numerous structures in the limbic system that are interconnected and mediate the different functions of cognitive emotions (sensory perception, attention, consciousness, movement, motivation, learning, memory, etc). However, brain circuitries such as the amygdala and prefrontal cortex are vital in sensing and regulating emotions (Lewis and Todd, 2007).

Based on the level of regulating emotions appropriately, individuals are classified into low-EQ and high-EQ personalities. The person with low EQ can be easily identifiable through certain visible traits or characteristics. They have sudden emotional outbursts and are ill-tempered, confrontational, and stressed, they have adjustment disorders, and they are poor listeners with difficult social relationships. Hence, low EQ personalities will struggle to perform better under pressure or crisis, which negatively affects their chances of getting hired and/or being promoted. A person who is weak in understanding emotions will fail to regulate their thinking and actions to complete the given task in time. On the other hand, people with high EQ can demonstrate better job performance, productivity, and leadership qualities. They are confident, optimistic, expressive, resilient, active listeners, considerate, and creative, having leadership and decision-making abilities. We humans are a highly complex living entity, and hence, some internal and behavioural adjustments are needed to manage the social complexities prevalent in schools and workplaces. Inferring information about the other's thoughts, feelings, and intentions is crucial in successful social interactions, and has for example been related to leadership skills. Therefore, the person with high EQ—along with technical proficiency—is the most preferred for hiring (Setyawan et al., 2017). It is apparent that negative emotions will greatly affect mental health, and also, the direct link between un-controlled stress and impaired physical health is well established. The main reason for the stress is unable to manage emotions, so those with better EI can better take care of their health.

32.6 Gender-based EQ

Like many common comparisons between males and females in performing different tasks, there has been a handful of research done to understand the EQ difference between them. Newer EQ tests such as EI and MSCEIT report that women have higher EI than men (Cabello et al., 2016). The test findings are also matched with self-report data, i.e., women have shown more empathy than men. However, when the samples are subjected to different hypothetical and experimental studies like reviews, behavioral analysis, physiological processes, and brain neuro-imaging, the results are highly varied and inconsistent (Baez et al., 2017; Christov-Moore, 2014; Kret and De Gelder, 2012). Social cognition is used as an important parameter to evaluate EI in gender-based studies. Social cognition is a term that denotes facial expression, body language, vocal expression, intention, emotion, expectations, etc. Different studies have stated that women tend to express more social cognition than men, whereas men have reduced ability in social judgments—but men can outsmart women in sensing the behavioral cues such as outbursts and threatening ones. The possible scientific explanation which can be given is the enhanced brain activity in the right temporal cortex of the female, which could act as a core for social cognition. Functional magnetic resonance imaging (fMRI) scanning images have revealed that the females have greater gray matter volumes in the posterior inferior frontal and anterior inferior parietal cortexes. This might result in elevated empathy and cognition in women (Zaidi, 2010).

Gender-Based EI: A Case Study

In general, it is hard to differentiate the level of intelligence between the genders, but some studies have demonstrated females having higher EI than men (Joseph and Newman, 2010; Patel, 2017). On the other hand, some studies report that there are no such common traits between the genders, and that they exhibit different personalities. Generally, males express assertiveness and females articulate empathy (Siegling et al., 2015). The EI can be measured by different methods such as self-reports, empathy quotient, emotional quotient inventory (EQ-i), emotional awareness (LEAS), and interpersonal reactivity index (IRI). To test whether EI is based on gender difference, the Bar-On emotional quotient inventory was conducted for 455 undergraduate students in Iran. Although the final test scores were not found to reveal significant differences between male and female students, females scored better in certain categories like self-awareness, self-esteem, empathy, and interpersonal relationships (Meshkat and Nejati, 2017). The emotional sensitivity hypothesis states that women can better comprehend non-verbal expressions and effectively read subtle emotions.

32.7 EI: An Innate and Learned Skill

EI does not comprise regular concept-based learning; rather, it is a part of the natural evolution and development occurring in human beings. Evolution is a scientific concept which explains the change in heritable traits that are transferred from one generation to successive generations. Previously, terms like 'empathy' and 'social cognition' were thought to be a natural and integral part of human development, but lately, humans are largely keen to improve solely the IQ part and firmly believe that it alone is essential to attain success. They fail to understand complete human growth and development; rather, they focus only on a particular domain of cognition. It is because they tend to spend more on-screen time than in face-to-face interaction which makes them less sensitive to emotions and more sensitive to non-verbal communications (Humphrey et al., 2007). Empathy is a result of a cascade of complex neurological reactions that takes place in one's brain, and it cannot be completely instructed or taught through programs—yet, one can passively implement certain practices or changes in the curriculum to learn and understand 'empathy'.

32.7.1 Improving EI in the Classroom

It is reported that an individual with controlled emotions has a high chance of academic success (Berenson et al., 2008). Social and emotional learning (SEL) programs have become standard parts of the curriculum in many schools to enhance EI. Other than implementing such programs or providing additional learning materials, the creation of knowledge spots or knowledge corners can help the students to think and learn about self-awareness in the academic setup. The role of metacognitive practices is well established in EI, as it improves the overall cognitive functioning of an individual, along with its enhancement. Unfortunately, most adults are unaware of how to learn such practices. It is relatively easy to enhance cognitive knowledge, but the appropriate regulation of the acquired knowledge is most challenging. Hence, teaching methods blended with metacognition strategies will help the students to regulate their emotions. Metacognitive techniques like concept mapping, thinking aloud, visual study tools, classroom assessment tools (CATS), and reflective writing will radically improve EI (Hunter et al., 2006; Weissberg et al., 2015).

The teacher or the instructor should provide the opportunities, viz., the real-life practice of empathy, conflict management, cooperative behavior, etc. Examples like sitting with someone new at lunch, interviewing classmates, or a classroom charity project would give them the space to improve mindfulness and thoughtfulness. The teacher should allow students to effectively communicate in the classroom to increase their value and make them feel confident. More than implementing changes in the curriculum level or providing any external help, EI can be better improved by individuals with slight internal changes. It is advised to focus on them and others, to do face reading, maintaining eye contact during the communication, decoding the vocal tone (as it will demonstrate the true and innate feeling), listening more, and labeling your emotions. In addition to that, practicing self-talk and recording it, and segregating and labeling one's thoughts and implementing control measures to the flow of thoughts, would be of great aid.

32.8 EI and Industry 4.0

> Industry 4.0 is a phenomenon that will come inevitably, whether we want it or not.
>
> **(Hermann et al., 2016)**

Industry 4.0 is increasingly important and relevant in the current scenario, as it offers a multitude of benefits. It mainly demonstrates the importance of interconnectivity between production, automation, and modern technologies to possibly reduce the industrial challenges. The main aim of Industry 4.0 is to enhance the communication between individuals, machines, and resources to complete the transformation of centralized production into an automatic model (Baena et al., 2017). Besides offering advanced technologies and tools, viz., robotics, artificial intelligence, Big Data, and IoT, producing a skilled workforce is also equally essential to meet the challenges of Industry 4.0. Hence, the students are expected to have extreme flexibility, a rapid decision-making process, and leadership qualities to confront the needs and challenges associated with the development of new technologies.

EI plays a vital role in determining the success of a person, whether being a student, teacher, parent, or leader. The qualities such as IQ, personality type, and EI together determine a person's way of thinking. Among these, EI is the only quality which can be improved by counseling and training (Stichler, 2006). Current research shows that people with high EI levels are associated with more career success, strong personal relationships, and improved health than those with low-level EI (Atta et al., 2013). Besides, high EI is less likely to be associated with negative behaviors such as smoking, alcoholism, drug abuse, and aggressive behavior with others (Mayer et al., 2004). Implementation of EI can enhance the productive outcome individually and at the organizational level (Stedman and Andenoro, 2007). In a technological view of Industry 4.0, an educational leader aims to transform the students and make them succeed in life according to changing learning styles by executing virtual reality, i.e., adapting to pressures and demands of the environment. Educational policies are the primary source of modeling of the human resources of tomorrow. Similarly, enhancing EI in the curriculum could help to forestall side effects of Industry 4.0 like technological unemployment (Campa, 2020).

32.9 Limitations of Implementing EI

Unlike kids and children, adults studying in colleges or universities are not very flexible or are less interested to learn about empathy, social cognition, self-awareness, etc. As EI has to be instructed from childhood, and further with it being a brain-based connection, enforced learning about EI will not effectively reach adults and help them regulate their emotions. Although EI can be improved to a certain extent through SEL programs or other relevant practices, the host institution has to arrange all the essentialities like extra tutors, facilities, cost factors, etc. Though SEL implementation is comparatively easy, the practice and measuring of its effectiveness and reachability in daily life is a daunting task. Learning EI outside the curriculum hours makes the students less interested—and ironically, learning emotions through digital learning will not be the ideal way to deliver and comprehend emotions or expressions. There is some criticism behind the concept of EI, and IQ is still vastly considered as the 'real' intelligence in many parts of the globe (Stough et al., 2009).

32.10 Summary

Due to rapid changes in human lifestyles, mainly because of technological advancements, certain innate characteristics like self-awareness, empathy, and social cognition have become weakened. Hence, an attempt to improve such innate abilities—viz., self-awareness, self-regulation, and empathy toward others—will intensify human knowledge and perception toward life and work. The overall improvement in the regulation of emotions is termed emotional intelligence (EI). Fostering and refining EI will facilitate the person's ability to increase their mental health and achieve the set goals. It is suggested that organizations should offer certain exclusive programs to identify the emotional or behavioral cues of the students, and provide a platform to represent them. Likewise, the family setup and the way it is (family) functioning should offer an ideal environment for effective emotional development and behavioral growth. Individuals with high EQ exhibit higher productivity and less vehemence. The high-EQ personalities and emotionally intelligent individuals are believed to resolve conflicts and skillfully maintain potential human connections. The author would like to insist on his take on 'emotional intelligence'—that EI is an innate characteristic that is present in every human being. What one needs to do is find time for oneself and doing nothing except observing the world. It is neither a skill that you need to acquire nor a method of teaching.

REFERENCES

Ashkanasy, N.M. and Daus, C.S., 2005. Rumors of the death of emotional intelligence in organizational behavior are vastly exaggerated. *Journal of Organizational Behavior*, 26(4), pp. 441–452.

Atta, M., Ather, M. and Bano, M., 2013. Emotional intelligence and personality traits among university teachers: Relationship and gender differences. *International Journal of Business and Social Science*, 4(17).

Bae, J., Jennings, P.F., Hardeman, C.P., Kim, E., Lee, M., Littleton, T. and Saasa, S., 2020. Compassion satisfaction among social work practitioners: The role of work—life balance. *Journal of Social Service Research*, 46(3), pp. 320–330.

Baena, F., Guarin, A., Mora, J., Sauza, J. and Retat, S., 2017. Learning factory: The path to industry 4.0. *Procedia Manufacturing*, 9, pp. 73–80.

Baez, S., Flichtentrei, D., Prats, M., Mastandueno, R., Garcia, A.M., Cetkovich, M. and Ibanez, A., 2017. Men, women . . . who cares? A population-based study on sex differences and gender roles in empathy and moral cognition. *PLoS One*, 12(6), p. e0179336.

Bar-On, R., 1988. The development of an operational concept of psychological well-being. Unpublished doctoral dissertation. Rhodes University, South Africa.

Berenson, R., Boyles, G. and Weaver, A., 2008. Emotional intelligence as a predictor of success in online learning. *The International Review of Research in Open and Distributed Learning*, 9(2).

Boyatzis, R. and Boyatzis, R.E., 2009. Competencies as a behavioral approach to emotional intelligence. *Journal of Management Development*, 28(9), pp. 749–770.

Cabello, R., Sorrel, M.A., Fernández-Pinto, I., Extremera, N. and Fernández-Berrocal, P., 2016. Age and gender differences in ability emotional intelligence in adults: A cross-sectional study. *Developmental Psychology,* 52(9), pp. 1486–1492.

Campa, R., 2020. Fourth industrial revolution and emotional intelligence: A conceptual and scientometric analysis. *Changing Societies & Personalities*, 4(1), pp. 8–30.

Chin, S.T.S., Raman, K., Yeow, J.A. and Eze, U.C., 2012. Relationship between emotional intelligence and spiritual intelligence in nurturing creativity and innovation among successful entrepreneurs: A conceptual framework. *Procedia-Social and Behavioral Sciences*, 57, pp. 261–267.

Chopra, P.K. and Kanji, G.K., 2010. Emotional intelligence: A catalyst for inspirational leadership and management excellence. *Total Quality Management*, 21(10), pp. 971–1004.

Christov-Moore, L., Simpson, E.A., Coudé, G., Grigaityte, K., Iacoboni, M. and Ferrari, P.F., 2014. Empathy: Gender effects in brain and behavior. *Neuroscience & Biobehavioral Reviews*, 46(4), pp. 604–627.

Di Fabio, A. and Saklofske, D.H., 2014. Comparing ability and self-report trait emotional intelligence, fluid intelligence, and personality traits in career decision. *Personality and Individual Differences*, 64, pp. 174–178.

Farahbakhsh, S., 2012. The role of emotional intelligence in increasing quality of work life in school principals. *Procedia-Social and Behavioral Sciences*, 46, pp. 31–35.

Gardner, H., 1983. *Frames of Mind.* New York: Basic Book, 440pp.

Goleman, D., 1995. *Emotional Intelligence.* New York: Bantam Books, 352pp.

Gragg, P., 2008. From theory to practice: Operation emotional intelligence. *Legal Reference Services Quarterly*, 27(2–3), pp. 241–253.

Hermann, M., Pentek, T. and Otto, B., 2016. Design principles for industrie 4.0 scenarios. In 2016 49th Hawaii International Conference on System Sciences (HICSS), IEEE, pp. 3928–3937.

Hernon, P. and Rossiter, N., 2006. Emotional intelligence: Which traits are most prized? *College & Research Libraries*, 67(3), pp. 260–275.

Humphrey, N., Curran, A., Morris, E., Farrell, P. and Woods, K., 2007. Emotional intelligence and education: A critical review. *Educational Psychology*, 27(2), pp. 235–254.

Hunter, D., Mayenga, C. and Gambell, T., 2006. Classroom assessment tools and uses: Canadian English teachers' practices for writing. *Assessing Writing*, 11(1), pp. 42–65.

Joseph, D.L. and Newman, D.A., 2010. Emotional intelligence: An integrative meta-analysis and cascading model. *Journal of Applied Psychology*, 95(1), pp. 54–78.

Kaya, H., Şenyuva, E. and Bodur, G., 2017. Developing critical thinking disposition and emotional intelligence of nursing students: A longitudinal research. *Nurse Education Today*, 48, pp. 72–77.

Kret, M.E. and De Gelder, B., 2012. A review on sex differences in processing emotional signals. *Neuropsychologia*, 50(7), pp. 1211–1221.

Lewis, M.D. and Todd, R.M., 2007. The self-regulating brain: Cortical-subcortical feedback and the development of intelligent action. *Cognitive Development*, 22(4), pp. 406–430.

Mayer, J.D. and Salovey, P., 1997. What is emotional intelligence? *Emotional Development and Emotional Intelligence: Educational Implications*, pp. 3–31.

Mayer, J.D., Salovey, P. and Caruso, D., 2004. Psychological inquiry: An international journal for the advancement of psychological theory. *Psychological Inquiry*, 15(3), pp. 197–215.

Mérida-López, S. and Extremera, N., 2020. The interplay of emotional intelligence abilities and work engagement on job and life satisfaction: Which emotional abilities matter most for secondary-school teachers? *Frontiers in Psychology*, p. 11.

Meshkat, M. and Nejati, R., 2017. Does emotional intelligence depend on gender? A study on undergraduate English majors of three Iranian universities. *SAGE Open*, 7(3), pp. 1–8.

Ogurlu, U., 2021. A meta-analytic review of emotional intelligence in gifted individuals: A multilevel analysis. *Personality and Individual Differences*, p. 110503.

Palmer, B.R., Gignac, G., Manocha, R. and Stough, C., 2005. A psychometric evaluation of the Mayer—Salovey—Caruso emotional intelligence test version 2.0. *Intelligence*, 33(3), pp. 285–305.

Patel, S.K., 2017. Emotional intelligence of college level students in relation to their gender. *The International Journal of Indian Psychology*, 4(2), pp. 2349–3429.

Payne, W.L., 1986. A study of emotion: Developing emotional intelligence; Self-integration; relating to fear, pain and desire. *Dissertation Abstracts International*, 47, p. 203A (University microfilms No. AAC 8605928).

Richardson, K. and Norgate, S.H., 2015. Does IQ really predict job performance? *Applied Developmental Science*, 19(3), pp. 153–169.

Rockstuhl, T., Seiler, S., Ang, S., Van Dyne, L. and Annen, H., 2011. Beyond general intelligence (IQ) and emotional intelligence (EQ): The role of cultural intelligence (CQ) on cross-border leadership effectiveness in a globalized world. *Journal of Social Issues*, 67(4), pp. 825–840.

Salovey, P. and Mayer, J.D., 1990. Emotional intelligence. *Imagination, Cognition and Personality*, 9(3), pp. 185–211.

Sánchez-Álvarez, N., Extremera, N. and Fernández-Berrocal, P., 2016. The relation between emotional intelligence and subjective well-being: A meta-analytic investigation. *The Journal of Positive Psychology*, 11(3), pp. 276–285.

Setyawan, I., Budiyono and Slamet, I., 2017, August. The comparison of Missouri mathematics project and teams games tournament viewed from emotional quotient eight grade student of junior school. In AIP Conference Proceedings (Vol. 1868, No. 1, p. 050013). AIP Publishing LLC.

Shelar, P.S., 2016. Conceptual study of relationship between emotional intelligence & work life balance in corporate world. *Human Resource Management*, pp. 117–121.

Siegling, A.B., Furnham, A. and Petrides, K.V., 2015. Trait emotional intelligence and personality: Gender-invariant linkages across different measures of the big five. *Journal of Psychoeducational Assessment*, 33(1), pp. 57–67.

Śmieja, M., Orzechowski, J. and Stolarski, M.S., 2014. TIE: An ability test of emotional intelligence. *PLoS One*, 9(7), p. e103484.

Stedman, N.L. and Andenoro, A.C., 2007. Identification of relationships between emotional intelligence skill and critical thinking disposition in undergraduate leadership students. *Journal of Leadership Education*, 6(1), pp. 190–208.

Stichler, J.F., 2006. Emotional intelligence. *Nursing for Women's Health*, 10(5), pp. 422–425.

Stough, C., Saklofske, D.H. and Parker, J.D., 2009. Assessing emotional intelligence. Theory, research, and applications. In *The Springer Series on Human Exceptionality*. Boston, MA: Springer, pp. 3–8.
Thorndike, E. L., 1920. Intelligence and its uses. *Harper's Magazine*, 140, pp. 227–235.
Wechsler, D., 1939. *The Measurement of Adult Intelligence*. Baltimore, MD: US. Williams & Witkins.
Weissberg, R.P., Durlak, J.A., Domitrovich, C.E. and Gullotta, T.P., 2015. *Social and Emotional Learning: Past, Present, and Future*. New York: Guilford, pp. 3–19.
Zaidi, J.F., 2010. Gender differences in human brain: An overview. *The Open Anatomy*, 2, pp. 37–55.

Appendix A

A. Syllabi for New Courses—Syllabi 4.0

The syllabi for various courses that deal with Industry 4.0 tools are given in this section.

A.1 Big Data Analytics

Unit I: Introduction

Data—Information—Data Terminologies—Database—Data Mining—Data Warehouse— Data Evolution Road Map—Big Data—Definition—Type of Data—Numeric—Categorical—Graphical—High Dimensional Data—Data Classification—Hot Data—Cold Data—Warm Data—Thick Data—Thin Data—Classification of Digital Data: Structured, Semi-Structured and Unstructured Data Sources—Time Series—Transactional Data—Biological Data—Spatial Data—Social Network Data

Unit II: Data Science

Data Science-A Discipline—Data Science vs. Statistics, Data Science vs. Mathematics, Data Science vs. Programming Language, Data Science vs. Database, Data Science vs. Machine Learning—Data Analytics—Relation: Data Science, Analytics, Big Data Analytics—Data Science Components: Data Engineering, Data Analytics Methods and Algorithms, Data Visualization

Unit III: Big Data

Digital Data: An Imprint: Evolution of Big Data—What Is Big Data—Sources of Big Data. Characteristics of Big Data 6Vs—Big Data Myths—Data Discovery: Traditional Approach, Big Data Technology: Big Data Technology Process—Big Data Exploration—Data Augmentation—Operational Analysis—360 View of Customers—Security and Intelligence

Unit IV: Big Data Technology Potentials

AI—Machine Learning—Cloud Computing—Mobile Communication—IoT—Big Data in Industry 4.0: Big Data Platforms—HADOOP—SPARK—No SQL Database Types—Big Data Challenges

Unit V: Big Data Use Cases

Big Data Roles Data Scientist, Data Architect, Data Analyst—Skills—Case Study: Big Data—Customer Insights—Behavioural Analysis—Big Data Industry Applications—Marketing—Retails—Insurance—Risk and Security—Health Care

Books

1. V. Bhuvaneswari, T. Devi, *Big Data Analytics*, Scitech Publisher, Chennai, India, 2018.
2. Han Hu, Yonggang Wen, Tat-Seng, Chua, Xuelong Li, *Toward Scalable Systems for Big Data Analytics: A Technology Tutorial*, IEEE, 2014.

3. P. Kaliraj, T. Devi, *Big Data Applications in Industry 4.0*, 2022, ISBN 9781032008110, CRC Press, Taylor & Francis Group, New York.

A.2 Data Analytics Using R

Unit I: Introduction to Data Analytics

Data Analysis vs. Data Analytics—Data Analytics—Types—Data Analytics—Framework—Data Analytics—Tool—R Language—Understanding R Features—Installing R and RStudio—Packages and Library—Importing and Exporting Files: CSV Files—JSON Files—.txt Files—Excel Files—Xml Files—Command Line vs. Scripts.—Data Pre-Processing—Missing Value—Omitting Null Values—Data Transformation—Data Selection—Data Integration

Unit II: Understanding R Features

Installing R and RStudio—Packages and Libraries—Importing and Exporting Files: CSV Files—JSON Files—.txt Files—Excel Filse—Xml Files—Command Line vs. Scripts Data Manipulation: Slicing—Subscripts and Indices—Data Subset—Dplyr Package: Select Function—Filter Function—Mutate Function—Arrange Function

Unit III: Data Summarization and Visualization

Mean—Median—Mode—Variability Measures—Variance—Range—IQR—Standard Deviation—Sum of Squares—Identifying Outliers using IQR. Data Visualization—Introduction—Datasets—Exploratory Data Analytics—Univariate Analysis—Histogram—Bivariate Analysis—Box Plot—Multivariate Analysis—Scatter Plot—MASS Package—Categorical Variable—Bar Chart—Mosaic Plot

Unit IV: Reporting Tool

Analyzing Gathering Information—Storytelling—R Markdown—R Markdown Framework—rmarkdown Package—Knit for Embedded Code: knitr Package—Convert Files: HTML,. pdf, MS Word—Markdown Formatted Text—ShinyApp—shiny Package: Built Shiny App—Control Widgets—Customize Reactions— Reactive Expressions—Customize Appearance—Deploy Shiny App

Unit V: Data Analytics Case Studies

Marketing—Logistic Management—Insurance—Behavioural Analytics—Data Analytics on Diamond Dataset

Books

1. V. Bhuvaneswari, *Data Analytics with R Step by Step*, Scitech Publisher, India, ISBN—978-81-929131-2-4, Edition 2016.
2. Roger D.Peng, *R Programming for Data Science*, Lean Publishing, 2014, [eBook].
3. Vignesh Prajapati, *Big Data Analytics with R and Hadoop*, Packt Publishing, Birmingham, UK, ISBN—978-1-78216-328-2, 2013.
4. Sholom Weiss, et.al, *The Text Mining Handbook: Advanced Approaches in Analysing Unstructured Data*, Springer, New York, Paperback 2010.
5. P. Kaliraj, T. Devi, *Big Data Applications in Industry 4.0*, 2022, ISBN 9781032008110, CRC Press, Taylor & Francis Group, New York.

A.3 Advanced Data Analysis Using R

Unit I: Introduction

Data Analytics —Data Analysis vs. Data Analytics—Big Data Analytics—Data Formats—Data Characteristics—Big Data Platforms—Applications—Data Analytics Use Case: Data Analytics—Health Care—Marketing

Unit II: Descriptive Data Analytics

Data Visualization: Lattice Package—Univariate Analysis: Histogram Features Mode—Skewness—Kurtosis—One Variable—Multiple Variable—Bivariate Analysis—Density Plot—Box Plot—Outlier Identification—Multivariate Analysis: Scatter Plot—Correlation—Cor() Function—Descriptive Analytics—Ships Dataset in MASS Package

Unit III: Regression Analysis

Linear Regression Analysis—Logistic Regression Analysis—Regression Analysis—Air Quality Dataset—Clustering Approaches: k-Means Clustering—Hierarchical Clustering—Clustering—Car Dataset

Unit IV: Text Pre-processing

Nature of Unstructured and Semi-Structured Text—Basic String Function: tolower()—toupper()—str-split()—gsub()—grep()- regexpr()—Converting Text to Document Standardization—Tokenization—Lemmatization—Stemming—Parsing Text—n-Gram—POS—Corpus Creation—tm Package—Text Visualization: word_cloud—word_cloud Package

Unit V: Inferential Analytics

Statistical Hypotheses—Parametric Test—Non-Parametric Test—Data Standardizing—Z Score—Negative Z Score—Chi-Square Test—Wilson's Score Interval

Unit VI: Dashboard and Reporting Tool

Analyzing Gathering Information—Story Telling—rmarkdown rmarkdown Framework—rmark-down Package—Markdown Formatted Text—Knit for Embedded Code: knitr Package—Convert File: HTML,. pdf, MS Word—Introduction Shiny Dashboard—shinydashboard Package—Shiny—HTML—Structure: Header—Sidebar—Body—Layouts—Use Cases—Social Analytics—Health Catalyst Prediction

Books

1. V. Bhuvaneswari, *Data Analytics with R Step by Step*, Scitech Publication, India, ISBN—978-81-929131-2-4, Edition 2016.
2. Roger D.Peng, *R Programming for Data Science*, Lean Publishing, 2014, [eBook].
3. Vignesh Prajapati, *Big Data Analytics with R and Hadoop*, Packt Publishing, Birmingham, UK, ISBN-978-1-78216-328-2, 2013.
4. Sholom Weiss, et.al, *The Text Mining Handbook: Advanced Approaches in Analysing Unstructured Data*, Springer, Paperback, New York, 2010.
5. Emmanuel Paradis, *R for Beginners*, France, 2005.

6. P. Kaliraj, T. Devi, *Big Data Applications in Industry 4.0*, 2022, ISBN 9781032008110, CRC Press, Taylor & Francis Group, New York.

A.4 Python for Data Analytics

Unit I: Python Introduction

History of Python—Python Features—Python Interpreter—Installation and Setup: Windows—Linux—macOS—Installing/Updating Python Packages—Essential Python Libraries—Basic Data Types—Python Built-In Functions—IDEs—Text Editors—IPython—Jupyter Notebook—Importing and Exporting Files:. csv Files—JSON Files—.txt Files—Excel Files—.xml Files—Delimited Formats

Unit II: Data Structures

Introduction—NumPy Package—Python List: Introduction—Accessing Values—List Manipulation—List Operations—Python Tuples: Creating Tuples—Operation in Tuples—Accessing and Functions in Tuples—Python Dictionary: Accessing—Functions in Dictionary—Functions—Namespaces—Indexing—Slicing—Matrices—Arrays Functions—Exception Handling—Global and Local Variables

Unit III: Data Manipulation

Pandas Package—Series—Data Frames—Combining Data Frames—Index Objects—Filtering—Renaming—Dealing with Outliers—Summarizing—Correlation—Covariance—Data Cleaning—Handling Missing Data—Data Transformation—String Manipulation—Regular Expressions—Data Wrangling—Reshaping—Combining—Merging—Indexing.

Unit IV: Data Visualization

Matplotlib Library—Seaborn Library—Configuration—Graphical Parameters—Plotting Function in Pandas: Line Plots—Bar Plots—Histograms—Density Plots—Scatter Plots—Facet Grids—Categorical Data

Unit V: Advanced Interactive Plot

Introduction Plotly Library—Data Understanding—Preparing Variables—Visualization—Distribution: Histogram—Boxplot—Correlation: Scatter Plot—Heat Map—Ranking Plot: Barplot—Boxplot—Wordcloud

Books

1. Fred L. Drake, Guido Van Russom, *An Introduction to Python*, Network Theory Limited, UK.
2. Wesley J. Chun, *Core Python Programming*, 2nd Edition, Pearson Education, USA.
3. Magnus Lie Hetland, *Beginning Python: From Novice to Professional*, 2nd Edition. Springer Nature, India.
4. Mark Summerfield, *Programming in Python*, Pearson Education, India.
5. Wes McKinney, *Python for Data Analysis*, 2nd Edition, O'Reilly Media, Inc., ISBN: 9781491957653, 2017. India.
6. P. Kaliraj, T. Devi, *Big Data Applications in Industry 4.0*, 2022, ISBN 9781032008110, CRC Press, Taylor & Francis Group, New York.

A.5 Robotic Process Automation

Unit I: Introduction to Automation and RPA

Basics of RPA—RPA Benefits—Processes That Can be Automated—Types of Robots—Automation and RPA Concepts: Business Models for Implementing RPA—Centre of Excellence—Types and Their Applications—Building an RPA Team—Approach for Implementing RPA Initiatives

Unit II: Understanding the Automation Cycle

Automation Stages and the Role of a Business Manager—Guidelines for Tracking the Implementation Success—Metrics/Parameters to be Considered for Gauging Success—Choosing the Right Licensing Option—Setting Up the UiPath Environment—Introduction to UiPath—The User Interface—Keyboard Shortcuts—Automation Projects and Debugging—Managing Activities—Reusing Automation Library

Unit III: Basic Concepts of RPA

Recording and UI Interaction—Data Scraping and Screen Scraping—Sequences, Variables and Control Flow—Selectors—Coding the Robot—Advanced Automation Concepts: Image-Based Automation—Keyboard-Based Automation—Email Automation—Information Retrieval—Advanced Citrix Automation Challenges

Unit IV: Data Persistence in RPA

Tables in RPA—Data Manipulation in Excel—Extracting Data from. pdf Files—Using Anchors in. pdf—Exceptional Handling: Debugging Tools—Strategies for Solving Issues—Catching Errors—Orchestrator: Introduction—Tenants—Authentication—Users—Roles—Robots—Environments—Queues and Transactions—Schedules

Unit V: RPA Projects

Sales Order Entry Robots—Robots for Transactions in Stock Markets—MySQL Backup Robot—Email Categorization Robots—Email Autoresponder Robots—Disk Monitoring and Clean-Up Robots

Reference Links

1. www.uipath.com/landing/academic-studio-download
2. https://www.uipath.com/rpa/robotic-process-automation
3. https://www.uipath.com/rpa/academy

A.6 Robotic Process Automation Design and Development

Unit I: Robotic Process Automation (RPA)

Programming Basics—Data and Data Structures—Algorithms—Software Development Guidelines—Compilers—Frameworks and Languages—Information Sharing—File Types—Access Control—Basic RPA Concepts—Applying RPA—RPA vs. Automation—Programming Constructs in RPA—RPA Deployments. Advanced RPA Concepts—Standardization of Processes—RPA Development—Robotic

Control Flow Architecture—RPA Business Case—Industries Best Suited for RPA—Risks and Challenges with RPA—RPA and Emerging Ecosystems

Unit II: UiPath Introduction

Installing UiPath Studio Academic Alliance Edition—The User Interface—Keyboard Shortcuts—Automation Projects—Automation Debugging—Managing Activities Packages—Reusing Automation Libraries—Variables within Studio—Namespaces—Control Flow—Loops—Flowcharts—Data Manipulation Techniques—Scalar Variables, Collections and Tables—Text Manipulation—Data Manipulation—Gathering and Assembling Data

Unit III: Recording and Advanced UI Interaction

Basic and Desktop Recording—Web Recording—Screen Scraping—Data Scraping—Selectors—Defining and Assessing Selectors—Customization—Debugging—Dynamic Selectors—Partial Selectors—RPA Challenges—UiPath Advanced Concepts and Application—Image, Text and Data Tables Automation in Studio—Automating Citrix,. pdf, and Email—Best Practices

Unit IV: Excel Data Tables and PDF

Data Tables in RPA—Data Manipulation in Excel—Extracting Data from. pdf—Anchors—Using Anchors in. pdf—Debugging and Exception Handling—Debugging Tools—Strategies for Solving Issues—Catching Errors—Project Organization—Best Practices—Avoiding Pitfalls—Invoke Activity

Unit V: UiPath

Orchestrator—Tenants—Authentication—Users and Roles—Robots—Environments—Queues and Transactions—Schedules—Artificial Intelligence and Machine Learning Implementation in RPA—Digital Assistants—Future of RPA—Basic RPA Projects: Sales Order Entry Robots—Robots for Transactions and Email Categorization—Advanced Projects: Email Autoresponder Robots—Disk Monitoring and Clean-Up Robots

Reference Links

1. www.uipath.com/landing/academic-studio-download
2. https://www.uipath.com/rpa/robotic-process-automation
3. https://www.uipath.com/rpa/academy

A.7 Robotic Process Automation for Business

Unit I: Introduction to RPA

Overview of RPA—Benefits of RPA in a Business Environment—Industries and Domains Fit for RPA—Identification of Processes for Automation—Types of Robots—Ethics of RPA and Best Practices—Automation and RPA Concepts—Different Business Models for Implementing RPA—Centre of Excellence—Types and Their Applications—Building an RPA Team—Approach for Implementing RPA Initiatives

Unit II: Role of a Business Manager in Automation Initiatives

Skills Required by a Business Manager for Successful Automation—The Importance of a Business Manager in Automation—Analyzing Different Business Processes—Process Mapping Frameworks—Role of a

Business Manager in Successful Implementation—Part 1—Understanding the Automation Cycle—First Three Automation Stages and Activities Performed by Different People

Unit III: Evaluating the Automation Implementation

Detailed Description of Last Three Stages and Activities Performed by Different People—Role of a Business Manager in Successful Completion—Part 2—Activities to be Performed Post-Implementation—Guidelines for Tracking the Implementation Success—Metrics/Parameters to be Considered for Gauging Success—Choosing the Right Licensing Option—Sending Emails—Publishing and Running Workflows

Unit IV: Ability to Process Information through Scopes/Systems

Understand the Skill of Information Processing and Its Use in Business—Leveraging Automation—Creating a Robot—New Processes—Establish Causality by Variable Behaviour—Understanding the Skill of Drawing Inference or Establishing Causality by Tracking the Behaviour of a Variable as It Varies across Time/Referenced Variable—Leveraging Automation for This Skill—Robots and New Process Creation

Unit V: Inference from Snapshots of Curated Terms

Omni-Source Data Curation—Multi-Source Trend Tracking—Understand the Skill of Drawing Inference from the Behaviour of Curated Terms by Taking Snapshots across Systems in Reference to Time/Variable(s)—Leveraging Automation for This Skill—Robot Creation and New Process Creation for this Skill

Reference Links

1. www.uipath.com/landing/academic-studio-download
2. https://www.uipath.com/rpa/robotic-process-automation
3. https://www.uipath.com/rpa/academy

A.8 Internet of Things

Unit I: Introduction to IoT

Evolution of IoT—Definition and Characteristics of IoT—Architecture of IoT—Technologies for IoT—Developing IoT Applications—Applications of IoT—Industrial IoT—Security in IoT

Unit II: Basic Electronics for IoT

Electric Charge, Resistance, Current and Voltage—Binary Calculations—Logic Chips—Microcontrollers—Multipurpose Computers—Electronic Signals—A/D and D/A Conversion—Pulse Width Modulation

Unit III: Programming Fundamentals with C Using Arduino IDE

Installing and Setting Up the Arduino IDE—Basic Syntax—Data Types/Variables/Constants—Operators—Conditional Statements and Loops—Using Arduino C Library Functions for Serial, Delay and Other Invoking Functions—Strings and Mathematics Library Functions

Unit IV: Sensors and Actuators

Analog and Digital Sensors—Interfacing Temperature Sensor, Ultrasound Sensor and Infrared (IR) Sensor with Arduino—Interfacing LED and Buzzer with Arduino

Unit V: Sending Sensor Data over the Internet

Introduction to ESP8266 NODEMCU WiFi Module—Programming NODEMCU Using Arduino IDE—Using WiFi and NODEMCU to Transmit Data from Temperature Sensors to an Open Source IoT Cloud Platform (ThingSpeak)

Books

1. Arshdeep Bahga, Vijay Madisetti, *Internet of Things: A Hands-On Approach*, 2014. ISBN: 978-0996025515.
2. Boris Adryan, Dominik Obermaier, Paul Fremantle, *The Technical Foundations of IoT*, Artech Houser Publishers, London, 2017.
3. Michael Margolis, *Arduino Cookbook*, O'Reilly, 2011. India.
4. Marco Schwartz, *Internet of Things with ESP8266*, Packt Publishing, Birmingham, UK, 2016.
5. Dhivya Bala, *ESP8266: Step by Step Tutorial for ESP8266 IoT, Arduino NODEMCU Dev Kit*, 2018.
6. P. Kaliraj, T. Devi, *Securing IoT in Industry 4.0 Applications with Blockchain*, 2022, ISBN 978–1032008103, CRC Press, Taylor & Francis Group, New York.

Reference Links

1. Introduction to IoT Part I—Lecture 1—https://nptel.ac.in/courses/106/105/106105166/
2. Introduction to IoTs Part I and Part II—Lectures 1 and 2 https://nptel.ac.in/courses/108108098/
3. Introduction to IoT—Lecture 1—https://ocw.cs.pub.ro/courses/iot/courses/01
4. Electronics for Internet of Things—Lecture II—https://ocw.cs.pub.ro/courses/iot/courses/02
5. Introduction to Arduino—I—Lecture 22—https://nptel.ac.in/courses/106105166/
6. Introduction to Arduino—II—Lecture 23—https://nptel.ac.in/courses/106105166/
7. Integration of Sensors and Actuators with Arduino—I—Lecture 24—https://nptel.ac.in/courses/106105166/
8. Integration of Sensors and Actuators with Arduino—II—Lecture 25—https://nptel.ac.in/courses/106105166/
9. www.youtube.com/watch?v=-nuBmJBvdog

A.9 Critical Thinking, Design Thinking and Problem Solving

Unit I: Critical Thinking

Definition, Conclusions and Decisions, Beliefs and Claims, Evidence—Finding, Evaluation, Inferences, Facts—Opinion, Probable Truth, Probably False, Venn Diagrams—Applied Critical Thinking: Inference, Explanation, Evidence, Credibility, Two Case Studies, Critical Thinking and Science, Critical Evaluation, Self-Assessment

Unit II: Applied Critical Thinking

Introduction: Need of Design Thinking, Problem to Question—Design Thinking Process—Traditional Problem Solving vs. Design Thinking—Phases of Design Thinking—Problem Exploration—Stakeholder Assessment—Design Thinking for Manufacturers—Smart Idea to Implementation

Unit III: Design Thinking

Thinking to Confidence: Fear Management, Duty vs. Passion—Team Management—Tools for Design Thinking—Prototype Design—Relevance of Design and Design Thinking in Engineering, Human-Centred Design, Case Study: Apply Design Thinking in Problems

Unit IV: Problem Solving

Problem Definition—Problem Solving Methods—Selecting and Using Information—Data processing—Solution Methods—Solving Problems by Searching, Recognizing Patterns, Spatial Reasoning, Necessity and Sufficiency—Choosing and Using Models—Making Choices and Decisions

Unit V: Reasoning

Deductive and Hypothetical Reasoning—Computational Problem Solving—Generating, Implementing, and Evaluating Solutions—Interpersonal Problem Solving—Advanced Problem Solving—Combining Skills: Using Imagination, Developing Models, Carrying Out Investigations, Data Analysis and Inference—Graphical Methods of Solution—Probability, Tree Diagrams and Decision Trees

Books

1. John Butterworth and Geoff Thwaites, *Thinking Skills: Critical Thinking and Problem Solving*, Cambridge University Press, Cambridge, 2013.
2. H. S. Fogler and S. E. LeBlanc, *Strategies for Creative Problem Solving*, 2nd edition, Pearson, Upper Saddle River, NJ, 2008.
3. A. Whimbey and J. Lochhead, *Problem Solving and Comprehension*, 6th edition, Lawrence Erlbaum, Mahwah, NJ, 1999.
4. M. Levine, *Effective Problem Solving*, 2nd edition, Prentice Hall, Upper Saddle River, NJ, 1994.
5. Michael Baker, *The Basics of Critical Thinking*, The Critical Thinking Co press, 2015. www.criticalthinking.com.
6. David Kelley and Tom Kelley, *Creative Confidence*, 2013, [eBook].

Reference Links

1. www.swyam.gov.in
2. www.nptel.ac.in
3. www.videolectures.net
4. www.ideou.com
5. www.creativeconfidence.com
6. www.ted.com/talks/tim_brown_urges/designers_to_think_big
7. www.ideo.com/work
8. www.designkit.org

A.10 Quantum Computing

Unit I: Introduction to Quantum Computing, Linear Operators and Spectral Decomposition

Unit II: Operator Functions and Tensor Products Postulates of Quantum Mechanics

Unit III: Computation, Quantum and Classical Deutsch-Jozsa, Fourier Transformation and Phase Estimation

Unit IV: Factor Simon's Algorithm, Factorization

Unit V: Grover Search, Query Complexity

Books

1. *Quantum Computation and Quantum Information*, M A Nielsen and I L Chuang, Cambridge University press, Cambridge, UK.
2. *An Introduction to Quantum Computing*, P Kaye, R Laflamme and M Mosca, Oxford University Press, Oxford, UK.
3. *Linear Algebra and its Applications*, G. Strang. ISBN 9788131501726, Cengage India Pvt Ltd, India.
4. *Matrix Analysis*, Bhatia. 1997, Springer, India.

A.11 Cybersecurity

Unit I: History of the Internet

Overview of Cybersecurity—The Security Environment—Threats: Cyber Crime, Warfare, Terrorism and Espionage—Vulnerabilities in Software, System Administration, Network Architectures, Open Access Data and Weak Authentication

Unit II: Cyberspace

Web Browsing and Browser Security—Email Security, Firewalls in Browsers—Security Certificate—Basic Security for HTTP Applications and Services—Password Security: Guidelines to Choose a Password, Two-Step Authentication, WiFi Security—Securing Social Media—Social Media Secure Networking—Smartphone Security: Android, iOS

Unit III:

Cyber Intrusion, Abuse of Privileges, Unauthorized Access, Malware Infection—Intrusion Detection and Prevention Techniques: Network Based and Host Based, Anti-Malware Software—Cybersecurity Regulations—Government and Private Organizations in Cyberspace—Cybersecurity Standards—National Cybersecurity Policy 2013

Unit IV: Introduction to Cryptography

Classifications of Cryptography: Symmetric Key and Asymmetric Key Cryptography—Applications of Cryptography—Firewalls: Types of Firewalls, VPN Security—Security Protocols: Application Layer Security, PGP and S/MIME, Transport Layer Security, SSL and TLS, Network Layer Security, IPSec

Unit V: Introduction to Cyber Forensics

Preliminary Investigations Procedures and Methods—Conducting Disk-Based Analysis—Tracing Internet Access—Tracing Memory—Recovering from Information Loss—Destroying Sensitive Information—CCleaner for Windows—Defensive Programming—Emerging Cybersecurity Threats

Books

1. Michael E Whitman and Herbert J Mattord, *Principles of Information Security*, 4th Edition, Vikas Publishing House, 2011, Singapore.

2. Atul Kahate, *Cryptography and Network Security*, McGraw Hill, 2013, New Delhi.
3. William Stallings, *Cryptography and Network Security Principles and Practices*, 7th Edition, Pearson, 2017, New Delhi, India.
4. Man Young Rhee, *Internet Security: Cryptographic Principles*, Wiley Publications, 2003.
5. Nelson, Phillips, Enfinger, Steuart, *Computer Forensics and Investigations*, Cengage Learning, India Edition, 2008.
6. P. Kaliraj, T. Devi, *Securing IoT in Industry 4.0 Applications with Blockchain*, 2022, ISBN 978–1032008103, CRC Press, Taylor & Francis Group, New York.

A.12 Ethical Hacking

Unit I: Introduction to Ethical Hacking

Hacker and Cracker—Fundamentals of Computer Fraud—Footprinting and Scanning—Malware Threats: Viruses and Worms, Trojans, Spyware—Malware Countermeasures: Ethics and Legality

Unit II: Security Testing

Introduction to Penetration Testing: Virtualization, VirtualBox, Vulnerable Machines, Target Machines and Beast Machines—Anonymous Hacking: Tor Browser—Proxychains: Proxy Servers, VPNs, MAC Addresses

Unit III: Web Attacks

Web Server Hacking—Application Hacking—Database Hacking—Wireless Technologies—Mobile Security and Attacks—Wireless LANs, Firewalls, Honeypots

Unit IV: Introduction to Information Gathering

Types, Tools, Methods, and Frameworks—DNS Footprinting—Email Footprinting—Vulnerability Scanning and Analysis: Network Vulnerability Scanning, Mobile Application Vulnerability Scanning

Unit V: Password Cracking Techniques

Importance of Using Passwords—Hashes and Encoders—Brute Force Attacks—Dictionary-Based Attacks—Cracking Online Services: SSH, FTP, Physical Security—Social Engineering—Cloud Computing—Session Hijacking—Cryptography

Books

1. Lakshay Eshan, *Ethical Hacking: A Beginners Guide to Learning the World of Ethical Hacking*, Shockwave Publishing, 2018, e-book.
2. Michael T.Simpson *Hands-On Ethical Hacking and Network Defense*, 2 Edition, by Cengage Learning, Boston.
3. Arnold Robbins, Elbert Hannab and Linda Lamb, *Learning the vi and vim Editors*, 7th Edition O"Reilly, Cambridge, 2008.
4. P. Kaliraj, T. Devi, *Securing IoT in Industry 4.0 Applications with Blockchain*, 2022, ISBN 978–1032008103, CRC Press, Taylor & Francis Group, New York.

A.13 Industry 4.0: Augmented Reality

Note: Numbers given below within the brackets denote the section numbers in the book for the course

Unit I: Introduction to Augmented Reality

History of AR (4-4.2.1) - Augmented reality characteristics (1-1.1.1) – Difference between Augmented Reality and Virtual Reality (1-1.1.2) – AR technological components (1-1.2.1.1) – Technologies used in AR– Feature Extraction (1-1.2.2) – Hardware components (1-1.3) – AR devices (1-1.3.3) – Importance of AR (2-.2.1) - Real world uses of AR – AR types (2-2.2.2) – Software tools available for AR (1-1.5)

Unit II: Need of technologies for Augmented Reality

Hardware technology (5-5.4) – virtual scenes (5-5.4) – 3D objects (5-5.4) – AR components (5-5.4.1) – Display (5-5.4.2) – HMD – Eyeglasses (5-5.4.4) – Contact Lenses(5-5.4.5) – significance of AR (5-5.5) – AR powered devices (7-7.4)– AR application development drawbacks (7-7.4) – Compatibility–Performance (7-7.4) – AR libraries (7-7.6) – Motion tracking (7-7.7) – Environmental understanding – Anchors (7-7.8)

Unit III: Technology Integration and Implementation of AR

Technology use and integration in industrial settings (5-5.6) – Assistive training to faculty members (5-5.7) – Planning and administration for implementation (5-5.8) – AR implications (5-5.8.1) – Practical data – AR labs (5-5.8.2) – Platforms to form AR content (5-5.10.2) – Coordinated utilization of AR applications – Hands-on preparation (5-5.11)

Unit IV: Augmented Reality and Virtual Reality for Micro Learning

Micro learning techniques (5-5.11 [9]) – Utilizing VR for learning – VR for Practical online assessment (5-5.11 [9 A])– VR info graphics (5-5.11)– Virtual case considerations (5-5.11) - Utilizing AR for learning (4-4.4) – Accessible learning (5-5.12) – sensible data (5-5.12) – elevated learner engagement (5-5.12) - VR technology (2-2.3) – Components of VR (2-2.3.1) – VR Hardware (2-2.3.2) – VR applications (2-2.3.3) – Civil Engineering (2-2.3.3) – Real Estate (2-2.3.3) – Biology and Medicine (2-2.3.3) – Virtual Mall (2-2.3.3) – VR in Education (2-2.3.3) – Virtual Laboratory – Factory Planning – Automobile Industry (2-2.3.3)

Unit V: Tools and Applications of Augmented Reality

Tools available for Augmented Reality and Recognition (1-1.5) – Software Tools (1-1.5.1) – Google Poly – Unity – software approaches – recognition types (1-1.5.2) – native software solutions (1-1.5.2.1) -– ARKit (7-7.6) – ARCore (7-7.6, 7.10.3) – software development kit - Cloud services - AR business applications (1-1.4) – weather prediction (1-1.4.2) – market prediction (1-1.4.3) – smart cities (1-4.4) - AR application for Education (4-4.3) - AR application for Healthcare sector (8-8.3) – Agriculture – Civil Engineering – Architecture – Archaeology – Crime and Security (2-2.2.7) – Games (6-6.2) – IoT (8-8.3.3) – Use cases (7-7.9) – Social Media (7-7.9.1) – Gaming (7-7.9.2) – Education (7-7.9.3) – Healthcare (7-7.9.4) – Shopping and Business (7-7.9.5)

Book

1. Kaliraj P, Devi T, (2021). Innovating with Augmented Reality: Applications in Education and Industry, First edition, Auerbach Publications, Boca Raton, https://doi.org/10.1201/9781003175896

A.14 Industry 4.0: Artificial Intelligence Applications

UNIT I: Artificial Intelligence Insight

Artificial Intelligence: What and Why (1-1.2) – History of AI (1-1.3) – What is AI – The Basics (5-5.1.1) - AI Environment (1-1.5) - Challenges in AI (1-1.8) – Current work in AI for environment (3-3.1) – Customer Experience (CX) and the use of AI (5-5.2) – Future of AI (5-5.6) – Future challenges in AI (7-7.5)

UNIT II: Influence of AI in Machine Learning

Definition (14-14.1) – What is Machine Learning (14-14.2) - Importance of Machine Learning (14-14.1.2) – Types of Machine Learning (14-14.3) – Approaches of Machine Learning (17-17.2) - Machine Learning Algorithm (14-14.4) – Programming Languages (14-14.5.1) – Frameworks (14-14.5.2) – Databases (14-14.5.3) – Deployment tools (14-14.5.4) – Methodology for Model Building (16-16.2) – Machine learning methods (16-16.6) – Statistical Measures (16-16.7) - Application areas of Machine Learning (14-14.6) – Medical Machine Learning (17-17.4) – Influence of AI and ML in Clinical and Genomic Diagnostics (17-17.5)

UNIT III: Artificial Intelligence in Healthcare sector & Assistive Technology (AT)

AI in diagnosis of Genetic Diseases (8-8.4) – Cancer (8-8.4.1) – Diabetes (8-8.4.2) – AI in Diagnosis of Syndrome (8-8.5) – AI in diagnosis of Psychiatric Disorders (8-8.6) – Depression (8-8.6.1) – Alzheimer's Disease (8-8.6.2) – Autism Spectrum Disorder (8-8.6.3) – Anxiety (8-8.6.4) – Parkinson's Disease (8-8.6.5) – AI in other Diagnosis (8-8.7) – Infectious Disease (8-8.7.1) – Lung and Brain Disease (8-8.7.2) - Case studies on AI in systems Biology (7-7.4) – AI technologies in Systems Biology towards Pharmacogenomics (7-7.4.1) – AI in Systems Biology for Cancer Cure (7-7.4.2) – Applications of AI for COVID-19 Pandemic (7-7.4.3) - Transformative impact of AI on AT (13-13.3) – AI experience and AT for disables people in India (13-13.5) – AI Powered technology for an inclusive world (13-13.6)

Unit IV: Artificial Intelligence in Agriculture (10)

Need of AI in Agriculture (10-10.3) – Emerging Agricultural Technologies (10-10.4) – Soil and water sensors (10-10.4.1) – Weather Tracking (10-10.4.2) – Satellite Imaging Agriculture (10-10.4.3) – Automation Systems (10-10.4.4) – RFID Technology (10-10.4.5) – Potential Agricultural Domain for Modernization (10-10.5) – AI transformation in Agricultural Scenarios (10-10.6)

Unit V: Artificial Intelligence in Radiotherapy (6)

Importance of Artificial Intelligence in Radiotherapy (6-6.2) – AI tools for automated treatment planning (ATP) (6-6.3) – Present ATP techniques (6-6.3.1) – AI applications, Advancements and Research Guidance in ATP (6-6.3.2) – AI challenges in ATP (6-6.3.3) – AI in Intensity modulated Radiotherapy (IMRT) (6-6.4) – AI for IMRT Dose Estimation (6-6.4.1) – AI for IMRT Planning Support (6-6.4.2) – AI for Modeling IMRT outcome and plan deliverability (6-6.4.3) – AI for AUTO-Segmentation of OAR in IMRT (6-6.4.4) – AI in Brachytherapy (6-6.5) – AI in Radiotherapy Quality Assurance (6-6.6) – Challenges associate with AI for Quality Assurance in RT (6-6.6.4) – Future directions to improve AI-based Quality Assurance in RT (6-6.6.5) – AI in Radiation Biology (6-6.7) – AI in Radiation Protection/Safety (6-6.8) – Motivations to develop AI-Based systems for Radiation protection (6-6.8.1)

Book

1. Kaliraj, P., & Devi, T. (Eds.). (2021). Artificial Intelligence Theory, Models, and Applications (1st ed.). CRC Press, Taylor & Francis Group, Boca Raton, ebook ISBN 9781032008097, Auerbach Publications. https://doi.org/10.1201/9781003175865

A.15 Industry 4.0: Big Data Applications

UNIT I: Introduction to Big Data Analytics and Data Science

Data: Terminologies (5-5.1.1) – Data Evolution (5-5.1.2) - Data Formats and sources (5-5.1.2.2) - Big Data Analytics (5-5.1) - Big Data concepts (4-4.2) – Big Data Components (5-5.2) – Big Data Characteristics (5-5.2.1) – Big Data vs. Statistics vs. Data Mining (5-5.1.3.3) – Big Data Approaches (13-13.1.3) - Data Lifecycle (13-13.2) – Data Science: A Definition (1-1.1.1) – Data Analysis (5-5.1.3.2) - Data Analytics types (1-1.1.3) – Data in the business (1-1.1.2) - Data Analytics Process, Implementation and Measurement (1-1.1.5)

UNIT II: Data Integration and Big Data Systems

Data Integration (2-2.2) – Data Integration Solutions (2-2.3) – ETL (2-2.3.2.1) – Data Integration Methodologies (2-2.4) – Big Data Processing: Architecture (5-5.2.2) – Traditional vs Big Data Framework (5-5.2.2.1) – Big Data related technologies (5-5.2.3) – Big Data Industry 4.0 Applications (5-5.2.4)

UNIT III: Business Statistical Methods for Big Data Analytics

Statistical methods and analytics techniques used across business (1-1.5) – Statistical methods and analytics techniques used in sales and marketing (1-1.6) – Data types generated in sales and marketing function (1-1.6.1) – Statistical Methods and Analytical Techniques (1-1.6.2) – Statistical Methods and Analytics Techniques used in Supply Chain Management (1-1.7) – Analytics use case in SCM (1-1.7.2)

UNIT IV: Big Data for Education 4.0

Education 4.0 in India (10-10.6) - Digital Revolution of Education 4.0 (8-8.2) – Education 4.0 (8-8.2.1) – Requirements of Education 4.0 in Industry (8-8.2.2) – Benefits of Education 4.0 for Business Sector (8-8.2.3) – Influence of Industrial Revolution 4.0 on Higher Education (8-8.2.4) – Conceptual Framework of Big Data for Industry 4.0 (8-8.3) – Need for Big Data Analytics in Education (10-10.2)

UNIT V: Applications using Big Data and Business Analytics

Big Data Analytics and Business Analytics: An introduction (8-8.1) – Business Analytics (8-8.4) – Business Analytics vs. Business Intelligence (8-8.4.1) – Business Intelligence (8-8.4.1.2) – Challenges of Big Data and Business Analytics (8-8.6) – Applications of Big Data (8-8.5) – Big Data Analytics in Finance Industry (9-9.4) – Applications of Big Data Analytics in Education (10-10.3) – Big Data in Biomedical Research (13-13.4) – Applications in Biomedicine (17-17-4) – Applications in Healthcare (17-17.5) – Big Data Use case: Warehouse Management and Supply Chain (5-5.4.2) – Automobile in Industry (5-5.4.2.2) – Pharmaceuticals (5-5.4.2.3) – Sport Analytics (5-5.4.2.4)

Book

1. Kaliraj, P. Devi, T. (2022). Big Data Applications in Industry 4.0, First edition, Auerbach Publications. Boca Raton. https://doi.org/10.1201/9781003175889

Index

F

M

N

O

S

W

X

Y

Z

www.ingramcontent.com/pod-product-compliance
Lightning Source LLC
LaVergne TN
LVHW080113011026
849160LV00013B/1085
9781032331416